The Chronicle of the Princes

Brut y Tywysogion

Rev. John Willams ab Ithel

The content of this publication is in the public domain.
This edition published in 2020
ISBN: 978-1-71651-628-3
Imprint: Lulu.com

BRUT Y TYWYSOGION;

OR,

THE CHRONICLE OF THE PRINCES.

EDITED

BY

THE REV. JOHN WILLIAMS AB ITHEL, M.A.,

RECTOR OF LLANYMOWDDWY, MERIONETHSHIRE.

PUBLISHED BY THE AUTHORITY OF THE LORDS COMMISSIONERS OF HER MAJESTY'S TREASURY, UNDER THE DIRECTION OF THE MASTER OF THE ROLLS.

LONDON:
LONGMAN, GREEN, LONGMAN, AND ROBERTS.
1860.

Printed by
EYRE and SPOTTISWOODE, Her Majesty's Printers.
For Her Majesty's Stationery Office.

CONTENTS.

	Page.
PREFACE	vii
BRUT Y TYWYSOGION; or, THE CHRONICLE OF THE PRINCES	2–3
GLOSSARY	377
INDEX	421

PREFACE.

THE voice of Tradition would not lead us to suppose that the ancient Britons paid any very particular attention to the study of chronology previous to the era of Prydain,[1] son of Aedd the Great, which is variously dated from the year 1780 to 480 before the nativity of Christ. Prior to that time the recollection of events depended upon the popularity of rude and inartificial songs, which were composed by the Gwyddoniaid, or Sages, and issued by them individually in their capacity of priests and local instructors. Whilst Prydain was engaged in the work of reforming the laws of the land, "he ordered diligent search to be "made throughout the island for any persons who "might possibly have retained in memory the pri- "mitive knowledge of the Cymry, so as to secure "the traditional preservation of it."[2] Three such were

The primitive system of British chronology, and memorials.

---

[1] Prydain is a character much referred to in ancient British documents, especially in the Triads, wherein he is represented as having introduced among the several states social reforms of such importance as to cause his own name to be given to the island, which ever after has been called "Ynys Prydain," the Isle of Prydain. There is reason to believe that the Trojan fable has been founded upon this name, the similarity which it bears to that of Brutus having led to the mistake.

[2] "The voice conventional of the "Bards of the Island of Britain," extracted from Meurug of Glamorgan's Book, at Rhaglan Castle, by Llywelyn John of Llangewydd, in Glamorgan, who flourished about A.D. 1580.

found, whose names were Plennydd, Alawn, and Gwron, and who belonged to the patriarchal order of the Gwyddoniaid. These having communicated what they knew, the whole, after due and proper notice, was recited publicly at the national sessions of the bards, which were now for the first time established; and the recitation was enjoined to be continued periodically on the occurrence of the bardic festivals, with the view of impressing the information on the public memory. And as time drew on, other events, according to the order in which they happened, were added to the series of memorials—being embodied either in vocal song or in triads.

Fitness of the system for the times. It cannot be denied that this system was admirably calculated, under the circumstances of the times, for effecting the desired object. Hence the "voice con-"ventional" was called the chief of the three modes of perpetuating memorials—the other two being "vocal "song," and "letters," as they existed of course in their primitive and isolated forms.[1]

Under the management and superintendence of the Bards. All this was entrusted to the Bards, who at this time were, for the sake of greater convenience, divided into three distinct classes—Bards, Druids, and

---

[1] "The three memorials of the "Bards of the race of the Cymry; "the memorial of the voice of "gorsedd, the memorial of vocal "song, and the memorial of books; "and the strongest of the three is "the memorial of the voice of "gorsedd, because it is preserved "in the memory and hearing of "country and nation, so that he "who sees cause may doubt it." (From the Book of Gutto the scholar, of Llanhari.) It may be proper to observe that most of the documents which relate to the Bardo-Druidic system hitherto exist only in manuscript. At the Grand Eisteddvod, which was held at Llangollen, last year, a prize of a Gold Bardic Tiara and thirty pounds in money, was offered for "the fullest illustration, from ori-"ginal sources, of the Theology, "Discipline, and Usages of the "Bardo-Druidic system of the "Isle of Britain." The prize was won by the editor of the present volume. The information thus brought together is such as will, when published, inevitably attract the attention of both British and Continental scholars.

Ovates, each having its own peculiar duties and privileges. It is to be remarked that Cæsar bears witness to the care with which the Druids in his day cultivated the art of memory; nor did it escape his observation that letters were but sparingly used for the purpose, which he concludes was the case partly lest the pupils, by trusting too much to letters, should become less attentive to the faculty of memory,[1] a conclusion which seems to concur with the Bardic statement, that the use of letters was of inferior importance to the voice conventional.

The first event ascertained by Plennydd, Alawn, and Gwron, was the arrival of the Cymry in the island of Britain, which, according to the "Rhol Cov a Chyv-"riv,"[2] or the roll of memorial and computation, took place eight hundred and forty-nine years before the time of Prydain, son of Aedd the Great. In other authorities the interval is somewhat differently and variously described: thus "Amseroedd Cov a Chyvriv,"[3] or the periods of memorial and computation, gives it at eight hundred and sixty-three years; "Cyvar-"wyddyd,"[4] or historical guide, nine hundred years; "Cov Cyvriv—Cov Gwlad,"[5] or the memorial of computation—the memorial of country, seven hundred years; and another manuscript, six hundred and fifty years.

Arrival of the Cymry in Britain.

---

[1] "Magnum ibi numerum versuum ediscere dicuntur; itaque annos nonnulli vicenos in disciplina permanent. Neque fas esse existimant, ea literis mandare, quum in reliquis fere rebus, publicis privatisque rationibus, Græcis utantur literis. Id mihi duabus de causis instituisse videntur; quod neque in vulgum disciplinam efferri velint, neque eos, qui discant, literis confisos, minus memoriæ studere; quod fere plerisque accidit, ut præsidio literarum diligentiam in perdiscendo ac memoriam remittant."—De Bell. Gall. Lib. vi. c. 14.

[2] Iolo MSS. p. 48. Copied by Meurug Davydd 1560–1600 from an old MS. in the Library of Rhaglan Castle.

[3] Iolo MSS. p. 36.

[4] Called also "Oes Lyvr," or Age Book. MS.

[5] MS.

PREFACE.

Era of Prydain, or the time of memorial.

But without laying much stress upon the statements of these authorities as to pre-historic memorials, or trying to reconcile apparent discrepancies, it is an undoubted fact that the Cymry in later ages were strongly impressed with the idea that the era of Prydain was the national era of chronology, which they termed "Amser Cov a Chyvriv," or "Oedran Cov a Chyvriv," that is, the time of memorial and computation, or the age of memorial and computation.

Documents referring to the subject.

Several fragments remain in manuscript which refer to this matter; and as they are in themselves highly curious, and also full of interest in respect of the subject of our inquiry, we will make no apology for making a few translated extracts:—

Conjecture and memory of country.

"This is the mode in which the primitive teachers "made a record of times:—From the arrival of the "nation of the Cymry to this island it was the con-"jecture and memory of country and nation, for there "was no privilege attached to the guidance of the "memorial of computation prior to the time of Pryd-"ain, the son of Aedd."

Memorial of computation.

"Before the time of Christ the Bards counted their "time from the era in which Prydain, the son of Aedd "the Great, existed, that is, seven hundred years before "Christ; and they would speak of the year of the "memorial of computation, as if they said, Christ "was born in the year of the memorial of computation "719, for it is true that that was the year. And "there was no memorial of computation before the "time of Prydain, the son of Aedd the Great, when "order and privilege were conferred upon Bards and "what the Bards knew. And when the faith in "Christ came, memorials were kept according to the "year of Christ."

Memorial and computation.

"The age of memorial and computation was counted "from the time of Prydain, the son of Aedd the "Great, namely, four hundred and eighty years before

"the time when Christ came in the flesh. And when
"Bran the Blessed, son of Llyr, introduced the faith
"in Christ to the nation of the Cymry, time began
"to be calculated according to the years of Christ.
"Some maintain that the periods of every proclama-
"tion of country and congress ought to be dated from
"the time of Prydain, according to the usage of the
"primitive Cymry; others will have that and the
"year of Christ together; others will have none but
"the year of Christ."[1]

It ought to be remarked that the latter portion of the preceding extract refers to practices or opinions as late as the middle of the last century.

"Before the time of Christ's advent in the flesh Memorial and computation.
"the Bards celebrated times according to the years of
"memorial and computation, that is to say, from the
"time of Prydain, the son of Aedd the Great, who
"was famous five hundred and sixty-six years before
"the birth of Christ in the flesh. From that period
"it is usual for the Bards to celebrate the time of
"memorial and computation in conjunction with the
"year of Christ. Prydain, the son of Aedd the Great,
"as far as it is remembered and known, existed the
"above mentioned time before the birth of Christ,
"and, according to the conjecture of the sages and well
"informed herald Bards, six hundred and fifty years
"after the first arrival of the nation of the Cymry
"in the isle of Britain, that is to say, one thousand
"two hundred and sixteen years before the birth of
"Christ, the nation of the Cymry first came into the
"isle of Britain, and this is called Brut's time, for
"the years of memorial and computation in old
"times were reckoned conjecturally from the time of
"Brut, which was about a thousand years after the
"demolition of the tower of Nimrod the Giant, and

---

[1] MS. of John Bradford, who flourished about 1760.

"about two thousand eight hundred years after the
"expulsion of Adam and Eve from Paradise, namely,
"five (*al.* nine) hundred years after God had created
"this world."

The following is from a record of Henry the
Seventh's time:—[1]

A record of Henry VII.'s time.
"This Howel [*i.e.* Howel the Good] gave wise and
"just laws to the nation of the Cymry, and ordained
"that chronological records should be dated from the
"year of Christ, the Son of God, and His coming in
"the flesh, as it is at this day."

Edict of Arthur.
We may add, on the authority of a scrupulously
faithful antiquary, and one that was deeply versed
in the traditions of his order—the late Iolo Morganwg, that king Arthur in his institutes of the
Round Table introduced the age of the world for
events which occurred before Christ, and the year of
Christ's nativity for all subsequent events.

Summary of the preceding authorities.
The summary of the preceding authorities, then,
as far as they bear upon the question we are investigating, is this;—that previous to the time of
Prydain there was no uniform and regular method
of recording occurrences—that subsequently periods of
time were computed from his era—that this mode
was continued until after the introduction of Christianity into the island, when, to some extent, the year
of Christ was adopted—that the Bards for the most
part adhered to the old rule of Cov a Chyvriv until
the time of Arthur, when events that occurred before
the Christian era were enjoined to be dated accord-

---

[1] Iolo MSS. p. 39. The date of this record may be ascertained from the following passage in it:— "From the time of Howel the Good "to *this present year of the coronation of King Henry the VII.,* "the son of Edmund, the son of "Owain Tudur (all of them being "genuine Britons of the primitive "royal lineage) five hundred and "forty-five years."

ing to the age of the world, and subsequent events from the Nativity—that Howel the Good ordained chronological records to be dated from the year of Christ's coming in the flesh.[1]—and that until a comparatively late period the Bards were in the habit of dating the holding of their congresses sometimes simply from the era of Prydain—sometimes from that and the year of Christ conjointly, though it would seem that other events were chronicled by them invariably after the Christian mode.

Though the language of these extracts would lead us to suppose that the Christian computation was more or less adopted by the Britons immediately upon their conversion to the faith, we can hardly conclude that such was really the case, for it was not even established in Italy before the sixth century. Perhaps we ought to consider the authorities in question as referring in general to the time subsequently to the introduction of Christianity, without intending to ascribe the change of chronological usage to that particular period—a view which receives support in some degree from what is said of Arthur, and his edict.

How their language is to be understood.

But have we any early records by which we could test the correctness of the above assertions? There is every reason to believe that a few of the Historical Triads are genuine memorials of Druidic times; for though they might not have been committed to writing until, perhaps, the twelfth century, yet it is very probable that they were respectively compiled, when the last event of each was still fresh in the memory. Internal evidence points to the remotest antiquity.[2]

The Historical Triads.

---

[1] It is not quite clear whether "dyfodiad ynghnawd," here literally translated *coming in the flesh*, was meant by the chroniclers to express the Annunciation, or simply the Nativity.

[2] "The Historical Triads have "been obviously put together at "very different times. Some allude "to circumstances about the first "population and early history of "the island, of which every other

Being thus framed, they would be publicly recited at the periodic festivals of the Bards, and the repeated recitation would be the sure means of preventing all interpolation and corruption. Indeed written literature might be more easily tampered with in those days than oral traditions, thus, as it were, nationally stereotyped. The only circumstance that would affect their transmission would be the impracticability of meeting in a national convention, as, no doubt, was the case during parts of the Roman domination. Whenever that difficulty offered itself, the duty of preserving such records devolved upon individual members of the Bardic Institute, meeting in groups of twos or threes, and interchanging communications, couched in the language of secrecy.

The Triads void of dates.

The Triads furnish only the *order* in which occurrences took place; they afford us no clue as to the exact date when they severally happened, nor as to the length of the interval that elapsed between each event. We may be allowed to suppose, however, that these particulars were in early times well known to the Britons from a reference to the Gorseddau, or Bardic congresses, which were held (efficiently) every three years, and that in this respect something like the Greek Olympiad was in vogue; but of this we have no intimation.

" memorial has perished. The Triads were noticed by Camden with respect. Mr. Vaughan, the antiquary of Hengwrt, refers them to the seventh century. Some may be the records of more recent date. I think them the most curious, on the whole, of all the Welsh remains."—*A Vindication of the Ancient British Poems, by Sharon Turner, Esq., F.A.S.*, 1803, p. 131.

" The Triades of the Isle of Britain, as they are called, are some of the most curious and valuable fragments preserved in the Welsh language. They relate of persons and events from the earliest times to the beginning of the seventh century."— *The Heroic Elegies, &c., of Llywarch Hen, by William Owen,* p. viii.

Great events alone were embodied in the triadic records. Particulars of minor importance were most probably recollected from their relative connection with the greater ones, but were entrusted to the less certain medium of song, or even to the unaided memory, and were consequently more liable to suffer perversion from the lapse of time. *Great events only recorded in the Triads.*

From the Triads we turn to the Poems of the sixth century, which are pronounced by all competent judges to be authentic productions of the times to which they are usually assigned.[1] Here again we fail to find anything like acknowledged chronology, though there are several allusions to the Triads, which prove that the triadic mode of perpetuating the memory of events was as old at least as the sixth century. *Poems of the 6th century.*

Gildas, who, though he wrote in Latin, was of Cymric extraction, being the son of Caw, lord of Cwm Cowlwyd in the North, leaves us in his Treatise "De Excidio Britanniæ" hardly any trace of a chronological computation. The only event to which he assigns a date is that of the composition of his work, which he particularizes as being the 44th year from the siege of Mount Badon,[2] thus confirming our theory as to minor events, that they were remembered from their association with national epochs. *Gildas.*

The Book, bearing the name of Nennius, contains several chronological modes:—it calculates from the Creation—from the Incarnation and Passion—and in reference to some prominent or well-known event. There are allusions made in it to the number of years by which one event preceded and another followed the nativity of Christ. All this variety *Nennius.*

---

[1] See especially Sharon Turner's "Vindication of the Ancient British Poems."

[2] Cap. xxvi. According to *Annales Cambriæ* the battle of Mount Badon took place A.D. 516.

plainly shows that the mode of registering occurrences was still in a very unsettled state.

<small>First edition of Nennius.</small> The earliest edition of Nennius, of which we have any account, was issued A.D. 674, as is inferred from the manner in which the Editor describes the then current year as the 647th from the Passion of Christ.[1] In this edition both the Nativity and the Passion are taken as points from which computations are made.

<small>Second edition.</small> The date of the second edition is said to concur with the fourth year of Mervyn, king of Britain;[2] that is about A.D. 823. In the Harleian Manuscript 3859, as well as others, we have a specimen of the chronology of this period, in the following passages:—
" Ab Adam vero usque ad Passionem Christi anni sunt
" quinque millia ducenti viginti octo; a Passione autem
" Christi peracti sunt anni 796, ab Incarnatione autem
" ejus anni sunt 832," intended probably for 823. Again:—" A primo anno quo Saxones venerunt in
" Britanniam usque ad annum quartum Mervini regis
" supputantur anni cccCXXIX."

<small>Third edition.</small> The date of the third edition is A.D. 858, which in Chapter XI. is marked as the current year in this way;—from our Lord's Incarnation to the Advent of St. Patrick into Ireland there are twenty-three cycles of nineteen years, and these make up 437 years; from the Advent of St. Patrick to the cycle in which

---

[1] Thus the "Historia" in the Vatican reads: "Quando Gratianus Æquantius Consul fuit in Roma, quia tunc a consulibus Romanorum totus orbis regebatur, Saxones a Guorthegirno, anno post Domini Passionem trecentesimo quadrigesimo septimo suscepti sunt: ad hunc quem (quo) nunc scribimus annum sexcentesimum quadragesimum septimum numeramus."

[2] According to the best known authorities, Mervyn Vrych, or the Freckled, son of Nest, daughter of Cadell of Vale Royal, prince of Powys, is said to have succeeded to the principality of Gwynedd in right of his wife Essyllt, daughter of Cynan Tindaethwy, about A.D. 818 or 819.

PREFACE. xvii

we now are there are twenty-two cycles and three years in ogdoad of another cycle, which make up 421 years; in all 858.

In fixing the date of the fourth edition, the Editor makes the following computation: "A Passione "autem Christi peracti sunt anni DCCCLXXX.[1] Ab "Incarnatione autem ejus anni sunt DCCCCVII[1] usque "ad tricesimum annum Anarauht[2] regis Moniæ, id "est, Mon, qui regit modo regnum Wenedotiæ re- "gionis, id est Guernet; fiunt igitur ab exordio "mundi usque in annum præsentem 6108;" which makes the current year to be A.D. 907.

Fourth edition.

The current year of the fifth edition is thus indicated:—"Ita simul fiunt ab Adam usque ad Prædi- "cationem Christi et 15 annum imperii Imperatoris "Tiberii 5228. A Passione Christi peracti sunt anni "946. Ab Incarnatione autem ejus sunt anni 977."

Fifth edition.

In the documents, to which we have thus adverted, we do not discover any direct indication of a Prydain chronology; at the same time they contain nothing which tends to contradict it. The usage might have been observed more especially by the Bardic fraternity. Indeed we are in possession of chronological notices which profess to be in reality portions of the Register called "Cov a Chyvriv;" one in particular is printed in the collection known as the Iolo MSS.; and though, in its present form, not older than A.D. 1485, it purports to have been compiled on the ancient model. Thus runs the heading:—"Here follow the periods of memorial and computation, according to

No traces of a Prydain chronology in any of the editions of Nennius.

Memorial and computation.

---

[1] The numerals vary in most manuscripts. Those here supplied are concurrent with the year of the world 6108, according to the Eusebian calculation.

[2] Anarawd was the eldest son of Rhodri the Great, and grandson of Mervyn the Freckled. He is said to have succeeded to the principality of Gwynedd, or North Wales, about A.D. 877.

"the old system of the Bards of the Isle of Britain, as they were recorded and computed before the nation of the Cymry obtained the faith in Christ, and after that were introduced memorial and computation in respect of the time of Christ's coming in the flesh, as is the case in every country in Christendom." And at its close is this sentence;— "And thus is the information relating to the periods of memorial and computation of years, and the events of those years, as verified by scrutinizing investigation in respect of well-known and particular years and times, which were warranted by memorials and records drawn up according to the direction, memorials, and sciences of ancient wise men, literary persons, and the sciences of letters."[1]

Chronology of the document. In this chronicle the number of years which elapsed between remarkable epochs only is recorded; so that the date of a distant event is not computed directly from Prydain, but is ascertainable in reference to him by the process of adding up the numerical lengths of the several stages, which make up the intermediate series. Thus, if we wished to know how many years after Prydain Beli the Great flourished, we should have to add up the following: —twenty-nine years, which happened between Prydain and Dyvnvarth; a hundred and twenty-eight between Dyvnvarth and Gwrgan Varvdrwch; two hundred and four between Gwrgan and Morydd; forty-seven between Morydd and the period of Owen and Peredur; a hundred and eighteen between the death of Peredur and Blegywryd; and seventy-nine years between Blegywryd and Beli the Great; and accordingly we should arrive at the year 605. In this respect, indeed, it countenances the supposition that

---

[1] See Iolo MSS. p. 36.

the mode of computing from remarkable eras, adopted in Gildas and Nennius, was in reality founded upon the Prydain chronology.

It is remarkable that the several editions of Nennius, occupying a little more than three hundred years, exhibit a great similarity one to the other in the manner of chronicling events. Perhaps, this may be accounted for on the supposition that the editors successively did not consider themselves at liberty to deviate to any considerable extent from the rule adopted by their respective predecessors,—that they were impressed with the opinion that the mode of chronology, as well as the language of the narrative should be disturbed as little as possible. We perceive, however, a general tendency in them all to make the Christian era the grand point of chronology, especially for events which happened subsequently to the Nativity, though without discarding the year of the world. Both being thus in some degree coupled together would seem to substantiate the tradition about Arthur and his royal edict. Even Asser,[1] who generally dates from the Incarnation, might have derived the usage principally from his native land. *Mutual similarity of the several editions of Nennius in point of chronology.*

We do not mean to insinuate that the Britons were in no respect influenced by foreign authorities in the matters of arranging their chronological system; on the contrary, as Wales was in the sixth century studded with schools and colleges, in which the most eminent of our native saints and philosophers received their education, we think it very likely that these would avail themselves of all means of knowledge within their reach, whether derived from the works of Eusebius, St. Jerome, Prosper of Aqui- *The Welsh not uninfluenced by foreign authorities.*

According to the Welsh pedigrees, Asser was the son of Tudwal, the son of Rhodri the Great.

xx   PREFACE.

taine, or from Irish books. Such a course would have been quite in unison with the object of the Bardic Institute, of which St. David, St. Teilo, and St. Padarn, were members.[1] There was nothing that they could borrow from the Anglo-Saxons before the time of Bede, who, however, was not born when the work usually assigned to Nennius was first issued.

<small>Borrowed from an Irish chronicle.</small> In the tenth century we find that they did borrow from an Irish chronicle, at least in the matter of events and transactions.

<small>Annales Cambriæ.</small> The "Annales Cambriæ" is the first approach to a regular register of Welsh occurrences that meets our notice, and is apparently the basis of all subsequent chronicles relative to the principality of Wales. The chronology of this document is designated by the repetition of the word "annus" for each successive year, whether blank or otherwise, whilst every tenth year is marked x. xx, &c. From a comparison of dates assigned to many of the events noticed in it by other writers, it would appear that the era on which its chronology rests would concur with the year 444 of the Incarnation. There is no reason given for this particular date; but if it refers to some incident in the apostleship of St. Patrick, it may be taken as an argument in favour of the Irish origin of the chronicle. The mission of St. Patrick was adopted as a chronological stage or epoch even in Nennius.

<small>When compiled.</small> The "Annales Cambriæ" is supposed to have been originally compiled in the year 954, at which date the chronicle ends in the oldest manuscript.

<small>By whom.</small> The writer was evidently a partisan of Owain, son of Howel the Good, as he affixes the pedigree of that Prince to his chronicle.[2]

---

[1] "The three blessed Bards of "Baptism of the Isle of Britain; "Dewi, Teilo and Padarn." Triads of the Bards (unpublished).

[2] The oldest copy of this chronicle is a manuscript in the Harleian collection, No. 3859.

PREFACE. xxi

After this there is a lapse of about two hundred years, during which little or no attention seems to have been paid to the History or Literature of Wales, the troublous state of the times being evidently unfavourable to the cultivation of the same.

An interval of two hundred years comparatively barren of Welsh literature.

Towards the middle of the twelfth century Walter de Mapes, archdeacon of Oxford, a diligent enquirer after the antiquities of his nation, while journeying in Armorica, met with a History of Britain, written in Welsh.[1] Of this he published a Latin translation, which, coming under the notice of his contemporary Geoffrey of Monmouth, was by him much enlarged and embellished.[2]

Walter de Mapes's Chronicle.

The popularity of this version, which professes to treat of national affairs from the era of Brutus down to the abdication of king Cadwalader, seems to have added a fresh impulse to the study of British History. Geoffrey himself took an active part in promoting the movement, as he was well able to do from his position and great learning. At the end of one of his

Geoffrey of Monmouth commissions Caradog of Llancarvan to write a History of Wales.

---

[1] In *Breton*, according to a MS. History of the Kings of the 12th century, in the Library of Corpus Christi College, Cambridge.

[2] At the end of the chronicle called "Brut Tysilio," printed in the *Myvyrian Archaiology*, vol. ii., occurs the following statement:—"I, Walter, Archdeacon of Oxford, translated this Book from Welsh into Latin, and in my old age I translated it a second time from Latin into Welsh." Such a proceeding may, perhaps, be explained in this way:—that the archdeacon translated the work in the first instance from the Armorican or Breton dialect into Latin, and finally translated this Latin version into Welsh. This view is confirmed by the difference of language used at the end of a copy of Geoffrey of Monmouth in the Red Book, and in the statements appended to two other copies in the *Myvyrian Archaiology*. In the former it is said, "they have "not the *Breton* Book, which Wal- "ter, Archdeacon of Oxford, trans- "lated from Breton into Latin," but in the two latter "they have "not that Welsh Book." Seeing that Breton and Cymraeg are kindred dialects, bearing very strong resemblance to each other, it is very possible that an enthusiastic Welsh writer should have considered the former as his own language.

chronicles of the kings, a copy of which is inserted in the Red Book of Hergest, his purpose in this respect is announced as follows:—" The kings that were from "that time forward in Wales, I shall commit to "Caradog of Llancarvan, my fellow student, to write "about; and the kings of the English to William "Malmesbury and Henry Huntington. I shall desire "them to be silent about the kings of the Britons, "since they do not possess this Breton Book, which "Walter, archdeacon of Oxford, translated from Breton "into Welsh, which is truly a collection of their his- "tories, in honour of the said princes."

<small>The commission differently worded in other copies.</small>
Two copies, which are printed in the *Myvyrian Archaiology*, vol. ii., have their endings somewhat differently worded from the above. Here the commission given to Caradog is spoken of in the past tense, in the one copy thus:—" The princes who were after- "wards successively over Wales, I committed to "Caradog of Llancarvan; he was my contemporary, "and to him I left materials for writing that book. "From henceforward the kings of the English and "their successors I committed to William of Malmes- "bury and Henry of Huntington, to write about; "but they were to leave the Welsh alone; for they "do not possess that Welsh book, which Walter, "archdeacon of Oxford, translated from Latin into "Welsh; and he narrated truly and fully from the "history of the aforesaid Welshmen." The close of the second copy is much to the same effect, though there is evidently an unintentional omission in respect of William of Malmesbury, and Henry of Huntington.

<small>Caradog supposed to have been dead before Geoffrey.</small>
It would appear from a comparison of these statements not only that Geoffrey had actually entrusted Caradog with the task of compiling the Chronicle of the Princes, before he himself had finished the copies, which are printed in the *Myvyrian Archaiology*, but

that Caradog was now dead. "He *was* my contem-
"porary," is the expression used. In that case
Caradog must have ended his life before 1152, which
is the year in which Geoffrey is said to have died.[1]

The particulars of Caradog's life are very few, drawn [Life of Caradog.]
from fragmentary sources of various degrees of credi-
bility. He was the son of Llevoed,[2] who was the
domestic bard of Gruffudd, son of Morgan, son of
Iestyn, prince of Glamorgan; his native place being
the present county of Brecon, where he was born
about the middle of the eleventh century. The first
time, however, that he attracts our particular atten- [Sides with Iestyn.]
tion is as a partisan of Iestyn, in whose services he
lost his lands; but whether this was before the return
of Rhys, son of Tewdwr, from Armorica, in 1077,
when that prince made war upon Iestyn, or at some
other time, is not clear. According to one account [In favour with Rhys. Quarrels with him and retires into a monastery.]
Caradog was high in favour with Rhys, until, owing
to some differences that arose between them, he took
offence, and retired into a monastery. Another and a
more probable account says, that, because of the losses
which he suffered under Iestyn, he transferred his alle- [Sides with Gruffudd, son of Rhys.]
giance to Gruffudd, the son of Rhys, son of Tewdwr,
but that a misunderstanding ensuing between Rhys,

---

[1] Gwentian Chronicle apud Myv. Arch. v. ii.

[2] Llevoed Wynebglawr, or with the Flat Face. One of his compositions, being a moral piece, entitled "Gosymdeith," or the Journey of Life, is printed in the first volume of the *Myvyrian Archaiology*. It would appear almost incredible that Llevoed should have been attached to the household of a grandson of Iestyn, and yet that his son should have served under Iestyn himself, did we not consider the great age of the prince of Glamorgan, when he died. He is said to have married his first wife A.D. 994, and to have died at the age of 111 (according to others 129) "leaving behind him nine "sons and daughters, sixty-six "grandchildren, one hundred and "forty-one great grandchildren, "two hundred and nine great "great, grandchildren, and fifteen "great, great, great grandchildren."

xxiv   PREFACE.

                    the son of Gruffudd, and himself, he forsook him also,
Possesses a   and became a monk. If we may judge from these
bad temper.   angry outbursts, he does not seem to have been endowed
                    with the best of tempers; on the contrary they indi-
                    cate a vindictive and selfish spirit; though, if the
                    latter account be the true one, he did not abandon the
                    cause of Iestyn, until it had become absolutely hope-
                    less. For the veteran, on being dispossessed of his
                    territory by the Normans, in 1089, retired from public
Death of   view, and died at Keynsham, at the patriarchal age
Iestyn.   of a hundred and twenty-nine years.[1]
Gruffudd,   Gruffudd, who had been brought up in Ireland,
son of   crossed over into Wales in 1113. His arms were di-
Rhys.   rected chiefly against the English, Normans, and
                    Flemings, whom he defeated in numerous battles.
                    Having at length succeeded in recovering his domi-
                    nions, he celebrated the event by a splendid feast
                    at his palace of Ystrad Towy, to which he invited all
                    who could come in peace from every part of Wales.
                    The remainder of his reign he spent in reforming and
                    enforcing the laws of his kingdom. His death took
Rhys, son   place in 1136, when he was succeeded by his son Rhys,
of Gruf-   with whom Caradog quarrelled, but for what reason,
fudd.   we are not told. It had the effect, however, of driv-
                    ing him to seek the monk's cowl in the church of
                    St. Teilo at Llandav; from thence he retired to the
                    desolate church of St. Kened, thence to St. David's,
                    where he was made priest. He finally ended his life
                    as abbot of St. Ishmael's, in the present county of
                    Pembroke.
Date of   The date of his death is usually placed in the year
Caradog's   1156. A chronicle in the Red Book of Hergest places
death.   it about three years later: but according to the tenor

---

[1] According to one authority, published in the Iolo MSS. p. 22, his age, when he died, was 111.

PREFACE.   XXV

of some of Geoffrey of Monmouth's announcements,
appended to his Chronicle of the Kings, he must, as
before observed, have died prior to the year 1152,
unless we suppose that this is incorrectly assigned as
the year of Geoffrey's death.[1]

Giraldus Cambrensis informs us that Caradog was buried in the north transept of St. David's Cathedral, near the altar of St. Stephen.[2] He was canonized by Innocent III., at the instance of Giraldus,[3] and miracles are said to have been wrought at his tomb. *His burial place and canonization.*

Caradog inherited the poetical genius of his father, and is said to have composed many good songs, according to the art which prevailed in his time. There is a poem, of which he is reputed the author, printed in the *Myvyrian Archaiology*, vol. iii. p. 144; it is addressed to his friend and contemporary Gwgan the Bearded, the bard of Iestyn, and is followed by Gwgan's answer, likewise in verse. "Englynion yr "Asswynau" and "Englynion y Gorugau" are also attributed to him; but according to some authors the latter were the production of his father Llevoed, whilst in the *Iolo MSS.*, where they are printed, they are said to have been composed by Geraint the Blue Bard. Be that as it may, Caradog is better known, and more particularly distinguished among men of letters, as the compiler of "Brut y Tywysogion," or the Chronicle of the Princes. *His poetical compositions.*

Geoffrey's acquaintance with Caradog might have originated from his connection with Walter, archdeacon *Geoffrey's acquaintance with*

---

[1] The learned editors of the *History and Antiquities of Saint David's*, referring to *Nova Legenda Angliæ*, fol. iv., as their authority, place the death of Caradog in 1124.

[2] " Et sic Meneviam corpus al-
" latum crebra miracula tam præ-
" sentium quam sequentium quoque
" coruscatione, in ecclesiam Sancti
" Andreæ Sanctique David ala si-
" nistra juxta altare Sancti proto-
" martyris Stephani, debita est
" celebritate tumulatum."—*Giraldus Itin. Cambriæ I.* c. ii.

[3] Anglia Sacra, 11, p. 547.

xxvi   PREFACE.

<small>Caradog accounted for.</small>   of Oxford, who became a resident at Llancarvan, according to a Welsh account, in the following manner. Walter de Mapes, chaplain to Henry the First, was the second son of Blondel de Mapes, who accompaniad Fitzhamon, and acquired the lands of Gweirydd, son of Seisyllt, lord of Llancarvan, but had the generosity to marry Flur, the only child of Gweirydd that was living, by whom he had two sons, Hubert and Walter. Hubert dying without heirs, Walter inherited after his brother, and built the village of Trev Walter, now Walterston, and a mansion for himself. He restored most of the lands which he became possessed of to the original proprietors, and built the present church of Llancarvan.[1]

<small>Considers him qualified to write a History of the Princes.</small>   Being thus introduced to him, and finding Caradog of a similar turn of mind to himself, and engaged in the same literary pursuits, for, as Pitsius observes, " uterque fuit natione Britannus, uterque etiam simi- " libus studiis deditus, uterque elegans Poeta, eloquens " Rhetor, Historicus non contemnendus;"[2] it is but

---

[1] Walter de Mapes, in addition to other benefits which he conferred upon his adopted country, wrote a very sensible treatise on agriculture in Welsh, which is extant in several manuscripts.

[2] Jó. Pitsius, de Illustribus Angliæ Scriptoribus, p. 215. ed. Paris. 1619. The author further enumerates the books which Caradog wrote;—" Nam scripsit de regibus Walliæ, qui regnare ultra montes cœperunt, postquam e reliqua Britannia per Anglos et Saxones expulsi fuerunt; incipiensque ab Idwalla primo post Cadwalladrum Venedotarum regulo, scripsit res gestas Britannorum per annos quadringentos circiter et sexaginta usque ad suam ætatem. Juxta disticon, *Historiam Britonum doctus scripsit Historiam Britonum, librum unum.* MS. Cantabrigiæ in Collegio S. Benedicti. *De situ orbis, librum unum. Commentarios in prophetias Merlini, librum unum.* Nondum autem ad hunc locum. *Vitam Gildæ Albanii, liorum unum.* Navus fit rex Pictorum nobil. Quem librum hoc sequente distico conclusisse perhibetur:

' *Historiæ veteris Gildæ luculentus
    arator
  Hæc retulit, parvo carmine plura
    notans.*'

Claruit Caradocus anno gratiæ 1150, sub perturbato in Anglia Steghan regno."

natural that Geoffrey should have considered the Welsh student of Llancarvan as eminently qualified to compile the work he had in view, and for which he in a great degree supplied him with materials.

There are several copies of the Chronicles of the Princes preserved in MS., all of which, whilst they differ more or less in style, generally agree in matter, with the exception of one, which differs so completely from the others, both in style and narrative of facts, as to lead to the belief of their being the works of different writers. General agreement of the chronicles attributed to Caradog.

We are informed by Guttyn Owain, a bard and herald, who flourished in the fifteenth century,[1] that Caradog terminated his labours in the year 1156, and that the successions and acts of the princes of Wales were subsequently registered in the monastic establishments of Strata Florida and Conway. The events thus recorded yearly were conferred together ordinarily every third year, when the bards attached to those two abbeys went from the one to the other in the time of their clera, or triennial visitation.[2] Testimony of Guttyn Owain.

These particulars, in addition to such other facts as may be supplied from an examination of the different compositions, must guide us in our efforts to discover the real authorship. We will now, therefore, cursorily review the principal characteristics of the various forms which have reached our times. Guides towards finding out the authorship of the Chronicle of the Princes.

The manuscript which differs so considerably from the others, was found in Glamorganshire, and has been published in the *Myvyrian Archaiology*, vol. ii. The Gwentian Chronicle.

---

[1] Guttyn Owain was historian and herald bard to the abbeys of Basingwerk and Strata Florida, and resided alternately in those two monasteries. He was the second person named by Henry VII. in the commission to enquire into the pedigree of his grandfather, Owain Tudor. He died about 1480.

[2] All the details of the Bardic visitation were regulated by statute.

xxviii   PREFACE.

It professes to relate "how wars and paramount 'occurrences, revenges, and remarkable incidents, "took place; extracted from the old preserved records, "and regularly dated by Caradog of Llancarvan."[1] From this heading we might expect satisfactory and conclusive grounds for pronouncing the work, or rather the former part of it, to be the genuine compilation of the historian of Llancarvan. The chronicle terminates in 1196; but here comes the difficulty, that no perceptible discrepancy enables us to trace the language of more than one writer. If, therefore, part is to be attributed to Caradog, for it is not reasonable to suppose that he was the compiler of the whole, a subsequent author has added an indefinite portion, not distinguishable from the prior part. The language, indeed, though modernised in its orthography, may well be considered as that of the twelfth century, which was, perhaps, the most resplendent period of Welsh literature. It may also be that of the sixteenth century, as in its orthographical form it undoubtedly is. It is very much the same as that of the Historical Triads, which are said to have been "taken from the "book of Caradog of Nantcarvan, and the book of "Ieuan Brechva."[2]

Want of uniformity in the manner of recording events.

But though the language is uniform throughout, there is a difference perceptible in the manner of recording events from about the year 1150 to the

---

[1] To this heading is added in the *Myvyrian Archaiology* the following statement relative to the source whence the copy in question was obtained:—"The above history was copied from the Book of George Williams of Aberpergwm, Esquire, by me Thomas Richards, curate of Llangrallo, in the year 1764. And I Iorwerth, son of Iorwerth Gwilym, copied it out of the Book of the Rev. Mr. Richards in the year 1790; and recopied it for Owain Myvyr, in the autumn of the year 1800."

[2] "These Triads were extracted from the Book of Caradog of Nantgarvan, and from the Book of Ieuan Brechva, by me, Thomas Jones of Tregaron; and this is all I could find of the three hundred—1601."

end. The narrative in this interval is much more meagre and cursory than that which occupies the former part of the work, and we fain would trace in it the finger of a different writer.

The year 1150 coincides so nearly with the date at which, according to Guttyn Owain, Caradog finished his chronicle, that we hesitate not to accept it as the true date, especially as we have another chronicle, purporting to have been "taken from the books of Caradog " of Llancarvan, and other old books of information," which absolutely terminates at that very period. *The date at which the chronicle of Caradog ends.*

It is not improbable, indeed, that some of his earlier copies ended in 1150, and that transcripts were made by him a little before his death, to which the intermediate events were added. *Different copies supposed to have ended at different times.*

We cannot from any internal evidence infer that this was a copy of the register, which was deposited either at Strata Florida or Conway, and yearly augmented by the inmates, there being no allusion whatsoever to either of those two establishments. *The Gwentian not one of the monastic Chronicles.*

It seems then that the only conclusion which we are warranted in arriving at is, that the chronicle in question is the real production of Caradog, but revised more or less, and thoroughly recast, as to the style of language, by a person living subsequently to A.D. 1196, who, moreover, added the entries of the last 46 years. *Inferred to be a revised edition of the work of Caradog, subsequently to 1196.*

Another chronicle, already alluded to, bears the title of "the Chronicle of Ieuan Brechva. A record of " princes, battles, remarkable events, revenges, and " other notable occurrences; taken from the books of " Caradog of Llancarvan and other old books of in- " formation."[1] It differs in some instances from the *The Chronicle of Ieuan Brechva.*

---

[1] "Out of the Book of Rhys Thomas, printer." Myv. Arch. vol. ii. p. 470. Ieuan Brechva was an eminent poet, historian, and herald of Caermarthenshire, who died about 1500.

xxx   PREFACE.

other chronicles, but in general agrees with the preceding one. The notices are very meagre, and the whole work is evidently an abridgment.

Date of its termination. Ieuan Brechva, the author, flourished in the sixteenth century. He concludes the epitome under consideration with the year 1150, a fact which, in conjunction with the difference to be perceived in the copy just examined, leads to the supposition that this also was founded upon the same basis.

Not the original or genuine work of Caradog. Indeed, if this chronicle had professed to have been extracted from the works of Caradog alone, there could have been but little difficulty in the matter; but the mention of "other old books of information" would indicate a certain amount of tampering with the original text of Caradog.

The Chronicle either of Strata Florida or of Aberconway. A chronicle, of which numerous copies of considerable antiquity are in existence, the most extensively diffused over Wales, and which must certainly have originated either from Strata Florida or Conway, demands attentive consideration. It has no proem, similar to the above, but immediately enters upon the subject, and the narrative is carried on in an uniform style to the year 1120. At this period a remarkable alteration is strikingly perceptible; the narrative of the events of the twenty years included between 1100 and 1120 occupies a space double to that devoted to the history of the period which elapsed between 1120 and 1164, the date of the foundation of the monastery of Strata Florida. The prior portion is written by a person favourable to the Normans, or fearful of giving offence to them. He remarks that "William defended " the kingdom of England in a great battle, with an " invincible hand, and his most noble army" (p. 47), and died " after a sufficiency of the glory and fame " of this transient world, and after glorious victories " and the honour acquired by riches" (p. 53). "A.D " 1091, Rhys, son of Tewdwr, king of South Wales,

" was killed by the French, who inhabited Brecheiniog,
" and then fell the kingdom of the *Britons*" (p. 55).
About 1113, Gruffudd, son of Rhys, aspired to his
father's possessions in South Wales, and at the commencement of his career destroyed some of the Norman
castles. This success, according to the historian,
incited "many foolish young men from every part to
" join him, being deceived by the desire of spoils, or
" seeking to repair and restore the British kingdom.
" But the will of man does not avail anything unless
" God assists him." (p. 125.) This has evident allusion to the transference of the " British kingdom "
to the English sovereigns on the death of Rhys, the
father of Gruffudd, intimated before. He then narrates
a successful expedition by Gruffudd against the garrison
of the castle of Caermarthen and the castle of William
de Londres in Gower; he observes, " that as Solomon
" says, the spirit becomes elevated against the fall
" of man," Gruffudd "prepared, being swollen with
" pride, and with the presumption of the unruly
" rabble and the silly inhabitants, to arrange foolish
" expeditions from Dyved into Ceredigion, and to take
" the part opposed to equity, being invited by Cedi-
" vor, son of Goronwy, and Howel, son of Idnerth,
" and Trahaiarn, son of Ithel, who were near in
" proximity of kindred and acquaintance, and who
" agreed that he should have dominion." And above
all, "fearing to offend King Henry, the man who
" had subdued all the sovereigns of the isle of Bri-
" tain by his power and authority, and who had
" subjugated many countries beyond sea under his
" rule, some by force and arms, others by innume-
" rable gifts of gold and silver; the man with whom
" no one could strive but God alone, from Whom
" he obtained the power." (pp. 128, 129.) He then
describes the progress of Gruffudd in Ceredigion, and
states "that the men of the country, instigated by

"the devil, flocked to him suddenly, and as it
"were of one accord," and spoiled and killed the
Saxons there (p. 131). They then "without setting up
"standards, a villain host, like a company of people
"without counsel and without a commander, took
"their course towards the castle of Aberystwyth,"
where they were defeated (p. 133). King Henry then
sent for Owain, son of Cadwgan, and addressed him:—
"My most beloved Owain, art thou acquainted with
"that thief Gruffudd, son of Rhys, who is like a
"fugitive before my commanders; for and because I
"believe thee to be a most loyal man to me, I
"will that thou be commander of an army with
"my son, to expel Gruffudd, son of Rhys, and I
"will make Llywarch, son of Trahaiarn, thy com-
"panion, because I place confidence in you two; and
"when thou returnest back I will properly reward
"thee" (p. 135). This arrangement is, however, rendered inoperative by Owain falling in with an army of Flemings, headed by Gerald, who kill him (p. 139).

Omissions. Although the narrative is very diffusive, and the occurrences of each year detailed at great length, we find not the slightest allusion to the conquest of Glamorgan by Fitzhamon,[1] or to the reverses which his successor Robert, earl of Gloucester, experienced when he attacked his uncle Gruffudd, or to this earl's capture by Ivor Petit, and constrained departure from Cardiff, occasioned by the indignant resistance of the native population to the tyranny of their oppressors. These incidents, the latter of which a Welshman, truly attached to his country, would have exulted in relating, we are left to gather from other sources; the author of this work has omitted them.

---

[1] The conquest of Glamorgan is detailed at considerable length in the Gwentian Chronicle.

PREFACE. xxxiii

Still, perhaps, we ought to regard the spirit manifested in respect of the Normans as arising more from a feeling of consciousness in his breast of their being necessary and irresistible instruments in the hands of Divine providence to punish the national iniquity of the Welsh, than from any spontaneous sympathy with them in their work of aggression. At times, indeed, sparks of patriotism do clearly burst out, as when the writer, observing the treacherous propensities of the Normans, indignantly indites, "as is the " manner of the French to deceive people by promises" (p. 121). His apparent partiality for the Normans accounted for.

About 1120 another writer, or else the same writer under the influence of another spirit, for a bias is manifestly observable in favour of the Welsh, takes up the subject. Under 1124 we read that the same Gruffudd, previously so vituperated, was deprived of the land which the king had given him, " after he had " been innocently and undeservedly accused by the " French" (p. 153). Some encomiastic expressions are generally applied to the Welsh princes at this period. Under 1129 we have a notice of the death of Maredudd, "the ornament and safety and defence of all " Powys, after undergoing salvatory penance of his " body and sanctity of repentance in his spirit, and " the communion of the body of Christ, and extreme " unction." (p. 157). These religious solemnities, mention of which is now for the first time introduced into the text, are henceforth repeatedly expressed to have taken place upon the demise of the princes of the three districts of the principality. In 1135, Owain and Cadwalader, the sons of Gruffudd, prince of North Wales, are said to be "the ornament of all " the Britons, their safety, their liberty, and their " strength; men who were two noble and two generous " kings, two dauntless ones; two brave lions; two " blessed ones; two eloquent ones; two wise ones; Difference of sentiments.

"protectors of the churches, and their champions;
"the defenders of the poor; the slayers of the foes;
"the pacifiers of the quarrelsome; the tamers of
"antagonists; the safest refuge to all who should flee
"to them; the men who were pre-eminent in energies
"of souls and bodies; and jointly upholding in unity
"the whole kingdom of the Britons." (p. 159.) A
battle which took place at Aberdovey in the same
year is described, in which, it is said, "the Flemings
"and the Normans took to flight, according to their
"usual custom," (p. 161). In 1136, the writer notices
the death of Gruffudd and styles him "the light and
"strength and gentleness of the men of South Wales,"
(p. 161).

Not inconsistent with the idea of Caradog being the author.

Having called attention to these facts, the question arises, are they inconsistent with the view which attributes to Caradog the authorship of this Chronicle? We think not: on the contrary the change of bias from one political body to another, which characterizes the text, is in perfect harmony with what we learn of Caradog in the scanty memorials that have come down to us, though it would be difficult, no doubt, to reconcile the order in which variations of this kind occur with that of his life.[1]

Difference in the style of composition.

But besides such variations as are indicated by a change of sentiments, there is a difference here and there perceptible in the style of composition. The chronicle commences A.D. 680. It does not give the events under each year, but under each decade as 690, 700, 710, &c., and registers a series of occurrences without comment until six or seven years prior to 1100. At that period it commences the use of the phrase "Y vlwydyn rac wyneb," (the ensuing year,)

---

[1] Thus, one would have naturally expected, from what is stated in his life that the reproaching of Gruffudd, son of Rhys, would have followed, rather than, as in the Chronicle, preceded his eulogy.

before each year, under which events are recorded, until the next decade, successively, and the narrative is carried on in an uniform style to the year 1120. At this period again a remarkable alteration is very perceptible. As before observed, the narrative of the events of the twenty years included between 1100 and 1120 occupies a space double to that devoted to the history of the period which elapsed between 1120 and 1164. There is nothing whatever to indicate a change of writers about the period which is usually assigned as the termination of Caradog's labours.

The first part—the portion taken up in registering events to about the year 1100, may be considered as the History of the Principality, current in the different divisions of Wales. From that date it enters into a detailed account or occurrences in Gwynedd or North Wales, and Dyved or West Wales, particularly of events in Cardiganshire, and but very cursorily notices those of Gwent. *Scope of the Chronicle.*

If Caradog is to be considered as the author of the chronicle down to about 1150, the variation in the style must be regarded as a reflection of the original draught or copy, which formed the basis of his compilation. And if no other writer could use a similar language in continuing the narrative, we are driven to suppose that the whole was a translation from the Latin. *Difference in style, and uniformity of language accounted for.*

In the absence of any Latin transcript of this form, it is difficult to decide whether the chronicle was indeed originally a Welsh compilation, or a translation. The language of the Welsh text, at least at the commencement, betrays a Latin origin; this is more strikingly apparent in the manuscript marked C., in which the rendering is frequently erroneous. Thus under 789, it has "gyd " ac Offa," for *cum* or *apud Offa*, which are the expressions used in the oldest copy of the *Annales Cambriæ.*[1] *The Chronicle supposed to be a translation from the Latin.*

---

[1] Another version has *ab Offa*. The proper Welsh would have been " gan Offa."

Under 827, "vwa Deganwy" is evidently a mistaken translation of *arx Deganhui*,[1] found in a later version of the *Annales*. Under 863, *Duta* seems to have been rendered "hono;" and under 1096, *Magnus* is translated "Mawrus."[2]

The Book of Conway quoted. We have already intimated that this chronicle must have come to us from either Conway or Strata Florida. In "British Antiquities Revived," by Mr. Robert Vaughan, we meet with quotations from a chronicle, styled by the illustrious author the Book of Conway;[3] these excerpts are found in that which we are now considering. A great similarity in the productions of both establishments may be inferred from what Guttyn Owain says, namely, that the annalists of those two monasteries ordinarily compared their entries, one with the other, every three years. No copies which have descended to us, profess to be derived from either of those places, but the preponderance of internal evidence is in favour of a Strata Florida emanation.

Reasons for supposing our Chronicle to be that of Strata Florida. The reasons which have led us to consider it as having been derived from Strata Florida, have been the following.—The prominent manner in which the foundation of the abbey is introduced to the reader;—"In "that year (1164), by the permission of God and

---

[1] "Bwa" (of which vwa is a mutate), is a *bow* or *arch*; in Latin *arcus*.

[2] From "mawr," *great*. L. magnus.

[3] "The rest he reserved to himselfe, saving Dywalwern, a little piece of Cyveiliog, which he gave the Lord Rees, because (according to the Book of Conway) the report went that it stood within the confines of the said Rees his dominions." *Br. Antiq. Revived*, Ed. 1834, p. 14. Compare this with what is said in the Chronicle under 1166. Again,

"And in the year of our Lord 1164 (just 20 yeares before the date of the former Charter) as witnesseth the Book of Conway, it [i.e. Strata Florida] was first covented." Br. Antiq. Rev. p. 37. See under that year in the Chronicle. Further, "Witnesse the office of being Justice of South Wales, which the king had given him three years before that peace at Gloucester, as the Book of Conway mentioneth." Br Antiq. Rev. p. 44. See Chronicle, p. 209.

" the inspiration of the Holy Spirit, *came* a con-
" vent of monks first to Strata Florida:" (p. 203),
and the brief way in which we are informed that
the establishment of Conway emanated from Strata
Florida; — "In the same year (1186), about the
" month of July, the convent of Strata Florida,"
or a society from Strata Florida, "went to Rhedynog Velen in Gwynedd," (p. 233). In the margin of
the manuscript marked E., this place is stated to be
" Maenan," to which the monks of Aberconway were
removed by Edward I.—The number of local events
narrated, interesting to the inmates; among which
we may class the burials of twenty-two distinguished
personages, including four abbots of the place; whereas
the number of similar occurrences, stated to have taken
place at Conway, amounts to only five.—The mention
of six abbots by name, one of whom, Gruffudd, made
his peace with king Henry, and compounded for his
dues (p. 335). We find no mention of an abbot of Conway but once, that is to say, when the body of prince
Gruffudd was delivered up to the abbots of Strata
Florida and Conway, in London, and conveyed by them
to Aberconway for burial (p. 335). We read, "1201,
" on the eve of Whitsunday, the monks of Strata
" Florida came to the new church; which had been
" erected of splendid workmanship," (p. 257). Under
1238, mention is made of the fealty sworn by the
chieftains of Wales to David, son of Llywelyn, at
Strata Florida," (p. 327). Under 1254, we have the
price of the great bell at Strata Florida; and 1280,
the burning of the monastery. Many other entries
might be adduced, to exemplify the great interest
taken in registering incidents which occurred at Strata
Florida, instances of which are rare in regard to Conway. The above have been selected as the most prominent, and elucidatory of the source of the work in
its present form.

The Chronicle of Caradog of Llancarvan the basis of it.

As there seems then no doubt that the record we have been discussing is the veritable chronicle of Strata Florida, we are obliged, in the absence of any evidence to the contrary, or which has not yet occurred to us, to accept the statement of Guttyn Owain, that the basis or groundwork is none other than that which was laid down by Caradog of Llancarvan, at the instance of Geoffrey of Monmouth. In other words, that he compiled the prior part, though we cannot tell exactly at what period his labours ended, or what amount of transformation, if any, it underwent at the hands of the monks, or bards attached to the establishment, who undoubtedly continued and completed the register.

Source of Caradog's materials.

But whence did Caradog obtain his materials? We are informed in the announcement appended to the Chronicle of the Kings that they were, at least some of them, supplied to him by Geoffrey, and that these were mainly contained in "the Breton Book, which Walter, "archdeacon of Oxford, translated from Breton into "Welsh, which is truly a collection of their histories, "in honour of the said princes." In addition to this book, Caradog might have availed himself of the *Annales Cambriæ*;[1] indeed, there is every reason to believe that he did so; also of, "other old books of in-"formation," which no doubt had been preserved in different parts of the country, whether in monasteries or among the Bards. The events that occurred between about 1077 and 1150 would come, more or less, under his own immediate notice. From 1164 to the end the entries were continued regularly by the annalists of Strata Florida, who, in all probability also supplied the registers of the interval between the death of

---

[1] This work is now being prepared for the press, and is intended to form one of the series of works published by the authority of the Lords Commissioners of Her Majesty's Treasury, under the direction of the Master of the Rolls.

Caradog and the foundation of their own society, from authentic sources.

The chronology of the Strata Florida Chronicle is regulated by decades. Down to nearly the close of the eleventh century, there is nothing whatever to distinguish the intermediate years. From that period forth they are discriminated respectively by the simple phrase "the ensuing year." This chronological arrangement seems to have been copied from the *Annales Cambriæ;* an attempt having been made by the compiler to adapt the decennary notation observed in that work to the era of the Incarnation. It has, however, been so carelessly executed that the intervals which, according to the *Annales,* should exhibit the events of ten years, at one time contain those of three, at another of sixteen years.

Chronology of the Strata Florida Chronicle.

The writer of the Gwentian version has, from some sources unknown to us, supplied the intermediate years throughout, which improving process of itself strongly indicates it to be of posterior date to the other.

Powel,[1] in the preface to his "Historie of Cambria," asserts the existence of upwards of a hundred

Number of copies.

---

[1] David Powel, lineally descended from Llywelyn Aurdorchog, was born in Denbighshire about the year 1552. Having completed his education at Oxford, and received holy orders, he was made vicar of Ruabon in his native country in 1570, and prebendary of St. Asaph, and in the following year he obtained the rectory of Llanvyllin, which latter he resigned on being preferred to the vicarage of Meivod in 1579. The sinecure rectory of Llansantfraid in Mechain was added to his preferments in 1588. He was now grown eminent for his learning, and took the degree of B.D. in 1582, and that of D.D. in 1583. In 1584 he became chaplain to Sir Henry Sidmouth, Lord President of the Marches of Wales, who had in his possession the unfinished translation of Caradog's Chronicle of the Princes by the eminent antiquary Humphrey Lwyd. At his lordship's solicitation Dr. Powel completed the translation, and enriched the work with many valuable additions. This was printed in 1584 in 4to, and is the work referred to above. He was also the author of "*Annotationes in Itinerarium*

copies of the Chronicle of the Princes, "whereof," he says, "the most part were written two hundred "yeares ago," that is, about 1384. Time has in the last two centuries and a half considerably lessened the number. Perhaps the assertion may have likewise been too unqualified, for it is evident that he did not accurately examine them, otherwise he would not have stated that these records ceased in 1270, most of those now remaining terminating in 1282; the events of the last twelve years being detailed at considerable length, which ought to have found a place in his compilation. The Chronicle of the Kings, at present, occurs much more frequently in libraries than the Chronicle of the Princes; and it is probable that this was the case at former periods, if we allow the proportion which obtains in the British Museum and Hengwrt Collections, where copies of the former greatly preponderate, to have been general. In the Museum we meet with no Chronicles of the Princes in the Welsh language, and but three Latin transcripts; at least such was the case a few years ago. Hengwrt library contains but three, and those Welsh which is the number inserted in the catalogue of that collection, drawn up in the time of Mr. Robert Vaughan,[1] the founder of it. The library of Glodd-

---

Cambriæ, scriptum per Sil. Giraldum Cambrensem." The same volume also contains " *Annotationes in Cambriæ descriptionem per S. Giraldum,"* and " *De Britannica Historica recte intelligenda Epistola."* He likewise published in 1585, "*Historia Britannica,*" or the British History, written by Ponticus Virunius, in six books. Dr. Powel also rendered essential service to Dr. Morgan in the translation of the Holy Scriptures into Welsh, which was completed and published in 1588. He died in 1598.

[1] Robert Vaughan was born in 1592 at Hengwrt, near Dolgelley, in Merionethshire. He entered the university as a commoner of Oriel College, in 1612, but he left without taking a degree, and retired to his patrimony at Hengwrt, where he cultivated those studies that have rendered his name so celebrated, and of such authority on all subjects connected with Welsh history and

aith, which has been unaffected by fluctuations, has three.

Nevertheless we have no reason to disbelieve the general statement of Powel as to the great number of copies which existed at one time in Wales, though they probably differed much in style and phraseology, owing to the variety of hands employed upon them. John Rhydderch, a poet and grammarian, who flourished from 1700 to 1730, hath given us a list of Welsh historians, who for the most part lived in the fifteenth and sixteenth centuries; it is as follows :— *Welsh historians in the 15th and 16th centuries.*

"Richard Broughton, one of the Councell of the
"Marches, writ concerning all England, and partes be-
"yond the seas: who had a commission to search the
"ancient records in White Hall (*the White Tower of*
"*London*) that were lost (*i.e. could not be found*)
"*per* the Gentlemen and Poets.

"George Owen, Lord of Kemmes, in Pembrook-
"shire, hath writ concerning all Britain.

"John Lewis, a Lawyer, hath write concerning all
"B.

"Evan Lewis, ap David ap John, Esqr., hath
"written concerning all England and Wales.

"Thomas Jones of Tregaron, gent., hath written
"concerning Great Britain.

"John Mil, of Tre'r Delyn, gent., hath written
"concerning Great Britain.

"Thomas ap Llewelyn ap Ithel, of Bodvary, in
"Flint, hath written concerning all Britain.

---

antiquities. To this end he was engaged in an extensive correspondence with persons of similar pursuits, among whom were Archbishop Usher, Sir S. D'Ewes, Selden, and other eminent antiquaries. He formed at Hengwrt an unrivalled collection of Welsh manuscripts, many of which are of very early date. This collection was recently bequeathed by the late Sir R. W. Vaughan, Bart. to W. W. E. Wynne of Peniarth, Esq. M.P. We have chosen, however, to retain the old designation, as being better known to the literary world. Robert Vaughan died in 1666.

"John ap William ap John,[1] of the same county, hath written concerning all Britain.

"Sir Edward Mansel, of Glamorgan, knt., hath written concerning Great Britain.

"Sir Edward Stradling, k^t., hath written concerning all Britain.

"Rees ap Meyrick, of Cottrel, gent., who was author of one of the fairest and most inquisitive books in all Wales, and he hath written concerning all England.

"Anthony Powel, of Tir yr Earle, hath written concerning Great Britain.[2]

"The names of the authorized Poets who hath written concerning England and Wales:

"Iolo Goch, Master of Arts, Poet Lawrell or Cheif Poet, who hath written concerning the 3 provinces of Wales, and he was the cheifest of Poets.

"Howel Swrdwal, Master of Arts, Poet Lawrel, or Cheif Poet, who hath written concerning the three provinces of Wales, and made a fair choronology in Latin, from Adam to Edward 1st, and write the Welsh Choronickle, which was with Owen Gwynedd, the Poet.

"Guttun Owen, Poet Lawrel, of Maelor, hath written concerning the three provinces, and his Books be very faire.

"Evan Brechva, of South Wales, hath written concerning the three provinces of Wales.

"David ap Edmond, Poet Lawrel, or Cheif Musician, who win'd the Gold Chair, at the Excellent Convocation or Sitting, South Wales. He lived at

---

[1] This was John Jones of Gelli Lyvdy, whose volumes of MSS. amounting to upwards of fifty, are now preserved in the Hengwrt library. Among them is an exact copy, written by himself, of the Strata Florida Chronicle, which in all probability, is the history alluded to here.

[2] This is probably the Chronicle of the Saxons, alluded to in note at page xlvi, *post.*

"Hanmer, and hath written concerning the three
"provinces of Wales.

"Gutto 'r Glynn, Poet Lawrel, Cheif Musician, one
"of the Bards or Poets that belong'd to W^m. Herbert,
"sen., Earl of Pembrook, and he hath written con-
"cerning the three provinces.

"David ap Howel ap Howel ap Evan Vaughan,
"Poet Lawrel, or Cheif Musician, hath written con-
"cerning the three Provinces.

"Howel ap Sir Mathew, Poet Lawrel, hath written
"concerning the three provinces.

"Griffith Hiraethog, Poet Lawrel, or Cheif Musician,
"and Deputy at Armes over all Wales, under the
"Garter; he hath written concerning all Britain, and
"his Disciples had his Books, viz.:

"W^m. Llyn, Poet Lawrel; Owen Gwynedd, Poet
"Lawrel; Simon Vaughan, Cheif Poet; John Tudur,
"Cheif Poet; W^m. Cynwal, Poet; and John Philip,
"Poet. And they all writt very industriously con-
"cerning Wales, as appeareth per their Bookes, to this
"very day.

"Lewis Morganwg, Poet Lawrel, or Cheife Musician;
"he hath written concerning the three provinces,
"and Meurig David, and David Benwyn, Glamorgan-
"shire, Poets, had his Books, and they were fairly
"written.

"John Brwywnog, Poet Lawrel, or Cheif Musician,
"of Anglesey, hath written concerning the 3 pro-
"vinces.

"John Wynn ap D. David ap Griffri, of Mont-
"gomeryshire, gent., hath written concerning all
"Wales.

"Robyn Achwr, of Northwales, hath written con-
"cerning the 3 provinces.

"Maurice ap Dackin ap Pierce Treven, of Betus
"Cadewen, in Powis, gent., hath written concerning
"all Wales.

xliv   PREFACE.

"Rees Cain, of Oswestree, who was Wm. Llyn's
"Disciple, and a perfect man, and he hath written
"concerning all Wales."[1]

The text of our Chronicle, whence taken.   The work now presented to the public is that which we believe to have come to us from Strata Florida. The text of it, marked A., has been taken from the Red Book of Hergest, now preserved in the archives of Jesus College, Oxford. At one time this manuscript was in the possession of the Mansell family, one of whom, Francis, was elected principal of Jesus College in 1620. It was lent by Lewis Mansell to Dr. John Davies, the author of the Welsh Grammar, who removed it from Glamorgan into North Wales. It subsequently passed into the hands of Thos. Wilkins, who presented it to the Welsh College, at Oxford, in 1701. The manuscript is a large folio, magnificently bound in morocco, of a colour to correspond with its designation of Red Book. The name Hergest refers to the place where it was originally found, in South Wales. It consists of 1442 columns, there being two columns in each page, thus making 721 pages in all. Count de la Villemarque in his "Notices des principaux Manuscrits "des Anciens Bretons,"[2] expresses his opinion that it was written at different times, the former portion about 1318, indicated in column 516, the latter about 1454, in which year died Gwladus, whose elegy is sung by Lewis Glyn Cothi, and is inserted in column 1409. The Chronicle of the Princes commences in column 230, and belongs therefore to the former portion of the manuscript.

Contents of the Red Book.   The volume contains a variety of subjects; chronicles, romances, popular tales, historic triads, treatises on

---

[1] The above list occurs at p. 91 of John Rhydderch's MS., and is printed among the notes at p. 331 of Lewis Dwn's "Heraldic Visitation of Wales," vol. 1.
[2] Paris. Imprimerie Impériale. 1856.

grammar, versification, and physic, as well as poems from the sixth century to the fifteenth, all of them being written in the Welsh language.

This manuscript has been selected on account of its being entire, and written throughout in the same dialect, the Dimetian, as the majority of existing copies. It has been collated with two manuscripts at Hengwrt, designated as B. and C., with the Cottonian manuscript Cleopatra, B. v., here marked D., and also with the book of Basingwerk, marked E., now belonging to T. T. Griffiths, Esquire, of Wrexham. Collated with other MSS.

The manuscript marked B. is a small quarto volume on vellum, in the Hengwrt library. It is imperfect at the commencement; but is the most correct of all the manuscripts, and written in purest Dimetian dialect. At the commencement of each decade a place has been left for the illuminated initial. It is evidently older than manuscript A., as may be inferred not only from the character of the handwriting, but also from certain expressions used; for instance, manuscript A. relates of a certain people "then they were dwelling about the " borders of the country " (p. 103), but the expression employed in manuscript B. is " they are still dwelling," which clearly points to an earlier period of time. It was probably written about the end of the thirteenth century. The variations in these two manuscripts are very few and unimportant, which makes it very probable that one is a direct copy of the other. Fac similes of both are given with the present edition. Description of manuscript B.

C. is a Venedotian manuscript on vellum, agreeing in matter with the preceding, but totally differing in phraseology. The chronicle is carried down to 1282, at which period there is a break to mark the termination of the copy before the writer. The narrative is then continued to 1332. In addition to the Chronicle of the Princes this volume contains a religious commentary, a Welsh grammar, and poetical institutes, Description of manuscript C.

d

xlvi   PREFACE.

with some Welsh poetry. It was written about the sixteenth century.

Description of manuscript D. — The manuscript marked D.[1] is a corrupted version of the preceding chronicle, amalgamated with the Annals of Winton, in order to connect, and detail, contemporaneous occurrences in England and Wales. The portion devoted to Welsh events is very carelessly constructed, the facts being in many instances perverted, and the language frequently obscure. This manuscript is in the Cottonian collection at the British Museum, and is there marked Cleopatra, B. v.; it is written on vellum, and may be ascribed to the latter end of the fifteenth century.

Description of manuscript E. — Manuscript E. is a compilation of a similar character. It was written by the celebrated bard and herald Guttyn Owain, and is styled in some catalogues, "The Book of Basing," on account of having been in the library of Basingwerk Abbey. The prior part of this manuscript contains an imperfect version of the Chronicle of the Kings, written about the end of the fourteenth century; to supply the deficiency Guttyn Owain added the remainder from a dissimilar copy. It was this manuscript that the Rev. Peter Roberts adopted as the foundation for his publication of the Chronicle of the Kings,[2] and he considers it to be alto-

---

[1] In the following extract this chronicle also is attributed to Caradog of Llancarvan:—" This is the History, called the Chronicle of the Saxons, composed by Caradog of Llancarvan, in Glamorgan, that is to say, a memorial of the kings of the Isle of Britain, who were Saxons, after the time of Cadwalader the Blessed, who was the last of the kings of the Britons, that had been kings of the island even from the time of Prydain, the son of Aedd the Great, until the time of the said Cadwalader, which was one thousand two hundred and fifty thee years, according to the Register of Memorials. And it was I Antony Powel of Tir Iarll in Glamorgan that wrote it from an old book at Plas y Bettws, which had been at Llwydarth. (The book of John Phillip of Treos)."—*Welsh MS.*

[2] A Chronicle of the Kings of Britain, translated from the Welsh of Tysilio, 4to. 1811.

gether a transcript by Guttyn Owain. He remarks the great change in the style at the part alluded to, but did not notice the variation in the handwriting and orthography, which distinction is sufficiently obvious. Guttyn Owain then adds the Chronicle of the Saxons, enlarging the genealogical notices, and carries it down to 1461. This differs in diction from manuscript D., but very little in matter; both are taken from a common source, adapted by each writer to the idiom and literary language of his province. It is written on vellum, and is now in the possession of Thos. T. Griffiths, Esquire, of Wrexham.

Inasmuch as manuscript B. is of older date, and therefore of greater antiquity than any of the other versions, it has been deemed advisable to notice all its variations, however slight, with the minutest care. Owing to the very close manner in which it agrees throughout with the text, the Editor has been enabled to do this without much inconvenience. No such accuracy, however, has been, nor indeed could well be, observed with the verbal peculiarities of the other copies, except in the case of proper names. Indeed the collation of the last two, in consequence of the very wide difference they exhibit from the text in point of phraseology, has been mainly confined to mere matters of fact. All these additional facts have been incorporated with the text, wherever they would conveniently cohere, being enclosed within brackets, but where this could not be well done, the variations form a second text.

Various readings.

The mere verbal variations are referred to by a small numeral, thus (¹); but such as form a second text are marked by a small Roman letter, thus (ᵃ). These, as well as the bracketted words, are referred to their respective copies by a numeral. There is also used another mark, called a tick, thus ('). In the body of the text this mark shows the end of a

How noticed.

passage, for which a various reading is to be found, and in the notes a corresponding tick has been placed immediately after the numeral. The brackets have not been introduced into the translation at all, the tick being made to serve instead.

The translation. As to the translation, it has been attempted to render this as literal as possible, without becoming obscure, or doing much violence to the idiom of the language. The copious Glossary, which has been added, will greatly assist the curious reader in testing the fidelity with which it has been executed.

Marginal chronology. The marginal chronology is taken for the most part from manuscript D., as far as that chronicle extends, that is, to about the year 1198. Afterwards it follows the arrangement of manuscript C., and thus continues to the end.

The Editor's obligations. It now remains that the Editor should tender his thanks to those kind friends who have in any way assisted him in preparing the present volume for the press. His special thanks are due to Lady Llanover, always foremost in every attempt to promote the literature of her native country, for access to valuable transcripts in her possession. He desires to express his great obligation to W. W. E. Wynne, Esq., of Peniarth, M.P. for the county of Merioneth, for leave to examine the Hengwrt MSS. at his house, when the late Sir R. W. Vaughan, Bart., was suffering from a severe domestic affliction;—to the Principal and Fellows of Jesus College, Oxford, for facilities afforded him in examining the Red Book of Hergest; and lastly to his friend Mr. Kenward, near Birmingham, for assistance in the tedious work of compiling an Index to the whole volume.

VARIOUS READINGS

REFERRED TO IN

The COPY of the CHRONICLE OF THE PRINCES, which is printed in the Second Volume of the *Myvyrian Archaiology*, and which professes to be a transcript of that in the Red Book of Hergest, made by "R. Davies," in the year 1780.[1]

	TEXT.	VARIOUS READINGS.
Page Line		
4, 22,	Góarchmaelaóc	Garthmaelawc, D.P. MS. Ll.
6, 5,	Maesydaóc	Magedaóc, P. Maes Edawc, Ll. MS.
„ 20,	Fferuaael	Ffermael, D.P. Ffernael, Ll. MS.
8, 16,	Rei	Run, D.P.
„ „	Dyued	Dyfed, MS. Ll.
10, 10,	Tryffin	Gruffyth, D.P.
„ „	Rein	Run.
„ 15,	Kynon	Conan, D.P.
„ 17,	Rywynyaó	Rhyvonioc, D.P.
12, 3,	Satubin	Saturbin, MS. Ll.
14, 3,	ymeith	Ymddeith, MS. Ll.
„ 7,	Nifer	Nifer, D.P.
„ 9,	Dubkynt	Dubert, D.P.
„ 24,	Dórngarth	Dwngarth, Ll. MS. Dungarth, D.P.
16, 7,	Dwy vlyned—Rufein.	Ac yna y bu farw Cadweithen, MS. Ll. Ac y bu farw Hywel yn Rhufein.
18, 1,	un	Rufein, Ib.

---

[1] These were not made use of in the body of the present work, because the Editor had no access to the MSS. from which they have been taken, and could not therefore vouch for their correctness.

THE CHRONICLE OF THE PRINCES.

		Text.	Various Readings.
Page	Line		
18,	5,	y Saesson	Y Saeson, MS. Ll.
,,	9,	Ros Meilon	Molerain, D.P.
,,	15,	Dumeirt	Dinneir, MS. Ll. Dinerth, D.P.
,,	19,	Coruabc	Carmot, D.P.
,,	20,	Guleuan	Gulenan, MS. Ll. Cukeman, D.P.
,,	21,	Keruallt	Kyrnalt, D.P.
,,	,,	Langesy	Lagmes, D.P.
,,	,,	keugant	Kengant, Ll. MS.
20,	7,	Uercu	Nercu, MS. Ll.
,,	16,	Hennyrth	Eunyth, D.P.
,,	22,	Arthual	Arthfael, MS. Ll. Arthuael, D.P.
,,	25,	Lônbert	Hubert, D.P.
,,	26,	Morcheis	Morcleis, MS. Ll. Marclois, D.P.
,,	28,	Chyngen	Conan, D.P.
,,	29,	Eueurys	Eneurys, MS. Ll.
22,	14,	Llanrwst	Llan Rwst, MS. Ll.
,,	20,	Hayardur	Yarthyr, D.P.
24,	7,	Tywyn[1]	Tywyn, MS. Ll.
,,	18,	dellis	Delis, MS. Ll.
26,	6,	ac y—Idwal	Ac y bu farw Idwallawn fab Einiawn, MS. Ll.
,,	18,	gorescynnbys kyuoeth.	Gorescynnbyt Cyfoeth, MS. Ll.
,,	21,	Custennhin	Custenhin Ddu, MS. Ll.
28,	3,	Llanwannabc	Llan Wenawc, MS. Ll.
,,	24,	diffeithbyt	Sic in MS. Ll.
,,	25,	Gotbric[2]	Gotbric.
,,	26,	Ynys	Yn ynys, MS. Ll.
,,	,,	dellit	Delid, MS. Ll.
30,	3,	holl	Deest in MS. Ll.
32,	11,	Arthmarcha	Arthmarchan, MS. Ll.

[1] *In the Myvyrian copy this is written* ty Wyn.

[2] *Gorbric in copy.*

VARIOUS READINGS.

	Text.		Various Readings.
Page	Line		
32,	23, Talarthi	- -	Talarchi, MS. Ll.
34,	4, ydaeth	- -	y doeth, MS. Ll.
,,	6, Eldryt	- -	Etheldryd, MS. Ll.
,,	12, Ac yn	- -	Yna yn, MS. Ll.
36,	3, y laƀ chun	-	alw, MS. Ll.
,,	5, a - -	-	ae, MS. Ll.
,,	6, goruchel	-	goruchaf, MS. Ll.
,,	17, aoryssant	-	oryssant, MS. Ll.
,,	21, y Gƀyndyt	-	or Gƀyndyt, MS. Ll.
,,	24, waradƀydus [1]	-	war adwydus.
38,	23, Lloeger	-	Lloeger a Skotland, MS. Ll.
,,	,, Germania	-	Norwaye, Ib.
40,	3, Y vlƀydyn	-	Yn y vlƀydyn, MS. Ll.
,,	8, Heurun	-	Hernun, D.P.
,,	15, honno	-	honno, MS. Ll.
,,	24, yna	-	yno, MS. Ll.
42,	1, dƀyll	-	brad, MS. Ll.
,,	26, tref	-	dref, MS. Ll.
46,	15, Minbo	-	Nimbo.
,,	17, hynaƀs y	-	hynaƀs wrth y, MS. Ll.
,,	21, genedloed	-	kenedloed, MS. Ll.
48,	16, rƀg Llywelyn	-	rhwng Gronw a Llywelyn meibon, MS. Ll.
50,	2, doeth	-	doethion, MS. Ll.
52,	12, oludoed	-	oludoed, ef a gladwyd yn nhref lan yn Normandi, MS. Ll.
,,	20, Llych Crei	-	Llechryd, D.P.
56,	8, brenhin	-	brenhin y Brytanieid, MS. Ll.
,,	16, anriethaƀ	-	anrheitheu, MS. Ll.
58,	16, heb	-	a heb, MS. Ll.
60,	15, Hu	-	Huw.
62,	2, brenhin	-	frenhin.
,,	27, arall	-	ddyn arall, MS. Ll.
64,	5, y	-	y am y, MS. Ll.
,,	16, aŷ—Gaer Wint	-	Ac e a gladdwyd yng Nhaer Wynt, MS. Ll.

---

[1] war anwydus *in copy.*

THE CHRONICLE OF THE PRINCES.

	Text.		Various Readings.
Page	Line		
64,	24,	gor	goron, MS. Ll.
,,	26,	Prydein	Picteit.
66,	20,	decem—gyntaf	neu o bobtu hynny, MS. Ll.
68,	11,	ynbyn	yn erbyn, MS. Ll.
,,	20,	urenhin [1]	urenhin.
,,	26,	ac	om., MS. Ll.
72,	10,	Mfirchath	Mwrthach, MS. Ll.
,,	15,	gfielet	gwybod, MS. Ll.
,,	24,	gastell	castell i'r brenhin, MS. Ll.
74,	26,	Ac—y brenhin [2]	Ac yna y gelwit Iorwoerth uab Bledyn y Amwythic drwy dwyll i cyghor y brenhin, MS. Ll.
76,	6,	kedernit	gedernid, MS. Ll.
,,	,,	ae hechyt	a iechyd, MS. Ll.
,,	16,	gychwynnafid	gylchynawdd, MS. Ll.
,,	9,	Gadfigafin	Gwgawn, MS. Ll.
,,	12,	nos	om., MS. Ll.
,,	20,	meint	faint, MS. Ll.
,,	,,	idi	iddaw, Ib.
,,	21,	llafi	llafi. Ac ychydic amser wedi hynny y gweled dwy leuad, y naill yn y dwyrein ar llall yn y gorllewin, MS. Ll.
80,	10,	darestygfiys	ddodes, MS. Ll.
,,	,,	diwed	niwedd, MS. Ll.
,,	12,	ac	gan, MS. Ll.
,,	24,	eu	om., MS. Ll.
,,	26,	gfilat	wlad, MS. Ll.
82,	11,	hedifi	heddyw, MS. Ll.
84,	8,	yndafi	ynddi, MS. Ll.
,,	12,	hi	om., Ib.
,,	,,	kanys	yng nghylch, MS. Ll.
,,	17,	firthafi	wrth.
,,	,,	yssyd	a oeddynt, MS. Ll.
,,	29,	y	yn, MS. Ll.

---

[1] *This word is omitted in copy.* | [2] *Omitted in copy.*

VARIOUS READINGS. liii

	TEXT.	VARIOUS READINGS.
Page Line		
88,	22, Cornnec	Corunec, MS. Ll.
,,	26, reig[1]	reig.
90,	9, ymgerydu	ymgredu, MS. Ll.
,,	10, dywedut	dyweddi, Ib.
,,	,, y neb	om., Ib.
,,	,, ymgedymdeithock-au.	ymgydymdeithaw, MS. Ll.
,,	19, offeirat	offeirieit, MS. Ll.
,,	20, agkyweithas	kyweithas, MS. Ll.
92,	4, Môrchath	Murtarch, MS. Ll.
,,	17, Ridit	Riddid, MS. Ll.
94,	11, ac ny—brenhin	ae ni lefasawdd neb arwein ei genadwri hyd at y brenhin, MS. Ll.
,,	18, daly	talu, MS. Ll.
,,	20, dalaôd	talawdd, Ib.
,,	17, ytyghetuen	dyngedfen, MS. Ll.
98,	15, mi[2]	mi.
102,	5, oedynt	a aethant, MS. Ll.
106,	27, ac adaô—tan	ae adaô Iorwoerth y tan, MS. Ll.
108,	11, hyrrôyd	herwyd, MS. Ll.
110,	19, Madave[3]	Madawc, MS. Ll.
,,	25, yspiwyr yno	anfon yspiwyr a wnaeth yno, MS. Ll.
,,	27, a dala	ae ddaly, Ib.
112,	2, Yna y deuth	Yn i ddoeth.
,,	8, Riô	Riô. Ac yng nghylch yr amser yma y bu ddaear grynn mawr yn Amwythic o fore hyd hwyr. A hefyd yr amser hwnnw yr ymddangoses seren gynffonnawc ac y bu aiaf caled yn ol hynny, a marwolaeth a phrinder, MS. Ll.

---

[1] Reing in copy.
[2] un in copy.
[3] Maredud in A.

	Text.	Various Readings.
Page Line		
112, 14,	tir	dir, Ib.
„ 23,	Cyrnẏw [1]	Kernyṽ.
„ „	Blataon	Blathaon.
114, 13,	Pennaeth	Pennant, D.P.
118, 15,	y Dyfet	i Ddyfed, MS. Ll.
„ 24,	Gṽyned	gwydd, MS. Ll.
122, 4,	beuafyeit	hennafieid, Ib.
„ 9,	aniben	am benn, MS. Ll.
124, 4,	dyn	dyn, MS. Ll.
126, 2,	Cafṽy	Cofwy. Tofwy, Ib.
„ 23,	Selyf	Selyf ddoeth, Ib.
„ „	aṽna	aṽna yr, MS. Ll.
„ 24,	dyn	dyn, Ib.
„ 26,	ynvydyon	deithiau, Ib.
„ 28,	gyfyaṽnder	cyfiawnder, MS. Ll.
128, 2,	chyfaduab	chyfadnabod, MS. Ll. Ib.
„ 3,	a dunnaṽ	addunaw, Ib.
„ „	arglṽydiaetheu	arglwyddiaethu, Ib.
„ 17,	ymoscryn	ymystrin, MS. Ll.
„ 22,	y deuth	yd oed, Ib.
„ 23,	y drigyaṽ	yn trigaw, Ib.
130, 12,	Anafrṽyd	Anaddasrṽydd, Ib.
132, 28,	thynnu	thynnu attunt, MS. Ll.
134, 2,	yggṽrthallt	nghwr allt, Ib.
„ 25,	coetir	ynial, Ib.
136, 2,	deuth	ddoethant, MS. Ll.
„ 3,	wyr	lu, Ib.
140, 27,	Maṽdṽy [2]	Mawddwy, MS. Ll.
142, 9,	y vrodyr	ae vrodyr, Ib.
144, 13,	luossogrṽyd	luoed, MS. Ll.
„ 24,	debygynt	debygid, MS. Ll.
146, 21,	y foynt	o doynt, Ib.
148, 17,	gṽyr	gwr, MS. Ll.
154, 8,	Blen	Paine, D.P.
156, 7,	Kadṽgaṽn	Cadwallawn, MS. Ll.
160, 11,	geith	gyweith, MS. Ll.

---

[1] Iwerdon *in A.*   [2] Madaṽc *in A.*

VARIOUS READINGS.

	TEXT.	VARIOUS READINGS.
Page Line		
162, 14,	Idnerth	Iorwerth, Ib.
164, 2,	ac	ac nas, MS. Ll.
166, 2,	o Gymry	o Gymru, MS. Ll.
,, 4,	Gemaron	Gemaeron, Ib.
,, 6,	kastell Colŵyn	Gastell Colwyn, Ib.
,, 12,	Aberteiui	Aberteifi, MS. Ll.
,, 25,	gyssegredigaeth	gyssegredic; Ib.
168, 1,	aghenn	angeu, Ib.
,, 21,	yn arueu	ac arueu, MS. Ll.
170, 18,	dyat	dyfiad, Ib.
,, 27,	chlaear	chlaer, Ib.
172, 2,	Yrŵydgruc	y Rwydgruc.
,, 19,	Gŵiss[1]	Gwiss, MS. Ll.
174, 14,	ydeuth[2]	y deuth.
,, 16,	ae galŵ	a galw, MS. Ll.
,, 23,	arŵydon	arwon, Ib.
,, 31,	vrenhin	frenhin, MS. Ll.
176, 26,	y Geredigyaŵn	o Geredigyaŵn, Ib.
180, 18,	gŵrthladyr Catwaladyr.	gwrthladwyd Cadwaladyr, MS. Ll.
182, 7,	Aberuyn	Aberavan, D.P.
184, 3,	ar offeren	a Rosser, MS. Ll.
,, 10,	hytt	hyd, Ib.
,, 22,	o	o.
186, 12,	amynet——Rudlan	a mynet hyt yn Rhuddlan, MS. Ll.
,, ,,	yn greulaŵn	om., Ib.
188, 9,	llogwyr	llongeu, MS. Ll.
190, 24,	Ac ny—hynny	Ac ni mynnawdd y brenhin beri iawn iddaŵ am hynny, MS. Ll.
192, 22,	ac	ydd, MS. Ll.
194, 16,	aghenn	angeu, Ib.
,, ,,	ŵylua	wyddfa, MS. Ll.
,, 28,	Wiceŵ	Wicew Wicwm, Ib.
196, 26,	ab Owein	a Owein, MS. Ll.

---

[1] Gŵiff *in copy.*   [2] yd aeth *in copy.*

THE CHRONICLE OF THE PRINCES.

Page	Line	Text	Various Readings
198,	14,	uuduchockau	ufuddoccau, Ib.
200,	14,	deuuab[1]	deu uab.
,,	,,	Idnerth[2]	Idnerth.
,,	15,	ef	wynt, MS. Ll.
204,	4,	Dieruut	Diermit.
,,	20,	dywetit	dyweid, MS. Ll.
206,	10,	Diernut	Diermit.
,,	,,	Mϭrchath	Mwrtach, MS. Ll.
,,	19,	ac—Kymry	a dewredd y Cymry, MS. Ll.
208,	7,	achledẏfeu	a chleddyfeu, Ib.
,,	8,	Terstig	Trist. Strisling.
,,	11,	Dieruut	Diermit.
214,	23,	daϭn	daϭn ac urdas, MS. Ll.
216,	5,	dyuot gwil	dyuot gwyl, MS. Ll.
211,	9,	ϭr	wyr, MS. Ll.
222,	8,	o bei vyϭ	a fei fwy, MS, Ll.
,,	9,	o bei vyϭ	a fei fwy, Ib.
224,	11,	wledychei — Caer Llion.	ac yna o ddeisyfyd gyrch y goresgyn y Ffreinc Gaer Llion, MS. Ll.
226,	28,	Reinys	Remys.
228,	5,	gerd arwest	genedloedd arwest.
234,	2,	Maelgϭn[3]	Maelgϭyn.
240,	15,	y Gamaron	yng Nghamaron, MS. Ll.
,,	18,	kymhydeu	kymhydeu o bobtu, MS. Ll.
242,	12,	traethu	saethu.
246,	2,	baed	yn wherun, MS. Ll.
254,	16,	drϭy dϭyll[4]	drwy dwyll, MS. Ll.
,,	22,	Oϭein	Oϭein Gwynedd, Ib.
,,	29,	a llaϭed	gan allwed.
260,	10,	meibon	meibon Gruffudd, MS. Ll.
268,	29,	laϭ	laϭy brenhin, MS. Ll.
270,	22,	castell	cestyll, MS. Ll.
272,	7,	ar Sarassinyeit	ac or Sarasinieid, MS. Ll.
282,	5,	a ieirll	ae ieirll, MS. Ll.

---

[1] Deunaϭ *in copy.*
[2] Iorwoerth *in copy.*
[3] Madaϭc *in copy.*
[4] *Not in copy.*

VARIOUS READINGS. lvii

	Text.		Various Readings.
Page	Line		
282,	16, idaỽ	-	*om.*, MS. Ll.
290,	17, echrestyr	-	chiaster, MS. Ll.
292,	30, mlyned	-	mlyned o oedran, MS. Ll.
298,	16, kymu	-	cymododd, MS. Ll.
316,	12, Kori	-	Keri, D.P.
318,	3, Camtaỽn	-	Camtwm.
,,	4, yn [1]	-	yn, MS. Ll.
320,	31, Bỽlch	-	Bwch, MS. Ll.
322,	18, uarchogyon [2]	-	uarchogyon.
,,	28, ygkabidyldy	-	senedd-dy, MS. Ll.
328,	2, yr brenhin	-	i Henri frenhin, MS. Ll.
,,	24, vrenhin	-	frenhin, MS. Ll.
334,	20, Damieta [3]	-	Damieta.
342,	10, Riỽ	-	Riwyn, MS. Ll.
,,	16, a rann [4]	-	Q. an. *a ran.*
344,	2, Toran	-	Coran.
,,	7, kymmodes	-	cyfodes, MS. Ll.
,,	22, kymydaỽd	-	cymodawdd, Ib.
,,	27, gan	-	dau, Ib.
350,	26, Leos	-	Lewes, MS. Ll.
370,	11, Etmỽnt [5]	-	Etmwnt.

[1] Y *in copy.*
[2] dywyssogyon *in copy.*
[3] Danneta *in copy.*
[4] Garan *in A.*
[5] Etwart *in copy.*

CORRIGENDA.

Page Line
41, 29, *for* Llandav *read* Llandaf.
59, 23, 24, *for* Uchtrud *read* Uchtryd.
74, 26, 27, *dele* brackets and reference.
93, 32, *after* Ceredigion *add* of the foreign nations to inhabit it.
95, 18, *for* Rickart *read* Rickert.
120, 15, *for* danyon *read* dynyon.
124, 3, *for* anoeitheu *read* anreitheu.
146, 12, *for* w eic *read* wreic.
148, 30, *for* ac *read* ae.
167, 17, *for* belonging to the son of Uchtryd *read* in Mabudrud.
192, 12, *for* arnen *read* aruei.
239, 13, 14, *for* Gwis *read* Gwys.
243, 6, and 283, l. 25, *for* Hyvaidd *read* Hyveidd.

BRUT Y TYWYSOGION;

OR

THE CHRONICLE OF THE PRINCES OF WALES.

BRUT Y TYWYSOGION.

DCLXXXI. Petwar ugeint mlyned a whechant¹ [ac vn] oed oet Crist pan vu y uarỽlyaeth uaỽr drỽy holl ynys Prydein. ²Ac o dechreu byt hyt yna yd oed blỽydyn eissieu o petwar ugeint mlyned ac ỽyth cant aphum mil.'

Ac yny vlỽydyn honno y bu uarỽ Kadỽaladyr uendigeit uab Kadwallaỽn uab Catuan brenhin y Brytanyeit yn Rufein y deudecuet dyd o Vei; megys y proffỽydassei Vyrdin kyn no hynny ỽrth Ỽrtheyrn gỽrtheneu: ac o hynny allan y colles y Brytanyeit goron y teyrnas ac yd ennillaỽd y Saeson hi.

DCLXXXIII. Ac yn ol Kadwaladyr y gỽledychaỽd Iuor uab Alan vrenhin Llydaỽ, yr honn a elwir Brytaen uechan; ac nyt megys brenhin namyn megys pennaeth neu tywyssaỽc. A hỽnnỽ agynhellis llywodraeth ar y Brytanyeit ỽyth mlyned a deugein, ac yna y bu uarỽ. Ac yny ol ynteu y gỽledychaỽd Rodri Maelỽynaỽc.

DCLXXXV. Ac yn oes hỽnnỽ ¹[ª dwy vlyned wedy hynny] y bu uarỽolyaeth yn Iỽerdon.

DCLXXXVII. Ac yna ¹[ᵇ³'r vlwydyn nessaf y honno] y crynaỽd y dayar yn ᶜLlydaỽ.

ª'⁴ Ac ýn ýr eil vlwýdyn gwedý dýuot Iuor ýr ýnýs honn,

ᵇ'⁴ petwýrýd vlwýdýn gwedý dýuot Ivor ýr ýnýs honn,   ᶜ⁴ Manaw.

---

¹ C. | ᵛ Not in C.

THE CHRONICLE OF THE PRINCES.

681. Six hundred and eighty [1] one was the year of Christ, when the great mortality took place through the whole island of Britain. [2] And from the beginning of the world until that period one year was wanting of five thousand eight hundred and eighty years.'

And in that year Cadwalader the Blessed, son of Cadwallon, son of Cadvan, king of the Britons, died at Rome, on the twelfth day of May; as Myrddin had previously prophesied to Vortigern of Repulsive Lips; and thenceforth the Britons lost the crown of the kingdom, and the Saxons gained it.

683. And after Cadwalader, Ivor, son of Alan, king of Armorica, which is called Little Britain, reigned; not as a king, but as a chief or prince And he exercised government over the Britons for forty-eight years, and then died. And after him Rhodri Molwynog reigned.

685. And in his time [a][1] two years subsequently,' there was a mortality in Ireland.

687. And then, [b] the year following,' there was an earthquake in [c] Armorica.

---

[a]' [4] And in the second year after Ivor came to this island,

[b] [4] the fourth year after Ivor came to this island,

[c] [4] Man.

---

[1] *In MS.* ar, and the. | [4] *D. E.*

DCLXXXVIII. Ac yna [1] [a pedeir blyned wedy hynny] y bu y glaƀ gwaet yn ynys Prydein ac Iwerdon.

DCXC. [2] Deg mlyned a phedwar ugein a whechant oed oet Crist yna,' ac yna yd ymchoelaƀd y llaeth ar emenyn yn waet.

DCXCII. [3] [Dwy vlyned wedy hynny] ar lleuat aymchoelaƀd yn waetaƀl liƀ.

DCCIV. [1] [Pedeir blyned a] seith cant mlyned oed oet Crist pan vu uarƀ [4] Elffryt brenhin y Saeson, [1] [ac y kladpwyd yn Damnan.]

[5] DCCX. [b] Deg mlyned a seithgant oed oet Crist' pan vu varƀ Pipin vƀyaf brenhin Ffreinc. Ac yna kyn oleuet oed y nos ar dyd.

DCCXVI. Ac yna [1] [blwydyn wedy hynny] y bu uarƀ [6] Osbric brenhin y Saeson.

DCCXVII. Ac [1] [blwydyn wedy hynny] y kyssegrƀyt eglƀys Lan Vihaggel.

DCCXX. Vgein mlyned a seithcant oed oet Crist pan vu yr haf tessaƀc.

DCCXXI. Ac yna [1] [blwydyn wedy hynny] y bu uarƀ Beli uab Elfin. Ac y bu vrƀydyr [7] Heilin [8] [a Rhodri Malwŷnawc] Ygkernyƀ, a gƀeit [9] Gƀarchmaelaƀc, achat Pen [10] Coet yn Eheubarth. Ac yn y teir brƀydyr hynny y goruu y Brytanyeit.

DCCXXVIII. [c] Deg mlyned ar hugeint a seith cant oed oet Crist,' pan vu vrƀydyr ym mynyd Carn.

DCCXXXV. [d] Deugeint mlyned' a seith cant oed oet Crist pan uu varƀ Beda offeirat.

---

a [11] blwýdỳn gwedý hýnný
b [12] Blwydyn wedy hynny
c [12] Dwy vlyned wedy hynny
d [12] Pymthec mlyned arhugeint

---

[1] C.
[2] Not in C. D. E.
[3] C. D. E.

[4] Elfric, C. Elfricus, D. E.
[5] DCCVIII. D.
[6] Osbrit, D. E.

688. And then, a¹ four years after that,' it rained blood in the island of Britain, and in Ireland.

690. ² Six hundred and ninety was then the year of Christ,' and then the milk and butter turned to blood.

692. ³ Two years after that,' and the moon turned of a bloody colour.

704. ¹ Four years and' seven hundred was the year of Christ, when ⁴ Elfryt, king of the Saxons, died, ¹ and was buried at Damnan.'

710. Seven hundred and ten was the year of Christ,' when Pepin the Elder, king of France, died. And then the night was as light as day.

716. And then, ¹ a year after that,' ⁶ Osbric, king of the Saxons, died.

717. And, ¹ a year after that,' the church of St. Michael was consecrated.

720. Seven hundred and twenty was the year of Christ, when the hot summer happened.

721. And then, ¹ a year after that,' Beli, son of Elfin, died. And the battle of ⁷ Heilin, ⁸ with Rhodri Molwynog,' took place in Cornwall; and the action of Garthmaelog, and the fight of Pencoed in South Wales. And in those three battles the Britons were victorious.

728. ᶜ Seven hundred and thirty was the year of Christ,' when there was a battle on Carn mountain.

735. Seven hundred and ᵈ forty' was the year of Christ, when Bede the priest died.

---

a ¹¹ A year after that
b′ ¹² A year after that
c′ ¹² Two years after that
d′ ¹² Thirty-five years

---

⁵ Heil, *D.* Huail, *E. Not in C.*
⁶ *D. E.*
⁷ Garthmaelawc, *C. D. E.*
¹⁰ Kwn, *C.*
¹¹ *D. E.*
¹² *C.*

DCCXXXVI. Ac yna ¹[blwydyn wedy hynny] y bu uarỏ Owein brenhin y Picteit.

DCCL. Deg mlyned a deugeint a seith cant oed oet Crist pan vu y vrỏydyr rỏg y Brytanyeit ar Picteit yg gỏeith ²Maesydaỏc, ac y lladaỏd y Brytanyeit Talargan brenhin y Picteit. Ac yna y bu uarỏ Teỏdỏr uab Beli.

DCCLIV. Ac ¹[pedeir blyned wedy hynny] y bu uarỏ Rodri ³[Maelwynawc] brenhin y Brytanyeit;

DCCLVII. Ac ¹[teir blyned wedy hynny] Etbalt brenhin y Saeson.

DCCLX. Trugein mlyned a seith cant oed oet Crist pan vu brỏydyr y rỏg y Brytanyeit ar Saeson yg gỏeith Henfford. Ac y bu uarỏ Dyfynwal uab Tewdỏr.

DCCLXVIII. ᵃDeg mlyned a thrugein a seith cant oed oet Crist' pan symudỏyt Pasc y Brytanyeit drỏy orchymyn Elbot gỏr y Duỏ.

DCCLXXIII. ¹[Teir blyned ardec athrugein a seith gant oed oed Krist,] ac yna y bu uarỏ ⁴Ffernuail uab Idwal ⁵[iwrch].

DCCLXXIV. ⁶[Blwydyn wedi hynny y bu varw Kymoyd vrenhin y Picteid;]

DCCLXXV. A Chubert abat ⁶[y vlwydyn nessaf wedy hynny].

DCCLXXVI. Ac yna ¹[y vlwydyn nessaf y honno] ᵇy bu distryỏ y Deheubarthwyr gan Offa vrenhin.'

ᵃ'⁷ Wyth mlyned wedy hynny,

ᵇ'⁸ gwŷr Debeubarth Kẏmre a diffeithassant ẏr ẏnys hŷd ar Offa brenhin Mers.

---

¹ C.
² Mictouc, C. Metgetawc, D. Magedawc, E.
³ D. E.
⁴ Ffermael, D. E.

736. And then, ¹ a year after that,' Owain, king of the Picts, died.

750. Seven hundred and fifty was the year of Christ, when the battle between the Britons and Picts took place, to wit, the action of ² Maesydog, and the Britons killed Talargan, king of the Picts. And then Tewdwr, son of Beli, died.

754. And, ¹ four years after that,' Rhodri ³ Molwynog, king of the Britons, died;

757. And, ¹ three years after that,' Edbalt, king of the Saxons.

760. Seven hundred and sixty was the year of Christ, when a battle between the Britons and Saxons took place, to wit, the action of Hereford. And Dyvnwal, son of Tewdwr, died.

768. ᵃ Seven hundred and seventy was the year of Christ,' when the Easter of the Britons was altered by the command of Elbod, a man of God.

773. ¹ Seven hundred and seventy-three was the year of Christ,' and then ⁴ Fernvail, son of Idwal ⁵ the Roe,' died.

774. ⁶ A year after that Cemoyd, king of the Picts, died;'

775. And abbot Cubert, ⁶ the next year after that.'

776. And then, ¹ the next year to that,' ᵇ the destruction of the South Wales men by king Offa took place.'

ᵃ' ⁷ Eight years after that,
ᵇ' ⁸ the men of the South part of Wales devastated the island as far as Offa, king of Mercia.

¹ E.   ² C.
⁶ C. D. E.   ⁸ D.

DCCLXXXIV. ªPedwar ugein mlyned a seith cant oed oet Crist pan diffeithaѡd Offa urenhin y Brytanyeit yn amser haf.'

DCCXCV. ᵇDeg' mlyned a phedѡar ugein a seith cant oed oet Crist pan deuth y Paganyeit gyntaf y Iwerdon, ¹[ac y distrywyd Rechrenn.]

DCCXCVI. Ac ²[blwydyn wedy hynny] y bu uarѡ Offa vrenhin; a Maredudd brenhin Dyfet ᶜac y bu' vrѡydyr yn Rudlan.

DCCXCVIII. ᵈWyth cant mlyned oed oet Crist' pan ladaѡd y Saeson Garadaѡc brenhin Gѡyned.

DCCCVII. ²[Seith mlyned ac wythgant oed oed Krist,] ac yna y bu uarѡ Arthen vrenhin Keredigyaѡn. Ac y bu diffyc ar yr heul.

DCCCVIII. Ac ²[blwydyn wedy hynny] y bu uarѡ Rei vrenhin ¹[Dyued] a Chadell brenhin Powys.

DCCCIX. Ac ²[blwydyn wedy hynny y bu varw] Elbot archescob Gѡyned.

DCCCX. Deg mlyned ac ѡyth cant oed oet Crist pan duaѡd y lleuat duѡ Nadolyc. Ac y lloscet Mynyѡ.

ᵃ/³ Teir blyned wedy hynny yr haf y distrywyd y Brytannyeid gyd ac Offa.

⁴'Yr haf ẏ diffeithws ẏ Kẏmre kẏuoeth Offa, ac ẏna ẏ peris Offa gwneuthur clawd ẏn deruẏn rẏngthaw a Chẏmre ual y bei haws ẏdaw gwrthnebu ẏ ruthẏr ẏ elẏnion, a hwnnw a elwit glawd Offa ẏr hẏnnẏ hẏd hedẏw.' ⁵Ac ef y sydd yn estynnv or mor yr llall nid amgen or dehev yn emyl Brvsto tv ar gogledd gorvwch y Fflint y rwng mynachloc ddinas Basing a mynydd y Glo.'

ᵇ/⁶Pump   ᶜ/⁶yny

ᵈ/⁶Dwy vlyned wedy hynny,

---

¹ C. D. E.   ᵛ C.
² C.   ᵛ' D.E.

784. ᵃ Seven hundred and eighty was the year of Christ, when king Offa spoiled the Britons in summer time.'

795. Seven hundred and ninety was the year of Christ, when the Pagans first came to Ireland, ¹ and Racline was destroyed.'

796. And, ² a year after that,' king Offa died; and Maredudd, king of Dyved; ᶜ and a ' battle took place at Ruddlan.

798. ᵈ Eight hundred was the year of Christ,' when the Saxons killed Caradog, king of Gwynedd.

807. ᵉ Eight hundred and seven was the year of Christ,' and then Arthen, king of Ceredigion, died. And there was an eclipse of the sun.

808. And, ² a year after that,' Rein, king of ¹ Dyved,' died; and Cadell, king of Powys.

809. And, ² a year after that, died ' Elbod, archbishop of Gwynedd.

810. Eight hundred and ten was the year of Christ, when the moon turned black on Christmas day; and

---

ᵃ/ ³ Three years after that, in the summer, the Britons were destroyed with Offa.

⁴ In the summer the Welsh devastated the territory of Offa, and then Offa caused a dike to be made, as a boundary between him and Wales, to enable him the more easily to withstand the attack of his enemies, and that is called Offa's dike from that time to this day.' ⁵ And it extends from one sea to the other, from the south, near Bristol, to the north, above Flint, between the monastery of Basingwerk and Coleshill.'

ᵇ/ ⁶ Five   ᶜ/ ⁵ in the

ᵈ/ ⁶ Two years after that,

ʸ E.   ᵍ C.

Ac y bu uarᴪolyaeth ¹[ar] yr anifeileit ªar hyt ynys Prydein.'

DCCCXI. Ac ¹[blwydyn wedy hynny] y bu uarᴪ Owein uab Maredud. Ac y lloscet Deganwy o tan myllt.

DCCCXII. Ac ¹[blwydyn wedi hynny] y bu vrᴪydyr y rᴪg Howel a Chynan, a Howel aoruu.

DCCCXV. Ac yna ¹[teir blyned wedi hynny] y bu daran uaᴪr ac y gᴪnaeth llawer o loscuaeu. Ac y bu uarᴪ ²Tryffin uab ³Rein. Ac y llas Griffri uab Kyngen ⁴[ap Kadell] o dᴪyll Elisse y uraᴪt. Ac y goruu Howel o ynys Uon. Ac y gyrraᴪd Gynan y uraᴪt o Von ymeith y gan lad llaᴪer oe lu.

DCCCXVII. Ac ¹[dwy vlyned wedy hynny] ᵇeilweith y gyrrᴪyt Howel o Von.' Ac y bu uarᴪ ⁵Kynon urenhin ⁶[Gwyned]. Ac y diffeithaᴪd y Saeson mynyded Eryri, ac y dugant urenhinyaeth Rywynyaᴪc.

DCCCXVIII. Ac ¹[blwydyn wedy hynny] y bu ⁷[ymlad yn Mon, yr hwn a elwit] weith Llan uaes.

DCCCXIX. Ac ¹[blwydyn wedy hynny] y diffeithaᴪd Genᴪlf brenhinyaetheu Dyfet.

DCCCXXIII. ¹[Teir blyned ar] ugein mlyned ac ᴪyth cant oed oet Crist pan distrywyt castell Deganwy gan y Saeson. Ac yna y duc y Saeson urenhinyaeth Powys yn eu medyant.

DCCCXXV. Ac ¹[dwy vlyned wedy hynny] y bu uarᴪ Hoᴪel, ⁷[brenhin Manaw.]

ª′ˢ drwẏ holl Kẏmrẏ.
ᵇ′ˢ ẏ deholet o Vanaw. ᴮy deholet Howel i Vanaw.

---

¹ C.
² Grufud, C. D. E.
³ Run, C.

⁴ E.
⁵ Cynan, C. D. E.

Menevia was burnt; and there was a mortality among the cattle ᵃ over the island of Britain.'

811. And, ¹a year after that,' Owain, son of Maredudd, died. And Dyganwy was burnt by lightning.

812. And, ¹a year after that,' a battle took place between Howel and Cynan; and Howel conquered.

815. And then, ¹three years after that,' there was a great thunder-storm, which caused many conflagrations; and ²Tryffin, son of ³Rein, died; and Griffri, son of Cyngen, ⁴son of Cadell,' was slain, through the treachery of his brother Elisse; and Howel subdued the isle of Mona; and expelled his brother Cynan from Mona, killing many of his army.

817. And, ¹two years after that,' ᵇHowel was a second time driven from Mona;' and ⁵Cynon, king ⁶of Gwynedd,' died; and the Saxons ravaged the mountains of Eryri, and took the kingdom of Rhuvoniog.

818. And, ¹a year after that,' ⁷a fight took place in Mona, called ' the action of Llanvaes.

819. And, ¹a year after that,' Cenulf ravaged the kingdoms of Dyved.

823. ¹Three and ' twenty and eight hundred was the year of Christ, when the castle of Dyganwy was destroyed by the Saxons. And then the Saxons took the kingdom of Powys into their possession.

825. And, ¹two years after that,' Howel, ⁷king of Man,' died.

ᵃ'⁸ through all Wales.
ᵇ'⁸ was driven from Man; ⁹Howel was driven to Man;

---

¹ E. | ³ D.
² D. E. | ⁴ E.

DCCCXXXI. ¹[Vn mlyned ar] deg mlyned ar hugein ac ẃyth cant oed oet Crist pan vu diffyc ar y lleuat ᵃ yr ẃythuet dyd o vis Racuyr.' Ac y bu varẃ ²Satubin escob Mynyẃ.

DCCCXL. Deugein mlyned ac ẃyth cant oed oet Crist pan wledychaẃd ᵇ Meuruc' escob ym Mynyẃ.

DCCCXLII. Ac ¹[dwy vlyned wedy hynny] y bu uarẃ Idwallaẃn.

DCCCXLIV. Ac ¹[dwy vlyned wedy hynny] y bu gẃeith ³Ketyll. Ac y bu varẃ Meruyn ⁴[urych].

DCCCXLVIII. Ac ¹[pedeir blyned wedy hynny] y bu weith Ffinant. Ac y llas ⁵Ithel brenhin Gẃent ygan wyr Brecheinaẃc.

DCCCXLIX. ᶜ Deg mlyned a deugein ac ẃythcant oed oet Crist' pan las Meuruc y gan y Saeson.

DCCCL. ¹[Dec mlyned a deugeint ac wythgant oed oet Krist,] ᵈ ac y tagẃyt Kyngen y gan y genedloed.'

DCCCLIII. Ac ¹[teir blyned wedy hynny] y diffeithẃydt Mon y gan y kenhedloed duon.

DCCCLIV. Ac ¹[blwydyn wedy hynny] y bu uarẃ Kyngen vrenhin Powys yn Rufein.

DCCCLVI. ⁶[Dwy vlyned wedy hynny y bu varw Kemoyth vrenhin y Picteid]. Ac y bu uarẃ Ionathal tywyssaẃc Abergeleu.

DCCCLX. ⁷[Trugein mlyned ac wythgant oed oet Krist pan vv varw Maelsalacheu.

    ᵃ ⁸ VIII. kł. Novembr.
    ᵇ ⁹ bonhedic
    ᶜ ¹⁰ Blwydyn wedy hynny,
    ᵈ ¹¹ pan ladawd y Paganyeid Gyngen.

---

¹ C.
² Saturbyn, C. D. E.
³ Kadell, E.
⁴ D. E.
⁵ Ithael, C.
⁶ C. D. E.

THE CHRONICLE OF THE PRINCES.   13

831. ¹One and' thirty and eight hundred was the year of Christ, when the eclipse of the moon happened on ᵃ the eighth day of the month of December.' And ²Satubin, bishop of Menevia, died.

840. Eight hundred and forty was the year of Christ, when ᵇMeurug, the' bishop, governed in Menevia.

842. And, ¹ two years after that,' Idwallon died.

844. And, ¹two years after that,' the action of ³Cetyll took place. And Mervyn ⁴the Freckled,' died.

848. And, ¹four years after that,' the action of Finnant took place. And ⁵Ithel, king of Gwent, was slain by the men of Brecheiniog.

849. ᶜEight hundred and fifty was the year of Christ,' when Meurug was killed by the Saxons.

850. ¹Eight hundred and fifty was the year of Christ,' ᵈand Cyngen was strangled by the Pagans.'

853. And, ¹three years after that,' Mona was ravaged by the black Pagans.

854. And, ¹a year after that,' Cyngen, king of Powys, died in Rome.

856. ⁶Two years after that Cemoyth, king of the Picts, died.' And Ionathal, prince of Abergeleu, died.

860. ⁷Eight hundred and sixty was the year of Christ, when Maelsalacheu died.

   ᵃ⸍ ⁸ the 8th of the calends of November.
   ᵇ⸍ ⁹ a noble
   ᶜ⸍ ¹⁰ A year after that,
   ᵈ⸍ ¹⁰ when the Pagans killed Cyngen.

---

⁷ *C. D.*   ⁹ *C. Not in D. E.*
⁸ *D. Not in C.*   ¹⁰ *C.*

DCCCLXII. Dwy vlyned wedy] trugein mlyned ac 6yth cant oed oet Crist ᵃ pan yrr6yt ¹ Kat6eitheu ymeith.'

DCCCLXIV. ² [ᵇ Dwy vlyned wedy hynny y diffeithyawd honno y Glyuyssic.']

DCCCLXV. Ac ²[blwydyn wedy hynny] y bu uar6 Kynan ᶜ Uant Nifer.'

DCCCLXVI. Ac ³[blwydyn wedy hynny] y diffeithwyt Kaer Efra6c ᵈ ygkat' Dubkynt.

DCCCLXIX. ᵉ Deg mlyned a thrugein ac 6yth cant oed oet Crist' pan vu kat ᶠ Kryn Onnen.

DCCCLXX. ³[Deg mlyned athrugeint ac wythgant oed oed Krist,] ac y torret Kaer Alclut y gan y Paganyeit.

DCCCLXXI. Ac ³[blwydyn wedy hynny] y bodes G6ga6n uab Meuruc brenhin Keredigya6n.

DCCCLXXIII. Ac ³[dwy vlyned wedy hynny] y bu weith Bangoleu ⁴[ac yno y llas Kynan:] a g6eith ⁵ Menegyd ym Mon. Ac y bu uar6 Meuruc escob bonhedic.

DCCCLXXIV. Ac ³[blwydyn wedy hynny] y kymerth ⁶ L6mbert escoba6t Vyny6.

DCCCLXXV. Ac ³[blwydyn wedy hynny] y bodes D6rngarth urenhin Kerny6.

DCCCLXXVI. Ac ⁷[blwydyn wedy hynny] y bu weith du6 Sul ym Mon.

ᵃ' ⁸ ẏ bu cat Gweithen.
ᵇ' ⁹ ẏ diffeithwẏt Glẏwẏsig ac ẏd alldudwẏd hwẏnt.
ᶜ' ¹⁰ nawd nifer.
ᵈ' ¹⁰ y gan gad ⁸ ac ẏ bu cat
ᵉ' ¹⁰ Teir blyned wedy hynny,   ᶠ'¹¹ brynn onnen.

---

¹ Katweithen, C.
² C. D.
³ C.
⁴ E.
⁵ Ynegyd, C. D. E.
⁶ Himbert, C. Lunberth, D. E.

THE CHRONICLE OF THE PRINCES. 15

862. Two years after' eight hundred and sixty years was the year of Christ, ᵃwhen Cadweithen was driven away.'

864. ²ᵇTwo years after that, he ravaged Glywysig.'

865. And, ²a year after that,' Cynan, ᶜof Nant Nyver,' died.

866. And, ³a year after that,' Caer Evrog was devastated ᵈin the battle' of Dubkynt.

869. ᵉEight hundred and seventy was the year of Christ,' when the battle of ᶠCryn Onen' took place.

870. ³Eight hundred and seventy was the year of Christ,' and Caer Alclut was demolished by the Pagans.

871. And, ³a year after that,' Gwgawn, son of Meurug, king of Ceredigion, was drowned.

873. And, ³two years after that,' the action of Bangoleu took place, ⁴and there Cynan was slain:' and the action of ⁵Menegyd in Mona. And Meurug, a bishop of noble lineage, died.

874. And, ³a year after that,' ⁶Lwmbert assumed the bishopric of Menevia.

875. And, ³a year after that,' Dwrngarth, king of Cornwall, was drowned.

876. And, ⁷a year after that,' the action on Sunday took place in Mona.

ᵃ′⁸ the battle of Gweithen took place.
ᵇ′⁹ Glywysig was ravaged, and they were banished.
ᶜ′¹⁰ the refuge of a multitude,
ᵈ′¹⁰ by the battle ⁸ and the battle took place
ᵉ′¹⁰ Three years after that,   ᶠ′¹¹ Ash Hill.

---

⁷ *D.*
⁸ *D. E.*
⁹ *D.*

¹⁰ *C.*
¹¹ *C. D. E.*

DCCCLXXVII. Ac ¹[blwydyn wedy hynny] y llas Rodri a Gŵryat y ᵃvraŵt y gan y Saeson.

DCCCLXXVIII. Ac ¹[blwydyn wedy hynny] y bu varŵ Aed uab Mellt.

DCCCLXXX. Pedwar ugein mlyned ac ŵyth cant oed oet Crist pan vu weith Conŵy y dial Rodri o Duŵ.

DCCCLXXXII. ²[Dwy vlyned wedy hynny y bu ᵇ varw Kadweithen.'

DCCCLXXXV. Teir blyned wedy hynny y bu varw Hywel yn Rufein.

DCCCLXXXVII. Dwy vlyned wedy hynny y bu varw ³ Cerball.]

DCCCLXXXIX. ᶜ Deg mlyned a phedwar ugein ac ŵyth cant oed oet Crist' pan vu uarŵ Subin y doethaf or Yscotteit.

DCCCXC. ¹[Dec mlyned a phedwar ugein ac wyth gant oed oed Krist,] ac yna y deuth y Normanyeit duon ᵈ eilweith y gastell Baldwin.'

DCCCXCI. Ac ¹[blwydyn wedy hynny] y bu uarŵ ⁴ Heinuth vab Bledri.'

DCCCXCIII. Ac yna ¹[dwy vlyned wedy hynny] y deuth Anaraŵt y diffeithaŵ Keredigyaŵn ac ystrat Tywi.

DCCCXCIV. Ac yna ¹[blwydyn wedy hynny] y diffeithaŵd y Normanyeit Loeger, a Brecheinaŵc, a Morganŵc, a Gŵent a ⁵ Buellt Gŵnllŵc.

DCCCXCV. Ac yna ¹[blwydyn wedy hynny] y diffygyaŵd bŵyt yn Iwerdon; kanys pryfet o nef a dygŵyd-

---
ᵃ ⁶ vab
ᵇ ⁷ cat Gweithen.   ⁸ — Gwytherin.
ᶜ ⁹ Dwy vlyned wedy hynny,
ᵈ ¹⁰ drachevýn hýt ar Gwinn.   ¹¹ y Wyned.

---
¹ C.
² C. D. E.
³ Kadell, E.

⁴ Henweith vab Bledric, C. Hennech vab Bledric, D. E.
⁵ Not in C. D. E.

877. And, 'a year after that,' Rhodri, and his ᵃbrother Gwriad, were killed by the Saxons.

878. And, ¹a year after that,' Aedd, son of Mellt, died.

880. Eight hundred and eighty was the year of Christ, when the action of Conwy took place, for God to avenge Rhodri.

882. ²Two years after that, ᵇCadweithen died.'

885. Three years after that, Howel died in Rome.

887. Two years after that, ³Cerball died.'

889. ᶜEight hundred and ninety was the year of Christ,' when Subin, the wisest of the Scots, died.

890. ¹Eight hundred and ninety was the year of Christ,' and then the black Normans came ᵈa second time to Castle Baldwin.'

891. And, ¹a year after that,' ⁴Heinuth, son of Bledri, died.

893. And then, ¹two years after that,' Anarawd came to devastate Ceredigion and the Vale of Tywi.

894. And then, ¹a year after that,' the Normans devastated England, Brecheiniog, Morganwg, Gwent, ⁵Buallt, and Gwenllwg.

895. And then, ¹a year after that,' provision failed in Ireland; for vermin of a mole-like form, each having

---
ᵃ ⁶ son
ᵇ′ ⁷ was the battle of Gweithen. ⁸— Gwytherin.
ᶜ′ ⁹ Two years after that,
ᵈ′ ¹⁰ again as far as Gwinn. ¹¹ to Gwynedd.

---
⁶ E.	⁹ C.
⁷ D.	¹⁰ D. E.
⁸ E.	¹¹ C.

aöd ar weith göad a deu dant y bop un, ar rei hynny a vöyttaaöd yr holl ymborth, a thröy vnpryt a göedi y görthladöyt.

DCCCXCVII. Ac yna ¹[dwy vlyned wedy hynny] y bu uarö ²Elstan brenhin ³[y Saesson];

DCCCXCVIII. Ac ¹[blwydyn wedy hynny] ⁴Alvryt urenhin ⁵Iwys.

DCCCC. Naö cant mlyned oed oet ⁶Crist pan deuth Igmönd y ynys Von, ac y kynhalyaöd maes ⁷Ros Meilon.

DCCCCI. Ac yna y llas mab Meruyn y gan y genedyl. Ac y bu uarö Llywarch uab ⁸Hennyth.

DCCCCII. Ac y llas penn ⁹Ryderch uab ¹⁰Hennyth ¹¹[yn Arwystli] duw Göyl Baöl.

DCCCCIV. Ac y bu weith ¹²Dumeirt ynyr hönn y llas Maelaöc cam uab Peredur. Ac yna y dileöyt Mynyö.

DCCCCV. Ac y bu uarö Gorchöyl escob. Ac y bu varö ¹³Coruaöc brenhin ac escob holl Iwerdon gör maör y grefyd ae gardaöt. ¹⁴Mab y Guleuan ¹alas ᵃoe vod y myön bröydyr.' ¹⁵Ac y bu uarö Keruallt uab Muregan brenhin Langesy ᵇo keugant diwed.'

DCCCCVI. Ac y bu uarö Asser archescob ynys Prydein;

DCCCCVII. A Chadell uab Rodri.

DCCCCXI. Deg mlyned a naö cant oed oet Crist pan deuth Other y ynys Prydein.

ᵃ' ¹⁶ ẏn ẏr ẏmlad hwnnw. ¹⁷yn y vlwyddyn hwnnw.
ᵇ' ¹⁶ ẏn diwed ẏr ẏmlad.

---

¹ C.
² Edelstan, C.
³ C. D. E.
⁴ Aldryd, C. Albrẏt, D. E.

⁵ Euwas, C. Gẏnoẏs, D. Gyndys, E.
⁶ *A leaf is here lost in C.*
⁷ Meleriaun, D. Meleriaum, E.
⁸ Hẏveid, D. E.

two teeth, fell from heaven, which devoured all the food; and through fasting and prayer they were driven away.

897. And then, ¹'two years after that,' Elstan, king ²'of the Saxons,' died;

898. And ¹'a year after that,' ⁴ Alvryd, king of the Gewissi.

900. Nine hundred was the year of ⁶ Christ, when Igmond came to the isle of Mona, and fought the battle of ⁷ Rhos Meilon.'

901. And then the son of Mervyn was killed by the Pagans. And Llywarch, son of ⁸ Hennyth, died.

902. And ⁹ Rhydderch, son of ¹⁰ Hennyth, was beheaded ¹¹ in Arwystli,' on the feast of St. Paul.

904. And the action of ¹² Dineirth took place, in which Maelog the Crooked, son of Peredur, was slain. And then Menevia was destroyed.

905. And bishop Gorchwyl died. And ¹³ Corvoc, king and bishop of all Ireland, died; a man eminent for faith and charity. ¹⁴ A son of Culeuan was slain ᵃ voluntarily in battle.' ¹⁵ And Cerwallt, son of Muregan, king of Leinster, died ᵇ of a fatal disorder.'

906. And Asser, archbishop of the isle of Britain, died;

907. And Cadell, son of Rhodri.

911. Nine hundred and ten was the year of Christ, when Other came to the island of Britain.

ᵃ' ¹⁶ in that fight.   ¹⁷ in that year.
ᵇ' ¹⁶ at the end of the fight.

---

⁹ Rodri, *D. E.*
¹⁰ Huueith, *D.*   Kyunerth, *E.*
¹¹ *D.*
¹² Duuneir, *D.*   Dinevwr, *E.*
¹³ Cormoc, *D.*   Corinoc, *E.*

¹⁴ Culennan, *D. E.*
¹⁵ *Not in E.*
¹⁶ *D.*
¹⁷ *E.*

DCCCCXIII. Ac y bu uarỼ AnaraỼt uab Rodri brenhin y Brytanyeit.

DCCCCXIV. Ac y diffeithỼyt Iwerdon a Mon y gan bobyl Dulyn. Ac y bu uarỼ Edelflet vrenhines.

DCCCCXVII. Ac y llas ClydaỼc uab Cadell ¹[ap Rodri mawr] y gan Ueuruc y vraỼt.

DCCCCXVIII. Ac y bu uarỼ ²Uercu escob ¹[da].

DCCCCXIX. Ac y bu weith y Dinas NeỼyd.

DCCCCXXVI. Ugein mlyned a naỼ cant oed oet Crist pan aeth Howel da vrenhin vab Kadell y Rufein: ac y bu uarỼ Elen.

DCCCCXXXIII. Deg mlyned arhugein a naỼcant oed oet Crist pan las Gruffud ap Owein y gan wyr KeredigyaỼn.

DCCCCXXXV. Ac y bu ryfel ³Brun.

DCCCCXXXVI. Ac y bu uarỼ ⁴Hennyrth uab ClydaỼc a Meuruc y vraỼt.

DCCCCXXXIX. Ac y bu uarỼ Edelstan brenhin y Saeson.

DCCCCXL. Deugein mlyned a naỼcant oed oet Crist pan vu uarỼ Abloyc vrenhin.

DCCCCXLI. A Chadell uab Arthuael a ỼenỼynỼyt, ac IdỼal uab Rodri ac Elised y ᵃvraỼt alas y gan y Saeson.

DCCCCXLII. Ac y bu uarỼ ⁵LỼnbert escob MynyỼ.

DCCCCXLIII. Ac Ussa uab LlaỼr; a ⁶Morcheis escob Bangor a vuant ueirỼ.

DCCCCXLIV. A Chyngen uab ⁷Elised a wenỼynỼyt, ac ⁸Eueurys escob MynyỼ a vu uarỼ. Ystrat Clut adiffeithỼyt y gan y Saeson.

ᵃ ⁹ vab

---

¹ E.
² Nercu, D. E.
³ Brune, D. Brynnev, E.

⁴ Hẏmeith, D. Kyfnerth, E.
⁵ LỼnberth, D. E.

913. And Anarawd, son of Rhodri, king of the Britons, died.

914. And Ireland and Mona were devastated by the people of Dublin. And queen Edelfled died.

917. And Clydog, son of Cadell, 'son of Rhodri the Great,' was killed by his brother Meurug.

918. And ²Uercu, a 'good' bishop, died.

919. And the action of Dinas Newydd took place.

926. Nine hundred and twenty was the year of Christ, when king Howel the Good, son of Cadell, went to Rome: and Elen died.

933. Nine hundred and thirty was the year of Christ, when Gruffudd, son of Owain, was slain by the men of Ceredigion,

935. And the battle of ³Brun took place.

936. And ⁴Hennyrth, son of Clydog, and his brother Meurug, died.

939. And Edelstan, king of the Saxons, died.

940. Nine hundred and forty was the year of Christ, when king Abloyc died.

941. And Cadell, son of Arthvael, was poisoned; and Idwal, son of Rhodri, and his ᵃbrother Elised, were killed by the Saxons.

942. And ⁵Lwmbert, bishop of Menevia, died.

943. And Ussa, son of Llawr; and ⁶Morcheis, bishop of Bangor, died.

944. And Cyngen, son of ⁷Elised, was poisoned; and ⁸Eueurys, bishop of Menevia, died. Strath Clyde was devastated by the Saxons.

ᵃ ⁹ son

---

¹ Morkleis, *D. E.*
⁷ Elisse, *D. E.*
⁸ Eneuris, *D. E.*
⁹ *D. E.*

DCCCCXLVIII. A Howel da uab Kadell vrenhin penn a molyant yr holl Vrytanyeit a vu uarỏ. A Chadỏgaỏn uab Owein alas y gan y Saeson. Ac yna y bu weith Carno rỏg meibon ¹[Ywain ap] Howel ² a meibon Idwal.

DCCCCL. Deg mlyned adeugein a nawcant oed oet Crist pan diffeithaỏd Iago a Ieuaf meibon Idwal Dyfet dỏyweith, ³[ac ỷ llas Dungwallaun ỷgan ev gwỷr wỷnt].

DCCCCLI. Ac yna y bu uarỏ ᵃDyfynỏal a Rodri meibon' Howel.

DCCCCLII. Ac yna ⁴[blwydyn wedy hynny] y bu ladua uaỏr ⁴[y] rỏg meibon Idwal a meibon Howel ᵇyg gweith Conỏy yn Llanrỏst. Ac y llas Hirmaỏr ac Anaraỏt y gan y pobloed, meibon oed y rei hynny y ỏryat.' A gỏedi hynny y diffeithỏyt Keredigyaỏn y gan ueibon Idwal. Ac y bu uarỏ Etwin uab Howel ¹[dda].

DCCCCLIII. Ac ⁴[blwydyn wedy hynny] y bodes ⁵Hayardur uab Mervyn.

DCCCCLIV. ⁴[Blwydyn wedy hynny y bu varw Edwin vab Hywel.] Ac y llas Congalach brenhin Iwerdon.

DCCCCLV. A ⁴[blwydyn wedy hynny y llas] Gỏgaỏn uab Gỏryat ¹[ap Rodri mawr.] Ac y bu yr haf tessaỏc.

DCCCCLVIII. ³[Teir blyned wedy hynny y diffeithyawd Ywein y ⁶Gorwyd.]

ᵃ/⁷ Rodri vab

ᵇ/⁷ yny lle a elwir Gwrgystu gweith Konwy ⁸hirmawr, ac y llas Anarawd vab Gwry.

---

¹ E.
² *Here C. resumes.*
³ C. D. E.
⁴ C.

948. And Howel the Good, son of king Cadell, chief and glory of all the Britons, died. And Cadwgan, son of Owain, was killed by the Saxons. And then the action of Carno took place between the sons of ¹Owain, son of' Howel, ²and the sons of Idwal.

950. Nine hundred and fifty was the year of Christ, when Iago and Ieuav, sons of Idwal, ravaged Dyved twice; ³and Dunwallon was slain by their men.'

951. And then ᵃDyvnwal and Rhodri, sons' of Howel, died.

952. And then, ⁴a year after that,' a great slaughter took place between the sons of Idwal and the sons of Howel, ᵇin the action of Conwy at Llanrwst. And Hirmawr and Anarawd were killed by the Pagans; they were sons of Gwriad.' And after that Ceredigion was devastated by the sons of Idwal. And Edwin, son of Howel ¹the Good,' died.

953. And, ⁴a year after that,' ⁵Hayarddur, son of Mervyn, was drowned.

954. ⁴A year after that, Edwin, son of Howel, died.' And Congalach, king of Ireland, was slain.

955. And, ⁴a year after that, was killed' Gwgawn, son of Gwriad, ¹son of Rhodri the Great.' And the hot summer happened.

958. ³Three years after that, Owain devastated the ⁶Gorwennydd.'

ᵃ/⁷ Rhodri, son.

ᵇ/⁷ in the place called Llanrwst the action of Conwy ⁸long and great, and Anarawd, son of Gwry, was slain.

---

⁵ Yardur, C.
⁶ Goryuŷd, D. E.
⁷ C. D. E.
⁸ C. D.

DCCCLIX. Ac ¹[blwydyn wedy hynny] ᵃ y bu diruaṽr ᵇ eira vis Maṽrth. A meibon Idwal yn gṽledychu.'
Ac y diffeithaṽd meibon Abloec Gaer Gybi a Lleyn.

DCCCLX. Trugein mlyned a naṽ cant oed oet Crist pan las Idwal uab Rodri.

DCCCLXI. Ac ²[blwydyn wedy hynny] y llas meibon Gṽynn. Ac y diffeithṽyt y Tywyn y gan y pobloed; ac y bu uarṽ Meuruc uab Catuan;

DCCCLXII. A ²[blwydyn wedy hynny] Ryderch escob;

DCCCLXIV. A ²[dwy vlyned wedy hynny] Chadṽallaṽn uab Owein ³[ap Howel dda.]

DCCCLXV. Ac yna ²[blwydyn wedy hynny] y diffeithaṽd y Saeson, ⁴ ac ⁵ Aluryt yn tywyssaṽc udunt vrenhinyaetheu meibon Idwal.

DCCCLXVI. Ac ²[blwydyn wedy hynny] y llas Rodri uab Idwal, ac y diffeithṽyt Aberffraṽ.

DCCCLVII. A ²[blwydyn] gṽedy hynny y ᶜ dellis Iago uab Idwal Ieuaf uab Idwal y vraṽt. Ac y carcharṽyt Ieuaf; ⁶ a gṽedy hynny y croget.'

DCCCLXVIII. Ac yna ²[blwydyn wedy hynny] y diffeithṽyt Gṽhyr y gan Einaṽn uab Owein.

DCCCLXIX. Ac ²[blwydyn wedy hynny] y diffeithaṽd ⁷ Marc uab Herald Benmon.

DCCCLXX. Deg mlyned a thrugein a naṽ cant oed oet Crist pan diffeithaṽd ⁸ Gotbric uab ⁹ Herald Von, ac o uaṽr ystryṽ y darestygaṽd yr holl ynys.

ᵃ ¹⁰ ỳ gwledỳchaud meibion Idwal drwỳ nerth diruaur mis Maurth.
ᵇ ¹¹ bla   ᶜ ¹² delis

---

¹ C. D. E.   ⁴ Not in D. E.
² C.   ⁵ Alfre, C.
³ E.   ⁶ Not in C. D. E.

959. And, 'a year after that,' a a great b snow happened in the month of March; the sons of Idwal reigning.' And the sons of Abloec devastated Caer Gybi and Lleyn.

960. Nine hundred and sixty was the year of Christ, when Idwal, son of Rhodri, was killed.

961. And, ²a year after that,' the sons of Gwyn were killed. And Towyn was devastated by the Pagans; and Meurug, son of Cadvan, died;

962. And, ²a year after that,' bishop Rhydderch;

964. And, ²two years after that,' Cadwallon, son of Owain, ³son of Howel the Good.'

965. And then, ² a year after that,' the Saxons, headed by ⁵Alvryd, ravaged the kingdoms of the sons of Idwal.

966. And, ²a year after that,' Rhodri, son of Idwal, was slain, and Aberfraw was devastated.

967. And, ²a year' after that, Iago, son of Idwal, c blinded his brother Ieuav, son of Idwal. And Ieuav was imprisoned; ⁶and after that hanged.'

968. And then, ²a year after that,' Gower was devastated by Einon, son of Owain.

969. And, ²a year after that,' ⁷Mark, son of Harold, devastated Penmon.

970. Nine hundred and seventy was the year of Christ, when ⁸Godfrey, son of ⁹Harold, devastated Mona, and by great craft subjugated the whole island.

---

a/ ¹⁰ the sons of Idwal ruled through great power in the month of March.
b ¹¹ plague   c ¹² captured

---

⁷ Madoc, *C.* Mactus, *D. E.*   ¹⁰ *D. E.*
⁸ Godfrid, *C.* Gotfrit, *D. E.*   ¹¹ *C.*
⁹ Harald, *C. D. E.*   ¹² *C. D. E.*

DCCCCLXXI. Ac yna ¹[blwydyn wedy hynny] y kynnullaôd ²[Edgar] brenhin y Saeson diruaôr lyges hyt Ygkaer llion ³ar ôysc.'

DCCCCLXXII. Ac ¹[blwydyn wedy hynny] y gôrthladôyt Iago oe gyfoeth, ac y gôledychaôd Howel drôy uudugolyaeth. Ac y ᵃclefychôyt Meuruc uab Idwal. Ac y bu varô Morgan.

DCCCCLXXIV. Ac yna ¹[dwy vlyned wedy hynny] y bu uarw Edgar brenhin y Saeson. Ac ydaeth Dônwallaôn brenhin Ystrat Clut y Rufein. Ac y bu uarô Idwallaôn uab ⁴Einaôn.

DCCCCLXXVI. Ac ¹[dwy vlyned wedy hynny] eil-. weith y diffeithaôd Einaôn ôbyr.

DCCCCLXXVII. Ac ¹[blwydyn wedy hynny] ᵇy diffeithwyt ᶜLlôyn Kelynaôc uaôr ⁵[yr eil weith] y gan Howel uab Ieuaf ar Saeson.'

DCCCCLXXVIII. Ac yna ¹[blwydyn wedy hynny] y delit Iago. Ac y goruu Howel uab Ieuaf ac y gorescynnôys ⁶[kyuoeth] Iago.

DCCCCLXXIX. Ac ¹[blwydyn wedy hynny] y llas Idwal. A gwedy hynny y diffeithaôd Custennhin uab Iago a ⁷Gotbric uab ⁸Herald Lyyn a Mon. A gwedy hynny y llas Custenhin uab Iago y gan Howel uab Ieuaf yn y vrôydyr a elwir gôeith ⁹Hirbarth.

ᵃ ¹⁰ dallwyd

ᵇ⸍ ¹¹ y diffeithyawd Gwrmid eilweith Leyn, ac y diffeithyawd Hywel vab Yeuaf ar Saesson Gyueilyawc vawr.

ᶜ ¹² Lleýn a

---

¹ *C.*
² *C. D. E.* Edward, *A.*
ᵛ *Not in C.*

⁴ Oweyn, *C. D. E.*
⁵ *D. E.*
⁶ *D.*

971. And then, ¹a year after that,' ²Edgar, king of the Saxons, collected a very great fleet at Caerleon ³upon Usk.'

972. And, ¹a year after that,' Iago was expelled from his territory, and Howel ruled in consequence of his victory. And Meurug, son of Idwal, ᵃfell sick.' And Morgan died.

974. And then, ¹two years after that,' Edgar, king of the Saxons, died. And Dunwallon, king of Strath Clyde, went to Rome. And Idwallon, son of ⁴Einon, died.

976. And, ¹two years after that,' Einon devastated Gower a second time.

977. And, ¹a year after that,' ᵇthe ᶜGrove of' Celynog the Great was devastated ⁵a second time' by Howel, son of Ieuav, and the Saxons.'

978. And then, ¹a year after that,' Iago was captured. And Howel, son of Ieuav, had the victory, and conquered ⁶the territory of' Iago.

979. And, ¹a year after that,' Idwal was slain. And after that Constantine, son of Iago, and ⁷Godfrey, son of Harold, devastated Lleyn and Mona. And after that Constantine, son of Iago, was killed by Howel, son of Ieuav, in the battle called the action of ⁹Hirbarth.

ᵃ ¹⁰ was blinded.

ᵇ/ ¹¹ Gwrmid a second time devastated Lleyn, and Howel, son of Ieuav, and the Saxons devastated Cyveiliog the Great.

ᶜ ¹² Lleyn and

⁷ Godfrid, *C.* Gotfrit, *D. E.*
⁸ Harald, *C. D. E.*
⁹ Hirbarwch, *C. D. E.*
¹⁰ *C. D. E.*
¹¹ *C.*
¹² *D. E.*

DCCCCLXXXI. ¹[Vn vlyned a] pedwar ugein mlyned a naỽ cant oed oet Crist pan diffeithaỽd ²Gotbric uab ³Herald Dyuet a Mynyỽ. ᵃAc y bu weith Llanwannaỽc.'

DCCCCLXXXII. Ac yna ¹[blwydyn wedy hynny] y diffeithỽyt Brecheinaỽc a holl gyfoeth Einaỽn uab Owein y gan y Saeson, ac ⁴Aluryt yn dywyssaỽc arnunt. A Howel uab Ieuaf ac Einaỽn aladaỽd llawer oe lu.

DCCCCLXXXIII. Ac yna ¹[y vlwydyn nessaf y honno] y llas Einaỽn uab Owein drỽy dỽyll ¹[y] gan uchelwyr Gỽent. Ac y bu uarỽ ¹[eu] bonhedic escob.

DCCCCLXXXIV. Ac ¹[blwydyn wedy hynny] y lladaỽd y Saeson Howel uab Ieuaf drỽy dỽyll. Ac y llas Iouaual uab Meuruc, a Chadỽallaỽn uab Ieuaf ae lladaỽd.

DCCCCLXXXV. ⁵[Blwydyn wedy hynny y llas ⁵Meyc vab Yeuaf, ᵇa Maredud ap Ywein a ladawd] Kadwallaỽn ab Ieuaf drỽy vudugolyaeth,' aoresgynnỽys y gyfoeth, nyt amgen noc ynys Von a Meiryonnyd; a holl wladoed Gỽyned o diruaỽr ystryỽ a challter a darestygaỽd.

DCCCCLXXXVI. Ac yna ¹[blwydyn wedy hynny] yd yspeilỽyt Llywarch ab Owein oe lygeit. Ac y diffeithỽyt ²Gotbric uab ³Herald ar llu du gantaỽ ac ef Ynys Von. Ac y ᶜdellit dỽy vil o dynyon, ar

---

ᵃ ⁷ a Llannweithenawc.

ᵇ ⁸ a Chatwallawn vab Ieuaf, ỹ gan Moredud vab Oweÿn

ᶜ ⁹ delit

---

¹ C.
² Godfrid, C. Gotfrit, D. E.
³ Harald, C. D. E.

⁴ Alfred, C. D. Not in E.
⁵ C. D. E.

THE CHRONICLE OF THE PRINCES.   29

981. ¹One year and' nine hundred and eighty was the year of Christ, when ²Godfrey, son of Harold, devastated Dyved and Menevia. ᵃ And the action of Llanwenog took place.'

982. And then, ¹a year after that,' Brecheiniog, and all the territory of Einon, son of Owain, were devastated by the Saxons, ⁴Alvryd being their leader. And Howel, son of Ieuav, and Einon killed many of his host.

983. And then, ¹the year next to that,' Einon, son of Owain, was killed through treachery by the nobles of Gwent. And ¹their bishop of noble lineage died.

984. And, ¹a year after that,' the Saxons killed Howel, son of Ieuav, through treachery. And Ionaval, son of Meurug, was killed, and Cadwallon, son of Ieuav, killed him.

985. ⁵A year after that, Maig, son of Ieuav, was killed, ᵇand Maredudd, son of Owain, killed' Cadwallon, son of Ieuav, victoriously,' and subjugated his territory, to wit, the isle of Mona and Meirionydd; and all the districts of Gwynedd he subdued by extreme craft and cunning.

986. And then, ¹a year after that,' Llywarch, son of Owain, was deprived of his eyes. And Godfrey, son of Harold, with the black host, devastated the isle of Mona. And two thousand men were ᶜblinded; and

---

ᵃ/⁷ and Llanweithenog.

ᵇ/⁸ and Cadwallon, son of Ieuav, by Maredudd, son of Owain.

ᶜ⁹ captured;

---

⁶ Mevric, E.   ⁴ D. E.
⁷ C. D. Not in E.   ⁵ C. D. E.

dryll arall o nadunt a duc Maredud uab Owein y gyt ac ef y Geredigyaͬn a Dyfet. Ac yna y bu uarͬolyaeth ar yr holl aniueileit yn holl ynys Prydein.

DCCCCLXXXVII. Ac yna ¹[blwydyn wedy hynny] y bu uarͬ Ieuaf uab Idwal, ac Owein uab Hoͬel. Ac y diffeithaͬd y kenedloed Lanbadarn a Mynyͬ a Llanulltut ²a Llangarban' a Llandydoch.

DCCCCLXXXVIII. Ac yna ¹[blwydyn wedy hynny] y llas ³[Glwmayn] mab Abloyc. Ac y talaͬd Maredud ¹[ap Ywein] yn deyrnget yr kenedloed duon geinaͬc o bop dyn. Ac y bu diruaͬr uarͬolyaeth ar y dynyon rac newyn.

DCCCCLXXXIX. Ac ¹[blwydyn wedy hynny] y llas Owein uab Dyfynwal.

DCCCCXC. ¹[Dec mlyned aphedwar ugeint a naw kant oed oet Krist,] ac y diffeithaͬd Maredud maes Hyfeid.

DCCCCXCI. ¹[Blwydyn wedy hynny] deg mlyned a phedwar ugein a naͬ cant oed oet Crist pan diffeithaͬd Etwin uab Einaͬn, ac ⁴Eclis uaͬr tywyssaͬc Seis y ar voroed y deheu' oll vrenhinyaetheu Maredud, nyt amgen Dyfet, Acheredigaͬn, Agͬhyr, Achedweli; ac eilweith y kymerth wystlon or holl gyfoeth; ar dryded weith y diffeithaͬd Vynyͬ. A Maredud a huryaͬd y kenedloed adathoedynt yny ewyllys gyt ac ef, ac a diffeithaͬd gͬlat Uorgan; a Chadwallaͬn y uab a uu uarͬ.

DCCCCXCII. Ac yna ¹[blwydyn wedy hynny] ᵃy duc meibon Meuruc kyrch hyt Yggͬyned,' ac y

---

ᵃ' ⁵ y bu o veibyon Meuryc wystlon Yngwyned,

---

¹ C.
² Not in E.

³ C. D. E.

the remainder Maredudd, son of Owain, took with him to Ceredigion and Dyved. And then a mortality took place among all the cattle over the whole island of Britain.

987. And then, ¹'a year after that,' Ieuav, son of Idwal, died, and Owain, son of Howel. And the Pagans devastated Llanbadarn, and Menevia, and Llanilltud, ²'and Llangarvan,' and Llandydoch.

988. And then, ¹'a year after that,' ³'Glumaen,' son of Abloec, was killed. And Maredudd, ¹'son of Owain,' paid to the black Pagans a tribute of a penny for each person. And a great mortality took place among the men through famine.

989. And, ¹'a year after that,' Owain, son of Dyvnwal, was slain.

990. ¹'Nine hundred and ninety was the year of Christ,' and Maredudd devastated Maes Hyveidd.

991. ¹'A year after that,' nine hundred and ninety was the year of Christ, when Edwin, son of Einon, with ⁴'Eclis the Great, a Saxon prince from the seas of the South,' devastated all the kingdoms of Maredudd, to wit, Dyved, and Ceredigion, and Gower, and Cydweli; and a second time took hostages from all the territory; and devastated Menevia a third time. And Maredudd hired the Pagans willing to join him, and devastated Glamorgan; and his son Cadwallon died.

992. And then, ¹'a year after that,' ᵃ'the sons of Meurug made an inroad into Gwynedd,' and the isle

---

ᵃ' ⁵ some of the sons of Meurug were hostages in Gwynedd,

ᵛ Edylfi seis, C. | ⁵ C.

diffeithŵyt ynys Von y gan y kenedloed duŵ Ieu Kyrchauel.

DCCCCXCIII. Ac yna ¹[blwydyn wedy hynny] y bu diruaŵr neŵyn ygkyfoeth Maredud. Ac y bu vrŵydyr y rŵg meibon Meuruc a Maredud yn ymyl Llangŵm, ac y goruu ueibon Meuruc; ac yno y llas Teŵdŵr uab Einaŵn.

DCCCCXCIV. Ac yna ¹[blwydyn wedy hynny] y diffeithŵyt Manaŵ y gan ²Yswein uab Herald.'

DCCCCXCV. Ac ¹[blwydyn wedy hynny] y llas Idwal uab Meuruc. Ac y diffeithŵyt ³Arthmarcha ac y lloscet.

DCCCCXCVIII. Ac ¹[teir blyned wedy hynny] y diboblet Mynyŵ y gan y kenedloet. Ac y llas Morgeneu escob y gantunt. Ac y bu varŵ Maredud uab Owein y clotuorussaf vrenhin y Brytanyeit.

DCCCCXCIX. ª Mil o vlŵynyded oed oet Crist' pan diffeithŵyt Dulyn y gan yr Yscoteit. Ac y gŵledychaŵd Kynan uab Howel Yggŵyned.

M. ¹[Mil o vlwydyned oed oet Krist,] ac y diffeithaŵd y kenedloed Dyfet.

MI. Ac ¹[blwydyn wedy hynny] y bu uarŵ ⁴Mor uab Gŵyn, ac Iuor ⁵Porth Talarthi.'

MIII. A ¹[blwydyn] gwedy hynny y llas Kynan uab Howel.

MIV. Ac ¹[blwydyn wedy hynny] y dallwyt Gŵlfac ac ⁶Vryat.

MV. ⁷[Blwydyn wedy hynny y bu y vlwydyn gyntaf a elwid ⁸decem nouennalis ⁹cicli II.']

ª' ¹⁰ Blwydyn wedy hynny,

---

¹ C.
² Ywein vab Harald, C
³ Athmatha, C. D.
⁴ Ivor, E.
⁵ Porthalarchi, C. D. E.
⁶ Vbiad, C. D. E.

of Mona 'was devastated by the Pagans on Ascension Thursday.

993. And then, ¹'a year after that,' a great famine happened in the territory of Maredudd. And a battle took place between the sons of Meurug and Maredudd near Llangwm, and the sons of Meurug conquered; and there Tewdwr, son of Einon, was slain.

994. And then, a ¹year after that,' the isle of Man was devastated by ²Swain, son of Harold.

995. And, a ¹year after that,' Idwal, son of Meurug, was killed. And ³Arthmarcha was devastated and burned.

998. And, ¹three years after that,' Menevia was depopulated by the Pagans. And bishop Morgeneu was killed by them. And Maredudd, son of Owain, the most celebrated king of the Britons, died.

999. ᵃA thousand was the year of Christ,' when Dublin was devastated by the Scots. And Cynan, son of Howel, reigned in Gwynedd.

1000. ¹A thousand was the year of Christ,' and the Pagans devastated Dyved.

1001. And, ¹a year after that,' ⁴Mor, son of Gwyn, died, and Ivor of ⁵Porth Talarthi.'

1003. And, ¹a year after that,' Cynan, son of Howel, was killed.

1004. And, ¹a year after that,' Gwlvac and ⁶Gwriad were blinded.

1005. ⁷A year after that was the first year called ⁸decem-novennalis ⁹cicli II.'

ᵃ/ ¹⁰ A year after that,

---

⁷ C. D. E.
⁸ The cycle of 19 years began in 1007.
⁹ D.
¹⁰ C.

MXI. ¹[Vn mlyned ar] mil adeg mlyned oed oet Crist pan diffeithöyt Mynyö y gan y Saeson ²nyt amgen y gan Entris ac Vbis.' Ac y bu uarö ³Hayarndrut' mynach o Enlli.

MXII. Ac yna ¹[blwydyn wedy hynny] ydaeth ³Yswein uab ⁴Herald y Loeger, ac y gyrraöd ⁵Eldryt uab Etgar oe deyrnas, ac y göledychaöd yny gyfoeth, ynyr hön y bu uarö yny vlöydyn honno.

MXIII. Ac yna y kyffroes Brian brenhin holl Iwerdon, a Mörchath y vab a lliaös o vrenhined ereill yn erbyn Dulyn, y lle ydoed Sitruc vab Abloec yn vrenhin. Ac yn eu herbyn y deuth göyr Largines, a Mael Mordaf yn vrenhin arnadunt, ac ymaruoll aorugant yn erbyn Brian vrenhin. Ac y huryaöd Sitruc gant yn erbyn Brian vrenhin, ac yna y huryaöd Sitruc llogeu hiryon aruaöc yn gyflaön o wyr llurugaöc a ⁶Derotyr yn tywyssaöc arnadunt. A göedy bot bröydyr y rygtunt agöneuthur aerua o bop tu y llas Brian ae vab or neilltu a thywyssaöc y llogeu ⁷ae vraöt,' a Mael Morda vrenhin or tu arall.

MXV. Ac yna ¹[dwy vlyned wedy hynny] y llas Owein uab Dyfynwal. Ac yna ¹[blwydyn wedy hynny] y gorescynnaöd Cnut uab ³Yswein vrenhinyaeth Loeger a Denmarc a Germania ¹[vawr].

MXVI. Ac yna ¹[blwydyn wedy hynny] y llas Aedan uab Blegyöryt ae bedwarmeib y gan Lywelyn uab Seisyll.

MXIX. Ac ¹[teir blyned wedy hynny] y llas Meuruc uab Arthuael.

---

a/ ⁸ Vbis Haeardur ⁹ Yardur

---

¹ C.
ʸ Eutris ac Ubis, C.
³ Ywein, C.

⁴ Harald, C. D. E.
⁵ Edelret, D. E.

1011. ¹One year and' one thousand and ten was the year of Christ, when Menevia was devastated by the Saxons, to wit, by Entris and Ubis. And ᵃHayarndrud,' a monk of Bardsey, died.

1012. And then, ¹a year after that,' ³Swain, son of Harold, came to England, and expelled Edelred, son of Edgar, from his kingdom, and reigned in his territory, in which he died in that year.

1013. And then Brian, king of all Ireland, and his son Mwrchath, and many other kings, were stirred up against Dublin, where Sitruc, son of Abloec, was king. And against them came the men of Leinster, headed by their king Mael Mordav; and they confederated against king Brian. And Sitruc hired a hundred men against king Brian; and then Sitruc hired armed long ships full of mailed men, headed by ⁶Derotyr; and after a battle between them, and slaughter made on both sides, Brian and his son were killed on one side, and the leader of the ships ⁷and his brother,' and king Mael Mordav, on the other side.

1015. And then, ¹two years after that,' Owain, son of Dyvnwal, was killed. And then, ¹a year after that,' Cnute, son of ⁸Swain, took possession of the kingdom of England, and Denmark, and Germany ¹the Great.'

1016. And then, ¹a year after that,' Aeddan, son. of Blegywryd, and his four sons, were killed by Llywelyn, son of Seisyll.

1019. And, ¹three years after that,' Meurug, son of Arthvael, was killed.

ᵃ' ⁸ Vbis Haearnddur ⁹ Iarddur

---

⁶ Brodr, *C. D. E.* ⁸ *D. E.*
⁷ *Not in C. D. E.* ⁹ *C.*

MXX. ¹[Vgein mlyned amil oed oet Krist,] ac yna y dechymygaōd neb un Yscot yngelōyd y uot yn vab y Varedud vrenhin, ac y mynnaōd y laō ehun yn vrenhin. Ac y kymerth gōyr y deheu ef yr arglōyd ac y deyrnas a henō un Rein. Ac yny erbyn yryfelaōd Llywelyn uab Seisyll goruchel vrenhin Gōyned a phennaf achlotuorussaf vrenhin or holl Vrytanyeit. Yny amser ef y gnotaei henafyeit y teyrnas dywedut bot y gyfoeth ef or mor py gilyd yn gyflaōn o amylder da a dynyon, hyt na thebygit bot na thlaōt nac eissiwedic yny holl wladoed na thref ōac na chyfle diffyc. Ac yna y duc Rein Yscot lu yn dilesc, a herwyd defaōt yr Yscoteit yn valch syberō, annoc awnaeth y wyr y ymlad, ac yn ymdiredus adaō a wnaeth udunt mae ef aorvydei. Ac ymgyfaruot aoruc yn ehofyn ae elynyon, ac ōynteu yn wastat diofyn aoryssant y chōydedic drahaus annogōr hōnnō. Ac ynteu yn hy diofyn agyrchaōd y vrōydyr, a gōedy gōeithaō y vrōydyr a gōneuthur kyffredin aerua o bop tu, a gōastat ymlad, drōy leōder y Gōyndyt, yna y goruuōyt Rein Yscot ae lu. A herōyd y dyōedir yny diareb. Annoc dy gi ac nac erlit. Ef agyrchaōd yn leō ehofyn, ac agilyaōd yn waradōydus o lōynogaōl defaōt. Ar Gōyndyt yn llidyaōc ae hymlynaōd drōy lad y lu a diffeithaō y wlat, ac yspeilaō pob mann, ae distryō hyt y Mars, ac nyt ymdangosses ynteu byth o hynny allan. Ar vrōydyr honno a vu yn Aber Gōyli. A gōedy hynny y deuth ²Eilad ªy ynys Prydein,' ac y̆ diffeithōyt Dyuet ac y torret Mynyō.

ª'³ y̆ dir Kẏmmre,

¹ C. | ² Eilaf, C. D. E.

1020. [1]'One thousand and twenty was the year of Christ,' and then a certain Scot falsely pretended to be the son of king Maredudd, and caused himself to be named king; and the men of the South received him as their lord, and to a kingdom; and his name was Rein. And Llywelyn, son of Seisyll, supreme king of Gwynedd, and the chief and most renowned king of all the Britons, made war against him. In his time it was usual for the elders of his kingdom to say, that his dominion was from one sea to the other, complete in abundance of wealth and inhabitants; so that it was supposed there was neither poor nor destitute in all his territories, nor an empty hamlet, nor any deficiency. And then Rein the Scot boldly led on his host, and, after the manner of the Scots, proudly and ostentatiously exhorted his men to fight, confidently promising them that he should conquer. And so he boldly approached his enemies, and they coolly and fearlessly awaited that vaunting and arrogant challenger. He, daring and fearless, repaired to the conflict, and after the battle was fought, with a general slaughter on both sides, and constant fighting, through the bravery of the Gwyneddians, victory was obtained over Rein the Scot and his host. And as it is proverbially said, 'Excite thy dog, but do not pursue;' he assaulted bravely and fearlessly, and retreated shamefully in a fox-like manner. And the Gwyneddians wrathfully pursued him, slaying his men, and devastating the country, pillaging every place, and destroying it as far as Mercia; and he never from henceforward made his appearance. And that battle took place at Aber Gwyli. And after that [2] Eilad came [a] to the island of Britain,' and Dyved was devastated, and Menevia was demolished.

---

a'[3] to the land of Wales,

MXXI. Ac yna ¹[blwydyn wedy hynny] y bu uarỏ Llywelyn uab Seisyll. Ac y kynhalyaỏd Ryderch uab Iestin llywodraeth y Deheu.

MXXIII. Ac yna ¹[dwy vlyned wedy hynny] y bu uarỏ ²Morgeneu escob ³[Mynyw.]

MXXIV. ⁴[Blwydyn wedy hynny y bu y vlwydyn gyntaf aelwid ⁵decem nouennalis.]

MXXV. Ac ¹[blwydyn wedy hynny] y llas Kynan uab Seisyll.

MXXXI. ¹[Vn mlyned ar] deg mlyned arhugeint a mil oed oet Crist pan las Ryderch uab Iestin y gan yr Yscottoeit. Ac yna y kynhalyaỏd Iago uab Idwal llywodraeth ỏyned wedy Llywelyn uab Seisyll. ᵃA Howel a Maredud veibon Etwin' a gynhalassant llywodraeth y Deheu.

MXXXII. Ac yna ¹[blwydyn wedy hynny] y bu weith ⁶Hiraethỏy ¹[y] rỏg meibon Etwin ⁴[a meibyon Ryderch.

MXXXIII. Blwydyn wedy hynny y llas Maredud ap Edwin] y gan ueibon Kynan. A Charadaỏc uab Ryderch a las y gan y Saeson.

MXXXVI. Ac yna y bu uarỏ Cnut uab ⁷Yswein vrenhin Lloeger a Denmarc a Germania. A gỏedy y varỏ ef y foes Eilaf hyt yn Germania.

MXXXVII. Ac yna ¹[pedeir blyned wedy hynny] ᵇy delis' y ⁸kenedloed Ueuruc uab Howel. Ac y llas Iago vrenhin Gỏyned; ac yny le ynteu y gỏledychaỏd Gruffud uab Llywelyn ab Seisyll, a hỏnnỏ oe dechreu hyt y diwed a ymlidyaỏd y Saeson, ar kenedloed

---

ᵃ'⁹ Ac Edwin a Howel meibion Moredud,
ᵇ'⁹ agŷnhaliassant

---

¹ C.
² Morgynnyd, C. D. E.
³ E.

⁴ C. D. E.
⁵ This was in 1026.

1021. And then, ¹a year after that,' Llywelyn, son of Seisyll, died. And Rhydderch, son of Iestin, assumed the government of the South.

1023. And then, ¹two years after that,' ²Morgeneu, bishop ³of Menevia,' died.

1024. ⁴A year after that was the first year called ⁵decem-novennalis.'

1025. And, ¹a year after that,' Cynan, son of Seisyll, was killed.

1031. ¹One year and' one thousand and thirty was the year of Christ, when Rhydderch, son of Iestin, was killed by the Scots. And then Iago, son of Idwal, held the government of Gwynedd after Llywelyn, son of Seisyll. ᵃAnd Howel and Maredudd, sons of Edwin,' held the government of the South.

1032. And then, ¹a year after that,' the action of ⁶Hiraethwy took place between the sons of Edwin ⁴and the sons of Rhydderch.

1033. A year after that, Maredudd, son of Edwin, was killed' by the sons of Cynan. And Caradog, son of Rhydderch, was killed by the Saxons.

1036. And then, Cnute, son of ⁷Swain, king of England, and Denmark and Germany, died. And after his death Eilav fled into Germany.

1037. And then, ¹four years after that,' the Pagans ᵇcaptured' Meurug, son of Howel. And Iago, king of Gwynedd, was slain; and Gruffudd, son of Llywelyn, son of Seisyll, governed in his stead: and he, from beginning to end, pursued the Saxons, and the other

---

ᵃ/⁹ And Edwin and Howel, sons of Maredudd,
ᵇ/⁹ supported

---

⁶ Irathwy, *C. D. E.*
⁷ Ywein, *C.*
⁸ bonhedigyon, *C.*
⁹ *D. E.*

ereill, ac ae lladaỏd, ac ae diuaaỏd, ac o luossogrỏyd o ymladeu ae goruu. Y vrỏydyr gyntaf awnaeth yn Ryt ¹ Groes ar Hafren, ac yno y goruu ef. Y vlỏydyn honno y dibobles ef Lanbadarn, ac y kynhelis ef llywodraeth Deheubarth, ac y gỏrthladaỏd Howel uab Etwin oe gyfoeth.

MXXXVIII. Ac yna ²[blwydyn wedy hynny] y bu uarỏ ³ Heurun escob Mynyỏ.

MXXXIX. Ac yna ²[blwydyn wedy hynny] y bu weith Pen Cadeir, ac y goruu Rufud ar Howel, ac y delis y wreic, ac ae kymerth yn wreic idaỏ chun.

MXL. Deugein mlyned a mil oed oet Crist pan uu vrỏydyr Pỏll Dyfach, ac yno y goruu Hoỏel y kenedloed aoedynt yn diffeithaỏ Dyfet. Yny vlỏydyn ²[honno] y delit Grufud y gan ªgenedloed Dulyn.'

MXLI. Ac yna ²[blwydyn wedy hynny] y bu varỏ Hoỏel uab ⁴ Etwin brenhin gỏlat Vorgan yny heneint.

MXLII. Ac yna ²[blwydyn wedy hynny] y medylyaỏd Hoỏel uab Etwin diffeithaỏ Deheubarth a llyges o genedyl Iwerdon gyt ac ef, ac yny erbyn y gwrthỏynebaỏd idaỏ Rufud ab Llywelyn. Agỏedy bot creulaỏn vrỏydyr a diruaỏr aerua ar lu Howel ar Gỏydyl yn Aber Tywi y dygỏydaỏd Howel ac y llas, ac yna y goruu Rufud. ⁵[Ac yna y bu varw Euilfre a Mactus vanach.]

MXLIII. Ac yna ²[blwydyn wedy hynny] y bu varỏ Iosef escob Teilaỏ yn Rufein. Ac y bu diruawr

---

ª/ ᵃ wyr Deheubarth.

---

¹ Groc, *C.*
² *C.*
³ Hermini, *D.* Iferinin, *E.*
⁴ Ywein, *C. D. E.*

nations, and killed and destroyed them, and overcame them in a multitude of battles. The first battle he fought at Rhyd y Groes on the Severn, where he was victorious. That year he depopulated Llanbadarn, and obtained the government of South Wales, and dispossessed Howel, son of Edwin, of his territory.

1038. And then, ²a year after that,' ³Heurun, bishop of Menevia, died.

1039. And then, ²a year after that,' the action of Pen Cadeir took place, and Gruffudd overcame Howel, and captured his wife, and took her to be his own wife.

1040. One thousand and forty was the year of Christ, when the battle of Pwll Dyvach took place, and there Howel vanquished the Pagans who were ravaging Dyved. In that year Gruffudd was captured by ᵃthe Pagans of Dublin.'

1041. And then, ²a year after that,' Howel, son of ⁴Edwin, king of Glamorgan, died in his old age.

1042. And then, ²a year after that,' Howel, son of Edwin, meditated the devastation of South Wales, accompanied by a fleet of the people of Ireland, and against him was opposed Gruffudd, son of Llywelyn. And after a cruel battle, and a vast slaughter of the army of Howel and of the Irish at Aber Tywi, Howel fell and was slain, and Gruffudd was victorious. ⁵And then Evilfre, and Mactus the monk, died.'

1043. And then, ²a year after that,' Joseph, bishop of Llandav, died at Rome. And exceeding treachery

---

ᵃ'⁶ the men of South Wales.

---

⁵ *C. D. E.* ⁶ *E.*

dȯyll gan Ruffud a Rys meibon Ryderch [1] [ap Iestin] yn erbyn Gruffud uab Llywelyn.

MXLV. Ac yna [2] [dwy vlyned wedy hynny] y dygȯydaȯd amgylch seith ugeinwyr o teulu Grufud drȯy dȯyll gȯyr Ystrat Tywi, ac y dial y rei hynny y diffeithaȯd Grufud Ystrat Tywi a Dyfet. Ac yna y bu diruaȯr eira duȯ kalan Ionaȯr, ac y trigyaȯd hyt [3] wyl Badric.

MXLVII. Ac [2] [dwy vlyned wedy hynny] y bu diffeith holl Deheubarth.

ML. Deg mlyned a deugein a mil oed oet Crist a pan ballaȯd llyges o Iwerdon yn [4] dyfot y Deheubarth.'

MLIV. Ac yna [2] [pedeir blyned wedy hynny] y lladaȯd Grufud uab Llywelyn Ruffud uab Ryderch. Agȯedy hynny y kyffroes Grufud ab Llywelyn lu yn erbyn y Saeson a chȯeiraȯ bydinoed yn Henford; ac yny erbyn y kyfodes y Saeson a diruaȯr bu gantunt, a [5] Reinȯlf yn tyȯyssaȯc arnunt; ac ymgyfaruot aorugant, a chȯeiraȯ bydinoed ac ymbarattoi y ymlad. Ae kyrchu aȯnaeth Grufud yndiannot, abydinoed kyȯeir gantaȯ, agȯedy bot brȯydyr chwerȯdost ar Saeson heb allell godef kynȯrȯf y Brytanyeit, yd ymchoelassant ar ffo, ac o diruaȯr ladua y dygȯydassant. Ae hymlit ynlut awnaeth Gruffud yr gaer, ac y myȯn y doeth, a dibobli y gaer aȯnaeth ae thorri a llosci y tref; ac odyna gyt a diruaȯr anreith ac yspeil yr ymchoelaȯd y wlat yn hyfryt uudugaȯl.

---

a/ [6] y periglawd llynghes o Iwerdon Dehavbarth.

---

[1] *E.*
[2] *C.*
[3] March 17.
[4] *Not in C. D.*

THE CHRONICLE OF THE PRINCES. 43

was practised by Gruffudd and Rhys, sons of Rhydderch, ¹son of Iestin,' against Gruffudd, son of Llywelyn.

1045. And then, ²two years after that,' about seven score men of the family of Gruffudd fell, through the treachery of the men of the Vale of Tywi, and to avenge them, Gruffudd devastated the Vale of Tywi and Dyved. And then there fell a great snow on the calends of January, which remained until the ³feast of St. Patrick.

1047. And, ²two years after that,' all South Wales lay waste.

1050. One thousand and fifty was the year of Christ, ª when a fleet failed coming from Ireland to South Wales.'

1054. And then, ²four years after that,' Gruffudd, son of Llywelyn, killed Gruffudd, son of Rhydderch. And after that Gruffudd, son of Llywelyn, raised an army against the Saxons, and arrayed his forces at Hereford; and against him the Saxons rose with a very great host, ⁵ Reinolf being commander over them; and they met together, arranged their armies, and prepared to fight. Gruffudd attacked them immediately with well-ordered troops, and after a severely hard battle, the Saxons, unable to bear the assault of the Britons, took to flight, and fell with a very great slaughter. Gruffudd closely pursued them to the fortress, which he entered, and depopulated and demolished the fortress, and burned the town; and from thence, with very great booty, he returned happily and victoriously to his own country.

ᵃ'⁶ a fleet from Ireland endangered South Wales.

ᵇ Randwlf, *C. D.*   ⁶ *E.*

44 BRUT Y TYWYSOGION.

MLVI. Ac yna ¹[dwy vlyned wedy hynny] y deuth ²Magnus uab ³Heralt brenhin Germania y Loeger, ac y diffeithaỏd vrenhinyaetheu y Saeson a Grufud vrenhin y Brytanyeit yn tyỏyssaỏc ac yn ganhorthỏy idaỏ.

MLVII. Ac yna ¹[blwydyn wedy hynny] y bu uarỏ Owein uab Grufud.

MLXI. ¹[Vn vlyned a] trugein mlyned a mil oed oet Crist pan dygỏydaỏd Grufud uab Llywelyn, penn atharyan ac amdiffynỏr y Brytanyeit drỏy dỏyll y wyr ehun; y gỏr a vuassei annorchyfegedic kynno hynny, yr aỏr honn aedewit y myỏn glynneu diffeithon, wedy diruaỏron anreitheu, adiuessuredigyon uudugolyaetheu, ac aneiryf oludoed eur ac aryant a gemmeu a phorfforolyon wiscoed. Ac yna y bu uarỏ Iosef escob Mynyỏ.

MLXII. ¹[Blwydyn wedy hynny y ⁴decem nouennalis gyntaf.]

MLXIV. Ac ¹[dwy vlyned wedy hynny] y bu uarỏ Dỏnchath uab Brian ᵃyn mynet y Rufein.'

MLXVI. Ac yna ¹[blwydyn wedy hynny] y medylyaỏd ³Heralt vrenhin Denmarc darestỏg y Saeson, yr hỏnn a gymerth ³Heralt arall uab Gotwin iarll aoed vrenhin yna yn Lloeger yndirybud diaryf, ac o deissyfyt ymlad drỏy ⁵wladaỏl dỏyll ae trewis yr llaỏr yny vu uarỏ. Ar Heralt hỏnnỏ a uuassei iarll yn gyntaf, trỏy greulonder gỏedy marỏ Edwart urenhin a ennillaỏd yn andylyedus uchelder teyrnas Loeger, a hỏnnỏ a yspeilỏyt oe teyrnas ae wyỏyt ygan Wilim bastard tyỏyssaỏc Normandi, kyt bocsachei or uudug-

ᵃ/⁶ ỳ Ruvein ac ỳno ỳ bu varw.

---

¹ *C.*
² Rodri Mawr *C.*
³ Harald, *C. D. E.*
⁴ A.D. 1064.

1056. And then, ¹'two years after that,' ²Magnus, son of Harold, king of Germany, came to England, and ravaged the dominions of the Saxons, Gruffudd, king of the Britons, being conductor and auxiliary to him.

1057. And then, ¹'a year after that,' Owain, son of Gruffudd, died.

1061. ¹'One year and' one thousand and sixty was the year of Christ, when Gruffudd, son of Llywelyn, the head and shield, and defender of the Britons, fell through the treachery of his own men. The man who had been hitherto invincible, was now left in the glens of desolation, after taking immense spoils, and after innumerable victories, and countless treasures of gold and silver, and jewels and purple vestures. And then Joseph, bishop of Menevia, died.

1062. ¹A year after that, the first ⁴decem-novennalis.'

1064. And, ¹'two years after that,' Dwnchath, son of Brian, ᵃdied on his way to Rome.'

1066. And then, ¹'a year after that,' Harold, king of Denmark, meditated the subjection of the Saxons; whom another Harold, the son of earl Godwin, who was then king in England, surprised, unwarned and unarmed, and by sudden attack, aided by national treachery, struck to the ground, and caused his death. That Harold who, at first earl, through cruelty after the death of king Edward unduly acquired the sovereignty of the kingdom of England, was despoiled of his kingdom and life by William the Bastard, duke of Normandy, though previously

---

ᵃ'⁶ went to Rome, and there he died.

---

³ dadawl, *C.* | ⁴ *D. E.*

olyaeth kynno hynny. Ar Gɤilim hɤnnɤ drɤy diruaɤr vrɤydyr a amdiffynnaɤd teyrnas Loeger o anorchfygedic laɤ ac uonhedickaf lu.

MLXVIII. Ac yna y bu weith Mechen rɤg Bledyn a Ruallaɤn veibon Kynfun, a Maredud ac Ithel veibyon Grufud. Ac yna y dygɤydaɤd meibon Grufud. Ithel a las yny vrɤydyr a Maredud a uu varɤ o annɤyt yn ffo; ac yno y llas Ruallaɤn uab Kynuyn. Ac yna y kynhellis Bledyn uab Kynfun Gɤyned a Phowys, a Maredud uab Owein uab Etwin agynhelis Deheubarth.

MLXX. Deg mlyned athrugein a mil oed oet Crist pan las Maredud uab Owein y gan Garadaɤc uab Grufud uab Ryderch ar Freinc ar lan avon [1] Rymhi. Ac yna y llas [2] Macmael Minbo clotuorussaf a chadarnaf urenhin y Gwydyl o deissyfyt vrɤydyr y gɤr a oed aruthur ɤrth y elynyon a hynaɤs y giɤtaɤtwyr, a gɤar ɤrth pererinyon adieithreit.

MLXXI. Yna [3] [blwydyn wedy hynny] y diffeithaɤd y Freinc Geredigyaɤn a Dyuet, a Mynyɤ a Bangor a diffeithɤyt y gan y genedloed. Ac yna y bu uarɤ Bleiddut escob Mynyɤ; ac y kymerth [4] Sulien yr escobaɤt.

MLXXII. Yna [3] [blwydyn wedy hynny] yr eilweith y diffeithaɤd y Ffreinc Geredigyaɤn.

MLXXIII. Ac yna [3] [blwydyn wedy hynny] y llas Bledyn uab Kynuyn y gan Rys [5] ab Owein drɤy dɤyll dryc ysprytolyon pennaetheu, ac uchelwyr Ystrat Tywi, y gɤr a oed gɤedy Grufud y uraɤt yn kynnal yn arderchaɤc holl deyrnas y Brytanyeit.

---

[1] Rympni, *D.*
[2] Deirmid, *C.*
[3] *C.*

vauntingly victorious. And that William defended the kingdom of England in a great battle, with an invincible hand, and his most noble army.

1068. And then the action of Mechain took place between Bleddyn and Rhiwallon, sons of Cynvyn, and Maredudd and Ithel, sons of Gruffudd; when the sons of Gruffudd fell. Ithel was killed in the battle, and Maredudd died of cold, in his flight; and there Rhiwallon, son of Cynvyn, was slain. And then Bleddyn, son of Cynvyn, held Gwynedd and Powys; and Maredudd, son of Owain, son of Edwin, held South Wales.

1070. One thousand and seventy was the year of Christ, when Maredudd, son of Owain, was killed by Caradog, son of Gruffudd, son of Rhydderch, and the French, on the banks of the river [1]Rymney. And then [2]Macmael Minbo, the most renowned and most powerful king of the Gwyddelians, was slain in a sudden onset;—the man who was terrible to his foes, friendly to his countrymen, and gentle towards pilgrims and strangers.

1071. Then, [3]'a year after that,' the French ravaged Ceredigion and Dyved, and Menevia and Bangor were laid waste by the Pagans. And then Bleiddud, bishop of Menevia, died; and Sulien assumed the bishopric.

1072. Then, [3]'a year after that,' a second time the French devastated Ceredigion.

1073. And then, [3]'a year after that,' Bleddyn, son of Cynvyn, was killed by Rhys, son of Owain, through the deceit of evil-minded chieftains and the noblemen of the Vale of Tywi—the man, who after Gruffudd his brother nobly supported the whole kingdom

---

[4] Sulgenius, *D.* | [5] uab, *D.*

Ac yny ol ynteu y góledychaód Trahayarn uab Karadaóc y gefynderó ar teyrnas ¹y Góndyt,' a Rys ²ab Owein a Ryderch uab Karadaóc agynhalassant ³Deheubarth. Ac yna yd ymladaód Grufud uab Kynan óyr Iago a ªMon, ac y lladaód y Góyndyt Kynóric uab Ruallaón. Ac yna y bu vróydyr yg Kaindór róg Goronó a Llywelyn meibion Kadógaón a Charadaóc uab Grufud gyt ac óynt, a Rys uab Owein a Ryderch uab Caradaóc ygyt ar rei hynny hefyt. Yny vlóydyn honno y bu vróydyr Bronn yr Eró róg Gruffud a Thrahayarn.

MLXXIV. Ac yna ⁴[blwydyn wedy hynny] y llas Ryderch uab Caradaóc y gan Meirchaón uab Rys uab Ryderch y gefynderó dróy dóyll.

MLXXV. Ac yna ⁴[blwydyn wedy hynny] y bu vróydyr ᵇGóennottyll róg Llywelyn a meibon Kadógaón a Rys uab Owein a Ryderch uab Karadaóc, y rei aoruuant eilweith.'

MLXXVI. Ac yna ⁴[blwydyn wedy hynny] y bu vróydyr Póll Gódyc, ac yna y goruu Trahayarn brenhin Góyned, ac y dialaód gʿaet Bledyn uab Kynuyn dróy rat Duó, yr hónn a uu waraf a thrugaroccaf or brenhined; ac nyt argyóedei y neb o ny chodit, a phan godit, oe anuod y dialei ynteu y godyant; góar

---

ª' ⁵ Manaw,

ᵇ' ⁶ Gweun ý nẏgẏl rwng meibion Cadwgawn ỳr eil veith, a Rys vab Oweỳn, ac ỳ goruuwýt ar Rýs ỳr eil weith. ⁷y rei y gorvvwyd eilweith arnunt.

---

¹ Wyned, C. 　　　　　³ y deheu, C.
² nab, D.　　　　　　⁴ C.

of the Britons. And after him Trahaiarn, son of Caradog, his cousin, ruled over the kingdom of the Gwyneddians; and Rhys, son of Owain, and Rhydderch, son of Caradog, held South Wales. And then Gruffudd, son of Cynan, fought against the men of Iago and of ᵃMona,' and the Gwyneddians killed Cynvrig, son of Rhiwallon. And then, a battle took place at Camddwr, between Goronwy and Llywelyn, sons of Cadwgan, and Caradog, son of Gruffudd, on the one side, and Rhys, son of Owain, and Rhydderch, son of Caradog, also on the other side. In that year the battle of Bron yr Erw took place between Gruffudd and Trahaiarn.

1074. And then, 'a year after that,' Rhydderch, son of Caradog, was killed by his cousin, Meirchion, son of Rhys, son of Rhydderch, through treachery.

1075. And then, 'a year after that,' ᵇthe battle of Gwennottyll took place between Llywelyn and the sons of Cadwgan, and Rhys, son of Owain, and Rhydderch, son of Caradog, who prevailed a second time.'

1076. And then, 'a year after that,' the battle of Pwll Gwdyg took place, when Trahaiarn, king of Gwynedd, prevailed, and, by the grace of God, avenged the blood of Bleddyn, son of Cynvyn, who was the mildest and most merciful of the kings, and who would injure no one unless offended, and when offended, it was against his will that he then avenged

---

ᵃ/⁵ the isle of Man,

ᵇ/⁶ the fight of Gweun y Nygyl took place between the sons of Cadwgan, the second time, and Rhys, son of Owain; and Rhys was overcome the second time. ⁷who were overcome a second time.

---

³ D.
⁴ D. E.

⁷ C.

oed ỽrth y gereint, ac amdiffynỽr ymdiueit a gỽeinon a gỽedwon, a chedernyt y doeth, ac enryded a grỽndwal yr eglỽysseu, a didanỽch y gỽlatoed, a hael ỽrth baỽp, aruthur yn ryfel a hegar ar hedỽch, ac amdiffyn y baỽb. Ac yna y dygỽydaỽd holl teulu Rys, ac ynteu yn ffoaỽdyr, megys karỽ ofnaỽc ym blaen y milgỽn drỽy y perthi ar creigeu. Ac yn diwed y vlỽydyn ¹[honno] yllas Rys ²[a] Howel y vraỽt y gan Garadaỽc ap Gruffud. Ac yna yd edewis ³ Sulyen y escobaỽt, ac y kymerth y ⁴ Uraham.

MLXXVII. Ac yna ⁵[blwydyn wedy hynny] y dechreuaỽd Rys ab Teỽdỽr wledychu.

MLXXVIII. Ac ⁵[blwydyn wedy hynny] y diffeithỽyt Mynyỽ yn druan y gan y kenedloed; ac y bu uarỽ y ⁴ Vraham escob Mynyỽ, ac y kymerth Sulyen yr escobaỽt eilweith oe anuod.

MLXXIX. Ac yna ⁵[blwydyn wedy hynny] y bu vrỽydyr ym mynyd Carn, ac yna y llas Trahayarn uab Karadaỽc, ᵃ uab' Gruffud ỽyr Iago, ar Yscotteit gyt ac ef yn ganhorthỽy idaỽ. Ac y llas Gỽrgeneu uab Seissyll drỽy dỽyll gan veibon Rys Seis. Ac yna ⁵[yn y vlwydyn honno] y deuth Gwilim vastard vrenhin y Saeson ar Freinc ar Brytanyeit ỽrth wediaỽ drỽy bererindaỽt y Vynyỽ.

MLXXX. ⁶[Y dechrewt edeiliat Caer Dŷf]

ᵃ⁄⁶ a meibion Riwallawn; Caradauc a Grufŷd a Meilir ŷ gan Rŷs vab Teudwr, canŷs

---

¹ D.
³ C. D. ap, A.

² Sulgenius, C.
⁴ Abraham, D. Euream, C.

the offence. He was gentle to his relations, and was defender of the orphans, the helpless, and the widows; was the supporter of the wise, the honour and stay of the churches, and the comfort of the countries; generous to all, terrible in war, and amiable in peace, and a defence to every one. And there all the family of Rhys fell, and himself became a fugitive, like a timid stag before the hounds, through the thickets and rocks. And at the end of that year Rhys, ²and Howel, his brother, were killed by Caradog, son of Gruffudd. And then Sulien resigned his bishopric, and it was assumed by Abraham.

1077. And then, ⁵'a year after that,' Rhys, son of Tewdwr, began to reign.

1078. And, ⁵'a year after that,' Menevia was miserably devastated by the Pagans; and Abraham, bishop of Menevia, died; and Sulien took the bishopric the second time against his inclination.

1079. And then, ⁵'a year after that,' the battle on Carn mountain took place, when were slain Trahaiarn, son of Caradog, ᵃ'the son of' Gruffudd, grandson of Iago, and with him the Scots, his auxiliaries. And Gurgeneu, son of Seisyll, was treacherously killed by the sons of Rhys the Saxon. And then, ⁵'in that year,' William the Bastard, king of the Saxons and the French and the Britons, came for prayer on a pilgrimage to Menevia.

1080. ⁶'The building of Cardiff began.'

ᵃ' ⁶ and the sons of Rhiwallon, Caradog and Gruffudd and Meilir, by Rhys, son of Tewdwr, for

---

⁵ *C.* ⁶ *D.*

MLXXXI. ¹[Un mlyned a phedwar ugeint a mil oed oet Krist pan oed y ² decem nouennalis gyntaf.]

MLXXXIII. Pedwar ugein mlyned a mil oed oet Crist pan edewis ³ Sulyen y escobaỽt y dryded weith, ac y kymerth Wilffre.

MLXXXIV. ⁴[Blwydyn wedy hynny y bu varw Terdelach brenhin Yscottieit nev y Gwydyl.]

⁵MLXXXV. Ac yna ⁶[blwydyn wedy hynny] y bu uarỽ Gwilim vastard, tywyssaỽc y Normanyeit a brenhin y Saeson ar Brytanyeit ar Albanwyr, wedy digaỽn o ogonyant a chlot y llithredic vyt yma, a gỽedy gogoneduson vudugolyaetheu ac enryded o oludoed; a gỽedy ef y gỽledychaỽd Gỽilim Goch y uab.

MLXXXVII. Ac yna ⁶[blwydyn wedy hynny] y gỽrthladỽyt Rys uab Teỽdỽr oe gyfoeth ae teyrnas y gan veibon Bledyn uab Kynuyn, nyt amgen Madaỽc a Chadỽgaỽn a ⁷ Ridit; ac ynteu a gilyaỽd y Iwerdon. Ac yny lle gỽedy hynny y kynhullaỽd ⁸[or Gwyddyl] ac y ymchoelaỽd drachefyn. Ac yna y bu vrỽydyr ⁹Llych Crei, ac y llas ᵃ meibon' Bledyn, ac y rodes Rys ab Teỽdỽr diruaỽr sỽllt yr llygheswyr Yscotteit ar Gỽydyl a deuthant yn borth idaỽ.

MLXXXVIII. Ac yna ⁶[blwydyn wedy hynny] y ducpỽyt yscrin Dewi yn lledrat or eglỽys ac yspeilỽyt

---

ᵃ' ¹⁰ wyrion ¹¹ deu vab ỳ Vledỳnt vab Kỳnvỳn nỳt amgen no Madoc a Ririt.

---

¹ C. D. '
² A.D. 1083.
³ Sulgenius, C.

⁴ C. D. E.
⁵ MLXXXVII., D.
⁶ C.

1081. ¹ One thousand and eighty-one was the year of Christ, when the first ² decem-novennalis occurred.'

1083. One thousand and eighty was the year of Christ, when Sulien resigned his bishopric the third time, and Wilffre took it.

1084. ⁴ A year after that, Terdelach, king of the Scots or Gwyddelians, died.'

1085. And then, ⁶ a year after that,' died William the Bastard, prince of the Normans, and king of the Saxons, the Britons, and the Albanians, after a sufficiency of the glory and fame of this transient world, and after glorious victories, and the honour acquired by riches; and after him William Rufus, his son, reigned.

1087. And then, ⁶ a year after that,' Rhys, son of Tewdwr, was expelled from his territory and his kingdom by the sons of Bleddyn, sons of Cynvyn, to wit, Madog, and Cadwgan, and Rhirid, and he himself retreated into Ireland. And immediately afterwards he collected a fleet ⁸ of the Gwyddelians,' and returned again. And then the battle of ⁹ Llych Crei' took place, and the ᵃ sons' of Bleddyn were slain. And Rhys, son of Tewdwr, gave an immense sum of money to the mariners, Scots and Gwyddelians, who had come to assist him.

1088. And then, ⁶ a year after that,' the shrine of St. David was taken by stealth out of the church,

---

ᵃ/ ¹⁰ grandsons ¹¹ two sons of Bleddyn, son of Cynvyn, to wit, Madog and Rhirid.

---

⁷ Ririt, *C. D.*
⁸ *E.*
⁹ Llech y Kreu, *C.* Llech Rẏt, *D.*

¹⁰ *E.*
·¹¹ *C. D.*

yn llόyr yn ymyl y dinas. Ac yna y crynaόd y dayar yn diruawr ᵃyn holl ynys Prydein.'

MLXXXIX. Ac yna ¹[dwy vlyned wedy hynny] y bu uarό ²Sulyen escob Mynyό, y doethaf or Brytanyeit ac arderchaόc o grefydus uuched, wedy clotuorussaf dysgedigaeth y disgyblon a chraffaf dysc y plόyfeu, y petwar ugeinuet vlόydyn oe oes, ar unvet eisseu o vgein oe gyssegredigaeth nos galan Ionaόr. Ac yna y torret Mynyό y gan genedyl yr ynyssed. Ac y bu uarw Kediuor uab Gollόyn. ᵇA Llywelyn y vab' ae vrodyr a όahaόdyssant Ruffud uab Maredud, ac yn y erbyn yd ymladaόd Rys ab Teόdόr ³[ac yn ymmyl Llandydoch y bu ymlat ryngthunt, ac y goruu Rys] ac ae gyrraόd ar ffo, ac yny diwed y lladaόd.

MXCI. ¹[Un mlyned ar] deg mlyned a phedwar ugein a mil oed oet Crist pan las Rys ab Teόdόr brenhin Deheubarth y gan y Ffreinc aoed yn pressόylaό Brecheinaόc. Ac yna y dygόydaόd teyrnas y Brytanyeit. Ac yna yd yspeilaόd Kadόgaόn uab Bledyn Dyuet ᶜyr eildyd o Vei.' Ac odyna deuvis wedy hynny amgylch kalan Gorffena y deuth y Ffreinc y Dyuet a Cheredigyaόn, y rei ae kynhallasant etwa, ac y gadarnhayssant y kestyll, a holl tir y Brytanyeit ¹[a achubasant.] Ac yna y llas y Moel Cόlόm ab Dόnchath brenin y Picteit ar Albanyeit y

---

ᵃ' ⁴ dros wẏneb Kẏmre.
ᵇ' ⁵ ay veibyon ynteu Llywelyn
ᶜ' ⁶ ẏchẏdic kẏn kalan Mei.

---

¹ C.
² Sulgenius, C.
³ C. D. E.
⁴ D.

and was completely despoiled close to the city. And then there was a dreadful earthquake ᵃin all the island of Britain.'

1089. And then, ¹two years after that,' Sulien, bishop of Menevia, the wisest of the Britons, and illustrious for his religious life, died,—after the most praiseworthy instruction of his disciples, and the most vigilant teaching of his parishes,—in the eightieth year of his age, and the twentieth but one of his consecration, on the eve of the calends of January. And then Menevia was demolished by the Pagans of the Isles. And Cedivor, son of Collwyn, died. ᵇAnd his son, Llywelyn,' and his brothers invited Gruffudd, son of Maredudd; and Rhys, son of Tewdwr, fought against him, ²and near Llandydoch a battle took place between them, and Rhys was victorious,' and drove him to flight, and at last slew him.

1091. ¹One year and' one thousand and ninety was the year of Christ, when Rhys, son of Tewdwr, king of South Wales, was killed by the French, who inhabited Brecheiniog; and then fell the kingdom of the Britons. And then Cadwgan, son of Bleddyn, despoiled Dyved ᶜon the second day of May.' And then, two months after that, about the calends of July, the French came into Dyved and Ceredigion, which they have still retained, and fortified the castles, and ¹seized upon' all the land of the Britons. And then Malcolm, son of Dwnchath, king of the Picts

---

ᵃ/ ⁴ over the face of Wales.
ᵇ/ ⁵ and his sons, Llywelyn
ᶜ/ ⁶ a little before the calends of May.

---

² *C. D. E.* | ⁶ *D.*

gan y Freinc, ac Edwart y vab. Ac yna y gϐediaϐd Margaret urenhines gϐreic y Moel Cϐlϐm ar Duϐ drϐy ymdiret yndaϐ gϐedy clybot llad y gϐr ae mab hyt na bei vyϐ hi yny varϐaϐl uuched yma; a gϐrandaϐ a oruc Duϐ y gϐedi, kanys erbyn y seithuet dyd y bu uarϐ.

MXCII. Ac yna ¹[blwydyn wedy hynny] yd aeth Gϐilim Goch brenhin yr hϐnn kyntaf aoruu ar y Saeson o glotuorussaf ryfel hyt yn Normandi y gadϐ ac y amdiffyn teyrnas Ropert yvraϐt, yr hϐnn aathoed hyt yg Kaerusalem y ymlad ar Sasinyeit a chenedloed ereill agkyfyeith, ac y amdiffyn ᵃy Cristonogyon,' ac y haedu mϐy o glot. A Gϐylim yn trigyaϐ yn Normandi y gϐrthladaϐd y Brytanyeit lywodraeth y Ffreinc heb allel godef eu creulonder, athorri y kestyll Yggϐyned, a mynychu anreithaϐ a lladuaeu arnunt. Ac yna y duc y Ffreinc luoed hyt Yggϐyned; ae kyuerbynyeit aoruc Kadϐgaϐn uab Bledyn, ae kyrchu a goruot arnunt, ac gyrru ar ffo ae llad o diruaϐr ladua. Ar vrϐydyr honno aϐnaethpϐyt ygkoet ²Yspϐys. Ac yn diwed y vlϐydyn honno y torres y Brytanyeit holl gestyll Keredigyaϐn a Dyuet, eithr deu, nyt amgen Penuro a Ryt y Gors. Ar bobyl a holl anifeileit Dyfet a dugant gantunt, ac adaϐ awnaethant Dyfet a Cheredigyaϐn yn diffeith.

MXCIII. Y vlϐydyn rac ϐyneb y diffeithaϐd y Ffreinc Gϐhyr a Chedweli ac Ystrat Tywi; ac y trig-

---

ᵃ'² y Gristonogaeth

---

¹ C. | ² Yspes, D. Yspys, E.

and Albanians, and Edward his son, were killed by
the French. And then queen Margaret, the wife of
Malcolm, prayed to God, trusting in Him, after she
had heard that her husband and son were killed, that
she might not survive in this mortal state; and God
hearkened unto her prayer, for by the seventh day
she was dead.

1092. And then, ¹ a year after that,' king William
Rufus, who first by a most glorious war prevailed
over the Saxons, went to Normandy to keep and defend the kingdom of Robert his brother, who had gone
to Jerusalem to fight against the Saracens and other
barbarous nations, and to protect ª the Christians,'
and to acquire greater fame. Whilst William remained in Normandy, the Britons resisted the domination of the French, not being able to bear their
cruelty, and demolished their castles in Gwynedd,
and iterated their depredations and slaughters among
them. And then the French led their armies into
Gwynedd; and Cadwgan, son of Bleddyn, went against
them, and attacked and prevailed over them, putting them to flight, and killing them with immense
slaughter. And that battle was fought in the wood
of ² Yspwys. And towards the close of that year the
Britons demolished all the castles of Ceredigion and
Dyved, except two, to wit, Pembroke and Rhyd y
Gors. And the people and all the cattle of Dyved
they brought away with them, leaving Dyved and
Ceredigion a desert.

1093. The ensuing year, the French devastated
Gower, Cydweli, and the Vale of Tywi; and the coun-

ª/ ³ Christianity,

² C.

yaỏd y gỏladoed yn diffeith. A hanher y cynhaeaf y kyffroes Gỏilim vrenhin lu yn erbyn y Brytanyeit, a-gỏedy kymryt or Brytanyeit eu hamdiffyn yny coetyd ar glynned yd ymchoelaỏd Gwilim adref yn orỏac heb ennill dim.

MXCIV. Y vlỏydyn rac ỏyneb y bu uarỏ Gỏilim uab Baldwin, yr hỏnn a rỏndỏalaỏd castell Ryt y Gors ¹[o arch brenhin Lloegyr. A gwedy y varw ef yr edewis y gwercheidweid y kastell yn wac.] Ac yna y gỏrthladaỏd Brytanyeit Brecheinaỏc a Gỏent a Gỏenllỏc arglỏydiaeth y Ffreinc. Ac yna y kyffroes y Ffreinc lu y Went, ac yn orỏac heb ennill dim ydymchoelassant, ac y llas yn ymchoelut drachefyn y gan y Brytanyeit yny lle aelwir ²Kelli Carnant. Gỏedy hynny y Ffreinc a gyffroasant lu y ᵃBrytanyeit;' a medylaỏ diffeithaỏ yr holl wlat heb allu cuplau eu medỏl yn ymchoelut drachefyn y llas gan veibon Idnerth ab Kadỏgaỏn, Grufud ac Iuor, yny lle aelỏir Aber Llech. Ar kiỏdaỏtwyr a drigyassant yn eutei yn ᵇdiodef yn diofyn' yr bot y kestyll etwa yn gyfan ar kastellwyr yndunt. Yny vlỏydyn honno y kyrchaỏd Vchtrut uab Etwin a Howel uab Goronỏ a llawer o bennaetheu ereill gyt ac ỏynt, ac ymlad ³o teulu Kadỏgaỏn uab Bledyn y gastell Penuro ae hyspeilaỏ oe holl anifeileit, a diffeithaỏ yr holl wlat, achyt a diruaỏr anreith ydymchoelassant adref.

MXCV. Y vlỏydyn rac ỏyneb y diffeithaỏd Geralt ystiwart yr hỏnn y gorchymynassit idaỏ ystiward-

ᵃ/ ⁴ Vrycheinyawc ;   ᵇ/ ⁵ ẏn ergrẏnedic

¹ C. D.   ²Kelli Caruawc, C. Carnawc, D. Gravoc, E.

tries remained a desert. And about the middle of harvest king William raised an army against the Britons; and after the Britons had taken to their fastnesses in the woods and glens, William returned home empty, without having gained anything.

1094. The ensuing year William, son of Baldwin, died, who founded the castle of Rhyd y Gors, ¹ by the command of the king of England. And after his death the custodians left the castle empty.' And then the Britons of Brecheiniog, Gwent, and Gwenllwg resisted the domination of the French. And then the French directed an army against Gwent, but empty, and without having gained anything, they retreated; and in returning back they were slain by the Britons, in the place called ² Celli Carnant. After that the French raised an army against ᵃ the Britons,' meditating the devastation of the whole country; without being able to fulfil their intention, on returning back, they were cut off by the sons of Idnerth, son of Cadwgan, Gruffudd and Ivor, in the place called Aber Llech. And the inhabitants remained in their houses, ᵇ confiding fearlessly,' though the castles were yet entire, and the garrisons in them. In that year, Uchtrud, son of Edwin, and Howel, son of Goronwy, with many other chieftains of the family of Cadwgan, son of Bleddyn, marched and fought against the castle of Pembroke, despoiled it of all its cattle, ravaged the whole country, and with an immense booty returned home.

1095. The ensuing year, Gerald the steward, to whom had been assigned the stewardship of the castle

---

ᵃ/⁴ Brecheiniog.   ᵇ/⁵ tremblingly,

²a, C.D.   ³ D.
⁴ C. D. E.

aeth castell Penuro ¹ teruyneu Mynyỏ. Ac yna yr eilweith y kyffroes Gỏilim vrenhin Lloeger aneiryf o luoed a diruaỏr uedyant a gallu yn erbyn y Brytanyeit. Ac yna y gochelaỏd y Brytanyeit eu kynnỏrỏf ỏynt, heb obeithaỏ yndunt e hunain namyn gan ossot gobeith yn Duỏ creaỏdyr pob peth drỏy ᵃ ymprydyaỏ agỏediaỏ ' arodi kardodeu a chymryt garỏ bennyt ar eu kyrff. Kanny leuassei y Freinc kyrchu y creigeu ar coedyd, namyn gỏibyaỏ yg gỏastadyon veussyd. Yny diwed yn orỏac yd ymchoelassant adref heb ennill dim; ar Brytanyeit yn hyfryt digrynedic a ymdiffynnassant eu gỏlat.

MXCVI. Y vlỏydyn rac ỏyneb y kyffroes y Ffreinc luoed y dryded weith yn erbyn Gỏyned, a deu dyỏyssaỏc yn eu blaen, a Hu ²[vras] Iarll Amỏythic yn bennaf arnunt. A phebyllyaỏ aorugant yn erbyn ynys Von ²[ỳ lle ỳ gelwỳt Aber Lliennauc, ac ỳ gwnaethant gastell ỳno]. Ar ³ Brytanyeit gỏedy kilyaỏ yr lleoed kadarnaf udunt oe gnotaedic defaỏt ac a gaỏssant yn eu kyghor achubeit Mon. A gỏahaỏd attunt ỏrth amdiffyn udunt llyges ar uor o Iỏerdon drỏy gymryt y rodyon ar gobreu y gan y Ffreinc. Ac yna yd edewis Kadỏgaỏn uab Bledyn a Grufud nab Kynan ynys Von, ac y kilyassant y Iwerdon rac ofyn tỏyll y gỏyr e hunein. Ac yna y deuth y Ffreinc y myỏn yr ynys, ac y lladassant rei owyr yr ynys. Ac ual ydoedynt yntrigyaỏ yno y deuth ⁴ Magnus brenhin ⁵ Germania a rei oe logeu gantaỏ

ᵃ ᵇ imprytyeu a gỏedieu

---

¹ The original word seems to have been *tremygu*; the other is written over it in another hand.
² *D.*
³ Gwindyd, *C. D.*

of Pembroke, ravaged the boundaries of Menevia.
And then, the second time, William, king of England,
assembled innumerable hosts, with immense means
and power, against the Britons. And then the Britons
avoided their impulse, not confiding in themselves,
but placing their hope in God, the Creator of all
things, by ᵃ'fasting and praying,' and giving alms, and
undergoing severe bodily penance. For the French
dared not penetrate the rocks and the woods, but
hovered about the level plains. At length they returned home empty, without having gained anything;
and the Britons, happy and unintimidated, defended
their country.

1096. The ensuing year the French, for the third
time, assembled their troops against Gwynedd, conducted by two leaders, with Hugh ²'the Fat,' earl of
Shrewsbury, as chief over them; and they encamped
against the isle of Mona, ³'in the place called Aber
Lliennog, where they built a castle.' And the
Britons, having retreated to their strongest places,
according to their usual custom, agreed in council to
save Mona. And they invited to their defence a fleet
that was at sea from Ireland, which had accepted
gifts and rewards from the French. And then Cadwgan, son of Bleddyn, and Gruffudd, son of Cynan,
left the isle of Mona, and retreated into Ireland, for
fear of the treachery of their own men. And then
the French entered the island, and killed some of the
men of the island. And whilst they tarried there,
⁴ Magnus, king of ⁵ Germany, came, accompanied by

ᵃ' ⁶ fasts and prayers,

---

⁴ Maurus, *C.*   ⁶ *C.*
⁵ Norwei, *D.*

hyt ym Mon drⱱy obeithaⱱ kaffel gorescyn ar wlatoed y Brytanyeit. A gⱱedy clybot o ¹Vagnus brenhin y Ffreinc yn mynych vedylyaⱱ diffeithaⱱ yr holl wlat, ae dⱱyn hyt ar dim, dyfryssyaⱱ aoruc y eu kyrchu. Ac ual yd oedynt yn ymsaethu y neill rei or mor ar rei ereill or tir y brathⱱyt Hu iarll yn y ⱱyneb, ac o laⱱ y brenhin ehun yny vrⱱydyr y digⱱydaⱱd. Ac yna ydedewis Magnus vrenhin drⱱy deissyfyt kyghor teruyneu y wlat. A dⱱyn aoruc y Freinc oll a maⱱr a bychan hyt ar y Saeson. A gⱱedy na allei y Gⱱndyt godef kyfreitheu a barneu a threis y Freinc arnunt, kyfodi aorugant eilweith yn eu herbyn, ac Owein uab Edwin yn dywyssaⱱc arnadunt y gⱱr adugassei y Freinc gynt y Von.

MXCVII. Y vlⱱydyn gⱱedi hynny yd ymchoelaⱱd Kadⱱgaⱱn uab Bledyn a Gruffud uab Kynan o Iwerdon. A gⱱedy hedychu ar Ffreinc o nadunt ran or wlat a achubassant. Kadⱱgaⱱn uab Bledyn a gymerth Keredigyaⱱn a chyfran o Bowys, a Gruffud agauas Mon. Ac yna y llas Llywelyn uab Kadⱱgaⱱn y gan wyr Brecheinaⱱc. Ac ydaeth Howel uab Ithel y Iwerdon. Yny vlⱱydyn honno y bu uarⱱ ²Rychmarch doeth mab ²Sulyen escob, y doethaf ᵃo doethon y Brytanyeit,' y dryded vlⱱydyn a deugein oe oes, y gⱱr ny chyfodaⱱd yn yr oessoed cael y gyffelyb kyn noc ef, ac nyt haⱱd credu na thybygu cael y gyfryⱱ gⱱedy ef. Ac ni chaⱱssei dysc gan arall eiryoet eithyr gan y dat

---

ᵃ/⁴ or Kymre,

---

¹ Maurus, *C.*   ² Rythemarch, *C.*

some of his ships, as far as Mona, hoping to be enabled to take possession of the countries of the Britons. And when king [1] Magnus had heard of the frequent designs of the French to devastate the whole country, and to reduce it to nothing, he hastened to attack them. And as they were mutually shooting, the one party from the sea, and the other party from the land, earl Hugh was wounded in the face, by the hand of the king himself. And then king Magnus, with sudden determination, left the borders of the country. So the French reduced all, as well great as small, to be Saxons. And when the Gwyneddians could not bear the laws and judgments and violence of the French over them, they rose up a second time against them, having, as their commander, Owain, son of Edwin, the man who had originally brought the French into Mona.

1097. The year after that, Cadwgan, son of Bleddyn, and Gruffudd, son of Cynan, returned from Ireland. And after they had made peace with the French, they retained part of the country; Cadwgan, son of Bleddyn, took Ceredigion and a portion of Powys; and Gruffudd obtained Mona. And then Llywelyn, son of Cadwgan, was killed by the men of Brecheiniog; and Howel, son of Ithel, went to Ireland. In that year died Rythmarch the Wise, son of bishop Sulien, the wisest [a] of the wise among the Britons,' in the forty-third year of his age; the man whose like had not appeared before for ages, and it is not easy to believe or to imagine that one similar shall be found after him; and who had never received

---

a'[4] of the Welsh,

---

[3] Sulgenius, *C.* | [4] *D.*

chun, gỽedy adassaf enryded y genedyl e hun, a gỽedy klotuorussaf ac atneỽydussaf ganmaỽl y gyfnessavyon genedloed, nyt amgen Saeson a Freinc a chenedloed eraill or tu draỽ y vor, a hynny drỽy gyffredin gỽynuan paỽb yn doluryaỽ eu callonneu y bu uarỽ.

MXCVIII. Yny vlỽydyn rac ỽyneb y llas Gỽilim Goch brenhin y Saeson, yr hỽnn a ỽnaethpỽyt yn urenhin gỽedy Gỽilim y dat. Ac ual yd oed hỽnnỽ dydgỽeith yn hela gyt a Henri y braỽt ieuaf idaỽ, a rei oe marchogyon gyt ac ỽynt y brathỽyt a saeth y gan ¹'Wallter Turel' marchavc idaỽ oe anuod, pan yttoed yn bỽrỽ karỽ y medraỽd y brenhin ac ae lladaỽd. A phan welas Henri y vraỽt ynteu hynny gorchymyn aoruc corf y vraỽt yr marchogyon aoed yny lle, ac erchi udunt gỽneuthur brenhinaỽl arỽylant idaỽ ²[aỷ dwỷn ỷ Gaer Wint.] Ac ynteu a gerdaỽd hyt yg Kaer Wynt yny lle yd oed sỽllt y brenhin ae vrenhinolyon oludoed. Ac achub yrei hynny a oruc. A galỽ ataỽ holl tylvyth y brenhin; a mynet odyna hyt yn Llundein ae gorescyn, yr honn y ssyd benhaf a choron ar holl vrenhinyaeth Loeger. Ac yna y kytredassant attaỽ Ffreinc a Saeson y gyt, ac o vrenhinaỽl gor y gossodassant ef yn vrenhin yn Lloeger. Ac yny lle y kymerth ynteu yn wreic briaỽt idaỽ ³Vahalt uerch y Moel Cỽlỽm, brenhin ᵃ'Prydein' o Vargaret urenhines y mam. A honno drỽy y phriodi a ansodes ef yn urenhines; kanys Gỽilim Goch y vraỽt ef yny vyỽyt a aruerassei o orderchadeu, ac

ᵃ'⁴ y Pictieit

¹ Sir Walter Tirel, *D.* | ² *D.*

instruction from any other but his own father,—after
the meetest honour of his own kindred, and after the
highest praise and renewed commendation of the
neighbouring nations, to wit, of the Saxons, the
French, and other nations beyond the sea—with universal lamentation, all being grieved in their hearts
that he died.

1098. In the ensuing year, William Rufus, king of
the Saxons, who had been made king after William,
his father, was killed; for, as he was on a certain
day hunting, along with Henry, his youngest brother,
accompanied by some of his knights, he was wounded
with an arrow by Walter Tyrell, a knight of his own,
who, unwittingly, as he was shooting at a stag, hit
the king and killed him. And when his brother Henry
saw that, he commended the body of his brother to
the charge of the knights who were present, and ordered them to make a royal funeral for him, ³'and to
convey it to Winchester;' and he himself proceeded to
Winchester, where the treasure and royal riches of the
king were deposited, which he secured; and he called to
him all the family of the king. And from thence he
went to London, and took possession of it, which is the
chiefest and crown of the whole kingdom of England.
Then the French and Saxons all flocked together
to him, and by royal council appointed him king in
England. And immediately he took for his wife
Mahalt, daughter of Malcolm, king of ᵃ Prydyn,' by
queen Margaret her mother. And she, by his mar-
rying her, was raised to the rank of queen; for
William Rufus, his brother, in his life time, had

ᵃ/ ⁴ the Picts,

---

³ Mahald, *C.* | ⁴ *C. D.*

orth hynny y buassei uarỽ heb etifed. Ac yna yd ymhoelaỽd Robert y braỽt hynaf udunt yn uudugaỽl o Gaerussalem, ac y bu uarỽ Tomas archescob Kaer Efraỽc. Ac yn y ol ynteu ydenessaỽd Gerrart a uuassei escob yn Herford kynno hynny; ac y derchafaỽd Henri urenhin ef, ar deilygdaỽt a oed vch yn archescob yg Kaer Efraỽc. Ac yna y kymerth [1]Ansel archescob Keint drachefyn y archescobaỽt drỽy Henri vrenhin yr hỽn a adaỽssei yn amser Gỽilim Goch vrenhin o achaỽs enwired hỽnnỽ ae greulonder. Kany welei ef hỽnnỽ yn gỽneuthur dim yn gyfyaỽn o orchymmyneu Duỽ, nac o lywodraeth vrenhinaỽl teilygdaỽt.

MXCIX. Blỽydyn gỽedy hynny y bu uarỽ Hu Vras Iarll Kaer Llion [2]ar Wysc; ac yny ol y dynessaỽd Roger y vab kyt bei bychan y oet. Ac eissoes y brenhin ae gossodes yn lle y dat a achaỽs meint y karei y dat. Ac yny vlỽydyn honno y bu uarỽ Gronnỽ uab Kadỽgaỽn ac [3]Owein uab Grufud.

MC. Can mlyned a mil oed oet Crist, [4][[5]decem nouenalis gyntaf] pan uu agkyttundeb rỽg Henri vrenhin a Robert Iarll Amỽythic [6][yr hwnn a elwid de Belen] ac Ernỽlf y vraỽt, gỽr a gauas Dyfet yn rann idaỽ, [4][o goelbren] ac awnaeth castell Penuro yn uaỽrurydus. A phan gigleu y brenhin eu bot yn gỽneuthur tỽyll yn y erbyn megys y deuth y chwedyl arnunt y galỽaỽd attaỽ y wybot gỽiryoned am hynny; ac ỽynteu heb allel ymdiret yr brenhin a geissassant achaỽs y vỽrỽ escus. Agỽedy gỽybot o nadunt adnabot or brenhin eu tỽyll ac eu brat, ny beidassant ymdangos ger bron y gendrycholder ef. Achub aorugant eu kedernit agalỽ porth o bob tu udunt, a gỽahaỽd attunt y Brytanycit aoedynt dares-

---

[1] Anselmus, *C.*   [3] Gwynn, *C. D.*
[2] *Not in C. D.*   [4] *D.*

consorted with concubines, and on that account had died without an heir. And then Robert, their eldest brother, returned victoriously from Jerusalem. And Thomas, archbishop of York, died, and Gerard succeeded him, who had been previously bishop of Hereford, and king Henry raised him to the higher dignity of archbishop of York. And then Anselm, archbishop of Canterbury, received back his archbishopric from king Henry, which he vacated in the time of king William Rufus, on account of the iniquity and cruelty of that monarch, for he could not see that he observed any of the commandments of God justly, nor the royal obligations of government.

1099. A year after that, died Hugh the Fat, earl of Caerleon ²upon Usk;' and to him succeeded Roger, his son; though he was but young of age, the king appointed him in the place of his father, for so greatly he loved his father. And in that year died Goronwy, son of Cadwgan, and ³ Owain, son of Gruffudd.

1100. One thousand and one hundred was the year of Christ, ⁵the first decem-novennalis,' when dissension arose between king Henry and Robert, earl of Shrewsbury, ⁶called de Belesme,' and Ernulf his brother, the person who had obtained Dyved for his share, ⁴by ballot,' and who magnificently built the castle of Pembroke. And when the king understood that they were practising deceit against him, as the report had come concerning them, he called them to him to know the truth of it. And they, not being able to trust to the king, sought for an occasion to make an excuse. And when they knew that the king was acquainted with their deceit and treachery, they dared not appear in his presence. They had recourse to their strong hold, and sought for assistance on every side; and invited

---

³ A.D. 1102. | ⁶ *C.*

tygedigyon udunt yn eu medyant, ac eu pennaetheu, nyt amgen Kadօgaօn, Iorwoerth a Maredud veibon Bledyn vab Kynuyn yn borth udunt. Ac au haruoll yn vaօrvrydic enrydedus udunt a orugant; ac adaօ llawer o da udunt; a rodi rodyon, a llaօenhau y gօlat o rydit. Ac ygkyfrօg hynny kadarnhau eu kestyll ae kylchynu o ffossyd a muroed, a pharattoi llaօer o ymborth, a chynullaօ marchogyon, a rodi rodyon udunt. Robert a achubaօd pedwar castell, nyt amgen Arօndel, a ¹ Blif, a ² Bryg ³ [ŷr hwnn ŷ bu rŷvel oe achos] ynbyn yr hօn yd oed yr holl twyll yndaօ yr hօn a rօndwallassei yn erbyn arch y brenhin, ac Amօythic. Ernօlf a achubaօd Penuro e hun. A gօedy hynny kynullaօ lluoed aorugant, a galօ y Brytanyeit y gyt, a gօneuthur ysclyfyaetheu, ac ymhoelut yn llaօen adref. A phan yttoedit yn gօneuthur y petheu hynny y medylyaօd Ernօlf hedychu ar Gօydyl ac erbynyeit nerth y gantunt. Ac anuon awnaeth kenadeu hyt yn Iwerdon, nyt amgen Geralt ⁴ystiwart, a llawer o rei ereill, y erchi merch ⁵Murtart urenhin ³[Iwerdon] yn briaօt idaօ. A hynny a gafas yn haօd; ar kenadeu adeuthant y eu gօlat yn hyfryt. A Murtart a anuones y verch a llawer o logeu aruaԑc gyt a hi yn nerth idaօ. A gօedy ymdyrchauael or Ieirll y myօn balchder o achaօs y petheu hynny, ac ny chymerassant dim hedօch y gan y brenhin Ac yna y kynnullaօd Henri vrenhin llu bob ychydic, ac yngyntaf kylchynaօd castell Arօndel drօy ymlad ahi. Ac odyna y kymerth castell ⁶Blif, a hyt yg gastell ⁷Brug: ac ympell y օrthaօ y pebyllyaօd. A chymryt kygor aoruc py vod y darestyghei ef y

---

¹ Blydense, *C. D.*
² Brugge, *D.* Brnche, *C.*
³ *D.*
⁴ dapifer, *D.*

the Britons, who were subject to them, in respect of
their possessions and titles, that is to say, Cadwgan,
Iorwerth, and Maredudd, sons of Bleddyn, son of
Cynvyn, to their assistance. And they received them
magnificently and honourably, and promised them much
property, and gave them gifts, and gladdened their
country with liberty. In the mean while they fortified their castles, surrounding them with ditches and
walls, prepared abundance of provisions, and assembled
cavaliers, giving them gifts. Robert seized upon four
castles, to wit, Arundel, and ¹Bliv, and ²Brygge, ³con-
cerning which there had been war,' against which the
whole deceit was perpetrated, and which he had founded
contrary to the order of the king, and Shrewsbury.
Ernulf seized upon Pembroke alone. Afterwards they
collected troops, and called the Britons together, and collected spoils, and joyfully returned home. And whilst
these things were being acted, Ernulf bethought him of
making peace with the Gwyddelians, so as to receive
assistance from them; and he sent messengers to Ireland, namely Gerald the steward and many others, to
demand the daughter of ⁵Murtart, king ³of Ireland,'
in marriage, which was easily obtained; and the messengers returned delighted to their country. Murtart
sent his daughter and many armed ships with her to
his assistance. After the earls had buoyed themselves
up in pride on account of those things, they would
accept no peace from the king. And then king
Henry gradually assembled an army, and in the first
place invested the castle of Arundel, fighting against
her, and then took the castle of ⁶Bliv, and proceeded to the castle of ⁷Brygge, and encamped at a
distance from it. There he took counsel, in what

---

⁵ Murcard, *C. D.*
⁶ Blydense, *C. D.*

⁷ Brugge, *D.* Brusys, *C.*

ieirll neu y lladedei, neu y gỏrthladei or holl deyrnas. Ac o hynny pennaf kyghor a gauas anuon kenadeu at y Brytanyeit, ac yn wahanredaỏl at Iorwoerth vab Bledyn, ae wahaỏd, ae alỏ ger y vronn, ac adaỏ mỏy idaỏ noc y gaffei y gan y ieirll, ar kyfran a berthynei y gael o tir y Brytanyeit. Hynny a rodes y brenhin ynryd y Iorwoerth uab Bledyn tra vei vyỏ y brenhin, heb tỏng a heb tal. Sef oed hynny Powys a Cheredigyaỏn a hanner Dyuet, kanys y hanner arall arodassit y vab Baldwin [1][git ac Ystrat Tŷwi] a Gỏhyr a Chedweli. A gỏedy mynet Iorwoerth uab Bledyn y gastell y brenhin anuon aoruc y anreithaỏ kyuoeth Robert y arglỏyd. Ar anuonhedic lu hỏnnỏ gan Iorwoerth gan gyfleỏni gorchymyn Iorwoerth aanreithasant gyfoeth Robert y arglỏyd drỏy gribdeilaỏ pob peth y gantunt a diffeithaỏ y wlat a chynullaỏ diruaỏr anreith gantunt or wlat. Kanys y iarll kyn no hynny aorchymynassei rodi cret yr Brytanyeit heb debygu caffel gỏrthỏyneb y gantunt, ac anuon y holl hafodyd ae anifeileit ae oludoed y blith y Brytanyeit heb goffau y sarahedeu a gaỏssei y Brytanyeit gynt y gan Rosser y dat ef, a [2]Hu vraỏt y dat. A hynny oed gudyedic gan y Brytanyeit yn vyuyr; Kadỏgaỏn uab Bledyn a Maredud y vraỏt aoedynt ettwa y gyt ar iarll heb ỏybod dim o hynny. Agỏedy clybot or iarll hynny anobeithaỏ aoruc, athebygu nat oed dim gallu gantaỏ o achaỏs mynet Iorwoerth y ỏrthaỏ, kanys pennaf oed hỏnnỏ or Brytanyeit, a mỏyaf y allu, ac erchi kygreir aoruc

---

[1] *C.D.*

manner he should overcome the earls or kill them, or expel them from the whole kingdom; and the result of the principal advice he obtained was, to send messengers to the Britons, and particularly to Iorwerth, son of Bleddyn, and invite and call him to his presence, and promise him more than he should obtain from the earls, and the portion he ought to have of the land of the Britons. The same the king gave to Iorwerth, son of Bleddyn, whilst the king should live, free, without homage and without payment; and that was Powys and Ceredigion, and the half of Dyved, as the other half had been given to the son of Baldwin, [1] with the Vale of Tywi' and Gower and Cydweli. And when Iorwerth, son of Bleddyn, had repaired to the castle of the king, he sent orders to despoil the territory of Robert his lord. And the army thus sent by Iorwerth, in fulfilling the command of Iorwerth, despoiled the territory of Robert his lord, carrying every thing away with them, ravaging the country, and collecting an immense booty. For the earl had previously commanded trust to be put in the Britons, not imagining he should experience any opposition from them; and so he had sent all his dairies and cattle and riches amongst the Britons, without reflecting upon the insults the Britons had received from his father Roger, and from Hugh, his father's brother, and which the Britons kept in mind. Cadwgan, son of Bleddyn, and his brother Maredudd, were still with the earl, without knowing any thing of what was passing. And when the earl had heard of the matter, he despaired, and thought he had no power left, since Iorwerth had gone from him; for he was the principal among the Britons, and the greatest in power; and requested

---

[1] Hvogyn, *D*.

ual y gallei y neill ae hedychu ar brenhin, ae adaƖ y
deyrnas o gƖbyl. YgkyfrƖg y petheu hynny yd athoed
ErnƖlf ae wyr yn erbyn y wreic ar llyges aruaƖc aoed
yn dyfot yn borth idaƖ, ac yn hynny y deuth [1] Magnus vrenhin Germania eilweith y Von. A gƖedy torri
llawer o wyd defnyd ymchoelut y VanaƖ drachefyn.
Ac yna herƖyd y dywedir gƖneuthur aoruc tri chastell,
[a] ae llenƖi' eilweith oe wyr ehun, [2] yrei adiffeithassei
kyn no hynny. [3] [Ac a anvones hyt yn Iwerdon]
ac erchi merch [4] MƖrchath oe vab, kanys pennaf oed
hƖnnƖ or GƖydyl a hynny a gafas yn llaƖen; agossot
aoruc ef y mab hƖnnƖ yn vrenhin ym ManaƖ; ac yno
y trigyaud y gaeaf hƖnnƖ. A gƖedy clybot o Robert
iarll hynny anuon kenadeu aoruc ar Vagnus, ac ny
chauas dim oe negesseu. AgƖedy gƖelet or iarll y
vot yn warchaedic o bop parth idaƖ, keissaƖ kennat a
fford y gan y brenhin y adaƖ y deyrnas. Ar brenhin
ae kanhataƖd. Ac ynteu drƖy adaƖ pob peth a vor-
dƖyaƖd hyt yn Normandi. Ac yna yd anuones y
brenhin at ErnƖlf y erchi idaƖ un or deu peth, ae
adaƖ y deyrnas a mynet yn ol y vraƖt, ae ynteu
adelei yny ewyllys ef [5] [ay benn yny arffed]. A
phan gigleu ErnƖlf hynny dewissaf vu gantaƖ vynet
yn ol y vraƖt. A rodi y gastell aoruc yr brenhin, ar
brenhin a dodes gƖercheitweit yndaƖ. GƖedy hynny
hedychu a oruc Iorwoerth [3] [vab Bledyn] ae vrodyr, a
rannu y kyfoeth y rydunt. AgƖedy ychydic o amser

[a'] [5] a llenwi Manaw

---

[1] Mawrus, C.
[2] honn, C.

[3] D.

a truce, that he might be enabled either to make peace with the king, or leave the kingdom altogether. In the midst of these things, Ernulf went with his men to receive his wife, and the armed fleet that was coming to his assistance ; and in the mean while [1] Magnus, king of Germany, came a second time to Mona. And after cutting down much building timber he returned back to the isle of Man; and there, according to the report, he built three castles, which theretofore he had demolished, and he ª filled them' the second time with his own men. He then [3] sent over to Ireland,' and demanded the daughter of [4] Murchath for his son; for that person was the chiefest of the Gwyddelians ; which he joyfully obtained; and he set up that son to be king in the isle of Man; and there he remained during that winter. When earl Robert had heard of this, he despatched messengers to Magnus, but his missions were unavailing. And when the earl perceived himself hemmed in on every side, he sought permission and way from the king to quit the kingdom; and the king granted them. And he, leaving every thing, went by sea into Normandy. And then the king sent to Ernulf, requiring of him one of two things, either to quit the kingdom and follow his brother, or else to be at his will [5] with his head in his lap.' When Ernulf heard that, he was most desirous of going after his brother; so he delivered his castle to the king, and the king placed a garrison in it. After that Iorwerth, [3] son of Bleddyn,' made peace with his brother, and shared the dominion between them. A little time afterwards Iorwerth took

---

ª/[5] filled the isle of Man

---

[4] Mwrcardi, *D.* Murcard, *C.* | [5] *C.*

y delis Iorwoerth Varedud y vraỼt, ac y carcharaỼd ygkarchar y brenhin. A hedychu aỼnaeth a ChadỼgaỼn y vraỼt, ac y rodi KeredigyaỼn a ran o PoỼys. Ac odyna mynet aỼnaeth Iorwoerth at y brenhin, a thebygu yr brenhin cadỼ y edewit ỼrthaỼ. Ar brenhin heb gadỼ amot ac ef aduc y gantaỼ Dyfet ¹[ar castell], ac ae rodes y neb un varchaỼc ¹[vrdaul] a elwit ²Saer; ac Ystrat Tywi a Chedweli a GỼhyr a rodes y ³Howel ᵃa GronỼ. Ac y kyfrỼg hỼnnỼ y delit GronỼ uab Rys ¹[o dwill] ac y bu uarỼ yny garchar.

MCI. Yny vlỼydyn rac Ỽyneb gỼedy dyrchauel o Vagnus vrenhin Germania hỼyleu ar ychydic o logeu, a diffeithaỼ aoruc tervyneu ᵇPrydein. A phan welas y ᶜPrydeinwyr hynny megys morgrugyon o dylleu y gogofeu y kyfodassant yn gadoed y ymlit eu hanreith. A phan welsant y brenhin ac ychydic o nifer y gyt ac ef, kyrchu yn ehofyn aorugant, a gossot brỼydyr yny erbyn. A phan welas y brenhin hynny kyweiryaỼ bydin a oruc, heb edrych ar amylder y elynyon a bychanet y nifer ynteu, herwyd moes ᵈyr AlbanỼyr' drỼy goffau y anneiryf uudugolyaetheu gynt kyrchu a oruc yn agkyfleus. A gỼedy gỼneuthur y vrỼydyr, allad llaỼer opob tu, yna o gyfarsagedigaeth lluoed ac amylder niferoed y elynyon y llas y brenhin. ⁴[Ac yna y gelwit Iorwoerth uab Bledyn y AmỼythic drỼy dỼyll kygor y brenhin.] Ac y dosparthỼyt y

---

a ⁵ vab   ᵇ⁶ Llẏchlẏn
c ⁶ Llẏchlẏnwyr   ᵈ'⁷ gwyr Denmarc

---

¹ D.
² Saher, D. *Not in E.*
³ Hywel, C. D.
⁴ C.

his brother Maredudd, and confined him in the king's prison; but made peace with his brother Cadwgan, and gave him Ceredigion and a part of Powys. Subsequently Iorwerth repaired to the king, supposing the king would keep his promise to him; but the king departing from his engagement with him, took Dyved ¹ and the castle' from him, and gave them to a certain cavalier called ²Saer; and the Vale of Tywi, Cydweli, and Gower he granted to Howel ᵃand Goronwy. And in that interval, Goronwy, son of Rhys, was taken ¹ through treachery,' and died in his prison.

1101. In the ensuing year, when Magnus, king of Germany, had hoisted sails on a few ships, he made depredations on the shores of ᵇBritain; and when the ᶜBritons saw that, they arose from the mouths of the caves in multitudes like ants in pursuit of their spoils. And when they saw the king had so few in number with him, they advanced boldly, and arranged in order of battle against him. And when the king observed that, he prepared his army, without looking upon the multitude of his enemies, and the smallness of his own number, according to the manner of the ᵈAlbanians; recollecting his innumerable victories of former times, he made a disadvantageous attack. And after the battle had proceeded, and many been killed on both sides; owing to the pressure and overpowering numbers of his foes, the king was killed. ᵉAnd at that time Iorwerth, son of Bleddyn, was cited to Shrewsbury, through the treachery of the

---

ᵃ ⁵ son of   ᵇ ⁶ Scandinavia
ᶜ ⁶ Scandinavians   ᵈ ⁷ men of Denmark

---

⁵ C. D.   ⁷ C.
⁶ D.

dadleuoed ac negesseu; a phan doeth ef yna ydymchoelaȯd yr holl dadleu yny erbyn e; ac ar hyt ydyd y dadleuȯyt ac ef, ac yny diwed y barnȯyd yn gamlyryus. A gȯedy hynny y barnȯyt y garchar y brenhin, nyt herȯyd kyfreith, namyn herȯyd medyant; ac yna y pallaȯd y holl obeith ae kedernit ae hechyt ae didanȯch yr holl Vrytanyeit.

MCII. Y vlȯydyn rac ȯyneb y bu uarȯ Owein uab Etwin drȯy hir glefyt. Ac yna yd ystores [1] Rickart uab Baldwin gastell [2] Ryt y Gors, ac y gyrrȯyt Howel uab Gronȯ ymeith oe gyfoeth, y gȯr aorchymynassei Henri vrenhin keitwataeth Ystrad Tywi a [2] Ryt y Gors. [a] Ac ynteu a gynnullaȯd anreitheu drȯy Iosci tei a diffeithaȯ hayach yr holl ȯladoed, allad llaȯer or Ffreinc aoedynt yn ymchoelut adref.' Ac ynteu a gychwynnaȯd y ȯlat o bop tu, ac ae hachubaȯd ar castell adrigyaȯd yn digyffro ae wercheitweit yndaȯ. Ygkyfrȯg hynny y gȯrthladaȯd Henri vrenhin [3] Saer marchaȯc o Penuro, ac y rodes keitwataeth y kastell ae holl teruyneu y [4] Heralt Ystiwert, yr hȯnn aoed dan Ernȯlf Ystiwert.

MCIII. [5] [Blwydyn wedy hynny] y vlȯydyn honno y llas Howel uab Gronȯ drȯy dȯyll y gan y Ffreinc aoedynt yn kadȯ Ryt y Gors. Gȯgaȯn uab Meuruc, y gȯr a oed yn meithryn mab y Howel [6] [a mwiaf gwr or bȳt ȳd ȳmdiriedev idau] aȯnaeth y urat ual

---

a/ [6] A llosgi ȳr ȳdev ar tei, ac adau ȳ tir ȳn diffeith, ac ȳmchwelut or Freinc adref drachevȳn heb argȳwed arnadunt.

---

[1] Ricard, *D.*
[2] Ryt Cors, *D.*
[3] Saher, *C. D. E.*
[4] Gerald, *D.*

king's council.' And his pleadings and claims were arranged; and on his having come, all the pleadings were turned against him, and the pleading continued through the day; and at last he was adjudged to be fineable, and was afterwards cast into the king's prison, not according to law, but according to power. Then failed all the hope, and the fortitude, and the strength, and the happiness, of all the Britons.

1102. The ensuing year Owain, son of Edwin, died after a long illness. And then Rickart, son of Baldwin, stored the castle of Rhyd y Gors; and Howel, son of Goronwy, was driven from his dominion,— the man to whom king Henry had deputed the conservancy of the Vale of Tywi and Rhyd y Gors. ᵃ Upon which he collected spoils, by burning houses and laying waste nearly all the districts, and killing many of the French who were returning home.' He also raised the country on every side, and repossessed it, and the castle remained undisturbed, and its garrison within it. In that interval king Henry expelled the cavalier ³ Saer from Pembroke, and granted the custody of the castle with all its boundaries to Gerald the steward, who had been under Ernulf the steward.

1103. ⁵ A year after that,' that year Howel, son of Goronwy, was killed, through treachery, by the French, who had the custody of Rhyd y Gors. Gwgawn, son of Meurug, the person who was nurturing a son of Howel, ⁵ and whom of all men he mostly trusted,' formed the

---

ᵃ′ ⁶ And he burnt the crops and houses, and left the land desolate; and the French returned home again without being molested.

---

³ *C.*   ⁶ *D.*

hynn. Galỽ a ỽnaeth Gỽgaỽn Howel y ty ae wahaỽd, ac anuon yr castell agalỽ a Ffreinc attaỽ, a menegi udunt eu teruynedic le, ac aros amser yny nos. Ac ỽynteu a deuthant amgylch pylgein, a chylchynu y dref ar ty yd oed Howel yndaỽ, a dodi gaỽr, ac aryr aỽr y duhunaỽd Howel yn dilesc, a cheissaỽ y arueu, a duhunaỽ y gedymdeithon, a galw arnunt. Ar cledyf arydaroed idaỽ y dodi ar benn y wely ae wayw is y traet arydygassei Gadỽgaỽn tra yttoed yn kyscu. A Howel a geisaỽd y getymdeithon ỽrth ymlad, a thebygu eu bot yn baraỽt. Ac neur daroed udunt ffo ar yr aỽr gyntaf or nos, ac yna y goruu arnaỽ ynteu fo. Agỽgaỽn ae hymlidyaỽd yngraff yn y delis megys y hedewis. A phan deuth kedymdeithon Kadỽgaỽn attaỽ tagu Hoỽel aorugant ; ar tagedic yn uarỽ haeach y dugant at y Freinc. Ac ỽynteu gỽedy llad y benn a ymchoelassant yr kastell. Yny vlỽydyn honno y gỽelat seren enryfed y gỽeletyat yn anuon paladyr o heni yn ol y chefyn, ac o brafftter colofyn y meint, a diruaỽr oleuat idi yn darogan yr hynn avei rac llaỽ. Kanys Henri amheraỽdyr Rufein gỽedy diruaỽryon uudugolyaetheu ; a chrefydussaf vuched y Grist a orffowyssaỽd ; ae vab gỽedy ynteu gỽedy cael llawer o enryded ac eistedua amherodraeth Rufein awnaethpỽyt yn amheraỽdyr. Ac yna ydanuones Henri vrenhin Lloeger marchogyon i darestỽg Normandi. A chyhỽrd ac ỽynt awnaeth [1] [Robert iarll ac Ernwlf ỹ vraut a] Robert iarll [2] o Vethlem' [1] [a William o [a] Moretania ỹ gevỹnderw] ; a

---

[a] [3] Vrytaen y ewythyr

---

[1] D. [2] de Belem, D.

plot in this wise: Gwgawn called Howel, and invited him into his house, and sent to the castle and called the French to him, and shewed them their appointed place, to wait till a certain time in the night. So they came about daybreak, and surrounded the hamlet and the house in which Howel was, and gave a shout; and with that shout Howel promptly awaked, and sought for his arms, and waked and called his companions. And the sword which he had placed on the top of his bed, and the spear at his feet, had been taken away by Cadwgan, whilst he was asleep. Howel sought for his companions to fight, supposing them to be ready; but they had fled, probably at the first hour of the night; and then he also was compelled to flee. And Gwgawn pursued him warily, till he had taken him, as he had promised. And when Gwgawn's companions came to him, they strangled Howel; and brought him, strangled and almost dead, to the French, who, after cutting off his head, returned to the castle. In that year there was seen a star of wonderful appearance, emitting a beam behind, and of the thickness of a column, of immense light, foreboding what would be in future. For Henry, emperor of Rome, after extraordinary victories, and a most religious life in Christ, went to his rest; and his son succeeding him, after having obtained much honour and the seat of the Roman empire, was made emperor. And then Henry, king of England, sent knights to subdue Normandy, and ¹ Robert the earl, with his brother Ernulf, and ' Robert, earl ² of Bethlehem,' ¹ and William of ᵃ Moretania, his cousin,' met them, and having prevailed

---

ᵃ/ ³ Brittany, his uncle,

---

³ *C.*

gŵedy gorfot arnunt eu gyrru ar ffo. A gwedy na rymheint dim anuon aorugant at y brenhin y geissaŵ nerth. Ac yna y brenhin ehun gyt ac amylder o varchogyon adiruaŵr lu a vordŵyaŵd drŵod. Ac yna y kyhyrdaŵd ar iarll yndilesc, ac ef ae ganhorthŵywyr ac yn gywarsagedic odra lluossogrŵyd y kymerth y ffo, ae ymlit or brenhin yny delis ac ef ¹ [a Gwilliam ẏ ᵃgevẏnderw] ae wyr. A gŵedy eu dala ae hanuones y Loeger y eu karcharu; a holl Normandi a darestygŵys ŵrth y vedyant e hun. Yn ¹ [diwed] y vlŵydyn honno y llas Meuruc a Griffri veibon Trahaearn vab Karadaŵc ᵇ ac Owein uab Kadŵgaŵn.

MCIV. Y vlŵydyn rac wyneb y diegis Maredud uab Bledyn oe garchar ac y deuth y wlat. ¹ [Ac ẏ bu varw Herwald escop Llandaf: ac ẏ doeth ẏnẏ le ẏntev Worgan Ancellin archescob aẏ kẏssegrwẏs ẏng Keint]. Ac yna y bu varŵ Edwart uab y Moel Cŵlŵm; ac yny le ef y kynhelis Alexander y vraŵt y deyrnas.

MCV. Y vlŵydyn gŵedy hynny ydanuonet neb un genedyl diadnabydus, herŵyd kenedlaeth a moesseu, ny wydit py le yd ymgudyssynt ynyr ynys dalym o vlŵynyded, y gan Henri vrenhin y wlat Dyfet. Ar genedyl honno aachubaŵd holl gantref Ros gyr llaŵ aber yr avon aelwir Cledyf, gŵedy eu gŵrthlad o gŵbyl. Ar genedyl honno, megys y dywedir, a hanoed o Fflandrys, y gŵlat yr honn yssyd ossodedic yn nessaf ger llaŵ mor y Brytanyeit. O achaŵs achub or mor agorescyn eugŵlat hyt yny ymchoelet yr holl wlat

---

² ewythyr   ᵇ ³ y gan

---

¹ *D.*   ² *C.*

over them, put them to flight. And since they could offer no resistance, they sent to the king to procure aid. And then the king himself, with a multitude of knights, and an immense army, sailed over; and then he met with the earl promptly, him and his abettors, who, overpowered by excess of numbers, took to flight, the king pursuing, until he secured him, ¹ and William his ᵃ cousin,' and his men. And having captured them he sent them to England, to be imprisoned; and he reduced the whole of Normandy into his own possession. Towards ¹ the close of ' that year were killed Meurug and Griffri, sons of Trahaiarn, son of Caradog, ᵇ and Owain, son of Cadwgan.

1104. The ensuing year Maredudd, son of Bleddyn, escaped from his prison, and returned to his country; ¹ and Herwald, bishop of Llandaf, died, and was succeeded by Worgan, who was consecrated in Kent by archbishop Ancellin.' Then died Edward, son of Malcolm; and Alexander, his brother, possessed the kingdom in his stead.

1105. The year after that, a certain nation, not recognised in respect of origin and manners, and unknown as to where it had been concealed in the island for a number of years, was sent by king Henry into the country of Dyved. And that nation seized the whole cantred of Rhos, near the efflux of the river called Cleddyv, having driven off the people completely. That nation, as it is said, was derived from Flanders, the country which is situated nearest to the sea of the Britons. This was on account of the encroachment of the sea on their country, the whole region having been reduced to disorder, and bearing

---

² uncle,   ᵇ ³ by

ᵃ *C. D.*

ar agkrynodeb heb dŵyn dim ffrŵyth gŵedy bŵrŵ o lanŵ or mor di ar tywot yr tir. Ac yny diwed gŵedy na cheffynt le y pressŵylyaŵ; kanys y mor a diueuassei ar draŵs yr aruordired ar mynyded yn gyflaŵn o dynyon hyt na allei baŵp bressŵylyaŵ yno a achaŵs amylder y dynyon a bychanet y tir, y genedyl honno a deissyuaŵd Henri vrenhin, ac ¹a adolygassant' idaŵ kaffel lle y pressŵylynt yndaŵ; ac ²[ÿna] yd anuonet ²[ŵynt] hyt yn Ros drŵy ŵrthlad odyno y priodolyon giŵdaŵtwyr, y rei agollassant eu priaŵt wlat ae lle yr hynny hyt ³[hediŵ]. ᵃYgkŵfrŵg hynny Geralt ystiwart Penuro a rŵndŵalaŵd kastell ⁴Kenarch Bychan,' ac ansodi awnaeth yno, a llehau yno y holl oludoed, ae wreic ae etifedyon ae holl annwylyt, ae gadarnhau awnaeth o glaŵd a mur ᵇ[a phort achlo arnav].

MCVI. Y vlŵydyn rac ŵyneb y paratoes Kadŵgaŵn uab Bledyn wled y bennaduryeit y wlat, ac y gŵahodes yr wled awnathoed Owein y vab o Powys. Ar wled honno a wnaeth ef y Nadolic yr enryded y Duw. A gŵedy daruot y wled, a chlybot o Owein vot Nest uerch Rys ab Tewdŵr gŵreic Geralt ystiwart yny dywededic gastell vry, mynet aoruc y ymwelet ahi ac ychydic o nifer y gyt ac ef megys ᵇachares' idaŵ ac velly ydoedynt, ⁵kanys Kadŵgaŵn uab Bledyn a Gŵladus uerch Riŵallaŵn mam Nest aoedynt gefynderŵ a chefnitherŵ, kanys Bledyn a Riŵallaŵn meibon Kynfyn aoedynt

---

ᵃ´ ⁶Ac ÿna ÿr adeiliawd Gerald gwasanaethwr ÿr eil weith castell Penvro ÿn lle ÿ gelwit Kengarth vachan.   ᵇ´ ⁷a chyueilles

---

¹ aadolygaŵd, B.
² D.
³ Supplied from other MSS.
⁴ Keugarth Vachaw, C.

no produce, owing to the sand cast into the land by the tide of the sea. At last, when they could get no space to inhabit, as the sea had poured over the maritime land, and the mountains were full of people, so that all could not dwell there on account of the multitude of men, and the scantiness of the land, that nation craved of king Henry, and besought him to assign a place where they might dwell. And ²then they were sent into Rhos, expelling from thence the proprietary inhabitants, who thus lost their own country and place from that time until ³the present day.' ᵃ In the meanwhile Gerald, the steward of Pembroke, founded the castle of ⁴'Little Cenarch,' where he settled; and there he deposited all his riches, with his wife, his heirs, and all dear to him; and he fortified it with a ditch and wall, ⁵and a gateway with a lock on it.'

1106. The ensuing year, Cadwgan, son of Bleddyn, prepared a feast for the chieftains of his country; and he invited to the feast, which he made, his son Owain from Powys. And that feast he made at Christmas in honour of God. And when the feast was ended, Owain hearing that Nest, daughter of Rhys, son of Tewdwr, and wife of Gerald the steward, was in the castle above mentioned, went, accompanied by a small retinue, to visit her as his ᵇkinswoman, and so she was; for Cadwgan, son of Bleddyn, and Gwladus, daughter of Rhiwallon, the mother of Nest, were cousins; as Bleddyn and Rhiwallon, sons of Cynvyn, were

---

ᵃ′ ⁶ And then Gerald the minister built a second time the castle of Pembroke, in the place called Little Cengarth.   ᵇ′ ⁷ friend

---

³ a, B.   ⁷ C.
⁶ D.

vrodyr o y Agharat uerch Varedud vrenhin. A gŵedy hynny o annoc ¹ᵃ[kythreul]' y doeth ef nossweith yr castell ac ychydic o nifer ᵇ y gyt ac ef' val amgylch pedwargŵyr ardec; a gŵedy gŵneuthur claŵd dan y trotheu yndirgel heb ŵybot y geitŵeit y kastell. Ac yna y doethant ¹[dros y mur ar fos' ²y mewn yn diarwybot] yr castell ydoed Geralt a Nest y wreic yn kysgu yndaŵ, a dodi gaŵr awnaethant ygkylch y castell, ac ennynu tan yn y tei ŵrth y llosgi. A dyhunaŵ a oruc Geralt pan gigleu yr aŵr ¹[hep ŵybot beth aŵnaei]. Ac yna y dyŵaŵt Nest ŵrthaŵ. Na dos allan heb hi yr drŵs, kanys yno y mae dy elynyon yth aros, namyn dyret ym ol i; a hynny a ³wnaeth ef. A hi ae harwedaŵd ef hyt yggeudy aoed gyssylltedic ŵrth ᶜy castell;' ac yno megys y dywedir y dihegis. A phan ŵybu Nest y dianc ef llefein aoruc a dywedut ŵrthaŵ y gŵyr yssyd allan beth a lefwch ⁴[chŵi] yn ofer, nyt yttiŵ yma y neb ageissŵch, neur dihegis. A gŵedy eu dyuot ⁵ŵynteu y myŵn, y geissaŵ aorugant ym pob man; a gŵedy nas kaŵssant, dala Nest aŵnaethant ae deu vab ae merch a mab ⁴[arall] idaŵ ynteu o garatwreic, ac yspeilaŵ y castell ae anreithaŵ. A gŵedy llosgi y kastell a chynullaŵ anreith a chytyaŵ a ⁶Nest ymchoelut ⁷aŵnaeth y' wlat. Ac nyt yttoed Kadŵgaŵn y dat ef yn gedrychaŵl yna yny wlat, kanys ef aathoed y Powys ŵrth hedychu y rei aoedynt yn anuhyn ⁸ac aathoedynt y ŵrth Owein.' A phan gigleu Kadŵgaŵn y gŵeithret hŵnnŵ kymryt ⁹y drŵc arnaŵ gan ¹⁰sorri

ᵃ' ¹¹ Duw ¹² gŷthreulaeth
ᵇ' ¹³ yny getymdeithas ᶜ' ¹³ yr ystauell;

¹ C.
² D.
³ oruc, B.
⁴ B.
⁵ ŵy, B.
⁶ hitheu, B.
⁷ a oruc drachenen yŵ, B.

brothers, from Angharad, daughter of king Maredudd. After that, instigated by ¹ᵃ the devil,' he came on a certain night to the castle, having ᵇ with him' a small number, about fourteen persons; and having privately excavated under the threshold, unknown to the keepers of the castle, they got ¹ over the wall and the ditch' ² unawares into' the castle, where Gerald and Nest were sleeping; and they set up a shout about the castle, and kindled a fire in the surrounding houses to burn them. Gerald awoke on hearing the shout, ¹ not knowing what to do;' and then Nest said to him, 'Go not out to the door, for there thy ene- 'mies wait for thee; but come and follow me.' And that he did, and she conducted him to a privy, adjoining ᶜ the castle,' whence, it is said, he escaped. And when Nest knew that he had escaped, she cried and said to the men outside, 'Why call ye out in 'vain? he is not here, whom ye seek; he surely has 'escaped.' And when they had entered, they searched for him everywhere; and not having found him, they took Nest, with her two sons and daughter, and also ⁴ another son that he had by a concubine; and spoiled and laid waste the castle. And after burning the castle, and collecting a booty, and having connexion with Nest, Owain returned to his country. But Cadwgan, his father, was not then in the country; for he had gone to Powys, to pacify those that were at variance, and had separated from Owain. And when Cadwgan became acquainted with that deed, he

---

a/ ¹¹ God,   ¹² devilry,
b/ ¹³ in his company   c/ ¹³ the room,

⁸ ac O6ein, ac a athoedynt   ¹¹ A.
yớrthaó, B.   ¹² D.
⁹ yn, B.   ¹³ B.
¹⁰ sorr, B.

aoruc ef hynny o achaὼs y treis kyt awnathoedit
a Nest verch Rys. Ac ¹[heuyt] rac ofyn llidyaὼ o
Henri vrenhin am sarhaet y ystiwart, ac yna ymchoelut aoruc acheissaὼ talu y wreic ae anreith y Eralt
ystiwart drachefyn y gan Owein, ac nys cafas. Ac
yna o ystryὼ y wreic a oed yndywedut ὼrth Owein
ual hynn. O mynny uygkael i yn ffydlaὼn ytt am
kynnal ¹[y] gyt athi, hebrὼg vym plant att eu tat.
Ac yna o dra serch a charyat y wreic, y gellygaὼd y
ᵃblant' yr ystiwart. A phan gigleu ²Rickart escob
Llundein hynny, y gὼr a oed yna ystiwart y Henri
vrenhin yn Amὼythic, medylyaὼ a oruc dial ar Oὼein
sarhaet Geralt ystiwart; a galὼ attaὼ ³awnaeth Ithel
a Madaὼc meibon ⁴Ridit uab Bledyn adywedut
ὼrthynt ual hynn. A vynnὼch chwi regi bod y Henri
vrenhin achaffel y garyat ae gedymdeithas yn dra-
gywydaὼl, ac ef ach maὼrhaa ¹[ac ach dyrcheif ynn
ych ac] yn bennach no neb och kyttirogyon, ac a
gyghorvynna ὼrthyὼch ych kyt teruynwyr och holl
genedyl. Ac atteb aὼnaethant mynnwn heb ὼynt.
Eὼch chὼitheu heb ef a delὼch Owein uab Kadὼgaὼn
os gellὼch ac onys gellὼch gὼrthbledὼch or wlat ef ae
dat; kanys ef awnaeth gam a sarhaet yn erbyn ⁵y
brenhin, a diruaὼr gollet y Eralt ystiὼart y wahan-
redaὼl gyfeillt am y wreic ae blant ae gastell, ac yspeil
ae anreith, a minheu ⁶arodaf gyt achὼi fydlonnyon
gedymdeithon nyt amgen Llywarch uab Trahaearn,

ᵃ' ⁷ y deu vab ar verch

---

¹ *B.*
² Richyard, *C.*
³ a oruc, *B.*
⁴ Ririt, *C. D.*

was sorry and displeased, because of the violation committed upon Nest, the daughter of Rhys, and ¹ also for fear king Henry should be enraged at the insult to his steward. Thereupon he returned, and endeavoured to prevail on Owain to restore to Gerald the steward, his wife and spoil; but he did not succeed. Then, through the finesse of the wife, who spoke thus to Owain, 'If thou will have me faithful 'to thee, and remain with thee, send my children to 'their father,' he then, from excess of love towards the wife, suffered ᵃ the children' to be returned to the steward. And when Rickart, bishop of London, who was steward to king Henry at Shrewsbury, heard of that affair, he thought of revenging upon Owain the insult done to Gerald the steward, and he called to him Ithel and Madog, the sons of Rhirid, son of Bleddyn, and addressed them thus: 'Would 'ye that you should please king Henry, and obtain 'his love and support for ever, and that he should 'magnify ¹ and exalt you higher than, and' above 'every one of your neighbours, and that your neigh- 'bours of your whole nation should envy you?' And they answered, 'We would.' 'Go ye then,' said he, 'and seize Owain, son of Cadwgan, if you can; and 'if you cannot, expel him and his father from the 'country; for he has committed wrong and insult 'against the king, and immense loss to Gerald the 'steward, his particular friend, in respect of his wife 'and children and his cattle, and the spoil and 'booty; and I will also procure you faithful ac- 'complices, to wit, Llywarch, son of Trahaiarn, the

---

ᵃ/⁷ two sons and daughter

---

³ Henri, *B*. | ⁷ *B. C. D.*
ᵃ chwanneccauf, *B*.

y gŵr a ladaŵd Owein y [a]vrodyr, ag Uchtryt uab Etwin. Ac [1]wynteu gŵedy credu yr edewidyon hynny a gynullassant lu, ac a [2]aethant y gyt ac agyrchassant y wlat. Ac Vchtryt a anuones kenadeu yr wlat y venegi yr [3]kiŵtaŵtwyr pŵy bynnac agilyei attaŵ ef y kaffei amdiffyn. A rei agilyassant attaŵ ef ereill y Arŵystli, ereill y Vaelenyd, ereill y Ystrat Tywi ar rann vŵyaf [4][ohonunt] y Dyfet ydaethant [5]yr lle yd oed Geralt yn vedyanus. A phan yttoed ef yn mynnu eu diua ŵynt ef adamŵeinaŵd dyuot Gŵallter [b]ucheluaer Kaer Loyŵ y gŵr aorchymynnassei y brenhin idaŵ llywodraeth [6][Kaerloyw] ac amdiffyn Lloeger hyt ygkaer Vyrdin. Aphan gigleu ef hynny eu hamdiffyn aoruc; a rei o nadunt a gilyaŵd y Arŵystli, ac y kehyrdaŵd gŵyr Maelenyd ac ŵynt ac y [7]lladassant; ar rei [8]agilyaŵd att Vchtryt adihagassant; ar rei [9]agilyaŵd y Ystrat Tywi Maredud uab Ryderch ae haruolles yn hegar. Kadŵgaŵn ac Owein a foassant y log aoed yn Aber Dyfi adathoed o Iwerdon ychydic kynno hynny a chyfnewit yndi. Ac yna y deuth Madaŵc ae vraŵt [c]yn erbyn' Vchtrut hyt yn [10]Ryt Cornnec,' ac yno pebyllyaŵ aorugant. Ac yny diwed y doeth Vchtrut attunt; a gŵedy eu hymgynullaŵ ygyt kerdet hyt nos aorugant a diffeithaŵ y gŵladoed yny [11]vu dyd. Ac yna ydywaŵt Vchtrut [12][ŵrthunt], o reig bod y chŵi nyt reit

[a] [13] vraut,   [b'] [13] escob   [c'] [13] ac

[1] vyntŵy, *B*.
[2] daethant, *B*.
[3] giŵdaŵt, *R*.
[4] *B*.
[5] ynny, *B*.
[6] *C*.
[7] lladyssant, *B*.
[8] a gilyassant, *B*.

'man whose ᵃbrothers' were killed by Owain, and
'Uchtryd, son of Edwin.' And they, confiding in
those promises, collected an army, and proceeded
together and entered the country; and Uchtryd sent
messengers about the country, to inform the inhabitants that whoever receded to him would find protection. Some did recede to him; others to Arwystli;
others to Maelienydd; others to the Vale of Tywi; and
the greater number ⁴'of them' went to Dyved, where
Gerald was in possession. And when he was intent
upon destroying them, Gwalter, the ᵇ'high constable'
of Gloucester, the person to whom the king had
committed the government ⁶'of Gloucester' and defence
of England, happened to come to Caermarthen, who,
hearing of that, protected them. Some of them withdrew to Arwystli, and were met by the men of
Maelienydd, who killed them, and those who retreated to Uchtryd escaped, and those who retreated
to the Vale of Tywi were kindly received by Maredudd, son of Rhydderch. Cadwgan and Owain
fled to a ship that was in Aberdovey, which a little
before had arrived with merchandize from Ireland.
And then Madog and his brother came ᶜ'to meet'
Uchtryd at Rhyd Cornnec, and there they encamped;
and at length Uchtryd came to them; and after
they had collected themselves together, they proceeded by night, and ravaged the countries until it
was day. Then Uchtryd addressed them, saying,
'If it be your will, that is not necessary; since

  ᵃ ¹³ brother   ᵇ' ¹³ bishop   ᶜ' ¹³ and

---

⁵ a gily6ys, *B.*
¹⁰ kastell Ryt Cornouet, *D.*
—Cornuec, *B. Not in E.*

¹¹ vei, *B. D.*
¹² *B.*
¹³ *D.*

hynny, kany dylyir tremygu Kadôgaôn ac Owein, kanys gôyr da grymus ynt a deôron, a medylyaô llawer y maent, ac ¹agatuyd y mae porth udunt hyt nas gôdam ni, ac ôrth hynny ny weda yni dyuot yn deissyfyt am ²eu pen namyn yn eglur dyd gyt ac ³urdassaôc gyôeirdeb nifer. Ac or geireu hynny bop ychydic yd hedychôyt ôynt ual ygallei dynyon y wlat dianc. Athrannoeth ydaethant yr wlat, a gôedy y gôelet yn diffeith, ymgerydu ehunein awnaethant a dywedut llyma wenyeith Vchtrut; a chuhudaô Uchtrut awnaethant a dywedut y neb ymgedymdeithockau ac ystryô ef. A gôedy gôibiaô pob lle yny wlat ny chaôssant dim namyn gre y Gadôgaôn; a gôedy ⁴cael ⁵honno a' llosgi y tei ar yscuboryeu ar ydeu awnaethant, ac ymchoelut aorugant y ᵃeu pebylleu' drachefyn, a diua rei or dynyon a ⁶ffoassynt y Lan Badarn, a gadel ereill heb eu diua. A phan yttoedynt uelly clybot awnaethant bot rei yn trigyaô yn nodua Dewi yn Llan Dewi Breui yn yr eglôys gyt ar ᵇoffeirat. Anuon awnaethant yno ᶜdrycysprytolyon agkyweithas' a llygru a ônaethant ⁷[y vynnôent a] yr eglôys ac diffeithaô o gôbyl. ᵈAgôedy hynny yn orwac hayach yd ymchoelassant eithyr cael anuolyanus anreith o gyfleoed

---

ᵃ' ⁸ gastell Ryd Gors ᵇ ⁹ offeireit.
ᶜ' ¹⁰ drycysprydolyaeth gyôeithas,
ᵈ' ¹¹ A gwedy hynny ymchwelud aorugant wedy diffeithyaw ac anreithyaw y wlad oll eithyr kyfleoed yseint ehunein Dewi a Phadern.

---

¹ atuyd, B.
² y, B.
³ urdassaôl, B.
⁴ kaffel, B.
⁵ hônnô, B.
⁶ ffoessynt, B.

'Cadwgan and Owain ought not to be slighted; for
'they are good and powerful men, and brave withal,
'and meditate much; and perhaps they may have
'assistance of which we are ignorant; and, therefore,
'it will not be prudent for us to come upon them
'suddenly, but in open day, with dignified com-
'pleteness of numbers.' And by those words they
gradually became pacified, so that the people of the
country were enabled to escape. The following morning they came into the country; and seeing it laid
waste, they blamed themselves, saying, 'Lo, the
'flattery of Uchtryd!' So they accused Uchtryd,
and said, 'Who would have any participation in his
'cunning?' And when they had traversed every
spot in the country, they found nothing except a stud
belonging to Cadwgan; and having found that, they
burned the houses, barns, and corn, and returned
back to ᵃ their tents,' and then they destroyed some
of the people who had fled to Llanbadarn, and
others they left without being destroyed. And whilst
they were thus engaged, they heard that some men
were staying in the sanctuary of Dewi, at Llanddewi
Brevi, in the church with the ᵇ priest. Then they
sent there certain ᶜ wicked and reckless spirits,' who
defiled ⁷ the churchyard and' the church, and completely laid them. waste; ᵈ and afterwards they
returned almost empty, with only an ignominious

ᵃ/ ⁸ the castle of Rhyd y Gors;   ᵇ ⁹ priests.
ᶜ/ ¹⁰ wicked spirits of society,
ᵈ/ ¹¹ and afterwards they returned, having devastated
and ravaged the whole country, except the precincts
of the saints themselves, Dewi and Padarn.

---

⁷ B. | ¹⁰ B.
⁸ E. | ¹¹ C.
⁹ B. D.

seint Dewi a Phadarn.' Agẃedy hynny y mordẃyaẃd Owein y Iwerdon gyt ac ychydic o gedymdeithon, ar rei yd oed achaẃs udunt trigyaẃ yny ol kanys ¹ buassynt ẃrth losgedigaeth y castell, ac y gan Mẃrchath ²[y] brenhin pennaf yn Iẃerdon yd aruollet ef yn hegar, kanys ef a vuassei gynt y gyt ac ef, a chyt ac ef y magyssit yn yr ryuel y diffeithwyt Mon y gan y deu iarll, ac yd anuonyssit ²[ef] y gan y vraẃt a rodyon y Murtart. Ac yna ydaeth Kadẃgaẃn yndirgel hyt Ympowys, ac anuon kenadeu ³ aẃnaeth y geissaẃ hedychu a Rickart ystiwart y brenhin, achael kygreir gantaẃ ⁴ awnaeth y geissaẃ hedychu ar brenhin py ẃed bynnac y gallei. Ae aruoll aoruc y brenhin a gadel idaẃ drigyaẃ ²[y] myẃn tref a gaẃssei y gan y ẃreic oed ⁵ Ffragges merch ⁶ Pictot Sage.' Ac yna ydachubaẃd Madaẃc ac Ithel meibon Ridit ⁷ [ab Bleddyn] ran Gadẃgaẃn ac Owein y vab o Powys y rei a lywassant yn anuolyanus; ac ny buant hedychaẃl y rygthunt ehunein. Ygkyfrẃg hynny gẃedy hedychu o Gadẃgaẃn ²[ar brenhin] y kafas y gyuoeth, nyt amgen Keredigyaẃn gẃedy y phrynu y gan y brenhin yr cant punt. A gẃedy clybot hynny ymchoelut a vnaeth paẃb or a ⁸ wascaryssit kylch o gylch; kanys gorchymyn y brenhin oed ᵃ na allei neb gynnal neb or rei

---

ᵃ/ ⁹ kynn no hynny na thrigei neb Yngheredigyawn na chiwdawdwyr gwyr dieithyr ac nachynnhalyei neb wynt. ¹⁰ Ac nat attalie neb or a doethassei ỳ Keredigiawn kỳn no hỳnnỳ ỳ ev chỳvanhedu o ỳstrawn genediloed; namỳn ev gellwng ỳn rỳd.

---

¹ buessynt, B.
² B.
³ aoruc at, B.

⁴ aoruc, B.
⁵ Ffranges, B.

booty from the precincts of St. Dewi and St. Padarn.'
And after that, Owain went on a voyage to Ireland,
with a few companions, and those who found it
necessary to follow him; for they had been at the
burning of the castle; and was kindly received by
Murchath, the supreme king in Ireland; for he had
been formerly with him, and had been educated with
him during the war in which Mona was ravaged by
the two earls, and had been sent by his brother,
with presents to Murtart. And then Cadwgan went
privately to Powys, and despatched messengers to endeavour to make peace with Rickart, the steward of
the king, and obtained his consent to try to make
his peace with the king in whatever way he could.
And the king received him, and suffered him to dwell
in a hamlet he had obtained with his wife, who
was a Frenchwoman, the daughter of [6]'Pictet Sage.'
And then Madog and Ithel, the sons of Rhirid, [7]'son
of Bleddyn,' seized the portion of Powys belonging
to Cadwgan and his son Owain, who had unworthily
governed, and who had not been at peace between
themselves. In that interval, after Cadwgan had made
his peace [9]'with the king,' he obtained his territory,
that is to say, Ceredigion, after purchasing it from
the king for a hundred pounds. And when that became known, all those who had been dispersed round
about returned, for it was the command of the king
[a]that no support was to be given to those who had

[a/9] previously, that none should dwell in Ceredigion,
whether natives or strangers, and that nobody should
support them. [10] And that he would not retain any
of those who had come to Ceredigion previously; but
let them go free.

---

[6] Piccot de Saii, *D.* Pigod o Saesis, *C.*
[7] *E.*
[9] Gesgeryset, *B.*
[9] *C.*
[10] *D.*

aoedynt ynpressŵylaŵ Keredigyaŵn, kyn no hynny na gŵr or wlat na gŵr dieithyr vei.' A rodi aoruc y brenhin y Gadŵgaŵn drwy yr ammot hynn yma; hyt nabei na chedymdeithas na chyfeillach y rygtaŵ ac Owein y uab, ac na adei idaŵ dyuot yr wlat, ac na rodei idaŵ na chyghor na nerth. Ac odyna ydymchoelaŵd rei or gwyr aathoed gyt ac Owein y Iwerdon, a llechu yn dirgeledic awnaethant heb ŵneuthur dim argŵywed. A gŵedy hynny yd ymchoelaŵd Owein, ac nyt y Geredigyaŵn y doeth namyn y Bowys; a cheissaŵ anuon kenadeu at y brenhin ¹[aŵmaeth] ²[ac ny lyuassaŵd neb arŵein y genadŵri hyt at y brenhin]. Ygkyfrŵg hynny y bu annuundeb rŵg Madaŵc ar Ffreinc, o achaŵs y lletradeu yd oed y Saesonn yn y wneuthur ar y tir, ac odyno yd oedynt yn gŵneuthwr cameu yn erbyn y brenhin ac yn dyuot at Vadaŵc. Ac yna yd anuones Rickert ystiwart at Vadaŵc y erchi ¹[idaŵ] ᵃdaly y gŵyr awnathoed y kam ᵇyn erbyn y' brenhin; ac ynteu aŵrthŵynebaŵd y hynny ac nys dalaŵd. Ac yn gamŵedaŵc heb wybot beth awnaei, namyn keissaŵ kyveillach gan Owein uab Kadŵgaŵn, a hynny a gavas; a gŵneuthur hedŵch rŵg a rei a oedynt yn elynyon kyn no hynny, ac ymaruoll vch benn creireu aŵnaethant hyt na hedychei vn ar brenhin heb y gilyd, ac na vredychei vn o nadunt y gilyd. Ac yna y kerdynt y gyt py le bynnac y dyckei ytyghetuen ŵynt; a llosci tref neb un ŵrda aorugant, a phy beth bynnac a ellynt y dŵyn gantunt nac yn veirch nac yn wiscoed ŵynt ae ducsant na neb ryŵ dim arall or a geffynt.

ᵃ ³ talu   ᵇ ³ yr

¹ B.   ² C.

been heretofore dwelling in Ceredigion, whether a man of the country or a stranger.' And the king made the grant to Cadwgan, on condition that there should be neither communion nor friendship between him and his son Owain, and that he should not allow him to enter the country, and that he should not afford him advice nor assistance. From that time, some of the men, who had gone with Owain into Ireland, returned, and concealed themselves, without committing any injury. And after that, Owain also returned, not to Ceredigion, but to Powys; and endeavoured to send messages to the king, ²and none dared to forward his business to the king.' Whilst that was passing, a discord arose between Madog and the French, on account of the robberies that the Saxons were committing upon the land; and thence they were committing wrongs against the king, and coming to Madog. And then Rickart the steward sent to Madog, desiring him to ᵃseize the men who had done the injury ᵇagainst' the king; and he objected to it, and did not seize them. And thus criminal, he knew not what he could do, other than seek the friendship of Owain, son of Cadwgan; and this he obtained; and so peace was made between those who before were enemies. And they mutually pledged upon the relics that neither should be reconciled to the king without the other, and that neither of them would betray the other. Then they wandered together wherever their destiny might lead them; and burned the hamlet of some gentleman, and carried off whatsoever they could with them, whether horses or clothes, or anything else they could find.

ᵃ ³ pay   ᵇ ³ to

² *B.*

MCVII. Y vl6ydyn rac 6yneb y koffaa6d Henri vrenhin garchar Iorwoerth uab Bledyn, ac anuon kennat atta6 y wybot beth arodei yr y ell6g oe garchar; kanys blin y6 bot yn hirgarchar. Ac ynteu aedewis m6y noc a allei [1] [y] dyuot ida6, adywedut [1] [aoruc ef] y rodei pob dim or [2] [aallei ac] a archei y brenhin; ac yn gyntaf [a] ynteu a' erchis g6ystlon [1] [y uap Ridit] o veibon goreug6yr y wlat; yr eilweith yd erchis [a] Ithel mab' Ridit y vra6t a thrychant punt o aryant py fford bynnac y gallei dyuot udunt, nac o veirch, nac o ychen nac o neb ry6 fford y gallei dyuot udunt. [b] Ac yna y rodet mab Kad6ga6n uab Bledyn yr h6nn a anyssit or Ffranges yr h6n a elwit Henri ac y tal6yt can morc drosta6.' Ac yna y rodet y 6lat idaw ef, a lla6er a dala6d. Ac yna y [3] gellyg6yt mab Kad6ga6n. Ac ygkyfr6g y petheu hynny y g6naeth Owein a Mada6c [4] ac eu' kedymdeithon lla6er o drygeu ygg6lat y Ffreinc ac yn Lloeger. A [5] pha beth bynnac a geffynt nac o ledrat nac o dreis, y dir Iorwoerth y dygynt. Ac yno y press6ylynt. Ac yna anuon kenad6ri a oruc Iorwoerth attunt yn garedic a dywedut 6rthynt ual hynn. Du6 anrodes ni yn lla6 [6] an gelynyon, ac an darestyga6d yn gymeint

---

[a/7] Yorwerth ac Ithel meibyon

[b/8] Ac o hẏnnẏ ẏ rodes ẏ brenhin ẏ vab Cadogon or Fraghes a dẏwedpwẏt vchot, Henri oed ẏ henw, cant morc.

---

[1] B.
[2] yd, B.
[3] gollyga6d ef, B.
[4] ae, B.

1107. The ensuing year king Henry remembered the imprisonment of Iorwerth, son of Bleddyn, and sent a message to him to know what he would give for liberating him out of his prison; for it is wearisome to be long in prison. And he promised more than he could compass, saying that he would give every thing ¹that he could, and' that the king might demand. And then he first demanded hostages from ¹his son Rhirid,' and from among the sons of the principal men of the country; and, secondly, he demanded ᵃIthel, son' of Rhirid, his brother, and three hundred pounds of silver, in whatsoever way he might obtain it, whether in horses, or in oxen, or in any way he could procure it. ᵇAnd then, the son of Cadwgan, son of Bleddyn, who had been born of the French woman, and whose name was Henry, was to be given up to him, and for him a hundred marks were paid.' And then his country was delivered up to him, for which he paid a great deal; and then the son of Cadwgan was set at liberty. And whilst these things were passing, Owain and Madog, with their companions, committed many crimes, in the country of the French, and in England; and whatsoever they obtained, whether by robbery or by force, they conveyed to the land of Iorwerth, and there they took up their abode. And then Iorwerth sent a kindly message to them, speaking to them thus, 'God has 'delivered us into the hands of our enemies, and

---

ᵃ' ⁷ Iorwerth and Ithel, the sons

ᵇ' ⁸ And thereupon the king gave to the son of Cadwgan by the French woman above mentioned, whose name was Henry, a hundred marks.

ˢ phy, B.
ᵉ yn, B.

ᵗ C. Not in D.
ᵉ D.

ac na allem gŵneuthur dim or auei ewyllys gennym. Gŵahardedic yŵ ynni baŵb or Brytanyeit hyt na chyffredino neb o honam ni a ¹chŵchŵi nac o vŵyt nac o diaŵt, nac o nerth, nac o ganhorthŵy, namyn ²aŵch keissaŵ ach ³hela ym pob lle, ach rodi yny diwed yn llaŵ y brenhin ⁴oc aŵch' carcharu neu ⁴oc aŵch' llad, neu ⁴ych ⁵dihenydyaŵ neu yr hynn a vynnei a chŵi. Ac yn bennaf y gorchymynŵyt imi a Chadŵgaŵn nat ymgredem achŵi. Kanys ny digaŵn neb tebygu na damunaŵ tat neu ewythyr da ⁶y eu' meibon ac nyeint. Kanys od ⁷ymgedymdeithŵn' ni a chŵi, neu vynet haeach yn erbyn gorchymynneu y brenhin, ni a gollŵn ⁸an kyfoeth, ac ankarcherir yny vom veirŵ neu anlledir. Ac ŵrth hynny mi aŵch gŵediaf megys ᵃkyueillt, a mi aŵch' gorchymynnaf megys ᵇarglŵyd, ac ach eirolaf megis ᶜkar nad eloch' ford ym kyuoeth i na ford y gyfoeth Kadŵgaŵn mŵy noc y gyfoeth gŵyr ereill yn kylch. Kanys mŵy o ⁹anuodedigaetheu a geissyr yn erbyn ni, noc yn erbyn ereill yn bot yn gylus. A thremygu hynny a ŵnaethant a mŵyvŵy eu kyfoeth a vynychynt, ¹⁰a breid y gochelynt kyndrycholder y gŵyr ehunein. A Iorwoerth a geissaŵd eu hymlit a chynnullaŵ llaŵer o wyr aoruc ¹¹ac eu ¹²hela. Ac ¹³ŵynteu ae gochelassant bob ychydic. Ac yn vn ¹⁴dorof ygyt y kyrchassant

---

ᵃ' ¹⁵ kyueillon ac ach   ᵇ ¹⁵ arglŵydi,
ᶜ' ¹⁵ kereint nath trossŵch

---

¹ chŵi, B.
² y ych, B.
³ hely, B.
⁴ y ŵch, B.

ᵇ diuetha, B.
ᵃ' yŵ, B.
⁷' ymgyffredinŵn dim, B.
⁸ yn, B.

'brought us down so much, that we could accomplish
'nothing of what might be our wish; it is inter-
'dicted to all of us Britons, to hold any intercourse
'with you, in respect of victuals, or drink, or aid, or
'support; but we must search and hunt for you in
'every place, and ultimately deliver you into the
'hands of the king, to imprison you, or to kill you,
'or to execute you, or to do unto you whatever he
'would wish. And specially has it been commanded
'me and Cadwgan, that we should have no fellowship
'with you; for no one can suppose but that a father,
'or an uncle, must desire the welfare of his sons and
'his nephews. Therefore, if we have communication
'with you, or in the least go contrary to the com-
'mand of the king, we shall lose our territory, and
'shall be imprisoned so that we die, or we shall
'be killed. Wherefore, I pray you, as ᵃa friend,
'and' command you, as ᵇyour lord,' and intercede
'with you, as ᶜa relative, that you go not into' my
'territory, nor into the territory of Cadwgan any
'more, nor into the territory of other men about us;
'because more causes of displeasure will be sought for
'against us, as being blameable, than against others.'
This they treated with contempt, and frequented their
territories the more; and scarcely would they avoid
even the presence of their men. And Iorwerth took
measures to pursue them, and collected many men,
and hunted after them; and the others step by step
avoided them, and in one combined body they pro-

---

a' ¹⁵ friends, and   b' ¹⁵ lords,
c' ¹⁵ relatives that ye pass not over

---

⁹ annogedigaethn, *B*.
¹⁰ ac a, *B*.
¹¹ y, *B*.
¹² hely, *B*.
¹³ Gynt, *B*.
¹⁴ Coryf, *B*.
¹⁵ *B*.

gyfoeth Vchtrut ¹[ap Edwin] hyt ym Meiryonyd. A phan gigleu veibon Vchtrut hynny ae teulu ²rei a ellygassant' Vchtrut y amdiffyn y tir, anuon a orugant y Veiryonyd y beri y baѡp dyuot attunt y ѡrthlad y gѡyr oc eu tir. Kanys yn gyntaf y dathoedynt y Gyfeilaѡc yny lle ydoed meibon Vchtrut. Ac ny allyssant ³eu gѡrthlad. Ac yna yd ymgynnullaѡd gѡyr Meiryonyd heb ohir ac y deuthant at veibon Vchtrut. Ac ual yd oed Owein a Madaѡc yn ⁴y lletyeu' Ygkyfeilaѡc, trannoeth y boreu aruaethu aorugant mynet y Veironnyd y ⁵letyaѡ heb wneuthur dim drѡc amgen. Ac ual ydoedynt yn dѡyn eu hynt, nachaf wyr Meiryonnyd ygkyfrѡg mynyded ac ⁶ynyalѡch yn' dѡyn y bydin gyweir yn kyfaruot ⁷[ac ѡynt], ac yn ⁸eu ruthraѡ, ac yn dodi gaѡr arnunt. Ac ⁹ѡynteu heb ¹⁰dybyaѡ dim ѡrthynt ar y kyrch kyntaf y ffoassant; ac y deuth Owein. ᵃA phan gѡelas gѡyr Meiryonnyd ef yn kyrchu yn ѡraѡl ac yn baraѡt y ymlad, ffo yn deissyfeit aorugant. Ac ⁹ѡynteu ac hymlidyassant ⁷[ѡynt] hyt eu gѡlat, a diffeithaѡ y wlat aorugant, a llosgi y tei ar ydeu allad yr yscrybyl kymeint ac a gaѡssant heb dѡyn dim gantunt.' A gѡedy hynny ydaeth Madavc y Bowys.

ᵃ' ¹¹ Agwedẏ gwelet o Oweẏn a Madoc ẏ gwẏr ẏn ẏmlad mor wrawl ac wẏnt, kẏmrẏt ev hẏnt ar fo a orugant, ac ev hẏmlit aoruc ẏ gwẏr ereill hẏt ev kẏvanhedev ac ẏna llosgi ẏ tei ar ẏdev a llad ẏr ẏsgrẏbẏl ẏn llwẏr.

---

¹ E.
ᵛ yrei aollygassei, B.
ᵃ y, B.

ᵛ' llettyu, B.
⁵ lettyv, B.
ᵛ' ynn anyallѡch, ynn, B.

ceeded towards the territory of Uchtryd, 'son of Edwin,' in Meirionydd. And when that became known to the sons of Uchtryd and their tribe, who were left by Uchtryd to defend their land, they sent to Meirionydd, ordering every body to join them to expel the men out of their land. For they had first come into Cyveiliog, where the sons of Uchtryd were stationed, who were not able to expel them; and thereupon the men of Meirionydd assembled without delay, and came to aid the sons of Uchtryd. And, as Owain and Madog were at their lodgings in Cyveiliog, they, early on the following day, purposed going into Meirionydd to take their quarters, without doing any mischief. And as they were pursuing their journey, behold the men of Meirionydd were, among the mountains and fastnesses, in well ordered array, coming to meet them, rushing upon them, and setting up a shout. And the others not suspecting any thing about them, fled on the first onset; and then Owain advanced. ᵃWhen the men of Meirionydd saw him coming bravely forward, and prepared to fight, they suddenly took to flight, and the others pursued them into their country; and they ravaged the country, and burned the houses and the corn, and killed all the cattle they could find, without taking any thing away with them.' After that Madog went into Powys;

ᵃ' ¹¹ And when Owain and Madog saw the men fighting so bravely with them, they took to flight, and the other men pursued them as far as their abodes, where they burned the houses and crops, and killed all the cattle.

---

⁷ B.
⁸ y, B.
⁹ 6y, B.

¹⁰ tybygu, B.
¹¹ D E.

Ac Owein a ymchoelaöd ef ae wyr y Geredigyaön y lle yd oed y dat yn göledychu ac yn pressöylaö; a thrigyaö aoruc ef ae gedymdeithon yny lle y mynnaöd, achoffau dyuodyat y dat kynno hynny yr kyfoeth. Kanys y ¹gedymdeith oedynt' y Dyfet ²y yspeilaö y wlat ³ac y dala' y dynyon, ac eudöyn ynröym hyt y llogeu adathoed gan Owein o Iwerdon. Ac ªyna ydoedynt' yn trigyaö yn teruyneu y wlat. Ac eilweith yd aethant y galö ynvydyon ⁴a chwanegi' eu rif, a chyrchu dros nos y ᵇwlat ae llosgi, allad paöb or a gaössant yndi, ac yspeilaö ereill, a döyn ereill gantunt ygkarchar, ac eu göerthu y eu dynyon neu eu hanuon yn röym yr llogeu. A göedy llosgi y tei a llad kymeint ac agaössant or annifeileit, a chymeint ac a gaössant a ⁵dugant gantunt, ac a ymchoelassant fford y Keredigyaön örth letyaö a thrigyaö a mynet a dyuot, heb edrych dim o achöysson Kadögaön nac o wahard y brenhin. A rei o nadunt dreilgöeith a oedynt yn kadö fford yd oed ⁶henafgör or Flemhissieit yn dyuot idi, aelwit Wiliam o ⁷Vreban, ae gyferbynieit a önaethant ae lad. Ac yna mynet o Gadögaön gyt a Iorwoerth y lys y brenhin y vynnu kael ymdidan ac ef. Ac ual ⁸y buant' yna nachaf braöt yr gör a ⁹ladyssit yny lle yn menegi yr brenhin ry lad o Owein ae gedymeithon y vraöt. Pan gigleu y brenhin hynny gofyn a oruc y Gadög-

---

ᵃ⸍ ¹⁰ etöa y mae   ᵇ⸍ ¹¹ dref o Dyued

¹⸍ getymdeithon aethant, *B.*   ⁴⸍ y chöanecau, *B.*
² ac, *B.*   ⁵ ducsant, *B.*
³⸍ a daly, *B.*   ⁶ hennefgöyr, *B.* esgob, *C.* primas, *D.*

and Owain with his own men returned to Ceredigion, where his father was reigning and dwelling; and he and his companions remained where he thought proper, calling to mind the coming of his father into the territory before; for his companions had gone into Dyved, to pillage the country and seize the people, and take them bound to the ships that had come with Owain from Ireland. And ᵃ then they were' dwelling about the borders of the country. And they went a second time to invite simpletons to augment their number, and entered ᵇ the country' by night, and burned it, and killed every body they found therein, and pillaged others, and took others with them as prisoners, and sold them to their people, or sent them bound to their ships. After burning the houses, and killing as many as they found of the cattle, and taking all they could bring with them, they returned to Ceredigion to lodge and abide, going and coming without at all minding the affairs of Cadwgan, or the interdiction of the king. And some of them, on a time, were watching the road along which an old man of the Flemings, called William of ⁷ Brabant, was travelling, and they intercepted and killed him. And then, Cadwgan and Iorwerth repaired to the court of the king, to obtain some conversation with him; and while they were there, behold the brother of the person that had been killed was present, informing the king how Owain and his companions had slain his brother. When the king heard that, he questioned Cadwgan,

---

a′ ¹⁰ they are still   b′ ¹¹ a town of Dyved

---

⁷ Brabawd, *C.* Vrebam, *B.*
⁸′ bydant, *B.*
⁹ ledissit, *B.*

¹⁰ *B.*
¹¹ *C. D. E.*

aỽn beth a dywedy am hynny. ¹ Nis gỽnn i' arglỽyd heb y Kadỽgaỽn. Yna ydyỽaỽt y brenhin kany elly di kadỽ dygyfoeth rac kedymdeithon dy vab hyt naladon vyggỽyr eilweith mi a rodaf dy gyfoeth yr neb ae kattỽo, a thitheu a drigy y gyt a mi drỽy yr amot hỽnn yma na sethrych di dy briaỽt wlat, a mi ath borthaf di om hymborth i yn y gymerỽyf gyghor ² am danat. A rodi aoruc y brenhin pedeir ar hugein idaỽ peunyd ygkyfeir y dreul. Ac ³ yna y trigyaỽd heb dodi ⁴ gefyn arnaỽ, namyn yn ryd y ford y mynnei eithyr ywlat e hun. A gỽedy clybot o Owein yspeilaỽ y dat oe gyfoeth, kyrchu Iwerdon aoruc ef a Madaỽc uab Ridit. A gỽedy hynny anuon aoruc y brenhin at Gilbert uab Rickert yr hỽnn a oed deỽr molyannus ⁵ galluus, a chyfeillt yr brenhin, agỽr arderchaỽc oed yny holl weithredoed ⁶ [y] erchi idaỽ dyuot attaỽ, ac ynteu y deuth. Ar brenhin a dywaỽt ỽrthaỽ, yd oedut yn wastat yn keissaỽ ran o tir y Brytanyeit y genyf, mi arodaf itt ⁷ yr aỽr honn' tir Kadỽgaỽn ⁸ [vab Bledyn] dos a goreskyn ef. Ac yna y kymerth yn llaỽen ygan y brenhin. Ac yna gan gynullaỽ llu gyt ae ⁹ gedymdeithon y deuth hyt yg Keredigyaỽn ac y gorescynnaỽd. Ac yd adeilaỽd deu gastell yndi, nyt amgen vn gyferbyn a Llan Badarn ynymyl aber yr auon aelwir Ystỽyth, ¹⁰ ar llall geir' llaỽ Aber Teifi, yny lle aelwir Dingereint, y lle ⁶ [y] grỽndwalassei Roger iarll kyn no hynny gastell. A gỽedy ¹¹ ychydic o amser yd ymchoelaỽd Madaỽc ab Ridit o Iwerdon heb allel godef andynolyon voesseu y Gỽydyl. Ac Owein a

---

ᵛ ny ỽn,' B.
² ym, B.
³ yno, B.
⁴ gefyneu, B.
⁵ galluaỽr, B.
⁶ B.

'What sayest thou concerning that?' 'I know not, 'my lord,' replied Cadwgan. Then said the king, 'Since thou canst not protect thy territory against the 'companions of thy son, to prevent them from killing 'my men a second time, I shall give thy territory to 'such as will protect it, and thou shalt remain with 'me under this condition, that thou tread not thy 'native soil; and I will support thee from my table, 'until I take counsel concerning thee.' And the king allowed him daily twenty-four pence towards his expenditure; and there he continued, without being put in fetters, having his liberty to go where he pleased, except to his own country. And when Owain heard how his father had been deprived of his territory, he, with Madog, son of Rhirid, went to Ireland. After that, the king sent to Gilbert, son of Rickert, who was brave, renowned, and powerful, and a friend of the king, and an honourable man in all his actions, desiring that he would come to him; and he came accordingly. The king said to him, 'Thou wert con-'tinually seeking for a portion of the land of the 'Britons from me, I will now give thee the land of 'Cadwgan, [8]son of Bleddyn;' go and possess it.' And he accepted it with pleasure from the king; and, having collected an army in concert with his companions, he proceeded to Ceredigion, and took possession of it; and built therein two castles, one opposite to Llanbadarn, near the efflux of the river called Ystwyth, and the other contiguous to Aberteivi, at the place called Dingeraint, where earl Robert had before then founded a castle. After a little time Madog, son of Rhirid, returned from Ireland, not being able to endure the savage manners of the Gwyddelians; but Owain

---

[7] yn aŵr, B.
[8] D.
[9] getymeithon, B.
[10] ac arall ger, B.
[11] ŵychydic, B.

drigyaỏd yno yn y ol dalym o amser. A Madaỏc aaeth y Powys; ac nyt aruollet nac yn hegar nac yn drugaraỏc y gan Iorwoerth y ªewythyr rac y gynnal yngylus y gan y brenhin herỏyd kyfreith a drycweithret ot ymgyffredinei ae nei o dim. Ac ynteu ynwibiaỏdyr a lechaỏd hỏnt ac yma gan ochel kydrycholder Iorwoerth. ¹[A] Iorwoerth aỏnaeth kyfreith hyt na bei ¹[neb] a veidei dywedut dim ỏrthaỏ ¹[ef dim] am Vadawc, na menegi dim am danaỏ gỏelit na welit. Ygkyfrỏg hynny aruaethu a wnaeth Madaỏc gỏneuthur brat Iorwoerth y ªewythyr. A ²dala kyveillach aoruc a Llywarch uab Trahaearn. Ac ymaruoll y gyt awnaethant yn dirgeledic; ac eissoes yr terỏyn hỏnnỏ ³ydaethant.

MCVIII. Y vlỏydyn rac ⁴ỏyneb ⁵[pan oed oet Crist mil achant ac wŷth mlŷned] y paratoes Madaỏc vrat Iorỏoerth ¹[a uedỏlyassei kynn o hynny], acheissaỏ amser achyfle a ⁶ỏnaeth y ⁷gyflenwi y ewyllys. A phan ymchoelaỏd Iorwoerth y ⁸Gaer Einaỏn' y kyrchaỏd Madaỏc a chedymdeithon Llywarch ygyt ac ef ynborth idaỏ kyrch nos am benn Iorwoerth. Adodi gaỏr a orugant ygkylch yty llo ydoed Iorwoerth; a dyhunaỏ awnaeth Iorwoerth gan yr aỏr, achadỏ y ty arnaỏ ef ae ⁹gedymdeithon ⁵[yn gadarn]; a llosgi y ty a ỏnaeth Madaỏc am ben Iorwoerth. A phan welas kedymdeithon Iorwoerth hynny kyrchu allan aorugant drỏy y tan, ¹[ac adaỏ Iorwoeth yn y tan]. Ac yntau pan welas y ty yndygỏydaỏ keissaỏ kyrchu allan aoruc ae elynyon ae kymerth ar vlaen ¹⁰gỏewyr, ac

---

a ¹¹ gevŷnderw

---

¹ B.
² daly, B.
³ y deuthant, B.

⁴ llaỏ, B.
⁵ D.
⁶ oruc, B.

remained there after him for some time. Then Madog proceeded to Powys; but was not received either kindly or mercifully by his ᵃuncle Iorwerth, lest he should be deemed culpable by the king, according to law, for the misdeed, if he connected himself with his nephew in any thing; and the other, a fugitive, skulked here and there, avoiding the presence of Iorwerth. A law was made by the king that none should dare say any thing to him about Madog, or speak about him, seen or not seen. Meanwhile, Madog formed a design of laying a plot against his uncle Iorwerth; and kept up an intimacy with Llywarch, son of Trahaiarn, and they privately pledged each other, and came to that resolution.

1108. The ensuing year, '⁵when the year of Christ was one thousand one hundred and eight,' Madog prepared the plot against Iorwerth, '¹which he had previously meditated,' and sought for time and opportunity to accomplish his design. When Iorwerth returned to ⁸Caereinion, Madog, with the assistance of Llywarch's accomplices, made a night attack upon Iorwerth. They set up a shout about the house, where Iorwerth resided; and Iorwerth awoke by the shout, and '⁵bravely' defended the house, aided by his companions. Then Madog set fire to the house about Iorwerth; and when the companions of Iorwerth saw that, they sallied out through the fire, ¹and left Iorwerth in the fire.' And he, seeing the house falling, attempted to get out, and his enemies received him on the points of their spears,

---

ᵃ ¹¹ cousin

---

⁷ gyfuleỏni, *B.*
⁹ Ynkeredigion, *E.*
⁸ getymeithon, *B.*

¹⁰ gỏayỏar, *B.*
¹¹ *D.*

yn atlosgedic y lad. A phan gigleu Henri vrenhin ry lad Iorwoerth rodi Powys a wnaeth y Gadȯgaȯn uab Bledyn. A hedychu ac Owein y vab. Ac erchi y Gadȯgaȯn anuon kenadeu yn ol Owein hyt yn Iwerdon. A gȯedy gȯybot a Vadaȯc ar rei aladyssynt Iorwoerth gyt ac ef rywneuthur agkyfreith o nadunt yn erbyn y brenhin llechu y myȯn coedyd aorugant, ac aruaethu gȯneuthur brat Kadȯgaȯn. A Chadȯgaȯn heb uynnu argȯedu y neb megys ydoed uoes gantaȯ adoeth hyt yn Trallȯg Llywelyn arvedyr trigyaȯ yno aphresȯylaȯ lle yd oed hyrrȯyd ac agos ¹[heuyt] y Vadaȯc. Ac yna anuon yspiwyr aoruc Madaȯc y ȯybot py le y bei Gadȯgaȯn. Ar rei hynny a doethant drachefyn ac a dywedassant y neb yd ²oedynt yny geissaȯ, ym pell y mae hȯnnȯ ac yn agos. Ac ynteu ae wyr yny lle a gyrchaȯd Kadȯgaȯn. A Chadȯgaȯn heb tybyaȯ dim drȯc a ymȯnaeth yn llesc heb vynny ffo, a heb allel ymlad, wedy ffo y wyr oll ae gael ynteu yn unic ae iad. A gwedy llad Kadȯgaȯn anuon kenadeu a ³wnaeth Madaȯc at ⁴Rickert escob Llundein y gȯr a oed yn kynhal lle y brenhin ac yn y lywyaȯ yn Amȯythic y erchi ¹[talu] idaȯ ef y tir y gȯnathoedit y kyflafaneu hynny ymdanaȯ. A gȯedy ⁵rac vedylyaȯ' or escob yn gynnil y achȯysson ef heb rodi messur ar hynny y oedi aoruc, ac nyt yr y garyat ⁶ef, namyn adnabot o honaȯ deuodeu gȯyr y wlat ¹[y] mae llad aȯnaei bop un o ⁷nadunt y gilyd. Ac gyfran a vuassei ⁸idaȯ ef ac y Ithel y ȯraȯt kyn no hynny a rodei idaȯ. A phan gigleu Varedud uab Bledyn hynny, kyrchu y brenhin aoruc y erchi idaȯ

---

¹ *B*. ³ oruc, *B*.
² oidem ni, *B*. ⁴ Richart, *D*.

greatly burnt, and killed him. And when king Henry heard that Iorwerth had been slain, he gave Powys to Cadwgan, son of Bleddyn, and was reconciled to Owain his son, and requested Cadwgan to send messengers after Owain to Ireland. Madog, and those who had joined him in killing Iorwerth, understanding that they had committed a breach of law against the king, lurked in the woods, intending to plot against Cadwgan. And Cadwgan, without intending to injure any one, as was his disposition, came to Trallwng Llywelyn, with the design of staying there, and dwelling where it was convenient, and near ¹ also to Madog. Thereupon Madog sent spies to learn where Cadwgan might be found; and they returned and said, that the person they were in search of was far and near. And he, with his men, immediately came upon Cadwgan; and Cadwgan, not imagining any mischief, conducted himself weakly, and would not flee, and without being able to fight, all his men having fled, he being found alone was put to death. After Cadwgan had been slain, Madog sent messengers to Rickert, bishop of London, the man who supplied the king's place, and was governing at Shrewsbury, to request that the land should be paid to him for which the crimes had been committed. And when the bishop had maturely considered the matter, he, without making a determination, delayed answering, not out of any love to him, but knowing the manners of the people of the country, that they would all be killing one another. But the portion that had been possessed by him and Ithel his brother before was given to him. When Maredudd, son of Bleddyn, became acquainted with this, he went to the king, to

---

⁵ gỽelet, *B.*
⁶ arnaỽ.

⁷ honunt, *B.*
⁸ eidaỽ, *B.*

tir Iorwoerth uab Bledyn y vraƀt, ar brenhin arodes kadƀryaeth y tir idaƀ, yny delei Owein uab Kadƀgaƀn yr wlat. Ygkyfrƀg hynny y deuth Owein ac yd aeth at y brenhin. A chymryt y tir ¹[y] gantaƀ trƀy rodi gƀystlon, ac adaƀ llaƀer o aryant. A Madaƀc ²[vab Ririt] aedewis llawer o aryant a gƀystlon ac amodeu ger bronn y brenhin. A gƀedy kymryt nodyeu ymoglyt aoruc pob vn rac y gilyd yny vlƀydyn honno hyt y diwed.

MCIX. Yny vlƀydyn rac ƀyneb ²[pan oed oet Crist MC. a nav mlyned] 'y delit Robert iarll uab ³Roser o Vedlehem' y gan Henri vrenhin, ac y carcharƀyt. Ac yryvelaƀd y uab yn erbyn y brenhin ¹[am yr achos hƀnnƀ].

MCX. Deg mlyned a chant a mil oed oet Crist pan anvones Maredud uab Bledyn y teulu y neb un gynhƀryf y tir Llywarch uab Trahaearn y dƀyn kyrch. Yna y damweinaƀd val yd oedynt yn dƀyn hynt drƀy gyfoeth ⁴[Madaƀc] uab Ridit, nachaf ƀr yn kyuaruot ac ƀynt a ⁵dala hƀnnƀ aorugant a gofyn idaƀ py le yd oed Vadaƀc uab Ridit y nos honno yn trigyaƀ. A gƀadu yn gyntaf aƀnaeth y gƀr hyt nas gƀydat ef. Ac odyna gƀedy y gystudyaƀ ae gymell adef aoruc y vot ynagos ²[attadunt]. A gƀedy rƀymaƀ ¹[y gƀr] hƀnnƀ ⁶yspiwyr a aroyssant' yno ᵃa llechu aƀnaethant yny oed oleu ¹[y] dyd drannoeth.' Agƀedy dyfot y bore o deissyfyt gƀnnƀryf y ⁷dugant kyrch idaƀ; a dala' a orugant ¹[idav] a llad llaƀer oe wyr, ae dƀyn

---

ᵃ⁄ ⁸ ac ynteu yn llechu yn agos yny vei dyd.

---

¹ B.   ³′ Roger de Belem, D.
² D.   ⁴ B. Maredud, A.

request that he would give him the land of his brother Iorwerth, son of Bleddyn; and the king granted him custody of the land, until Owain, son of Cadwgan, should return to the country. In that interval Owain came, and repaired to the king, and received the land from him, by giving pledges and promising much money; and Madog, ªson of Rhirid,' also promised much money and pledges, with conditions, in the presence of the king. And after taking securities, each of them avoided the other, unto the end of that year.

1109. The ensuing year, ʸwhen the year of Christ was a thousand one hundred and nine,' earl Robert, son of Roger of Bethlehem, was seized by king Henry, and imprisoned; and his son made war against the king ᶻon that account.'

1110. One thousand one hundred and ten was the year of Christ, when Maredudd, son of Bleddyn, sent his family on some enterprise to the land of Llywarch, son of Trahaiarn, to make an incursion. Then it happened, as they were taking their course through the territory of Madog, son of Rhirid, behold a man meeting them, whom they seized, and they questioned him where Madog, son of Rhirid, was abiding that night; and the man at first denied that he knew; and then, after torturing and urging him, he acknowledged that he was near ªthem. After binding the man, they sent spies to the place, ᵃand lurked till it was light the following morning.' And when the morning was come, by a sudden enterprise they made an attack upon him, caught him, killed many of his

---

ᵃ/ ᵃ he lurking near until it was day.

ᶻ daly, B.
ᵃ anuon yspiór a (naethant, B.
ʸ kyrchassant ef, ae daly, B.
ᵃ C.

ygkarchar at Uaredud, ae gymryt yn llaᵥen aoruc ac
gadᵥ y myᵥn gefyneu. Yna y deuth Owein ab Kadᵥg-
aᵥn yr hᵥn nyt yttoed gartref ¹[yna]. A phan gigleu
Owein hynny ar vrys y deuth; ac y rodes Maredud
ef yny laᵥ, ae gymryt ²a oruc' yn llaᵥen ᵃ ae dallu.'
A rannu ¹[y] rygtunt aᵥnaethant y rann ef o Powys,
sef oed hynny Kereinaᵥn a thraean Deudᵥr ac Aber
Riᵥ.

MCXI. Y vlᵥydyn rac ᵥyneb ³[pan oed oet Crist
MCXI.] y kyffroes Henri vrenhin ⁴ llu yn erbyn Gᵥyned,
ac yn bennaf ⁵y Powys. Agᵥedy barnu ar Owein
gᵥneuthur ⁶agkyfreith, y guhudaᵥ aoruc Gilbert uab
Rickert ᵥrth y brenhin, a dywedut bod gᵥyr Owein
yn gᵥneuthur lledrateu ar y wyr ef ac tir. Ar
⁷drygeu aᵥnelei ereill a dywedit ar ⁸ᵥyr Owein.' A
chredu aoruc y brenhin bot pob peth or a ⁹dyᵥaᵥt y
kyhudᵥr ynwir. Ygkyfrᵥg hynny kyhudaᵥ a ¹⁰wnaeth
mab ¹¹Hu iarll Kaer Llion Gruffud uab Kynan, a
Gronᵥ uab Owein. Ac aruaethu o gyttundeb mynnu
dileu yr holl Vrytanyeit o gᵥbyl hyt na ¹²cheffynt
Vrytanaᵥl enᵥ yn dragyᵥydaᵥl. Ac ᵥrth hynny y
kynullaᵥd Henri vrenhin llu or holl ynys ᵇo Penryn
Pengᵥaed yn ¹³[Cŷrnŷw] hyt ym Penryn Blataon yn
y Gogled' yn erbyn Gᵥyned a Phowys. A phan gigleu Varedud uab Bledyn hynny mynet awnaeth y

---

ᵃ′ ¹⁴ ac aberŷs ŷ dallu

ᵇ′ ¹⁴ or van eithiaf o Gyrnŷw lle gelwir Pengwaŷd,
hŷt ŷ vann eithiaf o Brŷdŷn lle gelwir Penblathaon.

---

¹ B.
²′ orugant, B.
³ D.
⁴ luyd, B.

⁵ ym, B.
⁶ agkyureitheu, B.
⁷ petheu, B.
⁸′ yᵥyr ef, B.

men, and brought him prisoner to Maredudd, who received him gladly, and kept him in fetters. Then Owain, son of Cadwgan, who was not at home, returned; and when Owain became acquainted with the affair, he came in haste, and Maredudd delivered him into his hand; and he took him with pleasure, ª and blinded him.' And they divided between them his share of Powys, which was Caereinion, and the third of Deuddwr and Aberrhiw.

1111. The ensuing year, 'when the year of Christ was a thousand one hundred and eleven,' king Henry led an army against Gwynedd, and principally to Powys. After Owain had been condemned of a breach of law, Gilbert, son of Rickert, accused him before the king, saying that the men of Owain were committing robberies upon his people and his land; and the crimes committed by others were charged to the men of Owain. And the king believed that every thing spoken by the accuser was true. Meanwhile, the son of Hugh, earl of Caerleon, accused Gruffudd, son of Cynan, and Goronwy, son of Owain, and purposed by a combination to exterminate all the Britons entirely, so that they should never more bear the British name. Accordingly, king Henry collected an army out of the whole island, ᵇ from the promontory of Pengwaed in Cornwall to the promontory of Blathaon in the North,' against Gwynedd and Powys. And when Maredudd, son of Bleddyn, became ac-

---

a' 14 caused him to be blinded.

b' 14 from the extreme point of Cornwall, a place called Pengwaed, to the extreme point of Prydyn, a place called Penblathaon.

ᵃ dybat, *B.* | ¹² chaffeit, *B.*
¹⁰ oruc, *B.* | ¹³ *D.* Iwerdon, *A.*
¹¹ Hywel, *E.* | ¹⁴ *D.*

geissaṽ kyfeillach y gan y brenhin. Agṽedy adnabot hynny o Owein kynullaṽ y holl wyr ae holl da a ¹ṽnaeth, a mudaṽ hyt ymynyded Eryri; kanys kadarnaf lle a diogelaf y gael amdiffyn yndaṽ rac y llu oed hṽnnṽ. Ygkyfrṽg hynny ²yd anuones' y brenhin tri llu. Un gyt a Gilbert tywyssaṽc o Gernyṽ, a Brytanyeit y Deheu, a Freinc a Saeson o Dyfet ar Deheu oll. Ar llu arall or Gogled ar Alban a deu tywyssaṽc arnunt, nyt amgen ³[noc] Alexander vab y Moel Cṽlṽm, a mab Hu iarll Kaer Llion. Ar trydyd gyt ac ef ehun. Ac ⁴yno y deuth y brenhin ae deulu y gyt ac ef, hyt y lle aelwir Mur Gastell. Ac Alexander ar iarll aaethant y ⁵Pennaeth Bachṽy. Ygkyfrṽg hynny ydanuones Owein genadeu at Ruffud ᵃac Owein y vab' y erchi udunt gṽneuthur ³[yn] kadarn hedṽch y rygtunt yn erbyn y gelynyon yrei yd oedynt yn aruaeth y dileu yn gṽbyl neu ⁶y gṽarchae yn y mor hyt nat enwit Brytanaṽl enṽ yn dragywydaṽl. Ac ymaruoll ygkyt awnaethant hyt na ṽnelei un heb y gilyd na thagnefed na chyfundeb ae gelynyon. Gṽedy hynny ydanuones Alexander uab y Moel Cṽlṽm ar iarll ³[y] gyt ac ef genadeu at Rufud, uab Kynan y erchi idaṽ dyuot y hedṽch y brenhin; ac adaṽ llawer idaṽ ae dṽyllaṽ y gyttuunaṽ ac ṽynt. Ar brenhin a anuones kenadeu at Owein y erchi idaṽ dyuot y hedṽch ac adaṽ y gṽyr ny ⁷aller gaffel na phorth na nerth y gantunt. Ac ny chyt-

---

ᵃ′⁸ ar Oronw vab Ywein ⁹ueibon

---

¹ oruc, B.
² ansodes, B.
³ B.
⁴ yna, B
⁵ Pennant, C. D.

quainted with that, he went to seek the friendship of the king. This having been made known to Owain, he collected together all his people, and all his property, and removed into the mountains of Eryri, for that was the strongest and safest place to make a defence against an army. In that interval the king sent out three armies; one under Gilbert, a prince of Cornwall, with the Britons of the South, and the French and English out of Dyved and all the South; and the other army was from the North and Alban, with two princes over them, to wit, Alexander, the son of Malcolm, and the son of Hugh, earl of Caerleon; and the third with himself. Then the king, with his retinue, came to the place called Mur Castell; and Alexander and the earl proceeded to ⁵Pennaeth Bachwy. In that interval Owain sent messengers to Gruffudd ᵃ and his son Owain,⁷ requesting of them to make a firm peace among themselves, against their enemies, who intended utterly to destroy them, or to hem them in by the sea, so that the British name should never more be uttered. They accordingly entered into a mutual agreement that no one should make any reconciliation or union with their enemies without the other. After that Alexander, son of Malcolm, in conjunction with the earl, sent messengers to Gruffudd, son of Cynan, to request him to make peace with the king, promising him a great deal; and cajoled him to enter into terms with them. The king also sent messengers to Owain, requiring him to make peace, and to quit the men from whom neither aid nor strength could be obtained; but

---

ᵃ/⁸ and to Goronwy, son of Owain, ⁹ his sons,

⁶ cu, *B.*
⁷ alle i, *B.*
⁸ *C.*
⁹ *B.*

synyaȯd Owein a hynny. Ac yny lle nachaf un yn dyvot attaȯ, ac yn dywedut ȯrthaȯ byd ovalus agȯna yn gall yr hyn aȯnelych. Llyma Rufud ᵃ ac Oȯein y uab ' gȯedy kymryt hedȯch gan uab y Moel Cȯlȯm ar iarll gȯedy rodi idaȯ o nadunt kael y tir yn ryd heb na threth na chyllit na chastell yndaȯ hyt tra vei vyȯ y brenhin. Ac ettwa ny chytsynyaȯd Owein a hynny. Ar eilweith yd ¹aruaethȯys y brenhin anuon kenadeu at Owein, a chyt ac ȯynt Maredud uab Bledyn y ᵇ ewythyr yr hȯnn pan welas Owein a dywaȯt wrthaȯ edrych na hȯyrheych dyuot at y brenhin rac raculaenu o ereill kael kedymdeithas y brenhin; ac ynteu agredaȯd hynny a dyfot a ȯnaeth at y brenhin. Ar brenhin ae haruolles yn llaȯen drȯy uaȯr garyat ac enryded ²[ef ae lu]. Ac yná y dywaȯt y brenhin ȯrth Owein ³ kan deuthost ti attaf i oth vod a ³ chan credeist ᶜ vygkenadeu' minheu ath vaȯrhaaf di ac ath dyrchavaf yn uchaf ac yn pennaf oth genedel di. A mi a dalaf it yn gymeint ac y kyghorvynho paȯb oth genedyl ȯrthyt. A mi a rodaf it dy holl tir yn ryd. A phan gigleu Grufud hynny ²[hedychu o Ywein ar brenhin] anuon kenadeu aoruc at y brenhin y geissaȯ hedȯch y gantaȯ. Ar brenhin ae kymerth ef y hedȯch drȯy dalu o honaȯ dreth uaȯr idaȯ. Ac ymchoelut aoruc y brenhin y Loegyr, ac erchi y Owein dyuot y gyt ac ef a dy-

---

ᵃ'⁴ a Goronw vab Ywein   ᵇ⁵ gevýnderw
ᶜ'⁶ kennadȯri vyg kennadi i   ⁵ geiriev vygkennadev ii

---

¹ aruaethaȯd, *B.*   ³ kanys, *B.*
² *B.*   ⁴ *C.*

Owain did not consent to that. And at the instant behold, there comes to him one, who says, 'Be careful, 'and what thou doest, do it discreetly. Here Gruf-'fudd ᵃand his son' have accepted terms of peace 'from the son of Malcolm and the earl, they hav-'ing granted him his land free, without either tri-'bute, or duty, or erection of a castle in it, so long 'as the king may live.' And yet Owain did not consent to it. And the second time did the king resolve to send messengers to Owain, and with them his ᵇuncle Maredudd, son of Bleddyn, who, when he saw Owain, said unto him, 'See that thou delay not 'coming to the king, lest others should be first 'to obtain the favour of the king.' He then believed that, and so came to the king. And the king received him gladly, with great courtesy and honour, ²him and his retinue.' Then the king said to Owain, 'Since thou hast willingly come to me, and since 'thou hast believed ᶜmy messengers,' I will dignify 'thee, and exalt thee to be the highest and the 'chiefest of thy nation; and I will pay thee so 'much that every one of thy nation shall envy 'thee; and I will give thee all thy land free.' When Gruffudd became acquainted with the circumstance ³that Owain had made his peace with the king,' he sent messengers to the king, to seek peace from him; and the king received him into terms of peace, upon payment of a large tribute. Then the king returned to England, requiring Owain to come with him, say-

---

ᵃ/ ⁴ and Goronwy, son of Owain   ᵇ ⁵ cousin
ᶜ/ ⁶ the message of my messengers,   ⁵ the words of my messengers,

---

⁵ D. | ⁶ B.

wedut ¹[idaw] y talei idaŵ a vei gyfyaŵn, a dywedut wrthaŵ hynn a dyŵedaf yt. Mi a af y Normandi ac o deuy di y gyt a mi, mi a ²gyweiraf itt bob peth or a edeweis it, a mi ath wnaf yn uarchaŵc urdaŵl. A chanlyn y brenhin aŵnaeth drŵy y mor. Ar brenhin a gywiraŵd idaŵ pob peth or a edewis idaŵ.

MCXII. Y vlŵydyn rac ŵyneb yd ymchoelaŵd y brenhin o Normandi, ac Owein uab Kadŵgaŵn ¹[y] gyt ac ef. Ac y bu varŵ ³Ieffrei escob Mynyŵ, ac yny ol ynteu y deuth gŵr o Normandi yr hŵnn aelwit Bernart yr hŵnn a dyrchafŵyt yn escob ym Mynyŵ y gan Henri vrenhin o anuod holl ysolheigon y Brytanyeit gan eu tremygu. Yghyfrŵg hynny y deuth Grufud uab Rys Teŵdŵr brenhin Deheubarth o Iwerdon ¹[y Dyfet] yr hŵnn aathoed yny vabaŵl oetran y gyt a rei oe gereint hyt yn Iwerdon. Ac yna y trigyaŵd yny bu ŵr aeduet. Ac yny diwed gŵedy diffygyaŵ o tra hir alltuded yd ymchoelaŵd y dref y dat. A hŵnnŵ a drigyaŵd amgylch dŵy vlyned gŵeitheu y gyt a Geralt, ᵃystiwart Castell' Penuro y daŵ gan y chŵaer; a honno oed Nest uerch Rys uab Teŵdŵr gŵreic ¹[y dyŵededic] Geralt Ystiwart ¹[megys y racdyŵetpŵyt uchot]: gŵeitheu ereill gyt ae gereint; gŵeitheu yg ᵇGŵyned; gŵeitheu yn absen o le y le. Yny diwed y cuhudŵyt ŵrth y brenhin. A dyŵedut bot medŵl paŵb or Brytanyeit gyt ac ef, drŵy ⁴y ryuygu' o vrenhinaŵl vedyant Henri vrenhin. A phan gigleu Gruffud y chwedleu hynny aruaethu awnaeth ar vynet at Ruffud uab Kynan y geissaŵ amdiffyn

ᵃ' ⁵ arglwẏd   ᵇ' ⁶ gŵyd

¹ B.
² gywiraf, B.
³ Geffrei, D.
⁴ ebryuygu, B.

ing that he would pay him what might be just, and saying to him, 'This I tell thee, I am going to 'Normandy, and if thou wilt accompany me, I will 'fulfil every thing I have promised thee; and I will '.make thee an honourable knight.' He accordingly accompanied the king over the sea; and the king fulfilled every thing he had promised him.

1112. The ensuing year the king returned from Normandy, and Owain, son of Cadwgan, along with him. Then died Jeffrey, bishop of Menevia; and after him came a man from Normandy, called Bernard, who was advanced to be bishop of Menevia by king Henry, against the will and in contempt of all the scholars of the Britons. In that interval Gruffudd, son of Rhys, son of Tewdwr, king of South Wales, came from Ireland ¹ to Dyved,' who, in his youth, had gone with some of his kindred to Ireland, where he remained until he arrived at maturity; and in the end, wearied with long estrangement, he returned to his patrimony. And he passed about two years, sometimes with Gerald, ᵃ steward of Pembroke Castle,' his brother in law, who had married his sister, Nest, the daughter of Rhys, son of Tewdwr, wife to ¹ the said' Gerald, the steward, ¹ as before mentioned;' at other times with his kindred; sometimes ᵇ in Gwynedd;' sometimes absent from place to place. At length he was accused to the king, and it was represented that the minds of all the Britons were with him, in contempt of the royal title of king Henry. And when Gruffudd heard of those reports he determined on going to Gruffudd, son of Cynan, to

---

a'⁵ lord of Pembroke,   b'⁶ present

---

⁵ D.   ⁶ B.

y hoedel. A gwedy anuon kenadeu ef aedewis [1] o deuei attaw y aruolli' yn llawen [2][iawn]. A gwedy clybot o Rufud uab Rys hynny [3] ef a Howel y vrawt aaethant' attaw; yr Howel honnw a vuassei ygkarchar Ernwlf uab Roser iarll [4] Castell Baldwin' yr honn y rodassei [5] Wilim vrenhin idaw kyfran o gyfoeth Rys uab Tewdwr. Ac yny diwed y diagassei yr Howel honnw yn annafus gwedy trychu y aelodeu or carchar. Ac yna ydaruollet [6] wynt ac ereill gyt ac wynt yn hegar y gan Rufud uab Kynan. Ac yghyfrwg hynny gwedy clybot or brenhin mynet Grufud ab Rys at Ruffud ab Kynan anuon kenadeu a wnaeth at Ruffud uab Kynan y erchi idaw dyuot attaw. Ac ufud vu Ruffud y vynet [7] at y brenhin.' Ac megys y mae moes y Ffreinc twyllaw danyon trwy edewidyon adaw llawer a [8] wnaeth Henri vrenhin idaw o chymerei arnaw [9] dala Grufud uab Rys ae anuon yn vyw attaw ef, ac ony allei y [9] dala y lad ac anuon y benn idaw. Ac ynteu drwy adaw hynny aymchoelawd y wlat. Ac yny lle gofyn a [10] wnaeth py' le ydoed Rufud uab Rys yn trigyaw. A menegi awnaethpwyt y Ruffud uab Rys dyuot Grufud uab Kynan o lys y brenhin ae geissaw ynteu yn ewyllys. Ac yna y dywawt rei wrthaw aoedynt yntrigyaw y gyt ac ef drwy ewyllys da, gochel y gedrycholder yny [11] wyper py fford y kerdo y [12] chwedyl. Ac [13] wynteu yn dywedut hynny nachaf vn yn dyuot ac yn dywedut. Llyma varchogyon yn dyuot ar vrys. A breid yd athoed ef dros y drws nachaf y marchogyon yn dyuot y geissaw.

---

[1]' yd artollei, *B*.
[2] *B*.
[3]' aeth ef a Howel y vraut, *B*.
[4]' Montgomeri, *D*.
[5] Gwilliam, *D*.
[6] wy, *B*.
[7]' attaw, *B*.

endeavour to save his life; and having sent messengers, the other promised that he would with great pleasure receive him if he came. After Gruffudd, son of Rhys, heard that, he and Howel, his brother, went to him. This same Howel had been in the prison of Ernulf, son of Roger, the lord of 'Castle Baldwin,' to whom king William had given a part of the territory of Rhys, son of Tewdwr; and subsequently this Howel had escaped, in a maimed state, with broken limbs, out of the prison. Thereupon, they and others along with them, were kindly received by Gruffudd, son of Cynan. And in that interval, when the king had heard that Gruffudd, son of Rhys, had gone to Gruffudd, son of Cynan, he sent messengers to Gruffudd, son of Cynan, requesting that he would come to him; and Gruffudd obeyed, and repaired to the king. And, as is the manner of the French to deceive people by promises, king Henry promised him much if he would undertake to secure Gruffudd, son of Rhys, and send him alive to him, and if he could not secure him, to kill him, and send his head to him; and he, promising that, returned to his country. And immediately he enquired where Gruffudd, son of Rhys, resided. And it was told Gruffudd, son of Rhys, that Gruffudd, son of Cynan, had come from the king's court, and was seeking to get him at his disposal. Then some who were dwelling with him, and wished him well, said, 'Do thou avoid his presence, until it be 'known which way the report travels.' And whilst they were telling this, behold, there comes one, saying: 'Here are horsemen coming in haste.' And he had scarcely passed the door, when the horsemen

---

⁸ oruc, B.
⁹ daly, B.
¹⁰ oruc pa, B.

¹¹ byppych, B.
¹² whedleu, B.
¹³ bynt, B.

Ac ni allaỏd amgen no chyrchu Eglwys Aber Daron arnaỏd. A gỏedy clybot o Ruffud uab Kynan y dianc yr eglwys anuon gỏyr aoruc y tynnu ef or eglỏys allan. Ac ny adaỏd ¹escyb a ²[henafyeit] beuafyeit y wlat hynny rac llygru naỏd yr eglỏys. A gỏedy y ellỏg or eglỏys ef a ffoes yr Deheu, ac a deuth y Ystrat Tywi. A gỏedy clybot ²[y petheu] hynny llawer aymgynullaỏd attaỏ o bop tu; ac ynteu a duc kyrch anhegar ³aniben y Ffreinc ar Flemhisyeit yny daruu y vlỏydyn honno.

MCXIII. Y vlỏydyn rac ỏyneb y kyrchaỏd y Grufud ab Rys a dywedassam ni uchot, yny vrỏydyr gyntaf y castell oed yn ymyl Arberth ac y llosges. Odyna ydaeth hyt yn Llan ym Dyfri lle yd oed gastell neb un tywyssaỏc aelwit Rickert ⁴[vab y] Pỏnsỏn y gỏr y rodassei Henri vrenhin idaỏ y Kantref Bychan, ac y profes y torri ae losgi, ac nys gallaỏd kanys ymỏrthlad ac ef awnaeth keitweit y kastell a chyt ac ỏynt Maredud uab Ryderch uab Cradaỏc y gỏr a oed yn kynnal ystiwerdaeth ⁵[Kantref Bychan] y dan y dywededic Rickert: y rac castell eissoes a losges. Agỏedy ymsaethu or tỏr ac ef abrathu llawer oe wyr a saetheu, allad ereill ydymchoelaỏd drachefyn. Agỏedy hynny y danuones y gedymdeithon y wneuthur kyrch a chynnỏrỏf ar gastell aoed yn ymyl Aber Tawy; a hỏnnỏ bioed iarll aelwit Henri Bemỏnd. A gỏedy llosgi y rac castell, ac amdiffyn or keitweit y tỏr a llad rei ⁶oe wyr ydymchoelaỏd drachefyn.

---

¹ preladyeid, *C.*
² *B.*
³ am benn, *B.*
⁴ *B. D.*

came in search of him; and he could do no more than flee to the church of Aberdaron for sanctuary. And when Gruffudd, son of Cynan, heard of his escaping to the church, he sent men to force him out of the church; but the bishops and the elders who owned that country, would not permit that, lest the sanctuary of the church should be violated. After he had been set at large from the church, he fled into the South, and came to the Vale of Tywi. And when those things became known, many collected to him from every side; and he made an untoward, pointless attack upon the French and the Flemings until the close of that year.

1113. The ensuing year, the Gruffudd, son of Rhys, whom we have mentioned above, made an attack, in the first battle, upon the castle that was near Arberth, and burned it. From thence he proceeded to Llanymddyvri, where there was a castle of a certain leader, called Rickert, [4]son of' Ponson, the person to whom king Henry had given Cantrev Bychan; and he essayed to breach and burn it, but was not able, for the garrison of the castle withstood him, with the aid of Maredudd, son of Rhydderch, son of Caradog, the person who held the stewardship of [5]Cantrev Bychan' under the said Rickert; the outwork of the castle, however, he burned. And after those on the tower and himself had been shooting at each other, and many of his men had been wounded with arrows, and others killed, he returned back. Afterwards he sent his companions to attack and to alarm a castle that was near Abertawy; and which belonged to an earl named Henry Beaumont. And after burning the outworks, the garrison defending the tower, and killing a few of his men, he retreated again. Hear-

---

[5] C.   [6] o, B.

A gôedy clybot hynny ac ymgynullaô attaô llauer o
ynvydyon ieueinc o bob tu wedy y dôyllaô o chôant
anoeitheu, neu o geissaô ¹[atgyôeiraô neu] atneôydu
Brytanaôl teyrnas. Ac ny thal ewyllys ¹[dyn] dim
o ny byd Duô yn borth idaô. Gôneuthur aoruc
² ysclyfaetheu maôr yn y gylch o gylch. Ar Ffreinc
yna y gymerassant gyghor agalô pennaetheu y wlat
attunt. Nyt amgen Owein ³uab Cradaôc' uab Ryderch
y gôr y rodassei Henri vrenhin idaô rann or Kantref
Maôr ⁴[yn Ystrat Tyôi]; a Maredud uab Ryderch yr
hônn a ¹[rac] dywedessam ni vry; a Ryderch uab
Teôdôr ae veibon ¹[nyt amgen] Maredud ac Owein.
Mam y rei hynny gôreic Ryderch ab Tewdôr oed
Hunyd uerch Bledyn ab Kynvyn y pennaf or Brytanyeit wedy Grufud ab Llywelyn yrei oedynt vrodyr
vn vam. Kanys Ygharat verch Varedud ⁵ vrenhin y
Brytanyeit oed y mam ell deu; ac Owein uab Kara-
daôc uab Gôenllian verch y dywededic Vledyn yrei
¹[hynn] a llaôer o rei ereill a deuthant y gyt. A
gofyn aoruc y Freinc udunt aoedynt oll fydlonyon y
Henri vrenhin; ac atteb awnaethant eu bot. A
dywedut awnaeth y Ffreinc ôrthynt od ydyôch ual
y dywedôch dagossôch ar aôch gôeithretoed yr hynn
yd yttyôch yn y adaô ar aôch tauaôt; reit yô yôch
gadô castell Kaer Vyrdin, yr hôn a bie y brenhin, pob
un ohonaôch yny ossodedic amser ual hynn. Cadô
y castell o Owein uab Cradaôc pythewnos; a˙ Ryderch ªuab Teôdôr' pythewnos arall; a Maredud uab
Ryderch ᵇab Tewdôr' pytheônos ¹[trydyd]. A ¹[c y]

ᵃ′ ⁶ aŷ veibion   ᵇ′ ⁷ vab Caradauc

¹ B.
² yscoluetheu, B.
³′ Not in D.
⁴ B. C.

ing this, many foolish young men from every part joined him, being deceived by the desire of spoils, or seeking to ¹repair and' restore the British kingdom. But the will ¹of man' does not avail any thing unless God assists him. He committed great depredations round about him. Then the French took counsel and summoned the chieftains of the country to them, that is to say, Owain, son of Caradog, son of Rhydderch, the person to whom king Henry had given a part of Cantrev Mawr ⁴ in the Vale of Tywi ;' and Maredudd, son of Rhydderch, whom we have mentioned above, and Rhydderch, son of Tewdwr, and his sons, ¹ to wit,' Maredudd and Owain. The mother of those, the wife of Rhydderch, son of Tewdwr, was Hunydd, daughter of Bleddyn, son of Cynvyn, the chiefest of the Britons, after Gruffudd, son of Llywelyn, and who were brothers by the same mother; for Angharad, daughter of Meredudd, king of the Britons, was the mother of both; and Owain, son of Caradog, by Gwenllian, daughter of the said Bleddyn. These, and many others, assembled together. The French asked them whether they were faithful to king Henry; and they answered that they were. Then the French said to them, ' If you be as you say, show by your deeds ' that which you promise by your tongue : you must ' keep the castle of Caermarthen, which belongs to ' the king, each one of you in his appointed time, ' in this manner: Owain, son of Caradog, is to keep ' the castle for a fortnight, and Rhydderch, ᵃ son of ' Tewdwr,' another fortnight; and Maredudd, son of ' Rhydderch, ᵇ son of Tewdwr,' a ¹third fortnight;

ᵃ⸍ ⁶ and his sons   ᵇ⸍ ⁷ son of Caradog

---

³ vrenhines, *B*.
⁴ *D*.
⁷ *B. C. D.*

¹Bledri uab Kediuor y gorchymynnỽyt castell Robert ²Laỽgan yn Aber ³Cafỽy. A gỽedy ansodi y petheu hynny, Gruffud ⁴ab Rys a bryderaỽd am anuon disgỽyleit am torri y castell neu y losgi. A phan gauas amser adas ual y gallei yn ⁵haỽd kyrchu y castell. Yna y damweinaỽd uot Owein uab Cradaỽc ⁶yn kadỽ ygkylch' y castell. Ac yna y duc Gruffud ab Rys kyrch nos am ben y castell. A phan gigleu Owein ae gedymdeithon kynnỽrỽf y gwyr ae geỽri yn dyuot, kyfot yn ebrỽyd or ty lle ydoed ef ae gedymdeithon a wnaethant. Ac yny lle y clywei yr aỽr ef e hun a gyrchaỽd ymblaen y vydin a thebygu bot y gedymdeithon yny ol, wynteu gỽedy y adaỽ ef e hunan a ⁷foassant, ac uelly y llas yna. A gỽedy llosgi y rac castell ᵃheb vynet y myỽn yr tỽr' yd ymchoelaỽd ac yspeileu gantaỽ yr notaedigyon goedyd. Odyna ydymgynullassant y ieueinc ynvydyon y ỽlat o bop tu attaỽ o debygu goruot o honaỽ ar bop peth o achaỽs y damwein hỽnnỽ; kanys castell a oed Yggỽhyr a losges ef o gỽbyl allad llawer o wyr yndaỽ. Ac yna ydedeỽis Gỽilim o Lundein y castell rac y ofyn ae holl aniueileit ae ⁸[holl annỽyl] oludoed. A gỽedy daruot hynny, ⁹megys y dyweit Selyf drychafel aỽna yspryt yn erbyn kỽymp ⁸[dyn].' Yna yd aruaethaỽd ⁸[ef] yn chỽydedic o valchder, ac o draha yr anosparthus bobyl ar ynvyt giỽtaỽt kyweiraỽ ⁸[hyntoed] ynvydyon o Dyfet y Geredigyaỽ. A chymryt ¹⁰gỽrthỽynebed yr gyfyaỽnder. Gỽedy ¹¹galỽ o Gediuor ab Gronỽ, a Howel

---

ᵃ/ ¹²adiang y tyreu

---

¹ Vledyn, *C. D.*
² laỽgam, *B.* Courtemayn, *D.*
³ Cofỽy, *B.* Korram, *C.* Commyn, *D.* Comwyn, *E.*
⁴ uab, *B.*
⁵ haỽs, *B.*
⁹ ar ygylch yn cadỽ, *B.*

' and Bledri, son of Cedivor, is appointed to keep
' the castle of Robert, the Crook-handed, at Aber
' Cavwy.' After settling these things, Gruffudd, son
of Rhys, bethought him of sending scouts to see how
to break the castle or burn it. And when he found
a good opportunity of approaching the castle easily, it
chanced that Owain, son of Caradog, was guarding
about the castle. Then Gruffudd, son of Rhys, made
a night attack upon the castle. And when Owain
and his companions heard the noise and shouting of
the men coming near, he and his companions suddenly
arose from the house they were in, and towards the
place where he heard the shout, advanced forward
himself before the troop, supposing his companions to
be close behind him; but they, leaving him alone,
had fled, and thus he was slain there. After burning the outer ward, ᵃ 'without entering the tower,' he
returned with his spoils to the accustomed woods.
Thereupon the foolish youths of the country on every
side collected to him, imagining that he was to overcome every thing, because of that event; for there
was a castle in Gower which he burned entirely,
killing many men therein. And then William of
London, through fear of him left his castle and all
his cattle and fond riches. When that was over, as
Solomon says, 'The spirit becomes elevated against
' the fall of man,' so he prepared, being swollen
with pride and with the presumption of the unruly
rabble, and the silly inhabitants, to arrange foolish
⁸expeditions from Dyved into Ceredigion, and to take
the part opposed to equity, being invited by Cedivor,

ᵃ ¹² and escaping the towers,

⁷ ffoyssant, *B*.
⁸ *B*.
ᵛ *Not in C*.

¹⁰ gọ́rthọ́yneb hynt, *B*.
¹¹ y alò, *B*.
¹² *C*.

uab Idnerth, a Thrahayarn ab Ithel, y rei a odynt yn dynessau o gyfnessafrṽyd gerennyd a ¹ chyfaduab a dunnaṽ arglṽydiaetheu idaṽ. Ar rei hynny aoedynt ²[y] gyt ac ef ymblaen hollwyr Keredigyaṽn ; ac nyt oed dim aallei uot yndireitach nor ᵃ Kediuor hṽnnṽ yr ṽlat agkyffredin kyn noc yt adaṽ Dyfet yn llaṽn o amryuaelon genedloed nyt amgen ' Flemissyeit a Ffreinc a Saeson ae guvtaṽt genedyl ehun, y rei kyt beynt vn genedyl agṽyr Keredigyaṽn eissoes gelynyon gallonneu oed gantunt o achaṽs ³ eu hanesmṽythdra ae hanundeb kyn no hynny. Ac yn vṽy no hynny rac ofyn y tremyc awnathoedynt y Henri vrenhin y gṽr a dofhaassei holl ⁴ bennaduryeit ynys Prydein oe allu ae vedyant, ac adarestygassei lawer o wladoed tramor ṽrth y lywodraeth, rei o nerth ²[ac] arueu ereill o aneiryf rodyon ²[o] eur ac aryant ; y gṽr nys dichaṽn neb ymoscryn ac ef eithyr Duṽ e hun y neb a rodes y ²[ryṽ] medyant idaṽ. A gṽedy dyuot Grufud uab Rys yn gyntaf ᵇ y deuth y Is Coet.' Ac yna y kyrchaṽd y lle a elwir blaen Porth ⁵ Hodnant, yr hwn a adeilassei neb un ²[teṽyssaṽc] Flemissṽr ⁶[aelṽit Gilbert vab Rickert]. Ac yno y deuth y Flemisseit ⁷ y drigyaṽ. A gṽedy ymlad dydgṽeith ar hyt y dyd, allad llaṽer o wyr y dref, a llad vn oe wyr ynteu, a llosgi y ran vṽyaf or dref, heb gael dim amgen no hynny ydymchoelaṽd drachefyn. Odyna y ruthraṽd gṽyr y wlat attaṽ o dieflic annogedigaeth

ᵃ' ⁸ kyghor hṽnnṽ yr ṽlat ac y gyffredin Kymry Nyt amgen noc adaṽ y Dyuet amrauaelon genedloed
ᵇ' ⁹ kyrchu Keredigion ẏs goit a oruc.

---

¹ chyfadnabot, B.   ⁴ penaetheu, B.
² B.   ⁵ Gwẏdni, D.
³ y, B.

son of Goronwy, and Howel, son of Idnerth, and Trahaiarn, son of Ithel, who were near in proximity of kindred and acquaintance, and who agreed that he should have dominion. And those were with him before all the men of Ceredigion; and none could be more mischievous than ᵃthat Cedivor, to the country in general, before he left Dyved, as he did, full of various nations, such as' Flemings, and French, and Saxons, and his own native tribe; who, though they were one nation with the men of Ceredigion, nevertheless, had hostile hearts, on account of their disquietude and discord formerly; and more than that, being in fear of offending king Henry, the man who had subdued all the sovereigns of the isle of Britain by his power and authority, and who had subjugated many countries beyond sea under his rule, some by force and arms, others by innumerable gifts of gold and silver; the man with whom no one could strive but God alone, from Whom he obtained the power. After the arrival of Gruffudd, son of Rhys, he first ᵇproceeded to Iscoed,' and there he attacked a place called Blaen Porth Hodnant, which had been built by a certain Fleming ²prince, ⁶named Gilbert, son of Rickert,' and where the Flemings were dwelling. And after fighting through the whole of a certain day, many of the men of the town being killed, and one of his own men being killed also, and the greatest part of the town burned, without effecting any thing more, he returned back. After this the men of the country,

---

ᵃ/ ⁸that counsel to the country and public of Wales, namely, to leave Dyved for the various nations,

ᵇ/ ⁹proceeded to Ceredigion Iscoed;

---

⁶ B. C.
⁷ yn, B.

⁸ B.
⁹ D.

BRUT Y TYWYSOGION.

yn gyfun megys yn deissyfyt. Ar Saesson a dugassei Gilbert kynno hynny y gyflenwi y wlat yr honn kyn no hynny o anamylder pobloed aoed wac ªvalch, adiffeithassant ac aladassant, ac [1] a yspeilassant, ac alosgassant y tei. Ae hynt ac kynhŵryf a dugant hyt Ymhenwedic. A chylchynu a orugant gastell [2] Razon Ystiwart [3] [y Gilbert] a oed ossodedic yn y lle [4] aelwir ystrad [5] Peithill, ac ymlad ac ef aorugant ae orchfygu. A gwedy llad llawer yndaw y losgi awnaethant. A phan deuth y nos pebyllyaw a [6] wnaeth yn y lle a elwir [7] [y] Glasgruc, megys ar villtir y ŵrth eglŵys Badarn. [8] Anafrŵyd a ŵnaethant ynyr eglŵys, dŵyn yr yscrubyl yn vŵyt udunt or ᵇeglŵys. [9] Ar bore drannoeth' ymaruaethu awnaethant ar castell aoed yn Aber Ystŵyth gan debygu y oruot. Ac yna ydanuones [2] Razon ystiwart gŵr aoed gastellŵr ar y castell hŵnnŵ. Ac alosgyssit y gastell ynteu kyn no hynny, ac y ᶜlladyssit y wyr yn gyffroedic o dolur am y wyr ac am y gollet ac yn ergrynedic rac ofyn kenhadeu hyt nos y gastell Ystrat Meuruc yr hŵnn awnathoed Gilbert y arglŵyd kyn no hynny y erchi yr castellwyr oed yno dyuot ar ffysc yn borth idaw. A gŵercheitŵeit y kastell a anuonassant attaw kymeint ac a [10] allyssant y gaffel; ac [7] [o] hyt nos y deuthant attaw. Trannoeth y kyuodes Gruffud uab Rys a Ryderch uab Teŵdŵr y ewythyr a Maredud ac Owein y veibon yu ansynŵyrus oc eu pebyll heb gyŵeiraw eu bydin,

---

ª' [11] hayach ogŵbyl   ᵇ [12] nawd.
ᶜ [11] dalassit

---

[1] ae, B.
[2] Rawlf, C.
[3] B. C.
[4] a elŵit, B.
[5] Pychyll, C.
[6] ŵnaethant, B.

instigated by the devil, flocked to him suddenly, and as it were of one accord. And the Saxons, who had formerly been brought by Gilbert to fill the country, which previously, from paucity of inhabitants, was ᵃ proudly empty, they ravaged and killed, and the houses they pillaged and burned. And they extended their course and tumult as far as Penwedig, and surrounded the castle of ² Razon, the steward ³ of Gilbert,' situated in the place called Ystrad ⁵ Peithyll, and they fought against it and overpowered it; and after killing many therein, they burned it. When night came, they encamped at the place called Glasygrug, about a mile from the church of St. Padarn; and committed indecencies in the church, and took the cattle for food for themselves out of the ᵇ church.' The following morning they formed a design against a castle that was at Aberystwyth, imagining that they could subdue it; and thereupon Razon the steward, who was castellaine of that castle, and whose own castle had been burned, and his men ᶜ killed, moved with sorrow for his men and his loss, and trembling with fear, sent messengers by night to the castle of Ystrad Meurug, which had been before erected by Gilbert his lord, requesting the garrison there to come in haste to his assistance. And the defenders of the castle sent him as many as they could procure; and they came to him by night. The following day Gruffudd, son of Rhys, and his uncle Rhydderch, son of Tewdwr, and his sons Maredudd and Owain, indiscreetly sallied from their tents, without putting

---

a ¹¹ almost entirely b ¹² sanctuary.
c ¹¹ captured,

---

² B.
³ Aadasrôyd, B.
⁵ Ac amtranoet y boreu, B.

¹⁰ gallassant, B.
¹¹ B.
¹² C.

ᵃa heb ossot arŵydon oc eu blaen namyn bileinllu,' megys cyweithas o giwtaŵt bobyl digygor heb lywyaŵdyr arnunt y kymerassant eu hynt parth a chastell Aber Ystŵyth, yn y lle yd oed ¹ Razon ystiwart ae gymhortheit gyt ac ef, heb ŵybot o nadunt hŵy hynny yny deuthant hyt yn Ystrat Antarron aoed gyfarŵyneb ar castell. Ar castell a oed ossodedic ar benn mynyd aoed yn llithraŵ hyt yn avon Ystŵyth, ac ar yr avon ydoed pont. Ac ual yd oedynt yn seuyll yno megys yn gŵneuthur magneleu, ac yn medylyaŵ pa ffuryf y torrynt y castell y dyd ²[a] lithraŵd haeach yny oed pryt naŵn. Ac yna ydanuones y castellwyr megys y mae moes gan y Ffreinc gŵneuthur pob peth drŵy ᵇystryŵ; ᶜgyrru saethydyon' hyt y bont y vickre ac ŵynt megys o delynt hŵy yn ansynhŵyraŵl ³ dros y bont y gallei uarchogyon llurugaŵc eu kyrchu yn deissyfyt ae hachub. A phan welas y Brytanyeit y saethydyon mor leŵ yn kyrchu yr bont yn ansynhŵyrus y redassant yn y erbyn gan ryuedu paham mor amdiredus y beidynt kyrchu y bont. Ac ual ydoed yneill rei yn kyrchu ar rei ereill yn saethu, yna y kyrchaŵd marchaŵc llurugaŵc yn gynhyruus y bont. A rei o wyr Gruffud ae kyferbynyaŵd ar y bont. Ac ynteu yn ⁴aruaethu eu kyrchu ⁵ŵynteu. Ac yna eissoes y torres y march y vynŵgyl. A gŵedy brathu y march y dygŵydaŵd. Ac yna yd aruaethod paŵb a gŵeŵyr y lad ynteu, ae luryc ae hamdiffynnaŵd yny doeth neb un or vydin ae ⁶thynnu. A phan gyfodes ynteu y ffoes. A phan welas y gedymdeithon ef yn

---

ᵃ⸍⁷ eithyr dodi yr ystondardeu or blaen
ᵇ⁷ astudrwyd achallder   ᶜ⸍⁸ saethu

---

¹ Rawlf, C. Rys, D.   ³ drŵy, B.
² B.   ⁴ aruaethas gynhyruus yn, B.

their troops in array; ^a and without setting up ensigns, a villain host,' like a company of people without counsel, and without a commander, they took their course towards the castle of Aberystwyth, where ¹ Razon the steward was with his supporters, they not knowing it, until they came to Ystrad Antarron, which was opposite the castle. The castle was situated upon the top of a hill that shelved down to the river Ystwyth, and over the river was a bridge. And as they were standing there, making engines, and devising by what means they might make a breach in the castle, the day glided away until it was afternoon. Then the garrison, as is the manner of the French to do every thing by ^b stratagem, ^c sent some archers' along the bridge to skirmish with them, that, in case they came imprudently over the bridge, the mailed cavalry might attack them suddenly and cut them off. And when the Britons saw the archers approaching the bridge so boldly, they indiscreetly ran to meet them, wondering that they should so confidently dare to come to the bridge. And as the one party was pressing on, and the other shooting, a mailed knight rushed violently to the bridge; and some of Gruffudd's men came to oppose him on the bridge. He essaying to attack them, his horse broke his neck, and the horse being wounded fell down; and then every body with spears endeavoured to kill him, but his coat of mail protected him, until some of his party came and dragged him away. And when he got up, he fled; and when his companions saw him

---

^a' ⁷ but placing the standards in front,
^b ⁷ study and prudence   ^c' ⁸ shot

---

⁵ hŵynt, *B*.
⁶ dynhu, *B*.
⁷ *C*.
⁸ *B*.

ffo y ffoassant ẃynteu holl. Ar Brytanyeit ae hymlidyaẃd ¹[hayach] hyt yggẃrthallt y mynyd. ªY doryf ol eissoes nys ymlidyaẃd, namyn heb geissaẃ na phont na ryt kymryt eu ffo aẃnaethant.' A phan welas y Ffreinc o benn y mynyd y ²rei hynny' ynffo kyrchu y doryf vlaen aẃnaethant allad kymeint ac agaẃssant ac yna y gẃasgarẃyt y giẃtaẃt bobyl ar draẃs y ³wlat o bop tu, rei ae hanifeileit gantunt rei ereill gẃedy adaẃ pop peth namyn keissaẃ amdiffyn eu heneideu yny edewit yr holl wlat yn diffeith. Yggyfrẃg hynny ydanuones Henri vrenhin kenadeu at Owein uab Kadẃgaẃn y erchi idaẃ dyuot attaẃ. Ac ynteu yny lle ⁴y deuth.' A phan doeth y dywaẃt y brenhin ẃrthaẃ. Vygkaredickaf Owein aatwaenost di y lleidryn gan Ruffudd uab Rys yssyd megys yn ᵇfoedic yn erbyn' vyn tywyssogyon i. Achaẃs achanys credaf i dyuot ti yn gyẃiraf gẃr ymi. Mi avynnaf dy uot ti yn dywyssaẃc llu gyt am mab i y ẃrthlad Grufud uab Rys. A mi awnaf Lywarch uab Trahaearn yn gedymdeith it, kanys ynaẃch chẃi aẃch deu yd ymdiredaf i. A phan ymchoelych drachefyn mi adalaf ¹[y] bẃyth it yn deilẃg. A llaẃenhau aoruc Owein or edeẃidyon hynny, a chynullaẃ llu a Llywarch gyt ac ef a mynet y gyt hyt yn Ystrat Tywi ¹[y] lle y ⁵tebygyd uot Grufud uab Rys yn trigyaẃ, kanys coetir ¹[ynnyal]

ª'⁶ Ac nyd ymlynawd y vydin ol eu kydymeithyon namyn kadw y ryd ar bont arnadunt o delei ymlid agatẃyd arnunt wac yn borth ywy kydmeithyon.

ᵇ'⁷ kyuodi yn erbyn

---

¹ B.
² gẃyr ereill, B.
³ gẃladoed ereill, B.
⁴ aaeth, B.

flee, they also all fled, and the Britons pursued them
¹almost to the declivity of the mountain. ᵃ The rear
body, however, did not pursue, but without seeking
either bridge or ford, they took to flight.' When
the French, from the top of the mountain, observed
these fleeing, they attacked the advanced body, and
killed as many as they could find; and the throng of
people was scattered about the country on every side,
some having their cattle with them, others having left
every thing, endeavouring to save their lives; so that
the whole country was left a desert. In that interval, king Henry sent messengers to Owain, son of
Cadwgan, desiring that he would come to him; and
he immediately came. When he was arrived, the king
said to him, 'My most beloved Owain, art thou
' acquainted with that thief Gruffudd, son of Rhys,
' who ᵇis like a fugitive before' my commanders? for
' and because I believe thee to be a most loyal man to
' me, I will that thou be commander of an army, with
' my son, to expel Gruffudd, son of Rhys; and I will
' make Llywarch, son of Trahaiarn, thy companion,
' because I place confidence in you two; and when
' thou returnest back, I will properly reward thee.'
And Owain rejoiced because of those promises. So he
collected an army, jointly with Llywarch, and they
proceeded together to the Vale of Tywi, where it was
supposed that Gruffudd, son of Rhys, was staying, as

ᵃ/ ⁶ But the rear army did not follow their companions, but kept the ford and bridge, in case pursuit
and distress should come upon them, clear, so as to be
a support for their companions.

ᵇ/ ⁷ rises against

ˢ tebygynt, *B.* | ⁷ *B.*
⁶ *C.*

oed, ac yn anaỏd y gerdet ¹ac yn' haỏd ruthraỏ gelynyaỏn yndaỏ. A phan ²[y] ³deuth y tervyneu yr wlat, holl ⁴wyr Owein a mab y brenhin ae kymhortheit ²[ỏynteu] a anuonassant ⁵eu bydinoed yr coedyd, paỏb ²[yny dut y] dan yr amot hỏnn hyt nat arbedei neb y gledyf nac y ỏr nac y wreic nac y vab nac y verch; a phỏy bynnag a delynt nas gochelynt heb y lad neu y grogi neu drychu y aelodeu. A phan gigleu giỏtaỏt bobyl y wlat hynny keissaỏ awnaethant ²[pa] ffuryf y ²gellynt gaffel' amdiffyn; ac uelly y gỏasgarỏyt ỏynt. Rei yn llechu yny coedyd, ereill yn ffo y wladoed ereill, ereill yn keissaỏ amdiffyn or kestyll nessaf y dathoedynt o ⁷honunt; megys y dywedir y myỏn Brytanaỏl diaereb, Y ki a lyha ⁸yr aryf' y brather ac ef. A gỏedy gỏasgaru yllu y dan y coedyd, ef adamweinaỏd y Owein ac ychydic o nifer ²[y] gyt ac ef kyrchu y coet o amgylch degwyr aphetwar vgein. Ac yn edrych a welynt oleu dynyon ²[yn ffo]. Nachaf y gỏelynt oleu dynyon ⁹[ac ysgrybyl] yn kyrchu ¹⁰parth achastell Kaer Vyrdin lle daroed udunt gỏneuthur eu hedỏch. Ac eu hymlit aỏnaeth hyt yn agos yr castell. A gỏedy eu ¹¹dala yno ymchoelut ²[hyt] at y gedymdeithon a oruc. Ygkyfrỏg hynny y damweinaỏd dyuot llu or Fflemisseit o Ros y Gaer Vyrdin yn erbyn mab y brenhin, a Geralt ¹²ystiwert gyt ac ỏynt. Nachaf y rei a ¹³diaghyssei yn dyuot dan llef tu ar castell, ac yn menegi y ²[ry] hyspeila o Owein uab Kadỏgaỏn ae hanreithaỏ. A phan gigleu y Fflemisseit hynny ennynnu awnaethant

---

¹' a, B.
² B.
³ deuthant, B.
⁴ lu, B.
⁵ y, B.
⁶' gallynt cael eu, B.
⁷ honaỏ, B.

it was a ¹wild woodland, and difficult to be traversed, and in which it was easy to rush upon enemies. When they had come to the borders of the country, all the men of Owain, and the king's son, with their abettors, sent their troops into the woods, every one ²to his own spot,' under this agreement, that no one was to spare his sword, either as to man, or woman, or boy, or girl; and that whomsoever they should lay hold of, they were not to refrain from slaying, or hanging, or cutting off his limbs. And when the common people of the country heard that, they sought in what manner they could obtain safety; and so they became scattered, some lurking in the woods, others fleeing to other countries; others seeking protection from the nearest castles, out of which they had come, as it is said in a British proverb, 'The dog 'will lick the weapon with which he is wounded.' After the army had been dispersed amid the woods, it happened that Owain, and with him a small number, about ninety men, entered the woods, and looking if they could see tracks of people ²in flight,' lo! they discovered tracks of men ⁹and cattle' in the direction of the castle of Caermarthen, where they had made their peace. And he pursued them to the vicinity of the castle; and having taken them there, he returned to his companions. In the mean while it happened that an army of Flemings was coming from Rhos to Caermarthen, to meet the son of the king, and Gerald the steward with them; when those who had fled were seen coming with a cry to the castle, and relating their having been pillaged and robbed by Owain, son of Cadwgan. When the Flemings heard that, they were kindled with hateful

---

⁹ y gŵaeyb, B. C.
⁸ D.
¹⁰ tu, B.

¹¹ daly, B.
¹² wasnaÿthwr, D.
¹³ diagassei, B.

o gassaől gyghoruynt yn erbyn Owein o achaős y mynych godyant awnathoed kedymdeithon Owein udunt kyn no hynny. Ac o annogedigaeth Geralt Ystiwert y gőr y llosgassei Owein y gastell ac adugassei y dreis Nest y wreic ¹[ae hysbeil] ae anreith. Y ymlit aorugant ²heb debygu bot gőrthőynebed idaő. Owein' a gymerth y hynt yn araf. Ac őynteu gan y ymlit ef adoethant yn ebrőyd hyt y lle yd oed ef ar anreith gantaő. A phan welas kedymdeithon Owein diruaőr luossogrőyd yn y hymlit, dyőedut a őnaethant őrthaő, llyma luossogrőyd yn ymlit heb allu o neb ym wrthlad ac őynt. ¹[Ac] atteb udunt a őnaeth nac ofynheőch heb ¹[ef] achaős, bydinoed y Flemisseit ynt. A gőedy dywedut hynny o neb vn gynnőryf eu kyrchu a wnaeth. A diodef y kynnőryf awnaethant yn őraől; gőedy bőrő saetheu o bop tu y dygőydaőd Owein yn vrathedic. A gőedy y dygőydaő ef ᵃyd ymchoelaőd y gedymdeithon ar ffo.' A phan gigleu Lywarch ab Trahaearn hynny ymchoelut ef ae wyr drachefyn awnaeth y wlat. A gőedy y lad ef y ³kynhalaőd y vrodyr y rann ef o Powys eithyr yr hynn a dugassei Owein kyn no hynny gan Maredud uab Bledyn, nyt amgen ⁴Kereinaőc yr hőnn oed eidaő Madaőc uab Ridit kyn no hynny. Ac enweu y vrodyr yw y rei hynn ¹[nyt amgen], Madaőc ab Cadőgaőn o Wenllian uerch Ruffud ab Kynan; ac Einaőn uab Kadőgaőn o Sanan uerch ⁵Dyfynwal; ar trydyd oed ⁶őrgan uab Kadőgaőn o ⁷Ellyő uerch Kediuor uab Gollwyn ᵇy gőr a vu bennaf arglőyd

---

ᵃ/ ⁸ ychŷdic adiengŷs or a oed gŷt ac ef.
ᵇ/ ⁸ týwýssawc Dývet.

---

¹ B.
² ac Yőein heb dybygu bot gőrthenebed idaő, B.
³ kynhelis, B.
⁴ Kereinaőn, B.

grudge against Owain, on account of the frequent vexations formerly caused to them by the friends of Owain; and incited by Gerald the steward, the man whose castle had been burned by Owain, and whose wife Nest had been violently carried away, ¹ with spoils' and booty, they went in pursuit. Not expecting any opposition, Owain took his course slowly; and they, in pursuing him, came speedily to the spot where he was with his booty. When the companions of Owain saw an immense multitude pursuing them, they said to him, 'Behold a multitude pursuing us, 'without our being able to oppose them.' ¹ And he replied to them, 'Fear not,' said he, 'for they are 'the troops of the Flemings.' And after he had said that, being in no way disturbed, he attacked them; and they bore the assault bravely. After discharging arrows on both sides, Owain fell wounded, and when he had fallen, ª his companions fled away.' When Llywarch, son of Trahaiarn, heard that, he returned with his men to his own country. After his death his brothers held his share of Powys, except what Owain had formerly taken from Maredudd, son of Bleddyn; to wit, Caereinion, which before then was the property of Madog, son of Rhirid. And these are the names of his brothers, to wit, Madog, son of Cadwgan, by Gwenllian, daughter of Gruffudd, son of Cynan; and Einon, son of Cadwgan, by Sanan, daughter of ⁵ Dyvnwal; and the third was ⁶ Gwrgant, son of Cadwgan, by Ellyw, daughter of Cedivor, son of Collwyn, ᵇ the man who was supreme lord over the country of

---

ᵃ' ⁸ a few that were with him made their escape.
ᵇ' ⁸ prince of Dyved.

---

⁵ Dyfnaval, *D*.
⁶ Morgant, *B. C. D.*
⁷ Ello, *D*.
⁸ *D.*

ar wlat Dyfet.' Petweryd uu Henri uab Kadôgaôn or Ffranges ¹[yôreic] uerch ²Pictot tywyssaôc or Ffreinc, ac o honno y bu uab arall idaô a elwit Gruffud. Y whechet vu Maredyd o Euron uerch Hoedlyô ab Kadôgaôn ab Elstan. A gôedy hynny yd ymaruolles Einaôn uab Kadôgaôn uab Bledyn, a Gruffud uab Maredud ab Bledyn y gyt y dôyn kyrch ambenn kastell Uchtrut uab Etwin a oed gefynderô y Vledyn vrenhin. Kanys Iweryd mam Owein ac Uchtrut ueibon Etwin ³[vrenin Tegingl], a Bledyn uab Kynfyn oedynt vraôt a chwaer un dat ac nyt vn vam. Kanys Agharat verch Varedud uab Owein oed vam Vledyn, a Chynvyn ab Gwerstan oed ⁴y tat ell deu. Ar castell rydywedassam ni a oed yny lle aelwit Kymer ym Meironyd. Kanys Kadôgaôn uab Bledyn a rodassei Veironnyd a Chefeilaôc y Uchtrut uab Etwin dan amot y uot yn gywir idaô ac y veibon ac yn ganhorthôy ynerbyn y holl elynyon. Ac ynteu oed ôrthôynebôr ac ymladgar ynerbyn Kadôgaôn ac veibon. A gôedy colli Owein heb debygu gallu dim o veibon Kadôgaôn awnaeth ef y dywededic castell. Ac ôynteu adywedassam ni vry drôy sorr a gyrchassant y castell, ac ae llosgassant. A gôedy fo rei or gôercheitweit adyuot ereill attunt hôynteu y hedôch, ¹[ac] achub aônaethant Ueironnyd a Chefeilaôc a Phenllyn ac rannu y rygtunt. Ac y Rufud uab Maredud y deuth Kefeilaôc, a ⁵[Maôdôy] a hanner Penllyn. ¹[Meiryonnyd] ⁶ar ranner arall y Penllyn' y veibon Kadôgaôn uab Bledyn. Ygkyfrôg hynny y teruynaôd y vlôydyn yn vlin ac yn atcas y gan baôp.

---

¹ B.
² Picot de Sai, D.
³ E.
⁴ eu, B.

Dyved;' the fourth was Henry, son of Cadwgan, by the French woman, ¹his wife,' daughter of ²Pictot, a French prince, and by her he had another son named Gruffudd; the sixth was Maredudd, by Euron, daughter of Hoedlyw, son of Cadwgan, the son of Elstan. After that, Einon, son of Cadwgan, son of Bleddyn, and Gruffudd, son of Maredudd, son of Bleddyn, joined together to make an attack upon the castle of Uchtryd, son of Edwin, who was cousin to king Bleddyn, for Iweryd, the mother of Owain and Uchtryd, the sons of Edwin, ³king of Tegeingl,' and Bleddyn, son of Cynvyn, were sister and brother, by the same father, but not by the same mother; as Angharad, daughter of Maredudd, son of Owain, was the mother of Bleddyn; and Cynvyn, son of Gwerystan, was the father of both. And the castle, of which we have spoken, was at Cymmer in Meirionydd; for Cadwgan, son of Bleddyn, had given Meirionydd and Cyveiliog to Uchtryd, son of Edwin, under an agreement that he should be faithful to him and to his sons, and come to his assistance against all his enemies; but he was an adversary and hostile to Cadwgan and his sons. It was when he lost Owain, not supposing that the sons of Cadwgan could accomplish any thing, that he made the said castle; and the others, mentioned by us above, in a pique, attacked the castle and burned it. And after some of the garrison had fled, and some had come to them in peace, they obtained Meirionydd, Cyveiliog, and Penllyn, and divided them among them; Cyveiliog came to Gruffudd, son of Maredudd, with ⁵Mawddwy and half of Penllyn; Meirionydd, and the other half of Penllyn, to the sons of Cadwgan, son of Bleddyn. In the mean while the year terminated vexatiously and untowardly to every body.

---

³ *B. C. E.* Machdwŷ, *D.* Madaŵc, *A.*   ⁰ *Not in D.*

mcxiv. Y vlŵydyn rac ŵyneb y bu uarŵ Gilbert uab Rickert ¹[ohir nychdaŵt a chleuyt]. A Henri vrenhin a drigyaŵd yn Normandi o achaŵs bot ryfel y rygtaŵ a brenhin Ffreinc. Ac velly y tervynaŵd y vlŵydyn honno.

mcxv. Y vlŵydyn rac ŵyneb y magŵyt annundeb y rŵg Howel uab Ithel aoed arglŵyd ar Ros a Rywynaŵc a meibon Owein uab Edwin, ²[nyt amgen], ᵃ Gronŵ a Ridit a Llywarch y vrodyr y rei ereill.' A Howel ³[ap Ithel] aanuones kenadeu at Varedud uab Bledyn ameibon Kadŵgaŵn uab Bledyn ²[nyt amgen] Madaŵc ac Einaŵn y eruynneit udunt ²[y] dyuot yn borth idaŵ. Kanys oe hamdiffyn ŵynteu ae kanhaledigaeth yd oed ef yn kynhal ²[yn] y gyfran or wlat ⁴adathoed yn ran idaŵ. Ac ŵynteu pan glyŵssant y ŵrthrymu ef ᵇo veibon Owein' a gynullassant ⁵eu gŵyr ae kedymdeithon y gyt, kymeint ac a gaŵssant yn baraŵt ual yn amgylch pedwar can ŵr. Ac ⁶yd aethant' yn y erbyn ²[ef] y Dyffryn Clŵyd yr hŵnn a oed wlat ᶜudunt hŵy.' Ac ŵynteu a gynnullassant y gŵyr gyt ac ᵈVchtrut eu hewythyr,' a dŵyn y gyt ac ŵynt y Ffreinc o Gaer Llion yn borth udunt ²[aorugant]. Ac ŵynteu agyfaruuant a Howel a Maredud a meibon Kadŵgaŵn ae kymhortheit: a gŵedy dechreu brŵydyr ymlad o bop tu aŵnaethant

---

ᵃ' ⁷ Ririt a Llywarch ac ev brodyr.   ⁸ y lleill meibyon Ywein ap Edwin ap Gronw.

ᵇ' ⁹ Gan Owein ap Edwin
ᶜ' ¹⁰ meibion Oweŷn ap Edwýn
ᵈ' ¹⁰ meibion Vchtrýt ev kefýnderw

---

¹ B. C.
² B.
³ D.

⁴ ae doeth, B.
⁵ y, B.
⁶' ydoethant, B.

THE CHRONICLE OF THE PRINCES. 143

1114. The ensuing year, Gilbert, son of Rickert, died ¹ of a long languishment and illness.' And king Henry remained in Normandy, because a war existed between him and the king of France. And thus ended that year.

1115. The ensuing year a dissension arose between Howel, son of Ithel, who was lord of Rhos and Rhyvoniog, and the sons of Owain, son of Edwin, ² namely,' ᵃ Goronwy, Rhirid, and Llywarch, and the other brothers.' And Howel sent messengers to Maredudd, son of Bleddyn, and to the sons of Cadwgan, son of Bleddyn, ² namely,' Madog and Einon, requesting them to come to his assistance, because by their protection and support he held that portion of the country, which had come to his share. They, when they heard that he was oppressed ᵇ by the sons of Owain,' collected their men and their friends together, as many as they found prepared, about four hundred men; and went against him to the vale of Clwyd, which was a district belonging ᶜ to them.' And the others assembled their men along with ᵈ their uncle Uchtryd,' bringing with them the French from Caerleon to aid them; and they met Howel and Maredudd, and the sons of Cadwgan, with their auxiliaries. When the battle had commenced, they fought bitterly on

---

ᵃ/ ⁷ Rhirid and Llywarch and their brothers.   ⁸ the others, the sons of Owain, son of Edwin, son of Goronwy.

ᵇ/ ⁸ by Owain, son of Edwin,

ᶜ/ ¹⁰ to the son of Owain, son of Edwin.

ᵈ/ ¹⁰ the sons of Uchtrud their cousin,

---

¹ *C. D. E.*   ⁹ *E.*
³ *C.*   ¹⁰ *D.*

yn ch6er6. Ac yny diwed y kymerth meibon Owein ae kedymdeithon ¹[eu ffo], 6edy llad Llywarch uab Owein a Iorwoerth uab Nud g6r de6r enwa6c oed, a g6edy llad llawer a brathu llia6s yd ymchoelassant yn orwac drachefyn. A g6edy brathu Howel ²[ap Ithel] yny vr6ydyr y ducp6yt adref. Ac ympenn y ³deugeinuet diwarna6t y bu uar6. Ac yna ydymchoela6d Maredud a meibon Kad6ga6n adref, heb lyuassu goresgyn y wlat rac y Ffreinc kyt ⁴keffynt y vudugolyaeth.

MCXVI. Y vl6ydyn rac 6yneb y bu uar6 ⁵M6rcherdarch, y brenhin pennaf o Iwerdon yn gyfla6n o ⁶luossogr6yd a budugolyaetheu.

MCXVII. Y vl6ydyn arall g6edy hynny yd aruaetha6d Henri vrenhin ymchoelut y Loeger wedy hedychu y rygta6 abrenhin Freinc, a gorchymyn a oruc yr ⁷mord6ywyr kyweira6 llogeu ida6. A g6edy parattoi y llogeu anuon a wnaeth y deu uab yn un or llogeu, un o honunt aanyssit or vrenhines y wreic pria6t. Ac o h6nn6 ydoed y tada6l obeith oe vot ¹[yn urenhin] yn g6ledychu yn ol y dat. A mab arall o orderch ida6, ae vn uerch a llawer o wyr ma6r gyt ac ⁸6ynteu. Ac o wraged arbennic amgylch deucant, y rei a ⁹debygynt eu' bot yn deilygaf o garyat plant y brenhin. Ac ef a rodeut udunt y llog oreu adiogelaf aodefei y mor donneu ar morolyon dymhestloed. A g6edy eu mynet yr llog dechreu nos dirua6r gyffroi aoruc y mor donneu dr6y eu kymell o dymhestla6l uord6y a drycdrum; ¹⁰ac yna y kyfaruu y llog a chreiga6l garrec aoed yn dirgel

---

¹ B.
² D.
³ deugeint, B.
⁴ caffont, B.
⁵ Murcherdach, C. D.
⁶ oludoed, B.

both sides; and in the end, the sons of Owain and their friends took to flight, after the slaughter of Llywarch, son of Owain, and Iorwerth, son of Nudd, a brave and renowned man; and after killing many, and wounding numbers, they returned back empty. Howel, ²son of Ithel,' having been wounded in the battle, was carried home, and at the end of the fortieth day he died. And thereupon Maredudd, and the sons of Cadwgan, returned home without daring to subdue the country, because of the French, though they had obtained the victory.

1116. The ensuing year died Murcherdach, the supreme king of Ireland, abounding in prosperity and victories.

1117. The next year after that, king Henry resolved upon returning to England, after peace had been made between him and the king of France; and he commanded the seamen to prepare ships for him. And after the ships had been made ready, he sent his two sons in one of the ships;—one of them born of the queen, his married wife, of whom he entertained the paternal hope that he would reign ¹ as king' after his father; the other son was by his concubine; also one daughter, and many great men along with them, and about two hundred principal women, who were deemed most worthy of the affection of the king's children. The best ship was assigned to them, and one which would most safely bear the sea-waves, and the maritime storms. After they had gone on board the ship at the beginning of night, the sea breakers were dreadfully agitated, being driven by the tempestuous current and broken surge, ¹⁰and in consequence the ship met with a

---

⁷ amheraódyr, B.
⁸ óynt, B.

⁹ tybygit y, B.
¹⁰ Not in D.

dan y tonneu heb ƀybot yr llogwyr, ac y torres y llog genti yn drylleu,¹ ac y bodes y meibon ar nifer aoed y gyt ac ƀynt hyt na diegis neb o nadunt. Ar brenhin aeskynassei y myƀn llog arall yn y hol. A chyt gyffroi o diruaƀryon dymhestleu y mordonneu, eissoes ¹ ef a diegaƀd' yr tir. A phan gigleu ryfodi y veibon drƀc ydaeth arnaƀ. Ac ygkyfrƀg hynny y ² teruynƀys y vlƀydyn honno.

MCXVIII. Y vlƀydyn rac ƀyneb y priodes Henri vrenhin merch neb un ³ dywyssaƀc or Almaen kanys kyn no hynny ᵃ gƀedy marƀ merch y Moel Cƀlƀm y w eic ⁴ a aruerassei yn wastat o ⁵ orderchu.' A phan doeth yr haf rac ƀyneb y kyffroes Henri diruaƀr greulaƀn lu yn erbyn gƀyr Powys, nyt amgen Maredud uab Bledyn ac Einaƀn ᵇ a Madaƀc a Morgan meibon Kadƀgaƀn uab Bledyn. A phan glywssant ƀynteu hynny, anuon kenadeu aorugant at Ruffud uab Kynan ᶜ aoed yn kynal ynys' Von, y eruynneit idaƀ vot yn gyt aruoll ac ƀynt yn erbyn y brenhin ual y gellynt warchadƀ yn diofyn ynyalƀch y gƀlat. Ac ynteu drƀy gynhal hedƀch ar brenhin, adywaƀt ⁶ y foynt hƀy y deruyneu y gyfoeth ef, y parei y hyspeilaƀ ae hanreithaƀ ac y gƀrthƀynebai. A phan ƀybu Uaredud a meibon Kadƀgaƀn hynny, kymryt kygor

---

ᵃ⸍⁷ ẏ buassei merch Moelculum ẏn orderch ẏdaw ac ẏ buassei varw.
ᵇ⁸ ap   ᶜ⸍⁷ arglwid

---

¹⸍ efe a dienghis, B. ³ duc, D.
² teruynaƀd, B. ⁴ yd, B.

rocky stone, that was concealed under the waves, unknown to the sailors, whereby the ship was broken in pieces;' and the children, with the retinue that accompanied them, were drowned, so that not one escaped. The king had embarked in another ship in its rear; and though the sea-breakers were agitated by dreadful tempests, nevertheless he escaped to land; and when he understood that his sons were drowned, he was grieved. And in the mean while that year terminated.

1118. The ensuing year, king Henry married the daughter of a certain prince of Germany, as before then, a after the death of his wife, the daughter of Malcolm, he had constantly accustomed himself to concubinage.' When the ensuing summer came, king Henry raised an immense and cruel army against the men of Powys, namely, Maredudd, son of Bleddyn, and Einon, b and Madog, and Morgan, sons of Cadwgan, son of Bleddyn. And when they heard that, they sent messengers to Gruffudd, son of Cynan, c who held the isle' of Mona, requesting that he would become confederate with them against the king, that they might be enabled, without fear, to guard the fastnesses of the country. Then he, to maintain peace with the king, said that, if they came to the borders of his dominion, he would cause them to be despoiled and plundered, and would oppose them. And when Maredudd, and the sons of Cadwgan, were made acquainted with that, they took

---

a' 7 the daughter of Malcolm had been his concubine, and had died.
b 8 son of   c' 7 lord

---

5 orderchadeu, *B.*   7 *D.*
6 o, *B.*   8 *B.*

awnaethant. Ac yn y kygor y kaŵssant ¹[gŵarch] adaŵ teruyneu y gŵlat ehunein, a chymryt eu hamdiffyn yndunt. Ar brenhin ae luoed adynessayssant y deruyneu Powys. Ac yna ydanuones Maredud uab Bledyn ychydic o saethydyon ²[o weisson] ieueinc y gyuerbynyeit y brenhin myŵn gŵrthallt goedaŵc ynyal fford ydoed yn dyuot, val y gellynt a saetheu ac ergydyeu wneuthur kynnŵryf ar y llu. Ac ef adamweinaŵd ynyr aŵr ydaethoed y gŵyr ieueinc hynny yr ŵrthallt ²[ynyal] dyuot yno y brenhin ae lu. Ar gŵyr ieueinc hynny a erbynnyassant yno y brenhin ae lu; ³drŵy diruaŵr gynnŵryf' ⁴gellŵg saetheu ²[ac ergydyon] ym plith y llu a wnaethant. A gŵedy llad ᵃllaŵer a brathu ereill, vn or gŵyr ieueinc a dynnaŵd y vŵa ac a ellygaŵd saeth ym plith y llu. A honno a dygŵydaŵd ygkedernit arueu y brenhin gyferbyn ae gallon, heb ŵybot yr ⁵gŵyr ae byryaŵd ac nyt argywedaŵd y saeth yr brenhin rac daet yr arueu, kanys llurygaŵc oed namyn treillaŵ aoruc y saeth ²[a datlamu] drachefyn ²[yar] yr arueu. Ac ofynhau yn uaŵr a wnaeth y brenhin, a diruaŵr ⁶aruthder a gymerth yndaŵ yn gymeint haeach a phei ⁷brethit trwydaŵ. Ac erchi yr lluoed a ŵnaeth bebyllyaŵ, agofyn ⁸aoruc py' rei a oedynt mor ehofyn ae gyrchu ef ⁹yn gyn leŵet' a hynny. A dywedut awnaethpŵyt idaŵ mae rai o wyr ieueinc a anuonassit y gan Varedud uab Bledyn awnaethoed hynny. Ac anuon awnaeth attunt genadeu y erchi udunt dyuot attaŵ drŵy gygreir. Ac ŵynteu a doethant. A gofyn a wnaeth udunt pŵy ac hanuonassei yno. A dywedut a ŵnaethant mae Maredud; a gofyn udunt

---

ᵃ ¹⁰ rei or llu

---

¹ C.
² B.
ᵛ athrŵy odŵrd achynnŵryf, B.

⁴ gollŵg, B.
⁵ gŵr, B.
⁶ aruthurder, B.

counsel; and in their counsel they resolved to guard the boundaries of their own country, and take up their defence within them. And the king with his hosts drew near to the boundaries of Powys. Then Maredudd, son of Bleddyn, sent a few archers, young ²men, to intercept the king, in a wild woody and steep cliff, the way he was to come, so as with arrows and missiles, to cause a disturbance in the army. And it happened, at the time when these young men had come to the ²wild cliff, that the king and his army arrived there; and these young men received the king and his army there; and with very great tumult they discharged arrows ²and missiles' among the army. And after killing ᵃmany, and wounding others, one of the young men drew his bow, and discharged an arrow among the army, which struck the armour of the king opposite his heart, unknown to the man who discharged it; but the arrow did no harm to the king, from the goodness of his armour, for he was mailed, and the arrow turned ⁹and rebounded' back from the armour. And the king became greatly frightened, and was almost as much astounded, as if he had been shot through. He then ordered the troops to encamp; and enquired who were those so bold as to attack him thus gallantly. They informed him, they were some young men, who had been sent by Maredudd, son of Bleddyn, that did it. He then despatched messengers to them, requesting them to come to him under a truce; and they came. He asked, who had sent them there; and they replied that it was Maredudd. He asked

---

ᵃ ¹⁰ some of the army,

---

⁷ brathassit, *B*.   ⁹ʹ mor leô, *B*.
⁸ pe, *B*.   ¹⁰ *B*.

aӧnaeth a wydynt ¹py le yd oed Uaredud yna. Ac atteb awnaethant y gӧydynt. Ac erchi awnaeth ynteu y Uaredud dyuot y hedӧch. Ac yna y doeth Maredud a meibon Kadӧgaӧn y hedӧch y brenhin. A gӧedy hedychu y rygtunt ²yd ymchoelaӧd y brenhin y Loeger drӧy adaӧ deg mil o warthec yn dreth ar Powys. Ac uelly y tervynaӧd y vlӧydyn honno.

MCXX. Ugein mlyned a chant a mil oet oed Crist pan ladaӧd Gruffud ab Rys ab Teӧdӧr Ruffud uab ³Trahaearn.

MCXXI. Y vlӧydyn rac ӧyneb y bu uarӧ Einaӧn uab Kadӧgaӧn y gӧr aoed yn kynhal rann o Powys a Meironyd y wlat adugassei ef y gan Uchtrut uab Etwin. ᵃAc ӧrth y agheu y kymynnaӧd y Varedud ⁴[y vrawt, aphan doeth y wereskyn y ӧlat y gӧrthladӧyt ef y gan Varedud] uab Bledyn y ewythyr. Ac yna y gellygӧyt Ithel uab Ridit o garchar Henri vrenhin. A phan doeth y geissaӧ ran o Powys ni chauas dim.' A phan gigleu Gruffud ab Kynan ry wrthlad Maredud ab Kadӧgaӧn o Varedud uab Bledyn y ewythyr, anuon a wnaeth ⁵Kadwalladyr ac Owein y ueibon a diruaӧr lu gantunt hyt ym Meironnyd, a dӧyn awnaethant holl dynyon y wlat ⁶o honei' ae holl da gyt ac ӧynt hyt yn Llyyn. Ac odyna kynullaӧ llu awnaethant ac aruaethu alldudaӧ holl wlat Powys. A heb allu ⁷kyfleӧni eu

---

ᵃ'⁸ Ac ẏ doeth Moredud ap Bledẏn ẏ gevẏnderw, ac Ithel ap Ririt ap Bledẏn a ellẏnghessit o garchar Henri vrenhẏn.

---

¹ pa, B.   ³ Sulhayarn, C. Talhaẏarn, D.
² yr, B.   ⁴ C.

them if they knew where Maredudd then was; and they answered that they did know. He then requested that Maredudd would come to make peace. Thereupon Maredudd and the sons of Cadwgan came under the king's peace. After peace had been made between them, the king returned to England, levying ten thousand head of cattle as a tribute upon Powys. And thus that year ended.

1120. One thousand one hundred and twenty was the year of Christ, when Gruffudd, son of Rhys, son of Tewdwr, killed Gruffudd, son of ³ Trahaiarn.

1121. The ensuing year, Einon, son of Cadwgan, died,—the person who held a part of Powys and Meirionydd, the country which he had taken from Uchtryd, son of Edwin, ᵃ and which at his death he bequeathed to Maredudd, ⁴ his brother; and when he came to take possession of the country, he was expelled by Maredudd,' son of Bleddyn, his uncle. And then Ithel, son of Rhirid, was liberated from the prison of king Henry; and when he came to claim a part of Powys, he obtained nothing.' When Gruffudd, son of Cynan, heard that Maredudd, son of Cadwgan, had been expelled by his uncle Maredudd, son of Bleddyn, he sent ⁵ Cadwalader and Owain, his sons, with a very large army into Meirionydd, and they took out of it all the men of the country, and all their property with them into Lleyn. And from thence they collected an army, intending to carry off the inhabitants of the whole country of Powys;

ᵃ'⁸ And Maredudd, son of Bleddyn, his cousin, came; and Ithel, son of Rhirid, son of Bleddyn, was liberated from the prison of king Henry.

---

³ Cat(valla(on, *B*. ⁷ kyflenwi, *B*.
ᵘ honno, *B*.   ⁸ *D*.

haruedyt ydymchoelassant drachefyn. Ac yna ydymaruolles Maredud uab Bledyn a meibon Kadʋgaʋn uab Bledyn y gyt ac y diffeithassant y rann vʋyaf o gyfoeth Llywarch uab Trahaearn, o achaʋs nerthu o honaʋ veibon Grufud ab Kynan ac ymaruoll ac ʋynt.

MCXXII. Y vlʋydyn rac ʋyneb y lladaʋd ¹ Grufud nab' Maredud ab Bledyn Ithel ab Ridit ab Bledyn y ᵃ gefynderʋ ² yggʋyd ᵇ Maredud y dat.' Ac ynol ychydic o amser wedi hynny y lladaʋd Catwallaʋn ab Grufud ab Kynan y tri ewythyr, nyt amgen Gronʋ a Ridit a Meilyr meibon Owein ab Edwin. Kanys Agharat uerch Owein ab Edwin oed wreic Ruffud ab Kynan, a honno oed vam Katwallaʋn ac Owein a Chatwaladyr, a llaʋer o verchet. Yny vlʋydyn honno y magʋyt teruysc y rʋg Morgan a Maredud meibon Katwgaʋn uab Bledyn. Ac yny teruysc hʋnnʋ y lladaʋd Morgan ac laʋ ehunan Varedud y vraʋt.

MCXXIII. Y vlʋydyn rac ʋyneb ³ yd ymchoelaʋd Henri vrenhin o Normandi wedy hedychu y rygtaʋ ⁴ ar neb y buassei tervysc ac ⁵ ʋynt kyn no hynny.

MCXXIV. Y vlʋydyn rac ʋyneb y gʋrthladʋyt Grufud uab Rys or kyfran o dir a rodassei y brenhin idaʋ wedy y gyhudaʋ yn wiryon heb y haedu o honaʋ or Ffreinc aoedynt yn kyt bressʋylaʋ ac ef. Yn diwed y vlʋydyn honno y bu uarʋ Daniel uab Sulyen escob Mynyʋ, y gʋr a oed gymodredʋr y rʋg Gʋyned

---

ᵃ ⁶ nai
ᵇ ⁷ tat Ithael a oed vrowt y Varedud.

ᵛ *Not in C.D.*　　　　　ᵃ *B.*
ᵛ *Not in E.*　　　　　⁴ *a rei, B.*

but without being able to fulfil their purpose, they returned back. And then Maredudd, son of Bleddyn, and the sons of Cadwgan, son of Bleddyn, combined together, and ravaged the greatest part of the territory of Llywarch, son of Trahaiarn, because he had assisted the sons of Gruffudd, son of Cynan, and combined with them.

1122. The ensuing year, [1]Gruffudd, son of' Maredudd, son of Bleddyn, slew his [a]cousin Ithel, son of Rhirid, son of Bleddyn, [2]in the presence of [b]his father Maredudd.' And, a little time afterwards, Cadwallon, son of Gruffudd, son of Cynan, slew his three uncles, to wit, Goronwy, Rhirid, and Meilyr, the sons of Owain, son of Edwin. For, Angharad, daughter of Owain, son of Edwin, was the wife of Gruffudd, son of Cynan; and she was the mother of Cadwallon and Owain and Cadwalader, and of many daughters. In that year, a disturbance arose between Morgan and Maredudd, the sons of Cadwgan, son of Bleddyn; and in that disturbance, Morgan killed Maredudd, his brother, with his own hands.

1123. The ensuing year, king Henry returned from Normandy, having made peace with those with whom he had had dissension previously.

1124. The ensuing year, Gruffudd, son of Rhys, was expelled from the portion of land which the king had given him, after he had been innocently and undeservedly accused by the French, who were jointly dwelling with him. In the end of that year died Daniel, son of Sulien, bishop of Menevia, the man who had been arbitrator between Gwynedd and

---

a [6] nephew

b [7] Ithel's father, who was brother to Maredudd.

---

[5] wynteu, *B.*
[6] *E.*
[7] *C.*

a Phowys yny teruysc a oed ¹[y] rygtunt. Ac nyt oed neb ¹[onadunt] a allei gael bei nac aglot arnaũ, kanys tangnefedus oed a charedic gan baũp. Ac archdiagon Powys oed.

MCXXV. Y vlũydyn rac ũyneb y bu uarũ Gruffud ²[ap Moredud] uab Bledyn. Ac yna y dellit Llywelyn ab Owein y gan Varedud uab Bledyn y ewythyr urawt y hendat a hũnnũ ae rodes yn llaũ Blen uab Ieuan y gũr ae hanuones ygkarchar hyt ygkastell ³Bruch. Yn diwed y vlũydyn ¹[honno] y bu uarũ Morgan ab Kadũgaũn yn Cipris yn ymchoelut o Gaerussalem wedy mynet o honaũ a chroes y Gaerussalem o achaũs rylad o honaũ kyn no hynny Varedud y vraũt.

MCXXVI. Y vlũydyn gũedy hynny ᵃy gũrthladũyt Maredud uab Llywarch oe wlat, y gũr a ladaũd mab Meuruc y gefynderũ. Ac a dallaũd meibon Griffri y deu gefynderũ ereill.' A Ieuaf uab Owein ᵇae gũrthladaũd ac yny diwed ae lladaũd.'

MCXXVII. Y vlũydyn rac ũyneb y llas Iorwoerth uab Llywarch ¹[y] gan Lyũelyn uab Owein ym Powys. Ychydic ũedy hynny y dyspeilũyt Llywelyn uab Owein oe lygeit ae geilleu y gan Uaredud uab Bledyn. Yn y vlũydyn honno y llas Ieuaf uab Owein

---

ᵃ⸍ ⁴ y lladawd Lliwelyn ap Ywein Varedud ap Llywarch wedy y dehol vy wlat y gwr aladassei Meuryc y geuynderw, ac a dynnassei lygeit Maredud a Griffri y deu geuyndyrw, ac adallasse y deu vroder.

ᵇ⸍ ⁵ a dallawt ỹ dev vroder ac aẏ deholas or wlat, ac ỹ llas wẏnt.

---

¹ B.
² D.
³ Brygge, D.

Powys, in the trouble between them; and there was none [1] of them' who could find blame or dispraise in him, for he was peaceful, and beloved by all; he was likewise the archdeacon of Powys.

1125. The ensuing year, Gruffudd, [2] son of Maredudd,' son of Bleddyn, died. And then Llywelyn, son of Owain, was blinded by his uncle, Maredudd, son of Bleddyn, brother to his grandfather, who delivered him into the hands of Blen, son of Ieuan, the man who sent him to prison to the castle of Brygge. At the end of that year, Morgan, son of Cadwgan, died at Cyprus, in returning from Jerusalem, after having taken the cross and gone to Jerusalem, on account of his having killed his brother Maredudd.

1126. The ensuing year, [a] Maredudd, son of Llywarch, was expelled from his country; the man who killed his cousin, the son of Meurug, and who blinded his two other cousins, the sons of Griffri.' It was Ieuan, son of Owain, [b] who expelled him, and ultimately killed him.'

1127. The ensuing year, Iorwerth, son of Llywarch, was killed by Llywelyn, son of Owain, in Powys. A little while afterwards, Llywelyn, son of Owain, was deprived of his eyes and testicles, by Maredudd, son of Bleddyn. In that year, Ieuav, son of Owain,

---

a/ [4] Llywelyn, son of Owain, slew Maredudd, son of Llywarch, after driving him to his country,—the man who had killed his cousin Meurug, and had put out the eyes of his two other cousins, Maredudd and Griffri, and had blinded his two brothers.

b/ [5] who blinded his two brothers, and expelled them from the country, and killed them.

---

[1] C.   [2] D.

y gan veibon Llywarch uab Owein y gefynderŵ. Yn diwed y vlŵydyn honno ᵃy llas Madaŵc uab Llywarch' y gan Ueuruc y gefynderŵ ¹uab Ridit.'

MCXXVIII. Yn diwed y vlŵydyn rac ŵyneb ydyspeilŵyt Meuruc uab Ridit oe deu lygat ae dŵy geill.

MCXXIX. Y vlŵydyn rac ŵyneb y llas Iorwoerth uab Owein. Yn y vlŵydyn honno y llas ²Kadŵgaŵn uab Gruffud ab Kynan ³[Ymanheudŵy] y gan Gadŵgaŵn uab Gronŵ ab Owein y gefynderŵ, ᵇac Einaŵn uab Owein. Ychydic wedy hynny y bu uarŵ Maredud ab Bledyn tegŵch a diogelŵch holl Powys ae hamdifyn wedy kymryt iachwyaŵl benyt ar y gorff, a gleindit ediuarŵch yny yspryt, a chymyn . corff Crist, ac oleŵ ac aghen.

MCXXX. ⁴[Yny pedair blyned wedy hynny, nyt amgen no] deg mlyned arhugein a chant a mil oed oet Crist pan vu bedeir blyned ar vn tu heb gahel neb ystorya or aellit y gŵarchadŵ ⁵[y] dan gof.

MCXXXIV. Ar vlŵydyn rac ŵyneb y bu uarŵ Henry uab Gŵilim bastard brenhin Lloegyr a Chymry ar holl ynys y am hynny yn Normandi ⁶y trydyd dyd o vis Racuyr.' Ac yny ol ynteu y kymerth Esteuyn o Blaes y nei goron y deyrnas y dreis, ac y darestygaŵd yn ŵraŵl idaŵ holl Deheu Lloegyr.

MCXXXV. Y vlŵydyn rac ŵyneb y llas Rickert uab Gilbert y gan Uorgan ab Owein; gŵedy hynny y kyffroes Owein a Chatwaladyr veibon Gruffud uab

ᵃ' ⁷ a Llỳwarch alas a Madoc ý vab
ᵇ ⁸ ap

---

¹ ap Owain, *E.*
² Cadwallawn, *C. D.*
³ *C.* ·yn nanhevdwy, *D.*
⁴ *C.*

was killed by the sons of Llywarch, son of Owain, his cousin. In the end of that year, ᵃ Madog, son of Llywarch, was killed' by his cousin Meurug, ¹ son of Rhirid.'

1128. In the close of the ensuing year, Meurug, son of Rhirid, was deprived of both his eyes, and both his testicles.

1129. The ensuing year, Iorwerth, son of Owain, was killed. In that year Cadwgan, son of Gruffudd, son of Cynan, was killed ³ at Nanheudwy' by his cousin Cadwgan, son of Goronwy, son of Owain, ᵇand Einon, son of Owain. A little after that Maredudd, son of Bleddyn, died—the ornament and safety and defence of all Powys, after undergoing salvatory penance of his body, and sanctity of repentance in his spirit, and the communion of the Body of Christ, and extreme unction.

1130. ⁴ Four years after that, that is to say,' one thousand one hundred and thirty was the year of Christ, when there were four successive years without any story to be found, that could be preserved in memory.

1134. And the ensuing year, Henry, son of William the Bastard, king of England and Wales, and of all the island besides, died in Normandy, on ⁶ the third day of the month of December.' And after him his nephew, Stephen of Blois, took the crown of the kingdom by force, and bravely brought all the South of England under his sway.

1135. The ensuing year, Rickert, son of Gilbert, was slain by Morgan, son of Owain. After that, Owain and Cadwalader, the sons of Gruffudd, son of Cynan,

---

ᵃ' ⁷ Llywarch was slain, and Madog his son,
ᵇ ³ son of

---

⁵ *B.*   ⁷ *D.*
⁶ iii. d. Noueb., *D.*   ⁸ *E.*

Kynan diruaόr greulaόn lu y Geredigyaόn y gόyr a ¹oed degόch yr holl Vrytanyeit ae diogelόch ae rydit ae kedernit, y gόyr a oedynt deu arderchaόc ²vrenhin a deu haelon. Deu diofyn deu leό deόron deu detwydyon. Deu huodron. Deu doethon. Diogelwyr yr eglόysseu ae ³hardemylwyr. Ac amdiffynnwyr y tlodyon; llofrudyon y gelynyon, hedychwyr y rei ymladgar; dofyodron y gwrthwynebwyr; y diogelaf naόd y baόp or afoei attunt; y gόyr a oedynt yn rac rymhau o nerthoed eneideu a chyrf. Ac yn kyt gynhal ynvn holl deyrnas y Brytanyeit. Y rei hynny ar yruthur gyntaf alosgassant gastell Gόallter ⁴[de Bec]. Ac yna wedy kyffroi ⁵eu hadaned ⁶yd ymladayssant a chastell Aber Ystόyth ac y llosgassant. A chyt a Howel uab Maredud a Madaόc uab Idnerth, a deu uab Howel nyt amgen Maredud a Rys a losgassant gastell Rickert Dylamar a chastell ⁷Dinerth, a chastell Kaer (ed)edros. Ac ⁸odyna yd' ymchoelassant adref. Yn diwed y vlόydyn honno y doethant eilweith y Geredigyaόn, a chyt ac όynt amylder lu o detholedigyon ymladwyr ual amgylch whemil o bedyt aduόyn ⁹[kant] a dόy vil o varchogyon llurugaόc. Ac yn borth udunt y deuth Gruffud uab Rys a Howel uab Maredud o Vrecheinaόc a Madaόc uab ¹⁰Idnerth, a deu uab Howel uab Maredud. Ar rei hynny oll yn gyfun a gyweirassant y bydinoed y Aber ¹¹Dyui. Ac yn y herbyn y deuth Ysteuyn gόnstabyl ⁴[y dref] a Robert uab Martin, a meibon Geralt ystiwert ¹²[a Gόilym ap Orc] ar holl Flemisseit, ar holl uarchogyon ar holl Ffreinc o

---

¹ oedynt, *B.*
² urenhined, *B.*
³ hardelόyr, *B.*
⁴ *D.*
⁵ y, *B.*
⁶ yd, *B.*

led a large and cruel army into Ceredigion ;—the men
who were the ornament of all the Britons, their safety,
their liberty, and their strength; the men who were
two noble and two generous kings; two dauntless ones;
two brave lions; two blessed ones; two eloquent ones;
two wise ones; protectors of the churches, and their
champions; the defenders of the poor; the slayers of
the foes; the pacifiers of the quarrelsome; the tamers
of antagonists; the safest refuge to all who should
flee to them; the men who were pre-eminent in
energies of souls and bodies; and jointly upholding
in unity the whole kingdom of the Britons. They on
the first onset burned the castle of Walter ⁴ de Bec ;'
and then, having moved their wings, they fought
against the castle of Aberystwyth and burned it;
and along with Howel, son of Maredudd, and Madog,
son of Idnerth, and the two sons of Howel, to wit,
Maredudd and Rhys, they burned the castle of Rickert
de la Mere, and the castle of Dinerth, and the castle
of Caerwedros; and afterwards they returned home.
In the close of that year they came a second time
into Ceredigion, having with them a numerous army
of choice combatants, about six thousand fine infantry,
and two thousand ⁹ one hundred' cavalry in armour.
And to their aid came Gruffudd, son of Rhys, and
Howel, son of Maredudd of Brecheiniog, and Madog,
son of ¹⁰ Idnerth, and the two sons of Howel, son of
Maredudd. And all those conjointly drew up their
troops at Aber ¹¹ Dyvi. And to oppose them came
Stephen the constable ⁴ of the town,' and Robert, son
of Martin, and the sons of Gerald the steward, ¹² and
William son of Orc,' and all the Flemings, and all
the marchers, and all the French from Aber Nedd

---

⁷ Dinyrth, B. Dineÿrth, D.
⁹ odyno yr, B.
⁹ D.E.

¹⁰ Ior, D.
¹¹ Teivi, B.C.D.
¹² B.

Aber Ned hyt yn Aber ¹Dyfi. A gŵedy kyrchu y vrŵydyr ac ymlad yn greulaŵn o bop tu y kymerth y Fflemisseit ar Normanyeit eu ffo herŵyd eu harueredic defaŵt. A gŵedy llad rei o nadunt, a llosgi ereill, ᵃa thrychu traet meirch ereill,' a dŵyn ereill ygkeithiwet a bodi y ran vŵyaf megys ynvydyon yn yr avon. A gŵedy colli amgylch teir mil oe gŵyr yn drist aflawen ²yd ymchoelassant ³y gŵlat. A gŵedy hynny yd ymchoelaŵd Owein a Chatwaladyr yŵ gŵlat yn hyfryt laŵen gŵedy ⁴kaffel y uudugolyaeth ⁵[yn anrydedus], a chael diruaŵr amylder o geith ac anreitheu a gŵiscoed maŵrweirthaŵc ac arueu.

MCXXXVI. Y vlŵydyn rac ŵyneb y bu varŵ Gruffud uab Rys, lleuuer a chedernit ac aduŵynder y Deheuwyr. ⁵[Yn] y vlŵydyn honno y bu uarŵ Gruffud ab Kynan brenhin a phennadur a thywyssaŵc ac amdiffynnŵr a hedychŵr holl Gymry. Gŵedy lliaŵs berigleu mor a thir. Gŵedy aneiryf anreitheu a budugolyaetheu ryueloed. Gŵedy goludoed eur ac aryant a dillat maŵrweirthaŵc. Gŵedy kynhullaŵ Gŵyned y briaŵt wlat y rei a daroed y gŵasgaru kynno hynny y ymrauaelon wlatoed, y gan Normanyeit. Gŵedy adeilat llawer o eglŵysseu yny amser ae kyssegru y Duŵ. ⁵[A] gŵedy gŵisgaŵ ymdanaŵ yn vynach, a chymryt cymun corff Crist, ac oleŵ, ac aghenn. Yny vlŵydyn honno y bu uarŵ Ieuan archoffeirat Llan Badarn y gŵr a oed doethaf or doethon. Gŵedy arwein y vuched yn grefydus heb pechaŵt marŵaŵl hyt agheu yny trydyd

---

ᵃ' ⁶ ac yssigaw ereill dan draet meirch

---

¹ Teivi, *E.*   ³ yŵ, *B.*
² yr, *B.*   ⁴ cael, *B.*

unto Aber ¹Dyvi. And after joining battle, with cruel fighting on every side, the Flemings and the Normans took to flight, according to their usual custom. And after some of them had been killed, and others burned, ᵃ'and the limbs of the horses of others broken,' and others taken captive, and the greater part, like fools, drowned in the river, and after losing about three thousand of their men, they returned exceedingly sorrowful to their country. After that, Owain and Cadwalader returned, happy and rejoicing, to their country, having obtained the victory ᵇ'honourably,' with an immense number of prisoners, and spoils, and costly garments and arms.

1136. The ensuing year, Gruffudd, son of Rhys, died—the light and strength and gentleness of the men of South Wales. In the same year Gruffudd, son of Cynan, died—the king and sovereign and prince and defender and pacifier of all the Welsh, after many dangers by sea and land, after innumerable spoils and victories in war, after riches of gold and silver and costly garments, after collecting together into Gwynedd, his own country, those who had been before scattered into various countries by the Normans, after building in his time many churches, and consecrating them to God, and after habiting himself as a monk, and receiving the communion of the Body of Christ, and extreme unction. In that year Ieuan, high priest of Llanbadarn, died—the man who was the wisest of the wise, after leading his life religiously, without committing mortal sin unto his dissolution, on the third day of the calends

---

ᵃ' ᵇ and bruised others under the feet of horses,

³ *B.*   ⁴ *C.*

dyd o galan Ebrill. Yny vlỽydyn honno hefyt y doeth meibon Gruffud ab Kynan y ᵃ dryded weith' y Geredigyaỽn, ac y llosgassant gastell Ystrat Meuruc, a chastell ¹Llan Ystyffan,' a chastell ²[Hỽmfre] ³[a] Kaer Vyrdin.

MCXXXVII. ⁴[Yn] y vlỽydyn rac ỽyneb y doeth yr amherodres y Loegyr yr darestỽg brenhinyaeth Loegyr y Henri y mab. Kanys merch oed hi y Henri gyntaf uab Gỽilim vastard. Ac yna y bu dyffic ar yr heul y deudecuet dyd o galan Ebrill.

MCXXXVIII. Y vlỽydyn rac ỽyneb y llas Cynwric ⁵[ap] Owein y gan deulu Madaỽc uab Maredud.

MCXXXIX. Y vlỽydyn wedy hynny y bu uarỽ Madaỽc uab Idnerth. Ac y llas Maredud uab Howel y gan ueibon Bledyn uab ⁶Kynuyn ⁴[y] Gỽyn.

MCXL. Y vlỽydyn rac llaỽ y llas Howel uab Maredud uab Ryderch or Cantref Bychan drỽy dychymic Rys uab Howel; ac ef e hun ae lladaỽd.

MCXLI. Deugein mlyned a chant a mil oed oet Crist pan las Howel uab Maredud ab Bledyn y gan ᵇneb un heb wybot pỽy ae lladaỽd.' Ac yna y llas Howel ae vraỽt ⁴[Chadỽgaỽn] meibon Madaỽc uab Idnerth.

MCXLII. Y vlỽydyn wedy hynny y llas Anaraỽt uab Grufud gobeith a chedernyt a gogonyant y Deheuwyr y gan deulu Kadwaladyr y gỽr yd ⁷oedynt yn

  ᵃ/ ⁸ eilweith
  ᵇ/ ⁹ y ỽyr ehun. ¹⁰ ẏr eidaw ehvn.

¹ Ystevyn, *D.*
² *B.* Sire Humfraẏ, *D.*
³ *C.*
⁴ *B.*
⁵ *B. C. D.* ac, *A.*
⁶ *Not in C. D.*

of April. In that year also, the sons of Gruffudd, son of Cynan, came the ᵃthird time' into Ceredigion, and burned the castle of Ystrad Meurug, the castle of Llanstephan, the castle ²of Humfrey,' ³and Caermarthen.

1137. ⁴In the ensuing year, the empress arrived in England, for the purpose of subduing the kingdom of England for Henry her son; for she was a daughter to Henry the first, son of William the Bastard. And then there was an eclipse of the sun on the twelfth day of the calends of April.

1138. The ensuing year, Cynvrig, ⁵son of' Owain, was killed by the family of Madog, son of Maredudd.

1139. The year after that, Madog, son of Idnerth, died; and Maredudd, son of Howel, was slain by the sons of Bleddyn, son of Cynvyn Gwyn.

1140. The forthcoming year, Howel, son of Maredudd, son of Rhydderch, of Cantrev Bychan, was slain by the machination of Rhys, son of Howel, and he himself slew him.

1141. One thousand one hundred and forty was the year of Christ, when Howel, son of Maredudd, son of Bleddyn, was killed by ᵇsome one, without its being known who killed him.' And then Howel and his brother ⁴Cadwgan, the sons of Madog, son of Idnerth, were slain.

1142. The year after that, Anarawd, son of Gruffudd, the hope, and strength, and glory of the men of South Wales, was killed by the family of Cadwalader—

ᵃ' ⁸ second time
ᵇ' ⁹ his own men.   ¹⁰ his own.

---

⁷ oed, B.   ⁹ B. C.
⁸ D.   ¹⁰ D.

ymdiret idaꞷ yn gymeint ac ofynhaei. A gꞷedy clybot o Owein y vraꞷt hynny drꞷc uu gantaꞷ. Kanys amot awnathoed rodi y verch y Annaraꞷt. A mynnu Kadwaladyr y vraꞷt awnaeth. Ac yna ydachubaꞷd Howel uab Owein ran Cadꞷaladyr o ¹Geinaꞷn, ac y llosges castell Cadꞷaladyr a oed yn Aber Ystꞷyth. Ac yna y llas Milo iarll Henfford asaeth neb un uarchaꞷc idaꞷ e hun aoed yn bꞷrꞷ karꞷ ²yn hela' y gyt ac ef.

MCXLIII. Y vlꞷydyn rac llaꞷ pan welas Catwaladyr uot Owein y vraꞷt yny ꞷrthlad oe holl gyfoeth kynullaꞷ llyges o Iwerdon aoruc, a dyuot y Abermenei yr tir. Ac yn dywyssogyon gyt ac ef ydoed ³Otter,' a mab Turkyll a mab ⁴Cherꞷlf. Ygkyfrꞷg hynny y kyttuunaꞷd Owein a Chatwaladyr megys y gꞷedei y vrodyr a thrꞷy gyghor y gꞷyr da y kymodassant. ᵃA phan ⁵glywyt' hynny y dellis ⁶[y] Germanꞷyr Cadwaladyr. Ac ynteu a amodes udunt dꞷy vil o ᵇgeith ac velly yd ymrydhaaꞷd y ꞷrthunt.' A phan gigleu Owein hynny a bot y vraꞷt yn ryd teruysgus gynnꞷrꞷf awnaeth arnunt ae kyrchu yn diennic a oruc. A gꞷedy llad rei a dala ereill ae kaethiꞷaꞷ yn warat-

---

ᵃ'⁷ A drwc oed gan y Gwydyl hynny canys oed amot ydunt dwy vil o vorkev yr dyvot gyt ac ef. A gwedy nas gavssant, wynt adalyassant llawer ac a dugassant gantunt yn attauel ev da.

ᵇ⁸ warthec,

---

¹ Geredigyaꞷn, B.C.
² ꞷrth hely, B.

³ Otter vab Octer, B.C. Occer vab Occer, D.

the man in whom they reposed as much confidence as he required. And when his brother Owain heard of it, he was sorry; for he had made a contract to give his daughter to Anarawd. And she would have his brother Cadwalader. Then Howel, son of Owain, seized Cadwalader's share of Ceredigion, and burned a castle of Cadwalader which was at Aberystwyth. At that time Milo, earl of Hereford, was killed by an arrow from a certain knight attached to himself, who was shooting a stag in hunting with him.

1143. The forthcoming year, when Cadwalader saw that his brother Owain was expelling him from all his territory, he collected a fleet from Ireland, and landed at Abermenai; and as leaders with him were ³Otter, and the son of Turkyll, and the son of ⁴Cherulf. In the meanwhile Owain and Cadwalader were reconciled, as became brothers, and it was through the advice of the good men that they were pacified. ᵃAnd when that became known, the Germans blinded Cadwalader; and he agreed to give them two thousand ᵇbondmen; and thus did he liberate himself from them.' And when Owain heard it, and that his brother was free, he became outrageous against them, and attacked them without mercy; and when some were killed, and others taken and confined, they ignominiously escaped by

---

ᵃ´ ⁷ And the Gwyddelians were sorry because of that, for there was an agreement that they should have two thousand marks for accompanying him. And when they did not receive them, they captured many, and took them away with them in pledge for their property.   ᵇ ⁸ cattle;

---

⁴ Yscherwlf, *C.*
ᵃ´ gigleu y Gwydyl, *C. B.*
⁷ *D.*
⁸ *C.*

wydus y diaghyssant ar ffo hyt yn Dulyn. Y vlóydyn honno y bodes ¹[o Gymry] pererinyon ar vor Groec yn mynet achroes y Gaerussalem. Yny vlóydyn honno ydatgyweiraód ²Hu uab ³Raólf gastell ⁴Gemaron ac y goreskynnaód eilweith Vaelenyd. Ac yna yd atgyweiróyt ⁵[kastell] ⁶Colóyn, ac y darestygóyt Eluael yr eilweith yr Ffreinc.

MCXLIV. Y vlóydyn rac óyneb y delis ⁷[Sir Hywe] o Mortemer Rys uab Howel ac y carcharaód myón carchar, wedy llad rei oe wyr a ⁸dala ereill. Ac yna y diffeithaód Howel uab Owein a Chynan y vraót ⁷[Aberteiui]. A góedy bot bróydyr aródost, a chael o nadunt y vudugolyaeth yd ymchoelassant drachefynn a diruaór anreith gantunt. Ac yna ydeuth Gilbert iarll uab Gilbert arall y Dyfet. Ac y darestygaód y wlat ᵃac ydadeilaód Gastell Kaer Uyrdin, achastell arall ym Mab Udrut.'

MCXLV. Y vlóydyn rac óyneb y bu uaró ⁹Sulyen ¹[vab] Richmarch mab y Seint Padarn mab maeth yr eglóys, a góedy hynny athro arbennic gór oed ⁵[ac] aeduet y geluydyt, ymadrodór dros y genedyl, a dadleuór ¹⁰kymedrodwyr, hedychór' amryuaelon genedloed, adurn o vrodyeu eglóyssolyon ar rei bydolyon y ᵇ decuet dyd o galan Hydref.' Góedy kymryt iachóyaól benyt ar y gyssegredigaeth gorff a chymyn corff

---

ᵃ' ¹¹ ac y goresgynnassant castell Caer Vyrdyn, ac edeiliat castell mab Vchtryt.

ᵇ' ¹² deu decuet dyd o galan mis Tachwed,

---

¹ C. D.
² Hugyn, D.
³ Randwlf, C.
⁴ Gymaeron, B.
⁵ B.
⁶ Kolunwy, C.

flight to Dublin. In that year, some pilgrims ¹ from Wales' were drowned on the sea of Greece, in going with the cross to Jerusalem. That same year, ² Hugh, son of Raulf, repaired the castle of ⁴ Gemaron, and conquered Maelienydd the second time. And then ⁵ the castle of' ⁶ Colwyn was repaired, and Elvael a second time was subjected to the French.

1144. The ensuing year, ⁷ Sir Hugh' de Mortimer seized Rhys, son of Howel, and confined him in prison, after killing some of his men, and taking others. And then, Howel, son of Owain, and his brother, Cynan, ravaged ⁷ Aberteivi; and after there had been a most severe battle, and they had obtained the victory, they returned back, with an immense booty. And then earl Gilbert, son of another Gilbert, came into Dyved, and subdued the country, ᵃ and erected the castle of Caermarthen, and another castle belonging to the son of Uchtryd.'

1145. The ensuing year died ⁹ Sulien, ¹ son of ' Rythmarch, son to St. Padarn, adopted son of the church, and afterwards an especial teacher, a man whose science was mature, a speaker in behalf of his nation, a pleader among arbitrators, the peace-maker of several nations, the ornament of ecclesiastical and civil decisions, on ᵇ the tenth day of the calends of October,' after undergoing salutary penance in his consecrated body, and taking the communion of the

---

ᵃ/ ¹¹ and conquered the castle of Caermarthen; and the castle of the son of Uchtryd was built.

ᵇ/ ¹² the twelfth day of the calends of the month of November,

---

⁷ D.
⁸ daly, B.
⁹ Sulgenius, C.

¹⁰′ kymrodedór hedychaůl, B.
¹¹ D.
¹² C.

Crist ac oleỡ ac aghenn. Ac yna y llas Meuruc uab Madaỡc uab Ridit ¹ yr hỡnn aelwit Meuruc Tybodyat trỡy vrat y gan eu wyr e hun.' Ac yna y llas Maredud uab Madaỡc uab Idnerth y gan Hu o Mortymer. ²[Yn] y vlỡydyn honno y goresgynnaỡd Cadell uab Grufud gastell Dinỡeileir yr hỡnn a wnathoed Gilbert iarll. ᵃ Ychydic wedy hynny y goruu ef a Howel ab Owein ³[gastell] Gaer Vyrdin drỡy gadarn ⁴ymrysson wedy' llad llawer oe gelynyon abrathu ereill. Ychydic o dydyeu wedy hynny y doeth yn deissyfyt diruaỡr luossogrỡyd or Ffreinc ar Fflemisseit y ymlad ar castell. Ac yn dywyssogyon yn y blaen meibon Geralt ystiwert, a Gwilim ab Aed; a phan welas Meredud uab Gruffud y ⁵[gỡr] y gorchymynnassit ⁶ udunt gadỡryaeth y castell ae amdifyn y elynyon yn dyuot mor deissyfyt a hynny gyrru callon yny gỡyr aoruc ae hannoc y ymlad, a bot yn drech gantaỡ y vryt noe oet. Kanys kyn bei bychan y oet eissoes yd oed gantaỡ weithret marchaỡc ac yn angrynedic dywyssaỡc yn annoc y wyr y ymlad, ac yn ᵇ kyrchu e hun y elynyon yn arueu.' A phan

---

ᵃ/ ⁷ A chastell Caer Vyrdyn drwý Howel ap Oweyn ar gwyr a oed yngarchar gyt ac ef. Ac odyna y doeth Cadell ay vrodyr Moredud a Rys y gastell Llan Ystiphan ac ymlad yn gadarn ac wynt a ⁸ ac y rodassant eu heneidyeu yr karcharoryon a odynt yno, ychydic wedy hynny ygoresgynnawd Kadell ay vrodyr Maredud a Rys kastell Llan Ystyffant

ᵇ/ ⁹ trychu e hun y elynyon ac arueu.

---

¹ Not in C. D.
² B.
³ C.

⁴ amrysson, B.
⁵ B. gỡyr, A.

Body of Christ, and extreme unction. And then
Meurug, son of Madog, son of Rhirid, ¹ who was called
Meurug Tybodiad, was killed through the treachery of
his own men.' And then Maredudd, son of Madog,
son of Idnerth, was killed by Hugh de Mortimer. In
that year Cadell, son of Gruffudd, reduced the castle
of Dinweileir, which had been erected by earl Gilbert. ᵃA little while afterwards, he and Howel, son
of Owain, overcame ³ the castle of' Caermarthen in a
severe struggle, after' killing many of their enemies,
and wounding others. A few days after that, an
immense multitude of the French and Flemings came
suddenly to attack the castle; and their commanders
to lead them were the sons of Gerald the steward,
and William, son of Aed. When Maredudd, son of
Gruffudd, the man to whom was assigned the custody of the castle and its defence, saw his enemies
coming so suddenly, he encouraged the men, and
urged them to fight, his mind being superior to
his age; for though he was young of age, nevertheless, he had the achievement of a knight, and as
an undaunted leader, he incited his men to fight, and
ᵇ himself assaulted his enemies in arms.' And when

ᵃ/ ⁷ and the castle of Caermarthen by the aid of
Howel, son of Owain, and the men who were in
prison with him. And from thence Cadell and his
brothers Maredudd and Rhys went to the castle of
Llanstephan and fought fiercely with them, ⁸ and
gave their lives to the prisoners who were there. A
little after that Cadell, and his brothers Maredudd
and Rhys, conquered the castle of Llanstephan,

ᵇ/ ⁹ himself mangled his enemies with arms.

---

⁶ idaỏ, *B*. | ⁸ *C*.
⁷ *D*. | ⁹ *B*.

welas y elynyon bychanet oed y nifer yn amdiffyn o
vyŵn y castell drychafael yscolyon ŵrth y muroed ¹[o
pop parth] aŵnaethant. Ac ynteu aodefaŵd y elynyon y yskynnu tu ar bylcheu. Ac yn dilesc ef ae
wyr a ymchoelassant yr yscolyon yny syrthaŵd y
gelynyon yny claŵd gan yrru ffo ar yrei ereill, ac
adaŵ lliaŵs o nadunt yn veirŵ; ar hynn a dangosses
idaŵ y detwyd dyghetuen rac llaŵ ar gaffel daŵn o
honaŵ ar wledychu yny Deheu. Kanys goruu ac ef
yn vab ar laŵer owyr profedic yn ymladeu. Ac ynteu
ac ychydic o nerth y gyt ac ef. Yn diwed y vlŵydyn honno y bu uarŵ Run uab Owein yn was ieuanc
clotuorussaf o genedyl y Brytanyeit, yr hŵn a ²uag-
yssei uoned yrieni yn arderchaŵc. Kanys tec oed o
ffuruf a drych, a hynaŵs o ymadrodyon, a huaŵdyr
wrth baŵb. Rac welaŵdyr yn rodyon. Vfud ymplith
y dylŵyth. Balch ymplith y estronyon, a therŵyn garŵ
urth y elynyon. Digrif ŵrth y gyfeillon; hir y dyat;
gŵynn y liŵ. Pengrych melyn y wallt; hir y ŵyneb.
³Goleisson y lygeit llydanyon a llawenyon. Mynŵgyl
hir praff. Dŵy vronn lydan. Ystlys hir. Mordŵydyd
praffyon. Eskeired hiryon; ac oduch y draet yn
veinon. Traed ⁴hiryon a byssed unyaŵn oed idaŵ. A
phan doeth y chŵedyl y irat agheu ef at y dat Owein
ef a godet ac a dristaaŵd yn gymeint ac na allei
dim y hyfrytau ef na thegŵch teyrnas na digrifŵch,
na chlaear didanŵch gŵyr da nac edrychedigaeth
maŵrweirthogyon betheu mamyn Duŵ rac welaŵdyr
pob peth a drugaraaŵd oe arueredic defaŵt a drug-
arhaaŵd ŵrth genedyl y Brytanyeit rac y cholli megys
llog heb ⁵lywyaŵdyr arnei ¹[ac] agedwis udunt
Owein yn tywyssaŵc arnunt. Kanys kyn kyrchassei
anniodefedic dristit vedŵl y tywyssaŵc, eissoes ef ae

---

¹ B.
² vagassei, B.
³ rudleissyon, C.

his enemies observed how small was the number within defending the castle, they raised ladders against the walls ⁴'on every side.' He suffered his enemies to ascend towards the embrasures, and then he and his men energetically pushed back the ladders, so that the foes fell into the ditch, putting the others to flight, many being left dead. In this was demonstrated his happy destiny in future of possessing merit for reigning in the South; for he, though a youth, overcame many tried men in combats, having with him only a small force. In the end of that year died Rhun, son of Owain, being the most praiseworthy young man of the British nation, whom his noble parents had honourably reared. For he was fair of form and aspect, kind in conversation, and affable to all; seen foremost in gifts; courteous among his family; high bearing among strangers, and fierce towards his enemies; entertaining to his friends; tall of stature, and fair of complexion, with curly yellow hair, long countenance; with eyes somewhat blue, full and playful; he had a long and thick neck, broad breast, long waist, large thighs, long legs, which were slender above his feet; his feet were long, and his toes were straight. When the report of his lamentable death came to his father Owain, he was afflicted and dejected so much, that nothing could cheer him, neither the splendour of a kingdom, nor amusement, nor the sprightly converse of good men, nor the exhibition of valuable things; but God, Who foreseeth all things in His accustomed manner, commiserated the British nation, lest it should perish like a ship without a pilot, and preserved Owain as a prince over it. For before insufferable sorrow had affected the mind of

---

⁴ hirueinyon, C.   ⁵ lywyaŵr, B.

drychafaöd, deissyfyt lewenyd dröy racweledigaeth Duö. Kanys yd oed neb un gastell a elwit Yröydgruc y buessit yn vynych yn ymlad ac ef heb dygyaö. A phan doeth göyr da Owein ae deulu y ymlad ac ef ny allaöd nac anyan y lle nae gedernit ymörthlad ac öynt yny losget y castell ac yny diffeithöyt, göedy llad rei or kastellwyr a ¹ dala ereill ae carcharu. A phan gigleu Owein yn tywyssaöc ni hynny y gellygöyt ef y gan bob dolur a phob medöl cöynuanus ac y doeth yn rymus ²[yn] yr ansaöd ³a oed arnaö gynt.

MCXLVI. Y vlöydyn rac öyneb ²[y] daeth Lowys urenhin Freinc ac amheraödyr yr Almaen ²[y] gyt ac ef a diruaör ⁴luossogröyd o ieirll a barömeit a thywyssogyon gyt ac öynt a chroes y Gaerussalem. ᵃ²[Yn] y vlöydyn honno y kyffroes Cadell ab Gruffud ae urodyr ²[nyt amgen] Maredud a Rys. A Göilim ab Geralt ae urodyr gyt ac öynt lu amben castell Göiss. A göedy annobeithaö o nadunt yn y nerthoed e hunein, galö Howel ab Owein a orugant yn borth udunt. Kanys gobeithaö ydoedynt oe deörleö luossogröyd ef parottaf y ymladeu ae doethaf

---

ᵃ′⁵ Yný vlwidýn ýd aeth Cadell ap Grufud aý vrodýr Moredud a Rýs am ben castell ý Wis; ac anvon ýn ol Howel ap Owein ýn borth ýdunt. A gwedý klýwet o Willam vap Geralt aý vrodýr hýnný, anvon ý wahawd Howel a orugant o barthret ý brenhin ac adaw llawer o da idav ýr dývot ýn borth ýdunt, ac ýntev adoeth ac a ýmdiffýnnawt ý castell oý nerth ef.

---

¹ daly, B. ³ yd, B.
² B.

the prince, he was restored to sudden joy, through the providence of God. There was a certain castle called Gwyddgrug, which had been frequently attacked, without its falling; and when the liege men of Owain and his family came to fight against it, neither the nature of the place nor its strength could resist them, till the castle was burned and destroyed, after killing some of the garrison, and taking others, and putting them in prison. And when Owain, our prince, heard of that, he became relieved from all pain, and from every sorrowing thought, and recovered his accustomed energy.

1146. The ensuing year, Louis, king of France, and the emperor of Germany, accompanied by an immense multitude of earls and barons and princes, took the cross and proceeded to Jerusalem. ᵃ In that same year, Cadell, son of Gruffudd, and his brothers, namely, Maredudd and Rhys, and William, son of Gerald, and his brothers with them, raised an army against the castle of Gwys. And after despairing of their own strength, they called Howel, son of Owain, to their aid; for they trusted from his courageous forces, who was the readiest in conflicts, and the wisest in council,

---

ᵃ'⁵ During the year Cadell, son of Gruffudd, and his brothers Maredudd and Rhys, went against the castle of Gwys; and sent for Howel, son of Owain, to their assistance. And when William, son of Gerald, and his brothers, heard that, they sent to invite Howel on the part of the king, promising him much property if he came to their aid, and he came and defended the castle with his own force.

---

⁴ luoessyd, *B.* | ⁵ *D.*

gyghor gaffel o nadunt y uudugolyaeth. A Howel
megys ydoed chϭannaϭc yn wastat y glot agogonyant
a beris kynullaϭ llu [1][agϭedy kynullaϭ y llu] gleϭaf
apharottaf yn enryded y harglϭyd; kymryt hynt
aoruc tu ar dywededic gastell [2][Gϭis]. A gϭedy y
aruoll yn enrydedus or [3]dyϭededigyon uarϭneit yno
pebyllyaϭ aϭnaeth. A holl negesseu y ryfel aϭneit oe
gygor ef ae dechymmic. Ac uelly [4]yd oed' baϭb or
aoed yno y oruchel ogonyant a budugolyaeth drϭy
oruot ar y castell oe gyghor ef gan diruaϭr ymrysson
ac ymlad. Ac odyno yd ymchoelaϭd Howel yn uud-
ugaϭl drachefyn;' ny bu bell gϭedy hynny yn y bu
teruysc y rϭg Howel a Chynan veibon Owein a
Chatwaladyr [1][y eϭythyr]. Ac odyna ydeuth Howel
or neilltu, a Chynan or tu arall hyt ym Meironnyd
[1]ae galϭ a ϭnaethant y laϭ gϭyr y wlat agilyassant y
noduaeu eglϭysseu gan gadϭ ac ϭynt y [5]noduaeu ac
enryded yr eglϭys. Ac odyna kyweiryaϭ eu bydin
awnaethant tu a Chynuael castell Cadwaladyr, yr
hϭnn awnathoed Katwaladyr kynno hynny yny lle yd
oed Moruran abat y ty Gϭyn yn ystiϭert yr hϭnn a
ϭrthodes rodi y ϭrogaeth udunt, kyt ysprofit weithen
drϭy [6]arϭydon vegythyeu, gϭeitheu ereill drϭy anneiryf [7]anregyon a' rodyon agynigyit idaϭ. Kanys
gϭell oed gantaϭ [1][y] uarϭ yn aduϭyn no dϭyn y
vuched yn dϭyllodrus. A phan welas Howel a Chynan
hynny dϭyn kyrch kynhyruus yr kastell aϭnaethant,
ac ennill a orugant y dreis. Ac o vreid y diegis
[8]ceitweit y castell drϭy nerth y kyfeillon wedy llad
rei oe kedymdeithon, a brathu ereill. Yny vlϭydyn
honno y bu uarϭ Robert iarll uab Henri [2][vrenhin]
gϭr agynhalassei ryfel ynerbyn Esteuyn vrenhin

---

[1] B.
[2] C.
[3] dywededic, B.
[4] y doeth, B.

that they should obtain the victory. And Howel, as he was always ambitious of fame and glory, caused to be assembled an army, 'and after assembling an army,' the bravest and most prepared in honour of his lord, he marched toward the said castle ² of Gwys ;' and after being honourably received there by the before mentioned barons, he encamped; and all the concerns of the war were executed from his counsel and design. In that manner every body there aspired to supreme glory and victory by overcoming the castle, through his advice, with extreme emulation and fighting. And from thence Howel returned back victorious.' It was not long afterwards before there was a commotion between Howel and Cynan, sons of Owain, and Cadwalader ¹ their uncle ;' and then Howel on one side, and Cynan on the other side, proceeded into Meirionydd, and called out the men of the country who had retired to the sanctuaries of the churches, preserving the sanctuaries and honour of the church. From thence they directed their force towards Cynvael, the castle of Cadwalader, which Cadwalader had formerly erected, in the place where Morvran, abbot of Whitland, was steward, who refused to do homage to them, though he was sometimes tried by severe threatenings, at other times by numberless presents and gifts offered to him; for he deemed it better to die reputably than to lead his life dishonourably. When Howel and Cynan found that, they made a violent attack upon the castle, and gained it by force; and hardly did the defenders of the castle escape through the aid of their friends, after some of their companions were killed, and others wounded. In that year died Robert, son of ² king Henry, the man who had maintained a war against Stephen for twelve

---

⁵ nadyeu, *B.*
⁶ aruon, *B.*

⁷ o, *B.*
⁸ keitbat, *B.*

deudeg mlyned kyn no hynny. ¹[Yn] y vlȯydyn honno y bu varȯ Gilbert iarll ²[vab Gilbert arall.]

MCXLVII. Y vlȯydyn rac ȯyneb y bu uarȯ Vchtrut escob Llan Daf gȯr maȯr y volyant ac amdiffynnȯr yr eglȯysseu, gȯrthȯynebȯr y elynyon yny berfeith heneint. Ac yny ol ynteu y bu escob ³Nicol uab Gȯrgant ¹[escob]. Yny vlȯydyn honno y bu uarȯ Bernart escob Mynyȯ yny dryded vlȯydyn ardec ar hugeint oe escobaȯt gȯr enryfed y ⁴volyant a dyȯaȯlder a' santeidrȯyd oed, wedy diruaȯryon lafuryeu ar vor a thir, ȯrth beri y eglȯys Vynyȯ y hen rydit. Ac yny ol ynteu y dynessaaȯd yn escob Dauyd uab Geralt archdiagaȯn Keredigyaȯn. Yny vlȯydyn honno y bu uarȯ Robert escob Henford gȯr ¹[a] oed herȯyd yn barnȯryaeth ni grefydys achyflaȯn oweithredoed cardodeu a hegar borthȯr y tlodyon, ac arbennic degȯch yr eglȯysseu yn gyflaȯn o dydyeu da hyt na lygrit cadeir ⁵yr ueint' brelat hȯnnȯ o anheilȯg erlynyaȯdyr. Yna yd urdȯyt Gilbert abat Kaer Loyȯ yn escob yn Henford. Yn y vlȯydyn honno y bu uaȯr uarȯolyaeth yn ᵃynys Prydein.'

MCXLVIII. Y vlȯydyn rac ȯyneb ydadeilaȯd Owein uab Grufud ab Kynan gastell yn Ial. ¹[Yn] y vlȯydyn honno yd adeilaȯd Kadwaladyr uab Grufud gastell ²[yn] Llan Rystut o gȯbyl ac y rodes y rann ef ⁶y Geredigyaȯn ⁷a Chadȯgaȯn y vab. Ygkylch diwed y vlwydyn honno yd adeilaȯd Madaȯc uab Maredud gastell Croes Hyswallt, ac yrodes ⁸ Gyfeilaȯc y Owein a Meuruc veibyon Grufud ab Maredud' y nyeint.

ᵃ' ⁹ Gẏmre.

---

¹ B.
² C.
³ Kadwgawn, C.

⁴ volyanrȯyd a dȯyȯaȯl y, B.
⁵ y veint, B.

years previously. In that same year died Gilbert, son of another Gilbert.'

1147. The ensuing year died Uchtryd, bishop of Llandaf, a man of high praise, the defender of the churches, and the opposer of his enemies, in the fulness of age. And after him came bishop Nichol, son of bishop Gwrgant. In that year Bernard, bishop of Menevia, died, in the thirty-third year of his episcopacy,—a man of extraordinary praise and piety and holiness,—after extreme exertions, upon sea and land, towards procuring for the church of Menevia its ancient liberty. And after him David, son of Gerald, archdeacon of Ceredigion, succeeded as bishop. In that year died Robert, bishop of Hereford; a man who was, according to our judgment, pious and abounding in works of charity, and the kind feeder of the poor, and the especial ornament of the churches,— full of good days, so that the chair of such a prelate was not polluted by an unworthy persecutor. Then Gilbert, abbot of Gloucester, was ordained bishop of Hereford. In the same year there was a great mortality in the isle of Britain.'

1148. The ensuing year, Owain, son of Gruffudd, son of Cynan, built a castle in Yale. In that same year, Cadwalader, son of Gruffudd, constructed a castle at Llanrhystud entirely, and gave his share of Ceredigion to his son Cadwgan. About the close of that year, Madog, son of Maredudd, built the castle of Oswestry, and gave Cyveiliog to his nephews, Owain and Meurug, the sons of Gruffudd, son of Maredudd.

---

a' 9 Wales.

---

6 o, B. D.
7 y, B. C. D.

8 Not in D.
9 D.

MCXLIX. Y vlȯydyn rac ȯyneb ydatgyweiraȯd Cadell ab Gruffud ¹gastell Caer Vyrdyn yr tegȯch a chedernit ²y deyrnas, ac y diffeithaȯd' Kedweli. Yny ulȯydyn honno y ᵃcarcharaȯd Owein vrenhin Gȯyned Cynan y uab.' Yny ulȯydyn honno y delis Howel uab Owein ³Gatuan uab' Kadwaladyr y ᵇgefynderȯ ac yd achubaȯd y tir ae gastell. Ny bu bell wedy hynny yny doeth meibon Gruffud uab Rys ⁴[nyt amgen], Cadell a Maredud a Rys a llu gantunt y Geredigyaȯn ae gorescyn hyt yn Aeron. Yny ulȯydyn honno y darparaȯd Madaȯc uab Maredud vrenhin Powys drȯy nerth Randȯlf iarll Kaer Lleon kyuodi yn erbyn Owein Gȯyned. A gȯedy llad ⁴[y] pobyl y ganhorthȯywyr ⁵[yn Konsyllt] ef yd ymchoelaȯd y rei eraill y kefyneu y ffo.

MCL. Deg mlyned a deugein a chant a mil oed oet Crist ᶜpan duc Cadell a Maredud a Rys veibon Gruffud ab Rys Geredigyaȯn oll y gan' Howel ab Owein eithyr un castell aoed yn Penn Gȯern yn Llan Vihagel. A gȯedy hynny y goreskynnassant gastell Llan Rustut o hir ymlad ac ef. A gȯedy hynny y cauas Hoȯel uab Owein y castell hȯnnȯ y dreis ac y llosges ⁶[wedy llad y castellyr] oll. Ny bu hayach

---

ᵃ′⁷ carcharȯyt Ywein vrenhin Gȯyned a Chynan y vab.

ᵇ⁸ ewythyr

ᶜ′⁹ Cadell, Moredud, a Rẏs, meibion Grufud aganatassant Keredigion ẏ

ᵛ *Not in D. E.*
² yr, *B.*
ᵂ *Not in D.*

⁴ *B.*
⁵ *B. C. D.*

1149. The ensuing year, Cadell, son of Gruffudd, repaired the castle of Caermarthen, for the ornament and strength of his kingdom; and ravaged Cydweli. In that year, ᵃ Owain, king of Gwynedd, imprisoned Cynan, his son.' In the same year, Howel, son of Owain, captured his ᵇ cousin, Cadvan, son of Cadwalader, and seized his land and castle. It was not long afterwards before the sons of Gruffudd, son of Rhys, 'to wit,' Cadell, and Maredudd, and Rhys, came with an army into Ceredigion, and subdued it as far as Aeron. In the same year, Madog, son of Maredudd, king of Powys, through the assistance of Randulf, earl of Caerleon, prepared to rise against Owain Gwynedd; and after the people of his auxiliaries had been slain ⁵ at Consyllt,' the others turned their backs to flee.

1150. One thousand one hundred and fifty was the year of Christ, ᶜ when Cadell and Maredudd and Rhys, the sons of Gruffudd, son of Rhys, took the whole of Ceredigion from' Howel, son of Owain, except one castle that was at Pengwern in Llanvihangel. And after that they conquered the castle of Llanrhystud, after long fighting with it. And subsequently Howel, son of Owain, obtained that castle by force, and burned it, ⁶ after killing the garrison wholly. It was but a short time after that when

---

ᵃ/⁷ Owain, king of Gwynedd, and Cynan, his son, were imprisoned.

ᵇ ⁸ uncle

ᶜ/⁹ Cadell, Maredudd, and Rhys, sons of Gruffudd, granted Ceredigion to

---

⁴ B. C.   ⁵ C.
⁷ B.   ⁹ D.

wedy hynny ¹[hyt] pan atgyweiraốd Cadell a Maredud ²[a Rys] veibon Gruffud ab Rys gastell Ystrat Meuruc. A gốedy hynny yd edewit Cadell uab Gruffud yn lletuarố wedy y yssigaố yn greulawn o rei o wyr Dinbych ac ef yn hela. Ac ychydic wedy hynny gốedy kynnullaố o Varedud a Rys veibon Gruffud ab Rys y kedernit ac yn gyfun y kyrchassant Whyr ac ymlad aốnaethant a chastell Aber Llychốr ae losgi adiffeithaố y wlat. Yn y vlốydyn honno yd atgyốeirassant ốy ³oll deu gastell ⁴Dinốeleir ac yd atgyweiryaốd Howel ab Owein gastell ¹[vab] Hốmffre yn nyffryn Clettốr.

MCLI. Yn y vlốydyn rac ốyneb ²[blwydyn o oed Krist dec a deugein a chant a mil] yd yspeilaốd Owein ⁵Gốyned ᵃGuneda uab Kadwallaốn y nei uab y vraốt oe lygeit ¹[ae geilleu].' Yn y vlốydyn honno y lladaốd ⁶Llywelyn ab' Madaốc ab Maredud Ystefyn uab Baldwin. Yn y vlốydyn honno y gốrthladyr ⁷[Catwaladyr] o ynys Von, ⁸[ẏgan Owein ẏ vraut] ac y bu uarố ⁹Simon archdiagon ¹⁰Keueilaốc gốr maốr y enryded ae deilygdaốt.

MCLII. Yn y vlốydyn rac ốyneb y kyweiraốd Maredud a Rys ueibon Gruffud uab Rys ¹¹[y bydinoed] y Penwedic. Ac ymlad aốnaethant a chastell Howel ae ᵇdorri. Ny bu uaốr gốedy hynny yny gyrchaốd

ᵃ' ¹² Cuneda ẏ nei, a Chatwallawn ẏ vraut oẏ lẏgeit aẏ geillieẏ rac bot etived ẏdunt.

ᵇ ¹³ darestốg

---

¹ B.
² C.
³ yll, B.
⁴ Dinevwr, C. E.
⁵ ap Grufud, C.
⁶ Not in D.
⁷ B. C. D.

THE CHRONICLE OF THE PRINCES. 181

Cadell and Maredudd ²and Rhys,' sons of Gruffudd, son of Rhys, repaired the castle of Ystrad Meurug. And subsequently Cadell, son of Gruffudd, was left half dead, having been cruelly bruised by some of the men of Tenby, whilst he was hunting. A little after that, Maredudd and Rhys, the sons of Gruffudd, son of Rhys, having collected their strength, conjointly entered Gower, and fought against the castle of Aberllychwr, burning it, and devastating the country. In the same year, both of them repaired the castle of Dinweileir; and Howel, son of Owain, repaired the castle of ¹the son of' Humfrey in the vale of Calettwr.

1151. In the ensuing year, ²the year of Christ one thousand one hundred and fifty,' Owain ⁵Gwynedd deprived ᵃhis nephew Cunedda, the son of his brother Cadwallon, of his eyes ¹and testicles.'' In that year, ⁶Llywelyn, son of' Madog, son of Maredudd, killed Stephen, son of Baldwin. In the same year, ⁷Cadwalader was expelled from the isle of Mona ⁸by Owain his brother;' and ⁹Simon, archdeacon of ¹⁰Cyveiliog, a man of great reputation and worth, died.

1152. The ensuing year, Maredudd and Rhys, sons of Gruffudd, son of Rhys, led ¹¹their forces' to Penwedig, and fought against the castle of Howel, and ᵇdemolished it. There was not much time after-

---

ᵃ' ¹² his nephew Cunedda, and Cadwallon his brother, of their eyes and testicles lest they should have an heir.

ᵇ ¹³ subdued

---

⁸ *C. D.*
⁹ Symeon, *B. D.* Einion, *E.*
¹⁰ Kelynnawc, *D. E.*
¹¹ *B. C.*
¹² *D.*
¹³ *B.*

ueibon Rys gastell Dinbych; a thrŵy urat nos wedy torri y ¹porth y goreskynnassant y castell, ac y dodassant ef ygkadŵryaeth Gŵilim ab Geralt; a gŵedy daruot hynny y diffeithaŵd Rys uab Gruffud adiruaŵr lu gyt ac ef gastell Ystrat Kyngen. A mis Mei wedy hynny y kyrchaŵd Maredud a Rys veibon Gruffud y gyt y castell ²Aberuyn, a gŵedy llad y castellwyr a llosgi y castell diruaŵr anreith ac anneiryf ᵃ oludoed adugant gantunt; odyno eilŵeith y diffeithaŵd Rys Gefeilaŵc drwy uudugolyaeth. ³[Yn] y vlŵydyn honno y bu uarŵ Davyd uab y Moel Cŵlŵm brenhin Prydein. ³[Yn] y vlŵydyn honno y doeth Henri tywyssaŵc y Loegyr ⁴[a y gŵledychaŵd holl Loegyr]. Y vlŵydyn honno y bu uarŵ Randŵlf iarll Kaer Llion. ³[Yn] y vlŵydyn honno ydaeth Cadell uab Gruffud y bererindaŵt, ac yd edewis y holl nedyant ae allu ygkatŵryaeth Maredud a Rys y vrodyr yny delei ef.

MCLIII. ⁵[Blwydyn wedy hynny] y ulŵydyn honno y bu uarŵ Ystefyn urenhin y gŵr a ⁶gynhelaŵd urenhinyaeth Loegyr y dreis yn ol Henri uab Gŵilim bastard. A gŵedy hŵnnŵ y doeth Henri uab yr amherodres y Loegyr ac y ⁷kynhalyaŵd holl Loeger. ³[Yn] y ulŵydyn honno y bu ŵarw ⁸Griffri ab Gŵynn.

MCLIV. Y vlŵydyn rac wyneb y bu uarŵ Maredud uab Gruffud ab Rys brenhin Keredigiaŵn ac Ystrat Tyŵi a Dyfet yn y bumet ulŵydyn arhugeint oe oet gŵr a oed diruaŵr y drugared ŵrth dlodyon, ac ard-

---

ᵃ ⁹ o luoed

---

¹ pyrth, *B.*
² Aber avyn, *B. D.* Aber auyn, *C.*
³ *B.*
⁴ *B. C.*
⁵ *C.*

wards before the sons of Rhys attacked the castle of Tenby, and by a night plot, after breaking the gate, they got possession of the castle, and delivered it into the custody of William, son of Gerald. And when that was accomplished, Rhys, son of Gruffudd, with an immense host, laid waste the castle of Ystrad Cyngen. And the month of May following, Maredudd and Rhys, sons of Gruffudd, jointly attacked the castle of ²Aberavan, and after killing the garrison and burning the castle, they brought from thence immense spoil and innumerable ᵃ riches. A second time Rhys victoriously ravaged Cyveiliog. ³ In that same year died David, son of Malcolm, king of Prydyn. ³ In that year prince Henry arrived in England, ⁴ and reigned over all England.' That year Randulf, earl of Caerleon, died. ³ In that year Cadell, son of Gruffudd, went on a pilgrimage, and left all his possessions and power in the keeping of his brothers, Maredudd and Rhys, until he should return.

1153. ⁵ A year after that,' that same year, king Stephen died,—the man who held the kingdom of England through usurpation, after Henry, the son of William the Bastard. And after him Henry, the son of the empress, came into England, and possessed the whole of England. ⁹ In that year ⁸ Griffri, son of Gwyn, died.

1154. The ensuing year, Maredudd, son of Gruffudd, son of Rhys, the king of Ceredigion and the Vale of Tywi and Dyved, died, in the twenty-fifth year of his age,—a man who was extremely compassionate to

---

ᵃ ⁹ forces

---

⁶ gynhelis, *B.*
⁷ kynhelis, *B.*

⁸ Grufud, *C. D.*
⁹ *B.*

erchaẃc y gedernit ẃrth y elynyon achyfoethaẃc ¹y gyfyaẃnder. ²[Yn] y ulẃydyn honno y bu uarẃ Geffrei escob Llan Daf ar offeren ³[ac y bu varw Roger] iarll Henford.

MCLV. Y ulẃydyn rac ẃyneb pan gigleu Rys uab Gruffud uot Owein Gẃyned y ewythyr yn dyuot a llu gantaẃ y Geredigyaẃn yn dilesc y kynnullaẃd ynteu lu ac y doeth hyt yn Aber Dyfi; ac yno y gorffẃyssaẃd ar uedyr ymlad arodi brẃydyr y Owein Gẃyned ae lu. Ac ny bu bell wedy hynny ²[hytt] pan wnaeth yno gastell. ²[Yn] y ulẃydyn honno y gẃnaeth Madaẃc uab Maredud arglẃyd Powys gastell Ygkaer Einaẃn yn ymyl Kymer. Yn y ulẃydyn honno y diegis Meuruc ⁴uab Gruffud nei yr dywededic Uadaẃc' oe garchar. Ny bu bell wedy hynny yny gyssegrwyt eglẃys Veir Ymeiuot. ²[Yn] y ulẃydyn honno y bu uarw Terdeilach vrenhin Conach.

MCLVI. Y ulẃydyn rac ẃyneb y duc Henri uab yr amherotres vrenhin Lloegyr, ẃyr oed hẃnnẃ y Henri uab Gẃilim bastard diruaẃr lu hyt ymaestir Kaer Lleon aruedyr darestẃg idaẃ holl Wyned; ac yno ⁵pebyllyaẃ a ẃnaeth.' Ac yna gẃedy galw ²[o] Owein tywyssaẃc Gẃyned attaẃ, y ueibon ae ⁶nerth ae lu' ae allu, ⁷pebyllyaẃ aoruc yndinas Basin ⁸y diruaẃr lu ²[y] gyt ac ef. Ac yno gossot oet brẃydyr ar brenhin awnaeth. Apheri drychafel clodyeu aruedyr rodi kat ar uaes y brenhin. Agẃedy clybot or brenhin hynny rannu y lu a oruc, ac anuon ieirll a ²[llaẃer ac anneiryf o] barẃneit gyt a chadarn luossogrẃyd o lu aruaẃc ar hyt y traeth tu ar lle ydoed Owein; ar brenhin e hun yn diergrynedic ac aruaẃc vydinoed

---

¹ o, B. ³ C. D. a Rosser, B.
² B.   ᵛ nei Madoc, D.

the poor, and of noble prowess against his enemies, and rich in righteousness. ²In that year died Jeffrey, bishop of Llandaf, at mass, ³and died Roger,' earl of Hereford.

1155. The ensuing year, when Rhys, son of Gruffudd, understood that his uncle, Owain Gwynedd, was leading an army into Ceredigion, he also collected an army without delay, and came as far as Aberdovey; and there he rested, with the intention of fighting and giving battle to Owain Gwynedd and his army. And it was not long afterwards before he made a castle there. ²In that year, Madog, son of Maredudd, lord of Powys, made a castle at Caereinion, in the vicinity of Cymmer. In that year, Meurug, son of Gruffudd, nephew to the said Madog, escaped from his prison. It was not long after that before the church of St. Mary was consecrated at Meivod. ²In that same year Terdeilach, king of Conach, died.

1156. The ensuing year, Henry, son of the empress, king of England, who was grandson of Henry, son of William the Bastard, brought an immense army into the champaign land of Caerleon, with the design of subjecting all Gwynedd to himself; and there he encamped. And then after Owain, prince of Gwynedd, had called to him his sons and his strength and his army and his power, he encamped at Basingwerk, having with him an immense host. And there he fixed an appointment for battle with the king, causing dykes to be raised, with the design of fighting a pitched battle with the king. When the king heard of that, he divided his army, and sent earls, ²many and innumerable' barons, with a powerful number of armed troops along the strand towards the place where Owain was. And the king himself undauntedly,

---

⁵ gossot pebylleu aoruc, *B.*
⁶ nerthoed, *B.*
⁷ pe pebyllu, *B.*
⁸ a, *B.*

parottaf y ymlad gyt ac ef a gyrchassant drѡy y coet ¹[aelwit Koet Kennadlaoc] aoed y rygtunt ar lle yd oed Owein ae gyferbynyeit aoruc ²Dauyd a Chynan' veibon Owein yny coet ynyal, a rodi brѡydyr chѡerѡdost yr brenhin. A gѡedy llad llawer ³oe wyr' breid y diegis yr maestir ⁴[dracheven]. A phan gigleu Owein bot y brenhin yn dyuot idaѡ or tu dra ⁵egefyn a gѡelet o honaѡ y ieirll or tu arall yn dynessau adiruaѡr lu ⁶aruaѡc gantunt' adaѡ y lle a oruc, a chilyaѡ aoruc hyt y lle a ⁷elwir Kil Owein. Ac yna kynullaѡ aoruc y brenhin y lu ygyt ⁴[amynet hyt yn Rudlan] ⁸yn greulaѡn.' Ac yna y pebyllyaѡd Owein yn Tal Llѡyn ᵃPina. Ac odyno yd argywedei ef yr brenhin dyd a nos. ᵇA Madaѡc uab Maredud arglѡyd Powys a ᶜdewissaѡd y le y bebyllyaѡ rѡg' llu y brenhin a llu Owein ual y gallei erbynyeit y kyrcheu kyntaf awnelei y brenhin. Ygkyfrѡg hynny y dyblygaѡd llyges y brenhin y Von. A gѡedy adaѡ yny llogeu y gѡyr ⁹noethon ⁴[diaryf] ar gѡassanaethwyr,' y kyrchaѡd tywyssaѡc y llogeu ¹⁰ar penllogwyr ⁴[y] gyt ac ef ⁴[ar ieuectit adas y ymladeu] ᵈy ynys Von,' ac

---

ᵃ ¹¹ Pennant ẏ vessuraѡ castell.

ᵇ/ ¹¹ Ac odẏna ẏdaeth Madoc tẏwẏssauc Powẏs a thalm o lu ẏ brenhin gẏt ac ef ar longhev hẏt ẏn Aber Menei, ac ẏno

ᶜ/ ¹² deissyuaѡd lle idaѡ y bebyllu rac

ᵈ/ ¹² yr ynys ymẏѡn

---

¹ C.
²′ Kynan a Danid, B.
³′ oѡyr y brenhin, B.

⁴ B.
⁵ chenen, B.
⁶′ gantunt ynn aruaѡc, B.

with armed troops, the most prepared for fighting,
accompanying him, proceeded through the wood,
¹called the Wood of Cennadlog,' that lay between
them and the place where Owain was; and ²David
and Cynan,' sons of Owain, intercepted them in the
trackless wood, and fought a severe battle with the
king; who after having many of his men killed,
scarcely escaped into the champaign land ⁴again.
And when Owain understood that the king was coming
upon him from behind, and saw the earls from the
other side approaching with an immense armed host,
he left the place and retreated into the place called
Cil Owain. And then the king collected his army
together, ⁴and proceeded to Rhuddlan' ⁸in a rage.'
Then Owain encamped in front of Llwyn ªPina; and
from thence he harassed the king day and night.
ᵇAnd Madog, son of Maredudd, lord of Powys,
ᶜselected his position for encamping between' the
army of the king and the army of Owain, so as to
enable him to meet the first attack made by the
king. In that interval the fleet of the king tacked
towards Mona; and after leaving in the ships the
naked ⁴unarmed men, and the servants,' the commander of the ships, with the head sailors, ⁴and the
youths fit for battles,' landed ᵈin the isle of Mona,'

ª ¹¹ Pennant, to measure a castle.

ᵇ ¹¹ And then came Madog, prince of Powys, with a
portion of the king's army, in ships to Abermenei;
and there

ᶜ ¹² requested a place for him to encamp in front of

ᵈ ¹² within the isle

---

² előit, *B.*
⁸ *Not in B.*
⁹ noeth, *B.*
¹⁰ a, *B.*
¹¹ *D.*
¹² *B.*

yspeilaỽ a ¹wnaethant eglỽys Ueir ac eglỽys Bedyr ²[yn Rossyr] a llaỽer o eglỽysseu ereill, ac am hynny y gỽnaeth Duỽ dial arnunt. Kanys trannoeth y bu vrỽydyr y rygtunt a gỽyr Mon. Ac yny vrỽydyr honno y kilyaỽd y Ffreinc herwyd ³eu gnottaedic defaỽt gỽedy llad llaỽer o nadunt a dala ereill a bodi ereill; a breid y diegis ychydic o nadunt yr llogeu wedy llad Henri uab Henri vrenhin a ⁴chanmỽyaf holl bennafduryeit y ᵃllogwyr. A gwedy daruot hynny yd hedychaỽd y brenhin ac Owein ac y kauas Kadwaladyr y gyfoeth drachefyn. Ac yna yd ymchoelaỽd y brenhin y Loegyr. Ac yna yd ᵇymchoelaỽd Iorwoerth Goch uab Maredud ᶜy gastell Ial ac y llosges.

MCLVII. Y ulỽydyn rac ỽyneb y llas Morgan ab Owein ⁵[Gwynedd] drỽy dỽyll y gan ỽyr ⁶Iuor uab Meuruc ⁷a chyt ac ef y llas y prydyd goreu, a honnỽ aelwit Gỽrgan uab Rys.' Ac yna y gwledychaỽd Iorỽoerth uab Owein uraỽt Morgan dir Kaer Llion a holl gyfoeth Owein. A gỽedy gwneuthur hedỽch o holl tywyssogion Kymry ar brenhin Rys uab Gruffud ehunan adarparaỽd gỽneuthur ryfel ac ef. A ᵈduunaỽ a wnaeth' holl Deheubarth ae holl ᵉannỽyleit ae holl da gantunt hyt ygcoedyd Ystrat Tywi. A phan gigleu y brenhin hynny anuon kenadeu a ⁸ỽnaeth at Rys y uenegi idaỽ uot yn gryno idaỽ

ᵃ ⁹ llogeu.   ᵇ ⁹ ymladaỽd   ᶜ ⁹ a
ᵈᶠ ⁹ mudaỽ a oruc   ᵉ ⁹ annuieileit

---

¹ orugant, B.   ⁴ No in D.
² E.   ⁵ E. ỽann, B.
³ y, B.

and pillaged the church of St. Mary, and the church of St. Peter, ²'in Rhoshir,' and many other churches; and because of that, God brought vengeance upon them, for on the following day there was a battle between them and the men of Mona. And in that battle the French, according to their accustomed manner, retreated, after many of them were killed, and others taken, and others drowned; and scarcely a few of them escaped to the ships, Henry, son of king Henry, and ⁴almost all the chief officers of the ᵃ seamen, having been slain. When that was accomplished, the king made peace with Owain; and Cadwalader had his territory restored to him; and then the king returned to England. Then Iorwerth the Red, son of Maredudd, ᵇreturned ᶜto the castle of Yale, and burned it.

1157. The ensuing year, Morgan, son of Owain ⁵Gwynedd, was killed through treachery by the men of ⁶Ivor, son of Meurug; ⁷and along with him was slain the best poet, who was called Gwrgant, son of Rhys.' Then Iorwerth, son of Owain, the brother of Morgan, governed the land of Caerleon, and all the territory of Owain. After peace had been made by all the Welsh princes with the king, Rhys, son of Gruffudd, alone prepared to wage war with him. And he ᵈconfederated all South Wales and all his ᵉfriends, with the whole of their property, as far as the woods of the Vale of Tywi. And when the king heard of this, he sent messengers to Rhys, to inform him that it would be well for him to repair to the court of the king,

---

ᵃ ⁹ ships, ᵇ ⁹ fought ᶜ ⁹ with
ᵈ ⁹ moved ᵉ ⁹ cattle

---

⁴ Iornerth, *B.* ⁵ oruc, *B.*
⁷ *Not in D. E.* ⁹ *B.*

vynet y lys y brenhin yn gynt noc y dygei Loegyr
a Chymry a Ffreinc am y benn ae nat oed neb
eithyr ef [1] ehunan yn [2] ymerbynyeit ar brenhin. A
gǔedy mynet yny gyghor ef ae wyrda ef aaeth y lys
y brenhin. Ac yno y goruu arnaǔ oe anuod hedychu
ar brenhin, [3] dan amot idaǔ gaffel y Kantref Maǔr
a chantref arall or auynhei y brenhin yrodi idaǔ yn
gyfan heb y wasgaru. Ac ni chynhelis y brenhin
ac ef hynny, namyn rodi dryll o dir [4] [idaǔ] yg
kyfoeth pob barǔn o amryuaelon uarǔneit. A chyt
dyallei Rys y [5] dǔyll honno' kymryt a [6] ǔnaeth y ran-
neu hynny ae kynnal yn hedychaǔl. Ac ygkyfrǔg
hynny kyt dyfryssyei Rosser iarll Clar mynet y
Geredigyaǔn; eissoes nys beidei kyn hedychu Rys
ar brenhin. A gǔedy hynny [a] dydgweith kyn' kalan
Mehevin y doeth y Ystrat Meuruc, a thrannoeth duǔ
kalan Mehevin [7] yd ystorres y castell hǔnnǔ a chastell
Hǔmfre, a chastell Aber Dyvi, a chastell Dineir, a
chastell Rystut. Ygkyfrǔg hynny y duc Gǔallter Clifford anreith o gyfoeth Rys ab Gruffudd, ac y lladawd
[4] [llaǔer] oe wyr [8] y wlat nessaf idaǔ. Kanys ef bioed
kastell Llan ym Dyfri. A gǔedy daruot hynny yd
danuones Rys genadeu att y brenhin [9] [y venegi hynny.
Ac ny mynnaǔd] y [10] [brenhin] beri iaǔn idaǔ am
hynny. Ac yna yd [b] ymchoelaǔd teulu Rys. [11] Ac y'
gastell Llan ym Dyfri [4] [ac] y doeth Rys attunt, ac y

---

a' [12] ar uldyd o   b [12] ymladaǔd

---

[1] ehun, B.
[2] ym erbyn, B.
[3] gann, B.

[4] B.
[5] tǔyll hǔnnǔ, B.
[6] oruc, B.

before he brought England and Wales and France about his head; and that there was none excepting himself in opposition to the king. After having taken counsel with his good men, he went to the king's court, and there he was compelled, against his will, to make peace with the king, under the stipulation of receiving the Cantrev Mawr, and such other cantrev as the king should be pleased to give him, whole and not scattered. Yet the king did not adhere to this, but gave ⁷him a piece of land in the territories of each out of several barons. And though Rhys understood that deceit, he accepted those portions, and held them peaceably. And in that interval, though Roger, earl of Clare, was intent upon entering Ceredigion, nevertheless, he dared not, before Rhys had made peace with the king. Afterwards, ᵃon a certain day before⁸ the calends of June, he came to Ystrad Meurug, and the day following the calends of June, he stored that castle, the castle of Humfrey, the castle of Aberdovey, the castle of Dineir, and the castle of Rhystud. In the meanwhile Walter Clifford carried a booty out of the territory of Rhys, son of Gruffudd, and killed ⁹many of the men of the country nearest to him; for the castle of Llanymddyvri was his property. When that was done, Rhys despatched messengers to the king ⁹to inform him of that; but the king would not⁹ cause satisfaction to be made to him for this. Then the family of Rhys ᵇreturned; and Rhys joined them at the castle of Llanymddyvri, and subdued the

---

ᵃ′ ¹² on a muggy day of   ᵇ ¹² fought

---

⁷ yr, *B.*
⁸ or, *B.*
⁹ *B. C.*

¹⁰ *C.*
¹¹′ *A, B.*
¹² *B.*

goresgynna6d y castell ; yna y kyrcha6d Eina6n uab Anara6t ¹[nei ap y] bra6t yr argl6yd Rys, ieuanc o oet a g6ra6l o nerth. Ac acha6s g6elet o hona6 bot Rys y ewythyr yn ryd or amot ac o bop ll6 ¹[or] a rodassei yr brenhin. Ac o acha6s y uot ynteu yn dolyrya6 kyvarsagedigaeth y bria6t genedyl gan d6yll ygelynyon. Yna y kyrcha6d am benn castell H6mfre ac y llada6d y marchogyon dewraf a cheitweit y kastell o g6byl. Ac duc holl anreith y castell ae holl yspeil oll ganta6. Ac yna pan welas Rys uab Gruffud na allei ef gad6 dim ganta6 or a ²rodassei y brenhin' ida6 namyn yr hynn aennillei oe arneu, kyrchu a ³wnaeth am benn y cestyll a darestygassei y ieirll ar bar6neit yg Keredigya6n ae llosgi. A g6edy clybot or brenhin hynny kyrchu Deheubarth a 6nnaeth a llu ganta6. ªA g6edy mynych 6rthynebu o Rys ae wyr ida6 ymchoelud awnaeth y Loegyr.' Ac odyno yd aeth dr6y y mor.

MCLVIII. Y ul6ydyn rac 6yneb y darestyga6d yr argl6yd Rys uab Gruffudd y cestyll a ⁴wnathoed y Freinc ar dra6s Dyfet ac y llosges ¹[6y]. Ygkyfr6g hynny yd arweda6d y lu y Gaer Vyrdin ac ymlada6d ac ef. Ac yna y doeth Reinalt uab Henri urenhin yny erbyn a chyt ac ef dirua6r luossogr6yd o Freinc a Normanyeit a Fflemisseit a Saeson a Chymry. Ac ada6 aoruc Rys y castell achynnulla6 y wyr y gyt hyt ym mynyd ⁵Kefyn Restyr.' Ac ⁶yno y pebyllya6d yg kastell ⁷Din6ileir. Reinallt iarll ¹[a iarll]

ª' ⁸ A gwedy rodi o Rys ydaw wystlon ef aymchwelawd y Loegyr.

---

¹ B.
² rossoedit, B.
³ oruc, B.

⁴ ry6naeth, B.
⁵ Kyneu Rychter mein, B. —a Rychter, E.

castle. Then Einon, son of Anarawd, ¹nephew, son of his' brother, to the lord Rhys, who was young of age, and manly in strength, seeing that his uncle Rhys was released from the agreement, and from every oath he had given to the king, also lamenting the subjection of his own nation, through the deceit of enemies, made an attack upon the castle of Humfrey, and slew the bravest knights, and all the garrison of the castle, and carried away with him the whole booty and spoil of the castle. And then, when Rhys, son of Gruffudd, perceived that he could not preserve any thing of what the king had given him, except what he could gain by his arms, he made an attack upon the castles that had been subdued by the earls and the barons in Ceredigion, and burned them. And when the king heard of this, he entered South Wales with an army; ᵃand after Rhys and his men had often opposed him, he returned to England;' and thence he proceeded beyond sea.

1158. The ensuing year, the lord Rhys, son of Gruffudd, subdued and burned the castles which the French had erected across Dyved. In the meanwhile, he conducted his army to Caermarthen, and fought against it; and thereupon Rheinallt, son of king Henry, came against him, with a vast multitude of French and Normans and Flemings and English and Welsh. And Rhys quitted the castle, and assembled his men together upon the mountain of ⁵'Cevn Rhestr.' And there encamped at the castle of ⁷ Dinweleir, earl Rheinallt, ¹ the earl of' Bristol, the earl of Clare, two

---

ᵃ'³ and when Rhys had given him pledges, he returned to England,

---

ᵃ yna, B.
⁷ Dinefŵr, B. Cornwyllon, E.

⁸ C.

Brustei a iarll Clar a deu iarll ereill, a Chatwaladyr uab Gruffud, a Hoŵel a Chynan veibon Owein Gŵyned, a diruaŵr lu o uarchogyon a phedyt gyt ac ŵynt a heb ueidaŵ kyrchu y lle ydoed Rys, ymchoelut adref a ¹ wnaethant yn ᵃ llaŵ segur.' Odyna kynnic kygreir y Rys a ² orugant ac ynteu ae kymerth. A chenattau y wyr a ³ ŵnaeth ymchoelut ⁴ y gŵlat.

MCLIX. Y ulŵydyn rac ŵyneb y bu uarŵ Madaŵc uab Maredud arglŵyd Powys, y gŵr a oed diruaŵr y uolyanrwyd yr hŵnn a ⁵ ffuruaŵd Duw ⁶ o gymmeredic' tegŵch. Ac ae ⁷ kyflanwaŵd o anhybygedic ᵇ hyder, ac ae hadurnaŵd oleŵder a molyanrŵyd vfud a hegar a hael ŵrth y tlodyon; huaŵdyr ŵrth ⁸ [yr] vfudyon. Garŵ ac ymladgar ŵrth y ⁹ alon. Gŵedy gŵneuthur iachŵyaŵl benyt a chymryt kymmun corff Crist, ac oleŵ, ac aghenn, ac Ymeiuot yny lle yd oed y ¹⁰ ŵylua yn eglŵys Tissiliaŵ sant y cladŵyt yn enrydedus. Ni bu uaŵr gŵedy hynny yny las Llyŵelyn y uab, y gŵr a oed unic obeith y holl wyr Powys. ᶜ Ac yna y delis Cadwallaŵn uab Madaŵc uab Idnerth Einaŵn Clut' y uraŵt ac ydanuones ygkarchar Owein Gŵyned. Ac Owein ae rodes yr Ffreinc a ᵈ throy y gedymdeithon ᵉ [ae deulu]' y diegis hyt nos o ¹¹ Wiceŵ yn ryd.

ᵃ' ⁸ ŵac laŵ.   ᵇ ⁸ bruder,
ᶜ' ¹² Ac ẏ dalpwẏt Cadwallawn ap Madoc ap Idnerth ẏgan Einaun Clut
ᵈ' ¹² ogẏghor ẏwẏr aẏ vrodẏr maeth

---

¹ orugant, B.   ⁴ yŵ, B.
² ŵnaethant, B.   ⁵ phurueidaŵd, B.
³ oruc, B.   ⁶' ae agkymaredic, B.

other earls, and Cadwalader, son of Gruffudd, and Howel and Cynan, with an immense host of cavalry and infantry; but not daring to approach the place where Rhys was, they returned home with ᵃ unemployed hands.' After that they offered a truce to Rhys, which he accepted; and he permitted his men to return to their country.

1159. The ensuing year died Madog, son of Maredudd, lord of Powys, the man who was of extraordinary celebrity, and whom God had endowed with acknowledged beauty, and filled with unmatched ᵇ confidence, and adorned with bravery and fame; being humble and kind, and generous to the poor; affable to the humble; and terrible and warlike towards his foes;—after undergoing salutary penance, and receiving the communion of the Body of Christ, and extreme unction; and at Meivod, where his burial place was, he was honourably interred. It was but shortly afterwards that his son Llywelyn was killed,— the person who was the only hope of all the men of Powys. ᶜ And then Cadwallon, son of Madog, son of Idnerth, seized Einon Clud' his brother, and sent him to the prison of Owain Gwynedd; and Owain delivered him to the French; and ᵈ by means of his friends and ⁸ his family,'' he escaped by night from ¹¹ Wiciew, and got his liberty.

ᵃ⁄⁸ empty handed.   ᵇ⁸ anxiety,

ᶜ⁄¹² And Cadwallon, son of Madog, son of Idnerth, was seized by Einon Clud

ᵈ⁄¹² by the advice of his men and his foster brothers,

---

⁷ kyflaȯnaȯd, *B.*
⁸ *B.*
⁹ ȯrthȯymebedigyon, *B.*
¹⁰ ȯydua, *B.*
¹¹ Weckȯm, *B.*
¹² *D.*

MCLXI. Trugein mlyned a chant a mil oed oet Crist pan ¹[ny bu dim. Blwydyn wedy hynny] uu uarw Agharat gῶreic Ruffud uab Kynan. ²[Yn] y ulῶydyn honno y bu uarῶ Meuruc escob Bangor. Yn y vlῶydyn honno y goreskynnaῶd Howel uab Ieuaf ³[ap Owain] o dῶyll gastell ⁴Daualwern Ygkeueilaῶc. Ac o achaῶs hynny y syrthaῶd Owein Gῶyned ygkymeint o dolur ac na allei na thegῶch teyrnas na didanῶch neb ryῶ dim arall y arafhau nae dynnu oe gymeredic lit. Ac eissoes kyt kyrchei anniodeuedic dristit uedῶl Owein ²[tyῶyssaῶc] deissyfyt lewenyd oracweledigaeth Duῶ ae kyfodes. Kanys yr un ryῶ Owein a gyffroes vn ryw lu y Arῶystli hyt yn Llan Dinan; a gῶedy ⁵kaffel diruaῶr anreith o nadunt yngynnullaῶ a oruc gῶyr Arῶystli amgylch trychan ῶr y gyt a Howel uab ⁶Ieuan y hargl῀yd y ymlit yr anreith ⁷[hyt yngordwr Hafren]. A phan welas Owein y elynyon yndyuot yn deissyfyt, annoc y wyr y ymlad aoruc, ar gelynyon a ymchoelassant ar ffo gan y llad o Owein ae wyr yn y bu vreid y diegis ⁸y traean adref ar ffo. A phan gyflenwis y llewenyd hῶnnῶ vedῶl ᵃOwein, yna yd ymchoelaῶd ar y gyssevin ansaῶd wedy y rydhau oe gymeredeic dristit, ac atgyweiraῶ y castell a oruc.

MCLXII. Y ulῶydyn rac ῶyneb y dygῶydaῶd ⁹Kaer Offa' y gan Owein ab Gruffud ab Owein ab Madaῶc, ᵇa Maredud uab Howel.' ²[Yn] y ulῶydyn honno y

---

a' ¹⁰ a bryt y tyῶyssaῶc,
b' ¹¹ a Moredud a Howel.   ¹²ap Moredud a Howel ap Madoc i vrawd.

¹ C.
² B.
³ E.

⁴ Walwern, C. D.
⁵ cael, B.
⁶ Ieuav, B.

1161. One thousand one hundred and sixty was the year of Christ, when ¹ nothing happened. A year after that,' Angharad, the wife of Gruffudd, son of Cynan, died. ² In that year, Meurug, bishop of Bangor, died. In the same year, Howel, son of Ieuav, ³ son of Owain,' got possession of the castle of ⁴ Tavalwern in Cyveiliog through treachery; and on that account, Owain Gwynedd fell into such grief, that neither the splendour of a kingdom, nor the consolation of any thing else, could assuage or draw him from his resentment. And nevertheless, though insupportable sorrow affected the mind of ² prince Owain, a sudden joy from the foreknowledge of God raised him up. For the same Owain moved an army into Arwystli, as far as Llandinam; and after they had obtained a vast booty, the men of Arwystli assembled together, being about three hundred men, under Howel, son of ⁶ Ieuan, their lord, to pursue after the booty ⁷ as far as the bank of the Severn.' And when Owain observed his enemies coming suddenly on, he incited his men to fight; and the enemies took to flight, and were killed by Owain and his men, so that scarcely a third of them escaped home. And when that joy had filled the mind ᵃ of Owain,' he returned to his former state, having been released from his sorrow; and he repaired the castle.

1162. The ensuing year, ⁹ Caer Offa' fell before Owain, son of Gruffudd, son of Madog, ᵇ and Maredudd, son of Howel.' ² In the same year king Henry

---

ᵃ/ ¹⁰ and thought of the prince,

ᵇ/ ¹¹ and Maredudd and Howel. ¹² son of Maredudd, and Howel son of Madog, his brother.

---

⁷ D	¹⁰ B.
⁸ a, B.	¹¹ D.
⁹ Karrekgoua, B. C. D. E.	¹² E.

kyffroes Henri vrenhin Lloegyr lu yn erbyn Deheubarth. Ac y doeth hyt ym Penn Cadeir. A g6edy rodi g6ystlon o Rys ida6 ymchoelut y Loegyr a wnaeth. Ac yna y llas Eina6n uab Anara6t yny ¹g6sc y gan Wallter ab Llywarch y 6r ehun, ac y llas Cad6ga6n ab Maredud y gan Wallter uab ²Ridit. Ac yna y kymerth Rys ab Grufud y Kantref Ma6r a chastell Dinef6r. ³[Yn] y ul6ydyn honno y bu uar6 Kediuor uab Daniel archdiagon Keredigya6n. Ac yna y bu uar6 Henri ab Arthen goruchel athro ar holl gyffredin yr holl yscolheigon.

MCLXIII. Y ul6ydyn rac 6yneb g6edy g6eled o Rys ab Gruffud nat yttoed y brenhin yn kywira6 ⁴dim 6rtha6' or a ada6ssei, ac na allei ynteu ⁵uuduchockau yn adu6yn kyrchu ⁶awnaeth yn wrawl' am benn cyfoeth Rosser iarll Clar y g6r y lladyssit Eina6n uab Anara6t y nei oe acha6s, a thorri ⁸[aoruc] castell Aber Reidawl, a chastell mab Wynya6n ac llosci, ac atoresgynn holl Geredigya6n ⁷[yr eilweith] a mynychu lladuaeu a lloscuaeu ar y Fflemisse, a d6yn mynych anreitheu y gantunt. A g6edy hynny yd ymaruolles yr holl Gymry ar ym6rthlad a cheitweit y Ffreinc a hynny yn gyfun y gyt.

MCLXIV. Y ul6ydyn rac 6yneb y diffeitha6d Dauyd uab Owein G6yned Tegigyl, ac y muda6d y dynyon ae hanifeileit y gyt ac ef hyt yn dyffryn Cl6yt ⁸[a oruc ef or holl wlad eithr dinas Basing y ty a seiliasai i dad]. A g6edy tebygu or brenhin y bydei ymlad ar y ᵃcastell aoed' yn Thegygyl kyffroi llu

---

ᵃ'⁹ gestyll a oedynt

---

¹ hun, B.
² Richard, C.D.
³ B.
⁴ ida6 din, B.
⁵ vuchodockau, B. D.

moved an army against South Wales; and he came to Pencader; and after Rhys had delivered hostages to him, he returned to England. And then, Einon, son of Anarawd, was slain in his sleep by Walter, son of Llywarch, his own man; and Cadwgan, son of Maredudd, was slain by Walter, son of ² Rhirid. Then Rhys, son of Gruffudd, took possession of Cantrev Mawr and the castle of Dinevwr. ³ In that year died Cedivor, son of Daniel, archdeacon of Ceredigion. And then died Henry, son of Arthen, the supreme teacher in general of all the scholars.

1163. The ensuing year, when Rhys, son of Gruffudd, saw that the king fulfilled nothing of what he had promised, and that he could not thus submit honourably, he manfully entered the territory of Roger, earl of Clare, the man on whose account his nephew Einon, son of Anarawd, had been slain; and dismantled and burned the castle of Aber Rheidiol, and the castle of the son of Gwynion, and reconquered ⁷a second time' the whole of Ceredigion, iterating slaughters and conflagrations among the Flemings, and taking from them many spoils. And after that, all the Welsh combined to expel the garrison of the French altogether.

1164. The ensuing year, David, son of Owain Gwynedd, ravaged Tegeingl, and removed the people, with their cattle, along with him into the Vale of Clwyd, ⁸ from all the country, except Basingwerk, the house which his father had founded.' And when the king supposed that there would be an attack made upon the ᵃ castle which was' in Tegeingl, he moved

---

ᵃ/⁹ castles which were

---

⁶ ynn (ra(l aoruc, B. | ⁸ D.
⁷ E. | ⁹ B.

aoruc dr6y diruaƀr vrys a dyuot hyt yn Rudlan ¹[a mynnassu gwneithur castell yno] a phebyllu yno deirnos. A g6edy hynny ymchoelut y Loegyr, a chynnulla6 diruaƀr lu y gyt ac ef a detholedigyon ymladwyr Lloegyr a Normandi a Fflandrys ac Angi6 a Gwasg6in a holl ª Brydein a dyuot hyt y Groes Oswallt, gan darparu alltuda6 a difetha yr holl Vrytanyeit. Ac yny erbyn ynteu y deuth Owein G6yned, a Chatwaladyr ueibon Grufud ab Kynan a holl lu G6yned y gyt ac 6ynt. Ar arlg6yd Rys ab Gruffud a holl Deheubarth y gyt ac ef; ac Owein Keveila6c a Iorwoerth Goch uab Maredud ²[o Voelmant] a meibon Mada6c uab Maredud a holl Powys y gyt ac 6ynt; a deuuab Mada6c uab Idnerth ae holl gyfoeth y gyt ac ³ ef. Ac ygyt yn gyfun diergrynedic y doethant hyt Yncideirna6n, a phebyllu a ⁴ wnaethant Yghoruaen. A g6edy trigya6 yn hir yny pebylleu yno heb arueida6 o vn gyrchu at y gilyd y ymlad, llidia6 aoruc y brenhin yn diruaƀr, a chyffroi y lu hyt yghoet Dyffryn Keiria6c; a pheri torri y koet ae b6r6 yr lla6r. Ac yno yd ymerbynya6d ac ef yn 6ra6l ychydic o Gymry etholedigyon y rei ny wydynt odef y goruot yn absen y tywyssogyon. A llawer or rei kadarnaf a dygwyda6d o bop tu. ⁵[Ac odena yduc y brenhin y lu hyt yn mynyd Berwyn]. Ac yna y pebyllya6d y brenhin ar bydinoed ⁶[blaen] y gyt ac ef ⁶[ymynyded Ber6yn]. A g6edy trigya6 yno ychydic odydyeu y kyfarsag6yt ef odiruaƀr dym-

---

ª ⁷ nerth ar Gogled

---

¹ *D.*   ³ 6ynt, *B.*
² *E.*   ⁴ oruc, *B*

an army with extreme haste, and came to Rhuddlan, ¹ and purposed to erect a castle there,' and encamped there three nights. After that he returned into England, and collected a vast army of the choice warriors of England, Normandy, Flanders, Anjou, Gascony, and all ᵃ Prydyn, and came to Oswestry, purposing to transport and destroy the whole of the Britons. And against him there came Owain Gwynedd and Cadwalader, the sons of Gruffudd, son of Cynan, and the whole force of Gwynedd with them; also the lord Rhys, son of Gruffudd, accompanied by the whole of South Wales; and Owain Cyveiliog, and Iorwerth the Red, son of Maredudd, ² of Moelmant,' and the sons of Madog, son of Maredudd, accompanied by the whole of Powys; also the two sons of Madog, son of Idnerth, and their whole country with them. And together, united and undaunted, they came into Edeyrnion, and encamped at Corwen. And after remaining there long in their tents, without one daring to attack the other, the king became extremely enraged, and moved his army into the woods of the Vale of Ceiriog, and ordered the woods to be cut and thrown down. And there a few chosen Welshmen came bravely to oppose him, who knew not what it was to be restrained in the absence of the princes; and many of the mightiest fell on each side. ⁵ And from thence the king led his army into the mountain of Berwyn,' and there the king encamped, with his ⁶ advanced troops, ⁶ in the mountains of Berwyn.' And after remaining there a few days, he was overtaken by a dreadful tempest of the sky, and extra-

---

ᵃ ⁷ the force of the North,

---

¹ *C. D.* ⁷ *C.*
⁶ *B.*

hestyl awyr a thra llifeireint glaƀogyd. A gƀedy
pallu ymborth idaƀ yd ymchoelaƀd y bebylleu ae lu y
vaestir ¹[gƀastatir] Lloegyr. Ac yn gyflaƀn odiruaƀr
lit y peris dallu y gƀystlon a vuassei ygkarchar gantaƀ, yr ystalym o amser kyn no hynny. Nyt amgen
deu uab Owein ᵃGƀyned Kadwallaƀn a Chynwric,
²[a Howel] a Maredud uab yr arglƀyd' Rys a
³[llawer or] rei ereill. A gƀedy kymryt kyghor y
symudaƀd y lu hyt yg Kaer Lleon, ac yno pebyllyaƀ
aoruc laƀer o dydyeu yny doeth llogeu o Dulyn ac
or dinassoed ereill ⁴o Iwerdon attaƀ. A gwedy nat
oed digaƀn gantaƀ hynny o logeu rodi rodyon aoruc
y logeu Dulyn ae gellƀg drachefyn, ac ynteu ae lu
a ymchoelaƀd y Loeger. Y ulƀydyn honno y kyrchaƀd
yr arglƀyd Rys kaer Aber Teiui ae chastell, ac y
torres, ac y llosges, adiruaƀr anreith a duc. Ac
achub castell Kil Gerran aoruc, a dala Robert ³[vab]
Ystefyn ae garcharu. ¹[Yn] y ulƀydyn honno drƀy
gennat Duƀ ac annoc yr Yspryt Glan y doeth koueint
o vyneich y Ystrat Fflur ⁵[gyntaf]. Ac yna y bu
uarƀ Llywelyn uab Owein Gƀyned y gƀr a ragores
mod paƀb o ⁶deƀred ¹[ar deƀred] ⁷a doethineb ar
doethineb o ymadrod, ar ymadrod o voesseu.

MCLXV. Y ulƀydyn rac ƀyneb y doeth y Ffreinc o
Benuro ar Fflemisseit y ymlad yn gadarn a chastell
Kil Gerran. A gƀedy llad llawer oe gƀyr ydymchoel-
assant adref yn llaƀ wac. Ac eilweith yd ymladassant

ᵃ/ ⁸ vrenhin, Catwallawn, a Kẏnwric a Moredud,
meibion

---

¹ B.
² E.

³ D.
⁴ yn, B.

ordinary torrents of rain. And when provisions had failed him, he removed his tents and his army to the open ¹ plains of England; and, full of extreme rage, he ordered the hostages, who had been previously long imprisoned by him, to be blinded; to wit, the two sons of Owain ᵃ Gwynedd, Cadwallon and Cynvrig, ² and Howel,' and Maredudd, son of the lord' Rhys, and ³ many others. After taking counsel, he removed his army to Caerleon, and there he encamped many days, until there came ships from Dublin, and other cities in Ireland, to him. And when he found the number of ships insufficient for him, he gave presents to the ships of Dublin, and discharged them; and himself and his army returned to England. The same year, the lord Rhys attacked the walls of Aberteivi and its castle, which he broke down and burned, and carried off a vast booty; and he seized the castle of Cilgerran, and took Robert, ³ son of' Stephen, and imprisoned him. ⁴ In that year, by the permission of God and the inspiration of the Holy Spirit, came a convent of monks ⁵ first to Strata Florida. And then died Llywelyn, son of Owain Gwynedd, the man who excelled every body in respect of bravery upon bravery, of wisdom upon wisdom, of conversation upon conversation, and of manners.

1165. The ensuing year, the French from Pembroke and the Flemings came to make a powerful attack upon the castle of Cilgerran; and after many of their men had been killed, they returned home empty

---

ᵃ/ ⁸ the king, Cadwallon, and Cynvrig, and Maredudd, the sons of

---

³ *B. D.*
⁶ deṍrder, *B.*
⁷ o, *B.*
⁸ *D.*

a Chilgerran yn over heb ¹gaffel y castell. ²[Yn] y
vlẃydyn honno y distrywyt dinas Basin y gan Owein
³Gẃyned. ²[Ac yn] y vlẃydyn honny y gẃrtladẃyt
⁴Dieruut uab ⁵Mẃrchath oe genedyl ac ydaeth hyt
yn Normandi at vrenhin Lloeger y erfynieit idaẃ y
dodi yny gyuoeth drachefyn wedy kẃynaẃ wrthaẃ. Ac
yn y vlẃydyn honno y gẃrthladẃyt Iorẃerth Goch
uab Maredud oe genedyl ac oe gyfoeth ym Mochnant
y gan y deu Owein. Ar deu Owein hynny y ran-
nassant Uochnant y rygtunt, ac ydeuth Mochnant vch
Raeadyr y Owein Keueilaẃc, a Mochnant is Raeadyr
y Owein Vychan.

MCLXVI. Y vlẃydyn rac wyneb y kyfunaẃd Owein a
⁶[Chatwaladyr] meibon Gruffud ab Kynan o Wyned
a Rys ab Gruffud ab Rys o Deheubarth yn erbyn
⁷[a gýrru fo ar] Owein Kefeilaẃc, ac y dugant y
gantaẃ ⁸Gaer Einaẃn,' ac y rodassant y Owein Vychan
uab Madaẃc uab Maredud ⁷[o Walwern]. Odyna yd
ennillassant Davalwern, a honno arodet yr arglẃyd
Rys kanys oe gyfoeth y dywetit y hanfot. Ny bu
uaẃr wedy hynny yny doeth Owein Keueilaẃc a llu
or Ffreinc y gyt ac ef am benn castell ⁸Kaer Einaẃn'
yr hẃn aẃnathoed Kymry kyn no hynny. A gẃedy
ennill y castell y dorri a ⁹ẃnaethant ae losgi a llad
yr holl ¹⁰gastellwyr. Yn diẃed y ulẃydyn honno y
kyrchaẃd Owein a Chatwaladyr tywyssogyon Gẃyned,
ar arglẃyd Rys tywyssaẃc o Deheubarth ae lluoed ²[y]
gyt ac ẃynt am benn castell Rudlan yn Tegeigyl,

---

¹ gael, *B.*
² *B.*
³ ab Grufud, *D.*
⁴ Diermit, *B.* Diermid, *D.*
⁵ Mwrchad, *D.*
⁶ *B. C. D.*

handed. And a second time they fought against Cilgerran in vain, without getting the castle. ² In that year, Basingwerk was destroyed by Owain Gwynedd. ³ And in' the same year, Diermid, son of Murchath, was expelled from his people, and went into Normandy, to the king of England, to request him to reinstate him in his dominion, having laid his complaints before him. And in that year, Iorwerth the Red, son of Maredudd, was driven from his people and his territory in Mochnant by the two Owains. And those two Owains divided Mochnant between them; Mochnant above the cataract came to Owain Cyveiliog, and Mochnant below the cataract to Owain the Little.

1166. The ensuing year, Owain and ⁶ Cadwalader, the sons of Gruffudd, son of Cynan, from Gwynedd, and Rhys, son of Gruffudd, son of Rhys, from South Wales, united against Owain Cyveiliog, ⁷ and put him to flight;' and they took from him Caereinion, and gave it to Owain the Little, son of Madog, son of Maredudd, ⁷ of Walwern.' From thence they won Tavalwern; and that was given to the lord Rhys, as it was said to have appertained to his dominion. It was not long afterwards before Owain Cyveiliog came, having an army of the French with him, against the castle of Caereinion, which the Welsh had previously erected; and having gained the castle, they broke it down and burned it, and killed all the garrison. In the close of that year, Owain and Cadwalader, princes of Gwynedd, and the lord Rhys, prince of South Wales, accompanied by their armies, came against the castle of Rhuddlan in Tegeingl;

---

⁷ *D.*
⁹ *Kereinavn, D.*

⁹ *ỏnaeth, B.*
¹⁰ *ỏarcheitỏeit, B.*

ᵃ ac eisted ẏrthaẇ trimis aorugant. A gẇedy hynny cael y castell ae dorri, ae losgi, a chastell arall ¹ [Prestattvn heuyt] y gyt ac ef yr ² molyant y Gymry yn hyfryt uudugaẇl paẇb yẇ gẇlat.'

MCLXVII. ¹ [Yn] y ulẇydyn rac wyneb y llas Gẇrgeneu abat a Llaẇden y nei y gan Gynan ᵇ ac Owein ³ [Gwynedd].

MCLXVIII. Y ulẇydyn rac ẇyneb y rydhaẇyt Robert uab Ystefyn o garchar yr arglẇyd Rys y gyveillt. Ac y duc ⁴ Diernut uab Mẇrchath ef hyt yn Iwerdon gyt ac ef. Ac yr tir y doethant y Lẇch Garmon, ac ennill y kastell awnaethant.

MCLXIX. Y ulẇydyn rac ẇyneb y llas Meuruc uab Adam ⁵ [o Buellt] drẇy dẇyll yn y gẇsc y gan Uaredud Bengoch y gefynderẇ. Yn diwed y ulẇydyn honno mis Tachẇed y bu uarẇ Owein Gẇyned uab Gruffud ab Kynan tywyssaẇc Gẇyned, gẇr diruaẇr y uolyant ac anueidraẇl y brudder ae uoned ae gedernit, ⁶ ae deẇred yg Kymry, ¹ [ynn anoruodedic oe uebyt] wedy anneuryf uudugolyaetheu, heb omed ⁷ neb eiryoet or arch a geissei, wedy kymryt penyt a chyffes ¹ [lan] ac ediuarẇch a chymun rinwedeu corff Crist, ac oleẇ ac aghenn.

MCLXX. Deg mlyned athrugein achant a mil oed oet Crist pan ladaẇd Dauyd ab Owein Howel uab Owein y braẇt hynaf idaẇ.

ᵃ′ ⁸ ac ẏno ẏbuant tri mis ẏn adeiliat castell gẇedẏ torri ẏ castell ẏ gafsant ẏno aẏ llosgi achastell Prestattvn ac ẏmchwelut adref ẏ ev gwlat ẏn hẏvrẏt lawen. ᵇ ⁹ ap

---

¹ B.
² ymchoelaẇd, B.
³ E.

⁴ Diermyt, D.
⁵ D.

ᵃand they sat before it three months. And then they got the castle, broke it, and burned it, with another castle, ¹Prestatyn also,' to the glory of the Welsh; and then every one, happy and victorious, to his own country.'

1167. ¹In the ensuing year, Gurgeneu the abbot, and Llawdden, his nephew, were slain by Cynan ᵇand Owain ³Gwynedd.

1168. The ensuing year, Robert, son of Stephen, was released from the prison of the lord Rhys, his friend; and Diermid, son of Murchath, took him with him to Ireland, and they landed at Lough Garmon, where they gained the castle.

1169. The ensuing year, Meurug, son of Adam ⁵of Buellt,' was killed, through treachery, in his sleep, by Maredudd Redhead, his cousin. In the end of that year, the month of November, died Owain Gwynedd, son of Gruffudd, son of Cynan, prince of Gwynedd, a man of great celebrity, and of the most extraordinary sagacity, nobleness, fortitude, and bravery in Wales, ⁶invincible from his youth,' after numberless victories,—who never denied any one the request he made,—after undergoing penance and ⁶holy confession, and repentance, and the communion of the sacraments of the Body of Christ, and extreme unction.

1170. One thousand one hundred and seventy was the year of Christ, when David, son of Owain, killed his eldest brother Howel, son of Owain.

ᵃ'⁸ and there they remained three months erecting a castle, after breaking down the castle which they found there, and burning it, with the castle of Prestatyn; and they returned happy and joyful to their country.   ᵇ⁹ son of

---

⁶ a, B. | ³ D.
⁷ dyn, B. | ⁹ B. C. D. E.

MCLXXI. Y vlẃydyn rac uyneb y llas Thomas archescob ¹[Keint] gẃr maẃr y grefyd ae santeidrẃyd ae gyfyaẃnder, ²ae gyghor, ac ³[o] annoc Henri urenhin Lloegyr y pumhet dyd gẃedy duẃ Nadolic ger bronn allaẃr y Drindaẃt yny gapel ehun yg Gheint ae escobaẃl wisc ymdanaẃ, a delẃ y groc yn y laẃ y llas ¹[achledỳfeu] ar diẃed yr efferen. Yn y vlẃydyn honno y mordẃyaẃd Rickert iarll Terstig uab Gilbert ⁴ vẃa kadarn' a chadarn varchaẃclu ³[y] gyt ac ef y Iwerdon. Ac yny kyrch kyntaf y kymerth Porth Lachi. A gẃedy gẃneuthur kyveillach a Dieruut vrenhin ᵃ ac erchi y verch' yn briaẃt, ac o nerth hẃnnẃ y cauas Dinas Dulyn drẃy wneuthur diruaẃr aerua. Ac yny vlẃydyn honno y bu uarẃ Ropert uab Llyẃarch. Ac y bu uarẃ Dieruut vrenhin Largines, ac y cladẃyt yn y dinas a elwit Fferna. Ac yny vlẃydyn honno y magẃyt teruysc y rẃg brenhin Lloegyr a brenhin Ffreinc amlad yr archescob. Kanys brenhin Lloegyr a rodassei yn veicheu y vrenhin Freinc Henri ⁵tywyssaẃc Bẃrgẃin a ⁶Thybaẃt ieuanc y vrawt meibon oed y rei hynny ⁷yr Tibaẃt tywyssaẃc Bẃrgẃin, a iarll Fflandrys a llaẃer o rei ereill pan wnaeth kymot ar archescob hyt na wnaei argyẃed idaẃ byth. A gẃedy clybot o Alexander bap rylad yr archescob anuon ³[y] llythyreu at urenhin Freinc a ẃnaeth, ac at y meicheu ereill. A gorchymyn udunt drẃy yscymundaẃt kymell brenhin Lloegyr y dyuot y lys Rufein y wneuthur iaẃn am ageu yr

---

ᵃ' ⁸ y verch agymerth

---

¹ D. | ² B.
³ o, B. | ⁴ Stragbow, D.

1171. The ensuing year, Thomas, archbishop ¹of
Canterbury,' was killed ¹with swords,' at the instigation of Henry, king of England,—a man great for his
piety, and his holiness, and his equity, and his counsel,
on the fifth day after Christmas Day, in front of the
altar of the Trinity, in his own chapel, at Canterbury,
clothed in his episcopal robe, having the image of
the cross in his hand, at the conclusion of the mass.
In that year, Rickert, earl of Terstig, son of Gilbert
Strongbow, having with him a powerful body of cavalry, sailed for Ireland. And in the first attack he
took Port Lachi; and after having formed a friendship
with king Diermid, ᵃ and demanded his daughter'
in marriage, with his aid he got possession of the
city of Dublin, through immense slaughter. In the
same year, Robert, son of Llywarch, died; and Diermid, king of Leinster, died, and was buried in the
city called Ferna. And in that year, a contention
was engendered between the king of England and
the king of France, on account of the murder of the
archbishop; for the king of England had delivered,
as pledges, to the king of France, Henry, duke of
Burgundy, and his brother ⁶Theobald the younger,
who were sons of Theobald, duke of Burgundy, and
earl of Flanders, with many others, when he made
a compact with the archbishop, that he would never
do him an injury. And after pope Alexander had
heard that the archbishop had been put to death,
he sent letters to the king of France, and the other
pledges, commanding them, on pain of excommunication, to compel the king of England to appear at
the court of Rome, to make satisfaction for the death

ᵃ' ³ he took his daughter

³ duc, *D.*
⁶ Theobaldus, *D.*
⁷ y, *B.*
⁸ *B.*

archescob. Ac ỽrth hynny anesmỽythaỽ a ỽnaethant o bop aruaeth ar y ¹ tremygu ef. A phan welas Henri vrenhin hynny dechreu gỽadu aoruc hyt nat oe gyghor ef y llas yr archescob, ac anuon kenadeu aỽnaeth ² at y pab' y venegi na allei ef vynet y Rufein drỽy yr achỽysson hynny. Ygkyfrỽg hynny y kilyaỽd ran uaỽr or ulỽydyn. A thra yttoedit yn hynny tu draỽ yr mor y kynullaỽd yr arglỽyd Rys uab Gruffud lu am benn Owein Keueilaỽc y daỽ ³[gan ẏ verch] ar vedyr y darestỽg. Kanys y genifer gỽeith y gallei Owein gỽrthỽynebu yr arglwyd Rys y gỽrthỽynebei ⁴[ynteu]. A Rys ae kymhellaỽd y darestỽg itaỽ. Ac y kymerth seith ỽystyl gantaỽ. Ygkyfrỽg hynny ofynhau aỽnaeth y brenhin yr ebostolaỽl ysgymundaỽt ac adaỽ gỽladoed Freinc ymchoelut y Loegyr, a dywedut y mynnei uynet y darestỽg Iwerdon. Ac ỽrth hynny ymgynnullaỽ a oruc ataỽ holl dyỽyssogyon Lloegyr a Chymry. Ac yna y deuth attaỽ yr arglỽyd Rys, or lle ydoed yn Llwyn Danet amgylch yrỽyl y ganet yr arglwydes Veir. Ac ymgyfeillaỽ a ⁵wnaeth ar brenhin drỽy adaỽ ⁴[idaỽ] drychan meirch; a phedeir mil o ychen a ᵃphetỽar gỽystyl ar hugeint.' ᵇA gỽedy hynny y denessaaỽd y brenhin y Deheubarth. Ac ynyr hynt honno ar auon ỽysc y duc gantaỽ' Iorwoerth uab Owein uab Cradaỽc uab Grufud. Ac o achaỽs hynny y distrywaỽd Iorwoerth ⁴[ap Yỽein] ac deu uab

---

ᵃ/ ⁶ xiiii o wẏstlon ar hẏnnẏ.

ᵇ/ ⁷ Odẏno ẏd aeth ẏ Gaerllion ar Wysc ac aduc ẏdinas ẏar

---

¹ teruyscu, *B.* ³ *D.*
²/ dat, *B.* ⁴ *B.*

of the archbishop. Thereupon they became uneasy
lest they should in any way treat him with contempt.
And when king Henry perceived this, he began to
deny that it was through his counsel the archbishop
had been killed; and despatched messengers to the
pope, declaring that he could not go to Rome because
of those matters. In the meanwhile, a great part of
the year had run out. During that transaction on
the other side of the sea, the lord Rhys, son of
Gruffudd, assembled an army against Owain Cyveiliog, his son in law, ³'by his daughter,' with the intention of subduing him; because as often as Owain
could resist the lord Rhys, he also resisted him.
And Rhys compelled him to submit; and he took
seven hostages from him. In that interval, the king
became alarmed at the apostolical excommunication,
and left the French territories, and returned to England, giving out that he would go and subdue Ireland.
Accordingly, he convoked to him all the princes of
England and Wales. And then the lord Rhys came
to him from the place where he was at Llwyn Danet,
about the feast on which was born the lady Mary.
And he entered into friendship with the king, by promising him three hundred horses, and four thousand
oxen, ᵃ'with twenty-four hostages.' ᵇAfter that the
king proceeded to South Wales; and in this journey,
upon the river Usk he took' Iorwerth, son of Owain,
son of Caradog, son of Gruffudd. And on that account
Iorwerth, ⁴'son of Owain,' with his two sons, Owain

---

a'⁶ with fourteen hostages besides.

b'⁷ From thence he proceeded to Caerleon upon
Usk, and took the city from

---

³ ornc. *B.*   ⁷ *D.*
⁴ *C. D.*

Owein a Howel a anyssit idaỽ o Agharat uerch
[1] Uchtrut escob Llan Daf. A Morgan uab Seisyll
uab Dyfynwal, o [2] Agharat uerch Owein chỽaer [3][y]
Iorwoerth uab Oỽein gyt a llawer o rei ereill dref
Gaer Llion ac y [4]llosget hyt y castell, ac y diffeithaỽd y wlat hayach o gỽbyl. Ac yna y deuth y
brenhin a diruaỽr lu gantaỽ hyt ym Penuro yr vnvet
dyd ar dec [5] o galan Hydref, ac y rodes yr arglỽyd
Rys Geredigyaỽn ac Ystrat Tyỽi ac [6]Ystlỽyf ac
[7] Euelfre. Ac ynyr haf hỽnnỽ yd adeilassei yr arglỽyd
Rys gastell Aber Teiui o vein a morter yr hỽnn
adistrywassei kyn no hynny pan y duc y ar iarll
Clar ac y [a] dileaỽd Robert uab Ystefyn o Nest
uerch Rys ab Teỽdỽr; ar Nest honno a oed vodrup
y Rys a Robert yn gefynderỽ idaỽ. A brodyr
Robert oed Dauyd escob Mynyỽ, a Gỽilim Bastard.
Meibon oed y rei hynny y Erald ystiwert. Ac yna
ydaeth Rys o gastell Aber Teiui hyt yggastell Penvro
y ymdidan ar brenhin y deudecuet dyd o galan
Hydref a duỽ Sadỽrn oed y dyd hỽnnỽ. Ac yd erchis
Rys gynullaỽ y meirch oll aadaỽssei yr brenhin y
Aber Teifi ual y beynt baraỽt ỽrth eu hanuon yr
brenhin. A thrannoeth duỽ Sul yd ymchoeles Rys
[8] ac ethol a ỽnaeth' whe meirch a phetwar ugeint
ỽrth eu hanuon drannoeth yr brenhin. A gỽedy dyuot
hyt y Ty Gỽynn clybot a [9] ỽnaeth ryvynet y brenhin
y Vynyỽ y bererinaỽ ac offrymaỽ a [9] ỽnaeth y brenhin

---

[a] [10] delhiis

---

[1] Vchrit, D. [4] llosces, B.
[2] Dudgu, C. D. [5] ar, B.
[3] B. [6] Arwistli, D.

and Howel, who had been born to him of Angharad,
daughter of ¹ Uchtryd, bishop of Llandaf, and Morgan,
son of Seisyll, son of Dyvnwal, by ²Angharad, daughter
of Owain, and sister to Iorwerth, son of Owain, and
many others, destroyed the town of Caerleon, and
burned all to the castle, and laid the whole country
nearly waste. Then the king proceeded with a vast
army into Pembroke, on the eleventh day of the
calends of October, and gave to the lord Rhys Ceredigion
and the Vale of Tywi, and ⁶Ystlwyv and
⁷Euelvre. And in that summer the lord Rhys built
the castle of Aberteivi, with stone and mortar, which
he had previously demolished, when he took it from
the earl of Clare, and ᵃremoved Robert, son of
Stephen by Nest, the daughter of Rhys, son of
Tewdwr. That Nest was aunt to Rhys, and Robert
was his cousin; and the brothers of Robert were
David, bishop of Menevia, and William the Bastard;
and those were sons to Gerald the steward. And
then Rhys went from the castle of Aberteivi to the
castle of Pembroke, to speak with the king, on the
twelfth day of the calends of October, and that day
was a Saturday. And Rhys ordered the horses, which
he had promised the king, to be collected at Aberteivi,
to be in readiness to be sent to the king. And
on the following day, Sunday, Rhys returned; and he
selected eighty-six horses, to be sent the following
day to the king. And having come to the White
House, he heard that the king had gone to Menevia,
on a pilgrimage; and in Menevia the king made an

ᵃ ⁷ captured

---

⁷ Elvael, D.
ᵇ⁷ adethol aoruc, B.

⁹ oruc, B.
¹⁰ B. C. D.

ym Mynyŵ deu ¹gappann cor' o bali ar vedyr cantoryeit y wassanaethu Duŵ ²[a Deŵi]. Ac offrymaŵ hefyt a ŵnaeth ³[dỳrneit o arÿant amgỳlch] dec swllt. Ac ervynneit aoruc Dauyd uab Geralt y gŵr aoed escob ym Mynyŵ yna yr brenhin vŵytta y gyt ac ef y dyd hŵnnŵ; a gŵrthot y gŵahaŵd aoruc y brenhin, o achaŵs gŵeglyt gormod dreul yr escob. Dyuot eissoes aoruc ef ar escob ªathrychanŵr' gyt ac ŵynt y ginaŵa, a Rickert iarll, gŵr a ⁴oed o Iŵerdon, y ymgyfeillaŵ ar brenhin. Kanys o anuod y brenhin y ᵇdathoed o Iŵerdon;' a llaŵer o rei ereill a ginaŵssant oc eu seuyll. Ac yn ebrŵyd gŵedy ⁵kinyaŵ ydysgkynnaŵd y brenhin ar y veirch. ⁶[A] glaŵ maŵr oed yn y dyd hŵnŵ, a duŵ gŵyl Vihagel oed. Ac yna ydymchoelaŵd y Benuro. A phan gigleu Rys hynny anuon y meirch yr brenhin aoruc ⁶[or blaen, val y gallei uynet at y brenhin yn ol kymryt y meirch]. A gŵedy dŵyn y meirch rac bronn y brenhin kymryt aŵnaeth vn ar bymthec ar hugeint a etholes, a dywedut nat ⁷y bot yn reit idaŵ ŵrthunt y kymerassei ŵynt, namyn yr talu ⁸diolŵch y Rys a vei vŵy no chynt. ᶜA gŵedy regi bod uelly yr brenhin dyuot aoruc Rys at y brenhin, a ⁹chael daŵn awnaeth gyr bron y ᵈbrenhin, a' rydhau aoruc y brenhin idaŵ Howel y uab, a vuassei gantaŵ yggŵystyl ynhir kyn no hynny ¹⁰[ÿn Lloegr], a rodi oet aoruc y brenhin idaŵ am y gŵystlon ereill adylyei Rys y dalu yr

---

ᵃ' ¹¹ a thri chanhonŵr   ᵇ' ¹² daeth y Iwerdon;
ᶜ' ¹³ Agwedỳ ev dỳuot hỳt ỳ Tỳ Gwin ỳgỳt
ᵈ' ¹¹ lygeit,

---

¹ cantelcop, *D.* cántel kop, *E.*
² *B. C.*
³ *B. D. E.*
⁴ dathoed, *B.*
⁵ kinnaŵha, *B.*
⁶ *B.*
⁷ yr, *B.*

offering of two choral caps of velvet, intended for the singers in serving God ²and St. David;' and he also offered ³ a handful of silver, about' ten shillings. Then David, son of Gerald, who at the time was bishop of Menevia, besought the king to eat with him on that day; but the king declined the invitation, in order to avoid an excess of expence to the bishop. Nevertheless he came to the bishop to dinner, attended ᵃ by three hundred men,' and earl Rickert, a man who came from Ireland to obtain the friendship of the king, for without the consent of the king ᵇ had he come from Ireland;' and many others also dined there standing. Shortly after dinner the king mounted his horses; and there was heavy rain on that day, which was Michaelmas day; and he returned to Pembroke. When Rhys heard of this, he sent the horses to the king, ⁶ before hand, that he might go to the king after he had received the horses.' And on the horses being brought before the king, he took thirty-six that he selected, saying, that it was not from want of them they were accepted, but to express his thanks to Rhys more than before. ᶜ And after having thus pleased the king, Rhys repaired to him, and obtained grace before ᵈ the king;' and' the king released his son Howel, who had been long before with him ¹⁰ in England' as hostage; and the king granted him time in respect of the other hostages, which Rhys was bound to deliver to the king;

ᵃ/¹¹ by three canons,   ᵇ/¹² had he come to Ireland; ᶜ/¹³ And when they had come together to the White House,   ᵈ/¹¹ his eyes;

---

⁸ diolch, *B.*   ¹¹ *B.*
⁹ chaffel, *B.*   ¹² *C. D.*
¹⁰ *D.*   ¹³ *D.*

brenhin. Ac am y dreth a dywetpŵyt ury yn y delei y brenhin o Iwerdon. Parattoi llyges aŵnaethpŵyt ac nyt oed adas y gŵynt udunt. Kanys amser nyŵlaŵc oed, a breid y keit yna yt aeduet yn un lle yg Kymry. A gŵedy dyuot [1][gwil] Galixtus bap, erchi aŵnaeth y brenhin gyrru y llogeu or borthua yr mor. Ar dyd hŵnnŵ ysgynnu [2] y llogeu aorugant. Ac etto nyt oed gymŵynassgar y gŵynt udunt. Ac achaŵs hynny ymchoelut aŵnaeth drachefyn yr tir, ac ychydic o nifer y gyt ac ef. Ar nos gyntaf wedy hynny ydyskynnaŵd y logeu gan [3] ŵylaŵ o honaŵ ef ehun ac o baŵp oe wyr ; a thrannoeth duŵ Sul oed yr vnuet dyd ar bymthec o galan Racuyr drŵy hyvrŵyd awel wynt y dyblygaŵd y logeu y dir Iwerdon. [4] [Ac yno ytrigyaŵd ef ygayaf hŵnnŵ hep ŵneuthur argyŵed y ŵyr Ywerdon].

MCLXXII. Y ulŵydyn rac ŵyneb y bu diruaŵr varŵolyaeth ar y llu [5][a] oed [5][y] gyt ar brenhin yn Iwerdon o achaŵs newydder y [a] diargrynedigyon wynoed,' ac o achaŵs kyfygdŵr o newyn. Am na allei y llogeu a newidyeu yndunt vordŵyaŵ attunt y gayaf, drŵy y dymestlaŵl gandared mor Iŵerdon. Y ulŵydyn honno y bu uarŵ Katwaladyr ab Grufud ab Kynan vis Maŵrth. Ac yny vlŵydyn honno yd ymchoelaŵd brenhin Lloegyr o Iwerdon, gan adaŵ yno uarŵneit a marchogyon urdolyon drostaŵ o achaŵs y kenadeu a dathoed attaŵ y gan y pab a Lowys urenhin Ffreinc. A duŵ Gŵener y Croglith y doeth [5][hyt] ym Penuro, ac yno y trigyaŵd y Pasc hŵnnŵ ; a duŵ Llun Pasc

---

[a] [5] diarueredigyon uŵydeu,

---

[1] B.D.
[2] yr, B.
[3] hŵylaŵ, B.

and also in respect of the tribute, that has been mentioned above, until the king should come from Ireland. A fleet was prepared, but the wind was not favourable for them; for it was a misty season, and then scarcely any ripe corn could be had in any part of Wales. And when ¹'the feast of' pope Calixtus had come, the king ordered the ships out of the port to sea; and on that day they went on board the ships. But yet the wind was not favourable to them, and on that account he, with a small retinue, returned to land. And on the first night after that he ascended the ships, himself and all his men steering; and the following day, being Sunday, the sixteenth day of the calends of December, with a fair gale, the ships bent their course to the land of Ireland. ⁴'And there he remained that winter, without doing any injury to the people of Ireland.'

1172. The ensuing year, there was a dreadful mortality among the army that was with the king in Ireland, on account of the ᵃ'newness and unfermented state of wines,' and because of the miseries of famine; the ships with merchandise not being able to sail to them during the winter, owing to the tempestuous violence of the Irish sea. That year Cadwalader, son of Gruffudd, son of Cynan, died, in the month of March. And in the same year the king of England returned from Ireland, leaving there barons and noble knights in his stead, and this on account of the messengers that came to him from the pope and Louis, king of France. And on Good Friday he arrived at Pembroke; and there he remained during that Easter.

ᵃ/ ⁵ unaccustomed meats,

---

⁴ B. C.   ⁵ B.

yd ymdidanaŵd a Rys yn Talacharn ar y fford. Ac odyno yd aeth y Loeger. A gŵedy mynet y brenhin o Gaer Dyf hyt y Castell Newyd ar Ŵysc anuon awnaeth y erchi y Iorwoerth uab Owein dyuot y ymwelet ac ef, ac y ymdidan am hedŵch. A rodi kadarn gygreir aoruc idaŵ ac oe veibon. A phan yttoed Owein uab Iorwoerth gŵas ieuanc grymus hegar yn parottoi o gyghor y dat ae wyrda y vynet ¹[y] gyt ae dat y lys y brenhin, y ᵃkyfaruu ŵr iarll Bristaŵ ac ef ar y fford yn dyuot a Gaer Dyf' ac y ²lladyssant. A gŵedy y lad ef yna y diffeithaŵd y dat a Howel y vraŵt a llaŵer o rei ereill heb ymdiret or achaŵs hŵnnŵ yr brenhin o neb un mod cyuoeth y brenhin hyt yn Henfford a Chaer Loyŵ drŵy lad a llosgi ac anreithaŵ heb drugared. Ac yna heb odric ydaeth y brenhin y Ffreinc wedy gossot yr arglŵyd Rys yn Iustus yn holl Deheubarth. ᵇYgkyfrŵg hynny y delit Seisyll ab ³Dyfynwal a' Ieuan uab Dyfynwal a Ridit drŵy dŵyll y gan wyr y brenhin, ac y carcharŵyt yg kastell Abergefenni.'

ᵃ⸍ ⁴ doeth gwŷr iarll Brustov o Caer Dỳf ford ỳ Castell Newỳd ar Wỳsg

ᵇ⸍ ⁴ Yn hỳnnỳ mỳs Aust ỳcavas Seissell a Dỳvỳnwal a Ieuan ap Seissill ap Ririt castell Aber Gevennỳ odwỳll ỳgan wỳr ỳ brenhin. ⁵A Ieuan vab Seissyll ap Riryt y mis Awst y gan wyr y brenhin drwy dwyll yn Abergeuenni.

¹ B.
² lladassant, B.
³ Seissyll ab, B.

On Easter Monday he had an interview with Rhys, on the road, at Talacharn; and from thence he went to England. After the king had gone from Cardiff as far as Newcastle upon Usk, he sent to require Iorwerth, son of Owain, to come to an interview with him, and to discourse about peace, giving a safe conduct to himself and to his sons. And as Owain, son of Iorwerth, a finely grown and amiable young man, was preparing, by the advice of his father, and liege men, to accompany his father to the court of the king, ᵃ a man of the earl of Bristol met him upon the road coming from Cardiff,' and killed him. And when he was killed, then his father, with his brother Howel, and many others, not trusting on that account to the king, destroyed by every means the territory of the king, as far as Hereford and Gloucester, by killing and burning and laying waste, without mercy. And then, without delay, the king proceeded to France, after appointing the lord Rhys to be justice over the whole of South Wales. ᵇ In that interval, Seisyll, son of ³ Dyvnwal, and' Ieuan, son of Dyvnwal, and Rhirid were seized treacherously by the king's men, and were imprisoned in the castle of Abergavenny.

ᵃ' ⁴ the men of the earl of Bristol came from Cardiff, by way of New Castle upon Usk,

ᵇ' ⁴ Then in the month of August, Seisyll, and Dyvnwal, and Ieuan, son of Seisyll, son of Rhirid, obtained the castle of Abergavenny through treachery from the men of the king. ⁵ And Ieuan, son of Seisyll, son of Rhirid, in the month of August, from the men of the king, through treachery, in Abergavenny.

---

⁴ *D.* | ⁵ *C.*

MCLXXIII. Y ulŵydyn rac ŵyneb y bu diruaŵr ardymer ¹ ar hinda ar hyt y gayaf ar gŵannŵyn a mis Mei hyt dyŵ Ieu ²kychavel. Ar dyd hŵnnŵ y kyuodes diruaŵr dymystyl yn yr aŵyr o ³ daraneu a myllt' a chorwynt a chawadeu kenllysc, a ⁴ glaŵ yrei adorres keigeu y gŵyd, ac a vyryaŵd y coedyd hyt y llaŵr; a ryŵ bryfet adoeth y ulŵydyn honno y yssu deil y gŵyd, yny diffrŵythaŵd hayach pob ryŵ prenn. ⁵[Yn] y vlŵydyn honno ar ulŵydyn kyn no hi y collet lliaŵs or dynyon ar anniueileit, ac nyt heb achaŵs. Kanys yn y ulŵydyn honno y ganet ⁶[Meuric] mab yr arglŵyd Rys ⁶[ap Grufud] o uerch Uarednd uab Gruffud y nith verch y uraŵt. Ygkyfrŵg hynny pan yttoed Henri urenhin hynaf y tu draŵ yr mor ydeuth y uab Henri ieuaf urenhin neŵyd attaŵ, y ofyn idaŵ beth adylyei y wneuthur. Kanys kyt bei urenhin ef llaŵer oed idaŵ o uarchogyon, ac nyt oed gantaŵ ford y dalu kyuarŵsseu ⁷ a rodyon yr marchogyon o nys kymerei ynechŵyn y gan y dat. Ar amser hŵnnŵ oed Raŵys. Ae dat a dywaŵt ŵrthaŵ y rodei idaŵ ugein punt o vŵnei y wlat honno beunyd yn dreul ac na chaffei mŵy. Ac ynteu a dywaŵt na chlyŵssei ef eiryoet bot brenhin yn ŵr pae ⁵[nac dan baes] ac na bydei ynteu. A gŵedy kymryt or mab gygor ef a aeth y dinas Tŵrs y geissaŵ aryant echŵyn y gan vŵrdeisseit y dinas. A phan gigleu y brenhin hynny, anuon kenadeu aoruc y brenhin at y bŵrdeisseit, y wahard udunt dan boen ⁸ y holl da, nat echwynynt dim oe uab ef. A heb ohir anuon aoruc wyr da y warchadŵ y uab rac y uynet odyno yn dirybud y un lle. A gŵedy adnabot

---

¹ a, *B.*
² kyfarchauel, *B.*
³ taran a mellt, *B.*
⁴ olaŵogyd, *B.*

1173. The ensuing year, there was an extraordinary season of fine weather throughout the winter and spring, and the month of May, until Ascension Thursday. And on that day there arose a most violent storm in the sky, of thunder and lightning, and whirlwind, and showers of hail and rain, which broke the branches of the timber, and threw the trees to the ground. And that year, some insects came to devour the leaves of the woods, so that every kind of tree was almost withered. ⁵In that same year, and the year before it, many people and animals were lost, and not without a cause; for, in that year was born ⁶Meurug, son of the lord Rhys, ⁶son of Gruffudd,' of the daughter of Maredudd, son of Gruffudd, his niece, the daughter of his brother. In that interval, when king Henry the eldest was beyond the sea, his son Henry the younger, the new king, came to him to enquire what he ought to do; for, since he was king, he had many knights, and he had no means of rewarding those knights with presents and gifts, unless he received a loan from his father; and this was in the time of Lent. And his father said to him that he would give him twenty pounds a day, of the money of that country, for expenditure, and that he should not have more. And he said that he had never heard of a king being a man on pay, ⁵or under wages,' and that neither would he be. After the son had taken advice, he went to the city of Tours, to obtain money on loan from the burgesses of the city; and when the king heard that, he sent messengers to the burgesses, to forbid them, under pain of losing all their property, to lend any thing to his son. And without delay he sent trusty men to watch his son, lest he should go anywhere without notice. And

⁵ B.
⁴ D.

⁷ o, B.
⁸ en, B.

or mab hynny peri aoruc medwi nossweith y gṽercheitweit aoed arnaṽ olys y brenhin. A gṽedy eu hadaṽ yn ¹ vedwon 'yn kysgu dianc a ² ṽnaeth ac ychydic o nifer y gyt ac ef hyt yn llys brenhin Ffreinc y whegrṽn. Ygkyfrṽg hynny yd anuones ³[Rŷs ap Grufud] Howel y uab hyt att yr hen vrenhin tu draṽ ⁴yr mor ar vedyr trigyaṽ yny llys a gṽassanaethu ar y brenhin ahaedu ⁵y gedymdeithas o bei vyṽ, ac' ual y gallei y brenhin ymdiret y Rys ⁶o bei vyṽ;' ar brenhin a aruolles y mab yn enrydedus, a diruaṽr diolch awnaeth y Rys. Ac yna aflonydu a oruc y brenhin ieuanc ar gyuoeth y dat drṽy nerth y whegrṽn, a ⁷Thybaṽt iarll Bṽrgṽyn, a ᵃiarll Fflandrys. A thra vyd y ᵇbrenhin yn ymrysson uelly tu draṽ yr mor y dechreuaṽd Iorwoerth uab Owein o Gṽynllṽg ymlad a Chaer Llion, y pymthecuet dyd o galan Aṽst duṽ Merchyr. Ac a ostygaṽd y dreis oe rym ae nerth. Duṽ Sadṽrn wedy hynny, gṽedy ⁸dala duṽ Gṽener y dyd kyn no hynny y gṽyr aoed yn kadṽ ⁹y baeli. A throstunt ṽynteu drannoeth y rodet y kastell. A gṽedy hynny yr eilweith yr eildyd ¹⁰[arbymthec] o vis Medi y kyrchaṽd Howel uab Iorwoerth Went is Coet. A thrannoeth duṽ Gṽener y darestygaṽd yr holl wlat eithyr y ᶜcastell ac y kymerth wystlon o vchelwyr y wlat. ¹¹[Yn] y ulṽydyn honno y goreskynnaṽd Dauyd uab Owein Gṽyned idaṽ ehun ynys Von gṽedy dehol o honaṽ Uaelgṽn uab Oṽein y vraṽt hyt yn Iwerdon.

ᵃ ¹² chŷghorwr   ᵇ ¹¹ brenhined   ᶜ ¹¹ kestyll

---

¹ veddṽeit, B.
² oruc, B.
³ D.
⁴ y, B.

⁵ʹ ketymeithas y brenhin a uei uṽy, B.
⁶ʹ a uei uṽy, B.
⁷ Theobaldus, D.

when the son became acquainted with this, he caused the guards that were over him from the palace to be made drunk on a certain night. Leaving them drunk and asleep, he escaped, accompanied by a small retinue, to the court of the king of France, his father in law. In that interval, ²Rhys, son of Gruffudd,' sent his son Howel to the old king, beyond the sea, with the intention of abiding at the court, and serving the king, so as to merit his favour if he should live, and that the king might confide in Rhys, if he should live. The king received the son honourably, and was extremely thankful to Rhys. And then the young king harassed the territory of his father, through the aid of his father in law, and ⁷Theobald, earl of Burgundy, and the ᵃ earl of Flanders. And whilst the ᵇ king contended thus beyond the sea, Iorwerth, son of Owain, of Gwenllwg, began to attack Caerleon, the fifteenth day of the calends of August, being Wednesday; and he forcibly reduced it by his power and strength. The Saturday afterwards, after having, on the previous Friday, captured the men who kept the outer court, the castle was delivered for their ransom. And after that, a second time, on the second day ¹⁰after the fifteenth' of the month of September, Howel, son of Iorwerth, attacked Gwent Iscoed; and the day following, Friday, he subdued the whole country, except the ᶜ castle, and took hostages of the chief men of the country. ¹¹ In that year David, son of Owain Gwynedd, subdued for himself the isle of Mona, after he had banished his brother Maelgwn, son of Owain, to Ireland.

---

a ¹² counsellor   b ¹¹ kings   c ¹¹ castles,

⁸ daly, *B.*
⁹ yr, *B.*
¹⁰ *B. C.*

¹¹ *B.*
¹² *D.*

MCLXXIV. Y ulẃydyn rac ẃyneb y goreskynnaẃd Dauyd uab Owein holl ẃyned gẃedy gẃrthlad o honaẃ y holl vrodyr ae holl ewythred. Y ulẃydyn honno y delis Dauyd uab Owein Vaelgẃn y vraẃt ac y karcharaẃd. Yn y vlẃydyn honno y bu uarẃ Kynan uab Owein Gẃyned.

MCLXXV. Yn y ulẃydyn gẃedy hynny y delis Howel ab Iorwoerth o Gaer Llion, heb ẃybot oe dat Oẃein Penn Carẃn y ᵃewythyr. A gẃedy tynnu y lygeit oe benn y peris y yspadu rac meithrin etifed o honaẃ a wledychei ¹[canys ef oed wir etived ar] ²[Caer Llion ẃedy hynny. Ac yna o deissyuyt gyrch duw Sadwrn rac wyneb y goresgynnaẃd Yffreinc] Gaer Llion. Ac y gyrrassant ymeith odyno Iorwoerth a Howel y vab. Yny ulẃydyn honno ³y hedychaẃd Henri vrenhin hynaf a Henri ieuaf, gẃedy diruaẃr distryẃedigaeth Normandi ae chyfnessafyeit wledyd. Ac yna y delis Davyd uab Owein drẃy dẃyll Rodri uab Owein y uraẃt un uam un dat ac ef, ac y carcharaẃd myẃn gefynneu ⁴[kyuyg] am geissaẃ cyfran o dref y dat gantaẃ. Ac yna y priodes y brenhin Dauyd hẃnnẃ ⁵Dam Em' chẃaer y vrenhin Lloeger drẃy debygu gallel o honaẃ kael y gyuoeth yn llonyd hedychaẃl or achaẃs hẃnnẃ. Ac yna y diegis Rodri o garchar Dauyd y vraẃt. A chyn diwed y ulẃydyn y gẃrthladaẃd ef Dauyd o Von ac o ẃyned, ᵇyny doeth drẃy auon' Gonẃy. Ac yna yd ymbarattoes yr arglẃyd Rys ab Gruffud ẃrth uynet y lys y brenhin ⁶[duw gwyl Iago apostol] hyt Ygkaer Loyẃ. Ac

---

ᵃ ⁷ gevynderw   ᵇ' ⁷ ewch

¹ D.   ³ yd, B.
² C.   ⁴ B.

THE CHRONICLE OF THE PRINCES.

1174. The ensuing year, David, son of Owain, got possession of the whole of Gwynedd, after he had expelled all his brothers and all his uncles. The same year, David, son of Owain, took his brother Maelgwn, and imprisoned him. In the same year, Cynan, son of Owain Gwynedd, died.

1175. In the year after that, Howel, son of Iorwerth, of Caerleon, seized Owain Pencarwn, his ᵃuncle, unknown to his father; and after taking his eyes out of his head, he caused him to be castrated, lest he should beget issue to govern, ¹for he would be the rightful heir to' ²Caerleon after that. And then by a sudden attack, the Saturday following, the French got possession of' Caerleon, and drove away from thence Iorwerth, and Howel his son. In that year, king Henry the elder was reconciled to Henry the younger, after vast destruction in Normandy, and its neighbouring countries. And then David, son of Owain, by treachery took Rhodri, son of Owain, his brother by the same mother and father, and confined him in ⁴strait fetters, for seeking to obtain from him a share of his father's patrimony. And then the same king David married ⁵dame Emma,' the sister of the king of England, imagining that he should be able to obtain his dominion quietly and peaceably on that account. And then Rhodri escaped from the prison of his brother David; and before the end of the year, he expelled David out of Mona, and out of Gwynedd ᵇuntil he passed through the river' Conway. And then, the lord Rhys, son of Gruffudd, prepared to go to the court of the king at Gloucester, ⁶on the feast of St. James the Apostle.'

ᵃ ⁷ cousin, ᵇ' ⁷ above

ᵛ Emme, *C. D.* ⁷ *D.*
⁶ *C. D.*

yduc ¹[y] gyt ac ef drȯy gygor y brenhin holl dywyssogyon y Deheu a uuessynt yggȯrthwyneb yr brenhin. Nyt amgen Katȯallaȯn uab Madaȯc o Vaelenyd y gefynderȯ, ac Einaȯn Clut o Eluael y daȯ gan y uerch, ac Einaȯn uab Rys o Werthrynyon y daȯ y llall. A Morgan ab Cradaȯc ab Iestyn o wlat Vorgan o Wladus y chwaer ²[a Grufud ap Iuor ap Meuryc o Seinhenyd ynei o Nest yhȯaer] a Iorwoerth uab Owein o Gaer Llion. A Seissyll uab Dyfynwal o Went uch Coet, y gȯr a oed yna yn briaȯt a Gȯladus chȯaer yr arglȯyd Rys. Hynny oll o dywyssogyon a ymchoelassant yw gȯladoed yn hedychaȯl gyt ar arglȯyd Rys y gȯr aoed garedickaf gyfeillt gan y brenhin yn yr amser hȯnnȯ, drȯy ymchoelut Kaer Llion drachefyn y Iorwoerth ab Owein. Yny lle wedy hynny y llas Seissyll uab Dyffynwal drȯy dȯyll arglȯyd Brecheinaȯc ³[ẏn castell Abergevenni] a chyt ac ef ⁴Ruffud y uab a llawer o bennaduryeit Gȯent. Ac yna y kyrchaȯd y Ffreinc lys Seissyll uab Dyfynwal, a gȯedy dala Gȯladus y wreic y lladyssant Gadȯaladyr y uab. Ar dyd hȯnnȯ y bu y druanaf aerua ar wyrda Gȯent. A gȯedy ygyhoededicka danllyȯychedic dȯyll honno ny beidaȯd neb or Kymry ymdiret yr Ffreinc. Ac yna y bu uarȯ Cadell uab Gruffud drȯy orthrȯm glefyt, ac y cladȯyt yn Ystrat Fflur wedy kymryt abit ycrefyd ymdanaȯ. Ac yna y llas ⁵Rickert abat ⁶Clerynaȯt myȯn manachlaȯc yn ymyl ⁷Reinys y gan neb vn anfydlaȯn uynach o vrath kyllell.

MCLXXVI. Y ulȯydyn rac ȯyneb y bu uarȯ Kynan abat y Ty Gȯynn a Dauyd escob Mynyȯ. Ac yny

¹ B.
² B. C. E.
³ D.
⁴ Geffrei, C. D.

And by the advice of the king he took with him all the princes of the South, who had been in opposition to the king; that is to say, Cadwallon, son of Madog, of Maelienydd, his cousin; and Einon Glud of Elvael, his son in law by his daughter; and Einon, son of Rhys of Gwerthrynion, his other son in law; and Morgan, son of Caradog, son of Iestin, by his sister Gwladus, of Glamorgan; ²and Gruffudd, son of Ivor, son of Meurug, of Senghenydd, his nephew by his sister Nest;' and Iorwerth, son of Owain, of Caerleon; and Seisyll, son of Dyvnwal, of Gwent Uchcoed, the man who was then married to Gwladus, sister of the lord Rhys. All those princes returned peaceably to their countries, along with the lord Rhys, the man who was the most beloved friend of the king at that time, after restoring Caerleon back to Iorwerth, son of Owain. Immediately after that, Seisyll, son of Dyvnwal, was slain, through the treachery of the lord of Brecheiniog, ³in the castle of Abergavenny,' and with him ⁴Gruffudd his son, and many of the chieftains of Gwent. And then the French repaired to the court of Seisyll, son of Dyvnwal; and after seizing Gwladus his wife, they killed his son Cadwalader. And on that day there was the most miserable slaughter of the good people of Gwent. And after that most open and flagitious treachery, none of the Welsh dared trust to the French. And then Cadell, son of Gruffudd, died of a severe disease, and was buried at Strata Florida, after taking the religious habit. And then ⁵Rickert, abbot of ⁶Clerynaut, was killed in a monastery near ⁷Rheims, by the stab of a knife from a faithless monk.

1176. The ensuing year died Cynan, abbot of the White House, and David, bishop of Menevia, after

---

⁵ Richard, *D.*
⁶ Clerval, *D.* Cleryuaüt, *B.*

⁷ Remys, *B. C.* Ramson, *D.*

ol y denessaaỗd ¹Pyrs ynescob. Ac yna y kynhalyaỗd yr arglỗyd Rys wled arbennic yn castell Aber Teiui, ac y gossodes deu ryỗ amrysson vn rỗg y beird ar ²prydydyon, ar llall' rỗg ³[y] telynoryon ⁴a chrythoryon a phibydyon ac amryuaelon gerd arwest; a dỗy gadeir a ossodes y vudugolyon yr amryssoneu. Ar rei hynny agyfoethoges ef o diruaỗryon rodyon. Ac yna y cauas gỗas ieuanc oe lys ³[ef] e hunan ⁵[mab i Cibon Grythwr] y uudugolyaeth o gerd arwest, a gỗyr Gỗyned agauas y uudugolyaeth o gerd dauaỗt. A phaỗb or kerdoryon ereill a gaỗssant y gan yr arglỗyd Rys kymeint ac a archyssant hyt na ỗrthladỗyt neb. Ar wled honno a gyhoedet vlỗydyn kyn y gỗneuthur ar hyt Kymry a Lloegyr a ⁶Phrydein ac Iỗerdon a llaỗer o wladoed ereill. Yn y ulỗydyn honno yny Graỗys ⁷yd ymgynullaỗd kyghor hyt yn Llundein ỗrth gadarnhau kyfreitheu yr eglỗysseu yno geir bronn kardinal o Rufein a dathoed yno ỗrth y neges honno. A gỗedy meithryn cynnỗryf y rỗg archescob Keint ac archescob Iorc y teruysgỗyt y kyghor. Kanys ydyd kyntaf or kygor ᵃyd achubassei archescob Iorc eistedua y gadeir or tu deheu yr cardinal yny lle y ⁸dylyer ac y gnottaei arch-

ᵃ/⁹ kýrchu aoruc archescop Keint lle delehe vot: athrannoeth ýd achubawt archescob Caer Efrauc ý lle hwnnw ýngwýd ý cardinaliet, ¹⁰kanys archesgob Keint a achubassei eisdedua yn gyntaf ac val yr oed y deu esgob drannoeth yn ymrysson am eu teilyngdodau yggwyd y kardinal,

¹ Perys, D.
²′ prydyon, ac arall, B.
³ B.
⁴ ar, B.
⁵ E.
⁶ Phrýdýn, D.

whom ¹ Pyrs succeeded as bishop. And the lord Rhys held a grand festival at the castle of Aberteivi, wherein he appointed two sorts of contention; one between the bards and poets, and the other between the harpers, fiddlers, pipers, and various performers of instrumental music; and he assigned two chairs for the victors in the contentions; and these he enriched with vast gifts. A young man of his own court, ⁵ son to Cibon the fiddler,' obtained the victory in instrumental song; and the men of Gwynedd obtained the victory in vocal song; and all the other minstrels obtained from the lord Rhys as much as they asked for, so that there was no one excluded. And that festival was proclaimed a year before it was held, throughout Wales and England and ⁶ Prydyn and Ireland, and many other countries. In that year, in Lent, a council was assembled in London, for confirming the laws of the churches there, in the presence of a cardinal who had come from Rome on that business. And a dispute having been fostered between the archbishop of Canterbury and the archbishop of York, the council was thrown into confusion. For on the first day of the council ᵃ the archbishop of York had secured the seat in the chair, on the right side of the cardinal, where it was due and customary for the arch-

ᵃ/³ the archbishop of Canterbury proceeded to the place where he ought to be; and the following day the archbishop of York secured that place in the presence of the cardinals, ² for the archbishop of Canterbury had first secured his seat, and as the two archbishops were the next day disputing for their privileges, in the presence of the cardinal,

---

⁷ yr, B.
⁸ dylyei, B.
⁹ D.
¹⁰ C.

escob Keint eisted. A thrannoeth pan doethant ger bronn y cardinal wedy amrysson yggѡyd yr holl lys am y teilygdodeu,' y deuth y rei or tu drachefyn y archescob Iorc ac ydymchoelassant y gadeir yny vyd gѡegil yr archescob yr llaѡr ar gadeir ar y vchaf ac ѡynteu ar y draѡs ef gan y sathru ae traet, ae ffustaѡ ae dyrneu ¹[yny vu]. A breid y dieghis yr archescob yn vyѡ odyno.

MCLXXVII. Y ulѡydyn rac ѡyneb y llas Einaѡn Clut, ac y llas Morgan uab Maredud. Ac yna yd adeilaѡd yr arglѡyd Rys gastell Rayadyr Gѡy.

MCLXXVIII. ¹[Yn] y ulѡydyn rac uyneb y ryfelaѡd meibon Kynan ²[ap Owein Gwynedd] yn erbyn yr arglѡyd Rys.

MCLXXIX. Ac yna y llas Kadwallaѡn. Ac y dechreuѡyt coueint y Manachlaѡc Gaer Llion ³[ar Wysg] yr honn aelwir Deuma ³[yn nant ⁴Teyrnon].

MLXXX. Pedwar ugein mlyned a chant a mil oed oet Crist pan uu varѡ Alexander bap. Ac yn y ol ynteu y doeth yn bap Lucius. Ac yna y bu uarѡ Adaf escob ⁵Llanelyѡ yn Ryt ychen, ac y cladѡyt y myѡn manachlaѡc ⁶Osnei.

MCLXXXI. ⁷[Ny bu dim or a dycket ar gof yny vlwydyn honno].

MCLXXXII. Y ulѡydyn rac ѡyneb y llas Randѡlff ⁸Depoyr a ᵃllawer o varchogyon y gyt ac ef y gan ieuenctit ⁹Caer Wynt.'

ᵃ ¹⁰ ychydic

---

¹ B.   ⁴ Thirnon, C.
² E.   ⁵ Llan elѡy, B. Seint Assaph, D.
³ D.   ⁶ Osyney, D.

bishop of Canterbury to sit. The following day, when they came into the presence of the cardinal, after disputing before the whole court for their privileges,' there came some persons behind the archbishop of York and overturned the chair, so that the back of the archbishop's head came upon the floor, with the chair upon him, and they across him, treading him with their feet, and cuffing him with their fists, ¹ while he was there,' so that the archbishop scarcely escaped from thence alive.

1177. The ensuing year, Einon Clud was slain; and Morgan, son of Maredudd, was slain. And then the lord Rhys erected the castle of Rhaiadr Gwy.

1178. ¹ In the ensuing year, the sons of Cynan, son of Owain Gwynedd, warred against the lord Rhys.

1179. And then Cadwallon was killed. And the society was established in the monastery of Caerleon ³ upon Usk,' which is called Deuma, ⁴ in the Glen of Teyrnon.'

1180. One thousand one hundred and eighty was the year of Christ, when pope Alexander died; and after him Lucius became pope. And then Adam, bishop of Llanelwy, died at Oxford, and was buried in the monastery of Osney.

1181. ⁷ There was nothing, which was put on record, in that year.'

1182. The ensuing year, Randulf De Poer, and ⁸ many knights with him, were killed by the youths ⁹ of Winchester.'

a ¹⁰ a few

---

⁷ C.
⁸ de Poer, D

⁹ o Went, D.
¹⁰ D.

MCLXXXIII. Y vluydyn rac 6yneb y bu uar6 Henri ¹ieuaf urenhin Lloegyr.' Ac y bu uar6 ²Rickert archescob Keint.

MCLXXXIV. Y ul6ydyn rac 6yneb y bu uar6 Ryderch abat y Ty G6yn. A Meuruc abat y Cwm Hir.

MCLXXXV. Y ul6ydyn rac 6yneb amgylch y Gara6ys y doeth padriarch Caerussalem hyt yn Lloegyr y eruynieit nerth y gan y brenhin rac distry6 or Ide6on ar Sarassinyeit holl Gaerussalem. A chyt ac amylder o varchogyon a phedyt ydymchoela6d drachefyn y Gaerussalem. Yny ul6ydyn honno du6 calan Mei y symuda6d yr heul y lli6, ac y dywa6t rei uot ³erni diffyc. ⁴[Yn] y vl6ydyn honno y bu uar6 Dauyd abat Ystrat Fflur. Ac y bu uar6 Howel uab Ieuaf ⁵[ap Owein] argl6yd Ar6ystli, ac y clad6yt yn enrydedus yn Ystrat Flur. Ac ⁶yna y bu uar6 Eina6n uab Kynan.

MCLXXXVI. Y ul6ydyn rac 6yneb y bu uar6 Lucius bap. Ac yny le yd urd6yt y trydyd Vrbanus yn bap. Yny vl6ydyn honno amgylch mis Gorffenna ydaeth cofeint Ystrat Flur y Redyna6c Velen Ygg6yned. Ac yna y bu uar6 ⁷Pedyr abat yn dyffryn Cl6yt.' Ac yna y llas Katwaladyr uab Rys ⁸[yn lledrat] yn Dyfet, ac y clad6yt yn y ⁹ty G6ynn ⁸[ar Daf]. Yn y ul6ydyn honno y bu uar6 Ithel abat ¹⁰Ystrat Marchell.' Ac yna y llas Owein uab Mada6c g6r ma6r y uolyant. Kanys cadarn oed athec, acharedic a hael, ac adurn o voesseu da ⁶[yn Garrec Gova] y gan deu uab Owein Kyveila6c, nyt amgen G6en6yn6yn a ¹¹Chatwalla6n, a hynny dr6y nossa6l urat ath6yll. Ac yna y delit Llywelyn uab Katwalla6n yn enwir y

---

¹' urenhin Lloegyr yr ieuhaf, *B*.
² Richard, *D*.
³ arnei, *B*.
⁴ *B*.
⁵ *E*.
⁶ odyno, *B*.

1183. The ensuing year, Henry the younger, king of England, died; and [2] Rickert, archbishop of Canterbury, died.

1184. The ensuing year died Rhydderch, abbot of the White House; and Meurug, abbot of Cwm Hir.

1185. The ensuing year, about Lent, the patriarch of Jerusalem came to England, to request aid from the king, lest the Jews and Saracens should destroy all Jerusalem; and with a multitude of cavalry and infantry he returned back to Jerusalem. In that year, on the calends of May, the sun changed its colour, and some said there was an eclipse of it. [4] In that year David, abbot of Strata Florida, died; and Howel, son of Ieuav, [5] son of Owain,' lord of Arwystli, died, and was honourably buried at Strata Florida; and then Einon, son of Cynan, died.

1186. The ensuing year, pope Lucius died; and in his stead Urbanus the Third was consecrated pope. In the same year, about the month of July, the convent of Strata Florida removed to Rhedynog Velen in Gwynedd. And then died [7] Peter, abbot, in the Vale of Clwyd.' And then Cadwalader, son of Rhys, was [8] privately killed in Dyved, and was buried in [9] the White House' [8] upon Tav.' In that year Ithel, abbot [10] of Ystrad Marchell,' died. And then Owain, son of Madog, was slain,—a man of great celebrity; for he was powerful and comely and amiable and generous, and a pattern of good manners—[8] at Careghova,' by the two sons of Owain Cyveiliog, to wit, Gwenwynwyn and [11] Cadwallon, and that by nocturnal treachery and plot. And then Llywelyn, son

---

[7] Perÿs abat Clervall, *D*.
[8] *D*.
[9] Ystrat Ffur, *E*.
[10] or Trallwng, *D*.
[11] Chaswallawn, *D. C.*

gan y vrodyr, ac y tynnȏyt y lygeit oe benn. Ac yna y diffeithaȏd ac y llosges Maelgȏn uab Rys ¹[o deheubarth] Dinbych. Y gȏr a oed ᵃ daryan achedernit yr holl Deheu. Kanys egluraf oed y glot a thec a charedic oed gan baȏp, kyt bei kymhedraȏl y ueint garȏ wrth y elynyon, hegar ȏrth y gedymdeithon, paraȏt y rodyon, budugaȏl yn ryuel. Ar holl tyȏyssogyon kyt amhinogyon ac ef ae hergrynynt, kyffelyb y leȏ yny weithredoed, ac megys keneu lleȏ aruthur yny helua, y gȏr a ladaȏd llaȏer or Flandraswyr ac ae gyrraȏd ar ffo.

MCLXXXVIII. Y ulȏydyn rac ȏyneb y doeth y ᵇ Sarassinyeit ar Ideȏon' y Gaerussalem gan dȏyn y groc gantunt duȏ Merchur y Lludȏ agoresgyn Kaerussalem, a chymeint ac agaȏssant o Gristonogyon yndi llad rei aȏnaethant a dȏyn ereill ygkeithiwet. Ac o achaȏs hynny y kymerth Phylip vrenhin Ffreinc, a Henri urenhin Lloegyr, ac ¹[Baldewẏn] archescob Keint ac anneiryf o luossogrȏyd Cristonogyon ac arȏydon Croes Crist arnunt.

MCLXXXIX. ²[Yn] y ulȏydyn rac ȏyneb y bu uarȏ Henri vrenhin, ac yny ol ynteu y coronet ³Rickert y uab yn vrenhin y marchaȏc goreu a gleȏaf. Y ulȏydyn honno y goresgynnaȏd yr arglȏyd Rys gastell ⁴Seint Cler,' ac Aber Coran, a Llan Yystyffan. Yn y ulȏydyn honno y delit Maelgȏn uab Rys ⁵[lleufer a thegwch ac adwyndra atharyan achdernyt holl deheubarth ay rydit

---

ᵃ ⁶ trayan
ᵇ' ⁷ Paganyeit ar Sarassinyeit

---

¹ *D.*   ³ Richard, *D.*
² *B.*   ⁴ Seinther, *D.*

of Cadwallon, was unjustly seized by his brothers, and his eyes were taken out of his head. And then Maelgwn, son of Rhys, ¹ from the South' ravaged and burned Tenby;—the man who was the ᵃ shield and strength of all the South; for his fame was most manifest, and he was comely, and beloved by all; though of middling size, he was fierce towards his enemies, amiable towards his friends, ready of gifts, victorious in war. And all the princes bordering upon him dreaded him, being like a lion in his actions, and like a dreadful lion's whelp in the chase—the man who slew many of the Flemings, and put them to flight.

1188. The ensuing year, the ᵇ Saracens and the Jews' came to Jerusalem, took possession of the Cross, on Ash Wednesday, and subdued Jerusalem; and of as many Christians they found therein, they killed some, and took the others into captivity. And on that account Philip, king of France, and Henry, king of England, and ¹ Baldwin, archbishop of Canterbury, with an innumerable host of Christians, took upon them the signs of the cross of Christ.

1189. ² In the ensuing year king Henry died; and after him Richard his son was crowned king—the best and bravest knight. That year the lord Rhys took possession of the castles of ⁴ St. Clare' and Aber Corran and Llanstephan. In that year Maelgwn, son of Rhys, ⁵ the light and beauty and courtesy and shield and strength and liberty of all the South, and

---

ᵃ ⁶ third part
ᵇ' ⁷ Pagans and Saracens

---

³ *C.*
⁶ *B.*

' *C. D.*

aruthder y Saesson ymarchoc goreu eil Gwalchmei] y gan y dat drôy gyghor Rys y uraôt ac y carcharôyt.

MCXC. Deg mlyned a phedwar ugein achant amil oed oet Crist pan aeth Phylip vrenhin Ffreinc, a ¹Rickert vrenhin Lloegyr ac ²[Baldewyn] archescob Keint a diruaôr luossogrôyd o ieirll abarôneit y gyt ac ôynt y Gaerussalem. Y ulôydyn honno yd adeilaôd yr arglôyd Rys gastell Ketweli. Ac y bu uarô Gôenllian uerch Rys vlodeu a thegôch holl Gymry.

MCXCI. Y ulôydyn rac ôyneb y bu uarô Gruffud Maelaôr ³[brenhin Powys] yr haelaf o holl tywyssogyon Kymry ⁴[ac y Meivod y kladpwyd ef yn anrydeddus]. Y ulôydyn honno hefyt y bu uarô Gôiaôn escob Bangor gôr maôr y grefyd ae enryded ae deilygdaôt. Ac y bu diffyc ar yr heul. Y ulôydyn honno y bu uarô ⁵[Baldewyn] archescob Keint. Ac yna y llas Einaôn or Porth y gan y vraôt. Ac y goresgynnaôd yr arglôyd Rys gastell ⁶Niuer. Ac y bu uarô Owein ⁷[ap Grufud] uab Rys yn Ystrat Flur.

MCXCII. Y ulôydyn rac ôyneb y diehegis ⁸Madaôc uab Rys o garchar ⁴[Rys i dad] arglôyd Brecheinaôc. Ac y gorescynnaôd yr arglôyd Rys gastell ⁹Llan y Hadein.' Ac y bu uarô Gruffud uab Cadôgaôn.

MCXCIII. Y ulôydyn rac ôyneb y delis neb un iarll ¹Rickert vrenhin Lloegyr ac ef yn dyuot o Gaerussalem, ac y dodet ygkarchar yr amheraôdyr. A thros y ellygdaôt ef y bu diruaôr dreth dros ôyneb holl Loegyr y gymeint ac nat oed ¹⁰yn helô ¹¹eglôysswyr na chrefydwyr nac eur nac aryant hyt yn oet y

---

¹ Richard, *D*.
² *B. C. D*.
³ *D*.
⁴ *E*.
⁵ *B. C. D. E*.
⁶ Dyneinir, *D*. Dineuwr, *E*.

the terror of the Saxons, the best knight, second to Gwalchmai,' was seized by his father, by the advice of his brother Rhys, and was imprisoned.

1190. One thousand one hundred and ninety was the year of Christ, when Philip, king of France, and Richard, king of England, and ²Baldwin, archbishop of Canterbury, with an immense multitude of earls and barons, went to Jerusalem. That year the lord Rhys built the castle of Cydweli. And Gwenllian, daughter of Rhys, died—the flower and ornament of all Wales.

1191. The ensuing year, Gruffudd Maelor, ³king of Powys,' died—the most generous of all the princes of Wales — ⁴and was honourably buried in Meivod.' That year also Gwion, bishop of Bangor, died—a man of great piety, and honour, and merit. And an eclipse of the sun occurred. The same year ⁵Baldwin, archbishop of Canterbury, died. And then Einon of Porth was killed by his brother. And the lord Rhys took the castle of ⁶Nyver. And Owain, ⁷son of Gruffudd,' son of Rhys, died at Strata Florida.

1192. The ensuing year, ⁸Madog, son of Rhys, escaped from the prison of 'Rhys his father,' the lord of Brecheiniog. And the lord Rhys took the castle of ⁹Llanuhadein. And Gruffudd, son of Cadwgan, died.

1193. The ensuing year, a certain earl seized Richard, king of England, as he was returning from Jerusalem; and he was confined in the prison of the emperor. And for his liberation, there was an extensive tax over all England; and such was its extent that there was not in the possession of churchmen or religious professors, either gold or silver, not even the

---

⁷ D. E.
⁸ Maelgwn, B. C. D.
⁹ Llanmadein, D.
¹⁰ ar, B.
¹¹ egl6yss6r, B.

¹ careclcu adotrefyn yr eglόysseu ar ny orffei y dodi oll ymedyant sόydogyon y brenhin ar deyrnas όrth y rodi drostaό ²[ef]. Y ulόydyn honno y darestygaόd Rodri uab Owein ynys Von drόy nerth ³[meibion] ⁴ Gόrthrych urenhin Manaό. A chyn penn y vlόydyn y gόrtladόyt y gan ueibon Kynan uab Owein ⁵[Gwynedd i neiaint]. Y ulόydyn honno nos Nadolic y doeth teulu Maelgόn uab Rys abliuieu gantunt y dorri castell Ystrat Meuruc, ac ᵃ yd ennillassant' y kastell. Y ulόydyn honno y kauas Howel Seis ab yr arglόyd Rys gastell Gόis drόy urat. Ac ydelis Phylip uab Gόis keitόat y castell ae wreic ae deu uab. A gόedy gόelet or dywededic Howel na allei ef gadό y kestyll oll heb vύrό rei yr llaόr, ef a ganhadaόd y deulu ac y deulu ²[Maelgόyn] y vraόt torri kastell Llan y Hadein ae distryό. A phan gigleu y Fflandrassyeit hynny kynnullaό a ⁶ όmaethant yn dirybud yn erbyn y deu uroder, ae kyrchu, a llad llawer oe gόyr, ae gyrru ²[όynteu] ar ffo. Ac yny lle gόedy hynny ymchoelut awnaeth y Kymry, ac ymgynnullaό ygkylch y castell, ac όrth y hewyllys y ⁷ distryόyt hyt y llaόr. Y ulόydyn honno y delis ⁸ Anaraόt ⁹[vab Rys o chwant y bydawl gyfoeth] Vadaόc a Howel y urodyr ac yd yspeilaόd ¹⁰ όynt oc eu llygeit.'

MCXCIV. ²[Yn] y ulόydyn honno y rodes Maelgόn uab Rys gastell Ystrat Meuruc ¹¹ y vraόt ³[dros y

---

ᵃ' ¹² ydryllassant

---

¹ caregyl, *B*.   ⁴ Godrich, *D*.
² *B*.   ⁵ *E*.
³ *D*.   ⁶ orugant, *B*.

sacred vessels and furniture of the churches, but was obliged to be all given into the hands of the officers of the king and the kingdom, to be applied for his ransom. That year, Rhodri, son of Owain, subjugated the isle of Mona, through the aid of ³the sons of' Godrich, king of Man; but before the end of the year he was expelled by the sons of Cynan, son of Owain ⁵Gwynedd, his nephews.' The same year, on Christmas eve, the family of Maelgwn, son of Rhys, brought missiles with them to break down the castle of Ystrad Meurug, and ᵃthey gained' the castle. That year, Howel the Saxon, son of the lord Rhys, obtained the castle of Gwis, through treachery; and he captured Philip, son of Gwis, the keeper of the castle, his wife, and two sons. And when the said Howel perceived he could not hold possession of all the castles, without throwing some of them down, he permitted his family, and the family of ²Maelgwn his brother, to demolish the castle of Llanuhadein. And when the Flemings heard of this, they assembled unexpectedly against the two brothers, attacked them, killed many of their men, and put them to flight. And immediately afterwards the Welsh returned and assembled about the castle, and, to their satisfaction, it was razed to the ground. That year, Anarawd, ⁹son of Rhys, from a desire of worldly territory,' seized Madog and Howel, his brothers, and deprived them of their eyes.

1194. ²In that year, Maelgwn, son of Rhys, gave the castle of Ystrad Meurug to his brothers, ³for

---

ᵃ/ ¹² they demolished

---

⁷ distryb, B.
⁸ Aranaut, D.
⁹ C.

¹⁰ oe llygeit bynt, B.
¹¹ ae, B.
¹² B.

wystlon]. Ac yd adeilaƀd yr arglƀyd Rys yr eilweith gastell Rayadyr Gƀy. Y vlƀydyn honno y delit yr ¹ arglwyd Rys y gan y ueibon ac y carcharƀyt. Ac y rydhaaƀd Howel Seis y dat gan dƀyllaƀ Maelgƀn uab Rys. ᵃ Ac yna y torres meibon Katƀallaƀn gastell ² [de Nỹuer ỹr hwn oed eidiaw Maelgwn a chastell] Rayadyr Gƀy.' Ac yd ymchoelaƀd Rickert urenhin o Gaerusalem. Ac yna kyfunaƀd Llywelyn ab Iorƀoerth ᵇ a Rodri uab Owein, a deu uab Kynan ab Owein, yn erbyn Davyd uab Owein' ³ [Gwynedd]. Ac y gƀrthladyssant ƀy holl gyfoeth Dauyd eithyr tri chastell.

MCXCV. Y ulƀydyn rac ƀyneb y deuth Roser Mortymer a llu gantaƀ y Uaelenyd. A gƀedy gƀrthlad ᶜ meibon Kadwallaƀn yd adeilaƀd' gastell y Gamaron. Ac yna y goreskynnaƀd Rys a Maredud meibon yr arglƀyd Rys drƀy dƀyll gastell Dinefƀr a chastell y Kantref Bychan drƀy gytsynnedigaeth gƀyr y kymhydeu. Arrei hynny y delit yny vlƀydyn honno drƀy dƀyll y gan y tat yn Ystrat Meuruc ac a garcharƀyt.

MCXCVI. Y vlƀydyn rac ƀyneb y bu uarƀ escob Bangor. Ac yny y kynnullaƀd yr arglƀyd Rys lu, ac y kyrchaƀd Kaer Vyrdin. Ac y llosges hyt y ᵈ prid eithyr y castell ehun.' Ac od yna y kych-

---

ᵃ' ⁴ Ac y kymerth kastell Nyner aoed eidaw Vaelgwn ac y llosges meibyon Kadwallawn kastell Rayadyr Gwy.
ᵇ' ⁵ a deu vab Kỹnan Rodri ac Owein
ᶜ' ⁵ deu uab Catwallawn o
ᵈ' ⁴ llawr wedy diang kwnstabyl y kastell ehunan.

---

¹ B. becomes imperfect here.   ³ E.
² D. E.

his hostages.' And the lord Rhys built the castle of Rhaiadr Gwy the second time. That year Rhys was seized by his sons and imprisoned; and Howel the Saxon released his father, by deceiving Maelgwn, son of Rhys. ᵃ And then the sons of Cadwallon demolished the castle ²of Nyver, which was the property of Maelgwn, and the castle' of Rhaiadr Gwy.' And king Richard returned from Jerusalem. And then Llywelyn, son of Iorwerth, ᵇ and Rhodri, son of Owain, and the two sons of Cynan, son of Owain, combined against David, son of Owain' ³ Gwynedd, and oppugned all the territory of David, except three castles.

1195. The ensuing year, Roger Mortimer came with an army into Maelienydd; and having expelled ᶜ the sons of Cadwallon, he built' the castle of Camaron. And then Rhys and Maredudd, the sons of the lord Rhys, subjected the castle of Dinevwr, and the castle of Cantrev Bychan, through treachery, by the consent of the men of the comots. And those were seized, through treachery, in the same year, by their father at Ystrad Meurug, and were imprisoned.

1196. The ensuing year the bishop of Bangor died. And then the lord Rhys collected an army, and attacked Caermarthen, and burned it to the ᵈ earth, except the castle itself.' From thence he marched

---

ᵃ' ⁴ And took the castle of Nyner, which was the property of Maelgwn, and the sons of Cadwallon burned the castle of Rhaiadr Gwy.

ᵇ' ⁵ and the two sons of Cynan, Rhodri and Owain

ᶜ' ⁵ the two sons of Cadwallon from

ᵈ' ⁴ ground, after the constable of the castle himself had escaped.

---

⁴ C. | ³ D.

wynnaȯd a diruaȯr lu gantaȯ oe wyr e hun ac o wyr arglȯydi ereill a odynt gyfun ac ef y ymlad a chastell ¹Colȯyn, ae gymell y ymrodi. A gȯedy y gael, ef ae llosges. Ac ynebrȯyd odyno y kychȯynnaȯd ae lu hyt Maes Hyfeid ae losgi. A gȯedy llosgi y dyd hȯnnȯ yny dyffryn yn gyuagos y kyweiraȯd Rosser Mortymer a ²Hu Dysai' yn vydinoed aruaȯc, o ueirch a llurugeu a helmeu a tharyaneu yn dirybud ynerbyn y Kymry. A phan welas y maȯrurydus Rys hynny ymwisgaȯ aȯnaeth megys lleȯ dyfal o gallon a llaȯ gadarn a chyrchu y elynyon yn wraȯl ae hymchoelut ar ffo ae hymlit ae traethu yn dielȯ kyt bei gȯraȯl, yny gȯynaȯd y marswyr yn diruaȯr yr ormod aerua or rei eidunt. Ac yny lle yd ymladadaȯd a chastell Paen yn Eluael a blifieu a magneleu. Ac y kymellaȯd y ymrodi. A gȯedy y gael y bu gyfundeb y rygtaȯ a Gȯilim Breȯys. Ac am hynny yd edewis y kastell hȯnnȯ ynhedȯch. Yny ulȯydyn honno yd ymladaȯd Henri archescob Keint iustus holl Loegyr, a hyt ac ef gynnulleitua o ieirll a barȯneit Lloegyr a holl tywyssogyon Gȯyned yn erbyn castell Gȯennȯynȯyn yn Trallȯg Llywelyn. ³[Ac ný thýgiawd ýdunt dým, canýs val ý bwrieýn ermýgýon ý ben ý castell ýdýuot ý mewn; pan deleint hýt ý býlchev ý bwrit wýnt hýt ýn waelawt clawd ýný dorrýnt eu mýnýglev eraill bodi.] A gȯedy llauurys ymlad ac ef ac amryuaelon peiranneu a dechymygyon ymladeu yny diȯed o enryued geluydyt ȯynt aennillassant y castell drȯy anuon mȯynwyr y gladu y danaȯ, ac y wneuthur ffossyd dirgeledic y dan y dayar. Ac uelly y kymbellȯyt

---

¹ Colȯnwys, C. Collwýnwý, D. | ²′ Hýgýn o Saý, D.

with a vast army of his own men, and of the men of other lords, who were joined with him, to attack the castle of ¹Colwyn, and compel it to surrender; and having obtained it, he burned it. And from thence he speedily marched with his army to Maes Hyvaidd, which he burned; and after burning it, on the same day, Roger Mortimer and ²Hugh de Say marshalled their armed forces of cavalry, equipped with mails and helmets and shields, unawares against the Welsh, in an adjoining valley. And when the magnanimous Rhys observed this, he accoutred himself, like a lion of furious heart, with a mighty hand, and gallantly attacked his enemies, and turned them to flight, pursued them, and dealt with them as of no account, though in a manly way; so that the marchers regreted extremely the excessive slaughter of their men. And then immediately, he attacked Pain's castle in Elvael with missiles and engines, and compelled it to surrender. After obtaining it, there was an agreement made between him and William Bruse, in consequence of which he relinquished that castle in peace. In the same year, Henry, archbishop of Canterbury, justice of all England, having with him an assemblage of the earls and barons of England, with all the princes of Gwynedd, made an attack upon the castle of Gwenwynwyn in Trallwng Llywelyn; ³and it availed them not, for as they flung their engines to the top of the castle in order to get in, when they got to the breaches, they were hurled to the bottom of the fosse, so as to break their necks, and others were drowned.' And after fighting severely against it with various instruments and devices of warfare, at length by wonderful science they gained the castle by sending miners to dig under it, and to make secret

³ *D.*

y kastellwyr y ymrodi. Ac eissoes ɓynt a diagyssant oll yn ryd ae gɓisgoed gantunt ae harueu eithyr vn allas. Ac odyna kyn diwed y ulɓydyn honno y kynullaɓd Gɓennɓynɓyn y wyr y gyt ac yd ymladaɓd yn wraɓl ar dywededic gastell ac ae kymhellaɓd y ymrodi idaɓ, drɓy amot hefyt rodi rydit yr castellɓyr y vynet yn iach ae dillat ae harueu gantunt. Y ulɓydyn honno y bu uarɓ Gruffud abat [1] Ystrat Marchell.'

MCXCVII. Y ulɓydyn rac ɓyneb y bu diruaɓr dymhestyl o uarɓolyaeth ar hyt ynys Prydein oll a theruyneu Ffreinc yny vu varɓ anneiryf or bobyl gyffredin, a diuessured or bonedigyon ar tywyssogyon. Ac yny ulɓydyn dymhestlaɓl honno yd ymdangosses Antropos oe chɓioryd y rei aelɓit gynt yn dɓywesseu y tyghetuennoed ykygoruynnus wenɓynic nerthoed yn erbyn y veint arderchaɓc dywyssaɓc hyt na allei ystoryau Ystas ystoryaɓr na chathleu Fferyll uard menegi y veint gɓynuan adolur a thrueni adoeth y holl genedyl y Brytanyeit pan dorres ageu yr emelldigedic ulɓydyn honno olɓyn y teghetuenneu y gymryt yr arglɓyd Rys ab Gruffud [2] [y pedweryd dyd galan Mei] dan y hadaned dan darestygedic uedyant ageu y gɓr aoed benn a tharyan a chedernit y Deheu a holl Gymry, a gobeith ac amdiffyn holl genedloed y Brytanyeit. Y gɓr hɓnnɓ a hanoed o vonhedicaf lin brenhined. Ef a oed eglur o amylder kenedyl, a grymuster y uedɓl a gyffelybaɓd ɓrth y genedyl. Kyghorɓr y dylyedogyon, ymladgar yn erbyn kedyrn, diogelɓch y darestygedigyon, ymladɓr ar geyryd. Ky-

---

[1] ỳ Trallwng, D.

passages under ground. And thus the garrison was compelled to surrender; and, nevertheless, they all escaped at large, with their clothes and arms, except one, who was killed. And then before the end of that year, Gwenwynwyn collected his men together, and fought manfully against the said castle, and compelled it to surrender to him, under an agreement also of granting liberty to the garrison to depart in safety with their clothes and arms. That year, Gruffudd, abbot of ¹ Ystrad Marchell,' died.

1197. The ensuing year there was a dreadful season of mortality over all the isle of Britain and the borders of France, so that innumerable of the common people died, and an immense number of the gentry and nobility. And in that troublous year did Atropos appear from among her sisters, who were formerly called the goddesses of destinies, with her maliciously malignant powers against that illustrious prince, in respect of whom neither the histories of Ystas the historian, nor the odes of Feryll the bard, could describe the extent of the lamentation and grief and misery that befel the whole nation of the Britons, when death, in that accursed year, broke the wheel of the destinies, to take the lord Rhys, son of Gruffudd, ²on the fourth day of the calends of May,' beneath its wings, under the subjected possession of death—the man who was the head and shield and strength of the South and of all Wales, and the hope and defence of all the tribes of the Britons—that man who was descended from the noblest line of kings, who was conspicuous for the extent of his race, and the energy of whose mind was assimilated with his race—the counsellor of the nobility, hostile against tyrants, the safety of the subjects, combatant upon the walls, an inciter in the

ffroŵr yn ryfeloed, kyweirŵr yny bydinoed ae reolŵr, cŵympŵr y toruoed, ac megys baed neu leŵ yn ruthraŵ uelly y dywalei y greulonder yn y elynyon. Och am ogonyant yr ymladeu, taryan y marchogyon, ymdiffynn y wlat, tegŵch arueu, breich y kedernit, llaŵ yr haelon, llygat y dosparth, echtyŵynnŵr yr aduŵynder, uchelder maŵrurytrŵyd, defnyd grymusder. Eil Achelarŵy o nerth cledyr y dŵyuron, Nestor o hynaŵster, Tideus o leŵder, Samson o gedernit, Ector o brudder, Ercŵlf o wychter, Paris o vryt, Ulixes o lauar, Selyf o doethineb, Aiax o uedŵl; a grŵndŵal yr holl gampeu ¹[iiii. kl. Maii]. ²[A llyma y gwerseu mydyr Lladin a wnaethpwyt pan vv varw yr arglwyd Rys:—

Nobile Cambrensis cecidit dyadema decoris
   Hoc est Resus obit Cambria tota gemit
Resus obit non foma perit sed gloria transit
   Cambrensis transit gloria, Resus obit
Resus obit decus orbis abit laus quoque tepescit
   Ingeniitum vivit Cambria Resus obit.
Semper Resus obit populo quo vivus amavit.
   Lugent corda tacent corpora, Resus obit.
Resus obit vexilla cadunt regalia signa
   Hoc jam nulla levat dextera Resus obit.
Resus obit ferrugo tegit galeam tegit ensem.
   Arma rubigo tegit Cambria Resus obit.
Resus abest inimitus adest Resus quia non est
   Jam t . . nil prodest Cambria Resus abest.
Resus obit populi plorant gaudent inimici.
   Anglia stat cecidit Cambria Resus obit.
Ora rigant elegi cunctis mea fletibus isti.
   Cor ferit omne ducis dira sagitta necis

---

¹ *D.*

wars, the arranger and ruler of the troops, the overthrower of hosts; and as a boar or a lion rushes onward, so raged his cruelty among his foes. Alas! for the glory of battles, the shield of the knights, the defence of the country, the ornament of weapons, the arm of strength, the hand of the generous ones, the eye of discrimination, the illustrator of courtesy, the summit of magnanimity, the substance of energy; like Achilles in the strength of his breast, Nestor in kindness, Tydeus in bravery, Sampson in strength, Hector in prudence, Hercules in gallantry, Paris in beauty, Ulysses in speech, Solomon in wisdom, Ajax in mind, and the foundation of all the excellencies — [1] on the fourth of the calends of May.' [2] And here are the Latin metrical verses, which were composed when the lord Rhys died:—

Nobile Cambrensis cecidit dyadema decoris,
   Hoc est Resus obit, Cambria tota gemit,
Resus obit, non foma perit, sed gloria transit,
   Cambrensis transit gloria, Resus obit,
Resus obit, decus orbis abit, laus quoque tepescit
   Ingeniitum vivit Cambria, Resus obit.
Semper Resus obit populo quo vivus amavit.
   Lugent corda, tacent corpora, Resus obit.
Resus obit, vexilla cadunt regalia signa,
   Hoc jam nulla levat dextera, Resus obit.
Resus obit, ferrugo tegit galeam, tegit ensem.
   Arma rubigo tegit Cambria, Resus obit.
Resus abest, inimitus adest, Resus quia non est
   Jam t . . nil prodest Cambria, Resus abest.
Resus obit, populi plorant, gaudent inimici.
   Anglia stat, cecidit Cambria, Resus obit.
Ora rigant elegi cunctis mea fletibus isti.
   Cor ferit omne ducis dira sagitta necis.

---

[2] *C.*

Omnis lingua canit Reso præconia nescit,
　Laudes insignis lingua tacere ducis.
Ploratu plene vite laxantur habene,
　Meta datur meri laus sine fine duci.
Non moritur sed subtraitur quia semper habetur
　Ipsuis egregium nomen in orbe novum.
Camber Locrinus Reso rex Albaquenactus
　Nominis et laudis inferioris erant.
Cesar et Arthurus leo fortis uterque sub armis
　Nil par vel similis Resus utrique fuit.
Resus Alexander duelli pari fuit alter
　Mundum substerni glistit uterque sibi.
Occasus solis testus Resi fuit armis
　Sensit Alexandri solis in orbe manum.
Laus canit . . . sancto cantet ab omni
　Celi laus regis debita spiritui.
Penna madet lacrimis quia scribit thema doloris
　Ne carcat forma littera cesset ea.

Llyma wedy hynny y gwerseu mydyr o Ladin y syd yn volyant ar y ved ef, ac a wnaethpwyt wedy daruot y gladu ef:—

Grande decus tenet iste locus si cernitur ortus,
　Siquis sit finis queritur ecce cinis.
Laudis amator honoris odor dulcedinis auctor,
　Resus in hoc tumulo conditur exiguo.
Cesaries qui congeries solis radiorum
　Principis et facies vertitur in cineres.
Hic tegitur sed detegitur quia fama perhennis
　Non sinit illustrem voce latere ducem.
Colligitur tumba cinis hac sed transvolat ultra
　Nobilitas claudi nestia fune brevi
Wallia jam viduata dolet ruitur a dolore.]

Góedy maró yr arglóyd Rys y dynessaaód Gruffud y vab yny ol yn y llywodraeth y kynoeth yr hónn adelis Maelgón y vraót pan doeth y dywededic Vaelgón wedy ryalltudaó kynno hynny oe gyfoeth ac wyr y

Omnis lingua canit Reso præconia, nescit
  Laudes insignis lingua tacere ducis.
Ploratu plene vite laxantur habene,
  Meta datur meri laus sine fine duci.
Non moritur sed subtraitur, quia semper habetur
  Ipsuis egregium nomen in orbe novum.
Camber Locrinus Reso rex Albaquenactus
  Nominis et laudis inferioris erant.
Cesar et Arthurus, leo fortis uterque sub armis,
  Nil par vel similis Resus utrique fuit.
Resus Alexander duelli pari fuit alter,
  Mundum substerni glistit uterque sibi.
Occasus solis testus Resi fuit armis,
  Sensit Alexandri solis in orbe manum.
Laus canit . . . sancto cantet ab ommi
  Celi laus regis debita spiritui.
Penna madet lacrimis quia scribit thema doloris
  Ne careat forma littera cesset ea.

Here after that are the Latin metrical verses, which are in his praise on his tomb, and which were made after he had been buried:—

Grande decus tenet iste locus, si cernitur ortus,
  Siquis sit finis queritur ecce cinis.
Laudis amator honoris odor dulcedinis auctor,
  Resus in hoc tumulo conditur exiguo.
Cesaries qui congeries solis radiorum
  Principis et facies vertitur in cineres.
Hic tegitur, sed detegitur, quia fama perhennis
  Non sinit illustrem voce latere ducem.
Colligitur tumba cinis hac, sed transvolat ultra
  Nobilitas claudi nestia fune brevi,
Wallia jam viduata dolet, ruitur a dolore.'

After the death of the lord Rhys, his son Gruffudd succeeded him in the government of the dominion, which was held by Maelgwn his brother, when the said Maelgwn, after being banished before from his

gyt ac ef, a theulu Gwenwynwyn y gyt ac wynt hyt yn
Aber Ystwyth. A goreskyn y dref ar castell, a llad
llawer oe bobyl, a dwyn ereill ygkeithiwet a goreskyn
holl Geredigyawn ae chestyll. A gwedy dala Gruffud y
urawt ydanuones y garchar Gwenwynwyn. A hwnnw herwyd y ewyllys ae hanuones y garchar Saeson. Ac yna
y goresgynnawd Gwenwynwyn Arwystli, ac y delis Llywelyn uab Iorwoerth ¹ a Dauyd ab Owein Gwyned. Y
vlwydyn honno y bu uarw Owein Kefeilawc yn Ystrat
Marchell ² [y vynachloc a seiliodd ef e hun] wedy
kymryt abit y crefyd ym danaw. Ac yna y bu uarw
Owein ab Gruffud Maelawr, ac Owein or Brithdir, ᵃ a
Howel uab Ieuaf ³ [ap Owein] a Maelgwn uab Kat-
wallawn a Vaelenyd. Y ulwydyn honno y delit Trahayarn Uychan o Vrecheinawc gwr arderchawc bonhedic
kadarn, ᵇ a nith yr arglwyd Rys yn briawt idaw' pan
yttoed yn dyuot drwy Lan Gors y lys ⁴ 'Wilim Brewys'
y arglwyd ac y gefynnwyt yn greulawn. Ac yn Aber
Hodni y llusgwyt wrth rawn meirch drwy yr heolyd hyt
y crocwyd, ac yno y llas y benn ac y croget herwyd
y draet; ac ar ycrocwyd y bu tridieu : ᶜ wedy dianc
y wreic ae vab ae vrawt ar ffo.'

ᵃ ³ vab.

ᵇ' ⁵ a nith verch chwaer ẏ Rẏs ap Grufud ẏn wreic
briawt ⁶ a nith yr arglwyd Rys verch y chwaer yn
wreic ydaw

ᶜ' ⁵ Ac ẏ dial ẏ vraut aẏ vab aẏ wreic, pan ẏw
ẏnẏ ford greulon ẏ divethawd.

---

¹ Not in C. D.
² E.
³ C. D. E.
⁴ William de Breusa, D.

territory, came, accompanied by his men, and also by the family of Gwenwynwyn, to Aberystwyth, and subjugated the town and castle, killing many of the people, and carrying others into bondage, and taking possession of the whole of Ceredigion with its castles. And after seizing his brother Gruffudd, he sent him to the prison of Gwenwynwyn, who agreeably to his desire sent him to an English prison. And then Gwenwynwyn subjugated Arwystli, and captured Llywelyn, son of Iorwerth ¹ and David son of Owain Gwynedd. That year, Owain Cyveiliog died at Ystrad Marchell, ² the monastery which he himself had founded,' after putting on the habit of religion. And then died Owain, son of Gruffudd Maelor, and Owain of Brithdir, ᵃ and Howel, son of Ieuav, ³ son of Owain,' and Maelgwn, son of Cadwalader of Maelienydd. The same year, Trahaiarn the Little of Brecheiniog, an illustrious, noble, and powerful man, ᵇ whose wife was niece of the lord Rhys,' was seized, when he was passing through Llangors to the court of William Bruse, and was cruelly fettered. And at Aberhodni he was dragged at the tails of horses through the streets to the scaffold; there his head was cut off, and he was hanged by his feet, and remained on the gallows three days, ᶜ after his wife, his son, and his brother had escaped by flight.'

ᵃ ³ son of

ᵇ' ⁵ whose wife was niece, sister's daughter, to Rhys, son of Gruffudd,- ⁶ whose wife was niece to the lord Rhys, his sister's daughter,

ᶜ' ⁵ and it was to take revenge upon his brother, his son, and his wife, that he was destroyed in that cruel way.

⁵ *D.* ⁶ *C.*

MCXCVIII. Y vlȯydyn rac wyneb y goreskynnaȯd Maelgȯn ab Rys Aber Teiui, ¹a chastell Ystrat Meuruc wedy mynet Gruffud y uraȯt yg karchar Saesson. Ac yna ydaeth coueint y Cȯm Hir y bressȯylaȯ y Gymer ²[y Nannav y Meirionydd]. Y vlȯydyn honno y goresgynnaȯd y meibon ieuaf yr arglȯyd Rys gastell Dinefȯr. Y ulȯydyn honno ²[ar ael gwyl Vair Vadlen] yd aruaethaȯd Gȯenȯynȯyn geissaȯ talu y hen deilygdaȯt yr Kymry, ae hen briodolder ae teruyneu. A gȯedy kytsynyaȯ ac ef ar hynny holl dywyssogyon Kymry kynullaȯ diruaȯr lu aoruc, a mynet y ymlad a chastell Paen. A gȯedy bot yn ymlad ac ef ³[heb na bliviav na magneleu] deir ȯythnos hayach heb wybot y damwein rac llaȯ. A phan ȯybu y Saesson hynny gellȯg awnaethant Rufud uab Rys aoed ygkarchar y gantunt a chynullaȯ kedernit Lloegyr y gyt ac ef ar vedyr hedychu ar Kymry. Ac yna ny mynnaȯd y Kymry hedȯch y gan y Saeson namyn gȯedy caffael y castell, bygythyaȯ awnaethant losgi y dinassoed a dȯyn y hanreitheu. A heb diodef or Saeson hynny ȯynt ae kyrchassant, ac yny vrȯydyr gyntaf ae kymellassant ar ffo drȯy wneuthur diruaȯr aerua o nadunt. Ac yna y llas Anaraȯt ²[ap Einiawn] ᵃab Owein ab Kadȯallaȯn, a Ridit ab Iestyn, a ⁴Rodri uab Howel, ac y delit Maredud uab Kynan ac y carcharȯyt. Ac uelly y deuth y Saesson drachefyn drȯy uudugolyaeth wedy y kyuoethogi o yspeil y Kymry. Y vlȯydyn honno

---

ᵃ ² ac

---

¹ *D. is imperfect here.* | ² *C. E.*

1198. The ensuing year, Maelgwn, son of Rhys, took Aberteivi [1] and the castle of Ystrad Meurug, after his brother Gruffudd had gone into an English prison. And then the convent of Cwm Hir removed, to settle at Cymmer, 'in Nannau of Meirionydd.' That year, the youngest sons of the lord Rhys took possession of the castle of Dinevwr. The same year, 'near the feast of St. Mary Magdalen,' Gwenwynwyn meditated endeavouring the restoration of their ancient rights to the Welsh, their original property, and their boundaries. And when all the princes of Wales had agreed with him thereon, he collected a vast army, and proceeded to attack Pain's castle; and after he had fought against it, 'without projectiles and engines of war,' for nearly three weeks, he was ignorant of the future issue. When the English had intelligence of that, they liberated Gruffudd, son of Rhys, whom they had in prison, and collected the strength of England to accompany him, with the intention of pacifying the Welsh. And then the Welsh would not accept peace of the English, but, after obtaining the castle, they threatened to burn the towns, and carry off their spoils; and the English, not brooking that, attacked them, and in the first battle put them to flight, making a vast slaughter of them. And then Anarawd, 'son of Einon,' a son of' Owain, son of Cadwallon, and Rhirid, son of Iestin, and Rhodri, son of Howel, were slain, and Maredudd, son of Cynan, was taken and imprisoned. And thus the English returned again victoriously, after being enriched with the spoils of the Welsh. That year,

---

a/ ² and

---

³ E. | ⁴ Rotpert, C. E.

y goreskynnaẅd Gruffud uab Rys yn ẅraẅl yran oe gyuoeth y gan Vaelgẅn y vraẅt eithyr deu gastell nyt amgen Aber Teivi ac Ystrat Meuruc. Ar neill o nadunt nyt amgen Aber Teivi a tygaẅd Maelgẅn uch benn amryvaelon greireu yggẅyd myneich ẅedy kymryt gẅystlon y gan Rufud dros hedẅch y rodei y castell, ar gẅystlon y gyt yn oet dyd y Ruffud. Ar llẅ hẅnnẅ a dremygaẅd ef heb rodi nar castell nar gẅystlon. Dẅywaẅl nerth eissoes a rydhaaẅd y gẅystlon o garchar Gẅenẅynẅyn. Y ulẅydyn honno y bu uarẅ Pyrs escob Mynyẅ.

MCXCIX. Y vlẅydyn rac ẅyneb y goresgynnaẅd Maelgẅn uab Rys gastell Dineirth a adeilassei Ruffud uab Rys, a chymeint ac a gauas yno o wyr llad rei awnaeth a charcharu ereill. Ac yna y goresgynnaẅd Gruffud ab Rys drẅy dẅyll gastell Kil Gerran. Y vlẅydyn honno ual yd oed Rickert urenhin Lloegyr yn ymlad achastell neb un uarẅn aoed ẅrth ẅyneb idaẅ y brathẅyt a chẅarel, ac or brath hẅnnẅ y bu uarẅ. Ac yna y drychafẅyt Ieuan y uraẅt yn vrenhin.

MCC. Deucant mlyned a mil oed oet Crist pan vu uarẅ Gruffud uab Kynan ab Oẅein yn Aber Conẅy wedy kymryt abit y creuyd ymdanaẅ. [1] [Y gwr a oed atnabodedic gan bawb o ynys Brydein o achaws helaethrwyd y rodyon ag hynawster ay dayoni ac nyt ryued kanys tra vo byw y gwyr y syd yr awr honn wynt a goffhant y glot ay volyant ay weithredoed]. Y vlẅydyn honno y gẅerthaẅd Maelgẅn uab Rys Aber Teiui a llaẅed holl Gymry yr ychydic werth y Saeson rac ofyn ac o gas Gruffud y uraẅt. Y ulẅydyn honno y grẅndwalẅyt [2] [Madoc ap Gruffydd

---

[1] C.

Gruffudd, son of Rhys, manfully got possession of his share of his territory from Maelgwn his brother, excepting two castles, namely, Aberteivi and Ystrad Meurug. As to one of them, namely, Aberteivi, Maelgwn swore upon several relics, in the presence of monks, after taking hostages for peace from Gruffudd, that he would deliver up the castle and hostages together to Gruffudd on a fixed day. And that oath he disregarded, giving up neither the castle nor the hostages; divine power, nevertheless, set the hostages free from the prison of Gwenwynwyn. That year, Pyrs, bishop of Menevia, died.

1199. The ensuing year, Maelgwn, son of Rhys, got possession of the castle of Dineirth, which Gruffudd, son of Rhys, had built; and of the men he found there some he slew, and others he imprisoned. And then Gruffudd, son of Rhys, possessed himself, through treachery, of the castle of Cilgerran. That year, as Richard, king of England, was fighting against the castle of a certain baron, who was opposed to him, he was wounded by an arrow, and of that wound he died; and then his brother John was advanced to be king.

1200. One thousand two hundred was the year of Christ, when Gruffudd, son of Cynan, son of Owain, died, after taking upon him the religious habit, at Aberconway,—[1] the man who was known by all in the isle of Britain for the extent of his gifts, and his kindness and goodness; and no wonder, for as long as the men who are now shall live, they will remember his renown, and his praise, and his deeds.' In that year, Maelgwn, son of Rhys, sold Aberteivi, the key of all Wales, for a trifling value, to the English, for fear of and out of hatred to his brother Gruffudd. The same year, [2] Madog, son of Gruffudd

---

[2] *E.*

Maelor] manachlaỼc Lenegwestyl ¹[yn ol yr hen groes] yn Ial.

MCCI. Y ulỼydyn rac Ỽyneb y goresgynnaỼd Llywelyn uab Iorwoerth gantref Llyyn wedy gỼrthlad Maredud ab Kynan o achaỼs y dỼyll. Y ulỼydyn honno nos wyl SulgỼyn ydaeth cofeint Ystrat Fflur yr eglỼys newyd a adeilyssit o aduỼynweith. Ychydic wedy hynny ygkylch gỼyl Bedyr a PhaỼl y llas Maredud uab Rys gỼas ieuanc aduỼyn campus ²[yn aruthder y wy elynyon karyat y gyueillyon megys lluchaden o dan y rwng toruoed aruawc gobeith y Deheuwyr agorouyn Lloegyr anryded y kaeroed athegwch y byt] YgkarnywyllaỼn a ²[Gruffud y vrawt aorysgynnawd] e gastell ynteu yn Llan ym Dyfri. Ar cantref yd oed yndaỼ a oresgynnaỼd Gruffud y uraỼt. Ac yny lle wedy hynny wyl Iago Ebostol y bu uarỼ Gruffud ab Rys yn Ystrat Fflur, wedy kymryt abit y crefyd ymdanaỼ, ac yno y cladỼyt. Y ulỼydyn honno y crynaỼd y dayar Ygkaerussalem.

MCCII. Y ulwydyn rac Ỽyneb y gỼrthladỼyt Maredud ab Kynan o Veironnyd y gan Howel ab Gruffud y nei ab y uraỼt ac yd yspeilỼyt yn llỼyr eithyr y varch. Y ulỼydyn honno yr Ỽythuet dyd gỼedy DuỼ GỼyl Bedyr a PhaỼl yd ymladaỼd y Kymry a chastell GỼerthrynyaỼn aoed eidaỼ Rosser Mortymer ac y kymhellassant y castellwyr y rodi y castell kyn penn yr Ỽythnos, ac y llosgassant ef hyt y prid. Y vlỼydyn honno amgylch gỼyl Ueir gyntaf yny kynhayaf y kyffroes Llywelyn uab Iorwoerth lu o Powys y

---

¹ E.

Maelor,' founded the monastery of Llanegwestl, ¹ near the old cross,' in Yale.

1201. The ensuing year, Llywelyn, son of Iorwerth, subdued the cantrev of Lleyn, having expelled Maredudd, son of Cynan, on account of his treachery. That year, on the eve of Whitsunday, the monks of Strata Florida came to the new church; which had been erected of splendid workmanship. A little while afterwards, about the feast of St. Peter and St. Paul, Maredudd, son of Rhys, an extremely courteous young man, ²the terror of his enemies, the love of his friends, being like a lightning of fire between armed hosts, the hope of the South Wales men, the dread of England, the honour of the cities, and the ornament of the world,' was slain at Carnwyllon; and ²Gruffudd, his brother, took possession of' his castle at Llanymddyvri. And the cantrev, in which it was situated, was taken possession of by Gruffudd, his brother. And immediately afterwards, on the feast of St. James the Apostle, Gruffudd, son of Rhys, died at Strata Florida, after having taken upon him the religious habit; and there he was buried. That year, there was an earthquake at Jerusalem.

1202. The ensuing year, Maredudd, son of Cynan, was expelled from Meirionydd, by Howel, son of Gruffudd, his nephew, son of his brother, and was despoiled of every thing but his horse. That year, the eighth day after the feast of St. Peter and St. Paul, the Welsh fought against the castle of Gwerthrynion, which was the property of Roger Mortimer, and compelled the garrison to deliver up the castle, before the end of a fortnight, and they burned it to the ground. That year, about the first feast of St. Mary in the autumn, Llywelyn, son of Iorwerth,

---

¹ *C.*

darestόg Gόenόynόyn idaό ac y oresgynn y όlat. Kanys kynn bei agos Gόenόynόyn idaό o gerennyd, gelyn oed idaό herόyd gόeithredoed. Ac ar hynt y gelόis attaό y tyόyssogyon ereill aoedynt gereint idaό y ymaruoll ar ryfelu y gyt yn erbyn Gόenόynόyn. A gόedy gόybot o Elisy ab Madawc [1] [ap Meredudd] hynny ymόrthod aόnaeth ar ymaruoll yggόyd paόb. Ac oe holl ynni aruaethu aόnaeth wneuthwr hedόch a Gόenόynόyn. Ac am hynny wedy hedychu o eglόyssόyr a chrefydwyr y rόg Gόenόynόyn a Llyόelyn a digyfoethet Elisy [1] [ap Madoc i ewythr]. Ac yn y diwed y rodet idaό ygkardaόt y ymborth gastell [2] [Krogen] a seith tref bychein y gyt ac ef. Ac uelly gόedy goresgyn castell y Bala yd ymchoelaόd Llywelyn drachefyn yn hyfryt. Y ulόydyn honno amgylch gόyl Uihangel y goresgynnaόd teulu Rys ieuanc ab Gruffud ab yr arglόyd Rys gastell Llan Ymdyfri.

MCCIII. Y ulόydyn rac όyneb y goresgynnaόd Rys ieuanc [1] [ap Gruffudd] gastell Llan Egόat. Ac yna y bu uarό Dauyd ab Owein yn Lloegyr wedy y dehol o Lywelyn ab Iorwoerth o Gymry. a Y ulόydyn honno y goresgynnaόd Gόenόynόyn a Maelgόn ab Rys

a/ 3 Yny vlwyddyn honn yr ynillwyd kastell Llan Ymddyfri a chastell Llan Gadoc i ar Vaelgwn ap Rys a Gwenwynwyn ap Owein Kyveilioc. Ynyr un amser y gorffennodd Maelgwn ap Rys gastell Dinerth.

[1] *E.* | [2] *C. E.*

raised an army from Powys, to bring Gwenwynwyn under his subjection, and to possess the country. For though Gwenwynwyn was near to him as to kindred, he was a foe to him as to deeds. And on his march he called to him all the other princes, who were related to him, to combine in making war together against Gwenwynwyn. And when Elise, son of Madog, [1]son of Maredudd,' became acquainted therewith, he refused to combine in the presence of all; and with all his energy he endeavoured to bring about a peace with Gwenwynwyn. And therefore, after the clergy and the religious had concluded a peace between Gwenwynwyn and Llywelyn, the territory of Elise, [1]son of Madog, his uncle,' was taken from him. And ultimately there was given him for maintenance, in charity, the castle [2]of Crogen,' with seven small townships. And thus, after conquering the castle of Bala, Llywelyn returned back happily. That year, about the feast of St. Michael, the family of young Rhys, son of Gruffudd, son of the lord Rhys, obtained possession of the castle of Llanymddyvri.

1203. The ensuing year, young Rhys, [1]son of Gruffudd,' subdued the castle of Llanegwad. And then died David, son of Owain, in England, after having been banished out of Wales by Llywelyn, son of Iorwerth. [a]That year Gwenwynwyn, and Maelgwn, son of Rhys, by devices got possession of the castle of

---

[a/3] In that year, the castle of Llanymddyvri and the castle of Llangadog were won from Maelgwn, son of Rhys, and Gwenwynwyn, son of Owain Cyveiliog. At the same time Maelgwn, son of Rhys, completed the castle of Dinerth.

---

[3] *E.*

drŵy dychymygyon gastell Llan ym Dyfri, a chastell Llan Gadaŵc; ac y cŵplaŵyt castell Dineirth.'

MCCIV. Y ulŵydyn rac ŵyneb y brathŵyt Howel Seis ab yr arglwyd Rys yg Kemeis drŵy dŵyll y gan wyr Maelgŵn y vraŵt, ac or brath hŵnnŵ y bu uarŵ, ac y cladŵyt yn Ystrat Flur, yn unwed a Grufud y vraŵt, wedy kymryt abit y crefyd ymdanaŵ. Y vlŵydyn honno y colles Maelgŵn ab Rys allwedeu y holl gyfoeth. Nyt amgen Llan Ymdyfri a Dinefŵr. Kanys meibon y vraŵt ae hennillaŵd arnaŵ yn ŵraŵl. Y ulŵydyn honno y deuth Gŵilim Marsgal adiruaŵr lu gantaŵ y ymlad a Chil Gerran, ac y goresgynnaŵd.

MCCV. Y ulŵydyn rac ŵyneb y bu uarŵ Hubert archescob Keint, y gŵr aoed ᵃlygat yr pab a phenn prelat holl Loegyr. Y ulŵydyn honno y peris Maelgŵn uab Rys ᵇy dyd kyntaf or gŵedieu yr haf' y neb un ŵydel ᶜAbŵell lad Kediuor ab ¹Griffri, gŵr da aduŵyn ae pedwar arderchogyon veibon gyt ac ef a hanhoedynt o dylyedaŵc voned. Kanys y mam oed Susanna verch Howel ²[ap Ievaf], o uerch Madaŵc uab Maredud ²[ap Bleddyn ap Kynvyn].

MCCVI. Y ulŵydyn rac ŵyneb y deuth Ieuan gardinal hyt yn Lloegyr, ac y kynnullaŵd attaŵ holl escyb ac abadeu Lloegyr, ac aneiryf o eglŵysŵyr a chrefydwyr ŵrth wneuthyr sened. Ac yny sened honno y kadarnhaaŵd kyfreith yr eglŵys drŵy yr holl

---

a ³ legat
b ³ duw Llun kynn difyeu Kyfarchauel
c ³ abwyall

---

¹ Gruffydd, C. | ² E.

Llanymddyvri, and the castle of Llangadog; and the castle of Dineirth was completed.'

1204. The ensuing year, Howel the Saxon, son of the lord Rhys, was stabbed at Cemaes, through treachery, by the men of Maelgwn, his brother, of which stab he died, and was buried at Strata Florida, in the same manner as his brother Gruffudd, after having taken upon him the habit of religion. That year, Maelgwn, son of Rhys, lost the keys of all his dominion, to wit, Llanymddyvri and Dinevwr; for the sons of his brother Gruffudd manfully won them from him. The same year, William Marshall came with a vast army to fight against Cilgerran, which he subdued.

1205. The ensuing year, Hubert, archbishop of Canterbury, died,—the man who was the ᵃ eye of the pope, and the head prelate of all England. That year, Maelgwn, son of Rhys, ᵇ on the first day of Rogations in the summer,' instigated a certain Irishman, ᶜ Abwell, to kill Cedivor, son of ¹ Griffri, a good benign man, and his four noble sons with him, who were descended of honourable lineage; for his mother was Susannah, daughter of Howel, ² son of Ieuav,' by a daughter of Madog, son of Maredudd, ² son of Bleddyn, son of Cynvyn.'

1206. The ensuing year, cardinal John arrived in England, and collected all the bishops and abbots of England, with innumerable churchmen and religious persons, to hold a senate; and in that senate he confirmed the church law through the whole kingdom.

ᵃ ³ legate
ᵇ ³ on the Monday before Ascension Thursday,
ᶜ ³ with an axe

---

³ *C.*

deyrnas. Y ulỽydyn honno y gỽnaeth Maelgỽn ab Rys gastell Aber Einaỽn. Ac yna y rodes Duỽ amylder o byscaỽt yn Aber Ystỽyth yn gymeint ac nabu y kyfryỽ kynno hynny.

MCCVII. Y ulỽydyn rac ỽyneb y gỽahardỽyt y Gristonogaeth y gan y pab yn holl teyrnas Loeger o achaỽs gỽrthỽynebu o Ieuan vrenhin etholedigaeth archescob Keint. Y ulỽydyn honno y gỽrthladaỽd Ieuan vrenhin Wilim Breỽys a Gỽilim ieuanc y vab ae gỽraged ae hỽyron o gyghoruynt achas hyt yn Iwerdon drỽy amarch a chollet ar yr eidunt. Y ulỽydyn honno y delis y brenhin Wenỽynỽyn yn Amỽythic. Ac y goresgynnaỽd Llywelyn uab Iorwoerth y holl gyfoeth ae gestyll ae lyssoed. A phan ỽybu Uaelgỽn ab Rys hynny rac ofyn Llywelyn ab Iorwoerth y byryaỽd gastell Ystrat Meuruc yr llaỽr a llosgi Dineirth ac Aber Ystỽyth. Ac nyt edewis eissoes Lywelyn y aruaeth namyn dyfot a ỽnaeth hyt yn Aber Ystỽyth ae hadeilat, achymryt cantref Penwedic idaỽ ehun, a rodi dryll arall o Geredigyaỽn vch Ayron y veibon Gruffud ab Rys y nyeint. Y vlỽydyn honno y goresgynnaỽd Rys Vychan uab yr arglỽyd Rys gastell Llan Gadaỽc, heb goffau yr amot awnaethoed ae nyeint pan rodyssynt idaỽ gastell Dineftr.

MCCVIII. Y ulỽydyn rac ỽyneb yd ymladaỽd Rys ac Owein meibon Gruffud a chastell Llan Gadaỽc ac y llosgassant gan lad rei or kastellwyr a charcharu ereill.

MCCIX. [1][Blwydyn wedy hynny] y vlỽydyn honno ydaeth Ieuan urenhin a diruaỽr lu gantaỽ hyt yn Iwerdon, ac y duc y ar neibon Hu Dylasai y tir

---

[1] C.

That year, Maelgwn, son of Rhys, constructed the castle of Abereinion. And then God bestowed an abundance of fish at Aberystwyth, so much that the like had not been before.

1207. The ensuing year, Christianity was interdicted by the pope in the whole kingdom of England, because king John had opposed the election of the archbishop of Canterbury. That year, king John banished William Bruse, and young William, his son, with their wives and grandsons, to Ireland, out of jealousy and hatred, to their disrespect and loss of property. The same year, the king seized Gwenwynwyn at Shrewsbury; and Llywelyn, son of Iorwerth, took possession of all his territory, his castles, and his courts. And when Maelgwn, son of Rhys, became acquainted therewith, from fear of Llywelyn, son of Iorwerth, he razed the castle of Ystrad Meurug to the ground, and burned Dineirth and Aberystwyth. But Llywelyn did not desist from his purpose; for he came to Aberystwyth and repaired it, and took the cantrev of Penwedig to himself, giving the other portion of Ceredigion above Aeron to his nephews, the sons of Gruffudd, son of Rhys. That year, Rhys the Little, son of the lord Rhys, took possession of the castle of Llangadog, without regarding the agreement which he had made with his nephews, when they delivered to him the castle of Dinevwr.

1208. The ensuing year, Rhys and Owain, sons of Gruffudd, attacked the castle of Llangadog, which they burned, killing some of the garrison, and imprisoning others.

1209. [1]'A year after that,' the same year, king John went with an immense army into Ireland; and he took from the sons of Hugh de Lacy their land and their

---

[1] *C.*

ae ᵃ kestyll. A g0edy kymryt g0rogaeth y gan ba0b
o Iwerdon, a dala g0reic Wiliam Brewys a G0ilim
ieuanc y uab ae wreic ae vab ae verch yd ym-
choela0d y Loegyr yn enrydedus. Ac yna y llada0d
ef Wilim ieuanc ae uam o anrugara0c agheu ygkastell Windylsor. Y ul0ydyn honno yd adeila0d
iarll Kaer Lleon gastell Degan0y, yr h0nn a dorryssei
Lywelyn uab Iorwoerth kynno hynny rac ofyn y
brenhin. Ac yna hefyd yd adeila0d y iarll h0nn0
gastell ¹ Terfynna0n, ac y diffeitha0d Llywelyn ab
Iorwoerth gyfoeth y iarll h0nn0. Ac yna g0edy
hedychu o Rys ᵇ Gryc ar brenhin, dr0y nerth y brenhin y goresgynna0d gastell Llan Ymdyfri. Kanys y
castellwyr wedy annobeitha0 o bop ford a rodassant
y castell, ac un am0s ar bymthec yuda0 du0 g0yl
Ueir y Medi dr0y amot kael or castellwyr y kyrff a
phob peth or eidynt yn iach. Y ul0ydyn honno
amgylch g0yl Andras y goresgynna0d G0en0yn0yn y
gyfoeth drachefyn dr0y nerth Ieuan urenhin. O lewenyd hynny yd hedycha0d Maelg0n ab Rys ar brenhin
heb goffau y ll0 ar aruoll a vuassei y rygta0 a Rys
ac Owein meibon Gruffud ab Rys y nyeint, kynnulla0
diruu0r lu o Ffreinc a Chymry y rygta0 a Phenwedic
ac y doeth hyt Ygkil Kennin, ac yno pebyllya0 aoruc.
Ac yna y kynulla0d Rys ac Owein meibon Gruffud
trychan0r o etholedigyon deuluoed a hyt nos kyrchu
llu Maelg0n aorugant a llad llawer a dala ereill
agyrru y dryll arall ar ffo. Ac yny ur0ydyr honno

ᵃ ² chastell. ᵇ ³ Vychan

---

¹ Trerfynna0n, *E*. | ² *E*.

a castles. After receiving homage of all in Ireland, and capturing the wife of William Bruse, and young William, his son, with his wife and his son and daughter, he returned with honour to England. He then put young William and his mother unmercifully to death in the castle of Windsor. That year, the earl of Caerleon built the castle of Dyganwy, which Llywelyn, son of Iorwerth, had previously demolished, for fear of the king. And then also, that earl built the castle of Holywell; and Llywelyn, son of Iorwerth, ravaged the territory of that earl. And then, after Rhys b the Hoarse' had made his peace with the king, he by the king's assistance obtained possession of the castle of Llanymddyvri; for the garrison, after despairing in every way, surrendered the castle, with sixteen steeds in it, on the feast day of St. Mary in September, under an agreement that the garrison should have their bodies safe, with every thing belonging to them. That year, about the feast of St. Andrew, Gwenwynwyn repossessed himself of his dominion, by the assistance of king John. Out of joy thereat, Maelgwn, son of Rhys, made peace with the king, without regarding the oath and engagement that existed between him and Rhys, and Owain, his nephews, the sons of Gruffudd, son of Rhys; and he collected a vast army of French and Welsh, directing his course towards Penwedig, and came to Cilcenin, where he encamped. And then, Rhys and Owain, the sons of Gruffudd, collected three hundred men out of select families, who by night attacked the army of Maelgwn, killed many, captured others, and put the remainder to flight. And in that battle,

---

a ² castle. b' ³ the Little

³ C. E.

ydelit [1] Kynan ab' Howel nei Maelgẃn, a Gruffud ab [2] Kynan penn kyghorẃr Maelgẃn, ac y llas Einaẃn ab Cradaẃc ac aneiryf o rei creill. Ac yna y diegis Maelgẃn ar y draet yn ffo yn waratwydus. Y ulẃydyn honno y cadarnhaaẃd [3] [Gelart] synyscal Kaer Loyẃ gastell Buellt, wedy llad or Kymry lawer oe wyr kyn no hynny. Y vlẃydyn honno [3] [gwyl Domas verthr] y bu uarẃ Mahallt y Brewys mam meibon Gruffudd uab Rys yn Llan Badarn Vaẃr, wedy kymryt kymun a chyffes a phenyt ac abit y crefyd ac y cladẃyt y gyt ae gẃr priaẃt yn Ystrat Fflur.

MCCX. Deg mlyned a deucant a mil oed oet Crist pan duc Llywelyn ab Iorwoerth greulonyon gyrcheu am benn y Saeson, ac am hynny y llidyaẃd Ieuan urenhin, ac aruaethu aẃnaeth digyfoethi Llywelyn o gẃbyl. A chynullaẃ diruaẃr lu aoruc tu a Gẃyned ar uedyr y distryẃ oll. A chyt ae lu ef y dyfynnaẃd attaẃ hyt Ygkaer Lleon hynn o dywyssogyon Kymry; Gẃenẃynẃyn o Powys, a Howel ab Gruffud ab Kynan [4] [o Wynedd], a Madaẃc ab Grufud Maelaẃr, a Maredud ab Rotbert o Gedewin, a Maelgẃn a Rys [a] Gryc meibon yr arglẃyd Rys. Ac yna y mudaẃd Llywelyn ae giwtaẃt y perued y ẃlat ae da hyt yn mynyd Eryri, a chiẃtaẃt Von ae da yn vnffunyt. Ac yna y daeth y brenhin ae lu hyt yg kastell Deganẃy. Ac yno y bu kymeint eisseu bẃyt ar y llu ac y

---

a [3] Vychan

---

[1] *Not in E.*   [2] *Kadwgon, C. E.*

¹ Cynan, son of ' Howel, nephew to Maelgwn, and Gruffudd, son of ² Cynan, Maelgwn's chief counsellor, were captured; and Einon, son of Caradog, and an immense number of others, were slain. And then, Maelgwn disgracefully fled, escaping on foot. That year, ³ Gelart, seneschal of Gloucester, fortified the castle of Buellt, after the Welsh had previously killed many of his men. That year, ³ on the feast of St. Thomas the Martyr,' Mahalt de Bruse, the mother of the sons of Gruffudd, son of Rhys, died at Llanbadarn the Great, after receiving the communion, and confession, and penance, and the habit of religion, and was buried with her husband at Strata Florida.

1210. One thousand two hundred and ten was the year of Christ, when Llywelyn, son of Iorwerth, made cruel attacks upon the English; and on that account king John became enraged, and formed a design of entirely divesting Llywelyn of his dominion. And he collected a vast army towards Gwynedd, with the view of utterly destroying it. And to join his army, he summoned to him at Caerleon these princes of Wales; —Gwenwynwyn of Powys, and Howel, son of Gruffudd, son of Cynan, ⁴ of Gwynedd,' and Madog, son of Gruffudd Maelor, and Maredudd, son of Robert, of Cydewain, and Maelgwn, and Rhys ᵃ the Hoarse,' the sons of the lord Rhys. And thereupon, Llywelyn moved with his forces into the middle of the country, and his property to the mountain of Eryri; and the forces of Mona, with their property, in the same manner. Then the king with his army came to the castle of Dyganwy. And there the army was in so great a want of provisions, that an egg was sold

---

ᵃ/ ³ the Little

---

³ *C. E.* | ⁴ *E.*

gỽerthit yr ỽy yr keinaỽc a dimei, a gỽled uoethus oed gantunt gael kic y meirch. Ac am hynny yd ymchoelaỽd y brenhin y Loegyr amgylch y Sulgỽyn ae neges yn amherffeith, wedy colli yn waradỽydus laỽer oe wyr ac oe da. A gỽedy hynny amgylch calan Aỽst yd ymchoelaỽd y brenhin y Gymry yn greulonach y vedỽl ac yn vỽy y lu. Ac adeilat llawer o gestyll Yggỽyned a wnaeth. A thrỽy auon Gonỽy ydaeth tu a mynyd Eryri. Ac annoc rei oe lu a wnaeth y losgi Bangor. Ac yno y delit Rotbert escob Bangor yny eglỽys, ac y gỽerthỽyt wedy hynny yr deu cant hebauc. Ac yna heb allel o Lywelyn diodef creulonder y brenhin drỽy gyghor y wyrda yd anuones y wreic at y brenhin yr honn oed verch yr brenhin y wneuthur hedỽch y rygtaỽ ar brenhin pa ffuryf bynhac y gallei. A gỽedy caffel o Lywelyn diogelrỽyd y uynet att y brenhin ac y dyuot ef aaeth attaỽ ac ahedychaỽd ac ef drỽy rodi gỽystlon yr brenhin o vonhedigyon y wlat, ac vgein mil o warthec a deugein emys; a chanhattau hefyt yr brenhin y berued wlat yn dragywydaỽl. Ac yna yd hedychaỽd ar brenhin holl dywyssogyon Kymry, eithyr Rys ac Owein meibon Gruffud ab Rys, ac yd ymchoelaỽd y brenhin y Loegyr drỽy diruaỽr lewenyd yn uudugaỽl. Ac yna y gorchymynnaỽd ef yr tywyssogyon hynny gymryt ygyt ac ỽynt holl lu Morgannỽc a Dyuet, a Rys Gryc, a Maelgỽn ab Rys ae lluoed, amynet am benn meibon Rys ab Gruffud ab Rys y gymell arnunt y dyuot y laỽ, neu gilyaỽ ar dehol or holl deyrnas. Ac yna y kymhellaỽd synyscal Kaer Dyf, gỽr a oed dywyssaỽc ar y llu, a Rys a Maelgỽn meibon yr arglỽyd Rys y lluoed ae kedernit achyrchu Pennwedic awnaethant. A gwedy na allei Rys ac Owein meibon Gruffud ymerbynyeit ar ueint allu hỽnnỽ, ac nat oed le ryd udunt yg

for a penny halfpenny; and it was a delicious feast to them to get horse flesh; and on that account the king returned to England about Whitsuntide, with his errand imperfect, after disgracefully losing many of his men and much property. After that, about the calends of August, the king returned to Wales, his mind being more cruel and his army larger, and he built many castles in Gwynedd. And he proceeded over the river Conway towards the mountain of Eryri, and incited some of his troops to burn Bangor. And there Robert, bishop of Bangor, was seized in his church, and was afterwards ransomed for two hundred hawks. Then Llywelyn, being unable to bear the cruelty of the king, by the advice of his liege men, sent his wife, who was daughter of the king, to the king, to make peace between him and the king, in any manner she might be able. After Llywelyn had obtained safe conduct to go to and from the king, he went to him and made his peace with him, by delivering hostages to the king of the nobles of the country, with twenty thousand cattle, and forty steeds, and consigning also the midland district to the king for ever. And thereupon all the Welsh princes, except Rhys and Owain, the sons of Gruffudd, son of Rhys, made peace with the king; and the king returned victoriously, and with extreme joy, to England. And then, the king commanded those princes to take with them all the troops of Morganwg and Dyved, with Rhys the Hoarse, and Maelgwn, son of Rhys, and their forces, and to go against the sons of Rhys, son of Gruffudd, son of Rhys, to compel them to surrender themselves into his hands, or to retire into banishment out of all the kingdom. And then the seneschal of Cardiff, the man who was the leader of the army, and Rhys, and Maelgwn, sons of the lord Rhys, urged their troops and their strength, and repaired to Penwedig. And since Rhys and Owain, the sons of Gruffudd, could not withstand a power of that magnitude, and there

Kymry y gyrchu idaỽ anuon kenadeu aorugant at Ffaỽcỽn y wneuthur y hedỽch. A hedychu ac ef awnaethant, a chanhattau awnaethant yr brenhin y kyfoeth rỽg Dyfi ac Aeron, ac adeilat aoruc Ffaỽcỽn gastell yr brenhin yn Aber Ystỽyth. Ac yna yd aeth Rys ac Owein meibon Gruffud ar gỽndit Ffaỽcỽnn y lys y brenhin, ae kymryt aoruc y brenhin yn gyfeillon idaỽ. A thra yttoedynt hỽy yn mynet y lys y brenhin, ediuarhau aoruc Maelgỽn uab Rys a Rys Gryc y uraỽt y hamodeu ar brenhin, a chyrchu aỽnaethant am benn y castell newyd yn Aber Ystỽyth ae dorri. A phan doeth Rys ac Owein veibon Gruffud ab Rys o lys y brenhin wedy hedychu ac ef kyrchu awnaethant Is Aeron cyuoeth Maelgỽn ª uab Rys' a llad allosgi ac anreithaỽ y kyuoeth aỽnaethant. Ac yno y llas gỽas ieuanc da deỽr oed hỽnnỽ ¹[Gruffydd ap Ivor, ac y bu varw Mredudd ap Karadoc].

MCCXI. Y ulỽydyn rac ỽyneb wedy na allei Lywelyn ab Iorwoerth dywyssaỽc Gỽyned diodef y genifer sarhaet awnaei wyr y brenhin idaỽ a edewyssit yn y castell newyd ²[yn Aber Konwy], ymaruoll aoruc a thywyssogyon Kymry nyt amgen Gỽenỽynỽyn a Maelgỽn ab Rys, a Madaỽc ab Gruffud Maclaỽr, a Maredud ab Rotbert; a chyfodi aoruc yn erbyn y brenhin, a goresgyn yr holl gestyll aỽnaethoed yg Gỽyned eithyr Deganỽy a Rudlan Marthaual ym Powys a wnathoed Robert Vepỽnt hỽnnỽ aoreskynnassant. A phan oedynt lyn goresgyn hỽnnỽ y doeth y brenhin a diruaỽr lu y gyt ac ef y gỽrth-

---

ᵃ' ² a Rys Gryc

---

¹ C.

was not a place open for them in Wales to repair to, they sent messengers to Foulke, to bring about a peace. And they made peace with him; and they consented that the king should have the territory between the Dyvi and Aeron; and Foulke built a castle for the king at Aberystwyth. And then, Rhys and Owain, the sons of Gruffudd, went, under the safe conduct of Foulke, to the court of the king; and the king received them as friends. And whilst they were repairing to the king's court, Maelgwn, son of Rhys, and his brother Rhys the Hoarse, repented of their terms with the king, and made an attack upon the new castle at Aberystwyth, and demolished it. And when Rhys and Owain, the sons of Gruffudd, son of Rhys, returned from the king's court, after making their peace with him, they entered Lower Aeron, the territory of Maelgwn, ᵃ son of Rhys,' and killed and burned and ravaged in the district. And there a good and brave young man was slain, [1] Gruffudd, son of Ivor; and Maredudd, son of Caradog, died.'

1211. The ensuing year, as Llywelyn, son of Iorwerth, prince of Gwynedd, could not brook the many insults done to him by the men of the king, who had been left in the new castle ²at Aberconway,' he confederated with the Welsh princes, namely, Gwenwynwyn, and Maelgwn, son of Rhys, and Madog, son of Gruffudd Maelor, and Maredudd, son of Robert; and rose against the king, subduing all the castles which he had made in Gwynedd, except Dyganwy and Rhuddlan; Mathraval, in Powys, made by Robert Vepont, they subdued, and whilst they were reducing that, the king, with a vast army, came to oppose

---

ᵃ/ ² and Rhys the Hoarse

---

² E.

lad ac ef ehun athan ae llosges. Y ulʋydyn honno y croges Robert Vepʋnt yn Amʋythic Rys ab Maelgʋn aoed yg gʋystyl y gan y brenhin, heb y uot yn seith mlʋyd etto. Ac yny ulʋydyn honno y bu uarʋ Robert escob Bangor.

MCCXII. Y vlʋydyn rac ʋyneb y bu urʋydyr ynyr Yspaen y rʋg y Cristonogyon ar Sarassinyeit; yny vrʋydyr honno y dyʋedir dygʋydaʋ deg mil o wyr a their mil o wraged. Y ulʋydyn honno y croget yn Lloeger trywyr arderchaʋc o genedyl a phrif tywyssogyon Kymry. Nyt amgen Howel ab Katwallaʋn, a Madaʋc uab Maelgʋn, a Meuruc Barach. Y ulʋydyn honno y rydhaaʋd Innossens bap y tri thywyssaʋc. Nyt amgen Llywelyn ab Iorwerth, a Gʋenʋynʋyn a Maelgʋn ab Rys or llʋ ar ffydlonder a rodassynt y urenhin Lloegyr. A gorchymyn udunt aʋnaeth yn uadeueint or pechodeu dodi gofalus garedicrʋyd y ryuelu yn erbyn enwired y brenhin. ᵃA gʋahard y Gristnogaeth a baryssei yr yspump mlyned kynno hynny yn Lloegyr a Chymry, y rydhaaʋd y pab y tri thywyssaʋc gynneu oe kyuoetheu' a phaʋb ar a uei vn ac ʋynt. Ac ʋynteu yn gyfun agyuodassant yn erbyn y brenhin. Ac a oreskynnassant ynʋraʋl ¹y arnaʋ y berued wlat, a dugassei ynteu kyn no hynny y ar Lywelyn ab Iorwoerth.

MCCXIII. Y ulʋydyn rac ʋyneb wedy gʋeled o Rys ieuanc y uot yn dirran o gyfoeth anuon kenadeu

---

ᵃ'² Ac ef a wahardawd yr eglwysseu pump mlyned yn holl Loegyr a Chymry eithur kyfoeth ytri tywyssawc hynny,

---

¹ B. resumes here.

them, and he himself burned it with fire. That year, Robert Vepont hanged, at Shrewsbury, Rhys, son of Maelgwn, who was a hostage to the king, not being yet seven years old. And in the same year, Robert, bishop of Bangor, died.

1212. The ensuing year, there was a battle in Spain between the Christians and Saracens. In that battle, it is said, ten thousand men, and three thousand women, fell. That year, three illustrious men, of the nation and chief princes of Wales, were hanged in England; that is to say, Howel, son of Cadwalader, and Madog, son of Maelgwn, and Meurug Barach. That year, pope Innocent absolved the three princes, namely, Llywelyn, son of Iorwerth, and Gwenwynwyn, and Maelgwn, son of Rhys, from the oath of fidelity which they had given to the king of England. And he commanded them, for the pardon of their sins, to give a sincere pledge of warring against the iniquity of the king. ᵃAnd the interdiction of Christianity, which he had ordered five years previously in England and Wales, was remitted by the pope to the three princes before mentioned, within their dominions,' and to all who were united with them. And they, with one consent, rose against the king, and bravely wrested from him the midland district, which he had previously taken from Llywelyn, son of Iorwerth.

1213. The ensuing year, when young Rhys saw that he had no portion of territory, he sent mes-

---

ᵃ'² And he had interdicted the churches five years in all England and Wales, except the territory of those three princes,

aoruc att y brenhin y eruynneit idaꝟ drꝟy y nerth ef peri idaꝟ rann o dref y dat. Ac yna ydanuones y brenhin att synyscal Henford, ac at ¹ Ffaꝟcꝟn synyscal Kaer Dyf, a gorchymmyn ²[vdunt] beri y Rys Gryc rodi castell Llan Ymdyfri ar wlat ³[y veibyon Gruffudd vab Rys] neu ynteu a gilyei ᵃo deruyneu y wlat' ar dehol. A gꝟedy dyfynnu Rys Gryc y atteb ꝟrth ⁴orchymynneu y brenhin. A dywedut aoruc yn atteb na rannei ef un erꝟ a Rys ieuanc. Ac yna llidiaꝟ aoruc Rys ieuanc, a chynnullaꝟ diruaꝟr lu o Vrecheinaꝟc, a dyfot y dreis aoruc y Ystrat Tywi, a phebyllyaꝟ yny lle aelꝟir Trallꝟc Elgan, ᵇ²[dyꝟ Ieu] wedy yr ꝟythuet dyd o wyl Seint Ilar.' A thrannoeth duꝟ Gꝟener y doeth attaꝟ Owein y vraꝟt, a ⁵Phaꝟcꝟn synysgal Kaerdyf ae lluoed. A thrannoeth kyrchu a orugant gyuoeth Rys Gryc a chyweiryaꝟ y bydinoed, a dodi Rys ieuanc ae vydin yny blaen, a ⁵Ffaꝟcꝟn ae vydin yn y canaꝟl, ac Owein ab Gruffud ae vydin yn ol. Ac ny bu bell yny gyuarvu Rys ᶜGryc ac ꝟynt. Ac yny vrꝟydyr ar vydin gyntaf y goruuꝟyt ar Rys Gryc ae wyr, ac y kilyaꝟd ar ffo wedy llad llaꝟer oe wyr a dala ereill. Ac yna yd aeth Rys ieuanc aruedyr ymlad

---

ᵃ'⁶ or teyrnas oll
ᵇ'⁷ athrannoeth diuyeu nessaf wedy gwyl Seint Yllari. ᶜ⁸ Vychan

---

¹ Fauk, B. ³ C.
² B. ⁴ orchymynn, B.

sengers to the king, to beseech him, that through his
power, he would cause him to have a share of his
father's inheritance. And thereupon the king sent to
the seneschal of Hereford, and to Foulke, seneschal
of Cardiff, commanding ²them to compel Rhys the
Hoarse to deliver up the castle of Llanymddyvri and
the district ³to the sons of Gruffudd, son of Rhys,' or
to retire ªfrom the borders of the country' into exile.
And after citing Rhys the Hoarse to answer to the
king's commands, he said in his reply that he would
not divide a single acre with young Rhys. Thereupon
young Rhys became enraged, and collected a vast army
out of Brecheiniog, and came in a hostile manner to
the Vale of Tywi, and encamped in the place called
Trallwng Elgan ᵇ²on the Thursday' after the octave
of the feast of St. Hilary.' And the following morning, being Friday, his brother Owain came to him,
and ⁵Foulke, the seneschal of Cardiff, with their forces.
The following day, they entered the territory of Rhys
the Hoarse, arrayed their troops, and placed young
Rhys with his force in the van, and ⁵Foulke with
his force in the centre, and Owain, son of Gruffudd,
with his force in the rear. And it was not long
before Rhys ᶜthe Hoarse' met them; and in the attack
with the first division, Rhys the Hoarse and his men
were overpowered, and he retreated and fled, after
having many of his men killed, and others taken.
And then young Rhys went, with the intention of

---

a′ ⁶ from all the kingdom
b′ ⁷ the following Thursday next after the feast of
St. Hilary.   c′ ⁸ the Little

---

³ Fabcoc, B.   ⁷ C.
⁴ B.   ⁸ C. E.

a chastell Dinefŵr. Ac eissoes Rys ªGryc ac raculaenaŵd ac a gadarnhaaŵd y gastell owyr ac arfeu. A gŵedy llosgi Llan Deilaŵ ¹kilyaŵ ymeith' aoruc Rys ªGryc. Ac eissoes Rys ieuanc a gyrchaŵd y castell, a thrannoeth dodi ²[a oruc] peiranneu a dechymygyon y ymlad ar castell. A gŵneuthur ystolyon ŵrth y muroed y wyr y drigaŵ dros y muroed, ac uelly y goresgynnaŵd ef y castell oll eithyr vn tŵr, ac yn hŵnnŵ ³yd ymgymerth y castellwyr ŵrth ymlad ac amdiffyn ac ergydyeu ac a pheiryanneu ereill; ac o dy allan yd oed saethydyon, ac arblastwyr, a mŵynwyr, a marchogyon yn ymlad ac ŵynt. Ac uelly y kymhellŵyt arnunt kynn y prynbaŵn talu y castell a rodi tri gŵystyl aŵnaethant ⁴[arodi y castell onny cheffynt nerth erbyn echŵyd trannoeth] drŵy amot cael ⁵y dillat ae harueu ae haeloden yn iach. Ac uelly y gŵnaethpŵyt. A gŵedy cael y castell ⁶[ac oresgyn tir y Kantrev Mawr] y kilyaŵd Rys ªGryc ae wreic ae veibon ae deulu att Vaelgŵn y vraŵt, wedy cadarnhau castell Llan Ymdyfri o wyr ac arueu ²[a bŵyt, a pheiryannev] ac aghenreiteu ereill. Ac eilweith ydaeth Rys ieuanc y Vrecheinaŵc. Ac yna kynullaŵ diruaŵr lu aoruc o Gymry a Ffreinc, achyrchu Llan Ymdyfri. A chynn pebyllu o nadunt ef a rodes y castellwyr y castell idaŵ drŵy amot cael y heneideu ae haelodeu yn iach. Y ulŵydyn honno y kymerth Ieuan urenhin benyt am y cameu aŵnath oed yn erbyn yr eglŵys, a galŵ drachefyn archescol

ª⁷ Vychan

¹′ y kilyaŵd ymdeith, *B.*
² *B.*
³ yr, *B.*
⁴ *B. C.*

attacking the castle of Dinevwr; however, Rhys ᵃ the Hoarse' preceded him, and strengthened his castle with men and arms; and after burning Llandeilo, Rhys ᵃ the Hoarse' retired hence. Nevertheless, young Rhys invested the castle; and the following day he placed engines and inventions for attacking the castle, and placed ladders against the walls, for men to climb over the walls, and thus did he possess himself of the castle altogether, save one tower; and in that the garrison secured themselves in fighting and defending, with missiles and other engines. And outside were the archers, and crossbowmen, and miners, and horsemen, fighting against them. And thus they were compelled, before the afternoon, to surrender the castle; and they delivered three hostages, ⁴ and gave up the castle, unless they should receive support by the evening of next day,' under an agreement to have their clothes and their arms, with the safety of their limbs; and thus it was concluded. And after they had got the castle, ⁵ and subdued the land of Cantrev Mawr,' Rhys ᵃ the Hoarse,' with his wife, his sons, and family, retired to his brother Maelgwn, having strengthened the castle of Llanymddyvri with men and arms, ² and food and engines,' and other necessaries. And a second time, young Rhys went to Brecheiniog; and there he collected a vast army of Welsh and French, and proceeded to Llanymddyvri; and before they had pitched their tents, the garrison gave up the castle, on condition of safety of lives and limbs. That year, king John did penance for the wrongs he committed against the church, and recalled

---

ᵃ⁷ the Little

---

¹ a, B.
⁵ C.

² C. E.

Kcint, ar esgyb ar yscolheigon a ymrodassynt y alltuded o achaṽs gṽahard yr eglṽysseu. Ac o achaṽs
y gṽrthrṽm godyant aṽnathoed yr eglṽys yd ymrṽym-
aṽd ef ae etiuedyon ae holl urenhinyaeth Lloegyr ac
Iwerdon y Duṽ a Phedyr a Phaṽl, ar pab ar pabeu
ereill yny ol yn dragywydaṽl. Ac ar hynny gṽneuthur
gṽrogaeth gan tyghu talu y baṽp or eglṽysswyr y
collet, a thalu mil o vorckeu bob blṽydyn y eglṽys
Rufein ¹[dros bop goddyant a gṽasanaeth dylyedus].
Y ulṽydyn honno gwedy ymadaṽ o Rys Gryc ar
Kymry a mynnu hedychu ac ṽynt eilweith herṽyd
y dyweit. Yna y delit ef yg Kaer Vyrdin ac y
dodet ²[ef] ygarchar y brenhin. Y ulṽydyn honno y
darestygaṽd Llywelyn uab Iorwoerth gastell Deganṽy
a chastell Rudlan.

MCCXIV. Y vlṽydyn rac ṽyneb y mordṽyaṽd Ieuan
urenhin ac ²[diruaṽr] amylder o ryfelwyr aruaṽc y
gyt ac ef hyt ym Pheitaṽ. Ac ymaruoll ac ef aoruc
iarll Fflandrys a ªBar a Henaṽnt. Ac anuon attunt
awnaeth ieirll Sarur y gyt ae vraṽt ac anneiryf a
uarchogyon, a gṽahaṽd attaṽ Otho amheraṽdyr Rufein
y nei, a chyfodi aoruc y ryfelu yn erbyn Phylip brenhin Freinc. Ac yna y magṽyt diruaṽr ryfel y rygtunt.
Otho amheraṽdyr Rufein ar iarll o parthret Flandrys
yn ryfelu, ar Ffreinc a Ieuan urenhin, o parthret
Peitaṽ yn aflonydu. Ac uelly o bop tu yd oedynt
yn kymhurthaṽ y Ffreinc. Ac yna ydanuones Phylip
arderchaṽc urenhin Ffreinc Lowys y uab y Peitaṽ a
llu y gyt ac ef y ymerbynyeit abrenhin Lloegyr.
Ac ynteu ehun ³ar Ffreinc y gyt ac ef a dynaṽd tu

ª⁴ yarll Bolwynn

---

¹ B. C. | ² B.

the archbishop of Canterbury, and the bishops and scholars, who had gone into exile, on account of the interdiction of the churches. And because of the oppressive vexation he had caused to the church, he bound himself, and his heirs, with his whole dominion of England and Ireland, to God and St. Peter and St. Paul, and the pope, and other popes successively for ever. And thereupon he did homage, swearing to pay to all the churchmen their loss, and to pay a thousand marks yearly to the church of Rome, ¹'for all vexation, and for every due service.' The same year, after Rhys the Hoarse had withdrawn himself from the Welsh, and sought a second time to make peace with them, as it is said, he was then seized at Caermarthen, and put in the king's prison. In that year, Llywelyn, son of Iorwerth, reduced the castle of Dyganwy and the castle of Rhuddlan.

1214. The ensuing year, king John, with a ³vast multitude of armed warriors, set sail for Poictou; and the earl of Flanders, and ᵃBar, and Hainault joined him. And the earl of Sarur, with his brother, and a great number of knights, sent to them, and invited to him Otho, emperor of Rome, his nephew; and he arose to make war against Phillip, king of France. And then a terrible war was kindled between them; Otho, emperor of Rome, and the earl warring on the part of Flanders, and the French and king John harrassing on the part of Poictou. And thus on every side they were distressing the French. Then Phillip, the noble king of France, sent his son Louis to Poictou, with an army to meet the king of England. And he himself, with the French, drew

---

ᵃ ⁴ the earl of Boleyn

---

³a, *B*.　　　　　|　⁴ *C*.

a Flandrys ynerbyn yr amheraỽdyr. A phan welas yr amheraỽdyr ar iarll hynny blỽg uu gantunt llauassu o vrenhin Freinc dynessau attunt, ae gyrchu yndic a [1] orugant. A gỽedy [a] yr ymlad ef a syrthyaỽd y nudugolyaeth y urenhin Freinc, ac a yrrỽyt yr amheraỽdyr ar ieirll ar ffo [b] o Fflandrys a Bar a Henaỽnt.' A phan gigleu brenhin Lloegyr y damỽein hỽnnỽ ofynhau a [2] wnaeth gynhal ryfel a vei vỽy, agỽneuthur kygreir seith mlyned aoruc a brenhin Ffreinc, ac ymchoelut y Loegyr, a thalu llawer oe colledeu yr eglỽysswyr. Ac yna y bu gyffredin ellygdaỽt yr eglỽysseu ar hyt Lloegyr a Chymry. Y ulỽydyn honno y bu uarỽ Geffrei escob Mynyỽ.

MCCXV. Y ulỽydyn rac ỽyneb y bu teruysc y rỽg Ieuan urenhin a Saesson y Gogled, a llaỽer o ieirll ereill a barỽneit Lloegyr, o achaỽs na chatwei Ieuan urenhin ac ỽynt yr henn gyffreith, a deuodeu da a [3] gaỽssynt gan Etwart a [4] Henri y brenhined kyntaf, a atygassei ynteu yr teyrnas pan rydhaaỽd rodi udunt y kyfreitheu hynny. Ar teruysc hỽnnỽ a gerdaỽd yn gymeint ac yd ymaruolles holl wyrda Lloegyr a holl dywyssogyon Kymry [5] [y gyt] yn erbyn y brenhin, hyt na mynnei neb o nadunt heb y gilyd y gan y brenhin na hedỽch na chyfundeb na chygreir yny dalei ef yr eglỽysseu y kyfreitheu ae [6] teilygdodeu, a

---

[a] [7] hir
[b] [8] adaly yarll Flandrys ayarll Bolwyn ayarll Sayrebus yn Vernwn.

---

[1] ỽnaethant, *B*.
[2] oruc, *B*.
[3] gossodynt, *B*.
[4] Alvryd, *E*.

towards Flanders, against the emperor. And when
the emperor and the earl saw that, it was galling to
them that the king of France should dare to approach
them, and they angrily attacked him. And after ᵃ the
fight, the victory fell to the king of France; and
the emperor and the earls were driven to flight, ᵇ from
Flanders and Bar and Hainault.' And when the
king of England heard of that event, he feared to
carry on war any longer, and so made a truce of
seven years with the king of France, and returned to
England; and paid many of their losses to the clergy.
And then there was a general remission to the
churches over England and Wales. That year, Jeffrey,
bishop of Menevia, died.

1215. The ensuing year, there was a disturbance
between king John and the English of the North,
and many others of the earls and barons of England,
because that king John would not keep with them
the old law and good customs which they had obtained from Edward and ⁴ Henry, the first kings, and
which he had withheld from the kingdom, when he
had released himself from giving them those laws.
And that disturbance extended so far that all the
good men of England, and all the princes of Wales
combined ⁵ together against the king, so that none of
them without the others would enter into peace or
agreement or truce with the king, until he restored
to the churches their laws and privileges, which he
and his ancestors had afore time taken from them;

ᵃ ⁷ a long

ᵇ ⁸ and the earl of Flanders, and the earl of Boleyn,
and the earl of Sayrebus, were captured at Vernon.

⁵ *B.*   ⁷ *B.*
⁴ teilygdaȯt, *B.*   ⁸ *C.*

dugassei ef aerieni kyn no hynny y gantunt ac yny ¹ dalei hefyt y wyrda Lloegyr a Chymry y tired ar kestyll a gymerassei wrth y ewyllys y gantunt heb na gwir na chyfreith. A gwedy ²eu dysgu o archescob Keint ac esgyb Lloegyr a ieirll ae barwneit a gofyn idaw arodei yr hen gyfreitheu da yr teyrnas y gomed aoruc a herwyd ³ryywespwyt rac y hofyn ⁴wynt, kymryt croes aoruc ac ual kynt y kyuodes y Gogledwyr yn y erbyn ⁵er neill tu, ar Kymry or tu arall. Ac yn y urwydyr gyntaf y ⁶duc y Gogledwyr y arnaw dinas Llundein. Ac yna y kyrchawd Llywelyn ab Iorwoerth ar Kymry y Amwythic. A heb wrthwynebed y rodet idaw y dref ar castell. Ac yna yd anuones Gilis o Brewys mab ⁷[y] Gwilim o Brewys Robert y urawt y Vrecheinawc. Ae gymryt yn enrydedus awnaeth gwyrda Brecheinawc idaw. A chynn penn y tri dieu y goreskynnawd castell Penn Kelli, ac Aber Gevenhi ar castell Gwyn ac ynys Gynwreid. Ar Gilis vry a oed escob yn Henford, ac auuassei vn or aruollwyr kyntaf yn erbyn y brenhin. A gwedy hynny ydaeth ynteu Gilis e hun y Vrecheinawc. Ac y goresgynnawd Aber Hodni a Maeshyfeid ar Gelli, a Blaen Llyfni, a chastell Buellt heb vn gwrthwynebed, castell Paen, a chastell Colwyn, a chantref Eluael wrthunt aedewis ef y Wallter ⁸[ap Gruffudd ap yr arglwydd Rys] uab Einawn Clut wrth y goresgynn. A thra yttoedit yn hynny ym Brecheinawc yd hedychawd Rys ieuanc ⁹[i nai] a Maelgwn uab Rys y ewythyr ac y kyrchassant Dyuet y gyt. Ac y goresgynnassant Gymry

---

¹ talei, *B.*
² y, *B.*
³ rydywespwyt, *B.*
⁴ hwy, *B.*
⁵ or, *B.*

and until he also restored to the good men of England and Wales their lands, and the castles, which he at his will had taken from them, without either right or law. And after they had been instructed by the archbishop of Canterbury, and the bishops of England, and his earls and his barons, they demanded whether he would restore the good old laws to the kingdom, but he refused them, as has been said before, from fear of them; and he took a cross; and, as before, the North men rose up against him, on one side, and the Welsh on the other side. And in the first battle, the North men took from him the city of London. And then Llywelyn, son of Iorwerth, with the Welsh, invested Shrewsbury; and without opposition the town and the castle were delivered up to him. Then Giles de Bruse, a son to William de Bruse, sent his brother Robert to Brecheiniog; and the good men of Brecheiniog received him honourably; and before the end of three days he took possession of the castles of Pencelli and Abergavenny, and the White Castle, and the isle of Cynwraid. The above Giles was bishop of Hereford, and had been one of the first confederates against the king. And after that, Giles himself also went to Brecheiniog, and obtained possession of Aberhodni, and Maes Hyvaidd, and Gelli, and Blaenllyvni, and the castle of Buellt, without any opposition; Pain's castle, and the castle of Colwyn, and the cantrev of Elvael attached to them, he left for Walter, ⁸ son of Gruffudd, son of the lord Rhys,' son of Einon Clud, who had subdued them. And whilst this was going on in Brecheiniog, young Rhys, ⁹ the nephew,' and Maelgwn, son of Rhys, his uncle, became reconciled, and they proceeded to Dyved together. And the Welsh obtained posses-

⁸ goresgynna(o)d, B.
¹ B.

⁸ C. E.
⁹ E.

a Dyfet oll eithyr Kemeis a honno aanreithassant, ¹[ac Arberth] ar Maen Clochaỗc a ²losgyssant. Ac ³odyna yd aeth Maelgỗn ac Owein ab Gruffud y Wyned att Lywelyn ab Iorwoerth, ac y kynnullaỗd Rys ieuanc lu diruaỗr y veint, ac y goresgynnaỗd Ketweli a Charnywyllaỗn, ac y llosges y castell, ac odyno y tynaỗd y Ghyr, ac yn gyntaf y goresgynnaỗd gastell Llychỗr. Ac odyno yd ymladaỗd achastell Hu. Ac yd aruaethaỗd y castellwyr gadỗ ¹[y castell] yny erbyn. Ac ynteu Rys agauas y castell y dreis gan ellỗg y castellwyr ar castell drỗy dan a haearn. Trannoeth y kyrchaỗd tu a ⁴[chastell Ystwm Llwyniarth yn] Sein Henyd, ac rac y ofyn ef y llosges y castellwyr y dref. Ac ⁵ỗynteu heb dorri ar y haruaeth agyrchassant gastell Ystumllỗynarth, a ⁶phebyllyaỗ yny gylch y nos honno a oruc, a thrannoeth y cauas y castell, ac y llosges ef ar dref. Ac erbyn penn y tri dieu y goresgynnaỗd holl gestyll Gỗhyr. Ac uelly yd ymchoelaỗd drachefyn yn hyfryt uudugaỗl. Ac yna y gellygỗyt Rys Gryc o garchar y brenhin gỗedy rodi y vab a deu wystyl ereill drostaỗ. Y ulỗydyn honno y gỗnaethpỗyt Iorỗoerth abat Tal y Llycheu yn escob ym Mynyỗ, a Chadỗgaỗn ᵃLlan Dyffei abat y Ty Gỗynn' yn escob Ymangor. Yna yd hedychaỗd Gilis escob Henford ar brenhin rac ofyn y pab, ac ar y fford ᵇynmynet att y brenhin' y clefychaỗd.

ᵃ/⁷ abat Llann Defit,
ᵇ/⁸ yn dyvod o lys y brenin   ¹ yn ymhoelut

¹ *B*.
² losgassant, *B*.
³ odyno, *B*.
⁴ *E*.

sion of all Dyved, with the exception of Cemaes, and that they ravaged, ¹and Arberth' and Maenclochog they burned. And from thence Maelgwn, and Owain, son of Gruffudd, proceeded to Gwynedd, to Llywelyn, son of Iorwerth. Young Rhys collected also an army of vast magnitude, and obtained possession of Cydweli, and Carnwyllon, and burned the castle. And from thence he drew to Gower; and he first reduced the castle of Llychwr, and afterwards he fought against the castle of Hugh, and the garrison essayed to keep ¹the castle' against him; but Rhys obtained the castle by force, passing the garrison and castle through fire and sword. The following day he marched towards ᵃthe castle of Ystum Llwynarth in' Senghenydd; and from fear of him, the garrison burned the town. And they, without being diverted from their purpose, proceeded to the castle of Ystum Llwynarth, and he encamped about it that night; and the following day he obtained the castle, which, with the town, he burned. And by the end of three days he reduced all the castles of Gower; and thus, happy and victorious, he returned home. And then, Rhys the Hoarse was liberated from the king's prison, after having given his son, and two other hostages for him. That year, Iorwerth, abbot of Tal y Llycheu, was made bishop of Menevia; and Cadwgan ᵃof Llandyfai, abbot of Whitland,' was made bishop of Bangor. Then Giles, bishop of Hereford, made peace with the king, from fear of the pope; and on the road, ᵇgoing to the king,' he was taken ill; and

---

ᵃ'⁷ abbot of Llandevid,
ᵇ'⁸ coming from the king's court, ¹ returning

ᵃ ynteu, B.
ᵉ phebyllu, B. Not in E.
⁷ C.
⁸ C. E.

Ac Ygkaer Loyỏ y bu uarỏ amgylch gỏyl Martin. ¹Ae dref tad' ef a gauas ²Reinald y Breỏys y uraỏt ³[ef]. A hỏnnỏ agymerth yn wreic idaỏ merch Lywelyn ab Iorwoerth tywyssaỏc Gỏyned. Y ulỏydyn honno y ᵃkynhalyaỏd y trydyd Innossens bap gyffredin gyghor or holl Gristonogaeth hyt yn eglỏys ⁴[Laterannis yn] Rufein. Ac yno yd atnewydỏyt kyfreitheu ⁵[a gossodedigaetheu] yr eglỏys, ac yd ymgyghoret am ᵇrydhau Kaerussalem adaroed ⁵yr Sarassinyeit y gywarsagu yr ysllawer o amseroed kynno hynny. Y ulỏydyn honno y kynnullaỏd Llywelyn ab Iorwoerth a chyffredin tywyssogyon Kymry diruaỏr lu hyt Ygkaer Uyrdin. A chynn penn y pumhet dyd y cauas y castell ac y byryaỏd yr llaỏr. Ac odyna y ⁶torryssant gastell Llan Ystyffan, a Thalacharn a Seint Cler. Ac odyna nos ỏyl Thomas ebostol ydaethant y Geredigyaỏn, ac ymlad ar castell ⁷[Emlyn] aorugant. Ac yna y gỏrhaaỏd gỏyr Kemeis y Lywelyn ab Iorwoerth, ac y rodet idaỏ gastell Trefdraeth. A hỏnnỏ o gyffredin gyghor a yssigỏyt. A phan welas castellwyr Aber Teifi na ellynt gynhal y castell y rodi awnaethant y Lywelyn ab Iorỏoerth duỏ gỏyl Ystyffan. A thrannoeth duỏ gỏyl Ieuan ebostol y rodet castell Kil Gerran idaỏ. Ac odyna yd ymchoelaỏd Llywelyn ab Iorwoerth, a holl tywyssogyon Kymry a oed y gyt ac ef yn hyfryt lawen ⁸y gỏlatoed drachefyn drỏy uudugolyaeth. A llyma ennỏeu y tywyssogyon a vuant ynyr hynt honno o ỏyned; Llywelyn ab Iorỏoerth tywyssaỏc Gỏyned, a Howel ab Grufud

---

ᵃ ³ kynullaỏd   ᵇ ³ nerthu

---

¹ Athref y tat, *B.*
² Reinallt, *B.*
³ *B.*
⁴ *B. C.*

he died at Gloucester, about the feast of St. Martin; and his patrimony came to his brother Rheinallt de Bruse, who took for his wife the daughter of Llywelyn, son of Iorwerth, prince of Gwynedd. That year, pope Innocent the third ᵃ held a general council of all Christendom at the ⁴ Lateran church in Rome. And there were the laws ³ and canons' of the church renewed; and it was resolved to ᵇ free Jerusalem, which the Saracens had oppressed for a long time before. That year, Llywelyn, son of Iorwerth, and the Welsh princes in general, collected a vast army to Caermarthen; and before the end of five days, he obtained the castle, and razed it to the ground. And then they demolished the castles of Llanstephan and Talacharn and St. Clare. And from thence, on the eve of the feast of St. Thomas the Apostle, they proceeded to Ceredigion, and fought against the castle ⁷ of Emlyn.' Then the men of Cemaes did homage to Llywelyn, son of Iorwerth, and the castle of Trevdraeth was delivered to him; which, by general consent, was shattered. And when the garrison of Aberystwyth saw that they could not maintain the castle, they delivered it up to Llywelyn, son of Iorwerth, on the feast of St. Stephen; and the following day, the feast of St. John the Apostle, the castle of Cilgerran was delivered to him. And then Llywelyn, son of Iorwerth, and all the Welsh princes that were with him, returned to their countries, happy and joyful with victory. And here are the names of the princes who were on that expedition from Gwynedd:— Llywelyn, son of Iorwerth, prince of Gwynedd, and

---

ᵃ ³ assembled   ᵇ ³ fortify

---

³ y, B.
⁴ torrassant, B.
⁷ C. E.
⁸ yó, B.

ab Kynan ¹[i ewythr], a Llyɓelyn ab Maredud ab Kynan. Ac o Poɓys Gɓenɓynɓyn ab Owein Kyueilaɓc, a Maredud ab Rotbert o Gedewein, a theulu Madaɓc ab Gruffud Madaɓc. A deu uab Maelgɓn ab Katwallaɓn. O Deheubarth Maelgɓn ab Rys a Rys Gryc y uraɓt, a Rys ieuanc ac Owein veibon Gruffud ab Rys. A llyma enɓeu y kestyll a oresgynnɓyt aryr hynt honno. Nyt amgen castell Sein Henyd, castell Ketweli Kaer Uyrdin, Llan Ystyffan, Seint Cler, Talacharn, Trefdraeth, Aber Teiui, Kil Gerran. Ac ar yr hynt ²honno y bu ᵃaraf hedɓch, a thegɓch hinon y gayaf, hyt na ɓelat ³[ac nachlyɓat] eiryoet kynno hynny y cyfryɓ hinda honno.

MCCXVI. ⁴[Blwydyn wedy hynny] ac yna y bu cyfran o tir y rɓg Maelgɓn ab Rys a Rys Gryc y uraɓt, a Rys ac Owein meibon Gruffud ab Rys, yn Aber Dyfi ger bron Llywelyn ab Iorwoerth gɓedy dyfynnu ³[yna] ygyt holl twyssogyon Kymry ³[gann mɓyhaf] a holl doethon Gɓyned. Ac y Uaelgɓn uab Rys y doeth tri chantref o Dyfet. Nyt amgen y cantref Gɓarthaf, a chantref Kemeis, a chantref Emlyn, a Phelunyaɓc, a chastell Kil Gerran, ac o Ystrat Tywi castell Llan Ymdyfri, a ᵇdeu gymɓt. Nyt amgen Hirfryn a Mallaen a Maenaɓr Vydfei. Ac o Gered-

---

ᵃ ³ arauɓch o   ᵇ ¹ thri

---

¹ E.   ² hɓnnɓ, B.

Howel, son of Gruffudd, son of Cynan, ¹his uncle,' and Llywelyn, son of Maredudd, son of Cynan; out of Powys, Gwenwynwyn, son of Owain Cyveiliog, and Maredudd, son of Robert of Cydewain, and the family of Madog, son of Gruffudd Madog, and the two sons of Maelgwn, son of Cadwallon; and out of South Wales, Maelgwn, son of Rhys, and Rhys the Hoarse, his brother, and young Rhys, and Owain, the sons of Gruffudd, son of Rhys. And these are the names of the castles which were subjugated in that expedition; that is to say, the castle of Senghenydd, the castle of Cydweli, Caermarthen, Llanstephan, St. Clare, Talacharn, Trevdraeth, Aberteivi, and Cilgerran. And during that expedition there was a ªgentle tranquillity, and fairness of winter atmosphere, such fine weather as had never been seen, ³or heard of' before.

1216. ⁴A year after that,' and then there was a partition of land between Maelgwn, son of Rhys, and his brother, Rhys the Hoarse, and Rhys and Owain, the sons of Gruffudd, son of Rhys, at Aberdovey, in the presence of Llywelyn, son of Iorwerth, when all the Welsh princes, ³for the most part,' and all the wise men of Gwynedd were summoned ³thither together. And to Maelgwn, son of Rhys, were allotted three cantrevs of Dyved, that is to say, the cantrev of Gwarthav, the cantrev of Cemaes, and the cantrev of Emlyn, with Penllwynog and the castle of Cilgerran; and of the Vale of Tywi, the castle of Llanymddyvri, with ᵇtwo comots, namely, Hirvryn and Mallaen, and the manor of Myddvai; and of Ceredigion, the two

---

ª ³ gentleness of   ᵇ ¹ three

---

³ *B.* | ⁴ *C.*

T

igyaẃn deu gymút, Gẃynyonyd a Mabwynyon. Ac y Rys ieuanc ac y Owein y uraẃt meibon Gruffud ab Rys y deuth castell Aber Teifi, a chastell Nant yr Aryant, athri cantref o Geredigyaẃn. Ac y Rys Gryc y doeth ¹[ynn rann] y Cantref Maẃr oll eithyr Mallaen, ar Cantref Bychan eithyr Hirvryn a Myduei. Ac idaẃ y deuth Ketweli a ²Charnywyllaẃn hefyt.' Yn y vlẃydyn honno ³yd hedychaẃd Gwenẃynẃyn arglẃyd Powys a Ieuan vrenhin Lloegyr, ⁴wedy tremygu y llẃ ar aruoll a rodassei y dyẃyssogyon Lloegyr a Chymry. A thorri yr ẃrogaeth a ⁵roessoed y Lywelyn ab Iorwoerth, a madeu y gẃystlon a rodassei ar hynny. ¹[A] gẃedy gẃybot o Lywelyn ab Iorwoerth hynny kymryt arnaẃ yn ẃrthrẃm a ⁶wnaeth, ac anvon attaẃ esgyb ac abadeu, a gẃyr ereill maẃr ⁷y haẃdurdaẃt ar llythyreu ar syartrasseu gantunt, ⁸ac echrestyr' yr aruoll ar ammot ar gẃrogaeth a ⁸ẃnathoed yndunt, o llauuryaẃ o bop medẃl acharyat a gẃeithret y alẃ drachefyn. A gẃedy nadygrynoei idaẃ hynny o dim, dygynnullaẃ llu aoruc, a galẃ canmẃyhaf tywyssogyon Kymry ygyt attaẃ, a chyrchu Powys y ryuelu ⁹ar Wenẃynẃyn, ae yrru arffo hyt yn sẃyd Kaer Lleon, a goresgyn y kyuoeth oll idaẃ e hun. Y ulẃydyn honno y doeth Lowys y mab hynaf y vrenhin Freinc hyt yn Lloegyr ¹[trẃy aruollẃyr Lloeger] gyt a lluossogrẃyd maẃr amgylch Sul y

a' ¹⁰ achraffter

---

¹ B.
²' Charnẃallaẃn, B.
³ y, B.
⁴ drẃy, B.
⁵ rodassoed, B.
⁶ oruc, B.

comots of Gwynionydd and Mabwynion. And to young Rhys, and his brother Owain, the sons of Gruffudd, son of Rhys, were allotted the castle of Aberteivi, and the castle of Nant yr Ariant, with three cantrevs of Ceredigion. And to Rhys the Hoarse were allotted, ¹ as his share,' the whole of Cantrev Mawr, except Mallaen, and the Cantrev Bychan, except Hirvryn and Myddvai; and to him likewise came Cydweli and ² Carnwyllon. In that year, Gwenwynwyn, lord of Powys, made peace with John, king of England, treating with contempt the oath and the engagement which he had plighted to the chieftains of England and Wales, and violating the homage which he had done to Llywelyn, son of Iorwerth, and surrendering the hostages that he had given thereon. ¹ And when Llywelyn, son of Iorwerth, became acquainted with this, he took it heavily upon him, and sent to him bishops and abbots and other men of great authority, bearing with them the letters and charters, ᵃ and the registers' of the compact and homage which he had made, and laboured by every thought and affection and deed to recal him back. And when that availed him nothing, he assembled an army, calling to him most of the princes of Wales, and entered Powys, to make war upon Gwenwynwyn, and compelled him to flee into the county of Caerleon, and took possession of his whole territory to himself. That year, Louis, the eldest son of the king of France, came to England, ¹ by means of English confederates, with a great multitude, about Trinity Sunday; and

---

ᵃ' ¹⁰ and the particulars

---

⁷ eu, *B*.
⁸ Gnaeth, *B*.
⁹ a, *B*.
¹⁰ *B*.

Drindaƅt, ac ofynhau aoruc Ieuan urenhin y dyuotyat ef, a chadƅ a oruc yr aberoed ar porthuaeu a diruaƅr gedernit o wyr aruaƅc ¹[y] gyt ac ef. A phan welas ef llyges Lowys yn dynessau yr tir, kymryt y ffo a oruc tu a Chaer Wynt a dyffryn Hafren. Ac ² yna y tynnaƅd Lowys tu a Llundein. Ac yna yd aruollet yn enrydedus, a chymryt aoruc gƅrogaeth y icirll ar barƅneit ac gƅahodassei, adechreu talu y kyfreitheu o baƅp o nadunt. A gƅedy ychydic o dydyeu wedy hynny yd aeth tu a Chaer Wynt. A phan ³ ƅybu Ieuan vrenhin hynny llosgi y dref aoruc, a gƅedy cadarnhau y castell kilyau ⁴ ymeith aƅnaeth. Ac ymlad aoruc Lowys ar castell, a chynn penn ychydic o dydyeu y ⁵ castell agauas.' A chyrchu a ⁶ oruc Ieuan urenhin ardal Kymry, a dyfot aoruc y Henford a llawer o wyr aruaƅc gyt ac ef. A galƅ attaƅ aoruc Reinalt y Breƅys a thywyssogyon Kymry y erchi udunt ymaruoll ac ef a hedychu. A gƅedy na rymhaei ¹[dim] idaƅ hynny kyrchu a ⁷ ƅnaeth y Gelli a Maes Hyfeid, a llosgi y trefyd a thorri y kestyll. Ac odyna llosgi Croes Hyswallt ae diffeithaƅ ae distryƅ. Yn y ulƅydyn honno amgylch gƅyl ¹[y kyuodet corff] Seint Benet y bu uarƅ y trydyd Innossens bap. Ac yn ol hƅnnƅ y bu bap y trydyd Honorius. Ac yna ygkylch gƅyl Luc euegylyƅr y bu uarƅ Ieuan vrenhin ⁸[yn Nieƅart ac y ducpƅyt odyna hut Ygkaer Yraggon], ac y cladƅyt Ygkaer Wyragon yn ymyl bed Dƅnstan Sant yn enrydedus. Ac yny lle wedy brenhinaƅl arƅylant y drychafƅyt Henri y mab hynaf idaƅ ⁹ naƅ mlyned' yn urenhin ar lyƅodraeth y deyrnas. A thrƅy ganmaƅl rei o wyrda Lloegyr ac hescyb y kyssegraƅd escob

---

¹ B.
² yno, B.
³ gigleu, B.

⁴ ymdeith, B.
⁵ gaffel aoruc, B.

king John dreaded his coming, and secured the rivers
and harbours, with a vast force of armed men. And
when he observed the fleet of Louis approaching the
land, he took flight towards Winchester and the Vale
of the Severn. Then Louis drew towards London,
and there he was honourably received; and he took
the homage of the earls and barons who had invited
him, and began to award to all of them their legal
claims. And at the end of a few days afterwards, he
proceeded towards Winchester; and when king John
knew this, he burned the town, and, having fortified
the castle, he went away. And Louis attacked the
castle, and before the end of a few days, he got the
castle. And king John proceeded to the border of
Wales, and came to Hereford, accompanied by many
armed men. And he summoned to him Rheinallt de
Bruse, and the princes of Wales, requiring them to
enter into compact with him, and make peace. And
when that did not avail him ¹ anything, he proceeded
to Gelli and Maes Hyveidd, and burned the towns,
and demolished the castles; and after that, he burned,
ravaged, and destroyed Oswestry. In that year,
about the feast of ¹ the Translation of' St. Benet,
pope Innocent the Third died; and after him the
third Honorius became pope. And then, about the
feast of St. Luke the Evangelist, king John died
⁸ at Newark, and was conveyed hence to Worcester,'
and was honourably buried at Worcester, near the
grave of St. Dunstan. And immediately after the
royal obsequies, his eldest son Henry, being nine
years of age, was raised to the government of the
kingdom; and through the commendation of some
of the good people of England and its bishops, the

---

⁶ ónaeth, *B.*
⁷ oruc, *B.*

⁸ *B. C.*
⁹ yn vab naó mlwyd, *C.*

Bad ef yn vrenhin drʊy aʊdurdaʊt cardinal o Rufein a
legat yr pab. Ac yna y coronet ac y kymerth y
groes. Y ulʊydyn honno y bu uarʊ Howel ab Gruffud
ab Kynan, ¹[yn was ieuanc arderchawc karedic gan
bawb] ac y cladʊyt yn Aber Conʊy.

MCCXVII. Y ulʊydyn rac ʊyneb y bu gyghor yn Ryt
Ychen y gan gyt ᵃ uaɾchogyon Henri urenhin. Ac
yno y traethʊyt amhedʊch a chygreir y rygtunt a
Lowys uab brenhin Freinc, a gʊyr y Gogled. A
gʊedy na dygrynoynt dim o hynny, mordʊyaʊ aoruc
Lowys y Freinc y geissaʊ kyghor y gan Phylip y
dat am y gʊeithretoed aʊnelei rac llaʊ yn Lloegyr.
Ygkyfrʊg hynny y kyfodes gʊyr y brenhin yn erbyn
y gyt aruollʊyr ef, a dʊyn llaʊer o gyrcheu arnunt.
Ac ²odyno dyuot awnaethant y Gaer Wynt, a
chymell y castellwyr y rodi y castell udunt, a goresgyn y kestyll ereill a rodyssit y Lowys ³[athynnu
attadunt laʊer ogyt aruollʊyr Leʊys]. Ygkyfrʊg hynny
yd ymchoelaʊd Lowys y Loeger ac ychydic o nifer
ygyt ac ef. Ac ⁴odyna o achaʊs y dyuotyat ⁵[ef] y
bu ehofnach y Gogledwyr ar Freinc, a chyrchu dinas
Lincol aʊnaethant ⁶ac oresgyn ac ymlad ar castellwyr. Ac eissoes y kastellwyr a ymdiffynnassant y
castell yn gywir ʊraʊl ac anuon kenadeu aorugant at
Wilim Varscal iarll Penuro y gʊr a oed yna hyneif
a phenkyghorʊr y deyrnas a gʊyrda ereill o Loegyr,
⁷ac erchi anuon porth udunt. ⁸Ar rei hynny ogyt

ᵃ ⁵ aruollʊyr

---

¹ C.
² odyna, B.
³ B. C.
⁴ yna, B.

bishop of Bath consecrated him king, by the authority of a cardinal from Rome, and the legate of the pope; and thereupon he was crowned, and received the cross. That year, Howel, son of Gruffudd, son of Cynan, ¹ being an excellent young man, and beloved by all,' died, and was buried at Aberconway.

1217. The ensuing year, there was a council at Oxford, held by the ᵃ co-knights of king Henry; and therein it was treated of peace and a compact between them and Louis, the son of the king of France, and the men of the North. And, since they came to no settlement, Louis sailed for France, to obtain advice of Phillip, his father, as to matters he might in future execute in England. In that interval, the men of the king rose against his allies, and made many attacks upon them. And from thence they proceeded to Winchester, and compelled the garrison to deliver the castle to them, and they took possession of the other castles, which had been delivered up to Louis, ⁸ and drew to them many of the confederates of Louis.' In that interval, Louis returned to England, accompanied by a small retinue. And then, on account of his coming, the North men and the French grew bolder, and proceeded to the city of Lincoln, which they got possession of, and fought against the garrison. However, the garrison defended the castle faithfully and bravely, and sent messengers to William Marshall, earl of Pembroke, the man who was then elder and chief counsellor of the kingdom, and to other good men of England, praying that assistance should be sent to them. And these, by common con-

---

ᵃ ⁵ entertainers

---

⁵ B.
⁶ ac at, B.
⁷ y, B.
⁸ Y, B.

gyghor ᵃa gynnullassant holl gedernit Lloegyr ygyt ac ỽynt y uynet y nerthockau' y castellwyr, kanys gỽell oed gantunt teruynu ¹eu bywyt yn ganmoledic dros rydit ¹eu teyrnas no chyt odef ac ᵇaghyfreitheu ²[ac an ordyuynedic geithỽet]' y Ffreinc. Ac yna tynnu aỽnaethant yn aruaỽc uarchaỽclu tu a Lincol. A cher bron y pyrth cyweiryaỽ ¹eu bydinoed ac gossot y ymlad ar gaer. Ac yna y Gogledwyr ar Freinc a ymwisgassant y ỽrthỽynebu udunt. Ac yscynnu y muroed ac amdiffyn yn ỽraỽl awnaethant. A gỽedy ymlad yn hir o bop tu, ef a ³diasgellaỽd bydin y ỽrth y llu yr honn ydoed iarll Kaer ⁴Loyỽ a Faỽcỽn Breỽys yny harỽein, a thrỽy drỽs dieithyr ar y castell y deuthant y myỽn, a chyrchu y dinas aỽnaethant a gỽneuthur diruaỽr aerua ⁵or Freinc ar Gogledwyr. Ac ỽynteu wedy ¹eu haruthraỽ agymerassant eu ffo, ⁶ac megys ynvydyon pob un o nadunt ⁷a ymgudyei yn y lle kyntaf y kaffei. Ac yna y kyrchaỽd gỽyr Henri urenhin y pyrth, ac y torrassant ac y deuthant y myỽn. Ac ymlit y ffoodron ac llad ae dala ae carcharu, ac yny vrỽydyr honno y delit iarll Caer Wynt a iarll Henford a Robert ab Gỽallter, ac y llas iarll ⁸Perffi y bonhedickaf ²[hayach] or Ffreinc, a Symỽnt ⁹Dypessi, a Hu Dyroc, a Gilbert iarll Clar, a Robert Derupel, a Reinald Dy Cressi

---

ᵃ' ¹⁰ agytssynyassant o vn vryt, ac vn eỽyllys ar gynullaỽ holl gerdennyt ykytaruollỽyr ygyt y vynet y nerthaỽ

ᵇ' ¹¹ anyledussyon ac andiodefedigyon dretheu a chyfreithyeu

---

¹ y, *B*.
² *B*.
³ diadellaỽd, *B*.
⁴ Llion, *B*.
⁵ ary, *B*.
⁶ a, *B*.

sent, ᵃ collected the whole strength of England, to
proceed to the support' of the garrison; for they
deemed it better to terminate their lives worthily for
the liberty of their country, than to bear with ᵇ the
unjust laws' ²and unaccustomed bondage'' of the
French. And thereupon they, as armed cavalry, drew
towards Lincoln, and in front of the gates they
arranged their forces, and placed them to fight against
the city. And then the North men and the French
arrayed themselves to oppose them, and ascended
the walls, and made a gallant defence. And after
long fighting on every side, a detachment made a
flank movement from the army that was led by the
earl of Caer ⁴Loyw and Foulke Bruse; and through
an unfrequented door they came in upon the castle,
and so attacked the city, and made immense slaughter
of the French and the North men, who, being terrified,
took to flight, and, like simpletons, every one of them
hid himself in the first place he could find. And then
the men of king Henry proceeded to the gates, which
they broke, and came in, pursuing and killing and
taking and capturing the fugitives. In that battle the
earl of Winchester and the earl of Hereford, and Robert
Fitz Walter were taken; and earl ⁸Percy, the noblest
²almost of the French, and Simon ⁹de Vescy,' and
Hugh de Roch, and Gilbert, earl of Clare, and Robert

ᵃ/¹⁰ agreed unanimously, and with one will, upon
assembling all the strength of his confederates to proceed to the support

ᵇ/¹¹ the unjust and unendurable taxations and laws

---

⁷ yr, B.
⁸ Perssi, B. Persia, E.
⁹ Depessi, B. de Persi, E.

¹⁰ B.
¹¹ C.

gσnstabyl Kaer Lleon, a Geralt ¹[Difσrneuaσs] iarll, a
llaσer o rei ereill ²[pennaf]. Ac anneiryf o nadunt
a vodes yn yr auon, ac uelly ydymchoelaσd gσyr y
brenhin yn llaσen ²[dracheuen] drσy uoli Duσ y gσr
a ³σnaeth rydit yr bobyl. Ac yna yn ofnaσc y peidy-
aσd Lowys ac ymlad ar castell ⁴[Kaunt], ac y bryssy-
aσd y Lundein. Ac anuon kenadeu aσnaeth y Ffreinc
yn ol nerth. Ac yna y kedσis gσyr y brenhin y
porthueyd a diruaσr lu gantunt. Ac yna y doeth y
Ffreinc y hσylaσ y moroed a diuessur ²[o] lyges gantunt; a chyr bronn Aber auon Temys y bu ymlad
llogeu y rσg y Saesson ar Ffreinc, a gσedy ᵃllad
llaσer or Freinc y syrthaσd y uudugolyaeth yr Saesson. Ac odyna yn hyfryt yd ymhoelassant drachefyn
wedy gσarchae Lowys yn Llundein. Ygkyfrσg hynny
o ⁵damwein y ⁶kymu Reinald y Breσys ar brenhin.
A phan welas Rys ieuanc ac Oσein meibon Gruffud
ab Rys ⁷[vod] y hewythyr yn mynet yn erbyn yr
aruoll aσnathoed σrth wyrda Lloegyr a Chymry.
Kyfodi yny erbyn a σnaethant a goresgyn Buellt
oll y arnaσ ᵇeithyr y ⁸kestyll.' Ac yna y llidiaσd
hefyt Llywelyn ab Iorwoerth ²[tyσyssaσc Gwyned]
yn erbyn Reinald y Breσys, ⁹a thorri yr' aruoll ac
yd ¹⁰aruaethaσd y lu hyt ym Brecheinaσc. Ac y
ᶜcychσynnaσd σrth ymlad ac Aber Hodni ac aruaethu
y distryσ oll. Ac yna ¹¹yd hedychaσd ᵈgσyr y dref a

---

a ² dala
c ² kyσeiraσd y vydinoed
ᵇ' ⁷ athri kastell.
d ² bσrdeisseit

---

¹ B. C.
² B.
³ σnathoed, B.
⁴ C. E.
⁵ damσeineu, B.
⁶ kymhodaσd, B.

de Rupel and Rheinallt de Cressy, constable of Caerleon, and earl Gerald ¹de Furneuale,' with many other ²chieftains, were killed; and a vast number of them were drowned in the river. And thus the king's men joyfully returned ²back, praising God, Who had wrought freedom for the people. And then, being in fear, Louis desisted from attacking the castle ⁴of Canterbury,' and hastened to London, from whence he despatched messengers to France for assistance. And then the king's men guarded the ports with a vast army. And the French came and navigated the seas with an immense fleet. And near the efflux of the river Thames there was a naval fight between the English and the French; and after many of the French had been ᵃkilled, the victory fell to the English, who joyfully returned from thence, having shut up Louis in London. In that interval, Rheinallt de Bruse and the king by chance became reconciled. And when young Rhys and Owain, the sons of Gruffudd, son of Rhys, saw that their uncle was going against the treaty which he had entered into with the good men of England and Wales, they rose up against him, and wrested the whole of Buellt from him, except ᵇthe castles.' Then also Llywelyn, son of Iorwerth, ²prince of Gwynedd,' became angry with Rheinallt de Bruse; and, breaking the treaty, he directed his army towards Brecheiniog; and he ᶜcommenced by attacking Aberhodni, which he designed totally to destroy. And thereupon, the ᵈmen of the town made peace with

---

ᵃ ² captured,
ᶜ' ² directed his troops

ᵇ' ⁷ three castles.
ᵈ ² burgesses

---

⁷ E.
⁸ castell, B.
⁹ am dorri y, B.

¹⁰ arбedaбd, B.
¹¹ y, B.

Llywelyn drôy Rys ieuanc oed gymeredic gymodrodôa y rygtunt gan rodi pum gôystyl y Lyôelyn o uonhedigyon y dref ar dalu can morc idaô kan ny ellynt y ôrthôynebu. Ac odyna yd arwedaôd y lu y Whyr dros y Mynyd Du, yny lle y periglaôd llaôer [1]o sômereu. Ac yna y pebyllyaôd yn Llan Giôc. A gôedy gôelet o Reinald [2][ac o ôiliam] y Brewys y diffeithôch ydoed Lywelyn yny wneuthur [3]yn y gyfoeth ef agymerth whech marchaôc urdaôl y gyt ac ef ac adoeth y ymrodi y Lywelyn ôrth y gyghor. Ac ynteu arodes castell Sein Henyd idaô a hônnô a orchymynnaôd Llywelyn dan gadôryaeth Rys Gryc. A gôedy trigyaô yno ychydic o dydyeu [a]arôein y uydinoed a [4]oruc [2][y] rygtaô a Dyfet yn erbyn y Fflandraswyr' yn eruyneit hedôch y gantaô. Ac nyt edeôis y tywyssaôc y aruaeth namyn tynu y Haôlfford a [5]wnaeth. A chyweiryaô y vydinoed ygkylch y dref ar uedyr ymlad a hi. Ac yna ydaeth Rys ieuanc a lleg o wyr y Deheu y gyt ac ef ydoed yn y harôein drôy avon Gledyf. A dynessau tu ar dref aônaeth ar niuer hônnô y gyt ac ef y ymlad yn gyntaf ar dref. Ac yna [6]ydoeth Iorôerth escob Mynyô a llaôer o grefydôyr ac eglôyssôyr y gyt ac ef yn dyuot att y tyôyssaôc, ac [7]yn aruaethu ffuryf [8]tagnefed ac ef. A llyma y ffuruf, nyt amgen rodi o nadunt yr tywyssaôc ugein [9][ôystyl Oros Aphenuro o rei bonedhicca ar talu mil] o vorkeu [2][idaô] erbyn gôyl Vihagel nessaf, neu ôynteu a ôrheynt idaô erbyn hynny,

a/ [10] adyuot aoruc hyt Ygkeuen Kynuarchan, ac yno ykyuaruu kennadeu ac ef ygan Yfflandrassôyr.

[1] ae, B.
[2] B.
[3] ar, B.
[4] ônaeth, B.
[5] oruc, B.
[6] nachaf, B.

Llywelyn, through young Rhys, who became an accepted arbitrator between them, by delivering five hostages to Llywelyn, of the gentlemen of the town, that they would pay him a hundred marks, since they could not oppose him. And from thence he conducted his army to Gower, over the Black Mountain, where many sumpters were endangered; and then he encamped at Llangiwg. When Rheinallt ²and William' de Bruse observed the devastation that Llywelyn was committing in his territory, he took six noble knights with him, and came to give himself up to the disposal of Llywelyn, who gave him the castle of Senghenydd, which Llywelyn had entrusted to the custody of Rhys the Hoarse. And after remaining there a few days, ᵃhe led his army towards Dyved, against the Flemings,' who were suing for peace from him. Yet the prince did not give up his purpose, but drew towards Haverford, and arranged his troops round the town, with the intention of fighting against it. And thereupon, young Rhys, at the head of a body of the men of the South, of whom he was leader, went through the river Cleddyv, and approached the town, having that retinue with him, in order to attack the town first. And then, Iorwerth, bishop of Menevia, accompanied by many of the religious and clergy, came to the prince, and proposed terms of peace to him. And these were the terms, namely, they were to give the prince twenty ⁹hostages from Rhos and Pembroke, of the noblest, that they would pay him a thousand' marks by next Michaelmas; or otherwise they were to

---

ᵃ/ ¹⁰ he came to Cevn Cynwarchan, where messengers met him from the Flemings,

---

⁷ y, B.
⁸ tagnef, B.

⁹ C. E.
¹⁰ C.

ac y kynhelynt y danaʋ yn dragywydaʋl. A gʋedy hynny ydymchoelaʋd paʋb y wlat. Ac ygkyfrʋg hynny y traethʋyt am dagnefed y rʋg Henri urenhin Lloegyr a Lowys uab brenhin Ffreinc. Ac ual hynn y bu y dagneved y rygtunt, nyt amgen talu o Henri vrenhin y ieirll a barʋneit y deyrnas y kyfreitheu ¹ ae gossodeu' y buassei ᵃ yr afreol' oe hachaʋs y rygtunt a Ieuan urenhin, a ² gellʋg paʋb or carcharoryon a dalyssit o achaʋs y ᵇ ryfel hʋnnʋ,' a thalu diruaʋr sʋmp o aryant y Loʋys uab brenhin Ffreinc, drʋy dyghu o honaʋ ynteu deyrnas Loegyr yn dragywydaʋl. Ac yna gʋedy cael sʋmp o aryant ac ellʋg ³[o] sentens yskymundaʋt y mordʋyaʋd yn Ffreinc. Ac yna y bu kyffredyn ellygdaʋt o wahardedigaeth yr eglʋysseu drʋy holl deyrnas Loegyr a Chymry ac Iʋerdon. Ygkyfrʋg hynny yd ymladaʋd Gʋilim Marscal a Chaer Llion, ac y goreskynnaʋd kany chytsynyassei y Kymry ar dagnefed uchot gan dybygu ³[y] ebrygofi ³[yn] y kymot ³[neu ydielʋi]. Ac yna y distryʋaʋd Rys Gryc gastell Sein Henyd a holl gestyll Gʋhyr ³[ae kedernit]. Ac y deholes y gibaʋt Saesson a oedynt yny wlat honno oll heb ⁴ obeithaʋ ymchoelut byth drachefyn gan gymryt kymeint ac afynaʋd ⁵ o da, a dodi Kymry y bressʋylaʋ yn y tired.

MCCXVIII. Y ulʋydyn rac ʋyneb y rydhaaʋd y Gristonogaeth y wyr y Deheu, ac y rodet Kaer Uyrdin ac Aber Teifi ³[y] dan gadʋryaeth Llywelyn uab Ior-

---

ᵃ′ ³ yryuel   ᵇ′ ³ ryueloed hynny,

---

¹′ oe gossodedigaethau, *B*. ³ *B*.
² gollʋg, *B*.

do homage to him by that time, and were to hold under him for ever. And after that every one returned to his country. And in that interval pacification was declared between Henry king of England, and Louis, son of the king of France. And the pacification was thus between them, namely, king Henry was to restore to the earls and barons of the kingdom the laws and institutions, on account of which ᵃthe disturbance' had taken place between them and king John; and each party was to liberate the prisoners taken on account of ᵇthat war;' and an immense sum of money was to be paid to Louis, the son of the king of France, he forswearing the kingdom of England for ever. Then, after obtaining the sum of money, and being absolved ⁴from the sentence of excommunication, he sailed for France. And then, there was an universal remission of the interdiction of the churches, through the whole kingdom of England and Wales and Ireland. In that interval, William Marshall fought against Caerleon, and took it; for the Welsh had not consented to the above pacification, supposing the agreement to have been forgotten, ⁵or disregarded.' And then Rhys the Hoarse destroyed the castle of Senghenydd, and all the castles of Gower, ⁵and their strength.' And he expelled the English population that were in that country entirely, so that they had no hope ever to return back, taking as much property as he chose, and placing Welshmen to dwell in the lands.

1218. The ensuing year, Christianity was rendered free to the men of the South; and Caermarthen and Aberteivi were put under the custody of Llywelyn,

ᵃ' ³ the war ᵇ' ³ those wars,

⁴ obeith, B.   ⁵ oe, B.

woerth. Ac yna ydaeth Rys ieuanc ¹e hunan' ²[a holl dywysogion—drwy gyngor Llywelyn] y lys y brenhin o Deheubarth y wneuthur gŵrogaeth idaŵ. Y ulŵydyn honno ydaeth llawer o groessogyon y Gaerussalem y rŵg y rei yd aeth iarll Kaer Lleon, a iarll Marscal ³[a Brian o ⁴Vilis], a llawer o wyrda ereill o Loegyr. Y ulŵydyn honno y mordŵyaŵd llud y Cristonogyyn hyt yn ⁵Dametta. Ac yny blaen yn tywyssogyon yd oed brenhin Kaerussalem a phadriarch Kaerussalem, a meistyr y demyl, a meistyr yr yspytty, a thywyssaŵc Aŵstria, ac ymlad ar dref a ⁶orugant ae goresgyn; a chastell a oed ygkanaŵl yr auon wedy adeilat ar logeu, hŵnnŵ a eskynnaŵd y pererinyaŵn ar yscolyon ac ⁷ae torrassant wedy llad llaŵer or Sarassinyeit a dala creill.

MCCXIX. Y ulŵydyn rac ŵyneb y priodes Rys Gryc uerch iarll Clar, ac y priodes Ion y Breŵys Vargaret verch Llywelyn uab Iorwoerth. Y ulŵydyn honno yrodes yr holl gyfoethaŵc Duŵ dinas ⁸Damiet yn yr Eifft a oed ar avon Nilus y lu y Cristonogyon aoed wedy blinaŵ o hir ymlad ar dinas; kanys dŵywaŵl racweledigaeth aberis y veint uarŵolyaeth ³[ary bopyl] yny dinas hyt na allei y rei buŵ gladu y rei meirŵ. Kanys y dyd y cahat y dinas ydoed mŵy no theirmil o gyrff y meirŵ ar hyt yr heolyd megys kŵn heb y cladu. Ar dyd hŵnnŵ yr molyant a gogonyant yr Creaŵdyr y creŵyt archescob yny dinas.

MCCXX. Ugein mlyned a deu cant a mil oed oet Crist pan dyrchafŵyt corff Thomas uerthyr y gan Ystyffan archescob Keint, a chardinal o Rufein, ac y dodet yn enrydedus y myŵn yscrin o gywreinweith

---

¹ ehun, B. ³ B.
² C. E. ⁴ Lile, C.

son of Iorwerth. And then young Rhys went himself, [2] and all the princes,—by the advice of Llywelyn,' to the court of the king, from South Wales, to do him homage. That year, many crusaders went to Jerusalem, among whom went the earl of Caerleon, and earl Marshall, [3] and Bryan de [4] Ville," with many other good men from England. That same year, an armament of Christians sailed to [5] Damietta, whose leaders were the king of Jerusalem, and the patriarch of Jerusalem, and the master of the Temple, and the master of the Hospital, and the prince of Austria. They attacked the town, and obtained possession of it; and there was a castle in the middle of the river, constructed upon ships; that was scaled by the pilgrims with ladders, and they demolished it, after killing many of the Saracens, and capturing others.

1219. The ensuing year, Rhys the Hoarse married the daughter of the earl of Clare; and John de Bruse married Margaret, the daughter of Llywelyn, son of Iorwerth. That year, the Almighty God delivered the city of [8] Damietta in Egypt, which was upon the river Nile, to the army of the Christians, who were wearied with long fighting against the city; for Divine providence caused such mortality [9] among the people' in the city, that the living could not bury the dead; as, on the day the city was obtained, more than three thousand dead bodies were found about the streets, like dogs, unburied. And on that day, to the praise and glory of the Creator, an archbishop was consecrated in the city.

1220. One thousand two hundred was the year of Christ, when the body of Thomas the Martyr was raised by Stephen, archbishop of Canterbury, and a cardinal from Rome, and was honourably deposited

---

[5] Dannetta, *B.*
[6] Gnaethant, *B.*
[7] a, *B.*
[8] Dannet, *B.*

eur ac aryant a mein gṽerthuaṽr ynegloys y Drindaṽt Ygkeint. Y ulṽydyn honno ¹[gwyl Ievan y kols nesaf ar hynny] y gelwis Llywelyn ab Iorṽoerth attaṽ ganmṽyaf tywyssogyon Kymry oll, a chynullaṽ diruaṽr lu aoruc am benn Fflandrasswyr Ros a Phenuro, am dorri onadunt yr hedṽch ar gygreir aṽnathoed wyr Lloegyr y rṽg y Saeson ar Kymry, drṽy wneuthur mynych gyrcheu ar y Cymry ac aflonydu arnunt. Ar dyd kyntaf y cyrchaṽd gastell Arberth yr hṽnn aadeilassei y Flandrasswyr wedy y distryṽ or Kymry kynno hynny. A chael y castell y dreis aṽnaeth ae vṽrṽ yr llaṽr, wedy llad rei or castellwyr a llosgi ereill acharcharu ereill. A thrannoeth y distryṽaṽd gastell Gṽis ac y llṽsges y dref. Y trydyd dyd y doeth y Haṽlfford ac y llosges y dref oll hyt ymporth y castell. Ac uelly y cylchynaṽd ef Ros a Deu Gledyf pump niṽarnaṽt drṽy wneuthur diruaṽr aerua ar bobyl y ṽlat. A gṽedy gṽneuthur kygreir ar Flandrasswyr hyt galan Mei yd ymchoelaṽd drachefyn yn llaṽen hyfryt.

MCCXXI. Y vlṽydyn rac ṽyneb ymagṽyt teruysc y rṽg Llyṽelyn ab Iorṽoerth a Gruffud y uab o achaṽs kantref Meironnyd a darestygassei Ruffud idaṽ. O achaṽs y sarhaadeu ² a ṽnathoed y kantref hṽnnṽ idaṽ ac ³y wyr. A llidyaṽc vu Lywelyn am hynny, a chynnullaṽ llu a chyrchu lle ydoed Ruffud drṽy ⁴vygṽth y' dial yr hynt honno arnaṽ ac ar y wyr. Ac aros awnaeth Gruffud yn ehofyn dyuotyat y dat wedy kyweiryaṽ y vydinoed ae lu. Ac yna ydedrych-

---

¹ C. E. ² ry, B.

in a shrine of curious workmanship of gold and silver and precious stones, in the church of the Trinity, at Canterbury. That year, [1] on the feast of S. Jean de Collaces next after that,' Llywelyn, son of Iorwerth, cited to him most of the princes of all Wales, and collected a vast army to go against the Flemings of Rhos and Pembroke, because of their breaking the peace and the treaty, which the men of England had made between the English and the Welsh, by their committing frequent depredations upon the Welsh, and harrassing them. On the first day he attacked the castle of Arberth, which the Flemings had built, after having been formerly destroyed by the Welsh; and he obtained the castle by force, and threw it to the ground, after killing some of the garrison, burning others, and capturing others. And the following day he destroyed the castle of Gwys, and burned the town. The third day he came to Haverford, and burned the whole of the town to the castle gate. And thus he went round Rhos and Deugleddyv in five days, making vast slaughter of the people of the country. And after making a truce with the Flemings until the calends of May, he returned back joyful and happy.

1221. The ensuing year, a dispute was engendered between Llywelyn, son of Iorwerth, and his son Gruffudd, on account of the cantrev of Meirionydd, which had been subjected by Gruffudd, because of the insults offered to him and his men by that cantrev. And Llywelyn became angry on that account, and collected an army, and proceeded to where Gruffudd was, threatening to revenge that proceeding upon him and upon his men. And Gruffudd boldly awaited the coming of his father, having arranged his troops and

---

[1] oe, B.   " vygythyaŵ, B.

aƀd doethon o bop tu meint y perigyl aoed yn
dyuot. Ac annoc awnaethant y Ruffud ymrodi ef
¹ ae da' yn ewyllys y dat, ac annoc ² hefyt awnaethant y Lywelyn kymryt y uab yn hedƀch ac yn
drugaraƀc amadeu idaƀ gƀbyl oe lit o ewyllys y gallon,
ac uelly y gƀnaethpƀyt ; ac yna yduc Llywelyn gantref Meironnyd y ar Ruffud, a chymƀt Ardudƀy. A
dechreu adeilat castell ² yndaƀ aƀnaeth idaƀ ehun.
Ygkyfrƀg hynny yllidyaƀd Rys ieuanc ƀrth yr arglƀyd
Lywelyn, ac yd ymedeƀis ac ef ac ydaeth att Wilim
Marscal iarll Penuro, o achaƀs rodi o Lywelyn Gaer
Uyrdin y Uaelgƀn ab Rys, ac na rodei idaƀ ynteu
Aber Teifi aoed yny rann pan rannƀyt Deheubarth.
Ac yna y deuth Llywelyn aelu hyt yn Aber Ystƀyth.
Ac y goresgynnaƀd y castell ar kyuoeth aoed ƀrthaƀ,
ac ae dodes dan y arglƀydiaeth ehun. Ac yna y
kyrchaƀd Rys ieuanc lys y brenhin, a chƀynaƀ aoruc
ƀrth y brenhin am y sarhaet awnathoed Lyƀelyn
idaƀ. A ᵃduunaƀ aƀnaeth y brenhin attaƀ Lyƀelyn a
ieirll a barƀneit y Mars hyt yn Amƀythic. Ac yny
kygor hƀnnƀ y ³kymodrodet Rys ieuanc a Llywelyn
ab Iorƀoerth, ac yd edewis Llywelyn idaƀ Aber Teiui
megys y rodassei Gaer Vyrdin y Vaelgƀn ab Rys. Y
ulƀydyn honno yd aeth llu y Cristonogyon ⁴Damieit
yn yr Eifft tu a Babilon ƀrth ymlad a hi, ac nys
gadaƀd dial Duƀ. Kanys llifaƀ aƀnaeth auon Nilus ar
y fford ⁵[yr wythuet dyd o wyl Veir diwoethaf or

ᵃ⁶ dyvynnu

¹ ar eidaƀ, B.
² yno, B.
³ kymydƀyt, B.
⁴ Dannet, B.

his host. And thereupon, the wise on both sides observed the impending danger, and exhorted Gruffudd to deliver himself and his property up to the will of his father. And they likewise exhorted Llywelyn to receive his son in peace and pity, and, from the bottom of his heart, to forego the whole of his anger; and thus was it accomplished. And thereupon, Llywelyn took the cantrev of Meirionydd, and comot of Ardudwy, from Gruffudd; and commenced building a castle therein for himself. In that interval, young Rhys became angry with the lord Llywelyn, and separated from him, and went to William Marshall, earl of Pembroke, because Llywelyn had given Caermarthen to Maelgwn, son of Rhys, and would not give Aberteivi to him, which fell to his share when South Wales was divided. Then Llywelyn, with his army, came to Aberystwyth, and obtained possession of the castle, with the territory attached to it, and placed it under his own dominion. And then young Rhys repaired to the court of the king, and complained to the king of the insult that Llywelyn had offered him. And the king [a] assembled Llywelyn and the earls and barons of the marches to Shrewsbury. And in that council young Rhys and Llywelyn, son of Iorwerth, were reconciled; and Llywelyn relinquished Aberteivi in his favour, as he had given Caermarthen to Maelgwn, son of Rhys. That year, the army of the Christians of [4] Damietta in Egypt proceeded towards Babylon, with the view of attacking it; but the vengeance of God suffered it not; for the river Nile flooded over their way, [5] the octave

---

a [6] summoned

---

[4] *C.* | [5] *B.*

kynhayaf], ae goarchei rog doy afon yny vodes anneiryf o [1] nadunt. [2] Ac yna keithiwao' ereill. Ac yna y goruu arnunt dalu [3] Damiet yr Sarassinyeit drachefyn dros y bowyt ac rydit y keith, a goneuthur kygreir oyth mlyned ac oynt. Ac [4] odyno y hebrygaod y Sarassinyeit oynt hyt yn Acrys lle ny wydit dim y orth groes Grist, namyn trugared Duo e hun ae talaod udunt. Y uloydyn honno [5] [am gylch gwyl Nicolaws] y kyoeiraod Ion y Breoys gastell [6] [Aber Tawy a] [7] Sein Henyd droy gennat a chyghor Llywelyn ab Iorwoerth.

MCCXXII. Y vloydyn rac oyneb y bu uaro Rys ieuanc [5] [ap Gruffud ap yr arglwyd Rys yn was ieuang arderchawc y volyant ay huolder ay synnwyr ay brudder ay doethineb yn oleuat yr henyon yn haelder a chlot agem yr ieueing yn anryded agogonyant athegwch achedernyt anorchyuygedic yr marchogyon yn golofyn athwr atharyan y wlat yndat abugeil athatmaeth yr ysgolheigyon yn wastadrwyd abonhed ahedwch. Achannawl yr pobloed yn long a phorthloed ac amdiffynwr yrgweinyeit yn sathrwr ac aruthder ac ouyn y elynyon yn vn gobeith y holl Deheubarth a hynny drwy hir nychdawt heint a dolur y mis Awst], ac y cladoyt yn Ystrat Fflur goedy kymryt penyt achymyn a chyffes ac abit [8] [y] crefyd ymdanao. A goedy hynny y kauas Owein ab Gruffud y vn braot ran oe gyfoeth, a ran arall arodes Llywelyn ab Iorwerth y Vaelgon ab Rys. Y vloydyn honno y mordoyaod Goilim Varscal iarll Penuro y Iwerdon.

[1] honunt, B.
[2]' a cheithiao, B.
[3] Dannet, B. Damacham, E.
[4] odyna, B.

of the feast of St. Mary, last in the autumn,' and they were hemmed in between two rivers, so that an immense number were drowned; and then the others were captured. And then they were compelled to restore ³Damietta back to the Saracens, to save their lives, and be freed from bondage, and to enter into a truce with them for eight years. And from thence the Saracens conveyed them to Acre, where nothing was known of the cross of Christ; but the mercy of God Himself rewarded them. That year, ⁵about the feast of St. Nicholas,' John de Bruse repaired the castle of ⁷Abertawy and' Senghenydd, by the permission and advice of Llywelyn, son of Iorwerth.

1222. The ensuing year, died young Rhys, ⁵son of Gruffudd, son of the lord Rhys, being a young man famous for his praise and bravery and sense and wisdom—the light of the old—the liberality and fame and gem of the young—the honour and glory and beauty and invincible strength of the knights—the pillar and tower of his country—the father and shepherd and fosterfather of the scholars,—constancy, gentility, and peace;—being a mediator for the people, a ship and harbour and a defender to the weak—the treader and admiration and terror of his enemies—the sole hope of all South Wales—and that after a long and lingering disorder, in the month of August;' and was buried at Strata Florida, after taking penance and communion and confession and the habit of religion. And after that, Owain, son of Gruffudd, his only brother, obtained part of his territory, and another part Llywelyn, son of Iorwerth, gave to Maelgwn, son of Rhys. That year, William Marshall, earl of Pembroke, sailed to Ireland.

⁵ *C.*
⁶ *E.*
⁷ *Not in C.*
⁸ *B.*

MCCXXIII. Y vlѡydyn rac ѡyneb y doeth Gѡilim Varscal o Iwerdon, alluossogrѡyd o varchogyon a phedyt gantaѡ ¹a diruaѡr lyges ²[y vynut] yr tir amgylch Sul y Blodeu. A duѡ Llun ³[Pasc] y kyrchaѡd Aber Teiui, ar dyd hѡnnѡ y rodet y castell idaѡ; a duѡ Merchyr rac ѡyneb y tynnaѡd y Gaer Uyrdin, ac y kauas y castell hѡnnѡ hefyt. A phan gigleu Llywelyn uab Iorwoerth hynny y gѡr ydoed gadѡryaeth y kestyll gantaѡ o blegyt y brenhin anuon Grufud y uab aoruc a diruaѡr luossogrѡyd o lu gantaѡ y ѡrthѡynebu yr iarll. A phan gigleu Grufud uot bryt y iarll ar dyuot y Getweli, kyrchu ⁴awnaeth adylyedogyon Kymry y gyt ac ef. ᵃA choffau aѡnaeth' Rys Gryc rac brat y gan y bѡrgeisseit, a cheissaѡ kyffroi y Kymry y diogelѡch y coedyd, ac nys ⁵gadyssant namyn kyrchu y dref aѡnaethant, a llosgi y dref ar eglѡys hyt y prid. A phan gigleu y iarll hynny kyrchu drѡy Tywi awnaeth y bont Gaer Vyrdin. Ac aros Gruffud ab Llywelyn yn ehofyn a ⁶ѡnaeth. A gѡedy hir ymlad y rann vѡyaf or dyd ymchoelut a wnaeth pob un or deu lu y ѡrth y gilyd y ⁷pebylleu wedy llad llawer o bop tu, a brathu ereill. Ac yna rac neѡyn ydymchoelaѡd Gruffud ab Llywelyn ᵇy wlat drachefyn.' Ac yna y kyweiraѡd y iarll gastell Kaer Vyrdin. Ac y dechreuaѡd adeilat kastell Kil Gerran. Ny bu bell ѡedy dechreu y gѡeith yny doeth llythyreu attaѡ y gan y brenhin,

---

ᵃ'⁸ Ac ofynhau aoruc   ᵇ'⁸ oe ѡlat.

¹ myѡn, B.
² B. C.
² B.
⁴ a oruc, B.

1223. The ensuing year, William Marshall returned from Ireland with a multitude of cavalry and infantry, and came ²up to land with a vast fleet about Palm Sunday. And on ³ Easter Monday he approached Aberteivi; and on that day the castle was delivered to him; and on the Wednesday following he drew to Caermarthen, and obtained that castle also. And when Llywelyn, son of Iorwerth, heard that,—the person who had the custody of the castles, on the part of the king,—he sent Gruffudd his son with a very numerous army to oppose the earl. And when Gruffudd understood that it was the intention of the earl to come to Cydweli, he proceeded towards it, accompanied by the nobility of Wales. And Rhys the Hoarse ᵃ reminded them that they were to guard' against the treachery of the burgesses, and endeavoured to excite the Welsh to seek the safety of the woods; but they did not give way, for they proceeded to the town, and burned the town and the church to the ground. When the earl heard of this, he proceeded through the Tywi by the bridge of Caermarthen, and boldly awaited Gruffudd, son of Llywelyn. And after continued fighting for the greater part of the day, each of the two armies separated and returned to their tents, after killing many on both sides, and wounding others. And then, for lack of provision, Gruffudd, son of Llywelyn, returned ᵇ back to his country.' Then the earl repaired the castle of Caermarthen; and began to build the castle of Cilgerran. It was not long after the work was commenced, before there came letters to him from the

---

ᵃ′⁸ was afraid   ᵇ′⁸ from his country.

---

⁵ gadassant, *B.*   ⁷ bepyllu, *B.*
⁶ oruc, *B.*   ⁸ *B.*

ac archescob Keint y erchi idaỽ dyuot yny briaỽt berson y atteb ger y bron ỽyntỽy ac y wneuthur iaỽn am aỽnathoed ac y gymryt iaỽn y gan y tywyssaỽc am bop cam or aỽnathoed idaỽ. Ar iarll a ufudhaaỽd yr ᵃgorchymynneu a mordỽyaỽ a ¹ỽnaeth y myỽn llog hyt yn Lloegyr gyt ac ychydic o nifer, ac adaỽ y lu Ygkilgerran y gynal y gỽeith dechreuedic ac y ²nerthockau y lle y ᵇgỽelynt berigyl. Ac ymdangos aỽnaethant y gyt yn Llỽtlaỽ y tywyssaỽc ³[ygyt] ar iarll gyr bron kyghor y brenhin ararchescob. A gỽedy naellit eu kymot aruaethu aỽnaeth y iarll drỽy nerth iarll Ferỽr, a Henri ⁴Pictot arglỽyd Euas dyuot drỽy gyuoeth ᶜy tywyssaỽc' tu ae wlat, ac nys gallaỽd. Kanys Llywelyn ab Iorwoerth ⁵a anuonassei' Ruffud y uab a diruaỽr lu y gyt ac ef, a Rys Gryc ae wyr hyt ⁶Ygkarnywyllaỽn y ragot y iarll ae wyr ⁷[ac yno y llas ef]. Ac ynteu Lyỽelyn ae holl allu adeuth hyt ym mab Udrut. Ac yno aros chỽedleu a wnaeth y ỽrth y wyr, ac y ỽrth dyuotedigaeth y iarll.

MCCXXIV. Y vlỽydyn rac ỽyneb yd aeth kofeint or Ty Gỽyn y bressỽylaỽ ⁷[yr brynn wylovus] y Gỽyndir yn Iwerdon.

MCCXXV. Y vlỽydyn arall rac llaỽ y bu uarỽ Kediuor abat Ystrat Fflur.

MCCXXVI. Y ulỽydyn rac llaỽ y bu uarỽ Lowys vrenhin Ffreinc.

ᵃ ³ gorchymun   ᵇ ³ gellynt
ᶜ ³ hỽnnỽ

¹ oruc, *B.*   ³ *B.*
² nerthaỽ, *B.*   ⁴ Rigot, *B.*

king and the archbishop of Canterbury, requiring him to come in his proper person to answer before them, and to make satisfaction for what he had done, and to receive satisfaction from the prince for every wrong he had done him. And the earl obeyed the ᵃcommands, and sailed with a small retinue in a ship for England, leaving his army at Cilgerran, to carry on the work commenced, and to strengthen the place where they might ᵇobserve danger. And the prince and the earl appeared together at Ludlow before the council of the king and the archbishop. And since they could not be reconciled, the earl designed through the aid of earl Ferers and Henry Pictot, lord of Ewias, to proceed through the territory of ᶜthe prince' to his own country; but he was not able, because Llywelyn, son of Iorwerth, had sent his son Gruffudd, and a large army with him, and Rhys the Hoarse, and his men, to Carnwyllon, to intercept the earl and his men, ⁷and there was he slain.' And Llywelyn himself, with all his power, proceeded to Mabudrud; and there he waited for tidings from his men, and as to the advance of the earl.

1224. The ensuing year, a convent went from the White House to dwell ⁷on the hill of lamentation' at Whitland in Ireland.

1225. The other forthcoming year, Cedivor, abbot of Strata Florida, died.

1226. The forthcoming year, Louis, king of France, died.

ᵃ ³ command,   ᵇ ³ be capable of
ᶜ ³ that person

ᵛ annones, *B*.   ⁷ *E*.
⁶ Ygkarn6alla6n, *B*.

MCCXXVII. Y ul6ydyn rac 6yn$b y delit Rys Gryc yn ¹Llanarthneu y gan Rys Vychan y vab, a thros gastell Llan Ymdyfri y gellygwyt. Y ul6ydyn honno y bu uar6 Maredud uab yr argl6yd Rys archdiagon Keredigya6n ym ²[eglwys Veir yn Llanbedyr Tal] Pont Ystyffan, ac y ducp6yt y gorff y Vyny6 ac y clad6yt yn enrydedus y gan Iorwoerth escob Myny6 yn egl6ys ³[De6i] gyr lla6 bed yr argl6yd Rys y dat.

MCCXXVIII. Y vl6ydyn rac 6yneb y doeth Henri ⁴[vrenhin] a chedernit Lloegyr y gyt ac ef y Gymry, ac aruaethu darest6g Llywelyn ab Iorwoerth a holl dywyssogyon Kymry ida6. Ac yny lle aelwir ⁵Kori y pebyllya6d; ac or tu arall yr coet yd ymgynulla6d y Kymry y gyt a Lly6elyn ab Iorwoerth ⁶eu tywyssa6c y 6rth6ynebu yr brenhin. Ac yna kyrchu ⁷y gelynyon awnaethant ac ymlad ac 6ynt yn duruig, a g6neuthur dirua6r aerua arnunt. Ac yno y delit G6ilim Bre6ys ieuanc yn vrathedic, ac y carchar6yt; a thros y ellygda6t ef y rodet y Lywelyn ab Iorwoerth gastell Buellt ar wlat a dirua6r s6mp o aryant. Ac yna yd ymhoela6d y brenhin y Loegyr yn ge6ilydyus, eithyr cael g6rogaeth o hona6 y gan y ty6yssogyon aoedynt yno, a ⁸ffurua6 tagnefed y rygta6 a Llywelyn ab Iorwoerth.

MCCXXIX. Y ul6ydyn rac 6yneb y bu uar6 Iorwoerth escob Myny6.

MCXXX. Deg mlyned arhugeint adeucant a mil oed Crist pan ⁹uord6ya6d Henri urenhin a dirua6r lu arua6c y gyt ac ef y Ffreinc ar uedyr euill y dylyet o Normandi ar Angi6, a Pheitta6. Ac yn

---

¹ Llanarth, *E*.
² *C.* Llanbedr Tal, *E*.
³ *B. C.*
⁴ *B*.
⁵ Keri, *B*.

1227. The ensuing year, Rhys the Hoarse was captured at [1] Llanarthneu by his son, Rhys the Little; and for the castle of Llanymddyvri was liberated. That year, Maredudd, son of the lord Rhys, archdeacon of Ceredigion, died [2] in the church of St. Mary, at Llanbedr Tal' Pont Stephan, and his body was conveyed to Menevia, where he was honourably buried by Iorwerth, bishop of Menevia, in the church [3] of St. David,' near the grave of the lord Rhys, his father.

1228. The ensuing year, [4] king Henry, having with him the strength of England, came to Wales, intending to subjugate Llywelyn, son of Iorwerth, and all the Welsh princes; and encamped in the place called Ceri; and on the other side of the wood, the Welsh, with Llywelyn, son of Iorwerth, their prince, assembled to oppose the king. And there they attacked their enemies, and fought with them furiously, making vast slaughter of them. And there young William Bruse was taken wounded, and imprisoned; and for his liberation the castle of Buellt, with the district, and a vast sum of money, was given to Llywelyn, son of Iorwerth. And then the king returned to England with shame, only he obtained the homage of the princes, who were there, and formed a pacification between him and Llywelyn, son of Iorwerth.

1229. The ensuing year, Iorwerth, bishop of Menevia, died.

1230. One thousand two hundred and thirty was the year of Christ, when king Henry, having with him a vast armed host, sailed for France, with the intention of obtaining his right as to Normandy and Anjou and Poictou. And soon after that, on account

---

[6] y, B.
[7] eu, B.

[8] phuruahu, B.
[9] vorbydabd, B.

ebrŵyd wedy hynny o achaŵs tymhestyl a marŵolyaeth drŵy y dŵyllaŵ oe aruaeth yd ymchoelaŵd y Loegyr. Y vlŵydyn honno y bu varŵ Gŵilim Camtaŵn o Gemeis. Ac yna y bu uarŵ Llywelyn ab Maelgŵn ieuanc yn gyuoeth Yggŵyned, ac y cladŵyt yn Aber Conŵy yn enrydedus. Y vlŵydyn honno y croget Gŵilim Breŵys ieuanc y gan Lywelyn ab Iorwoerth wedy y dala yn ystauell y tyŵyssaŵc gyt a ¹[dwysoges Sioned] merch Ieuean urenhin gŵreic y tywyssaŵc.

MCCXXXI. Y vlŵydyn rac ŵyneb y bu uarŵ Maelgŵn uab Rys yn Llanerch Aeron, ac y cladŵyt yn y cabidyldy yn Ystrat Fflur. Y vlŵydyn honno yd adeilaŵd Henri urenhin gastell Paen yn Eluael. Odyna ²[o] achaŵs ᵃ teruysc a vuassei' y rŵg Llywelyn ab Iorŵoerth ar brenhin y llosges Llyŵelyn dref y castell Baldwin a Maeshyfeid ar Gelli ac Aber Hodni, ac a distryŵaŵd y kestyll hyt y llaŵr. ³Odyna y tynnaŵd y Went ac y gŵnaeth Gaer Llion yn lludŵ kyt collit bonedigyon yno. Ac odyna y ᵇkychŵynnaŵd y gestyll Ned a chastell Ketweli ac y byryaŵd yr llaŵr.' Y ulŵydyn honno y llosges Maelgŵn ieuanc ⁴[ap] Maelgŵn ab Rys Aber Teiui hyt ymporth y castell ac y lladaŵd yr holl ⁵ vŵrgeisseit, ac ⁶a ymchoelaŵd yn vudugaŵl wedy cael diruaŵr anreith ac amylder o yspeil. Ac odyna ydymchoelaŵd ac y torres pont Aber Teiui. Ac ³odyna y doeth ²[ef] att Owein ab Gruffud ¹[ap yr arglwydd Rys i gefnderw] a gŵyr

---

ᵃ′ ⁷ teruysgeu avagyssit
ᵇ′ ⁷ kyfuchaŵd kestyll Ned achastell Ketŵeli ar llaŵr.

---

¹ E.
² B.
³ Yna, B.
⁴ B. a, A.

of a storm and mortality, being disappointed of his purpose, he returned to England. That year, William Canton of Cemaes died. Then young Llywelyn, son of Maelgwn, died, on his estate in Gwynedd, and was honourably buried at Aberconway. That year, William Bruse was hanged by Llywelyn, son of Iorwerth, kaving been caught in the chamber of the prince, with ¹ the princess Jannet,' daughter of king John, and wife of the prince.

1231. The ensuing year, Maelgwn, son of Rhys, died at Llanerch Aeron, and was buried in the chapter house at Strata Florida. That year, king Henry built Pain's Castle in Elvael. Then, on account of the ᵃ dispute which had taken place' between Llywelyn, son of Iorwerth and the king, Llywelyn burned the town and castle of Baldwin, and Maes Hyveidd, and Gelli, and Aberhodni, and razed the castles to the ground. From thence he drew into Gwent, and reduced Caerleon to ashes, whilst some gentlemen were lost there. And from thence he ᵇ started for the castle of Nedd, and the castle of Cydweli, and cast them to the ground.' That year, young Maelgwn, 'son of' Maelgwn, son of Rhys, burned Aberteivi to the gate of the castle, and slew all the burgesses, and returned victoriously, after obtaining vast spoil and a profusion of booty. And then he returned, and broke down the bridge of Aberteivi. And from thence he came to Owain, son of Gruffudd, ¹ son of the lord Rhys, his cousin,' and the men of Llywelyn,

---

ᵃ′⁷ disputes which had been fostered

ᵇ′⁷ levelled the castles of Nedd, and the castle of Cydweli, with the ground.

---

⁵ vôrdeisseit, B.
⁶ yd, B.

⁷ B.

Llywelyn ab Iorwoerth y ymlad ar castell, a chyn penn ychydic o dydyeu y torrassant y castell amagneleu. Ac y goruu ar y castellwyr adaỽ y muroed arodi y castell.

MCCXXXII. Y ulỽydyn rac ỽyneb y bu uarỽ Ion ¹[y] Bretỽys o greulaỽn ageu wedy y essigaỽ oe varch. Ac yna y bu uarỽ iarll Kaer Llion. Ac y bu uarỽ ²Ybraham escob Llan ³Elỽy.

MCCXXXIII. Y ulỽydyn rac ỽyneb ydatgyweiryaỽd Rickert iarll ⁴Penuro braỽt Henri urenhin gastell Maessyfeid yr hỽnn adistrywassei Lywelyn ab Iorwoerth yr ysdỽy vlyned kyn no hynny. Y ulỽydyn honno a kyrchaỽd Llywelyn ab Iorwoerth Vrecheinaỽc, ac y distryỽaỽd holl gestyll athrefyd y wlat, drỽy anreithaỽ ac yspeilaỽ pop lle. Ac ymlad achastell Aber Hodni vis a ⁵ỽnaeth gyt a blifieu a magneleu, ac yny diwed ⁶peidyaỽ drỽy ymchoelut y dref ¹[oll] yn lludỽ. Ac ⁷yna ar y ymhoel y llosges dref Golunỽy ac y darostygaỽd Dyffryn ⁸Teueityaỽc. Ac odyno ⁹[llosgi y Trallwng] y kyrchaỽd y Castell Coch ac y byryaỽd yr llaỽr. Ac y llosges dref Croes Oswallt. Y ulỽydyn honno y bu teruysc rỽg Henri urenhin a Rickert Marscal iarll Penuro. Ac yna y kytaruolles y iarll a Llywelyn uab Iorwoerth ac athyỽyssogyon Kymry. Ac yny lle kynullaỽ diruaỽr lu aoruc ef ac Owein ab Gruffud ⁰[ap yr arglwyd Rys], a chyrchu am ben Aber ¹⁰Mynyỽ aỽnaethant ae losgi a gỽneuthur aerua o wyr y brenhin aoedynt yno yn kadỽ. Odyna yn ebrỽyd y goresgynnassant hynn o ⁹[drevi a] gestyll, ¹[nyt amgen] Kaer Dyf, ac Aber Gefenni, Penn Kelli, Blaen Llyfni, Bỽlch y

---

¹ B.
² Efream, B.
³ Elyỽ, B.

⁴ Kernyt, B.
⁵ oruc, B.
⁶ y peidaỽd, B.

son of Iorwerth, to fight against the castle, and before the end of a few days, they broke the castle with engines; and the garrison was compelled to quit the walls, and to deliver up the castle.

1232. The ensuing year, John [1] de Bruse died of a cruel death, having been bruised by his horse. Then the earl of Caerleon died. And [2] Abraham, bishop of Llanelwy, died.

1233. The ensuing year, Rickert, earl of '[4]Pembroke, brother to king Henry, repaired the castle of Maes Hyveidd, which had been destroyed by Llywelyn, son of Iorwerth, two years previously. That year, Llywelyn, son of Iorwerth, proceeded to Brecheiniog, and destroyed all the castles and towns of the country, ravaging and despoiling every place. And he fought against the castle of Aberhodni for a month, with missiles and engines, and in the end desisted, after reducing [1] all the town to ashes. And then, on his return, he burned the town of Colunwy, and subjugated the Vale of Teveidiog. And after that, '[9]having burned Trallwng,' he proceeded to the Red Castle, and razed it to the ground, and burned the town of Oswestry. That year, there was a dispute between king Henry and Rickert Marshall, earl of Pembroke. And then the earl entered into treaty with Llywelyn, son of Iorwerth, and the Welsh princes; and immediately he, and Owain, son of Gruffudd, '[9]son of the lord Rhys,' assembled a vast army, and proceeded against Aber Mynyw, and burned it, and slaughtered the king's men, who were there in garrison. Afterwards, they soon reduced these '[9]towns and' castles, to wit, Cardiff and Abergavenny, Pen Gelli, Blaen Llyvni, and Bwlch y Dinas, and razed

---

[7] odyna, *B.*
[8] Teueidat, *B.*
[9] *E.*
[10] Mynyby, *B.*

x

dinas, ac ae byryassant oll yr llaŵr ¹eithyr Kaer Dyf. Y ulŵydyn honno ydymgynullaŵd Maelgŵn Vychan ab Maelgŵn ab Rys, ac Owein ab Gruffud ²[ap yr arglwydd Rys] ³[a] Rys ᵃGryc ⁴ae meibon hŵynteu, a llu Llywelyn ab Iorŵoerth, a llu iarll Penuro am benn Kaer Uyrdin. Ac ymlad a hi trimis agŵneuthur pont ar Tywi aorugant. Ac yna y doeth y llogwyr yn aruaŵc y gyt ar llanŵ y dorri y bont. A gŵedy gŵelet or Kymry na ffrŵythei y hynt udunt ymchoelut aŵnaethant y gŵlatoed. Y vlŵydyn honno y bu uarŵ Rys Gryc yn Llann Deilaŵ vaŵr, ac y cladŵyt ym Mynyŵ yn ymyl bed y dat. Y ulŵydyn honno y gorffennaŵd Maelgŵn Vychan ⁵[ap Maelgwn ap Rys] adeilat castell Tref Ilan yr hŵnn a dechreuassei Uaelgŵn y dat kynno hynny.

MCCXXXIV. Y ulŵydyn rac ŵyneb y brathŵyt Rickert iarll Penuro y myŵn brŵydyr yn ⁶[y] Iwerdon wedy y adaŵ oe uarchogyon yn dŵyllodrus, a chyn penn y pytheŵnos y bu uarŵ. Y ulŵydyn honno y gellygŵyt Grufud ab Llyŵelyn ab Iorwoeth wedy y vot ygkarchar whe blyned. Y vlŵydyn honno y bu uarŵ Katwallaŵn uab Maelgŵn o Vaelenyd yny Cwm Hir.

MCCXXXV. Y vlŵydyn rac wyneb y bu uarŵ Owein ab Gruffud ²[ap yr arglwydd Rys' ⁷gwr bonhedic o genedyl ac adwyn o deuodeu doeth a hael a chloduawr] yn Ystrat Fflur duŵ Merchyr wedy yr ŵythuet dyd o Ystŵyll, ac ycladŵyt ygyt a Rys ²[ap yr arglwydd Rys] y vraŵt ygkabidyldy y myneich. Y

ᵃ ⁶ Vychan

---

¹ namyn, *B.*   ³ *B.* ab, *A.*
² *E.*   ⁴ eu, *B.*

them all to the ground, except Cardiff. That year, Maelgwn the Little, son of Maelgwn, son of Rhys, and Owain, son of Gruffudd, ²son of the lord Rhys,' ³and Rhys ᵃthe Hoarse,' with their sons, and the army of Llywelyn, son of Iorwerth, and the army of the earl of Pembroke, assembled against Caermarthen. They fought against it for three months, and made a bridge over the Tywi. And then the sailors came armed, with the flood tide, to break down the bridge. When the Welsh perceived that their expedition prospered not, they returned to their respective countries. That year, Rhys the Hoarse died at Llandeilo the Great, and was buried in Menevia, near the grave of his father. The same year, Maelgwn the Little, ⁵son of Maelgwn, son of Rhys,' completed the building of the castle of Trev Ilan, which had previously been commenced by his father Maelgwn.

1234. The ensuing year, Rickert, earl of Pembroke, was stabbed in a battle in Ireland, after having been treacherously deserted by his knights; and before the end of a fortnight he died. That year, Gruffudd, son [of Llywelyn, son of Iorwerth, was liberated, after having been six years in prison. The same year, Cadwallon, son of Maelgwn, of Maelienydd, died at Cwm Hir.

1235. The ensuing year, Owain, son of Gruffudd, ²son of the lord Rhys,' ⁷'a gentleman by race, and courteous in manners, wise, generous, and praiseworthy,' died at Strata Florida, on the Wednesday after the octave of the Epiphany, and was buried with Rhys, ²son of the lord Rhys,' his brother, in

---

ᵃ/ ⁶ the Little,

---

⁵ *C. E.*
⁶ *B.*

| ¹ *C.*

ulvydyn honno y priodes Henri vrenhin verch iarll Prouins, ac y gvnaeth y neithavr yn Llundein y Nadolic gvedy ¹[ym] kynnullav escyb a chanmvyaf ieirll a barvneit Lloeger y gyt.

MCCXXXVI. Y ulvydyn rac vyneb y bu uarv Madavc ab Gruffud Maelavr ²[y gwr a ragorei rac pawb o volyanrwyd y deuodeu ahaelyoni a chreuyd, kanys ef noed grwndwalwr gwahanredawl y manachlogoed, ef a oed kynnheilyat yr anghanogyon ar tlodyon ar essewydyon], ac y cladvyt yn enrydedus ymanachlavc Llanegvestyl yr hon arvndwalassei ¹[ef] kyn no hynny. Y ulvydyn honno y bu uarv Owein ab Maredud ab Rotbert o Gedewein. Ac yna y bu uarv escob Llundein, ac escob Caer Wyragon, ac escob Lincol. Ac un nos kyn nos Nadolic y kyuodes diaerebus wynt y torri aneiryf o dei ac eglvysseu ac essigav y koetyd a ²[llad] llaver o dynyon ac anifeileit. Y ulvydyn honno y gellygavd y navvet Gregori bap Gadvgavn escob Bangor oe escobavt, ac y kymervyt yn enrydedus yny crefyd gvynn ymanachlavc Dor, ac yno y bu uarv ac y cladvyt. Ac yna y cauas Gilbert iarll Penvro drvy dvyll gastell Morgan ab Howel ³Ymachein. A gvedy y gadarnhau ydatueravd drachefyn rac ofyn Llywelyn ab Iorwoerth.

MCCXXXVII. Y ulvydyn rac vyneb y bu uarv ¹[dam] ⁴Giwan uerch Ieuan urenhin gvreic Lywelyn ab Iorwoerth vis Whefravr yn llys Aber, ac y cladvyt myvn ᵃ myntent newyd' ar lan y traeth, a gyssegrassei Howel escob Llan Elyv. Ac y henryded hi ydadeilavd

---

ᵃ' ² gard gyssegredic,

¹ B. | ³ C.

the chapter house of the monks. That year, king Henry married the daughter of the earl of Provence, and held his nuptial solemnities in London, at Christmas, after having assembled the bishops, and most of the earls and barons of England together.

1236. The ensuing year, Madog, son of Gruffudd Maelor—²the man who surpassed all in the celebrity of his manners, his generosity, and religion, for he was the special founder of monasteries, and was the supporter of the needy and poor and indigent,' died, and was honourably buried in the monastery of Llanegwestl, which he had previously founded. That year, Owain, son of Maredudd, son of Robert of Cydewain, died. And then the bishop of London, and the bishop of Worcester, and the bishop of Lincoln, died. And one night before Christmas Eve there arose a remarkable wind to break down an immense number of houses and churches, and to injure the trees, and ²kill many men and animals. That year, pope Gregory the ninth released the bishop of Bangor from his diocese, and he was honourably received into the white religious society in the monastery of Dor; and there he died and was buried. And then Gilbert, earl of Pembroke, obtained, through treachery, the castle of Morgan, son of Howel, in Mechain; and when he had fortified it, he restored it back, for fear of Llywelyn, son of Iorwerth.

1237. The ensuing year, ¹Dame ⁴Joan, daughter of king John, and the wife of Llywelyn, son of Iorwerth, died in the month of February, at the court of Aber, and was buried in a ᵃ new cemetery,' on the side of the strand, which Howel, bishop of

---

ᵃ'² consecrated garden,

---

² Ymeichein, *B.* | ⁴ Siwan, *B.* Signed, *E.*

Llywelyn ab Iorwoerth yno vanachlaȯc troetnoeth aelwis Llan Vaes ym Mon. Ac yna y bu uarȯ Ieuan iarll Kaer Lleon a Chynwric uab yr arglȯyd Rys. Y ulȯydyn hono ydeuth attaȯ gardinal o Rufein y Loegyr yn legat y gan y naȯuet Gregori bap.

MCCXXXVIII. Y ulȯydyn rac ȯyneb tranhoeth [1] o duȯ' gȯyl Luc euegylyȯr y tygaȯd holl tywyssogyon Kymry ffydlonder y Dauyd ab Llywelyn ab Iorwoerth yn Ystrat Fflur. Ac yna y duc ef y gan y uraȯt [2] [Grufud] Arȯystli a Cheri a Chyfeilaȯc, a Maȯdȯy a Mochnant, a Chaer Einaȯn; ac [3] ny adaȯd idaȯ dim namyn kantref Llyyn e hun. Ac yna y lladaȯd Maredud ab Madaȯc ab Gruffud Maelaȯr Ruffud y uraȯt. Ac yny lle y digyfoethes Llywelyn ab Iorwoerth ef am hynny.

MCCXXXIX. Y ulȯydyn rac ȯyneb y bu uarȯ Maredud [a] dall ab yr arglwyd Rys, ac y cladȯyt yny Ty Gȯynn. Ac yna y bu uarȯ escob Kaer Wynt, ac y ganet mab y Henri urenhin aelwit Etwart, ac y delis Dauyd ab Llywelyn Ruffud y vraȯt gan dorri aruoll ac ef, ac y carcharaȯd ef aeuab Ygrugyeith.

MCCXL. Deugein mlyned a deucant a mil oed oet Crist pan uu uarȯ Llywelyn ab Iorwoerth tywyssaȯc Kymry gȯr a oed anaȯd menegi y weithredoed da, ac y cladȯyt yn Aber Conȯy, wedy kymryt abit [2] [y] crefyd ymdanaȯ; ac yny ol ynteu y gȯledychaȯd Dauyd y uab o Siwan uerch Ieuan urenhin y uam. M s

---

[a] [4] goec

---

[1] ȯedy, B. | [2] B.

Llanelwy, had consecrated. And in honour of her, Llywelyn, son of Iorwerth, built there a monastery for barefooted monks, which is called Llanvaes in Mona. And then Ieuan, earl of Caerleon, and Cynvrig, son of the lord Rhys, died. That year, there came again a cardinal from Rome to England, sent, as his legate, by pope Gregory the ninth.

1238. The ensuing year, on the morrow after the feast of St. Luke the Evangelist, all the princes of Wales sware fidelity to David, son of Llywelyn, son of Iorwerth, at Strata Florida. And then he took, from his brother ² Gruffudd, Arwystli and Ceri and Cyveiliog and Mawddwy and Mochnant and Caereinion; leaving to him nothing but the cantrev of Lleyn itself. And then Maredudd, son of Madog, son of Gruffudd Maelor, slew his brother Gruffudd; and immediately Llywelyn, son of Iorwerth, divested him of his territory on that account.

1239. The ensuing year, Maredudd ᵃ the Blind,' son of the lord Rhys, died, and was buried at Whitland. Then also the bishop of Winchester died; and a son was born to king Henry, called Edward. And David, son of Llywelyn, seized his brother Gruffudd, breaking the compact with him, and imprisoned him and his son at Cricciaeth.

1240. One thousand two hundred and forty was the year of Christ, when Llywelyn, son of Iorwerth, prince of Wales, died—the man whose good works it would be difficult to enumerate—and was buried at Aberconway, after taking the habit of religion. And after him David, his son, by Joan, the daughter of king John, his mother, reigned. The month of

---

ᵃ/⁴ the Empty

³ nyt, *B.* | ⁴ *C. E.*

Mei rac ỽyneb ydaoth Dauyd ab Llywelyn a barỏneit Kymry y gyt ac ef hyt yg Kaer Loyỽ y ỏrhau ᵃ yr brenhin y ewythyr, ac ygymryt y gantaỽ y gyfoeth yn gyfreithaỏl. Ac yna yd anuones y Saeson Wallter Marscal a llu y gyt ac ef y gadarnhau Aber Teiui.

MCCXLI. Y ulỏydyn rac ỏyneb ydaeth Otto gardinal o Loeger, ac y delit ef allawer o archescyb ac escyb ac abadeu ac eglỏysỏyr ereill ygyt ac ef y gan Ffrederic amheraỏdyr gỏr a oed yn yskymun yn ryuelu yn erbyn Gregori bab. A gỏedy mynet y cardinal o Loegyr y kynnullaỏd y brenhin lu, ac y doeth y darestỏg tywyssogyon Kymry, ac y kadarnhaaỏd gastell y Garrec yn ymyl y Disserth yn Tegeygyl, ac y kymerth ỏystlon y gan Dauyd ab Llywelyn y nei dros ỏyned, ar talu o Dauyd y Ruffud ab Gỏenỏynỏyn y holl dylyet ym Powys, ac y veibon Maredud ab Kynan y holl dylyet ym Meironnyd, a chan dyfynnu Dauyd y Lundein yr cỏnsli, a dỏyn ygyt ac ef Ruffud y uraỏt, ar holl garcharoryon aoed y gyt ac ef ygkarchar y brenhin y Lundein. Ac yna y bu uarỏ y naỏuet Gregori bab.

MCCXLII. Y ulỏydyn rac ỏyneb ychydic wedy ¹ y Pasc y ² mordỏyaỏd Henri urenhin y Peitaỏ y geissaỏ ³ gan y' ⁴[vrenhin] Ffreinc y dylyet ar ydired adugassei urenhin Ffreinc y gantaỏ kyn no hynny ac nys cauas y ulỏydyn honno, namyn gỏedy gellỏg y ieirll drachefyn y trigyaỏd ef ar urenhines Ymmỏrdyỏs. Y vlỏydyn honno y kadarnhaỏyt hynn o gestyll Ygkymry, y gan Vaelgỏn Uychan Garthgrugyn, y gan

---

ᵃ ⁴ y Henri

---

¹ yr, B. | ² morỏydaỏd, B.

May following, David, son of Llywelyn, having with him the barons of Wales, went to Gloucester, to do homage to ᵃ the king his uncle, and to receive from him his territory lawfully. And then the English sent Walter Marshall, and an army with him, to fortify Aberteivi.

1241. The ensuing year, Otto, the cardinal, went from England, and he and many archbishops and bishops and abbots, and other churchmen were seized by the emperor Frederick, a man who, being excommunicated, was making war against pope Gregory. And after the cardinal had left England, the king assembled an army, and came to subdue the princes of Wales; and he fortified the castle of Carreg, near Diserth in Tegeingl, and took hostages from David, son of Llywelyn, his nephew, on account of Gwynedd, that David should pay to Gruffudd, son of Gwenwynwyn, his whole claim to Powys; and to the sons of Maredudd, son of Cynan, their whole claim in Meirionydd. And he cited David to London before the council, and he was to bring with him his brother Gruffudd, and all the prisoners that were with him in the prison of the king, to London. And then pope Gregory the ninth died.

1242. The ensuing year, a little after Easter, king Henry sailed for Poictou, to obtain from the ᵈ king of France his right as to his lands, which the king of France had taken from him previously. But he did not obtain it that year, but, after letting his earls return, he and the queen remained at Bourdeaux. That same year, these castles in Wales were strengthened; by Maelgwn the Little, Garthgrugyn,

---

ᵃ ᵈ Henry

ʸ y gann, *B*. | ᵈ *B*.

Ion ¹Mynyʘ ²[a] Buellt, y gan Roser Mortymer Maelenyd. Ac ²[yna] y bu uarʘ Gruffud ab Maredud ab yr arglʘyd Rys archdiagon Keredigyaʘn.

MCCXLIII. Y vlʘydyn rac ʘyneb ydymchoelaʘd Henri urenhin o Vʘrdyʘs, ac y ³kyfarsagʘyt y Kymry a llaʘer orrei ereill yn agkyfreithaʘl.

MCCXLIV. Y vlʘydyn rac ʘyneb y bu uarʘ Rys Mechyll uab Rys Gryc ⁴[ap yr arglwydd Rys]. Y vlʘydyn honno y keissaʘd Gruffud ab Llywelyn dianc o garchar y brenhin yn Llundein wedy bʘrʘ raff drʘy ffenestyr y tʘr allan a diskynnu arhyt y raff, a thorri y raf, ae syrthaʘ ynteu yny dorres y vynʘgyl. Ac yna y llidyaʘd Dauyd ab Llywelyn a dyuynnu aoruc holl wyrda y gyt, a ruthraʘ y elynyon ²[gurru] oe holl deruyneu eithyr aoedynt y myʘn kestyll. Ac anuon kenadeu allythyreu a ⁵ʘnaeth a dyuynnu attaʘ holl dywyssogyon Kymry, a phaʘb a gyuunaʘd ac ef eithyr Gruffud ab Madaʘc a Gruffud ab Gʘenʘynʘyn, a Morgan ab Howel, a llaʘer o golledeu awnaeth efe yr rei hynny, ae kymhell ae hanuod y darestʘg idaʘ. Y ulʘydyn honno y bu uarʘ Maredud ab Rotbert penn kyghorʘr Kymry wedy kymryt abit crefyd yn Ystrat Fflur.

MCCXLV. Y ulʘydyn rac ʘyneb ⁶[y kauas etuedyon Gwilyam Marscal eu tref tat yn hedwch] y kynnullaʘd Henri urenhin gedernit Lloeger ac Iwerdon ar uedyr darestʘg holl Gymry idaʘ, ac y doeth hyt yn Teganʘy. A gʘedy kadarnhau y kastell ac adaʘ marchogyon yndaʘ yd ymchoelaʘd y Loegyr gan adaʘ aneirif oe lu yn galaned heb y cladu wedy llad rei a bodi ereill.

---

¹ Mynʘy, *B*. Mynw, *E*. ³ kyʘaresagaʘd, *B*.
² *B*.   ⁶ *E*.

Menevia ² and Buellt by John, Maelienydd by Roger Mortimer. And ³ then, Gruffudd, son of Maredudd, son of the lord Rhys, archdeacon of Ceredigion, died.

1243. The ensuing year, king Henry returned from Bourdeaux; and the Welsh with many others, were unlawfully oppressed.

1244. The ensuing year, Rhys Mechyll, son of Rhys the Hoarse, ⁴son of the lord Rhys,' died. That year, Gruffudd, son of Llywelyn, attempted to escape from the king's prison in London, by throwing a rope through the window of the tower, and descending along the rope, but the rope breaking, he fell, and broke his neck. And then David, son of Llywelyn, became enraged, and summoned all his good men to him, and attacked his foes, ²and drove them' from all their borders, except such as were in castles. And he sent messengers with letters, summoning to him all the princes of Wales; and every body joined him, except Gruffudd, son of Madog, and Gruffudd, son of Gwenwynwyn, and Morgan, son of Howel; and to those he caused many losses, and compelled them against their will to submit to him. That year died Maredudd, son of Robert, the chief counsellor of Wales, after taking the religious habit at Strata Florida.

1245. The ensuing year, ⁶the heirs of William Marshall obtained their patrimony in peace.' And king Henry assembled the power of England and Ireland, with the intention of subjecting all Wales to him, and came to Dyganwy. And after fortifying the castle, and leaving knights in it, he returned to England, having left an immense number of his army dead and unburied, some having been slain and others drowned.

---

⁵ oruc, *B.* | ⁶ *C.*

MCCXLVI. Y ulѳydyn rac ѳyneb ¹[blwydyn glawawc oed] y bu uarѳ Dauyd ab Llywelyn yn Aber vis Maѳrth, ac y cladѳyt gyt ae dat yn Aber Conѳy. A gѳedy nat oed ²etiued o gorff idaѳ' y gѳledychaѳd Owein Goch a Llywelyn y nyeint meibon Gruffud ab Llywelyn y vraѳt yny ol. Y rei hynny o gyghor gѳyr da a ranassant y kyuoeth yn deu hanner ³[y rygthunt]. Y ulѳydyn honno ydanuones Henri urenhin Nicolas dy Mulus ⁴[vstus Kaer Vyrddin] a Maredud ab Rys ⁵[Gryc], a Maredud uab Owein y digyuoethi Maelgѳn Vychan. Ac yna y goruu ar Vaelgѳn ae eidaѳ ffo hyt Yggѳyned, ac Owein a Llywelyn veibon Gruffud ab Llywelyn gan adaѳ y kyuoeth y estronyon. Ac o achaѳs bot brenhinaѳl allu yndyuynnu paѳb or a vei gyfun ar brenhin yn erbyn Owein a Llywelyn, a Maelgѳn ⁴[Vychan] a Howel ab Maredud owlat Uorgan aoed yna y gyt ac ѳynt Yggѳyned wedy y digyuoethi ⁶yn gѳbyl o iarll Clar. A gѳedy gѳybod o nadunt hynny yd ymgadwassant yny mynydoed ar ynyalѳch. Y vlѳydyn honno y bu uarѳ ⁷Raѳlff Mortymer, ac yny le y kyuodes Roser y uab.

MCCXLVII. Y ulѳydyn rac ѳyneb y bu uarѳ Howel escob Llan Elyѳ yn Ryt Ychen ac yno y cladѳyt. Ac yna y bu uarѳ ⁸[Anseul Vras] escob Mynyѳ. Y ulѳydyn honno yr ugeinuet dyd o vis Whefraѳr ¹[y deudecvet dyd o brif y lleuat ar llythyren honn F yn kadw y Sul am gylch pryt gosper] y crynaѳd y dayar yn aruthur yn gyffredin ar draѳs yr holl deyrnas.

MCCXLVIII. Y ulѳydyn rac ѳyneb y kymerth arderchaѳc vrenhin Ffreinc ae dri broder ac anneiryf o luoed

---

¹ C.
²' oe gorff idaѳ etiued, B.
³ B.
⁴ E.

1246. The ensuing year ¹ was a rainy year.' David, son of Llywelyn, died at Aber, in the month of March, and was buried with his father at Aberconway. And since he had no issue of his body, his nephews Owain the Red, and Llywelyn, the sons of Gruffudd, son of Llywelyn, his brother, reigned after him. Those, by the advice of good men, divided their dominion ³ between them' into two halves. That year, king Henry sent Nicholas de Myles, 'justice of Caermarthen,' and Maredudd, son of Rhys ⁵ the Hoarse,' and Maredudd, son of Owain, to dispossess Maelgwn the Little. And thereupon, Maelgwn, with his family, was compelled to flee into Gwynedd, and to Owain and Llywelyn, the sons of Gruffudd, son of Llywelyn, leaving his territory to strangers; because the royal power summoned all that joined with the king against Owain and Llywelyn, and Maelgwn ⁴ the Little,' and Howel, son of Maredudd of Glamorgan, who were then along with them in Gwynedd, being entirely dispossessed by the earl of Clare. And when they became acquainted with that, they kept themselves in the mountains and the wilds. That same year ⁷ Ralph Mortimer died, and in his stead arose Roger his son.

1247. The ensuing year, Howel, bishop of Llanelwy, died at Oxford; and was there buried. And then ⁸ Anselm the Fat,' bishop of Menevia, died. The same year, the twentieth day of the month of February, ⁷ the twelfth day of the prime of the moon, and this letter F. denoting Sunday, about the time of vespers,' there was a dreadful earthquake generally throughout the whole kingdom.

1248. The ensuing year, the noble king of France, and his three brothers, having with them immense

---

³ *C. E.*
⁴ *o, B.*

⁷ Randwlff, *E.*
⁸ *B. C.*

Cristonogyon ¹[y] gyt ac ȏynt eu hynt hyt Ygkaerussalem. Ac am diwed y ulȏydyn y mordȏyssant y mor maȏr. Y ulȏydyn honno vis Gorfennaf y gȏnaeth Grufud abat Ystrat Fflur hedȏch a Henri vrenhin am dylyet a ²dylynt yr uanachlaȏc yr ys ³llaȏer o amser kyn no hynny gan uadeu yr abat ar cofeint ⁴[hanner y dylyet nyt amgen] deg morc adeugein morc, a thrychan morc a dalaȏd, a thalu y gymeint arall myȏn teruyneu gossodedic herwyd ¹[val] y keffir ⁵ynyaelaes y vanachlaȏc. Y ulȏydyn honno y kauas Owein ab Rotbert Gedewein y dylyet, ac y cauas Rys Vychan ab Rys Mechyll gastell Karrec Kennen drachefyn a rodassei ᵃy vam' yn dȏyllodrus ym medyant y Ffreinc o gas ar y mab. Y ulȏydyn honno y kanhataȏd Henri vrenhin y abat Ystrat Fflur ac abat Aber Conȏy gorff Gruffud ab Llywelyn, ac y dugant gantunt o Lundein y Aber Conȏy yny lle y mae yn gorwed.

MCCXLIX. Y vlȏydyn rac ȏyneb ydaeth Lowys vrenhin ae dri broder ar urenhines hyt yn dinas Damieta, ac y rodes Duȏ idaȏ yn rȏyd wedy adaȏ or Sarasinyeit. Yrhaf rac ȏyneb yd ymchoelaȏd y dyghetfen yny gȏrthȏyneb, ac y delit y brenhin y gan y Sarassinyeit wedy llad Robert y uraȏt, ac amgylch degmil arhugeint ⁶or Cristonogyon, a thros y ellygdaȏt ef ae hebrygyat ef ae wyr hyt yn Acris y goruu arnaȏ rodi Damieta drachefyn yr Sarassinyeit a ⁷[diruaȏr sȏmp o aryant y gyt a hynny ac ychydic] gȏedy hynny y

ᵃ' ¹ Ieuan

¹ B.
² dylyit, B.
³ hir, B.
⁴ C.

armies of Christians, took their course towards Jerusalem; and about the end of the year they sailed over the great sea. That year, the month of July, Gruffudd, abbot of Strata Florida, made peace with king Henry, in respect of a debt which the monastery owed for a long time previously, he forgiving to the abbot and convent 'half the debt, namely,' fifty marks; and three hundred marks the other paid, and was to pay as much more, under settled limitations, as may be found in the Register of the monastery. That year Owain, son of Robert, obtained Cydewain his right; and Rhys the Little, son of Rhys Mechyll, obtained the castle of Carreg Cennen back again, which ᵃhis mother' had deceitfully given into the possession of the French, from hatred towards her son. That year, king Henry permitted the abbot of Strata Florida, and the abbot of Aberconway, to have the body of Gruffudd, son of Llywelyn; and they brought it with them from London to Aberconway, in which place he lies.

1249. The ensuing year, king Louis, with his three brothers, and the queen, went to the city of Damietta; and God easily granted it to him, the Saracens having left it. The ensuing summer, the fates became adverse, and the king was taken by the Saracens, after Robert his brother had been killed, with about thirty thousand of the Christians; and for his liberation, and transport of himself and men to Acre, he was constrained to restore Damietta to the Saracens, and ⁷to pay an immense sum of money besides, and shortly'

ᵃ' ¹ John

---

⁵ ynyr annyales, *B.*
⁶ o, *B.*
⁷ *B. C.*

rodes Duꝏ idaꝏ ynteu uudugolyaeth y dial ar elynyon Crist y sarhaet. Kanys ef a anuones y deu uroder hyt yn Ffreinc y gynnullaꝏ nerth idaꝏ o sollt a goyr aruaꝏc tra ¹drickyei ynteu' ar urenhines yn Acrys. Ac odyna ydennillaꝏd ef dinas Damieta ²[dracheuen] gan lad anneiryf or Sarassinyeit.

MCCL. Dec mlyned a deugein a ²[deu] chant a mil oed oet Crist pan uu uarꝏ brenhin ³Prydein wedy adaꝏ y vn mab yn etiued idaꝏ.

MCCLI. Y vloydyn rac ꝏyneb y bu uarꝏ Goladus Du uerch Llywelyn ab Iorwoerth ⁴[Drwyndwn gwraic briod syr Randwlff Mortimer]. Ac yn diwed y vloydyn honno y bu uarꝏ Morgan ab yr argloyd Rys, wedy kymryt abit crefyd ymdanaꝏ yn Ystrat Fflur.

MCCLII. Y uloydyn rac ꝏyneb y bu gymeint gores yr heul ac y ⁵dissychaꝏd yr holl dayar gantho hyt na thyfaꝏd dim froyth ar y coet ⁶na maes, ac na ⁷chahat pysgaꝏt mor nac auonyd. Ac yndiwed y kynhayaf ⁸y vloydyn honno' y bu gymeint y glaꝏ-ogyd ac y kudyaꝏd llifdyfred ꝏyneb y dayar hyt na allei ᵃor mod sychdor' y dayar lygku y dyfred. Ac y llifhaaꝏd yr auonyd yny dorres y pynt ar melineu ar tei kyfagos yr afonyt achribdeilaꝏ y coedyd ar perllanneu a goneuthur llaꝏer o golledeu ereill yn yr haf. Y uloydyn honno yduc Goilim ab Gorwaret y

---

ᵃ ⁹ drasychedoed

---

¹ʹ drigyaꝏd ef, *B.*
² *B.*
³ Prydyn, *E.*

⁴ *E.*
⁵ sychaꝏd, *B.*

THE CHRONICLE OF THE PRINCES. 337

after that, God granted to him victory to revenge his insult on the enemies of Christ, for he sent his two brothers to France, to collect for him strength in money and armed men, whilst he and the queen remained at Acre. And from thence he gained the city of Damietta ²again, killing an immense number of the Saracens.

1250. One thousand ²two hundred and fifty was the year of Christ, when the king of Prydyn died, leaving one son as his heir.

1251. The ensuing year, Gwladus the Dark, the daughter of Llywelyn, son of Iorwerth ⁴ the Broken-nosed, and wife of Sir Randulph Mortimer,' died. And in the end of that year, Morgan, son of the lord Rhys, died, after taking the religious habit at Strata Florida.

1252. The ensuing year, the heat of the sun was so great, that all the earth became so dry therefrom, that no fruit grew on the trees or the fields, and neither fish of the sea nor of the rivers were obtained. And at the end of the harvest of that year, so great were the rains, that the water floods covered the face of the earth, since the ᵃ excess of the dryness' of the earth could not absorb the waters; and the rivers flooded so that the bridges and the mills and the houses adjoining the rivers were broken, and the woods and orchards were stripped, besides many other losses during the summer. That same year, William, son of Gwrwared, the person who was se-

---

ᵃ'⁹ excessive thirsts

---

⁶ nar, *B.*
⁷ chaffat, *B.*

⁸' hônnó, *B.*
⁹ *B.*

Y

gỏr a oed synysgal y brenhin ar dir Maelgỏn ieuanc
drỏy orchymynn y brenhin y ar wyr Eluael anreith
am ¹eu bot yn keissaỏ aruer o boreyd Maelenyd
megys o vreint.

Y ulỏydyn rac ỏyneb y ²mordỏyaỏd Henri urenhin y Vỏrdyỏs a diruaỏr lu gantaỏ, a gorchymyn y
vrenhinyaeth ³[aỏnaeth] y Etwart y uab ⁴a Rickert
iarll Kernyỏ y uraỏt ar vrenhines. Y ulỏydyn honno
y Grawys yd ymchoelaỏd Thomas escob Mynyỏ o lys
Rufein.

MCCLIII. Y ulỏydyn rac ỏyneb ydymchoelaỏd Loỏys
urenhin Freinc oe bererindaỏt wedy y vot whe blyned
yn ymlad ar Sarassinyeit. Y vlỏydyn ³[rac ỏyneb]
honno yd ymchoelaỏd Henri vrenhin o Wasgỏin
gỏedy adaỏ yno Etwart y vab yn kadỏ a diruaỏr lu
y gyt ac ef. Ac yna y bu uarỏ Gỏenllian uerch
Vaelgỏn ieuanc yn Llan Vihagel Gelynrot, ac y cladỏyt ⁵[ygkabidyldy ymyneich] yn Ystrat Fflur.

MCCLIV. Y ulỏydyn rac ỏyneb y bu uarỏ Maredud
ab Llywelyn o Veironyd, gan adaỏ vn mab yn etiued
idaỏ o Wenllian uerch Vaelgỏn. Ac ynebrỏyd gỏedy
gỏyl Ieuan y bu uarỏ Rys vn mab Maelgỏn ieuanc
wedy kymryt abit crevyd yn Ystrat Flur ac yno y
cladỏyt ⁵[yn emyl y chỏaer ygkabidyldy y mynyeich].
Yn y dydyeu hynny o annoc ᵃy kythreul' y magỏyt
teruysc ³[maỏr] y rỏg meibon Gruffud ab Llywelyn, nyt
amgen Owein Goch a Dauyd ⁶or neill tu, a Llywelyn

ᵃ'³ kyureith

---

¹ y, B.
² morỏyaỏd, B.

³ B.
⁴ ac y, B.

neschal to the king over the land of young Maelgwn, by the command of the king, took spoil from the men of Elvael, because they sought the custom of the pasturage of Maelienydd as of privilege.

The ensuing year, king Henry sailed for Bourdeaux, having with him an immense army; and he commended the kingdom to the care of Edward his son, and Rickert, earl of Cornwall, his brother, and the queen. The same year, in Lent, Thomas, bishop of Menevia, returned from the court of Rome.

1253. The ensuing year, Louis, king of France, returned from his pilgrimage, after having been for six years fighting with the Saracens. That ³ ensuing year, king Henry returned from Gascony, having left his son Edward there, to guard it, with an immense army along with him. And then Gwenllian, daughter of young Maelgwn, died at Llanvihangel Gelynrod, and was buried ⁵ in the chapter house of the monks,' at Strata Florida.

1254. The ensuing year, Maredudd, son of Llywelyn, of Meirionydd, died, leaving one son as his heir, by Gwenllian, the daughter of Maelgwn. And soon after the feast of St. John, Rhys, only son of young Maelgwn, died, after taking the habit of religion at Strata Florida, and there he was buried, ⁵ near his sister, in the chapter house of the monks.' In those days, by the instigation of ᵃ the devil,' ³ a great ' dissension was engendered between the sons of Gruffudd, son of Llywelyn, namely, Owain the Red and David, on the one side, and Llywelyn on the other side,

---

ᵃ/³ fate,

---

⁵ B. C. | ⁵ o, B.

or tu arall. Ac yna yd aruolles Llywelyn ae wyr yn diofyn ym Bryn Derwin drwy ymdiret y Duw creulawn dyuotyat y vrodyr a diruawr lu gantunt, a chyn penn vn awr y delit Owein Goch, ac y foes Dauyd wedy llad llawer ¹ or llu a dala ereill a ffo y dryll arall. Ac yna y carcharwyt Owein Goch, ac y goresgynnawd Llywelyn gyfoeth Owein a Dauyd ²[hep wrthwynep idaw]. Y vlwydyn honno y bu warw ³ Mararet uerch Vaelgwn, gwreic Owein ab Rotbert ⁴[ap Mredudd o Gydewain]. Ac y prynwyt y gloch uawr yn Ystrat Fflur yr ᵃtrugein a dwy vorc ar bymthec arhugeint' a dwy vu. Ac yny lle y drychafwyt ac y kyssegrwyt ygan escob Bangor. Ac yna amgylch diwed ²[yr] haf y bu warw Thomas Walis escob Mynyw.

MCCLV. Y vlwydyn rac wyneb ydoeth Etwart uab Henri urenhin iarll Kaer Llion ⁴[Awst nessaf ar hynny] y edrych y gestyll ae dired Yggwyned. Ac yna ⁵[val amgylch Awst agwedy y ymchwelut ef y Loegyr] y doeth dylyedogyon Kymry att Lywelyn ab Gruffud wedy y hyspeilaw oe rydit ae keithiwaw, a menegi ²[idaw] yn wynuanus bot yn well gantunt eu llad yn ryfel dros y rydit, no godef y sathru gan estronyon drwy geithiwet. A chyffroi aoruc Llywelyn wrth y dagreuoed, am eu hannoc ⁶wynt ae kyghor kyrchu y beruedwlat ae goreskynn oll kynn penn yr wythnos, achyt ac ef Maredud uab Rys Gryc. Ac odyna y

---

ᵃ' ⁴ saith mork ar hugain

---

¹ oe, *B*. ³ Margret, *B*.
² *B*.   ⁴ *E*.

And thereupon, Llywelyn and his men awaited, without fear, confiding in God, at Bryn Derwin, the cruel coming of his brothers, accompanied by a vast army; and before the end of one hour, Owain the Red was taken, and David fled, after many of the army were killed, and others captured, and the other part had taken to flight. And then Owain the Red was imprisoned; and Llywelyn took possession of the territory of Owain and David, ²without any opposition.' That year, Margaret, daughter of Maelgwn, and wife of Owain, son of Robert, ⁴son of Maredudd of Cydewain, died. And the great bell at Strata Florida was bought for ᵃthree score and thirty-seven marks,' and two kine; and it was immediately put up, and consecrated by the bishop of Bangor. And then, about the end of the summer, died Thomas Wallis, bishop of Menevia.

1255. The ensuing year, Edward, son of king Henry, earl of Caerleon, came, ⁴in August next after that,' to take a survey of his castles and lands in Gwynedd. And then, ⁵as it were about August, and after he had returned to England,' the nobles of Wales came to Llywelyn, son of Gruffudd, having been robbed of their liberty, and made captives, and complainingly declared ²to him' that they would rather be killed in war for their liberty, than suffer themselves to be trodden down by strangers in bondage. And Llywelyn was moved at their tears; and by their incitement and advice, he, with Maredudd, son of Rhys the Hoarse, invaded the midland country, and subdued it all before the end of the week. And then he took

---

ᵃ'⁴ twenty-seven marks,

---

³ C. ⁶ by, B.

kymerth Veironnyd idaỽ ehun. Ar rann a oed eidaỽ Etwart o Geredigyaỽn ef ae rodes y Varedud ab Owein ¹[ap Gruffydd ap yr arglwydd], a Buellt gyt a hynny. A thalu y Uaredud ab Rys Gryc y gyfoeth gan ỽrtlad Rys y nei oe gyfoeth, ᵃa rodi y kyfoeth' y Uaredud uab Rys heb gynhal dim idaỽ e hun or tired goreskynn ᵇoll eithyr clot agobrỽy. Ac odyna y goresgynnaỽd Werthrynyon y gan Roser Mortymer yny laỽ e hun. Ac yna y kyssegrỽyt yr athro ᶜRys o Gaer' Riỽ y gan y pab yn escob Mynyỽ.

MCCLVI. Y ulỽydyn rac ỽyneb y kyrchaỽd Llywelyn ab Grufud, a Maredud uab Rys ¹[Gryc], a Maredud uab Owein, a llawer o dylyedogyon ereill y gyt ac ef y gynoeth Gruffud ab Gỽennỽynỽyn, ac y goresgynnaỽd oll eithyr castell y Trallỽg ²[a rann] o dyffryn Hafren ac ychydic o Gaereinaỽn. A distryỽ aỽnaeth gastell ³Bydydon. Ygkyfrỽg hynny y kynnullaỽd Rys Uychan uab Rys Mechyll aoed yn Lloegyr ar dehol diruaỽr borth achedernit o varỽneit a marchogyon ⁴[o] Lloegyr ygyt ac ef. Ac y doeth hyt Ygkaer Vyrdin. Ac ⁵odyna yn ỽythnos y Sulgỽyn y duc hynt y Dineftỽr. A gỽedy ⁴[y] dyuot y myỽn yr castell y delis y castellỽyr ef, a chyrchu aỽnaethant y llu a dala y barỽneit ar marchogyon urdolyon, a llad mỽy no dỽy vil or llu ⁴[pann llas ygỽyr yny kymereu oed hynny]. Ac yna y kyrch-

---

ᵃ′⁴ ae rodi   ᵇ⁴ hynn
ᶜ′⁶ meistyr Richard de Kaerin

---

¹ E.   ² Vydydon, B.
³ B. Garan, A.   ⁴ B.

Meirionydd to himself; and that part of Ceredigion, which belonged to Edward, he gave to Maredudd, son of Owain, ¹son of Gruffudd, son of the lord,' with Buellt in addition; and he restored to Maredudd, son of Rhys the Hoarse, his territory, by expelling his nephew Rhys from his territory, ᵃ and gave the territory' to Maredudd, retaining nothing to himself of ᵇ all the conquered lands, other than fame and reward. And afterwards, he wrested Gwerthrynion from Roger Mortimer, and held it in his own hand. And then the doctor ᶜ Rhys, of Caer' Rhiw, was consecrated by the pope bishop of Menevia.

1256. The ensuing year, Llywelyn, son of Gruffudd, and Maredudd, son of Rhys ¹the Hoarse,' and Maredudd, son of Owain, accompanied by many other nobles, entered the territory of Gruffudd, son of Gwenwynwyn, and subdued the whole, except the castle of Trallwng, ² and part' of the Vale of Severn, with a little of Caereinion; and he destroyed the castle of Bydydon. In that interval, Rhys the Little, son of Rhys Mechyll, who was under banishment in England, collected vast aid and strength of the barons and knights ⁴ from England, and came to Caermarthen. And from thence, in Whitsun week, he took his course to Dinevwr; and when he had entered the castle, the garrison seized him; and then they proceeded with a body of men, and took the barons and the noble knights, and slew upwards of two thousand of the army, ⁴ that was, when the men were slain in mutual engagement.' And then the

ᵃ'⁴ and gave it   ᵇ⁴ these
ᶜ'⁶ master Richard de Caerin

⁵ odyno, B. | ⁶ C.

aᏮd y tywyssogyon ¹[y] Dyfet, a distryᏮ awnaethant gastell Aber Toran, a Llan Ystyffan, ac Arberth, ar Maen ClochaᏮc, a llosgi y dref ar trefyd.

MCCLVII. Y ulᏮydyn rac Ꮾyneb y goresgynnaᏮd Llywelyn ab Gruffud Gemeis. ²[A gwedy hynny ef a doeth Llywelyn uab Gruffud y Deheubarth amgylch gwyl Ieuan Vedydwr]. Ac y ᵃkymmodes Varedud ³[ap Rys] a Rys Vychan ⁴[Mechyll] y nei. Ac odyno yngyfun y kyrchassant Drefdraeth, ac y briwassant y castell. Ac odyno y kymerassant Uaredud ab Owein y gyt ac Ꮾynt. Ac y kyrchassant Ros, ac y llosgassant y wlat oll eithyr HaᏮlford. Ac odyno yd hᏮylassant y wlat Vorgan. A gᏮedy ¹[y] goresgyn a chael ¹[y] castell Llan ⁵ Geneu ydymhoelassant adref, wedy llad ilaᏮer a dala ereill. Ac yna ybu uarᏮ MaelgᏮn ieuanc ac y cladᏮyt ⁶[ygkabidyldy ymyneich] yn Ystrat Flur. Y ulᏮydyn honno amgylch gᏮyl Ueir yn AᏮst y deuth Henri urenhin a llu maᏮr gantaᏮ hyt yn TeganᏮy. Ac yno y trigyaᏮd hyt Ꮾyl Veir Ymedi. Ac yna ydymchoelaᏮd y Loegyr. Yn yr amser hᏮnnᏮ y llosges eglᏮys Lan Badarn VaᏮr. Ac y kymydaᏮd Llywelyn ab Gruffud a Gruffud ab MadaᏮc ⁴[ap Gruffydd Maelor], ac y gyrraᏮd Gruffud ab GᏮennᏮynᏮyn ar dehol oe gyfoeth.

MCCLVIII. Y vlᏮydyn rac Ꮾyneb y rodes kynnulleitua o dylyedogyon ¹[Kymry] lᏮ ffydlonder y Lywelyn ab Grufud gan boen ysgymundaᏮt. Ac ni chetᏮis Maredud

---

ᵃ¹ gᏮnaeth gymot rᏮg

---

¹ B.   ³ B. C. E.
² C.   ⁴ E.

princes marched to Dyved; and destroyed the castle of Aber Torran, and Llanstephan, and Arberth, and Maenclochog, and burned the town and towns.

1257. The ensuing year, Llywelyn, son of Gruffudd, subdued Cemaes. ²And after that, Llywelyn, son of Gruffudd, came to South Wales about the feast of St. John the Baptist.' And Maredudd, ³ son of Rhys' ᵃ was reconciled to' Rhys ⁴ Mechyll the Little, his nephew. And jointly from thence they attacked Trevdraeth, and demolished the castle. And then they took Maredudd, son of Owain, along with them, and invaded Rhos, and burned all the country, except Haverford. And from thence they marched to Glamorgan; and after reducing and taking the castle of Llan ⁵ Geneu, they returned home, having killed many, and captured others. And then young Maelgwn died, and was buried ⁶ in the chapter house of the monks,' at Strata Florida. That year, about the feast of St. Mary in August, king Henry came, with a large army, to Dyganwy; and there he tarried until the feast of St. Mary in September; and then he returned to England. At that time the church of Llanbadarn the Great was burned; and Llywelyn, son of Gruffudd, was reconciled to Gruffudd, son of Madog, ⁴ son of Gruffudd Maelor;' and Gruffudd, son of Gwenwynwyn, was driven from his territory into banishment.

1258. The ensuing year, a body of the nobles ¹ of Wales' made an oath of fidelity to Llywelyn, son of Gruffudd, under pain of excommunication; Maredudd,

---

ᵃ' ¹ made reconciliation with

---

³ Gynen, E.   ⁶ B. C.

ab Rys y llŵ honnŵ, namyn mynet yny erbyn yn agkywir. Y ulŵydyn honno y bu teruysc yn Lloegyr y rŵg yr estronyon amgylch gŵyl Ieuan Vedydyŵr. Y ulŵydyn honno ydaeth Dauyd ab Grufud a Maredud ab Owein a Rys Vychan, ᵃa Rys Mechyll y ymdidan a Maredud ab Rys ¹[Gryc], ac a Phadric ᵇDysaes synysgal y brenhin Ygkaer Vyrdin hyt yn Emlyn, pan welas Maredud a Phadric y gŵyr ereill torri kygreir aŵnaethant ae hachub. Ac yna y llas Padric a llaŵer o varchogyon a phedyt y gyt ac ef. Yn diwed y vlŵydyn honno y ²mordŵyaŵd Henri vrenhin y ymdidan a brenhin Ffreinc.

MCCLX. Trugein mlyned a deu cant a mil oed oet Crist pan aeth Llywelyn ab Gruffud y Vuellt, a dŵyn Buellt oll y gan Roser Mortymer eithyr y castell. Ac odyna drŵy ymdeith ar draŵs Deheubarth heb wneuthur drŵc y neb yd ymchoelaŵd y Ŵyned. Ac ³[gŵedy hynny] ᶜyny lle y kauas gŵyr Llyŵelyn o gyrch nos heb un ergyt ymlad gastell Buellt.' A gŵedy dala y castellŵyr achael y meirch ar arueu ar dotrefyn ar yspeil oll y distryŵassant·y castell. Ac yna ydoeth Owein ab Maredud o Eluael y hedŵch yr arglŵyd Lywelyn.

ᵃ⁴ ap   ᵇ⁵ dwysoc
ᶜ⁄⁶ val yr oed wyr or kastell yn egori ypyrth yr rei ereill aoedynt allan ynychaf wyr Llywelyn yn neittyaw ymywn o hyt nos.

---

¹ E.
² morŵydaŵd, B.
³ B. C.
⁴ B. E.

son of Rhys, however, did not keep that oath, but disloyally went against it. That year, there was a disturbance in England among the strangers, about the feast of St. John the Baptist. The same year, David, son of Gruffudd, and Maredudd, son of Owain, and Rhys the Little, [a] and Rhys Mechyll, went as far as Emlyn to speak with Maredudd, son of Rhys [1] the Hoarse,' and with Patrick [b] de Sayes,' the seneschal of the king at Caermarthen. When Maredudd and Patrick saw the other men, they broke the truce, and seized them; and then Patrick was slain, and many knights and infantry along with him. In the close of that year, king Henry made a voyage so as to have a conference with the king of France.

1260. One thousand two hundred and sixty was the year of Christ, when Llywelyn, son of Gruffudd, entered Buellt, and took the whole of it from Roger Mortimer, except the castle. And from thence, proceeding across South Wales, without doing harm to any one, he returned to Gwynedd. And 'after that' [c] immediately the men of Llywelyn, by a night onset, without a single stroke of fighting, got the castle of Buellt;' and after taking the garrison prisoners, and securing the horses and the arms and the furniture and all the spoil, they destroyed the castle. And then Owain, son of Maredudd of Elvael, made peace with the lord Llywelyn.

---

[a] [4] son of [b] [5] prince
[c] [6] as men from the castle were opening the gates to the others, who were without, lo, the men of Llywelyn leaped in by night.

---

[1] E.   [2] C.

MCCLXI. Y vlͧydyn rac ͧyneb y bu uarͧ Gͧladus verch Rufud ab Llywelyn gwreic ¹ᵃ yr arglͧyd Rys' ab Rys Mechyll. Ac yna amgalan gayaf y bu uarͧ Owein uab Maredud arglͧyd Kedewein.

MCCLXII. Y vlͧydyn rac ͧyneb y bu uarͧ ²[Rikert] iarll Clar. Y ulͧydyn honno amgylch gͧyl Andras y doeth rei o gyghor gͧyr Maelenyd yr castell newyd aoed y Roser Mortymer ym Maelenyd. A gͧedy dyuot y myͧn ³[drͧy] dͧyll y lladassant y porthoryon, ac y dalyssant Howel ab Meuruc a oed gͧnstabyl yno, ae wreic ae veibon, ae verchet, a menegi hynny aͧnaethant y synysgal a chͧnstabyl yr arglͧyd Lywelyn. A bryssyaͧ aoruc y rei hynny yno y losgi y castell. A phan gigleu y dywededic Rosser hynny dyuot a ⁴ͧnaeth a diruaͧr gedernit ³[y gyt ac ef] yn borth idaͧ hyt ³[yn lle] y dywededic gastell, a phebyllyaw o vyͧn y muroed ychydic o dydyeu. A phan ͧybu Lywelyn hynny kynnullaͧ llu aoruc adyuot hyt ym Maelenyd a chymryt gͧrogaeth gͧyr Maelenyd. A gͧedy ennill deu gastell ereill rodi kennat awnaeth y Roser Mortymer y ymchoelut drachefyn. Ac ynteu drͧy arch gͧyr da Brecheinaͧc aeth y Vrecheinaͧc, a gͧedy kymryt gͧrogaeth y wlat ydymchoelaͧd y ͧyned

MCCLXIII. Y ulͧydyn rac ͧyneb ⁵[ychydic y kynn y Pasc] y kyrchaͧd Ion ⁶Ystrog ieuanc aoed vaeli ³[yna] ygkastell Baldwin gyrch nos a diruaͧr lu

---

ᵃ'⁷ Rys ieuangk

ʸ yr Rys arglͧyd. ² B.
³ C. E.   ⁴ oruc, B.

1261. The ensuing year, died Gwladus, the daughter of Gruffudd, son of Llywelyn, the wife of ᵃ the lord Rhys,' son of Rhys Mechyll. And then, about the calends of winter, Owain, son of Maredudd, lord of Cydewain, died.

1262. The ensuing year, ² Rickert, earl of Clare, died. The same year, about the feast of St. Andrew, some men, by the counsel of the people of Maelienydd, came to the new castle that Roger Mortimer had in Maelienydd. And after having entered, through treachery, they killed the porters, and seized Howel, son of Meurug, who was constable there, with his wife and his sons and his daughters. And they informed the seneschal and constable of the lord Llywelyn thereof; and those hastened there to burn the castle. And when the aforesaid Roger heard of that, he came with vast strength to support him to ³ the place' of the said castle, and pitched his tents within the walls for a few days. And when Llywelyn became acquainted with that, he collected an army, and came into Maelienydd, and received the homage of the men of Maelienydd. And after gaining two other castles, he gave permission to Roger Mortimer to return back; and he, by the request of the good men of Brecheiniog, went to Brecheiniog, and, after taking the homage of the country, he returned to Gwynedd.

1263. The ensuing year, ⁵ a little before Easter,' John ⁶ Strange the younger, who was ⁸ then bailiff of Castle Baldwin, made a night attack with a vast

---

ᵃ ⁷ young Rhys,

---

⁵ *C.*
⁶ Ystrans, *B.* Ystrains, *C. E.*

⁷ *B. C.*

gantaƀ ar draƀs Keri ᵃ a Chedewein.' A gƀedy kynnullaƀ diruaƀr anreith o honaƀ ymchoelut aoruc drachefyn ¹[yƀaert' ²ford Gedewein Ydanad]. A phan gigleu y Kymry hynny y ymlit aƀnaethant, a llad y dyd hƀnnƀ or Saeson mƀy no ᵇ deudec kant y rƀg ar y meyssyd, ac yn yscubaƀr Aber Miƀl. Ac yny lle wedy hynny y llosges Ion ³Ystrog yr yscubaƀr ¹[o] achaƀs y lladua honno, ac ychydic wedy hynny y llas y Kymry yn ymyl Colunƀy. Yr amser hƀnnƀ ydoed Edwart yn ymdeith ardal Gƀyned, ac yn llosgi rei or trefyd. A gƀedy hynny yd ymchoelaƀd y Loeger. Ac yna o annoc y kythreul yd ymedewis Dauyd a chedymdeithas Llywelyn y vraƀt. Ac yd aeth y Loegyr arei oe aruollwyr y gyt ac ef. Ar amser hƀnnƀ y kyfodes barƀneit Lloegyr a rei o ieirll y gyt ar Kymry yn erbyn Etwart ar estronyon, ac aruaethu ⁴ eu gƀrthlad ⁵ oc eu' plith ac o holl Loegyr a darestƀg y ⁶dinassoed ᶜ kedyrn o nadunt o distryƀ y kestyll, a llosgi y llysoed. Ac yna y distrywaƀd Llywelyn y kestyll aoed Yggƀyned yny gyfoeth. Nyt amgen Deganƀy a ⁷Chaer Faelan.' A Gruffudd ab Gƀennƀynƀyn a distryƀaƀd castell yr ƀydgruc.

MCCLXIV. Y ulƀydyn rac ƀyneb y bu gouadƀy deruysc y rƀg Henri urenhin ac Etwart y uab. Ac kymhorthƀyr or neilltu. Ar ieirll ar barƀneit or tu arall. Ac yn hynny y doeth hyt ym maes Leos brenhin Lloegyr ¹[ae deu vap] a brenhin yr Almaen ae deu vab wedy ymmaruoll y gyt ar dala y ieirll ar barwn-

ᵃ' ¹ hyt Ygkedeƀein.   ᵇ ⁸ ddav.
ᶜ ¹ kadarnnhaf

¹ B.
² C.
³ Ystrans, B.
⁴ y, B.
⁵ oe, B.
⁶ dinessyd, B.

force upon Ceri ᵃ and Cydewain;' and after collecting immense spoil, he returned back, ¹down ²by way of Cydewain to the Tanad.' And when the Welsh got information of this, they pursued them, and slew on that day, of the English, upwards of ᵇ twelve hundred, including those on the fields and in the barn of Aber Miwl. And immediately after that, John ³Strange burned the barn on account of that slaughter; and a little afterwards he killed the Welsh near Colunwy. At that time, Edward was traversing the region of Gwynedd, and burning some of the towns. And after that he returned to England. And then, by the instigation of the devil, David forsook the society of his brother Llywelyn, and went to England, with some of his confederates. At that time, the barons of England, and some earls, rose with the Welsh, against Edward and the strangers, purposing to expel them from amongst them, and out of all England, to subdue the ᶜ strong cities, and to destroy the castles that were in Gwynedd, in his territory; to wit, Dyganwy and ⁷ Caer Vaelan.' And Gruffudd, son of Gwenwynwyn, destroyed the castle of Gwyddgrug.

1264. The ensuing year, there was a memorable disturbance between king Henry and Edward his son, with their supporters on the one side, and the earls and barons on the other side. And upon that occasion, the king of England ¹and his two sons,' and the king of Germany, and his two sons, came to the plain of Lewes, having agreed together upon seizing

ᵃ' ¹ as far as Cydewain;   ᵇ ⁸ two
ᶜ ¹ strongest

⁷ Karec Ffaelan, *E.* Charrec   ⁸ *C. E.*
—, *B*

eit aoedynt yn mynnu kyfreitheu a deuodeu da
Lloegyr. Ac eissoes y dyghetuen aymchoelaẃd yny
gẃrthẃyneb. Kanys y ieirll ar barẃneit adelis yno y
brenhined, a deu vab Henri vrenhin nyt amgen
Etwart ac Etmwnt, a phump ar hugein or barẃneit
pennaf aoed y gyt ac ẃynt, a llawer or marchogyon
bonhedickaf o nadunt, wedy llad mẃy no deg mil o
wyr y brenhined, herwyd y dywaẃt rei or gẃyr a vu
yny vrẃydyr. A gẃedy hynny o gyghor y gellygaẃd
y ieirll vrenhin Lloegyr gan garcharu yrei ereill. Y
vlẃydyn honno y trigyaẃd y Kymry yn hedẃch y gan
Ysaeson, a Llywelyn ab Gruffud yn dywyssaẃc ar
holl Gymry. Ac yna y bu uarẃ Llyẃelyn ab Rys ab
Maelgẃn ¹[ap yr arglwydd Rys ap Gruffydd ap Rys
ap Tewdwr] yr ẃythuet dyd or Ystẃyll.

MCCLXV. Y ulẃydyn rac ẃyneb duẃ Ieu kyn gẃyl y
Drindaẃt y diegis Etwart uab Henri vrenhin o garchar
Simẃnt Mẃnford o gastell Henford drẃy ystryẃ Roser
Mortymer. A gẃedy hynny y kynnullaẃd Edwart
diruaẃr lu o ieirll a barẃneit a marchogyon aruaẃc
yn erbyn Simẃnt Mẃnford ae gyt aruollẃyr, a duẃ
Maẃrth nessaf wedy Aẃst y doethant y gyt hyt ym
maes Efsam. A gẃedy bot ᵃdarestẃg y' vrẃydyr y
rygtunt a llad llaẃer o bop tu y dygẃydaẃd Simẃnt
Mẃnford ae vab, a lluossogrẃyd or rei ereill. Y ulẃydyn honno vis Maẃrth y bu uarẃ Maredud ab Owein
²[ap Gruffudd ap yr arglwydd Rys,' ³amdiffynwr
holl Deheubarth achynghorwr holl Gymry] yn Llan

ᵃ'⁴ garẃ dost

---

¹ E.   ² E.

the earls and barons, who were seeking to obtain the good laws and customs of England. Yet, nevertheless, fate turned adverse; for the earls and barons there seized the kings and the two sons of king Henry, namely, Edward and Edmund, with twenty-five of the principal barons who were with them, and many of the noblest knights among them, after more than ten thousand men had been killed on the side of the kings, as some of the men who were in the battle say. And after that, by advice, the earls liberated the king of England, and imprisoned the others. That year, the Welsh enjoyed peace from the English; Llywelyn, son of Gruffudd, being prince of all Wales. And then, Llywelyn, son of Rhys, son of Maelgwn, [1] son of the lord Rhys, son of Gruffudd, son of Rhys, son of Tewdwr,' died on the octave of Epiphany.

1265. The ensuing year, the Thursday before the feast of the Trinity, Edward, son of king Henry, escaped out of the prison of Simon Montford, in the castle of Hereford, through the scheme of Roger Mortimer. And after that, Edward collected a vast army of earls and barons and armed knights, against Simon Montford and his confederates; and on the Tuesday next after August, they came together to the field of Esham. And when the battle between them had [a] abated, and many been killed on both sides, Simon Montford and his son fell, with a multitude of others. That year, the month of March, Maredudd, son of Owain, [2] son of Gruffudd, son of the lord Rhys, the defender of all South Wales, and counsellor

---

[a] [4] been severely sharp,

[1] *C.*   [4] *B.*

Badarn Vaʋr ac y cladʋyt ¹[ygkabidyldy ymyneich] yn Ystrat Fflur. Ac yna ydetholet ²y pedwyryd Clemens' yn bap.

MCCLXVI. Y vlʋydyn rac ʋyneb y dihegis deu vab Simʋnt Mʋnford o garchar y brenhin. A gʋedy kadarnhau castell Kelli ʋrda o wyr ac arueu ac ymborth ³mordʋyaʋ aʋnaeth' y Freinc y geissaʋ nerth y gan y kereint ae ⁴kedymdeithon. A phan gigleu Henri urenhin hynny kynnullaʋ diruaʋr lu aoruc o holl Loegyr y ymlad ar castell wedy gʋyl Ieuan Vedydyʋr. Ar castellwyr yn ʋraʋl a gynhalassant y castell hyt nos ʋyl Thomas ebostol. Ac yna ⁵o eisseu ymborth y rodassant y castell drʋy gael o honunt ⁶[yn yach] y hencideu ae haelodeu ae harueu yn ryd.

MCCLXVII. Y ulʋydyn rac ʋyneb yd ymaruolles Llywelyn ab Grufud a iarll Clar. Ac yna y ᵃkyrchaʋd y iarll Lundein a diruaʋr lu gantaʋ,' a thrʋy dʋyll y bʋrgeisseit y goresgynnaʋd y dref. A phan gigleu Henri vrenhin ac Etwart y vab hynny kynnullaʋ diruaʋr lu aorugant achyrchu Llundein ac ymlad ahi, a thrʋy amodeu kymell y iarll ar bʋrgeisseit y ymrodi udunt. A gʋedy hynny duʋ gʋyl Galixto bab y ffuryfhaʋyt hedʋch y rʋg Henri vrenhin a Llywelyn ab Gruffud drʋy Octo Bonus legat y pab yn ⁷gymodrodʋr y rygtunt yg kastell Baldwin, a thros y kyfundeb hʋnnʋ yd edewis Llywelyn ab Gruffud yr

---

ᵃ/⁸ kynnyllaʋd yiarll diruaʋr lu,

---

¹ B. C.
²ʹ Clemens pedʋeryd, B.

²ʹ morʋydaʋ aʋnaethant, B.
⁴ ketymeithon, B.

of all Wales,' died at Llanbadarn the Great, and was
buried ¹in the chapter house of the monks,' at Strata
Florida. Then the fourth Clement was elected pope.

1266. The ensuing year, the two sons of Simon
Montford escaped from the prison of the king. And
after fortifying the castle of Celli Wrda, and supply-
ing it with men and arms and provisions, he sailed
for France, to seek aid from his relations and friends.
And when king Henry had information of that, he
collected a vast army from all England to attack the
castle, after the feast of St. John the Baptist; and the
garrison manfully defended the castle until the eve of
the feast of St. Thomas the Apostle. And then, for
want of provision, they delivered up the castle on
their having their lives and limbs ⁶safe, and retaining their arms.

1267. The ensuing year, Llywelyn, son of Gruffudd,
confederated with earl Clare. And then ᵃ the earl
marched with an immense army to London;' and
through the treachery of the burgesses he possessed
himself of the town. And when king Henry and his
son Edward was informed of this, they collected an
immense army, and marched to London, and attacked
it; and upon conditions they compelled the earl and
the burgesses to submit to them. After that, on the
feast of pope Calixtus, peace was confirmed between
king Henry and Llywelyn, son of Gruffudd, by Octobonus, the pope's legate, as arbitrator between them
at Castle Baldwin; and on account of that compact, Llywelyn, son of Gruffudd, promised the king

---

ᵃ/⁸ the earl collected an immense army,

---

⁵ rac, B.   ⁷ gymeruedyr, B.
⁶ B.   ⁸ B.

brenhin ᵃ deg mil arhugeint o uorceu o ysterligot. Ar brenhin agenhataaȯd idaȯ ynteu gȯrogaeth holl varȯneit Kymry, ac ymgynhal or barȯneit ¹yr eidunt y danaȯ ynteu byth, ac eu galȯ yn dywyssogyon Kymry o hynny allan. Ac yn tystyolaeth ar hynny y ᵇkynhalyaȯd y brenhin y siartyr ef y Llywelyn o gytsynnedigaeth ac y etiuedyon yn rȯymedic oe inseil ef, ac inseil y dywededic legat, a hynny a gadarnhaȯyt o awdurdaȯt y pap. Yny vlȯydyn honno y lladaȯd Charles vrenhin Cisil Coradin wyr ²[y] Ffredric amheraȯdyr a mab Ffredric y myȯn brȯydyr ar Uaes ³y Pȯyl. Y ulȯydyn honno y darestygaȯd Sȯdan Babilon dinas Antiochia gȯedy llad y gȯyr ar gȯraged a diffeithaȯ gȯlat Armenia ac eu dȯyn y geithiwet.

M.CCLXVIII. ²[Yn] y ulȯydyn rac ȯyneb y bu uarȯ Gronȯ ab Eidnyuet ⁴[distein yr tywyssawc noswyl Luc' ⁵euengylwr gwr arderchawc yn aruen a hael o rodyon doeth y gyngor achywir y weithret adigrif y eiryeu] a Ioab abat Ystrat Flur.

MCCLXIX. Y ulȯydyn rac ȯyneb ⁶[y vii dydd] ym mis Racuyr y bu uarȯ Grufud ab ²ᶜ[Madoc arglȯyd Maelaȯr a] Madaȯc Uychan y uraȯt' ac y cladȯyt yn Llan Egȯestyl.

MCCLXX. Deg mlyned athrugeint a deu cant a mil oed oet Crist pan uu varȯ Maredud ab Grufud arglȯyt

---

ᵃ⁷ dair   ᵇ² canhadaȯd
ᶜ'⁹ Gruffydd ap Maredudd ap Gruffydd Maelor a Maredudd Vychan i vrawd

---

¹ or, B.   ²yn, C.
²B.   ⁴E.

ᵃ ten and twenty thousand sterling marks. And the king granted that he should have the homage of all the barons of Wales, and that the barons should hold under him their property for ever; and they were thenceforth to be called princes of Wales. And in testimony thereof, the king ᵇ confirmed his charter to Llywelyn, with the consent of his heirs, bound by his seal, and the seal of the said legate, and that was established by the authority of the pope. In that year Charles, king of Sicily, killed Conradin, the grandson of the emperor Frederick, and the son of Frederick, in a battle on the plain of Poland. That year, the soldan of Babylon reduced the city of Antioch, after slaying the men and women, and ravaging the country of Armenia, and carrying the inhabitants into bondage.

1268. ²In the ensuing year died Goronwy, son of Ednyved, ⁴steward of the prince's household, on the eve of St. Luke' ⁵the Evangelist, a man illustrious in arms, and generous in gifts, wise in council, and upright in deed, and humorous in words,' and Joab, the abbot of Strata Florida.

1269. The ensuing year, ⁶the seventh day' of the month of December, Gruffudd, son of ² ᶜ Madog, lord of Maelor, and' Madog the Little, his brother' died, and were buried at Llanegwestl.

1270. One thousand two hundred and seventy was the year of Christ, when Maredudd, son of Gruffudd,

---

ᵃ ⁷ three ᵇ ² granted
ᶜ ⁹ Gruffudd, son of Maredudd, son of Gruffudd Maelor, and Maredudd the Little, his brother,

---

³ C. ⁷ E.
⁶ C. E. ⁹ C. E.

Hirvryn trannoeth o duƀ gƀyl ¹Lucy wyry ygkastell
Llan Ymdyfri, ac y cladƀyt ²[ygkabidyldy y myneich]
yn Ystrat Flur. Y ulƀydyn honno ³[mis Hydref]
y goresgynnaƀd Llywelyn ab Gruffud gastell Gaer
Filii. Yn y ulƀydyn honno y bu uarƀ Lowys vrenhin
Freinc ae vab, alegat ⁴[ypab] y gyt ac ef ar y ford
yn mynet Ygaerussalem, ar Lowys hƀnnƀ yssyd sant
enrydedus yny nef.

MCCLXXI. ⁴[Yn] y vlƀydyn rac ƀyneb y whechet dyd
ƀedy Aƀst y bu varƀ ⁵Maredud ab' Rys Gryc ygkastell
⁴[yn] y Dryslƀyn, ac y cladƀyt yn y Ty Gƀynn ⁶[yn
yr eglwys vawr ar y gradeu] rac bron yr allaƀr vaƀr.
Ym penn ⁴[y] teir ƀythnos gƀedy hynny ⁷[yr wythved
dydd wedy gwyl Sain Lowrans] y bu uarƀ Rys ieuanc
uab Rys Mecyll ³[ap Rys Gryc] ygkastell Dinefƀr, ac
y cladƀyt yn Tal y Llycheu.

MCCLXXII. ⁴[Yn] y ulƀydyn rac ƀyneb y bu uarƀ
Henri vrenhin duƀ gƀyl ⁸Filie wyry gƀedy gƀledychu
wythnos amis ac vn vlƀydyn arbymthec adeugein, ac
ycladƀyt yny vanachlaƀc neƀyd yn Llundein. A gƀedy
ef y gƀledychaƀd y mab hynaf idaƀ ⁴[ef], a gƀeith-
redoed hƀnnƀ yssyd ⁴[yn] yscriuenedic ynystoryaeu y
brenhined. Y ulƀydyn honno gƀyl Sein Denis yd
etholet y decuet Gregori bap.

MCCLXXIII. Y vlƀydyn rac ƀyneb yd atueraƀd Owein
a Grufud veibon Maredud ab Owein ³[ap Gruffydd
ap yr arglwydd Rys] y kymƀt perued y Gynan ⁹y
braƀt amgylch gƀyl Veir y canhƀylleu.

MCCLXXIV. Y vlƀydyn rac ƀyneb amgylch y Pasc
bychan y gofƀyaƀd Llyƀelyn ab Gruffud gastell Dol
Vorƀyn. A dyvynu attaƀ aoruc Ruffud ab Gƀenƀyn-

---

¹ Luc, *B.*
² *B. C.*
³ *E.*

⁴ *B.*
⁹ *Not in C. E.*

lord of Hirvryn, died, on the morrow of the feast of St. ¹ Lucy, Virgin, in the castle of Llanymddyvri, and was buried ²in the chapter house of the monks,' at Strata Florida. That year, ³in the month of October,' Llywelyn, son of Gruffudd, possessed himself of the castle of Caerphili. The same year died Louis, king of France, and his son, and ⁶the pope's' legate with him, on the road going to Jerusalem; and that Louis is an honourable saint in heaven.

1271. ⁴In the ensuing year, the sixth day after August, died ⁵Maredudd, son of' Rhys the Hoarse, in the castle at Dyryslwyn, and was buried at Whitland, ⁶in the great church, on the steps' in front of the high altar. At the end of three weeks afterwards, ⁷on the octave of the feast of St. Laurence,' young Rhys, son of Rhys Mechyll, ⁸son of Rhys the Hoarse,' died in the castle of Dinevwr, and was buried at Tal y Llychau.

1272. ⁴In the ensuing year, king Henry died, on the feast of St. Cicily, Virgin, after reigning fifty-six years, one month, and one week, and was buried in the new monastery in London. And after him his eldest son reigned; his acts are written in the histories of the kings. The same year, on the feast of St. Denis, the tenth Gregory was elected pope.

1273. The ensuing year, Owain and Gruffudd, sons of Maredudd, son of Owain, ⁹son of Gruffudd, son of the lord Rhys,' restored the middle comot to their brother Cynan, about Candlemas day.

1274. The ensuing year, about Low Easter, Llywelyn, son of Gruffudd, visited the castle of Dolvorwyn. And he summoned to him Gruffudd, son of

---

⁶ *C.*
⁷ *C. E.*

⁸ Cicilie, *B.* Sissil, *C. E.*
⁹ ey, *B.*

ởyn, ac ymliỡ ac ef amy tỏyll ar agkyỡirdeb aỡnathoed idaỡ, a dỡyn y arnaỡ Arỡystli ᵃ atheir tref ar dec o Gefeilaỡc yssyd tu draỡ Ydyfi yn Riỡ Helyc,' a dala Owein y mab hynaf idaỡ ae dỡyn y gyt ac ef hyt Yggỡyned. Y ulỡydyn honno y gỡnaeth y decuet Gregori bap kyffredin gỡnsli yn ¹ Liỡn duỡ kalan Mei. Y ulỡydyn honno duỡ Sul gỡedy duỡ gỡyl Veir yn Aỡst y kyssegrỡyt yn Llundein Etwart uab y trydyd Henri yn vrenhin yn Lloegyr. Yn y ulỡydyn honno amgylch gỡyl Andras ydanuones Llywelyn genadeu at Ruffud ab Gỡennỡynnỡyn hyt ygkastell y Trallỡg. Ac ynteu ae haruolles ² ỡynt yn llaỡen ac aeduc yr castell, ac ae porthes yn anhỡyl. ³ Ar nos honno ydaeth ef y Amỡythic ac y gorchymynnaỡd yr castellwyr attal y kenadeu ygkarchar. A phan gigleu y tywyssaỡc hynny kynnullaỡ holl Gymry aỡnaeth y ymlad ar castell. A gỡedy dyuot yno ⁴ [ef] ae lu y rodes y castellwyr idaỡ y castell. A gỡedy rydhau ohonaỡ y kastellwyr ar kenadeu y llosges y castell ⁴ [ac y distryỡaỡd] hyt y llaỡr. Ac odyna y goresgynnaỡd holl gyuoeth Grufud ab Gỡenỡynỡyn heb ⁵ ỡrthỡynebed, ac y gossodes y sỡydogyon e hun ynyr holl gyfoeth. Yny vlỡydyn honno y bu gyfnewit deu gymỡt y rỡg Kynan ⁶ [ap Mredudd ap Owein] a Rys ᵇ ieuanc ⁶ [i vrawd] ac y deuth ⁷ Pennard y Gynan, ar kymỡt perued y Rys Vychan.

ᵃ'⁸ ac vn kantref ar ddec rwng Riw a Helygi a rann o Gyveilioc,
ᵇ⁴ Vychan.

---

¹ Liuỡn, *B.* ³ Ac y, *B.*
² hỡy, *B.*   ⁴ *B.*

Gwenwynwyn, whom he upbraided for the deceit and
disloyalty he experienced from him; and he took from
him Arwystli, ᵃ and thirteen townships of Cyveiliog,
which are on the further side of the Dyvi, in Rhiw
Helyg,' and took Owain, his eldest son, and carried
him along with him to Gwynedd. That year, pope
Gregory the tenth held a general council in Lyons,
on the calends of May. That year, the Sunday after
the feast of St. Mary in August, Edward, son of the
third Henry, was consecrated king of England. In
that year, about the feast of St. Andrew, Llywelyn
sent messengers to Gruffudd, son of Gwenwynwyn, to
the castle of Trallwng; who on his part received them
joyfully, brought them into the castle, and entertained
them lavishly. And on that night he went to Shrewsbury, and commanded the garrison to detain the messengers in prison. And when the prince heard that,
he assembled all Wales to fight against the castle.
And when he had arrived there with his army, the
garrison delivered up the castle to him; and when he
had liberated the garrison and the messengers, he
burned the castle,⁴ and destroyed it' to the ground.
After that he subdued all the territory of Gruffudd,
son of Gwenwynwyn, without opposition, and placed
his own officers in all the territory. In the same
year, there was an exchange of comots between Cynan,
⁵son of Maredudd, son of Owain,' and ᵇyoung Rhys
⁶his brother ;' and thus Penardd came to Cynan, and
the middle comot to Rhys the Little.

ᵃ/⁸ and eleven cantrevs between Rhiw and Helygi,
and a portion of Cyveiliog,
  ᵇ ⁴ little

ᵃ Orthôynep, *B*.   ¹ Pennarth, *B*.
⁵ *E*.   ³ *C. E.*

MCCLXXV. ¹[Yn] y vlẃydyn rac ẃyneb ychydic ²ar Ieu ³Kychafel y gossodes Etwart vrenhin gẃnsli yn Llundein. Ac yna y gossodes ⁴ef gossodeu' neẃyd ⁵ar yr holl deyrnas. Yny ulẃydyn honno yny pymthecuet dyd o Aẃst y bu uarẃ ⁶[Yẃein] ab Maredud ab Owein ⁷[ap Gruffydd ap yr arglwydd Rys] ac y cladẃyt yn Ystrat Fflur ⁸[yny cabidyldy ymyneich] geir llaẃ y dat. Y ulẃydyn honno amgylch gẃyl Veir Ymedi y deuth Etwart urenhin o Lundein hyt Ygkaer Lleon, ac ⁹a dyunnaẃd attaẃ Lywelyn ab Gruffud tywyssaẃc Kymry y wneuthur idaẃ gẃrogaeth. Ar tyẃyssaẃc a dyfynnaẃd attaẃ ynteu holl varẃneit Kymry, ac o gyffredin gyghor nyt aeth ef at y brenhin o achaẃs vot y brenhin yn kynhal y ffoodron ef, nyt amgen Dauyd ab Gruffud, a Gruffud ab Gẃennẃynẃyn. Ac or achaẃs hẃnnẃ yd ymchoelaẃd y brenhin yn llidyaẃc y Loegyr, ac yd ymchoelaẃd Llyẃelyn y Gymry. ¹[Yn] y ulẃydyn honno yr ẃythuet dyd o ẃyl Veir Ymedi y crynaẃd y daear Ygkymry amgylch aẃr echẃyd. Y ulẃydyn honno ⁷[wedy gwyl Vilhangel] y ¹⁰mordwyaẃd Emri uab Simẃnt Mẃnford, ac Elianor ychwaer tu a Gẃyned. Ac ar yr hynt ¹¹honno y delit ¹²ẃynt y gan porthmyn ¹³Haẃlfford. Ac y hanuonet ygkarchar Etẃart urenhin. Ar Elianor honno a gymerassei Lyẃelyn yn ẃreic priaẃt idaẃ drẃy eireu kyndrychaẃl. A honno drẃy wedieu ac annoc Innosens bap a bonhedigyon Lloegyr a rydhaẃyt. Ac yna ¹⁴[gwyl Saint Edward] y gẃnaethpẃyt priodas Llywelyn ac Elianor Ygkaer Wynt, ac Etwart vrenhin Lloegyr yn costi y wled ar neithaẃr ehun yn ehelaeth. Ac or

---

¹ B.
² kynn, B.
³ kyfachauel, B.
⁴ gossodedigaetheu, B.
⁵ yn, B.
⁶ C.
⁷ E.
⁸ B. C.

1255. ¹In the ensuing year, a little before Ascension Thursday, king Edward appointed a council in London; and then he established new institutions over the whole kingdom. In that year, on the fifteenth day of August, ⁶Owain, son of Maredudd, son of Owain, ⁷son of Gruffudd, son of the lord Rhys,' died, and was buried at Strata Florida, ⁸in the chapter house of the monks,' near his father. That year, about the feast of St. Mary in September, king Edward came from London to Caerleon, and summoned to him Llywelyn, son of Gruffudd, prince of Wales, to do homage to him. And the prince summoned unto him all the barons of Wales; and by general consent, he did not go to the king, because the king harboured his fugitives, namely, David, son of Gruffudd, and Gruffudd, son of Gwenwynwyn. And on that account the king returned to England in anger, and Llywelyn returned to Wales. ¹In that year, the octave of the feast of St. Mary in September, there was an earthquake in Wales, about the hour of evening tide. That year, ⁷after the feast of St. Michael,' Emri, son of Simon Montford, with Eleanor his sister, sailed for Gwynedd. And upon that journey they were seized by the gate keepers of Haverford, and conveyed to the prison of king Edward. And this Eleanor had been betrothed to Llywelyn for his wife by representative words. And she, through the intercession and advice of pope Innocent and the gentry of England, was set at liberty. And then, ¹⁴on the feast of St. Edward,' the marriage of Llywelyn and Eleanor was solemnized at Winchester, Edward, king of England himself bearing the cost of the banquet and nuptial

---

⁹ y, B.
¹⁰ morόydaόd, B.
¹¹ hόnnό, B.

¹² hόy, B.
¹³ Haόrfforth, B.
¹⁴ C. E.

Eilanor honno y bu y Lywelyn verch aelwit Gŵenllian. ᵃ Ac Eilanor a vu uarŵ y ar etiued, ac y ¹cladŵyt ²[ymanacheloc y brodyr troetnoeth] yn Llan Vaes Ymmon. Ar dywededic Wenllian wedy marŵ y that a ducpŵyt ygkeithiwet y Loegyr, a chyn ᵇ bot yn' oet y gŵnaethpŵyt yn uanaches oe hanuod. Ac Emri a rydhaŵyt o garchar y brenhin, ac aduc hynt y lys Rufein.

MCCLXXVI. Y vlŵydyn rac ŵyneb yd anuones yr arglŵyd Lywelyn mynych genadeu y lys y brenhin wrth furfaŵ tagnefed y rygtunt, ac ny rymhaaŵd idaŵ. Ac yny diwed amgylch gŵyl ᶜ Ueir y kanŵylleu' y gossodes y brenhin gŵnsli Ygkaer Wyragon. Ac ³ yno yd ansodes trillu yn erbyn Kymry. Vn y Gaer Lleon ac ef ehun yn y blaen, arall y gastell Baldwin, ac yny blaen iarll Lincol, a Roser Mortymer. ᵈ Y rei hynny adodes Gruffud ab Gŵenŵynŵyn ⁴ y goreskyn oe gyfoeth agollassei kynno hynny, gan attal yr brenhin Gedewein a Cheri a Gŵerthrynyon a Buellt.' Ac yno y goresgynnaŵd iarll Henford Vrecheinaŵc. Y trydyd llu a anuones y Gaer Vyrdin a Cheredigyaŵn, ac yn y blaen Paen ⁵ uab Padric Dysaŵs.

MCCLXXVII. Y ulŵydyn rac ŵyneb y kylchynaŵd iarll Lincol a Roser Mortymer gastell Dol Vorŵyn ac

ᵃ ⁶ Ar dyŵededic   ᵇ′ ⁶ amser
ᶜ′ ⁷ Sanffraid,
ᵈ′ ⁸ Ar llu hwnnw a oresgynnodd Powys i Ruffydd ap Gwenwynwyn. A Chydewain Acheri a Gwerthrynion a Bullt i Rocher Mortmer.

---

¹ hagkladŵyt, *B.*   ² odyno, *B.*
² *C.*   ⁴ yn, *B.*

festivities liberally. And of that Eleanor there was a daughter to Llywelyn, called Gwenllian; ᵃ and Eleanor died in childbirth, and was buried ² in the chapter house of the barefooted friars,' at Llanvaes in Mona. The said Gwenllian, after the death of her father, was taken as a prisoner to England, and before ᵇ she was' of age, she was made a nun against her consent. Emri was liberated from the king's prison, and he took a journey to the court of Rome.

1276. The ensuing year, the lord Llywelyn sent frequent messengers to the court of the king about forming a peace between them, but he did not succeed. And at length, about the feast of ᶜ Candlemas,' the king appointed a council at Worcester; and there he designed three armies against Wales; one for Caerleon, and himself to lead it; another for Castle Baldwin, led by the earl of Lincoln and Roger Mortimer. ᵈ Gruffudd, son of Gwenwynwyn, had fixed upon them to reconquer his territory, which he had previously lost, by refusing Cydewain and Ceri and Gwerthrynion and Buellt to the king.' And then the earl of Hereford got possession of Brecheiniog. The third army he sent to Caermarthen and Ceredigion, led by Pain, son of Patrick de Says.

1277. The ensuing year, the earl of Lincoln and Roger Mortimer besieged the castle of Dolvorwyn,

---

ᵃ ⁶ and the said   ᵇ' ⁶ the time
ᶜ' ⁷ St. Bridget,
ᵈ' ⁸ which host subdued Powys for Gruffudd, son of Gwenwynwyn, and Cydewain and Ceri and Gwerthrynion and Buellt for Roger Mortimer.

---

⁵ ap, *B.*   ⁷ *E.*
⁶ *B.*   ⁸ *C. E.*

ympenn y pytheȯnos y kaȯssant ef o eisseu dyfȯr. Yna y kyfunaȯd Rys ab Maredud ¹[ap Owain ap Gruffydd ap yr arglwydd Rys], a Rys Wyndaȯt ¹[ap Rys ievangk ap Rys Mechell ap Rys Gryc ap yr arglwydd Rys] nei ¹[ap chwaer] y tywyssaȯc, a Phaen ²uab Padric ª Llyȯelyn y vraȯt a Howel, ²a Rys Gryc' aadaȯssant ³y kyuoeth ac a aethant y Wyned at Lywelyn. Rys ab Maelgȯn ¹[ap yr arglwydd Rys] a aeth at Roser Mortymer ac arodes darestygedigaeth yr brenhin yn llaȯ Roser. Ac yn diwethaf oll o Deheubarth y kyfunaȯd Gruffud a Chynan veibon Maredud ab Owein ¹[ap Gruffydd ap yr arglwydd Rys a Llywelyn ab Owein y nei ar brenhin. Ac uelly y darestygȯyt holl Deheubarth yr brenhin. Ac yna y darestygaȯd Paen uab Padric yr brenhin tri chymȯt o Vch Aeron; ⁵Anhunyaȯc a Meuenyd ar kymȯt Perued. Ac ydaeth Rys uab Maredud, a Rys Wyndaȯt, a deu uab Varedud ab Owein ¹[ap Gruffydd ap yr arglwydd Rys ⁴o Geredigyawn] ylys y brenhin y hebrȯg gȯrogaeth a llȯ kywirdeb idaȯ. Ar brenhin aoedes gymryt y gȯrogaeth hyt y kȯnsli nessaf gan ellȯg adref Rys ab Maredud a Grufud ab Maredud ac attal y gyt ac ef Gynan ab Maredud ¹[ap Owain] a Rys Wyndaȯt. Ac yna y ⁶dodes Paen Lywelyn ab Owein yn uab

---

ª' ⁷ a Llywelyn brawd Rys Wyndawd a Howel ap Rys Gryc,

---

¹ E.
² ap, B.
³ eu, B.
⁴ C.

and at the end of a fortnight they obtained it, through want of water. Then Rhys, son of Maredudd, ¹ son of Owain, son of Gruffudd, son of the lord Rhys,' and Rhys Wyndod, ¹ son of young Rhys, son of Rhys Mechell, son of Rhys the Hoarse, son of the lord Rhys,' nephew, ¹ sister's son,' to the prince, became reconciled to Pain, son of Patrick. ᵃ Llywelyn, his brother, and Howel, and Rhys the Hoarse,' quitted their territory, and went to Gwynedd, to Llywelyn; Rhys, son of Maelgwn, ¹ son of the lord Rhys,' went to Roger Mortimer, and made submission to the king, by the hand of Roger. And last of all, from South Wales, Gruffudd, and Cynan, the sons of Maredudd, son of Owain, ¹ son of Gruffudd, son of the lord Rhys,' and Llywelyn, son of Owain, his nephew, became reconciled to the king. And thus all South Wales became subjected to the king. Then Pain, son of Patrick, subjugated to the king three comots of Upper Aeron—⁵ Anhunog, and Mevenydd, and the middle comot. And Rhys, son of Maredudd, and Rhys Wyndod, and the two sons of Maredudd, son of Owain, ¹ son of Gruffudd, son of the lord Rhys,' ⁴ from Ceredigion,' went to the court of the king, to offer their homage and oath of allegiance to him. But the king delayed accepting their homage until the next council; sending Rhys, son of Maredudd, and Gruffudd, son of Maredudd, home, and retaining with him Cynan, son of Maredudd, ¹ son of Owain,' and Rhys Wyndod. And then Pain placed Llywelyn, son of Owain, as a youth in guardianship,

---

ᵃ/⁷ and Llywelyn, brother of Rhys Wyndod, and Howel, son of Rhys the Hoarse,

---

⁵ Nanhvniawc, *C. E.*   ⁷ *C. E.*
⁶ rodes, *B.*

ygkadoryaeth o achaus diffyc oet. Guedy hynny yr uythuet dyd o uyl Ieuan y gunaeth Rys ab Maelgun ar pedwar barun vry urogaeth yr brenhin yny kunsli Ygkaer Wyragon. Y vluydyn honno uyl Iago ebostol ydeuth Etmunt brauft y brenhin allu gantau hyt yn Llan Badarn, a dechreu adeilat castell Aber Ystwyth aunaeth. Ac yna y deuth y brenhin ᵃ ae gedernit' gantau yr Beruedwlat, a chadarnhau ᵇllys idau a ¹ unaeth yny Fflint o diruaur glodyeu yny chylch. Odyno y doeth hyt yn Rudlan ae chadarnhau hefyt o glodyeu yny chylch, a thrigyau yno dalym o amser a unaeth. Y uluydyn honno duu Sadurn wedy Aust yd enkilyaud Rys ab Maelgun ² [ap yr arglwydd Rys] y uyned at Lywelyn rac ofyn y dala or Saeson ³ [a] oed yn Llan Badarn. Ac yna y goresgynnaud y Saeson y holl gyfoeth. A chyt ac ef yd enkilyaud guyr Geneu yr Glyn oll y uyned, ac adau y tir ae hydeu oll yn diffeith. A nos wyl Vatheu yd aeth Etmunt a Phaen y Loegyr, ac adau Rosser Mulus yn gunstabyl yn Aber Ystuyth ac y uarchadu y ulat. A thrannoeth guedy guyl Seint Ynys yd ymchoelaud Rys uyndaut a Chynan ab Maredud o lys y brenhin ⁴ y eu gulat. Y uluydyn honno ⁵ yn dechreu y kynhayaf ydanuones y brenhin rann uaur oe lu y Von y losgi llawer or wlat ⁶ a dwyn llauer oe hydeu. A ⁷ [chalan gaiaf] guedy hynny y deuth Llywelyn at y brenhin y Rudlan, ac yd hedychaud

---

ᵃ′³ a diruaur lu   ᵇ⁸ kastell

---

¹ oruc, *B.*
² *E.*
³ *B.*
⁴ yu, *B.*
⁵ ygkylch, *B.*

because of a deficiency of age. After that, on the octave of the feast of St. John, Rhys, son of Maelgwn, and the four above named barons, did homage to the king in the council at Worcester. The same year, the feast of St. James the Apostle, Edmund, the king's brother, came with an army to Llanbadarn; and began to build a castle at Aberystwyth. And then the king, having ᵃ his force' with him, came to the Midland District, and fortified a ᵇ court at Flint, surrounded with vast dykes. From thence he proceeded to Rhuddlan, and this he also fortified, by surrounding it with dykes; and there he tarried some time. That year, the Saturday after August, Rhys, son of Maelgwn, ²son of the lord Rhys,' retired to Gwynedd, to Llywelyn, for fear of being taken by the English who were at Llanbadarn; and thereupon the English took possession of his whole territory. And along with him the men of Genau y Glyn all retreated to Gwynedd, leaving the whole of their corn and land waste. On the eve of St. Mathew, Edmund and Pain went to England, and left Roger Myles to be constable at Aberystwyth, and to protect the country. The day after the feast of St. Ynys, Rhys Wyndod, and Cynan, son of Maredudd, returned from the court of the king to their own country. That year, in the beginning of harvest, the king sent a great part of his army into Mona, which burned much of the country, and took away much of the corn. And ⁷on the calends of winter' after that, Llywelyn came to the king at Rhuddlan, and made his peace

---

ᵃ'³ an immense army   ᵇ⁸ castle

---

⁶ ac y, *B.*   ⁹ *E.*
⁷ *C. E.*

ac ef. Ac yna y gỽahodes y brenhin ef y Nadolic y Lundein, ac ¹ynteu aaeth yno. Ac yno y rodes y wrogaeth yr brenhin. A gỽedy y drigyaỽ pythewnos yn Llundein yd ymchoelaỽd y Gymry. Ac ygkylch gỽyl Andras y gollygỽyt Owein Goch ac Owein ab Gruffud ²[ap Llywelyn ap Iorwerth a Gruffydd] ab Gỽenỽynỽyn o garchar Llywelyn drỽy orchymyn y brenhin. Ac yna y cauas Owein Goch y gan Lywelyn y vraỽt oe gỽbyl uod gantref Llyyn.

MCCLXXVIII. Y ulỽydyn rac ỽyneb gỽyl Etwart urenhin y rodes Etwart urenhin ac Etmỽnt y uraỽt Elianor y kefnitherỽ merch Simỽnt Mỽnford ²[kanis Elenor verch Ievan vrenin oedd vam Simwnt Mwnffordd] y Lywelyn ar drỽs yr eglỽys vaỽr Ygkaer ỽyragon, ac yno y priodes, ar nos honno y gỽnaethpỽyt y neithaỽr. A thrannoeth yd ymchoelaỽd Llywelyn ac Elianor yn llaỽen y Gymry.

MCCLXXIX. Y vlỽydyn rac ỽyneb y peris Etwart vrenhin ffuruaỽ mỽnei newyd, a gỽneuthur y dimeiot ar ffyrlligot yn grynyon. Ac uelly y cỽplaỽyt prophỽytolyaeth Vyrdin pan dywaỽt. Ffuryf y gyfnewit ahólltir, ar hanner a vyd crỽn.

MCCLXXX. Petwar ugeint mlyned adeucant amil oed oet Crist pann uu uarỽ Rickert o Gaer Riỽ escob Mynyỽ ᵃduỽ kalan Ebrill.' Ac yny le ynteu ydurdỽyt Thomas Beg yn escob. Y ulỽydyn honno y bu uarỽ

ᵃ/ ᵇ duw Llun nessaf kynn gwyl Seint Ambros kalan Ebrill.

---

¹ ef, B. | ² E.

with him; and then the king invited him to come to London at Christmas, and he went there, and there he made his homage to the king. And after he had remained in London a fortnight, he returned to Wales. About the feast of St. Andrew, Owain the Red, and Owain, son of Gruffudd, [2] son of Llywelyn, son of Iorwerth, and Gruffudd,' son of Gwenwynwyn were released from the prison of Llywelyn, by the command of the king. And then Owain the Red obtained from his brother Llywelyn the cantrev of Lleyn, with his full consent.

1278. The ensuing year, the feast of St. Edward the king, king Edward and Edmund his brother, bestowed their cousin Eleanor, daughter of Simon Montford, [2] for Eleanor daughter of king John was the mother of Simon Montford,' on Llywelyn, at the door of the great church in Worcester, and there were they married; and on that night the nuptials were solemnized. And the next day Llywelyn and Eleanor joyfully returned to Wales.

1279. The ensuing year, Edward ordered the coining of new money; and that the halfpennies and farthings should be made round. And thus was fulfilled the prophecy of Myrddin, when he says, "The "symbol of the exchange shall be split, and the half "shall be round."

1280. One thousand two hundred and eighty was the year of Christ, when Rickert, of Caer Rhiw, bishop of Menevia, died [a] on the calends of April;' and in his stead Thomas Beck was consecrated bishop.

---

a/[3] on the Monday next before the feast of St. Ambrose, the calends of April;

---

[2] C.

Phylip Goch y trydyd abat ardec o Ystrat Fflur. A gŵedy ef y bu abat Einaŵn Seis. Ac yn oes hŵnnŵ y llosges y vanachlaŵc. Gŵedy hynny nos ŵyl ᵃVeir y kanhŵylleu' y cant escob Mynyŵ offeren yn Ystrat Fflur, a honno vu yr offeren gyntaf a ganaŵd ynyr escobaŵt, a duŵ gŵyl Dewi rac ŵyneb yd eistedaŵd yny gadeir yn eglŵys Vynyŵ.

MCCLXXXI. Y vlŵydyn rac ŵyneb y goresgynnaŵd Dauyd ab Grufud gastell ¹ Penhardlech ŵyl Seint Benet abat, ac y lladaŵd y kastellwyr oll eithyr Rosser Clifort arglŵyd y castell a Phaen ²Gameis. Y rei hynny a delis ac agarcharaŵd.

MCCLXXXII. Y vlŵydyn rac ŵyneb gŵyl Ueir y gehyded y goresgynnaŵd Gruffud ab Maredud ³[ap Owein ap Gruffydd ap yr arglwydd Rys], a Rys ab Maelgŵn ³[Vychan ap Maelgwn ap yr arglwydd Rys] dref Aber Ystŵyth arcastell, ac y llosgassant y dref ar castell, ac y distryŵassant y gaer aoed ygkylch y castell ar dref drŵy arbet y heneideu yr castellwyr, o achaŵs dydyeu y diodeueint aoedynt yn agos. Ar dyd hŵnnŵ y goresgynnaŵd Rys ab Maelgŵn gantref Penwedic, a Gruffud ab Maredud gymŵt Meuenyd.

Benedicamus Domino. Deo gracia.

ᵃ' ³ Sanffraid

¹ Pennardd alave, *E*. | ² Degomeres, *E*.

That year died Philip the Red, the thirteenth abbot of Strata Florida; and after him Einon the Saxon became abbot, and in his lifetime the monastery was burned. After that, on the eve of the feast of ᵃ Candlemas, the bishop of Menevia sang mass in Strata Florida; and that was the first mass that he sang in the diocese; and on the feast of St. David ensuing he sat in the chair in the church of Menevia.

1281. The ensuing year, David, son of Gruffudd, reduced the castle of ¹ Penharddlech, on the feast of St. Benet the abbot, and slew the whole of the garrison, except Roger Clifford, the lord of the castle, and Pain Gamage; those he took and imprisoned.

1282. The ensuing year, the feast of St. Mary of the equinox, Gruffudd, son of Maredudd, ³ son of Owain, son of Gruffudd, son of the lord Rhys,' and Rhys, son of Maelgwn ³ the Little, son of Maelgwn, son of the lord Rhys,' possessed themselves of the town and castle of Aberystwyth; and they burned the town and the castle, and destroyed the rampart that was round the castle and the town; sparing the lives of the garrison, because the days of the passion were near. And on that day, Rhys, son of Maelgwn, conquered the cantrev of Penwedig, and Gruffudd, son of Maredudd, the comot of Mevenydd.

Benedicamus Domino. Deo gratia.

ᵃ ³ St. Bridget,

---

³ E.

GLOSSARY.

INTRODUCTORY NOTE.

THIS Glossary may be useful to such as are desirous of satisfying themselves as to the correctness of the translation. The leading words are written in the orthographical style of the present day, followed, however, where any difference exists, by that form which they in general respectively assumed during the middle ages. This form, together with the etymological analysis of the particular word explained, is enclosed within brackets. In old Welsh documents it is not generally an easy task to discover the radical form of words, not only because of the mutation to which initial consonants, under certain circumstances, are subject, as well as of the changes of cases and tenses, but more especially because of the way in which prepositions and other particles are prefixed to them. This last mode is peculiar to old writings, and it would require no inconsiderable time and practice to get familiar therewith, so as to be able to distinguish and separate the words. The rule for the formation of numbers and tenses was formerly much more capricious than that which prevails in our own times. On this point the Editor begs to refer the reader to *Dosparth Edeyrn Davod Aur*, or the Ancient Grammar of Wales, which was recently published under the auspices of the

Welsh MSS. Society. As to mutable consonants, the subjoined table will show their modifications at one view.

		Radical.	Soft.	Nasal.	Aspirate.
1st Class	C	Câr	Gâr	Nghâr	Châr.
	P	Pen	Ben	Mhen	Phen.
	T	Tad	Dâd	Nhâd	Thâd.
2nd Class	B	Brawd	Frawd	Mrawd.	
	D	Dant	Ddant	Nant.	
	G	Gwr	Wr	Ngwr.	
3rd Class	Ll	Llaw	Law.		
	M	Mam	Fam.		
	Rh	Rhaw	Raw.		

Though this table is strictly applicable only to the present style of writing, nevertheless, as far as the orthographical capabilities of the ancients went, the tendency of their mutations was invariably in the same direction.

GLOSSARY.

A.

A. And; with; who; which.
AB (ap). A son.
ABAD (abat). An abbot.
ABER (ab-er). A confluence of water; a junction of rivers; the fall of a lesser river into a greater, or into the sea.
ABIT (L. *habitus*). Habit; dress.
ABSEN (ab-sen). Absent.
AC = A (the former being used before a vowel, the latter before a consonant). And.
ACHAWS (a-caws). Cause; because.
ACHUB (a-cub; L. *occupo*). To save; to defend; to seize upon; to intercept.
ACHWYS (a-caws). A cause, or reason.
ADEILAW (adeiliaϭ; ad-ail). To wattle; to build.
ADEN (ad-en). A wing.
ADFERU (atueru; admer). To restore.
ADGAS (atcas; ad-cas). Odious; hateful; unlucky.
ADGYWEIRIAW (atgyϭeiraϭ; ad-cywair). To repair.
ADLOSGEDIG (atloscedic; adlosg). re-scorched; burning again.
ADNABOD (adnabot; ad-nabot). To know; to recognize.

ADNABODEDIG (atnabodedic; adnabod). Known; recognized.
ADNEWYDDU (atneϭydu; adnewydd). To renew.
ADNEWYDDUS (atneϭyduss; adnewydd). Renewed.
ADORESGYN (atorescyn, atoreskyn; ad-goresgyn). To reconquer; to repossess.
ADREF (at-tref). Homewards; home; back again.
ADDAS (adas; a-das). Meet; suitable.
ADDAW (adaϭ; a-daw). To promise; to engage.
ADDEF (adef; a-def). To acknowledge; to confess.
ADDEWID (edeϭid; addaw). A promise.
ADDFED (aeduet; add-med). Ripe; mature.
ADDFWYN (aduϭyn; add-mwyn). Meek; gentle; courteous.
ADDFWYNDER (aduϭynder; addfwyn). Meekness; courtesy.
ADDURN (adurn; add-gurn). Ornament.
ADDURNAW (adurnaϭ; adurn; L. *adorno*). To adorn; to ornament.
ADDWYNDRA (adϭyndra; addfwyn). Meekness; courtesy.

ADDWYNWAITH (adŏynŏeith; addwyn-gwaith). Elegant workmanship.

AEL. A brow; a skirt, or border.

AELAWD (aelot; ael-awd); a limb.

AERFA (aerua; aer). A slaughter; place of slaughter.

AFLAWEN (an-llawen). Not merry; exceedingly.

AFLONYDDU (aflonydu; aflonydd). To disquiet; to disturb.

AFON (auon; aw-on). A river.

AFREOL (an-rheol). Irregularity; disorder; misrule.

AGATFYDD (agatuyd; ag-at-bydd). Peradventure.

AGAWR (egor; ag). To open; to expand; to unfold.

AGOS (a-caws). Near.

ANGEN (aghen; an-geni). Necessity; extreme unction.

ANGENRHAID (aghenreit; angen=rhaid). Necessity.

ANGEU (agheu; ageu; ang). Liberation; death.

ANGHLOD (aglot; an-clod). Dispraise; dishonour.

ANGHRYNEDIG (angrynedic, agkrynedic; anghryn). Intrepid.

ANGHRYNODEB (agkrynodeb; anghryno). Incompactness; diffuseness.

ANGHYFIAITH (agkyfyeith; an-cyfiaith.) Of different speech.

ANGHYFRAITH (agkyfreith; an-cyfraith.) Lawlessness; lawless.

ANGHYTTUNDEB (agkyttundeb; an-cyttundeb). Disagreement.

ANGHYWEITHAS (agkyŏeithas; an-cywaith.) Untoward; uncivil.

ANGHYWIR (agkyŏir; an-cywir). Incorrect; unjust.

ANGHYWIRDEB (agkyŏirdeb; an-cywirdeb). Incorrectness; dishonesty.

AIL (eil). Second; like.

ALBRYSIWR (arlblastŏr; albrys-gwr). A cross-bow-man.

ALLAN (all). Out; without.

ALLAWR (a-llawr). An altar.

ALLTUDAW (alltud). To banish; to alienate, or reduce to the state of a stranger.

ALLWEDD (allŏed; all-gwedd). A key.

AM. Round; for.

AMDDIFFYN (amdiffyn; am-diffyn). Defence; protection.

AMDDIFFYNU (amdiffynu; amddiffyn). To defend; to protect.

AMDDIFFYNWR (amdiffynŏr; amddiffyn-gwr). A defender; a protector.

AMDDIRIEDUS (amdiredus; amddiried). Confiding; trusting.

AMGEN (can). Otherwise; on the contrary; different; also; but.

AMGYLCH (am-cylch). Around; about.

AMHERAWDR (amheraŏdyr; L. *imperator*). Emperor.

AMHERODRAETH. Empire.

AMHERODRES (amherotres). Empress.

AMLDER (amylder; aml). Frequency; multitude.

AMMHARCH (amarch; an-parch). Disrespect; disgrace; reproach.

AMMINIAWG (amhinaŏg; ammin). Abutting upon; conjoining; bordering.

Ammod (amot; am-bod). A covenant, or contract.
Ammodi (ammod). To covenant.
Amrafael (amrauael; ymrauael; amry-mal). Several.
Amryfal (amryuael; amryw-mal). Divers; sundry.
Amryson (am-rhy-son). Contention; to contend.
Amser (am-ser). A revolution of the stars; time; season.
Amws (am-ws). A stallion; a steed.
Anafrwydd (anafrŵyd; anafrhwydd). Indecency.
Anafus (annafus; annaf). Maimed; mangled; hurt.
Anamlder (anamylder; anaml). Paucity; fewness.
Aneirif (aneiryf; anneuryf; aneirif). Innumerable; numberless.
Anesmwythaw (anesmwyth). To become uneasy; to disturb.
Anfeidrawl (anueidraŵl; anmeidrawl). Immense; infinite.
Anfodd (anuod; an-bodd). Against one's will.
Anfoliannus (anuolyanus; anfoliant). Void of praise; ignominious.
Anfon (anuon; an-mon). To send.
Anfonedig (anuonhedic). Sent.
Anfyn (anuhyn; an-myn.) Without gentleness; morose.
Anhawdd (anaŵd; an-hawdd). Not easy; difficult.
Anheilwng (anheilŵg; an-teilwng). Unworthy.
Anhwyl (an-hwyl). Out of order.
Anial (ynnyal; an-ial). Wild; uncultivated; a desert.

Anialwch (ynyalŵch; anial). Wilderness.
Anian (anyan; an). Nature; natural instinct.
Anifail (anifeil; aniueil; L. *animal*). Animal.
Annhebygedig (anhybygedic; anhebyg). Unlike; dissimilar.
Annhrugarawg (anrugaraŵc; antrugarawg). Unmerciful.
Annioddefedig (anniodefedic; anniodeuedic; annioddef). Insufferable.
Annog (annoc; an-dog; Gr., ἀνάγω). To incite; to provoke; to exhort.
Annogedigaeth (annogedig). Incitement; exhortation.
Annosparthus (annosparth). Unruly; void of system.
Annwyd (ahnŵyt; an-nwyd). A cold; a chillness.
Annyledus (annyled). Undue.
Annynawl (andynol; an-dynawl). Inhuman; unmanly.
Anobeithiaw (anobeithaŵ; anobaith). To despair.
Anorchfygedig (annorchfygedic; an-gorchfygedig). Unconquered; invincible.
Anorfodedig (anoruodedic; angorfodedig). Unconquered; invincible.
Anrhaith (anreith; an-rhaith). Spoil; pillage; illegal property.
Anrheithiaw (anreithaŵ; anrhaith). To spoil; to plunder; to act illegally.
Anrhydedd (enryded; an-rhydedd). Honour.
Anrhydeddus (enrydedus; anrhydedd). Honourable.

ANRHYFEDD (enryfed; an-rhyfedd). Without wonder; wonderful.
ANSAWDD (ansaỽd; an-sawdd). State; quality; condition.
ANSODDI (ansodi; ansawdd). To place; to establish.
ANSYNWYRAWL = ANSYNWYRUS (ansynwyr). Indiscreet; unreasonable.
ANUNDEB (annundeb; an-undeb). Disunion; disagreement.
ANWIREDD (enỽired; an-gwiredd). Falsehood; iniquity.
ANWYL (an-gwyl). Dear.
APOSTOL (ebostol; L. *apostolus*). An apostle.
APOSTOLAWL (ebostolaỽl; apostol). Apostolic.
AR. On; upon.
A'R (ar; a yr). And the; with the.
ARAF (a-rhaf). Slow; soft; still.
ARAFHAU (araf-hau). To make slow; to assuage.
ARALL (ar-all). Another; other; not the same; different.
ARAWS (aros; ar-aws). To stay; to wait.
ARBED (ar-ped). To spare; to save.
ARBENIG (arbennic; arben). Principal; special.
ARCHDIACON (archdiagon; arch-diacon). Archdeacon.
ARCHESGOB (archescob; archescop; arch-esgob). Archbishop; primate.
ARCHESGOBAWD (archescobaỽt; arch-escobawd). Archbishopric.
ARCHOFFEIRIAD (arch-offeiriad). High priest.

ARDDERCHAWG (arderchaỽc; ardderch). Excellent; exalted; illustrious.
ARDYMHER (ardymer; ar-tymher). Temperature.
ARF (aryf). A weapon; a tool.
ARFAETH (aruaeth; ar-maeth). A design; a purpose.
ARFAETHU (aruaethu; arfaeth). To design, or purpose.
ARFAWG (arfaỽc, aruaỽc; arf). Armed.
ARFEIDDIAW (arueidaỽ; arfaidd). To adventure; to dare.
ARFER (aruer; ar-mer). Use; custom.
ARFEREDIG (arueredic; arfer). Accustomed; usual.
ARFERU (arueru; arfer). To use; to habituate.
ARFOLL (aruoll; ar-moll). Entertainment; a reception; a welcome; a contract.
ARFOLLI (aruolli; arfoll). To entertain hospitably; to welcome; to make a contract.
ARFOLLWR (aruollỽr; arfoll-gwr). A confederate, or one who unites himself to another.
ARFORDIR (aruordir; arfor-tir). Maritime land.
ARFFED (ar-ffed). The lap.
ARGLWYDD (arglỽyd; ar-clwyd). Lord, governor; master.
ARGLWYDDES (arglỽydes; ar-glwydd). Lady.
ARGLWYDDIAETH (arglỽydyaeth; arglwydd). Lordship, dominion.
ARGYWEDDU (argyỽedu; argy-wedd). To oppress; to hurt.
ARIANT (aryant). Silver.

GLOSSARY.

Arnadunt (ar-nadunt). On, or upon them.
Arnaf, Arno, Arnynt (arn). Upon me, him, them.
Aruthder (aruthr). Amazement; terror.
Aruthr (aruthur; ar-uthr). Marvellous; prodigious; dire.
Arwain (arŵein; ar-gwain). To lead; to conduct; to bear.
Arweddu (arŵedu; arwedd). To bear; to lead.
Arwest (ar-gwest). Music.
Arwydd (arŵyd; ar-gwydd). Sign; ensign.
Arwyliant (arŵylant; arwyl). Funeral solemnities; a funeral.
Astudrwydd (astudrŵyd; astudrhwydd). Studiousness; diligence.
At. To.
Attadunt (at-at-hwynt). To them.
Attal (ad-dal). To stop; to restrain; to retain.
Attaw (at-o) To him.
Atteb (at-ebu). To answer.
Attunt (at-hwynt), To them.
Athraw (athro; ad-traw). Teacher; master.
Athu (ath). To go.
Aur (eur). Gold.
Awdurdawd (aŵdurdaŵt; awdur; L. *auctoritas*). Authority.
Awel (aw-el). A gale; a current of air.
Awr. An hour.
Awst (L. *Augustus*). August.
Awyr (aw-yr; Gr. αὴρ, L. *aer*). Air; sky.

B.

Baedd (baed; aedd). A boar.
Baeli. Bailiff.
Balch (bal). Prominent; superb; proud.
Balchder (balch). Pride; pomp.
Bardd (bard; bar). A bard.
Barn (bar). Judgment; sentence.
Barnu (barn). To judge; to adjudicate.
Barnwriaeth (barnŵryaeth; barnwr). Judgment.
Baron (barŵn; bar). A baron.
Bastardd (bastard; bas-tardd). A bastard.
Bedd (bed; edd). A grave, or sepulchre.
Beiddiaw (beidaŵ; baidd). To dare; to adventure.
Beili (baeli; bal; L. *ballium*). An outlet; a mound; a bailey.
Bendigaid (L. *benedictus*). Blessed.
Bicra (bickre; bicre). To skirmish; to bicker.
Bileinllu (bilain-llu). A villain host.
Blaen (bal). A point; the extremity; the top; the foremost part; priority.
Blif (bal-if). A warlike engine to throw stones, or other things; a catapulta.
Blin (bal). Troublesome; weary, tired.
Blinaw (blin). To trouble; to weary; to become fatigued.
Blodau (blodeu; blawd). Flowers; blossoms.

BLWNG (blŵg; bal-wng). A frown; frowning; angry; obdurate.
BLWYDDYN (blŵydyn; blwydd). A year.
BLYNEDD (blyned; llynedd).= Blwyddyn.
BOCSACHU (bocsach). To puff out the cheeks; to boast; to envy.
BOD (bot). Existence; residence; to be; to exist.
BODDI (bodi; bawdd). To drown; to immerse.
BONEDD (boned; bon). Stock; pedigree; nobleness of birth.
BONEDDIG (bonedic; bonedd). Having a stem, or origin; genteel; noble.
BRAD (brat; bar). Treachery; perfidy; treason.
BRADYCHU (bradwch). To betray; to deceive.
BRAICH (breich; bar; L. *brachium*). An arm.
BRAIDD (breid; bar). Near; scarcely.
BRAINT (breint; brai). Privilege; prerogative. In the Welsh Laws it is the rank, or condition of an individual; so peers were denominated *unfraint*, of one dignity.
BRAS (bar). Fat; thick; large.
BRATH (bar-ath). A bite; a stab.
BRATHEDIG (brathedic; brath). Bitten; stung; stabbed.
BRATHU (brath). To bite; to sting; to stab.
BRAWD (brawt; rhawd). A brother; a friar.
BRENHIN (braint). A king.

BRENHINAWL (brenhin). Royal; kingly.
BRENHINES (brenhin). A queen.
BRENHINIAETH (brenhinyaeth; brenhin). A kingdom.
BRIWAW (briw). To bruise; to hurt.
BRON (bar). A breast. *Ger bron, rhag bron*; in presence.
BRUD (brut; bar). A chronicle; also a prophecy. The word may have a reference to Prydain, Brut, or Brutus, from whose era the Britons formerly computed dates. "A hynny a elwir *Amser Brut;*" that is called the chronology of Brut. *MS*.
BRWYDYR (brwyd). A battle.
BRY (bar). High; above.
BRYCH (brwch). Brindled; freckled.
BRYD (bryt; rhyd). Mind; thought; purpose; resolution.
BRYN (rhyn). A hill.
BRYS (rhys). Haste; quick, hasty.
BRYSIAW (brys). To make haste; to hasten; to shoot with a crossbow.
BRYTANAWL (Prydain). British.
BU. A being; a cow.
BUCHEDD (buched; buch). Life; manner of living; condition of life.
BUCHEDDOCAU (buchedockau; buchedd). To lead a life.
BUDDUGAWL (budugawl; buddug). Victorious.
BUDDUGOLIAETH (budugolyaeth; buddugawl). Victory.
BUGAIL (bugeil; bu-cail). A herdsman; a shepherd.

GLOSSARY.

Bwa (bw). A bow; an arch.
Bwgwth (begôth; bw-gwth). A threat; to threaten.
Bwlch (bwl). A breach; a gap; a defile; a notch.
Bwrdais (bôrdeis; bwr-tais). A burgess; a freeman; a citizen.
Bwrgais (bôrgeis; bwr-cais)= Bwrdais.
Bwrw (bwr). To cast; to thrust; to suppose.
Bwyd (bôyt, byw). Meat; food.
Bwytta (bwyd). To eat.
Bychan (bach). Little, small.
Byd (byt; bod). A world.
Bydawl (byd). Worldly; secular.
Byddin (bydin; bydd). A snare; a party for an ambuscade, or secret enterprize; now a band, or troop, drawn up in array; an army.
Bys (ys). A finger.
Byw (yw). To live; alive.
Bywyd (byôyt; byw). Life, existence; animation.

C.

Cabidyldy (kabidyldy; L. *capitulum*). A chapter-house.
Cad (cat). A battle.
Cadair (kadair; cad-gair). A chair; a seat of authority.
Cadarn (kadarn; cad-arn). Strong; compact.
Cadarnhau (kadarnhau; cadarn). To strengthen; to fortify, to confirm.
Cadernid (kedernyt; cadarn). Strength.
Cadw (kadô; cad). To keep; to guard.

Cadwraeth (kadôryaeth; cadw). Keeping; guardianship.
Cael (kael; cae). To have; to obtain; to find.
Caer (kaer; cae). A wall or mound for defence; a fortress; a city.
Caeth (kaeth; cae). Bondman; a captive; bound, captive.
Caethiwaw (keithiôaô; caeth). To enslave; to lead into captivity.
Caethiwed (keithiôet; caethiw). Bondage; captivity.
Caffael (kaffel)=Cael.
Caill (keill; cai). A testicle.
Cainc (keig; cang). A branch.
Calan (kalan; L. *calendæ*). Calends; the first of each month.
Calon (kalon; cal). The heart; the middle; the womb.
Callder (kallter; call). Prudence; circumspection.
Cam (kam). Crooked; wrong; injury.
Camlyryus (kamlyryus; camlwrw). Incurring a penalty.
Campus (kampus; camp). Excellent.
Camweddawg (kamôedaôc; cam-wedd). Iniquitous.
Can (kan). For; since.
Caniattau (kanatau; caniad). To permit; to consent; to concede.
Canmawl (kanmaôl; can-mawl). Commendation; recommendation; to commend; to praise.
Canmoledig (kanmoledic; can-mawl). Commended; praised; praiseworthy.
Canmwyaf (kanmôyaf; can-mwyaf). For the most part.

B B

CANOL (kanaől ; cant-ol). Middle.
CANONWR (kanhonőr ; canon-gwr). A canon.
CANT. A circle ; a hundred.
CANTREF (kantref ; cant-tref). A canton, or hundred. "The num-"ber of acres in a cantrev is "twenty-five thousand six hun-"dred, not more, not less."— *Welsh Laws.*
CANTWR (kantor ; can-gwr). A singer.
CANWYLL (kanhőyll; can-gwyll). A candle. *Gwyl Fair y Canhwyllau;* the Feast of St. Mary of the Candles, Candlemas, Feb. 2.
CANYS (kanys ; can-ys). For, because ; since.
CAPAN (kappan ; cap). A cap. *Capan cor;* a canonical cap.
CARCHAR (karchar ; carch ; L. *carcer*). A prison.
CARCHARU (karcharu ; carchar). To imprison.
CARCHARWR (karcharőr ; carchar= gwr). A prisoner.
CARDAWD (kardaőt ; car-dawd). Charity; alms.
CARDINAL (kardinal; L. *cardinalis*). A cardinal ; an ecclesiastical prince in the Romish church.
CAREDIG (karedic ; car). Beloved ; kind.
CAREDIGRWYDD (karedicrőyd ; caredig.) Kindness.
CAREGL (karecyl ; car). A sacred vessel.
CARENNYDD (kerennyd ; carant). Friendship ; alliance of kindred.
CARES (kares ; car). Kinswoman.

CARIAD (karyat; car). Attachment; love ; charity.
CARIADWRAIG (karatőreic ; cariad= gwraig). A love-wife ; a concubine.
CARREG (karrec ; car). A stone.
CARU (karu; car). To love.
CARW (karő ; car). A stag.
CAS (kas). Hatred ; hateful.
CASAWL (kassaől ; cas). Hateful.
CASTELL (kastell ; cae-asdell; L. *castellum*). A castle.
CASTELLWR (kastellőr; castell-gwr). A castellan.
CATHL (kathyl; ca-tyl). A song or hymn ; melody.
CAWAWD (kaőad; caw). A shower.
CEFN (kefyn ; caf). The back ; a ridge ; the upper side.
CEFNDERW (kefynderő; cefn-derw). A cousin.
CEIDWAD (keitőat ; cadw). Keeper; guardian.
CEIDWADAETH (keitőataeth ; ceidwad). Keeping ; guardianship.
CEINIAWG (keinaőg ; cant). A penny ; ring money.
CEISIAW (keissaő ; cais), To seek.
CELANEDD (kelaned ; celan). A heap of dead carcases ; a carnage.
CELFYDDYD (keluydyt ; celfydd). Art.
CELWYDD (kelőyd ; cel-gwydd). Falsehood.
CENAD (kenad ; kennat ; can). A mission ; a messenger ; an ambassador.
CENADU (kanhadu ; cenad). To permit ; to bear tidings.
CENADWRI (kenadőri ; cenad). Embassy ; mission.

CENAU (kenau; can). A cub or whelp.
CENEDL (kenedyl; can). A kindred; clan or tribe; a nation.
CENHEDLAETH (kenedlaeth; cenedl). Race; generation.
CENLLUSG (kenllysc; can-llusg). Hail.
CERAINT (kereint; car). Kindred; relatives.
CERDD (kerd; cer). A song.
CERDDAWR (kerdor; cerdd). A songster; a minstrel.
CERDDED (kerdet; cerdd). To walk; to go.
CEUGANT (keugant; cau-cant). An enclosing circle; vacuity; infinity; a term used by the Bards to denote the vast expanse where God alone exists; certain.
CI (ki). A dog.
CIG (kic). Flesh.
CILIAW (kilyaʋ; cil). To retreat; retire; to withdraw; to go away.
CINIAW (kinyaʋ; cin). A meal; a dinner.
CINIAWA (kinyaʋa; ciniaw). To dine.
CIWDODWR (kiʋtaʋtʋr; ciwdawd-gwr). A citizen; a member of society.
CIWED (kiʋaʋt; ciw). A multitude, or rabble.
CLADDU (kladu; cladd). To bury.
CLAUAR (klaear; clau). Lukewarm; temperate; gentle; mild.
CLAWDD (klaʋd; cy-llawdd). A dyke; an embankment.
CLEDDYF (kledyf; cledd). A sword.
CLEFYCHU (kleuychu; clafwch). To fall sick.

CLEFYD (klefyt; claf). Sickness; disease.
CLO (klo). A lock.
CLOD (klot). Praise; commendation.
CLODFORUS (klotuorus; clodfawr). Commendable; praiseworthy.
CLYBOD (klybot; cly-bod). To hear.
CLYWED (klyʋet; clyw). To hear.
CNOTAU (knotau; cnawd). To be accustomed, or used.
CODDI (kodi; cawdd). To straiten; to vex.
CODDIANT (kodyant; cawdd). Straitness; vexation.
COED (coet). Wood.
COEG (coec; co-oeg). Empty; vain; saucy.
COELBREN (koelbren; coel-pren). A piece of wood used in balloting, on which was cut the name of the candidate; a lot.
COETTIR (koetir; coed-tir). Woodland.
COFADWY (couadʋy; cof). Memorable.
COFEINT (koueint; L. *conventus*). A convent; a religious assembly.
COFFHAU (koffhau; cof). To remind; to remember.
COLOFN (kolouyn; colof; L. *columna*). A column, or pillar.
COLS (kols; L. *decollatio*). A beheading. *Gwyl Ieuan y Cols;* the Feast of the beheading of St. John, August 29.
COLLED (kollet; koll). A loss.
COLLI (koll). To lose.
COR (kor). A choir.
CORFF (korff; L. *corpus*). A body.

CORON (cor). A crown.
CORONI (koroni ; coron). To crown.
CORWYNT (korŵynt ; cor-gwynt). A whirlwind.
CRAFF (kraff ; craf). Fast ; keen.
CRAIG (kreic ; crai). A rock.
CRAIR (kreir ; cra). A relic.
CREAWDWR (kreaŵdyr ; creawd= gwr). Creator.
CRED (kret; cre). Belief; credence.
CREDU (kredu ; cred). To believe; to trust.
CREFYDD (kreuyd ; cref). Religion.
CREFYDDUS (kreuydus ; crefydd). Religious.
CREFYDDWR (krefydŵr ; crefydd= gwr). A religious man; a devotee.
CREIGIAWL (kreigaŵl; craig). Rocky.
CREU (kreu ; cre). To create ; to make.
CREULAWN (kreulaŵn ; crau-llawn). Cruel.
CREULONDER (kreulonder ; creulawn). Cruelty.
CRIBDDEILIAW (cribdeilaŵ ; cribddail). To extort.
CRIST (Gr. ΧΡΙΣΤΟΣ). Christ.
CRISTIONOGAETH (kristonogaeth ; cristion). Christianity.
CROES (kroes ; cro). A cross ; adversity ; contrary.
CROESAWG (kroessaŵc ; croes). Crusader.
CROGI (krogi ; crog). To hang.
CROGLITH (kroglith ; crog-llith). The service of the cross.
CROGWYDD (krocŵyd; crog-gwydd). Gallows.
CRWN (krŵn). Round, circular.

CRYNO (kryno ; crwn). Compact; compendious ; neat ; well-set.
CRYNU (kryn). To quake ; to tremble.
CRYTHWR (krythor ; crwth-gwr). One who plays on a crwth ; a crowder ; a violinist.
CUDDIAW (kudyaŵ ; cudd). To hide or conceal.
CUDDIEDIG (kudyedic ; cudd). Hidden, concealed ; secret.
CWBL (kŵbyl ; cwb). A whole ; entire, all.
CWBLHAU (kuplau ; cwbl). To fulfil ; to finish.
CWMWD (kymŵt ; cwm). A subdivision of a cantrev or hundred ; a comot; a wapentake. "Twelve " manors and two hamlets there " are in a comot."—*Welsh Laws.*
CWNDIT (kŵndit ; cwn ; L. *conductus*). Conduct.
CWNSLI (kŵnsli ; L. *consilium*). Council.
CWNSTABL (kŵnstabyl ; L. *constabularius*). A constable.
CWSG (kŵsc). Sleep.
CWYMP (kŵymp ; cy-gwymp). A fall.
CWYMPWR (kŵympŵr ; cwymp-gwr). Feller ; overthrower,
CWYNAW (kŵynaw ; cwyn). To complain.
CWYNFAN (kŵynuan ; cwyn-ban). A lamentation.
CWYNFANUS (kŵynuanus; cwynfan). Complaining ; wailing.
CYCHWYN (kychŵyn; cy-cwyn). To start ; to commence a journey.
CYD (kyt). Joint ; while ; forasmuch.

CYDARFOLLI (kytaruolli; cyd-arfoll). To confederate.

CYDARFOLLWR (kytaruollŵr ; cyd-arfollwr). A confederate.

CYDIAW (kytyaw ; cyd). To join ; to copulate.

CYDSYNIAW (kytsynyaü ; cyd-synyaw). To consent.

CYDSYNIEDIGAETH (kytsynnedigaeth ; cydsynied). Concurrence, or mutual accordance.

CYDYMDAITH (kedymdeith ; cyd-ymdaith). A companion, or fellow traveller.

CYFADNAB (kyfadnab; cyd-adnab). Acquaintance.

CYFAGOS (cyuagos ; cyd-agos). Near ; adjoining.

CYFAILL, CYFAILLT (kyueill ; kyueillt ; cyd-aill, aillt). A friend.

CYFAN (kyuan ; cyfa). Whole, entire, complete.

CYFANNEDD (kyuanned ; cyd-annedd). Habitation, abode.

CYFANNEDDU (kyuanedu ; cyfannedd). To inhabit.

CYFARFOD (kyuaruot ; cyd-arf). To meet.

CYFARSANGEDIG (kyuarsagedic ; cyfarsang). Mutually trodden, oppressed.

CYFARSANGEDIGAETH (kyuarsagedigaeth ; cyd-arsang). A mutually treading ; a being oppressed or subdued.

CYFARSANGU (kyuarsagu ; cyd-arsang). To mutually tread; to oppress.

CYFARWYS (kyuarüys ; cywar-gwys). A gift, grant, or favour, conferred on a public occasion; honorary reward ; a present.

CYFEILLACH (kyueillach ; cyfaill). Friendship ; fellowship.

CYFEILLES (kyueilles ; cyfaill). A female friend.

CYFER (kyuer ; cyd-ar). An opposite situation.

CYFERBYN (kyuerbyn; cyd-erbyn). Opposite.

CYFERBYNU (kyuerbynu ; cyd-erbyn). To oppose.

CYFIAWN (kyfyaün ; cyd-iawn). Just.

CYFIAWNDER (kyfiaünder ; cyfiawn). Justice; equity.

CYFLAFAN (kyflauan ; cyd-llafan). A heinous deed ; felony ; also, massacre or slaughter.

CYFLAWN (kyulaün ; cyd-llawn). Full, complete.

CYFLAWNI (kyfleüni ; cyflawn ; cyd-llawn). To fulfil.

CYFLE (kyfle ; cyd-lle). Place ; convenience ; opportunity.

CYFLENWI (kyflenüi ; cyd-llenwi). To fulfil.

CYFNESAFIAD (kyfnessafiad ; cyfnesaf). The next of kin ; a near relation.

CYFNESAFRWYDD (kyfnessafrüyd ; cyfnesaf). Nearness.

CYFNEWID (kefneüit ; cyd-newid). To exchange.

CYFNITHERW (kefnitherü ; cyfnith; cefn-nith). A female cousin-german.

CYFODI (kyuodi; cyd-bod). To arise.

CYFOETH (kyuoeth ; cy-moeth). Power ; dominion ; wealth.

CYFOETHAWG (kyuoethawc; cyf-oeth). Mighty; rich.
CYFOETHOGI (kyuoethogi; cyfoeth-awg). To enrich; to grow rich.
CYFRAITH (kyureith; cyd-rhaith). Law.
CYFRAN (kyuran; cyd-rhan). A portion.
CYFREITHIAWL (kyureithaŵl; cyf-raith). Legitimate.
CYFRWNG (kyfrŵg; cyd-rhwng). An interval; between.
CYFRYW (kyfryŵ; cyd-rhyw). Similar; such.
CYFUCHAW (kyfuchaŵ; cyfuwch). To level.
CYFUN (kyun; cyd-un). United, accordant.
CYFUNAW (kyuunaŵ; cyfun). To unite, to join.
CYFUNDEB (kyundeb; cyd-undeb). Unity; confederacy.
CYFYNG (kyuyg; cyfwng). Narrow, straight.
CYFFELYB (kyffelyb; cyfal). Like, or similar.
CYFFES (kyffes; L. *confessio*). A confession.
CYFFREDIN (kyffredin; cyd-rhed). Universal, common. *Y cyffredin;* the commonalty.
CYFFREDINAW (kyffredinaŵ; cyff-redin). To make common; to have intercourse.
CYFFROEDIG (kyffroedic; cyffro). Moved, roused.
CYFFROI (kyffroi; cyffraw). To agitate, to move or stir.
CYFFROWR (kyffroŵr; cyffro). Agitator.

CYGLYU (kigleu; cy-cly). To hear.
CYNGHOR (kyghor; cyd-cor). Counsel, advice.
CYNGHORFYNNUS (kygoruynnus; cynghorfynt). Malicious; envious.
CYNGHORFYNT (kyghoruynt; cyng-hor-myn). Malice; envy.
CYNGHORFYNU (kyghorvynnu; cynghor-mynu). To bear malice; to envy.
CYNGHORWR (kyghorŵr; cynghor-gwr). Counsellor.
CYNGRAIR (kygreir; cy-crair). A covenant or agreement by oath; a treaty; a truce; an alliance.
CYHOEDDEDIG (kyhoededic; cy-hoedd). Public; open.
CYHOEDDI (kyhoedi; cyhoedd). To publish; to proclaim.
CYHUDDAW (kuhudaŵ; cy-hudd). To accuse; to impeach.
CYHUDDWR (kyhudŵr; cyhudd). Accuser.
CYHWRDD (kyhŵrd; kehŵrd; cy-hwrdd). To come in contact, to meet.
CYLCH (kylch; cyl). A circle; a circuit; a course or turn; about; concerning. *Cylch o gylch;* round about.
CYLCHYNU (kylchynu; cylch). To surround.
CYLUS (kylus; cwl). Culpable; blameworthy.
CYLLELL (kyllell; cwll). A knife.
CYLLID (kyllit; cwll). A contribution of provision; income, rent, or tax.
CYMDEITHAS (ketymdeithas; cyd-ymdaith). Society.

GLOSSARY.   391

CYMEDRAWL (kymhedraŵl; cymedr). Moderate.
CYMEDRODDWR (kymedrodŵr; cymedr-rhodd-gwr). A moderator, an arbitrator.
CYMHELL (kymell; cyd-pell). To compel.
CYMHORTHAW (kymhorthaŵ; cymhorth). To support.
CYMHORTHIAD (kymhorthat; cyd=porth). A succouring; assistance; assistant.
CYMHORTHWR (kymhorthŵr; cymhorth-gwr). An assistant.
CYMMAINT (kymeint; cyd-maint). So much; so many.
CYMMEREDIG (kymeredic; cymmer). Accepted.
CYMMERYD (kymeryd; cyd-mer). To take; to accept.
CYMMODI (kymodi; cymod). To reconcile.
CYMMODRODDI (kymodrodi; cymmod-rhoddi). To reconcile.
CYMMODRODDWR (kymodrodŵr; cymmod-rhodd-gwr). A reconciler, or mediator.
CYMMUN (kymun; cyd-un). Communion.
CYMWYNASGAR (kymŵynasgar; cymwynas-car). Good natured; courteous.
CYMYNU (kymynu; cymyn). To commend; to bequeath.
CYN (kyn). Before; as.
CYNDDRYCHIAWL (kedrychaŵl; cynddrych). Present, face to face.
CYNHAL (kynhal; kynnal; cyd-dal). To sustain; to support; to maintain.
CYNHALEDIGAETH (kanhaledigaeth; cynhal). Maintenance; preservation.
CYNHAUAF (kynhayaf; kynhaeaf; cyn-gauaf). Autumn; harvest.
CYNHWRF (kynŵrŵf; kynnŵryf; cy-twrf). Commotion; tumult; trouble.
CYNHYRFUS (kynhyruus; cynhwrf). Provocation; agitated.
CYNNIFER (keniuer; cyd-nifer). Of even number; so many, or as many.
CYNNIL (kynnil; cyn-dil). Skilful; frugal.
CYNNORTHWY (kanhorthŵy; cynnorth). Succour; help; support.
CYNNRYCHIAWL (kyndrychaŵl; cynrych). Present.
CYNNRYCHIOLDER (kendrycholder; cynnrych). Presence.
CYNNULL (kynhull; cyd-dull). To collect, to gather.
CYNNULLEIDFA (kynnulleitua; cynnull). An assembly; a congregation.
CYNNYG (kynig; cyn-dyg). To offer; to tender, propose, or make an overture; to attempt.
CYNTAF (kyntaf; kynt). First.
CYRCH (kyrch; cwr). A centre; tendency towards a centre; an inroad or invasion; an onset.
CYRCHAFAEL (kyrchauel; cyrch). Ascension.
CYRCHU (kyrchu; cyrch). To approach; to resort to; to assault.
CYSGU (kysgu; cwsg). To sleep.
CYSSEFIN (kysseuin; cysaf). Primary; first, or primitive.
CYSSEGREDIG (kyssegredic; cyssegr). Consecrated.

CYSSEGREDIGAETH (kyssegredigaeth; cyssegr). Consecration; a consecrated state.
CYSSEGRU (kyssegru; cysegr). To consecrate.
CYSSYLLTIEDIG (kyssylltedic; cyswllt). Conjoined.
CYSTUDDIAW (kystudyaƀ; cystudd). To afflict; to distress.
CYTTIRAWG (kyttiraƀc; cyd-tir). A partner that hath a share of land in common with another; a borderer, one that dwelleth hard by, a near neighbour.
CYTTUNAW (kyttunaƀ; cyttun). To coincide; to agree; to assent to; to become pacified.
CYTTUNDEB (kyttundeb; cyd-undeb). Unity; confederacy.
CYTHRAUL (kythreul; cyd-traul). The devil.
CYWAIR (kyƀeir; cy-gwair). Orderly.
CYWEIRDEB (kyƀeirdeb; cywair). Correctness; completeness; good order.
CYWEIRIAW (kyƀeiraƀ; cywair). To put in order; to correct; to equip; to prepare.
CYWEIRIWR (kyƀeirƀr; cywair). One who puts in order; an arranger.
CYWEITHAS (kyƀeithas; cywaith). Society, fellowship, or alliance; commerce or dealing; courteous.
CYWIR (kyƀir; cy-gwir). Sincere; true; faithful.
CYWIRAW (kyƀiraƀ; cy-gwir). To perfect; to fulfil a promise or trust; to be sincere.
CYWIRDEB (kyƀirdeb; cywir). Perfection; sincerity; uprightness.

CYWREINWEITH (kyƀrcinƀeith; cywrain-gwaith). Curious workmanship.

CH.

CHWAER. Sister.
CHWANEGU (chwaneg). To increase; to add.
CHWANNAWG (chƀannaƀc; chwant). Desirous, ambitious, covetous.
CHWANT (chwan). Desire, longing, appetite, lust.
CHWAREL (chwar). A dart or javelin.
CHWECH (ƀhech). Six.
CHWECHANT (ƀhechant; chwechcant). Six hundred.
CHWECHED (ƀhechet; chwech). Sixth.
CHWEDL (chƀedyl; chwed). A saying; a fable; a tale or story; report.
CHWEFRAWR (ƀhefraƀr; chwefr). February.
CHWEGRWN (ƀhegrƀn; chwegr). A father-in-law.
CHWEMIL (ƀhemil; chwech-mil). Six thousand.
CHWERW (chwar). Bitter; sharp, or severe.
CHWERWDOST (chwerw-tost). Exceedingly severe.
CHWI. You.
CHWYDDEDIG (chƀydedic; chwydd). Swollen; pompous.

D.

DA. A produce; a good; wealth, goods, or chattels; good.
DADLAMU (datlamu; dad-llamu). To rebound.

DADLEU (dadl). A debate ; a pleading ; to argue ; to plead.
DADLEUWR (dadleu-gwr). An advocate ; a pleader.
DAEAR (dayar ; daiar ; dai-ar). Earth.
DAGR (dag). A tear.
DANGAWS (daghos ; dan-caws). To give proximity ; to show ; to explain.
DAIONI (dayoni ; da). Goodness.
DAL (dy-al). To hold ; to detain ; to catch.
DALL (all). Blind.
DALLU (dall). To blind; to become blind.
DAMUNAW (dam-unaw). To wish; to desire ; to ask.
DAMWAIN (damûein ; dam-gwain). An accident ; chance.
DAMWEINIAW (damwain). To happen.
DANFON (danuon ; dy-anfon). To send ; to convey.
DANT (dan). A tooth ; a tusk.
DARFOD (daruot ; dar-bod). To cease ; to conclude.
DAROGAN (dar-gogan). A foreboding ; to predict ; to forebode.
DAROSTWNG (darestwg ; dar-gostwng). To subdue ; to subjugate ; to bring under.
DAROSTYNGEDIG (darestygedic ; darostwng). Subject.
DAROSTYNGEDIGAETH (darestygedigaeth ; darostwng). Subjection.
DARPARU (darpar). To prepare ; to provide.
DAU (deu). Two.
DAW (da). A son-in-law.
DAWN (daw). A gift; virtue; grace.

DEALL (dyali ; de-gall). To understand.
DECEM. Ten. *Decem novennalis* is a revolution of nineteen years, at the end of which time the various aspects of the moon are, within an hour, the same as they were on the same days of the month nineteen years before. This cycle was adopted on the 16th of July, B.C. 433.
DECHREU (dechre). A beginning ; to begin.
DEDWYDD (detôyd ; dad-gwydd). Recovery of intelligence ; bliss ; happy.
DEFAWD (deuaôt ; def). Usage ; manner; custom, or established rule.
DEFNYDD (deunyd ; defn). Matter, or substance of which anything is made ; material ; element.
DEG (dec). Ten.
DEGFED (decuet ; deg). Tenth.
DEGWR (deg-gwr). Ten men.
DEHEU (de-heu). The right ; the south; because that quarter of the world is on the right hand to those that look towards the east, as the Bards used to do in their circles.
DEHEUBARTH (deheu-parth). The southern part ; South Wales.
DEHEUBARTHWR(deheu-parth-gwr). A South Walian.
DEISYFU (deissyuu ; deisyf). To request ; to beseech ; to desire.
DELW (del). An image ; a form.
DEOL (dehol ; de-ol). Exile ; to separate ; to banish.
DETHOL (dy-ethol). To select ; to choose ; to elect.

DETHOLEDIG (dethol). Select; chosen.
DEUDDEG (deudec; dau-deg). Twelve.
DEUDDEGFED (deudecuet; deuddeg). Twelfth.
DEUFIS (deuvis; dau-mis). Two months.
DEUGAIN (deugein; deugeint; dau=ugain). Forty.
DEUGEINFED (deugeinuet; deugain). Fortieth.
DEWIS (dew). A choice; choice; to choose.
DEWR (dew). Valiant, brave.
DEWREDD (deƀred; dewr). Valour.
DEWRLEW (dewr-glew). Brave and valiant.
DIAL (dy-al). Vengeance; punishment; revenge; to avenge; to punish; to revenge.
DIANC (diag; di-anc). To escape; to avoid; to deliver; to be delivered; to retreat.
DIANNOD (diannot; di-annod). Without suspension or delay.
DIAREB (di-areb). What is incontrovertible; a proverb; unanswerable.
DIAREBUS (diareb). Proverbial.
DIARF (diaryf; di-arf). Weaponless; unarmed.
DIARFEREDIG (diarueredic; diarfer). Unhabituated.
DIARGRYNEDIG (diargrynedic; diargryn). Intrepid; unfermented.
DIARWYBOD (diarƀybot; di-arwybod). Unknowing; unknown.
DIASGELLU (diasgell). To divest of a wing or wings.

DIAWD (diaƀt; dy-iawd). Drink; beverage.
DIBOBLI (dibobl). To depopulate.
DICHAWN (dig). To be able; to effectuate.
DIDDANWCH (didanƀch; diddan). Consolation.
DIEFLIG (dieulic; diafl). Devilish; diabolical.
DIEITHR (dieithyr; di-eithr). Without exception; strange.
DIELW (di-elw). Worthless; vile.
DIELWI (dielw). To contemn; to despise.
DIENIG (diennic; dien). Deadly.
DIENYDDIAW (dihenydyaƀ; dienydd). To disanimate; to execute.
DIERGRYNEDIG (diergrynedic; diergryn). Intrepid; undaunted.
DIFA (diua; dif). To consume; to destroy; to devour; to waste
DIFESUR (diuessur; di-mesur). Immense; without measure.
DIFESUREDD (diuessured; difesur). Immensity.
DIFESUREDIG (diuessuredig; difesur). Unmeasured; immense.
DIFFAITH (di-ffaith). Wilderness; wild.
DIFFEITHIAW (diffaith). To devastate; to lay waste.
DIFFEITHWCH (diffaith). Wilderness.
DIFFYG (diffyc; diff; L. *defectus*). A defect; a want; an eclipse.
DIFFYGIAW (diffygyaƀ; diffyg). To fail; to be wearied.
DIGAWN (dig). Enough; sufficient.
DIGRIF (crif). Amusing; merry.
DIGRIFWCH (digrif). Amusement; mirth.

DIGRYNEDIG (digrynedic ; digryn). Intrepid, undaunted.

DIGWYDDAW (dygwydaԑ; digwydd). To fall ; to befal, to happen.

DIGYFOETHI (digyfoeth). To spoil of wealth.

DIGYFFRAW (digyffro ; di-cyffraw). Undisturbed, composed.

DIHUNAW (dyhunaԑ; dihun). To wake ; to awake.

DILESG (dilesc ; di-llesg). Not weak, unfeeble.

DILEU (dile). To divest of place ; to abolish ; to exterminate.

DILLAD (dillat ; dill). Apparel or clothes.

DIM. Nothing ; anything

DIMAI (dimei; dim). A halfpenny.

DINAS (din-as). A fortress ; a fortified town ; a city.

DIOED (dioet ; di-oed). Without delay.

DIOFN (diofyn; di-ofn). Fearless.

DIOGEL (di-gogel) Unexposed ; secure.

DIOGELRWYDD (diogelrԑyd; diogel). Security ; safe conduct.

DIOGELWCH (diogel). Security, safety.

DIOGELWR (diogel-gwr). A securer; a protector.

DIRAID (direit; di-rhaid). Useless.

DIRAN (di-rhan). Portionless.

DIRFAWR (diruaԑr ; dir-mawr). Very large, vast.

DIRGEL (dir-cel). Secret.

DIRGELEDIG (dirgeledic ; dirgel). Concealed.

DIRYBUDD (dirybud ; di-rhybydd). Without warning ; sudden.

DISGYBL (L. *discipulus*). A disciple.

DISGYNU (diskynnu ; disgyn). To descend ; to dismount.

DISTRYW (dy-ystryw). Destruction.

DISTRYWEDIGAETH (distryw). Destruction.

DISTRYWIAW (distryw). To destroy.

DISYFYD (deissyuit; di-syfyd). Void of stay ; sudden.

DIWARNOD (diԑarnaԑt ; diw-arnod). A day.

DIWEDD (diԑed ; di-gwedd). Completion ; end.

DODI (dawd). To put ; to appoint; to give.

DODREFN (dotrefn ; dy-godrefn). Furniture.

DOETH (dy-oeth). Wise; prudent ; eloquent.

DOETHINEB (doeth). Wisdom.

DOFHAU (dof). To tame.

DOFIAWDR(dofyaԑdyr; dof). Tamer.

DOL (dy-ol). A dale ; a mead.

DOLUR (dy-golur). Anguish, pain; sorrow.

DOLURIAW (doluryaԑ ; dolur). To ache; to be in pain ; to cause anguish or pain.

DOS ; *v. imper.* Go thou.

DOSBARTHU (dosparthu ; dosbarth). To distribute ; to distinguish ; to analyse.

DRINGAW (drigaԑ, dring). To climb.

DRWG (drԑc; dy-rhwg). Evil; bad.

DRWS (dy-rhws). A passage; a doorway ; a door.

DRYCH (dry). Aspect, form.

DRYGDRUM (drycdrum; drwg-trum). Bad ridge, or surge.

DRYGWEITHRED (drycԑeithret ; drwg-gweithred). Evil deed.

DRYGYSPRYDOL (drycysprytol; drwg-yspryd). Evil-spirited.

DRYLL (dy-rhyll). A piece; a fragment, a part.

DU. Black; dark.

DUAW (du). To blacken; to darken; to become black; to become dark.

DURFING (duruig; durf.) Close; hard; austere.

DUW (dy-yw). God.

DUWIES (dóyões; duw). A goddess.

DUWIOLDER (dyõawlder; duwiol). Godliness.

DWFR (dwfyr; dwf). Water.

DWRN (dy-gwrn). A fist.

DWY (dy-wy). Two.

DWYFAWL (dóyuaõl; dwyf). Divine, godly.

DWYFRON (dóyuron; dwy-bron). The breast. *Cledr y ddwyfron;* the chest.

DWYN (dy-gwyn). To bring; to take away; to steal.

DWYWAITH (dóyõeith; dwy-gwaith). Twice.

DYBLYGU (dyblyg). To double; to fold.

DYCHYMYG (dechymic; dy-cymyg). Invention; imagination.

DYCHYMYGU (dechymygu; dychymyg). To devise; to conjecture.

DYDD (dyd; dy-ydd). A day.

DYDDGWAITH (dydgõeith; dydd=gwaith). A certain day.

DYFAL (dyual; dy-bal). Sedulous; diligent.

DYFETHA (difetha; dyfeth). To destroy, to waste.

DYFOD (dyuot; dy-bod). To be, to exist; to come to pass; to come.

DYFODEDIGAETH (dyuotedigaeth; dyfodedig). Arrival.

DYFODIAD (dyuodyat; dyfod). A coming; arrival; advent.

DYFRYSIAW (dyfryssyaõ; dyfrys). To hasten.

DYFU (dyuu; dwf). To glide, or to move forward; to come.

DYFYNU (dyfyn). To draw to; to cite.

DYFFRYN (dwfr-hynt). A vale through which a river flows.

DYGYNNULLAW (dygynnull). To assemble; to collect.

DYLYED (dylyet; dyly). Duty; debt; claim.

DYLYEDAWG (dylyedaõc; dylyed). Entitled to property; noble; a proprietor.

DYLYEDUS (dylyed). Due; obligatory.

DYLYU (dyl). To be bound in duty; to owe.

DYN (dy-yn). A person; a human being, a man or woman.

DYNESAU (denessu; dy-nesau). To approach, to draw near.

DYODDEF (diodef; dy-goddef). To suffer, to endure, to allow.

DYODDEFAINT (diodeuaint; dyoddef). Suffering, passion.

DYOLWCH (diolõch; dy-golwch). Gratitude.

DYRCHAFAEL (dyrchauel; dyrchaf). To elevate; to ascend.

DYRCHAFU (derchafu; dyrchaf). To raise; to ascend.

DYRNAID (dyrneit; dwrn). A handful.

DYSG (dysc, dy-ysg). Learning.

DYSGEDIGAETH (dysgedig). Learning.
DYSGU (dysg). To learn; to teach.
DYSGWYL (disgŵyl; dys-gwyl). To look for, to expect, to wait for.
DYSYCHU (dissychu ; dysych). To dry ; to become dry.
DYUNAW (dunnaŵ ; dyun). To agree ; to unite.
DYWALU (dywal). To become furious.
DYWEDEDIG (dyŵededic ; dywed). Said.
DYWEDYD (dyŵedut ; dy-gwedyd). To speak, to say.

E.

EBARGOFI (ebrygofi ; ebargof). To forget.
EBRILL (eb-rhill; L. *Aprilis*). April.
EBRWYDD (ebrŵyd ; eb-rhwydd). Quick ; hasty ; soon.
ECHRESTR (ech-rhestr). A register.
ECHTYWYNWR (ech-tywynwr). An illustrator.
ECHWYDD (echŵyd ; ech-cwydd). The evening.
ECHWYN (e-cwyn). What is taken or given for use ; a loan.
ECHWYNAW (echwyn). To borrow; to lend.
EDIFARHAU (ediuarhau; edifar). To repent.
EDIFARWCH (ediuarŵch ; edifar). Penitence.
EDRYCH (e-drych). To look ; to see.
EDRYCHEDIGAETH (edrychedig). The act or state of looking ; appearance ; sight.
EF. Him.

EFENGYLWR (euegylŵr ; efengyl= gwr). Evangelist.
EGLUR (eg-llur). Clear ; plain ; visible.
EGLWYS (glwys ; L. *ecclesia*). A church.
EGLWYSAWL (eglwys). Ecclesiastical ; belonging to the church.
EGLWYSWR (eglwys-gwr). A churchman ; an ecclesiastic ; a clergyman.
EHELAETH (helaeth). Extensive ; large ; abundant.
EIDDAW (eidaw ; aidd). One's own ; possession ; chattel.
EILDYDD (eildyd ; ail-dydd). The second day.
EILWAITH (eilŵeith ; ail-gwaith). Twice.
EIRA (air). Snow.
EIRIAWL (eiryol; eiraŵl; air-iawl). To entreat ; to intercede ; to persuade.
EISEWYDD (esseŵyd ; eisiw). Want; indigent.
EISIEU (es). Want.
EISIWEDIG (eissiŵedic ; eisiwed). Needy ; indigent ; poor.
EISOES (es-oes). Nevertheless ; however ; moreover ; likewise ; already.
EISTEDD (eisted ; eiste). To sit. *Eistedd wrth* ; to sit down by ; to besiege.
EISTEDDFA (eistedua ; eistedd-ma). A sitting place; a seat ; a station.
EITHR (eithyr ; aith). Except ; besides ; but.
ELW (el). Property ; profit, gain.
EMELLDIGEDIG (emelldigetic; melldigedig). Accursed.

ENAID (eneit; en-aid). A soul; life.
ENCILIAW (enkilyaw; encil). To retreat; to retire; to withdraw.
ENNILL (en-nill). Gain; profit; to gain.
ENNYNU (ennyn). To kindle; to inflame; to be inflamed.
ENW (nw). A name.
ENWAWG (enŵaŵc; enw). Having a name; renowned.
ENWI (enw). To name.
EOFN (ehofyn; e-ofn). Fearless; bold; daring; confident.
ERAILL (ereill; arall). Others.
ERBYN (pyn). Against; opposite; to receive.
ERBYNIAD (erbynyeit; erbyn). To receive.
ERCHI (arch). To ask; to demand.
ERFYNIED (eruynneit; erfyn). To request; to entreat.
ERGRYNEDIG (ergrynedic; ergryn). Made to tremble; trembling.
ERGRYNU (ergryn). To tremble; to fear.
ERGYD (er-cyd). A throw; a shot; a charge; a stroke.
ERIOED (eiryoet; er-oed). From the beginning; ever; never. It is used always of the time past.
ERLID (erlit; eryl). To pursue; to prosecute; to persecute; to chase.
ERLYNIAWDWR (erlynyaŵdŵr; er-lyn). One who pursues; a persecutor; a prosecutor.
ERMIG (ermyg; er-mig). An instrument.
ERW (ar-w). An acre; a measure applied exclusively to arable lands; it appears to have contained about 4,320 yards.
ESGAIR (eskeir; esg). A shank; a leg; a limb.
ESGOB (escob; L. *episcopus*). A bishop.
ESGOBAWD (escobaŵt; esgob.) A bishopric; a diocese.
ESGYN (eskyn; es-cyn; L. *ascendo*). To ascend; to mount; to rise.
ESTRAWN (es-trawn). One of a separate community; a stranger; a foreigner.
ESTYN (es-tyn). To extend; to reach; to hold out.
ETIFEDD (etiued; e-tifedd). A birth; an infant; an heir.
ETWA (ed-gwa). Yet; still; again.
ETHAWL (ethol; e-tawl). To elect; to choose; to select.
ETHOLEDIG (ethawl). Elect; chosen.
ETHOLEDIGAETH (etholedig). Election.
EU. Their; them.
EWCH; *imperative mood, second person plural of* MYNED. Go ye.
EWYLLYS (ewyll). Will; inclination; desire.
EWYTHR (ewythyr; e-gwythr). An uncle.

Ff.

FFO. A flight, or retreat; to flee.
FFOADUR = FFOAWDR (ffoaŵdyr; ffoad). A fugitive.
FFOEDIG (ffoedic; ffoi). Fled.
FFOI (ffo). To flee.
FFORDD (fford; ffor). A passage; a road, a way.

Ffos (ffy-os). A fosse, a ditch.
Ffrwyth (ffrwy; L. *fructus*). Fruit.
Ffrwythaw (ffrwyth). To fructify, to bear fruit.
Ffurf (ffuryf; ffur; L. *forma*). Form; manner.
Ffurfiaw (ffuruaỏ; ffurf). To form, to shape.
Ffustiaw (ffustaỏ; ffust). To thresh, to beat.
Ffyddlawn (ffydlon; ffydd-llawn). Faithful.
Ffyddlonder (ffydlonder; ffydd-lawn). Fidelity.
Ffysg (ffysc). A quick course; impetuosity; sudden; quick; impetuous.

G.

Gadael (gad). To part from, to leave; to forsake.
Gadaw (gad). To leave.
Gair (geir; ga-ir). A word.
Gal (ga-al). An enemy.
Galw (gal). To call; to invoke; to name.
Gallel (gall). To be able; to be possible.
Gallu (gall). Power; to be able.
Galluus (gallu). Able; powerful.
Gan (can). With; by; because; since.
Garw (gar). Rough; severe.
Garwdost (garw-tost). Sharply severe.
Gauaf (gau-af). Winter.
Gawr (awr). A shout; a tumult; a conflict.
Gefyn (geuyn; gaf). A fetter, a gyve; a shackle.

Gefynu (geuynu; gefyn). To fetter, to shackle.
Gelyn (gal). A foe, or enemy.
Gem (em; L. *gemma*). A gem, a jewel.
Geni (gan). To be born.
Ger (cer). By, or at; near to.
Geudy (gau-ty). A privy.
Gilydd (cil). Mutual selves; one another, each other.
Glan (llan). The brink, side, or bank of a river, or any water.
Gleindid (gleindit; glan). Purity, holiness.
Glew (llew). A hero; brave, valiant; sharp, acute.
Glewder (glew). Bravery; sharpness.
Glo. Coal.
Glyn (llyn). A deep vale through which a river runs; a glen.
Gnotaedig (gnotaedic; gnawd). Accustomed, usual.
Gobaith (gobeith; go-paith). Hope; a common, or an open wild.
Gobeithiaw (gobeithaỏ; gobaith). To hope.
Gochel (go-cel). To avoid; to beware.
Goddef (godef; go-def). To bear; to suffer.
Godrig (gotric; go-trig). A delay.
Gofalus (goualus; gofal). Careful; solicitous; anxious.
Gofwyaw (gofwy). To visit.
Gofyn (go-myn). To ask, to inquire.
Gogelu (gỏeglu; gogel). To eschew; to shelter; to protect.
Gogledd (gogled; go-cledd). The

north, which is to the left (cledd) of a person looking eastward.

GOGOF (ogof). A cave, a cavern.

GOGONEDDUS (gogonedus; gogon-edd). Glorious; illustrious.

GOGONIANT (gogonyant; co-coniant). Glory.

GOHIR (go-hir). A delay.

GOLAS (go-glas.) Of a faint blue, bluish.

GOLEU (gawl). Light.

GOLEUAD (goleuat; goleu). Light.

GOLUD (golut; go-llud). Wealth, or riches.

GOLLWNG (gellŵg; go-llwng). To loosen; to dismiss; to absolve.

GOLLYNGDAWD (gellygdaŵt; gollwng). Dismissal; release; absolution.

GOMMEDD (gomed; gom-medd). To refuse; to deny.

GORCHFYGU (gorchfyg). To overcome, to conquer.

GORCHYMMYN (gor-cymmyn). A command; to command.

GORDDERCH (gorderch; gordd-erch). A paramour; a concubine.

GORDDERCHAD (gorderchat; gordderch). A concubine.

GORDDERCHU (gorderchu; gordderch). To woo; to play the wanton.

GORESGYN (goreskyn; gor-esgyn). To super-ascend; to come upon; to take possession; to subdue.

GOREU (gor). Best.

GOREUGWR (goreu-gwr). Best man; principal man.

GORFOD (goruot; gor-bod). To get superior; to cause submission; to overcome.

GORMOD (gorm). Excess; too much.

GORPHEN (gorffen; gor-pen). To finish.

GORPHOWYSAW (gorffoŵysaŵ; gor-powys). To rest, to repose.

GORPHWYSAW (gorffŵysaŵ; gorphwys)=Gorphowys.

GORTHRWM (gor-trwm). Very heavy; depressive.

GORTHRYMU (gŵrthrymu; gorthrwm.) To oppress.

GORU (gor). To cause; to accomplish.

GORUCHEL (gor-uchel). Supreme; very high.

GORUWCH (gor-uwch). Above.

GORWAG (gorŵac; gor-gwag). Supremely empty; vain; pompous.

GOSAWD (gosot, gosaŵt; go-sawd). A statute, or ordinance; to place; to appoint; to set upon.

GOSODEDIG (gosodedic; gosawd). Placed; appointed.

GOSODEDIGAETH (gosodedig). A position; an ordinance; a constitution.

GOSTWNG (gestŵg; gos-twng). To lower; to humble; to descend; to become low.

GRADD (grad; L. *gradus*). A step; a degree.

GRAWYS (gra-gwys). Lent.

GRE (rhe). A flock; a herd; a stud, which consisted of fifty mares and a stallion.

GRWNDWAL (grwnd-gwal; S. groundwall). A foundation.

GRWNDWALU (grwndwal). To found.

GRWNDWALWR (grwndwal-gwr). A founder.

GRYMHAU (grym). To avail; to be powerful; to strengthen.

GRYMUS (grym). Powerful; energetic.

GRYMUSDER (grymuster; grymus). Strength; mightiness.

GWADU (gwad). To deny.

GWADD (gŵad; gwa). A mole.

GWAED (gŵaet; gwa-ed). Blood.

GWAEDAWL (gŵaetaŵl; gwaed). Bloody.

GWAERED (gŵaeret; gwaer). The bottom of a descent, or declivity. *I waered;* downward.

GWAEW (gŵayŵ; gwae). Pang, agony; a lance, or spear.

GWAG (gŵac; gwa; L. *vacuum*). Empty.

GWAHANREDAWL (gwahanred). Distinctive; particular.

GWAHARDD (gŵahard; gwa-hardd) To forbid; to prohibit.

GWAHARDDEDIG (gŵahardedic; gwahardd). Forbidden.

GWAHAWDD (gŵahaŵd; gwa-hawdd). To invite.

GWAITH (gŵeith; gwai). Action; work; course, turn, or time.

GWALLT (gwall). The hair of the head.

GWAN (gwa). Weak; faint; poor.

GWANWYN (gwan-gwyn). Spring.

GWAR (gwa-ar). Placid; gentle; mild, or tame.

GWARADWYDDUS (gŵaratŵydus; gwaradwydd). Scandalous; disgraceful.

GWARCHADW (gwar-cadw). To keep; to ward; to look after.

GWARCHAE (gwar-cae). A siege; a hemming in; to hem in; to besiege; to pound.

GWARCHAEDIG (gŵarchaedic; gwarchae). Hemmed in; confined; besieged.

GWARCHEIDWAD (gŵercheitŵad; gwarchadw). A guardian.

GWARTHEG (gŵarthec; gwarth). A medium of exchange; cattle.

GWAS (gwa-as). What is of a smooth or even quality; a youth; a servant.

GWASANAETH (gwasan). Service.

GWASANAETHU (gwasanaeth). To serve.

GWASANAETHWR (gwasanaeth-gwr). A server; a minister.

GWASGARU (gwasgar). To scatter; to disperse.

GWASTAD (gŵastat; gwast). A plain; even; level, continued; constant.

GWASTADTIR (gŵastatir; gwastadtir). Level ground; plain.

GWEDI (gŵedy; gwed). After, later than.

GWEDDI (gŵedi; gwedd). A prayer, a supplication.

GWEDDIAW (gŵediaŵ; gweddi). To pray, to supplicate.

GWEDDU (gŵedu; gwedd). To render orderly; to submit; to yoke; to wed; to become orderly; to befit.

GWEGIL (gwe-cil). The hinder part of the head; the bottom of the back part of the skull.

GWEITHIAW (gŵeithaŵ; gwaith). To work; to labour.

c c

Gweithred (gŵeithret; gwaith). An act.

Gweladwr (gŵelaŵdyr; gwel). A seer, a beholder.

Gweled (gŵelet; gwel). To see, to behold.

Gwelediad (gŵlediat; gweled). A seeing; vision, sight.

Gwely (gwal). A bed, or couch; a family.

Gwell (gwe-ell). Better.

Gwener (gwen). Venus. *Dydd Gwener;* dies Veneris, Friday.

Gweniaith (gŵenyeith; gweniaith). Flattery.

Gwenwynaw (gwenwyn). To poison; to fret; to feel envious.

Gwenwynig (gŵenŵynic; gwenwyn). Poisonous.

Gwers (gwer; *L. versus*). A lesson; a verse.

Gwerth (gwer). Value, worth, price; sale.

Gwerthfawr (gŵerthuaŵr; gwerth=mawr). Precious; valuable.

Gwerthu (gwerth). To sell; to traffic.

Gwewyr (gwew). What is pungent; what causeth pain; a spear.

Gwibiaw (gŵibyaŵ; gwib). To wander; to hover.

Gwin (gŵyn; gw-in; *L. vinum*). Wine.

Gwir (gw-ir; *L. verum*). Truth; true.

Gwirionedd (gŵiryoned; gwiriawn). Verity, truth.

Gwisg (gwise; gw-isg). A garment.

Gwisgaw (gwisg). To dress; to wear.

Gwlad (gŵlat; gw-llad). A country.

Gwladawl (gŵlataŵl; gwlad). Belonging to a country; national.

Gwlaw (gwl-aw). Rain.

Gwlawiawg (gwlaw). Rainy.

Gwledychu (gwledwch). To exercise dominion; to reign.

Gwledd (gŵled; gw-lledd). A banquet.

Gwnaeth (*pret.* of Gwn). Has made; has done.

Gwobr (gŵobr; gobr). A reward; a fee; a bribe.

Gwobrwy (gwobr), A reward.

Gwr (gw-wr; *L. vir*). A being endowed with power, will, or liberty; a man; a husband.

Gwraig (gŵreic; gwr). A woman; a wife.

Gwrandaw (gwr-andaw). To listen, to hearken, to hear.

Gwrawl (gwr). Manly; valiant.

Gwrda (gwr-da). A man of quality; a gentleman.

Gwrhau (gwr). To render homage; to be manly.

Gwriogaeth (gŵrogaeth; gwriawg). Homage.

Gwrthallt (gwrth-gallt). A cliff running contrary to another.

Gwrthenau (gŵrthenou; gwrthgenau). Repulsive lips.

Gwrthladd (gŵrthlad; gwrthlladd). To oppugn; to prevent; to drive off.

Gwrthod (gŵrthot; gwrth). To refuse; to object.

Gwrthwyneb (gwrth-wyneb). A contrary face; opposition; contrary; adverse.

GWRTHWYNEBEDD (gŵrthŵnebed; gwrthwyneb). Contrariety; opposition.
GWRTHWYNEBU (gwrthwyneb). To confront; to oppose.
GWRTHWYNEBWR (gwrthwyneb=gwr). An adversary.
GWYBOD (gŵybot; gwydd-bod). Knowledge; to know.
GWYDD (gwyd; gwy-ydd). Trees; shrubs; wood; presence.
GWYDDAW (gŵydaŵ; gwydd). To give knowledge; to know.
GWYDDFA (gŵydua; gwydd-ma). A place of presence; an eminence where Bardic meetings were held; an artificial mound, or tumulus, which served to teach the people from, and also as a sepulchre.
GWYL (gwel; L. vigil). A feast, or festival.
GWYLFA (gwyl-ma). A watching place; a watch.
GWYN (gwy). White; fair; blessed.
GWYNEB (gwyn-eb). A face, aspect, or countenance.
GWYNT (gwyn; L. ventus). Wind.
GWYSTL (gŵystyl; gwyst). A pledge; surety; hostage.
GYD (mutate of CYD). With.
GYRRU (gyr). To drive; to enforce; to send.

H.

HAEDDU (haedu; haedd). To deserve.
HAEL (hy-ael). Generous, liberal.
HAELIONI (haelyoni; haelion). Generosity, liberality.
HAF (ha). What spreads out; summer.
HAFOD (hafot; haf-bod). A summer dwelling; a dairy.
HAIACH (hayach; hai). An instant; instantly; almost.
HAIARN (hayarn; hai-arn). Iron.
HAINT (heint; hain). A disease, sickness; pestilence.
HANNER (han-der). A half, a moiety; half.
HANU (han). To proceed from, to emanate.
HAUL (heul; ha-ul). The sun.
HAWDD (haŵd; hy-awdd). Feasible, easy.
HEB (hy-eb). Without.
HEBOG (hebauc; heb). A hawk.
HEBRWNG (hebrŵg; heb-rhwng). To go with; to conduct; to accompany; to send onward.
HEDDWCH (hedŵch; hedd). Peace.
HEDDYCHAWL (hedychaŵl; heddwch). Peaceable.
HEDDYCHU (hedychu; heddwch). To make peace; to pacify.
HEDDYCHWR (hedychŵr; heddwch=gwr). A peacemaker, a pacifier.
HEDDYW (hedyŵ; hedd). To day.
HEFYD (heuyt; haf). Also, likewise.
HELA (hel). To gather; to hunt.
HELAETH (hel). Extensive, abundant.
HELAETHRWYDD (helaethrŵyd; helaeth). Extensiveness, abundance.
HELFA (helua; hel). A collected heap; a hunt.

HEN (hy-en; L. *senex.*) Age; aged, old.
HENAFGWR (henaf-gwr). The eldest man, the chief man; an elder.
HENAFIAD (henafyat; henaf). Ancestor; elder.
HENAINT (henain). Old age.
HENDAD (hendat; hen-tad). A grandfather.
HEOL (he-ol). A course; a street; a road.
HERWYDD (herbyd; her-gwydd). Because, for, with respect to; according to; by, with.
HI. She.
HINDDA (hinda; hin-da). Fair or calm weather.
HINON (hin). Serene weather, a clear atmosphere; the weather, the atmosphere.
HIR (hy-ir). Long; prolix; dilatory.
HIRGARCHAR (hir-carchar). Long imprisoned.
HIRMAWR (hir-mawr). Long and great.
HOEDL (hoedel; hoed). Life, the duration of life.
HOLL (oll). All, the whole of.
HOLLTI (hollt). To split.
HON (hy-on). This, *fem.*
HONOF, HONOT, HONAW, HONEI (honi), HONOM, HONOCH, HONYNT; following the preposition O. of. Me, thee, him, her, us, you, them.
HONNO (*fem.* of HWNNW). That one.
HUAWDR (huodr, huabdyr; huawdr). A guide; affable; eloquent.

HUN (hy-un). Self, the same person.
HURIAW (huryab; hur). To hire; to take hire.
HWN (hy-wn). This one, *mas.*
HWNNW (hwn). That one.
HWY (by; hy-wy). They; them.
HWYL (hwy). A course; order; progress; a sail.
HWYLIAW (hwylab; hwyl). To direct; to progress; to sail.
HWYNT (bynt)=Hwy.
HWYNTAU (bynteu; hwynt). They likewise; them also.
HWYRHAU (hwyr). To become late; to delay.
HYD (hyt; hy-yd). Length; as far as; until.
HYDER (hy). Confidence; trust.
HYFRWYDD (hyurbyd; hyf-rhwydd). Unimpeded.
HYFRYD (hyfryt; hy-bryd). Having the mind at liberty; happy; cheerful; delightful.
HYFRYDHAU (hyfrytau; hyfryd). To delight; to cheer.
HYGAR (hegar; hy-car). Amiable, lovely; pleasing.
HYN. This.
HYNAF (hyn). Ancestor; an elder, a senator.
HYNAWS (hy-naws). Good natured; kind; gentle.
HYNAWSDER (hynabster; hynaws). Good nature; gentleness.
HYNNY (hyn). That.
HYNT (hwnt). A way; a career; a journey.
HYOLDER (huolder; hyawl). Boldness; bravery.
HYRWYDD (hyrbyd; hy-rhwydd)= Hyfrwydd.

I.

I. I.
I. To.
IACH (ia-ach). Sane, sound, healthy; unhurt.
IAR (i-ar). From off; off the top; off.
IARLL (iar). An earl; a noble.
IAU (Ieu; au). Jupiter. *Dydd Iau*; dies Jovis, Thursday.
IAWN (awn). Right; satisfaction; just, very.
IDDAW, IDDI, IDDYNT (idaỽ, idi, idynt). To him, her, them.
IECHYD (iechyt; iach). Soundness; health.
IEUANGC (ieuanc; iau-anc). Young.
IEUENCTID (ieuegtit; ieuangc). Youth.
INSEL (inseil; in-sel). A mark, a seal.
IRAD (irat; ir). Pungency; affliction; pungent, grievous, terrible.
Is. Lower; below; inferior to.
IWRCH (wrch). A roebuck.

L.

LEGAT (L. *legatus*). A legate; a cardinal or bishop, whom the pope sends as his ambassador to sovereign princes.

LL.

LLADD (llad; lly-ad). To cut; to slay.
LLADDFA (lladua; lladd). Slaughter.
LLAETH (lly-aeth; L. *lac*.) Milk.
LLAFASU (llauassu; llafas). To venture, to dare.
LLAFUR (llauur; llaf; L. *labor*). Labour; husbandry.
LLAFURIAW (llauuryaỽ; llafur). To labour.
LLAFURUS (llauurus; llafur). Laborious.
LLALL (lly-all). The other.
LLAN (lly-an). An inclosure; a village; a church.
LLANW (llan). Fulness; the flowing in of the tide; the tide.
LLAW (lly-aw). A hand. *Rhag llaw*; henceforth. *Ger llaw*; near, at hand.
LLAWEN (lla-gwen). Merry, joyful.
LLAWENHAU (llawen). To gladden; to rejoice.
LLAWENYDD (llaỽenyd; llawen). Joy; mirth; pleasure.
LLAWER (lla-gwer). Many; a diversity.
LLAWN (lly-awn). Full; complete.
LLAWR (lly-awr). A floor, the ground, the earth.
LLE. A place; where; stead.
LLECHU (llech). To lurk.
LLEDFARW (lletuarỽ; lled-marw). Half dead, partly dead.
LLEDRAD (lledrat; lled-rhad). Stealth, or theft.
LLEF (lly-ef). A voice, a cry.
LLEFAIN (llefein; llef). A loud cry; to cry aloud; to weep.
LLEHAU (lle). To make a place; to place.
LLEIDRYN (lleidr). A petty thief.
LLENWI (llanw). To fill; to become full; to flow, as the tide.

LLESG (llesc; lly-esg). Feeble, faint.
LLETTYAW = LLETTYU (lletty). To lodge.
LLEUAD (lleuat; lleu). The moon.
LLEUFER (lleuuer; lleu-mer). Splendour.
LLEW (lly-ew). A lion.
LLIAWS (lli-aws). A multitude.
LLID (llit; lly-id). Wrath; anger; inflammation.
LLIDIAW (llidyaḃ; llid). To raise anger, to inflame; to be angry, to be enraged; to be inflamed.
LLIDIAWG (llidyaḃc; llid). Wrathful, angry; inflamed.
LLIFAW (lliuaḃ; llif). To flow.
LLIFDDWFR (llifdḃr; llif-dur). A stream of water, a torrent.
LLIFEIRIANT (llifeireint; llifer). A torrent; an inundation.
LLIN (lly-in) A line, a lineage.
LLITHRAW (llithr). To glide away; to slip.
LLITHREDEG (llithredic; llithred). Slippery; gliding.
LLIW (lli). Colour; form.
LLONG (llog; llwng). A ship.
LLONGWR (llogḃr; llong-gwr). A ship-man; a sailor.
LLONYDD (llonyd; llawn). Tranquil, calm.
LLOSGEDIGAETH (llosgedig). A burning, conflagration.
LLOSGFA (llosgua; llosg). A burnt or burning place.
LLOSGI (llosg). To burn; to be burning.
LLU. A throng; an army; a host.

LLUCHEDEN (lluchaden; lluched). A flash of lightning; a fit of fever.
LLUDW (llud). Ashes.
LLUN (llu-un). The moon. *Dydd Llun;* dies Lunæ, Monday.
LLUOSOGRWYDD (lluossogrḃyd; lluosawg). Multitude.
LLURYGAWG (llurugaḃc; lluryg). Wearing a coat of mail, mailed.
LLUSGAW (llusg). To drag, to pull.
LLW. An oath.
LLWYNOGAWL (llwynog). Like a fox, foxy.
LLWYR (llw-yr). Quite, complete. *Yn llwyr;* utterly.
LLYDAN (lly-tan). Broad, wide.
LLYFASU (llyuassu; llyfas). To dare, or to attempt.
LLYFU (llyuu; llyf). To lick with the tongue.
LLYGAD (llygat; llwg). The eye.
LLYGRU (llwgr). To corrupt, to pollute, to spoil.
LLYNGCU (llygku; llwngc). To swallow.
LLYNGES (llyges; llong). A fleet, a navy.
LLYNGHESWR (llygheswr; llynges=gwr). A navigator, a sailor.
LLYMA (lly-ma). Lo here, behold.
LLYS (lly-ys). A court; a palace.
LLYTHYR (llyth-yr; L. *litera.*) A letter.
LLYWIAW (llyḃaḃ; llyw). To guide; to rule, to govern.
LLYWIAWDR (llyḃyaḃdḃr; llywiawd). A director; a ruler.
LLYWODRAETH (llywawdr). Government.

M.

MAB (ma-ab). A boy; a son.
MABAWL (mab). Like a child; filial.
MACH (ma-ach). A bail, a surety.
MADDAU (madeu; madda). To dismiss; to forgive.
MADDEUANT (madeuant; maddau). Forgiveness.
MAEN (ma-en). A stone.
MAES (ma-es). A plain, a field.
MAESDIR (maes-tir). Champaign land.
MAETH (my-aeth). Cherishment; fosterage. *Mab maeth;* foster son.
MAGNEL (maen). A warlike engine, a battering ram.
MAGU (mag). To rear; to breed.
MAI (ma; L. *Maius*). May.
MAIN (mein; my-ain). Slender, thin.
MAINT (meint; main). Magnitude; quantity.
MAL (my-al). Like; as.
MAM (ma-am). A mother.
MAN (my-an). A place, a spot.
MARCH (my-arch). A horse.
MARCHAWG (marchaŵc; march). A horseman, a knight.
MARCHAWGLU (marchaŵclu; marchawg-llu). A mounted host; cavalry.
MARSWR (mars-gwr). Marcher.
MARW (mar). A dead one; dead; to die.
MARWOL (marw). Deadly; mortal.
MARWOLAETH (marwol). Death; mortality.

MAWR (my-awr). Great, large; greatly.
MAWRFRYDIG (maŵrurydic; mawrfryd). Magnanimous.
MAWRFRYDRWYDD (maŵrurydrŵyd; mawrfryd). Magnanimity.
MAWRFRYDUS (maŵrurydus; mawrfryd)=Mawrfrydig.
MAWRHAU (mawr). To magnify.
MAWRTH (mawr; L. *Mars*). March.
MAWRWERTHIAWG (maŵrŵeirthaŵc; mawr-gwerthawg). Of great value.
MEBYD (mebyt; mab). Childhood.
MEDI (med). A reaping; September.
MEDR (medyr; med). Skill; capability.
MEDRU (medr). To be able; to accomplish; to take aim; to hit.
MEDDIANNUS (medyannus; meddiant). Possessive.
MEDDIANT (medyant; medd). Possession; authority.
MEDDWI (medŵi; meddw). To get drunk; to make drunk.
MEDDWL (medŵl; medd). Mind; to think; to intend.
MEDDYLIAW (medylyaŵ; meddwl). = *v.* Meddwl.
MEGYS (meg-ys). As, like as.
MEISTR (meistyr; maist). A master.
MEITHRIN (maeth-trin). To nourish, to rear.
MELIN (mal). A mill.
MELYN (mel). Yellow.
MELLTEN (mellt). A lightening.
MELLDIGEDIG (emelldigedic; melldith. L. *maledictus*). Accursed.
MERCH (my-erch). A woman; a daughter.

MERCHUR (merchyr; march). Mercury. *Dydd Merchur;* dies Mercurii, Wednesday.
MESUR (mes-ur). A measure; a rule; a metre.
MESURAW (mesur). To measure.
MEWN (me-wn). Within, in.
MIL (my-il). A thousand.
MILGI (mil-ci). A grey-hound.
MILLTIR (mil-tir). A mile.
MIS (my-is). A month.
MODRYB (modrup; mod-rhyb). An aunt.
MODD (mod; my-od; L. *modus*). A mode; a form, or fashion.
MOES (my-oes). Civility; manner.
MOETHUS (moeth). Delicate; nice; dainty.
MOLIANNUS (molyannus; moliant). Commendable.
MOLIANRWYDD (molyanrŵyd; moliant). Celebrity; praiseworthiness.
MOLIANT (molyant; mawl). Praise; adoration.
MOR (mo-or). What is boundless; the sea.
MOR (my-or). How, so, as.
MORC. A mark.
MORDON (mor-ton). Sea wave.
MORDWYAW (mordwy). To sail.
MORDWYWR (mordwy-gwr). A sailor.
MORDDWYD (morddŵyt; morddgwyd). A thigh.
MORGRUG (morgruc; mor-crug). Ants.
MORTER (S. *mortar*). Mortar, cement.

MUDAW (mud). To remove; to change an abode.
MUR (mu-ur; L. *murus*). A wall, a rampart.
MWNAI (mwnei; mwn). Money, coin.
MWNWGL (mônŵgyl; mwnwg). The neck.
MWYNWR (mwyn-gwr). A miner.
MYDR (mydyr; myd). A metre.
MYFYR (myuyr; myr). Contemplation; contemplative.
MYNACH (manach; mwn; L. *monachus*). A monk.
MYNACHLOG (manachloc; mynachllog). A monastery.
MYNED (mwn-ed). To go; to depart.
MYNEGI (menegi; mynag). To express, to tell.
MYNU (myn). To exercise the will; to seek; to insist; to will; to obtain.
MYNWENT (mynw; L. *monumentum*). A sepulchre; a churchyard.
MYNYCH (mwn). Frequent.
MYNYCHU (mynych). To frequent.
MYNYDD (mynyd; mwn). A mountain.

N.

NA=NAC. The former being used before consonant initials, the latter before vowel initials. Nor; neither; either.
NAD (na). A conditional negative. That; that not.
NADOLIG (L. *natalis*). Christmas; the Nativity.

NAI (nei ; na). A nephew.
NAMYN (nam). Except; but.
NANT (nan). A hollow formed by water ; a ravine ; a brook.
NAW (ny-aw). Nine.
NAWCANT (naw-cant). Nine hundred.
NAWDD (nawd ; naw). Refuge ; patronage ; privilege.
NAWFED (naḃet; naw-med). Ninth.
NEGES (neg-es). An errand ; business.
NEIDIAW (neidyaḃ ; naid). To leap.
NEILLDU (naill-tu.) One of two sides ; one side.
NERTH (ner). Might ; strength ; aid.
NERTHOCCAU (nerthockau ; nerthawg). To strengthen.
NERTHU (nerth). To strengthen.
NESAF (nes). Nearest.
NEWID (new). A change; cheapness.
NEWYDD (neḃyd ; new). New.
NEWYDDER (neḃyder ; newydd). Newness.
NEWYN (ne-gwyn). Hunger ; famine.
NID (nyt ; ny-id). Not.
NIFER (niuer ; nif). A number ; a host.
NITH (ny-ith). A niece.
NIWLIAWG (nyḃlaḃc; niwl). Misty.
No=Noc ; the former being used before consonant initials, the latter before vowel initials. Than.
NODDFA (nodua ; nawdd-ma). A place of refuge; a sanctuary.
NOETH (ny-oeth). Naked.

Nos (ny-os). Night.
NOSAWL (nos). Nightly ; nocturnal.
NOSWAITH (nosḃeith ; nos-gwaith). A certain night.
NOSWYL (nos-gwyl). Eve; a vigil.
NOTAEDIG (notaedic; nawd). Usual; accustomed.
NOVENNALIS. See DECEM.
NYCHA (nachaf ; na-ycha). Behold ! lo !
NYCHDAWD (nychdaḃt ; nych). A lingering disorder ; a pining away ; a consumption.

O.

O. From ; of, out of ; by.
ODDIYNA (odyna ; oddi-yna). From there ; from thence.
ODDIYNO (odyno; oddi-yno). From there ; from thence—speaking of a distant place or time.
OED (oet ; o-ed). Age ; a delay ; a day of assignation.
OEDRAN (oetran ; oed). Age.
OES (o-es). A period of time ; an age ; life.
OFER (of-er). Vain; useless.
OFN (ofyn ; of-yn). Fear, or dread.
OFNAWG (ofnaḃc ; ofn). Timid ; fearful.
OFNHAU (ofynhau; ofn). To become fearful; to render fearful.
OFFEIRIAD (offeirat ; offer). A priest.
OFFEREN (offeren; offer). Mass.
OFFRYMU (offrymaḃ ; offrwm). To offer; to sacrifice.
OL. A mark, trace ; the rear.

OLEW (ol-ew; L. *oleum*). Oil.
OLL. All; the whole of.
ONEN (on). An ash tree.

P.

PA. What; which.
PAB (pa-ab; L. *papa*). A father; the pope.
PABELL (pab-ell). A tent.
PAE (S. *pay*). A pay; wage.
PAGAN (L. *paganus*). A pagan.
PALADR (paladyr; palad). A ray; a shaft; a pole.
PALI (pal). Satin; velvet.
PALLU (pall). To fail; to cease; to perish.
PAN (pa-yn). When; whence; since; for which cause.
PARAWD (parabt; par). Ready; prepared.
PAROTTOI (parawd). To prepare.
PARTH (par). A part; a division; a division; a region.
PARTHRED (parthret; parth). Distinction; a side; a party.
PASG (pasc; H. פסח). The passover, Easter.
PE. If.
PEBYLLIAW (pabell). To pitch tents.
PEBYLLU=Pebyllaw.
PECHAWD (pechabt; pech; L. *peccatum*.) Sin.
PEDWAR (petbar; ped-gwar). Four.
PEDWARGWR (petwargbr; pedwar=gwr). Four men.
PEDWERYDD (petberyd; pedwar). Fourth.

PEDYD (pedyt; ped; L. *pedes*). The foot; the infantry.
PEIDIAW (peidyab; paid). To cease, to desist.
PEIRIANT (par). An instrument, or tool.
PELL (py-ell). An extreme limit; far.
PEN (py-en). An extremity, end; the head; a chief; a summit; supreme.
PENADUR (penad). A sovereign.
PENAETH (pen). A chieftain.
PENAFDUR (penaf). Chief-officer.
PENCYNGHORWR (penkyghorbr; pen-cynghorwr). Chief counsellor.
PENGOCH (pen-coch). Red-headed.
PENGRYCH (pen-crych.) Rough-headed; curly-headed.
PENLLONGWR (penllogbr; pen=llong-gwr). Head sailor; captain of a ship.
PENYD (penyt; pan). Penance.
PERERIN (per-er). A pilgrim.
PERERINDAWD (pererindabt; pererin). Pilgrimage.
PERERINIAW (pererinab; pererin), To go on a pilgrimage.
PERFEDD (perued; per-medd). The middle region; the bowels.
PERFFAITH (perffeith; per-ffaith; L. *perfectus*). Perfect.
PERI (par). To cause; to bid.
PERLLAN (per-llan). An orchard.
PERSON (per-son; L. *persona*). A person.
PERTH (py-erth). A thorn bush.
PERYGL (perigl; perig; L. *periculum*). Peril, danger.

PERYGLU (periglu; peryg). To endanger; to become dangerous.
PETH (py-eth). A thing.
PEUNYDD (peunyd; pae-dydd). Daily, every day.
PIAU (pieu; pi). To own, to possess.
PIEUFOD (pieuot; piau-bod). To be possessed of.
PLA (py-lla). A plague.
PLANT (plan). Children.
PLITH (py-llith). The state of being blended or amongst.
PLWYF (plwy; L. *plebs*). A complete body of people; a parish; a diocese.
POB (po). Each, every.
POBL (pobyl; pawb). A people.
PONT (pon). A bridge.
PORFA (porua; pawr-ma). Pasture.
PORPHORAWL (porfforol; porphor). Purple.
PORTH (por). Support; provision; a passage; a porch, or gateway; a ferry.
PORTHAWR (porth). A porter.
PORTHFA (porthua; porth-ma). A port, a harbour.
PORTHI (porth). To aid; to provide with food.
PORTHMON (porth-mon). A dealer in provisions; a drover; a porter.
PORTHWR (porth-gwr). A supporter; a porter; a provisioner; a ferry-man.
PRAFF (pra). Large, thick.
PRELAD (prelat). A prelate, a bishop.
PREN (pre). A tree.
PRESWYLIAW (preswyl). To dwell, to reside.

PRIAWD (priaöt; pri). Peculiar, proper; a married person.
PRIF (pri). The first day of the new moon; the golden number; prime; principal.
PRIODAWL (priawd). Appropriate; peculiar; legitimate; married.
PRIODI (priawd). To marry.
PRIODOLDER (priodawl). Appropriateness; property; the right or title to a thing.
PROFEDIG (prouedic; prawf). Proved, approved.
PROFI (prawf). To prove; to try.
PROPHWYDAW (proffőydaő; prophwyd). To prophesy.
PROPHWYDOLIAETH (proffőytolyaeth; prophwydawl). A prophecy.
PRUDDEDD (pruded; prudd). Discreetness; sadness.
PRYD (pryt). Time; the favour of the countenance; an aspect; also comeliness, beauty.
PRYDER (prw). Anxiety, solicitude.
PRYDERU (pryder). To be anxious; to consider.
PRYDNAWN (prytnaön; pryd-nawn). Afternoon.
PRYDYDD (prydyd; pryd). A poet.
PRYF (pry). A worm; a vermin.
PRYNU (pryn). To buy; to redeem.
PUMED (pumet; pump-med). Fifth.
PUMP (pum). Five.
PUNT (pun). A pound.
PWY (pw). Who, what.
PWYTH (pwy-yth). A point; a retaliation.
PY. What, which.

PYLGAIN (pylgein; pwl-cain). The morning twilight; matins.
PYMTHEG (pymthec; pump-deg). Fifteen.
PYMTHEGFED (pymthecuet; pymtheg-med). Fifteenth.
PYNAG (pynac; py nag). Soever.
PYSGAWD (pyscaƿt; pysg). Fish.
PYTHEFNOS (pytheƿnos; pymtheg=nos). A fortnight.

R.

RHAD (rat; rha-ad). Grace, favour; a blessing; free; gratuitous; cheap.
RHAG (rac). A front; a van; before; from; for; lest.
RHAGAWD (ragot; rhag). To go before; to prevent; to go against; to stop, to hinder.
RHAGDDYWEDYD (racdyƿedyt; rhag-dywedyd). To predict.
RHAGFLAENU (raculaenu; rhagflaen). To anticipate.
RHAGFYR (racuyr; rhag-byr). December.
RHAGORI (ragori; rhagor). To surpass, to excel.
RHAGWELEDIGAETH (racƿeledigaeth; rhagweled). Foresight; providence.
RHAI (rei; rha). Some.
RHAID (reit; rha-id). Necessity; it is necessary.
RHAN (ran; rha). A part; division.
RHANU (ranu; rhan). To part, to divide; to distribute.
RHAWN (raƿn; rhy-awn). The hair of a horse's tail.

RHEDEG (redec; rhed). To run.
RHEOLWR (rcolƿr; rheol). A ruler.
RHIENI (rieni; rhiant). Parents.
RHIF (rif; rhi-if). A number.
RHINWEDD (rinƿed; rhin). Virtue; a sacrament.
RHODD (rod; rho). A gift.
RHODDI (rodi; rhodd). To give.
RHUTHR (ruthyr; rhuth). A rush; an assault.
RHUTHRAW (ruthraƿ; rhuthr). To rush; to attack.
RHWNG (rƿg; rhy-wng). Between.
RHWYMEDIG (rƿymedic; rhwym). Bound, obliged.
RHY. Excess; excessively. Also a verbal particle.
RHYD (ryt; rhy-yd). A passage; a ford.
RHYDD (ryd; rhy-ydd). Free.
RHYDDHAU (rydau; rhydd). To free, to set at liberty.
RHYDDID (rydit; rhydd). Liberty; immunity; licence.
RHYFEDD (ryued; rhy-medd). Wonderful, strange.
RHYFEDDU (ryuedu; rhyfedd). To wonder.
RHYFEL (ryuel; rhy-bel). War, or warfare.
RHYFELA (ryuela; rhyfel). To war, to wage war.
RHYFELWR (ryuelƿr; rhyfel-gwr). A warrior.
RHYFYGU (ryuygu; rhyfyg). To presume; to act arrogantly.
RHYNGU (rygu, regi; rhwng). To intervene; to content.
RHYW (ryƿ; rhy-yw). A kind; a sex; some.

S.

SADWRN (sad-gwrn; L. *Saturnus*). Saturn. *Dydd Sadwrn;* dies Saturni, Saturday.
SAETH (sa-aeth). An arrow.
SAETHYDD (saethyd; saeth). An archer.
SAITH (seith; sa-ith). Seven.
SANT (san; L. *sanctus*). A saint.
SANTEIDDRWYDD (sancteidrŵyd; santaidd). Holiness.
SARHAD (saraat; sarhau). An insult; a reproach.
SARHAU (sar). To insult; to affront.
SATHRU (sathr). To tread; to trample.
SATHRWR (sathr-gwr). A treader; a trampler.
SEFYLL (seuyll; saf). A standing; to stand.
SEGUR (cur; L. *securus*). Void of trouble; idle.
SEILIAW (sail). To found; to lay a foundation.
SEITHFED (seithuet; saith-med). Seventh.
SENEDD (señed; sen; L. *senatus*). A senate; a synod.
SENESGAL (synyscal). A seneschal.
SENTENS (L. *sententia*). A sentence.
SEREN (ser). A star.
SIART (siartyr; L. *charta*). A charter.
SOR (sy-or). Sullenness; sullen.
SORI (sor). To chafe; to displease; to become displeased; to grow sullen.
SUL (su-ul; L. *sol*). The sun. *Dydd Sul;* dies Solis, Sunday.

SULGWYN (sul-gwyn). Whitsunday.
SWLLT (swll). A shilling; money; treasure.
SWM (sŵmp; sw-wm.) A sum.
SWMER (swm). A sumpter horse.
SWYDD (sŵyd; swy). Office; shire.
SWYDDAWG (sŵydaŵc; swydd). An officer.
SYBERW (syber). Stately; courteous; haughty; elegant.
SYCHDWR (sych). Drought.
SYMMUD (sy-mud). To move; to remove.
SYMMUDAW = Symmud.
SYNWYR (syn-gwyr). Sense.
SYRTHIAW (syrthyaŵ; syrth). To fall.

T.

TACHWEDD (tachŵed; tach-gwedd). November.
TAD (tat; ta-ad). A father.
TADAWL (tad). Fatherly.
TADMAETH (tad-maeth). A foster father.
TAFAWD (tauaŵt; taf). A tongue.
TAGEDIG (tagedic; tag). Strangled, choked.
TAGU (tag). To strangle, to choke.
TANGNEFEDD (tagneued; tangnef). Celestial tranquillity; peace.
TANGNEFEDDUS (tagneuedus). Tranquil.
TAIR (ta-ir). Three, *of the feminine gender.*
TAL (ta-al). Pay; reward.
TALM (talym; tal). A while.
TALU (tal). To pay; to reward; to be worth.
TAN (ta-an). A fire.

TARAN (tar). A thunder.
TARAW (tar). To strike.
TARIAN (tar). A shield.
TEBYGU (tebyg). To render similar; to compare; to presume; to conjecture.
TEG (tec; te-eg). Fair; beautiful.
TEGWCH (teg). Fairness; beauty; fine weather.
TEILWNG (teilôg; tal-wng). Worthy; merited.
TEILYNGDAWD (teilygdaôt; teilwng). Merit, worthiness.
TEIRMIL (tair-mil). Three thousand.
TEIRNOS (tair-nos). Three nights.
TELYNAWR (telyn). A harpist.
TEML (temyl; tem; L. *templum*). A temple.
TERFYN (teruyn; terf; L. *terminus*). An extremity; a limit.
TERFYNEDIG (teruynedic; terfyn). Limited; ended.
TERFYNU (teruynu; terfyn). To determine, to end.
TERFYNWR (teruynôr; terfyn-gwr). One who concludes; a boundary man.
TERFYSG (teruysc; ter-mysg). Confusion; tumult.
TERFYSGU (teruyscu; terfysg). To raise a tumult; to become tumultuous.
TERFYSGUS (teruysgus; terfysg). Tumultuous.
TERWYN (ter-gwyn). Ardent; strong.
TESAWG (tesaôc; tes). Sunny; hot.
TEULU (tau-llu). A family; a clan.

TEYRNAS (teyrn). A kingdom.
TEYRNGED (teyrnget; teyrn-ced). A tribute.
TIR (ty-ir). Land; earth.
TLAWD (tlaôt; tylawd). Poor.
TON (*fem.* of TWN). A wave.
TORF (toryf, torof; tor). A crowd; a multitude; a host.
TORRI (tor). To break; to cut; to become broken.
TRA (ty-rha). Beyond; whilst.
TRACHEFN (tracheuyn; tra-cefn). Behind the back; again.
TRAETH (tra-eth; L. *tractus*). A tract; shore, strand.
TRAETHU (traeth). To treat, to relate.
TRAGYWYDDAWL (tragyôydaôl; tragywydd). Eternal.
TRAHAUS (traha). Arrogant; haughty.
TRAIAN (traean; tri). The third part.
TRAIS (treis; tra-is). Violence; oppression.
TRAMOR (tra-mor). Transmarine; foreign.
TRANOETH (tra-noeth). The day after; the next morning.
TRASYCHED (tra-syched). Extreme drought.
TRAUL (treul; tra-ul). Waste; expense, charge, or disbursement.
TRAWS (tra). Adverse; cross.
TRECH (tre-ech). Of superior power.
TREF (tre). A dwelling place; a homestead; a township; a town.

TREFTAD (tref-tad). Patrimony; heritage.
TREILLIAW (traill). To turn; to roll; to traverse; to dredge.
TREMYG (tremyc; tram). Contempt; disparagement.
TREMYGU (tremyg). To contemn; to slight.
TRETH (tre-eth). Rate, or tax; tribute.
TREULGWAITH (treilgŵeith; traulgwaith). A certain day.
TRI (ty-rhi). Three.
TRICHANT (trychant; tri-cant). Three hundred.
TRIDIAU (tridieu; tri-diau). Three days.
TRIGAW (trig). To stay; to tarry; to starve.
TRIST (ty-rhist; L. *tristis*). Sad; sorrowful.
TRISTHAU (trist). To become sad; to sadden.
TRISTYD (tristyt; trist). Sadness, or sorrow.
TROED (troet; tro). A foot.
TROEDNOETH (troed-noeth). Barefooted.
TROS (tro-os). Over; for; instead of.
TROSI (tros). To turn out; to send over; to move onward.
TROTHWY (troth). A threshold.
TRUAN (tru). Wretched, miserable.
TRUENI (truan). Misery.
TRUGAIN (trugein; tri-ugain). Sixty.
TRUGARAWG (trugar). Merciful.
TRUGAREDD (trugared; trugar). Mercy.
TRUGARHAU (trugar). To be merciful, to commiserate.

TRWY (trw). Through; by.
TRYCHU (trwch). To cut; to lop.
TRYDYDD (trydyd; tryd-ydd). Third.
TU. A side, a part.
TWLL (tw-wll). A hole, a pit.
TWNG (tŵg; ty-wng). A plight, an oath; a pledge of homage; a yearly acknowledgment due to the lord of the soil, according to the Welsh laws. Also a certain ration of corn due from the tenant to the landlord.
TWR (tw-wr). A heap; a tower.
TWYLL (twy). Deceit, fraud.
TWYLLAW (twyll). To deceive; to cheat.
TWYLLODRUS (twyllawdr). Deceitful; fraudulent; crafty.
TY. A house.
TYBIAW (tybyaŵ; tyb). To suppose.
TYCIAW (twg). To prosper, to succeed.
TYFU (twf). To grow; to cause to grow.
TYNGEDFEN (tyghetuen; tyngedmen). Fate, destiny.
TYNGU (tygu; twng). To swear, to adjure.
TYLWYTH (ty-llwyth). A household, a family; a tribe.
TYMHESTL (tymhestyl; tymhest; L. *tempestas*). A storm, a tempest.
TYMHESTLAWL (tymhestl). Stormy, tempestuous.
TYNNU (tyn). To pull; to draw.
TYSTIOLAETH (tystyolaeth; tystiawl). Testimony.
TYWOD (tyŵaŵt; tyw). Sand.
TYWYSAWG (tyŵyssaŵc; tywys). A prince, a leader.

U.

Uch (ych). Higher.
Uchelder (uchel). Loftiness, height.
Uchelwr (uchel-gwr). A gentleman; a freeholder.
Uchod (uchot; uch). Above.
Ufudd (ufud; uf-ydd). Humble, obedient.
Ufuddhau (ufudhau; ufudd). To obey.
Ugain (ugein; ug). Twenty.
Ugaint (ugeint) = Ugain.
Ugeinfed (ugain-med). Twentieth.
Un. One.
Unfed (unuet; un-med). First.
Uniawn (un-iawn). Right; just.
Unweddun) ŵed; un-gwedd). Similar; alike.
Urddaw (urdaŵ; urdd). To ordain; to graduate.
Urddasawg (urdassaŵc; urddas). A dignitary.
Urddawl (urdaŵl; urdd). Dignified; honourable.

W.

Wedi (wedy; gwedi). After; afterwards.
Wrth (wr). Close to; by; with; compared with; while.
Wylaw (wyl). To wail, to weep.
Wylofus (wylof). Wailing; doleful.
Wyneb (wyn-eb). A face.
Wyr (wy-yr). A grandson.
Wyth (wy ŷth). Eight.
Wythfed (wyth-med). Eighth.
Wythnos (wyth-nos). A week.

Y.

Y. The, being used before consonant initials. It is also a verbal particle.
Ych. An ox.
Ychydig (ychydic; cyd). A little; a few.
Yd. A verbal particle, answering to *it, that, doth*.
Yd. Corn.
Ymadaw (gadaw). To depart; mutually to leave.
Ymadrawdd (ymadraŵd; adrawdd). Discourse; a sentence.
Ymadroddwr (ymadrodŵr; ymadrawdd-gwr). A discourser.
Ymaith (ymeith; maith). Hence, away.
Ymarfaethu (ymaruaethu; ymarfaeth). To form a design.
Ymarfoll (ymaruoll; arfoll). To receive one another; to confederate.
Ymarfolli = Ymarfoll.
Ymbarottoi (parottoi). To prepare one's self.
Ymborth (porth). Sustenance, support.
Ymchwelyd (ymchwel). To return.
Ymdaith (ymdeith; taith). A journey.
Ymddangos (ymdagos; dangos). To appear.
Ymddiddan (ymdidan; diddan). To converse.
Ymddifad (ymdiuat; difad). Destitute; fatherless or motherless.
Ymddiffyn (ymdiffyn; diffyn). A defence; to defend, to protect.

YMDDIRIED (ymdiret; diried). Mutual dependence; confidence; to trust.

YMDDIRIEDUS (ymdiredus; ymddiried). Confiding.

YMDDYRCHAFAEL (ymdyrchauael; dyrchafael). A self-exalting; to exalt one's self; to exalt mutually.

YMENYN (ymen). Butter.

YMERBYNU (erbynu). To be in opposition; to receive mutually.

YMGADW (cadw). To keep one's self; to refrain, to forbear.

YMGERYDDU (ymgerydu; ymgerydd). To self rebuke; to reprehend mutually.

YMGREDU (ymgred). To enter into mutual belief; to give mutual pledge.

YMGUDDIAW (ymgudyaƕ; ymgudd). To hide one's self; to hide mutually.

YMGYDYMDEITHOCCAU (ymgedymdeithockau; ymgydymaith). To accompany, to participate.

YMGYFARFOD (ymgyuaruot; cyfarfod). To meet.

YMGYFEILLIAW (ymgyueillaƕ; ymgyfaill). To enter into friendship.

YMGYFFREDINAW (ymgyffredin). To intercommunicate.

YMGYNGHORI (ymgyghori; cynghori). To consult mutually; to consult one's self.

YMGYMDEITHIAW(ymgedymdeithaƕ; ymgydymaeth). To associate.

YMGYNNAL (cynnal). Self support; to support one's self.

YMLADD (ymlad; lladd). A battle; to fight.

YMLADDGAR (ymladgar; ymladd=car). Addicted to fighting; pugnacious.

YMLADDWR (ymladƯr; ymladd-gwr). A fighter.

YMLID (ymlit; llid). A pursuit; to pursue.

YMLIW (lliw). A reproach; to reproach, to find fault, to expostulate.

YMLYNU (glynu). To cling; to adhere.

YMOSGRYN (ymoscryn; gosgryn). To concuss mutually; to give a shock.

YMOSGRYNU=Ymosgryn.

YMPRYD (ympryt; pryd). A fast.

YMPRYDIAW (ymprydyaƕ; ympryd). To fast.

YMRODDI (ymrodi; rhoddi). To resign one's self; to surrender.

YMRWYMAW (rhwymaw). To bind one's self, to engage.

YMRYDDHAU (ymrydhau; rhyddhau). To liberate one's self.

YMRYSON (rhyson). Mutual dispute; contention; to dispute.

YMSAETHU (saethu). To shoot mutually.

YMWELED (ymƕelet; gweled). A visitation; to visit.

YMWISGAW (gwisgaw). To dress one's self.

YMWNEUD (ymƲneut; gwneud). To have to do; to interfere.

YMWRTHLADD (ymƲrthlad; gwrthladd). Self opposition; to oppose one's self.

YMWRTHOD (ymƲrthot; gwrthod). To renounce.

D D

YMYL (byl). Side; a margin; a brim.
YN. In, at; in the way of; for, for the use of; into.
YNA (yn-a). There; then.
YNFYD (ynuyt; yn-myd). A fool; foolish.
YNNI (wn). Energy; vigour.
YNTAU (ynteu; wn-tau). Him also.
YNYS (wn-ys). An island.
YR. The. Used before vowel initials.
YSBYTTY (ysbyd-ty; L. *hospitium*). A hospital.
YSGLYFAETH (ysclyuaeth; ysglyf). Depredation.
YSGOL (col). A ladder; a school.
YSGOLHAIG (ysgolheic; ysgol). A scholar.
YSGRIFENEDIG (yscriuenedic; ys-grifen). Written.
YSGRIN (ys-crin). A shrine.
YSGRUBL (yscrybyl; crubl). A beast.
YSGUBAWR (yscubaẃr; ysgub). A barn.
YSGYMMUN (ys-cymmun). Excommunicate; accursed.
YSGYMMUNDAWD (yscymundaẃt; ysgymmun). Excommunication.
YSGYNU (ysgyn). To ascend, to mount.

YSIGAW (ysig). To bruise.
YSPAIL (yspeil; ys-pail; L. *spolium*). A spoil, or prey.
YSPEILIAW (yspeilaẃ; yspail). To spoil; to ravage.
YSPIWR (yspio-gwr). A spy.
YSPRYD (yspryt; ys-pryd; L. *spiritus*). A spirit, a ghost.
YSPRYDAWL (ysprytaẃl; yspryd). Spiritual.
YSTAFELL (ystauell; ystaf). A chamber, a room.
YSTAWL (tawl). A stool.
YSTERLING (ysterlig; S. *sterling*). Sterling.
YSTIWARD (ystiẃart; S. *steward*). A steward.
YSTIWARDAETH (ystiẃerdaeth; ystiward). Stewardship.
YSTLYS (ystyl). A side, a flank.
YSTONDARD (S. *standard*). A standard.
YSTORIA (ystorya; ysdawr; L. *historia*). A story, history.
YSTORIAW (ystor). To store, to treasure up.
YSTRAD (ystrat; ys-trad). A flat, a vale formed by the course of a river.
YSTRYW (ys-tryw). Subtilty; stratagem; a trick.
YSTWYLL (ys-twyll). Epiphany.

INDEX.

INDEX.

A.

[*The references are to the Welsh pages only.*]

Aber, dame Joan, daughter of king John, and wife of Llywelyn, son of Iorwerth, dies at the court of, 324.
David, son of Llywelyn, dies at, 332.
Aberavan, the castle of, burnt by Maredudd and Rhys, sons of Gruffudd, 182.
Aber Cavwy, Bledri, son of Cedivor, appointed to keep the castle of Robert the Crookhanded at, 126.
Aberconway, Gruffudd, son of Cynan, son of Owain, dies at, after taking the religious habit, 254.
Llywelyn, son of Iorwerth, insulted by king John's men in the new castle of, 270.
Howel, son of Gruffudd, son of Cynan, dies and is buried at, 294.
Llywelyn, son of Maelgwn, buried at, 318.
Llywelyn, son of Iorwerth, buried at, 326.
David, son of Llywelyn, buried at, 332.
the abbot of, obtains permission of king Henry to have the body of Gruffudd, son of Llywelyn, 334.
the body of Gruffudd, son of Llywelyn, conveyed to, 334.
Aber Corran, Rhys, son of Gruffudd, takes possession of the castle of, 234.

Aberdaron, Gruffudd, son of Rhys, flies for sanctuary to the church of, 122.
Aber Dyvi, (or Aberdovey,) Cadwgan and Owain flee to a ship at, 68.
Owain and Cadwalader, sons of Gruffudd, son of Cynan, with confederate princes, draw up their troops at, 158.
Rhys, son of Gruffudd, comes to, with an army, to give battle to Owain Gwynedd, 184.
Roger, earl of Clare, stores the castle of, 190.
partition of land at, between Maelgwn, son of Rhys, and Rhys the Hoarse and others, 288.
Abereinion, the castle of, constructed by Maelgwn, son of Rhys, 262.
Aberfraw, devastated, 24.
Abergavenny, the castle of, obtained through treachery by Seisyll and others from the men of king Henry II., 218.
Seisyll, son of Dyvnwai, slain in the castle of, through treachery of the lord of Brecheiniog, 226.
the castle of, taken by Robert de Bruse, 282.
reduced by Rickert Marshall and Owain, son of Gruffudd, 320.
Abergeleu, Ionathal, prince of, dies, 12.
Aber Gwyli, battle of, between Llywelyn, son of Seisyll, and Rein the Scot; the latter defeated, 36.
Aberhodni, Trahaiarn the Little, of Brecheiniog, is killed at, 250.
taken by Giles de Bruse, 282.

Aberhodni—*cont.*
  attacked by Llywelyn, son of Iorwerth, 298.
  the men of, make peace with Llywelyn, 300.
  burnt by Llywelyn, son of Iorwerth, 318.
  Llywelyn, son of Iorwerth, fights against the castle of, 320.
Aber Llech, the French cut off at, by the sons of Idnerth, son of Cadwgan, 58.
Aber Lliennog, the French encamp and build a castle at, 60.
Aberllychwr, the castle of, burnt by Maredudd and Rhys, sons of Gruffudd, son of Rhys, 180.
Abermenai, Cadwalader, son of Gruffudd, lands at, defending himself against his brother Owain, 164.
  Madog, prince of Powys, comes in ships to, 186.
Aber Miwl, the barn of, burnt by John Strange, on account of a great slaughter which had taken place in it, 350.
Aber Mynyw, burnt by Rickert Marshall and Owain, son of Gruffudd, 320.
Aber Nedd and Aberdovey, the French from between, oppose Owain and Cadwalader, sons of Gruffudd, with their confederates, 158.
Aber Rheidiol, the castle of, dismantled and burnt by Rhys, son of Gruffudd, 198.
Aberrhiw, divided between Owain, son of Cadwgan, and Maredudd, son of Bleddyn, 112.
Abertawy, a castle near to, attacked by Gruffudd, son of Rhys, belonging to Henry Beaumont, 122.
  the castle of, repaired by John de Bruse, 310.
Aberteivi, ravaged by Howel and Cynan, sons of Owain, 166.
  the walls and the castle of, attacked by Rhys, son of Gruffudd, 202.
  the castle of, rebuilt by Rhys, son of Gruffudd, 212.

Aberteivi—*cont.*
  grand festival held in the castle of, by Rhys, son of Gruffudd, 228.
  taken by Maelgwn, son of Rhys, 252.
  Maelgwn, son of Rhys, swears to deliver the castle of, to Gruffudd, his brother, 254.
  is sold by Maelgwn, son of Rhys, to the English, 254.
  the castle of, subjugated by Llywelyn, son of Iorwerth, and his allies, 288.
  the castle of, allotted to young Rhys and Owain, sons of Gruffudd, son of Rhys, 290.
  put under the custody of Llywelyn, son of Iorwerth, 304.
  relinquished by Llywelyn, son of Iorwerth, in favour of young Rhys, 308.
  the castle of, delivered up to William Marshall, 312.
  burnt by Maelgwn, son of Maelgwn, 318.
  the burgesses of, slain, 318.
  the bridge of, broken down, 318.
  the English send Walter Marshall to fortify, 328.
Aber Torran, the castle of, destroyed by Llywelyn, son of Gruffudd, 344.
Aber Tywi, battle of, between Howel, son of Edwin, and Gruffudd, son of Llywelyn; the latter victorious, 40.
Aberystwyth, expedition of Gruffudd, son of Rhys, against the castle of, 130.
  the castle of, burnt by Owain and Cadwalader, sons of Gruffudd, son of Cynan, 158.
  a castle at, belonging to Cadwalader, son of Gruffudd, burnt by Howel, son of Owain, 164.
  the town and castle of, subjugated by Maelgwn, son of Rhys, son of Gruffudd, 250.
  abundance of fish at, 262.
  burnt by Maelgwn, son of Rhys, 262.
  repaired by Llywelyn, son of Iorwerth, 262.

INDEX.   423

Aberystwyth—*cont.*
   a castle at, built by Foulke for king John, 270.
   demolished by Maelgwn, son of Rhys, and Rhys the Hoarse, 270.
   delivered up to Llywelyn, son of Iorwerth, 286.
   Llywelyn, son of Iorwerth, and his army, obtain possession of the castle of, 308.
   Edmund, the king of England's brother, begins to build a castle at, 368.
   taken and burnt by Gruffudd, son of Maredudd, and Rhys, son of Maelgwn the Little, 372.
Abloec, the sons of, devastate Caer Gybi and Lleyn, 24.
Abloyc, king, dies, 20.
Abraham, assumes the bishopric of Menevia, 50.
   his death, 50.
Abraham, bishop of Llanelwy, dies, 320.
Abwell, an Irishman, instigated by Maelgwn, son of Rhys, to kill Cedivor, son of Griffri, 260.
Achilles, the lord Rhys compared to, 246.
Acre, the Christians conveyed to, 310.
   Louis, king of France, and his queen remain at, 336.
Adam, bishop of Llanelwy, dies at Oxford, 230.
Aedd, son of Mellt, dies, 16.
Aeddan, son of Blegywryd, with his four sons, killed by Llywelyn, son of Seisyll, 34.
Aeron, Lower, the district of, ravaged by Rhys and Owain, sons of Gruffudd, son of Rhys, 270.
Ajax, the lord Rhys compared to, 246.
Albanians (the people of Alban or Scotland), the French kill Malcolm, son of Dwnchath, king of the Picts and, 54, 56.
Alexander, son of Malcolm, succeeds his brother Edward, in the kingdom of Scotland, 80.
   commands an army against the Britons under king Henry I., 114.

Alexander, son of Malcolm—*cont.*
   sends messengers to Gruffudd, son of Cynan, to request him to make peace with king Henry I., 114.
Alexander, pope, cites Henry I. to appear at Rome, to make satisfaction for the death of archbishop Becket, 208.
   his death, 230.
Alvryd, king of the Gewissi, dies, 18.
Alvryd, at the head of the Saxons, ravages the kingdom of the sons of Idwal, 24.
Anarawd, son of Einon, son of Owain, son of Cadwallon, slain, 252.
Anarawd, son of Gruffudd, killed by the family of Cadwalader, 162.
Anarawd, son of Gwriad, killed by the Pagans, 22.
Anarawd, son of Rhodri, comes to devastate Ceredigion and the vale of Tywi, 15.
   his death, 20.
Anarawd, son of Rhys, deprives his brothers, Madog and Howel, of sight, 238.
Ancellin, archbishop, consecrates Worgan, bishop of Llandaf, 80.
Angharad, daughter of Owain, son of Edwin, her relationship, 152.
   her death, 196.
Anhunog, the comot of, subjugated by Pain, son of Patrick, 366.
Anjou, king Henry II. collects an army from, to oppose the Welsh, 200.
   king Henry III. endeavours to establish his right to, 316.
Anselm, archbishop of Canterbury, receives back his archbishopric, 66.
Anselm the Fat, bishop of Menevia, dies, 332.
Antioch, the soldan of Babylon, reduces the city of, 356.
Arberth, the castle near, burnt by Gruffudd, son of Rhys, 122.
   burnt by young Rhys, and Maelgwn, son of Rhys, 284.
   the castle of, won by Llywelyn, son of Iorwerth, 306.

Arberth—*cont.*
  destroyed by Llywelyn, son of Gruffudd, 344.
Archbishop, an, consecrated in the city of Damietta, 304.
Archbishops, many, seized by the emperor Frederick, 328.
Ardudwy, the comot of, taken from Gruffudd, son of Llywelyn, 308.
Armenia, the country of, ravaged by the soldan of Babylon, 356.
Armorica, called Little Britain, 2.
  earthquake in, 2.
Arthen, king of Ceredigion, dies, 8.
Arthmarcha, devastated and burnt, 32.
Arundel, the castle of, seized by Robert de Belesme, earl of Shrewsbury, 68.
  the castle of, invested by king Henry I., 68.
Arwystli, the men of, under Howel, son of Ieuan, pursue after the booty taken by Owain Gwynedd, 196.
  subjugated by Gwenwynwyn, son of Owain Cyveiliog, 250.
  taken by David, son of Llywelyn, from his brother, Gruffudd, 326.
  taken from Gruffudd, son of Gwenwynwyn, by Llywelyn, son of Gruffudd, 358, 360.
Ash Hill, the battle of, 14.
Asser, archbishop of the Isle of Britain, dies, 18.
Atropos, 244.
Austria, the prince of, a leader of the armament of Christians sailing to Damietta, 304.

B.

Babylon, the army of the Christians of Damietta proceeds to attack, 308.
  the soldan of, reduces the city of Antioch, 356.
Bala, the castle of, conquered by Llywelyn, son of Iorwerth, 258.
Baldwin, the half of Dyved given by king Henry I. to the son of, 70.
Baldwin, the archbishop of Canterbury, preaches a crusade, 234.
  leads an immense multitude to Jerusalem, 236.
  his death, 236.
Baldwin, the town and castle of, burnt by Llywelyn, son of Iorwerth, 318.
Bangoleu, the battle of, in which Cynan was slain, 14.
Bangor, laid waste by the Pagans, 46.
  king John incites some of his troops to burn, 268.
Bangor, the bishop of, dies, 240.
  the bishop of, received into the monastery of Dor, 324.
  dies, and is buried, 324.
Bar, the earl of, accompanies king John to Poictou, 278.
Bardsey, Hayarndrud, a monk of, dies, 34.
Basingwerk, Owain, prince of Gwynedd, encamps at, 184.
  destroyed by him, 204.
Bath, the bishop of, consecrates Henry III. king of England, 292, 294.
Beaumont, Henry, owner of a castle near Abertawy, 122.
Bec, Walter de, the castle of, burnt by Owain and Cadwalader, the sons of Gruffudd, son of Cynan, 158.
Beck, Thomas, consecrated bishop of Menevia, 372.
Bede, the priest, dies, 4.
Belesme, Robert de, earl of Shrewsbury, quarrels with king Henry I., 66.
  seizes upon the castles of Arundel, Bliv, Brygge, and Shrewsbury, 68.
Beli, son of Elfin, dies, 4.
Bell, the great, at Strata Florida, is bought, 340.
  consecrated by the bishop of Bangor, 340.
Bernard, a man from Normandy, advanced by king Henry I. to be bishop of Menevia, 118.
  his death, 176.
  his great merit, 176.
Berwyn mountains, king Henry II. leads his army to, and encamps in, 200.

INDEX. 425

Bethlehem, Robert, earl of, puts to flight the knights sent by Henry I. to subdue Normandy, 78.

Bishop, a, of Gwent, of noble lineage, dies, (A.D. 983), 28.

Bishop, the, of Bangor, dies, (A.D. 1196), 240.

Black Mountain, Llywelyn, son of Iorwerth, leads his army over the, 300.

Blaenllyvni, Giles de Bruse, bishop of Hereford, obtains possession of, 282.
reduced by Rickert Marshall and Owain, son of Gruffudd, 320.

Blaen Porth Hodnant, attacked by Gruffudd, son of Rhys, son of Tewdwr, 128.

Bledri, son of Cedivor, appointed to keep the castle of Robert the Crookhanded, at Aber Cavwy, 126.

Bleddyn, son of Cynvyn, action of Mechain between him and his brother Rhiwallon on one side, and Maredudd and Ithel, sons of Gruffudd, on the other side, 46.
holds Gwynedd and Powys, 46.
killed by Rhys, son of Owain, 46.
avenged by Trahaiarn, king of Gwynedd, 48.
character of, 48.

Bleddyn, son of Cynvyn Gwyn, Maredudd, son of Howel, slain by the sons of, 162.

Bleiddud, bishop of Menevia, dies, 46.

Blen, son of Ieuan, sends Llywelyn, son of Owain, to prison to the castle of Brygge, 154.

Bliv, the castle of, seized by Robert de Belesme, earl of Shrewsbury, 68.
taken by king Henry I., 68.

Blois, Stephen of, takes the crown of England by force, 156.

Blood, rains, in Britain and Ireland, 4.
the milk and butter turned to, 4.

Bloody colour, the moon turns of a, 4,

Boleyn, the earl of, captured at Vernon, 280.

Bourdeaux, king Henry III. and his queen tarry at, 328.

Bourdeaux—cont.
king Henry III. returns from, 330.
the same king sails again for, 338.

Brabant, William of, is intercepted and killed, 102.

Brecheiniog, Ithel, king of Gwent, slain by the men of, 12.
devastated by the Normans, 16.
devastated by the Saxons, 28.
the French of, kill Rhys, son of Tewdwr, 54.
the Britons of, resist the domination of the French, 58.
the men of, kill Llywelyn, son of Cadwgan, 62.
the lord of, causes Seisyll, son of Dyvnwal, to be slain in Abergavenny castle, 226.
the men of, receive Robert de Bruse honourably, 282.
they pay homage to Llywelyn, son of Gruffudd, 348.
taken possession of by the earl of Hereford, 364.

Brian, king of all Ireland, stirred up against Dublin, 34.
killed in battle with Sitruc, son of Abloec, 34.

Bristol, the earl of, encamps at the castle of Dinweleir, against Rhys, son of Gruffudd, 192.
a man of, kills Owain, son of Iorwerth, 218.

Britain, Armorica called Little, 2.
death of Asser, archbishop of, 18.

Britons, lose the crown of the kingdom, 2.
victorious in three battles, Heilin, Garthmaelog, and Pencoed, 4.
engage in the battle of Maesydog against the Picts, and kill Talargan, king of the Picts, 6.
engage in the battle of Hereford against the Saxons, 6.
their Easter altered, 6.
spoiled by king Offa, 8.
their kingdom falls, on the death of Rhys, son of Tewdwr, 54.

Britons—*cont.*
    their land seized by the French, in Dyved and Ceredigion, 54.
    resist the domination of the French, 56.
    demolish the castles of Ceredigion and Dyved, 56.
    fruitless campaign of William I. against the, 58.
    resist the domination of the French, 58.
    slay the French at Celli Carnant, 58.
    defeat the French again, 58.
    attacked a second time by William I. with a great army, 60.
    a third time, 60.
    defeat the invasion of Magnus, king of Norway, 74.
    a bishop appointed for Menevia by king Henry I., in contempt of all the scholars of the, 118.
    a battle between the French in the reign of Henry I., and the, 134.
    God's commiseration of the, 170.
    N.B. Other references to the Britons are classified under the heads of the various princes and chiefs.
Bron yr Erw, the battle of, between Gruffudd, son of Cynan, and Trahaiarn, son of Caradog, 48.
Brun, the battle of, 20.
Bruse, Foulke, leads an army against the French and the North men in Lincoln, 296.
Bruse, Giles de, bishop of Hereford, sends his brother Robert on an expedition to Brecheiniog, 282.
    his own successes there, 282.
    makes peace with king John, 284.
Bruse, John de, marries Margaret, daughter of Llywelyn, son of Iorwerth, 304.
    repairs the castle of Abertawy, and Senghenydd, 310.
    dies a cruel death, 320.
Bruse, Mahalt de, mother of the sons of Gruffudd, dies at Llanbadarn, 266.
Bruse, Rheinallt de, inherits the patrimony of his brother Giles, 286.

Bruse, Rheinallt de—*cont.*
    marries a daughter of Llywelyn, son of Iorwerth, 286.
    summoned to Hereford by king John, 292.
    is reconciled to king Henry III., 298.
    Llywelyn, son of Iorwerth, becomes angry with him, 298.
    gives himself up to the disposal of Llywelyn, 300.
    receives the castle of Senghenydd, 300.
Bruse, Robert de, sent by his brother Giles to Brecheiniog, 282.
    takes possession of several castles there, 282.
Bruse, William, agrees with Rhys, son of Gruffudd, for the relinquishment by the latter of Pain's castle in Elvael, 242.
    banished to Ireland, by king John, 262.
    his wife and son captured, and put to death by John in Windsor castle, 264.
    gives himself up to Llywelyn, son of Iorwerth, 300.
    taken and imprisoned, 316.
    liberated for the castle of Buellt, with the district, and a sum of money, 316.
    hanged by Llywelyn, son of Iorwerth, 318.
Bryan de Ville, joins the crusade to Jerusalem, 304.
Brygge, the castle of, seized by Robert de Belesme, earl of Shrewsbury, 68.
    king Henry I. encamps before, 68.
    Llywelyn, son of Owain, imprisoned in, 154.
Bryn Derwin, Llywelyn awaits the hostile approach of his brothers at, 340.
Buallt (or Buellt), devastated by the Normans, 16.
    the castle of, fortified by Gelart, seneschal of Gloucester, 266.
    the castle of, obtained by Giles de Bruse, 282.

INDEX. 427

Buallt (or Buellt)—*cont.*
    wrested from their uncle by young Rhys and Owain, sons of Gruffudd, 298.
    the castle of, given for the liberation of William Bruse, 316.
    the castle of, fortified by John, 330.
    given by Llywelyn, son of Gruffudd, to Maredudd, son of Owain, 342.
    taken, except the castle, by Llywelyn, son of Gruffudd, from Roger Mortimer, 346.
Bwlch y Dinas, reduced by Rickert Marshall and Owain, son of Gruffudd, 320.
Bydydon, the castle of, destroyed by Llywelyn, son of Gruffudd, 342.

C.

Cadell, son of Arthvael, poisoned, 20.
Cadell, son of Gruffudd, reduces the castle of Dinweileir, 168.
    overcomes the castle of Caermarthen, 168.
    conquers the castle of Llanstephan, 168.
    raises an army against the castle of Gwys, 172.
    repairs the castle of Caermarthen, 178.
    ravages Cydweli, 178.
    subdues Ceredigion as far as Aeron, 178.
    takes the whole of Ceredigion, except one castle, from Howel, son of Owain, 178.
    conquers the castle of Llanrhystud, 178.
    repairs the castle of Ystrad Meurug, 180.
    cruelly bruised by the men of Tenby, while hunting, 180.
    goes on a pilgrimage, 182.
    dies, and is buried at Strata Florida, 226.
Cadell, king of Powys, dies, 8.

Cadell, son of Rhodri, dies, 18.
Cadvan, son of Cadwalader, captured by Howel, son of Owain, 178.
Cadwalader the Blessed dies at Rome, 2.
Cadwalader, son of Gruffudd, son of Cynan, sent by his father on an expedition into Meirionydd and Lleyn, 150.
    leads a large and cruel army into Ceredigion, 156, 158.
    eulogium of, and of his brother Owain, 158.
    burns the castle of Walter de Bec, 158.
    burns the castle of Aberystwyth, of Rickert de la Mere, of Dinerth, and of Caerwedros, 158.
    returns home, 158.
    comes a second time into Ceredigion with an army, 158.
    joined by other princes, 158.
    invests Aber Dyvi, 158.
    routs the Flemings and Normans, 160.
    returns home victorious, 160.
    his share of Ceredigion seized by Howel, son of Owain, 164.
    his castle at Aberystwyth burnt by the same, 164.
    collects a fleet from Ireland, and lands at Abermenai, 164.
    reconciled to his brother Owain, 164.
    blinded by his incensed allies, 164.
    liberates himself from them by ransom, 164.
    commotion with his nephews, Howel and Cynan, sons of Owain, 174.
    his castle of Cynvael taken by them, 174.
    constructs a castle at Llanrhystud, 176.
    gives his share of Ceredigion to his son, Cadwgan, 176.
    expelled from Mona by Owain, his brother, 180.
    his territory restored to him, 188.
    encamps at the castle of Dinweleir, 192.

Cadwalader, son of Gruffudd—*cont.*
defends Gwynedd against Henry II., 200.
unites with his brother Owain, and Rhys, son of Gruffudd, against Owain Cyveiliog, 204.
invests the castle of Rhuddlan in Tegeingl, 204.
burns it, and the castle of Prestatyn also, 206.
dies, in the month of March, 216.

Cadwalader, son of Rhys, privately killed in Dyved, 232.
buried in the White House upon Tav, 232.

Cadwalader, son of Seisyll, son of Dyvnwal, killed by the French, 226.

Cadwallon, son of Gruffudd, son of Cynan, slays his three uncles, Goronwy, Rhirid, and Meilyr, 152.
mutilated by his brother Owain, 180.

Cadwallon, son of Ieuav, kills Ionaval, son of Meurug, 28.
killed by Maredudd, son of Owain, 28.

Cadwallon, son of Madog, son of Idnerth, seizes Einon Clud, his brother, and imprisons him, 194.

Cadwallon, son of Madog, of Maelienydd, taken by Rhys, son of Gruffudd, to the court of king Henry II., at Gloucester, 226.
killed, 230.

Cadwallon, son of Maelgwn, of Maelienydd, dies at Cwm Hir, 322.

Cadwallon, son of Maredudd, son of Owain, dies, 30.

Cadwallon, son of Owain Cyveiliog, slays Owain, son of Madog, at Careghova, 232.

Cadwallon, son of Owain, son of Howel the Good, dies, 24.

Cadwallon, son of Owain Gwynedd, deprived of his sight by command of Henry II., king of England, 202.

* Cadwallon, the sons of, demolish the castle of Nyver, 240.

Cadwallon—*cont.*
the sons of, expelled by Roger Mortimer, 240.
the sons of, burn the castle of Rhaiadr Gwy, 240.

Cadweithen, is driven away, 14.
ravages Glywysig, 14.
his death, 16.

Cadwgan, son of Bleddyn, expels Rhys, son of Tewdwr, from his territory, 52.
despoils Dyved, 54.
goes against the French, attacks and conquers them, 56.
many chieftains of his family fight against the castle of Pembroke, and ravage the whole country, 58.
retreats into Ireland for fear of the treachery of his own men, 60.
returns from Ireland, 62.
takes Ceredigion and a portion of Powys, 62.
invited by Robert, earl of Shrewsbury, and his brother Ernulf, to assist them against king Henry I., 68.
is reconciled to his brother Iorwerth, 74.
prepares a great feast for the chieftains of his country, 82.
is displeased with his son Owain's conduct in respect of Nest, 86.
endeavours to prevail upon Owain to restore his wife and spoil to Gerald the Steward, 86.
makes his escape from Ithel and Madog, the sons of Rhirid, on board a ship that was at Aberdovey, 88.
goes privately to Powys, and despatches messengers to Rickert, the steward of the king, with the view of making peace with the king, 92.
his portion of Powys seized by Madog and Ithel, sons of Rhirid, 92.
having made his peace with the king, he obtains his territory of

INDEX.   429

Cadwgan, son of Bleddyn—*cont.*
    Ceredigion, on certain conditions, 92, 94.
    repairs to the court of the king, 102.
    is dispossessed of his territory by Gilbert, son of Rickert, 104.
    obtains Powys of the king of England, 108.
    is put to death by Madog, son of Rhirid, 108.
Cadwgan, son of Cadwalader, receives his father's share of Ceredigion, 176.
Cadwgan, son of Goronwy, kills his cousin, Cadwgan, son of Gruffudd, 156.
Cadwgan, son of Gruffudd, is killed by his cousin, Cadwgan, son of Goronwy, 156.
Cadwgan, of Llandyfai, abbot of Whitland, made bishop of Bangor, 284.
Cadwgan, son of Madog, is slain, 162.
Cadwgan, son of Maredudd, slain by Walter, son of Rhirid, 198.
Cadwgan, son of Owain, killed by the Saxons, 22.
Caer Alclut, demolished by the Pagans, 14.
Caereinion, divided between Owain, son of Cadwgan, and Maredudd, son of Bleddyn, 112.
    a castle made at, by Madog, son of Maredudd, lord of Powys, 184.
    taken from Owain Cyveiliog by Owain and Cadwalader, the sons of Gruffudd, and Rhys, son of Gruffudd, and given to Owain the Little, 204.
    Owain Cyveiliog comes against the castle of, takes and destroys it, killing the garrison, 204.
    taken by David, son of Llywelyn, from his brother Gruffudd, 326.
Caer Evrog, devastated in the battle of Dubkynt, 14.
Caer Gybi, devastated by the sons of Abloec, 24.
Caerleon (Chester), king Henry II. encamps in the plains of, 184.
    the land of, governed by Iorwerth, son of Owain, 188.

Caerleon (Chester)—*cont.*
    king Henry II. encamps for many days at, 202.
Caerleon (upon Usk). Edgar, king of the Saxons, collects a large fleet at, 26.
    king Henry II. takes the city of, from Iorwerth, son of Owain, 210.
    Iorwerth, son of Owain, destroys the town of, 212.
    attacked by Iorwerth, son of Owain, of Gwenllwg, 222.
    the French get possession of, 224.
    restored to Iorwerth, son of Owain, 226.
    the monastery of Deuma established at, 203.
    is taken by William Marshall, 302.
Caerleon, the earl of, builds the castle of Dyganwy, 264.
    builds the castle of Holywell, 264.
    goes to Jerusalem to fight the crusade, 304.
    his death, 320.
Caer Loyw, a flank movement made from the army of the earl of, 296.
Caermarthen, the castle of, burnt by the sons of Gruffudd, 162.
    the castle of, erected by earl Gilbert, 166.
    the castle of, subdued by Cadell, son of Gruffudd, and Howel, son of Owain, 168.
    the castle of, repaired by Cadell, son of Gruffudd, 178.
    Rhys, son of Gruffudd, fights against, 192.
    Rhys, son of Gruffudd, attacks and burns, 240.
    Llywelyn, son of Iorwerth, and other Welsh princes, collect a large army to, 286.
    placed under the custody of Llywelyn, son of Iorwerth, 302.
    the castle of, repaired by William Marshall, 312.
    Maelgwn the Little and others, fight against it for three months, 322.

Caer Offa, is taken by Owain, son of Gruffudd, and Maredudd, son of Howel, 196.
Caerphili, the castle of, taken by Llywelyn, son of Gruffudd, 358.
Caerwedros, the castle of, burnt by Owain and Cadwalader, the sons of Gruffudd, Howel, son of Maredudd, and Madog, son of Idnerth, 158.
Calettwr, Howel, son of Owain, repairs the castle of the son of Humfrey, in the Vale of, 180.
Camaron, Roger Mortimer builds the castle of, 240.
Camddwr, a battle at, between Goronwy and Llywelyn, sons of Cadwgan, and Caradog, son of Gruffudd, on the one side, and Rhys, son of Owain, and Rhydderch, son of Caradog, on the other side, 48.
Canterbury, a dispute between the archbishop of, and the archbishop of York, 228.
 Louis, king of France, desists from attacking the castle of, 298.
Canton, William, of Cemaes, dies, 318.
Cantrev Bychan, the castle of, reduced by Rhys and Maredudd, the sons of the lord Rhys, 240.
 allotted to Rhys the Hoarse, 290.
Cantrev Mawr, Rhys, son of Gruffudd, in making peace with king Henry II. stipulates that he should receive, 190.
 is taken possession of by Rhys, son of Gruffudd, 198.
 allotted to Rhys the Hoarse, 290.
Caradog, son of Gruffudd, kills Maredudd, son of Owain, 46.
 kills Rhys, and Howel, his brother, 50.
Caradog, king of Gwynedd, killed by the Saxons, 8.
Caradog, son of Rhiwallon, slain in the battle on Carn Mountain by Rhys, son of Tewdwr, 50.
Caradog, son of Rhydderch, killed by the Saxons, 38.

Cardiff, is begun to be built, 50.
 the seneschal of, leads an army to Penwedig, 268.
 reduced by Rickert Marshall, 320.
Carreg, the castle of, fortified by Henry III., 328.
Carreg Cennen, the castle of, recovered by Rhys the Little, 334.
Careghova, Owain, son of Madog, slain at, 232.
Carn Mountain, a battle on, 4, 50.
Carno, the battle of, between the sons of Owain, son of Howel, and the sons of Idwal, 22.
Carnwyllon, Maredudd, son of Rhys, slain at, 256.
 young Rhys obtains possession of, 284.
 allotted to Rhys the Hoarse, 290.
Castle Baldwin, the Black Normans come a second time to, 16.
 burnt by Llywelyn, son of Iorwerth, 318.
 peace formed at, between king Henry III. and Llywelyn, son of Gruffudd, 354.
Cedivor, son of Collwyn, dies, 54.
Cedivor, son of Daniel, archdeacon of Ceredigion, dies, 198.
Cedivor, son of Goronwy, invites Gruffudd, son of Rhys, to act lawlessly, 126.
Cedivor, son of Griffri, killed by an Irishman, 260.
Cedivor, abbot of Strata Florida, dies, 314.
Ceiriog, king Henry II. leads his army into the Vale of, 200.
Celynog the Great, the grove of, devastated by Howel, son of Ieuav, and the Saxons, 26.
Celli Carnant, the French slain by the Britons at, 58.
Celli Wrda, the castle of, fortified by Simon Montford, 354.
Cemaes, ravaged by the Welsh, 284.
 the men of, do homage to Llywelyn, son of Iorwerth, 286.
 the cantrev of, allotted to Maelgwn, son of Rhys, 288.

INDEX.

Cemoyd, king of the Picts, dies, 6.
Cemoyth, king of the Picts, dies, 12.
Cennadlog, king Henry II. marches through the wood of, 186.
Cenulf, ravages the kingdoms of Dyved, 10.
Cerball, death of, 16.
Ceredigion, devastated by Anarawd, 16.
    the men of, kill Gruffudd, son of Owain, 20.
    devastated by the sons of Idwal, 22.
    Maredudd, son of Owain, goes to, 30.
    devastated by Edwin, son of Einon, and Eclis the Great, 30.
    devastated twice by the French, 46.
    the French take possession of, 54.
    the Britons demolish the castles of, 56.
    left a desert, 56.
    given by king Henry I. to Iorwerth, son of Bleddyn, 70.
    given by Iorwerth to his brother, Cadwgan, 74.
    obtained of king Henry I. by Cadwgan, after purchasing it for a hundred pounds, 92.
    given by king Henry I. to Gilbert, son of Rickert, 104.
    Gilbert, son of Rickert, takes possession of, and builds castles in, 104.
    Owain and Cadwalader, the sons of Gruffudd, lead an army into, 156-8.
    they come a second time to, 158.
    David, son of Gerald, archdeacon of, made bishop of Menevia, 176.
    subdued as far as Aeron by Cadell, Máredudd, and Rhys, the sons of Gruffudd, 178.
    taken entirely by them, 178.
    reconquered by Rhys, son of Gruffudd, 198.
    given by king Henry II. to the lord Rhys, 212.
    taken possession of by Gruffudd, son of Rhys, 250.
    above Aeron, given by Llywelyn, son of Iorwerth, to his nephews, the sons of Gruffudd, 262.

Ceredigion—*cont.*
    the comots of Gwynionydd and Mabwynion in, allotted to Maelgwn, son of Rhys, 288-290.
    three cantrews of, allotted to Rhys and Owain, the sons of Gruffudd, 290.
Ceri, king Henry III. encamps at, 316.
    taken by David, son of Llywelyn, from his brother Gruffudd, 326.
    attacked in the night by John Strange, 348, 350.
Cerwallt, son of Muregan, king of Leinster, dies, 18.
Cetyll, the battle of, 12.
Cevn Cynwarchan, messengers from the Flemings meet Llywelyn, son of Iorwerth, at, 300.
Cevn Rhestr, Rhys, son of Gruffudd, assembles his men on the mountain of, 192.
Charles, king of Sicily, kills Conradin, 356.
Cherulf, the son of, commands a fleet under Cadwalader, son of Gruffudd, 164.
Christianity, interdicted in England by the pope, 262.
    rendered free to the men of the South, 302.
Christians, Robert of Normandy goes to protect the, at Jerusalem, 56.
    a battle between the, and Saracens, 272.
    an armament of, sails to Damietta, 304.
Cibon the fiddler, a son to, obtains the victory in instrumental song at the grand festival held by the lord Rhys in the castle of Aberteivi, 228.
Cilcenin, Maelgwn, son of Rhys, encamps at, 264.
Cilgerran, Rhys, son of Gruffudd, seizes the castle of, 202.
    the French from Pembroke and the Flemings make an attack upon the castle of, 208.

Cilgerran—*cont.*
    Gruffudd, son of Rhys, possesses himself through treachery of the castle of, 254.
    subdued by William Marshall, 260.
    the castle of, delivered up to Llywelyn, son of Iorwerth, 286.
    the castle of, allotted to Maelgwn, son of Rhys, 288.
    William Marshall begins to build the castle of, 312.
Cil Owain, Owain Gwynedd retreats to, 186.
Clare, the earl of, encamps at the castle of Dinweleir, 192.
    confederates with Llywelyn, son of Gruffudd, 354.
Cleddyv, the Flemings seize the country near the efflux of, 80.
Clement IV., elected pope, 354.
Clifford, Walter, spoils the territory of Rhys, son of Gruffudd, and kills many men, 190.
Clwyd, Peter, abbot, dies in the Vale of, 232.
Clydog, son of Cadell, killed by his brother Meurug, 20.
Cnute, son of Swain, takes possession of the kingdom of England, Denmark, and Germany, 34.
    his death, 38.
Colunwy, the town of, burnt by Llywelyn, son of Iorwerth, 320.
Colwyn, the castle of, repaired, 166.
    Rhys, son of Gruffudd, attacks and burns the castle of, 242.
    the castle of, left by Giles de Bruse for Walter, son of Gruffudd, 282.
Congalach, king of Ireland, is slain, 22.
Conradin, killed by Charles, king of Sicily, 356.
Constantine, son of Iago, devastates Lleyn and Mona, 26.
    killed by Howel, son of Ieuav, in the battle of Hirbarth, 26.
Consyllt, the auxiliaries of Madog, son of Maredudd, slain at, 178.

Conwy, the battle of, to avenge Rhodri, 16.
    a great slaughter takes place between the sons of Idwal and the sons of Howel in the battle of, 22.
Corvoc, king and bishop of all Ireland, dies, 18.
    his virtues, 18.
Corwen, Owen Gwynedd and Cadwalader, the sons of Gruffudd, Rhys, son of Gruffudd, Owen Cyveiliog, Iorwerth the Red, the sons of Madog, son of Maredudd, and the two sons of Madog, son of Idnerth, encamp with their forces at, 200.
Council, a, assembled in London, for the purpose of confirming the laws of the churches, 228.
Cressy, Rheinallt de, constable of Caerleon, killed in battle, 298.
Cricciaeth, David, son of Llywelyn, imprisons his brother Gruffudd at, 326.
Crogen, the castle of, given to Gwenwynwyn for his maintenance, 258.
Crusaders, many, proceed to Jerusalem, 304.
Cryn Onen, the battle of, 14.
Cubert, abbot, dies, 6.
Culenan, a son of, slain in battle, 18.
Cunedda, son of Cadwallon, mutilated by his uncle Owain Gwynedd, 180.
Cwm Hir, Meurug, abbot of, dies, 232.
    the conventual society of, removes to Cymmer in Meirionydd, 252.
Cydewain, attacked by John Strange, 348, 350.
Cydweli, devastated by Edwin, son of Einon, with Eclis the Great, a Saxon prince, 30.
    devastated by the French, 56.
    given to the son of Baldwin, 70.
    granted by king Henry I. to Howel and (son of, *C.D.*), Goronwy, 74.
    ravaged by Cadell, son of Gruffudd, 178.
    Rhys, son of Gruffudd, builds the castle of, 236.

Cydweli—*cont.*
  obtained possession of by young Rhys, 284.
  the castle of, subjugated by Llywelyn, son of Iorwerth, and his auxiliaries, 288.
  allotted to Rhys the Hoarse, 290.
  Gruffudd, son of Llywelyn, proceeds to, 312.
  Llywelyn, son of Iorwerth, destroys the castle of, 318.
Cymmer in Meirionydd, Einon, son of Cadwgan, and Gruffudd, son of Maredudd, make a joint attack upon the castle of Uchtryd at, 140.
  the convent of Cwm Hir removes to, 252.
Cynan, a battle takes place between him and Howel, 10.
  is expelled from Mona by his brother Howel, 10.
Cynan, is slain in the battle of Bangolen, 14.
Cynan, son of Howel, reigns in Gwynedd, 32.
  is killed, 32.
Cynan, son of Howel, captured, 266.
Cynan, son of Maredudd, obtains Penardd, 360.
  is reconciled to king Edward I., 366.
  goes to the king to offer his homage and oath of allegiance, 366.
  is retained at the king's court, 366.
  returns from the king's court, 368.
Cynan, of Nant Nyver, dies, 14.
Cynan, son of Owain, ravages Aberteivi, 166.
  a dispute between him and his uncle Cadwalader, 174.
  attacks and takes Cynvael, the castle of Cadwalader, 174.
  is imprisoned, 178.
  fights against king Henry II. in the wood of Cennadlog, 186.
  encamps at the castle of Dinweleir, 192.
  slays Gurgeneu, the abbot, 206.
  dies, 224.

Cynan, son of Owain—*cont.*
  his sons war against Rhys, son of Gruffudd, 230.
  they expel Rhodri, son of Owain, 238.
  the two sons of, combine with Llywelyn, son of Iorwerth, and Rhodri, son of Owain, against David, son of Owain Gwynedd, 240.
Cynan, son of Seisyll, is killed, 38.
Cynan, Maredudd, son of Edwin, killed by the sons of, 38.
Cynan, abbot of the White House, dies, 226.
Cyngen, is strangled by the Pagans, 12.
Cyngen, son of Elised, is poisoned, 20.
Cyngen, king of Powys, dies in Rome, 12.
Cynon, king of Gwynedd, dies, 10.
Cynvael, Howel and Cynan, sons of Owain, attack the castle of, 174.
Cynvrig, son of Owain, killed by the family of Madog, son of Maredudd, 162.
Cynvrig, son of Owain Gwynedd, ordered to be deprived of his sight by king Henry II., 202.
Cynvrig, son of Rhiwallon, killed by the Gwyneddians, 48.
Cynvrig, son of Rhys, son of Gruffudd, dies, 326.
Cynwraid, Robert de Bruse takes possession of the isle of, 282.
Cyveiliog, devastated by the Saxons, 26.
  obtained by Einon, son of Cadwgan, and Gruffudd, son of Maredudd, 140.
  granted by Madog, son of Maredudd, to his nephews, Owain and Meurug, the sons of Gruffudd, 176.
  ravaged a second time by Rhys, son of Gruffudd, 182.
  taken by David, son of Llywelyn, from his brother Gruffudd, 326.
  thirteen townships of, taken by Llywelyn, son of Gruffudd, from Gruffudd, son of Gwenwynwyn, 360.

D.

Damietta, an armament of Christians sails to, 304.
  is delivered up to the Christians, 304.
  an archbishop consecrated in, 304.
  the Christian army of, proceeds to attack Babylon, 308.
  restored to the Saracens, 310.
  given up to Louis, king of France, 334.
  restored to the Saracens, 334.
  regained by Louis, king of France, 336.
Damnan, Elfryt, king of the Saxons, buried at, 4.
Daniel, son of Sulien, bishop of Menevia, dies, 152.
David, son of Gerald, archdeacon of Ceredigion, is appointed bishop of Menevia, 176.
  his death, 226.
David, son of Gruffudd, disputes with his brother Llywelyn, 338.
  takes to flight, 340.
  proceeds to Emlyn to speak with Maredudd, son of Rhys the Hoarse, and with Patrick de Sayes, 346.
  forsakes the society of his brother Llywelyn, and goes to England, 350.
  reduces the castle of Penharddlech, 372.
David, son of Llywelyn, receives the homage of all the princes of Wales, 326.
  takes Arwystli, Ceri, Cyveiliog, Mawddwy, Mochnant, and Caereinion from his brother Gruffudd, 326.
  succeeds his father, 326.
  goes to Gloucester to do homage to king Henry III., 328.
  gives hostages to the king, 328.
  is cited before a council in London, 328.
  summons to him all the princes of Wales, 330.
  causes many losses to Gruffudd, son of Madog, Gruffudd, son of Gwen-

David, son of Llywelyn—*cont.*
  wynwyn, and Morgan, son of Howel, who had disregarded his summons, 330.
  dies at Aber, 332.
David, son of Malcolm, king of Prydyn, dies, 182.
David, bishop of Menevia, dies, 226.
David, son of Owain, fights against king Henry II. in the wood of Cennadlog, 186.
  ravages Tegeingl, and removes the inhabitants and their cattle to the Vale of Clwyd, 198.
  kills his eldest brother, Howel, 206.
  subdues the isle of Mona, having banished his brother Maelgwn to Ireland, 222.
  gets possession of all Gwynedd, having expelled his brothers and uncles, 224.
  takes his brother Maelgwn and imprisons him, 224.
  takes his brother Rhodri and confines him in fetters, 224.
  marries Emma, sister of the king of England, 224.
  expelled from Mona and Gwynedd by his brother Rhodri, who had escaped from prison, 224.
  combined against by Llywelyn, son of Iorwerth, Rhodri, son of Owain, and the two sons of Cynan, son of Owain, 240.
  captured by Gwenwynwyn, 250.
  dies in England, 258.
David, abbot of Strata Florida, dies, 232.
Decem-novennalis, 32, 38, 44, 52, 66.
Denmark, Cnute, son of Swain, takes possession of the kingdom of, 34.
  Harold, king of, meditates the subjection of the Saxons, 44.
Derotyr, commands a fleet under Sitrac, son of Abloec, 34.
Deuddwr, the third of, divided between Maredudd, son of Bleddyn, and Owain, son of Cadwgan, 112.

Deugleddyv, Llywelyn, son of Iorwerth, puts many to the sword in, 306.
Deuma, the religious society of, established, 230.
Dewi, certain persons take refuge in the sanctuary of, 90.
Diermid, king, forms a friendship with Rickert, earl of Terstig, son of Gilbert Strongbow, 208.
Diermid, king of Leinster, dies, 208.
Diermid, son of Murchath, is banished from his people, 204.
— gains the castle of Lough Garmon, 206.
Dinas Newydd, the battle of, 20.
Dineir (Dinerth, Dineirth), the battle of, 18.
— the castle of, burnt by Owain and Cadwalader, the sons of Gruffudd, son of Cynan, and their auxiliaries, 158.
— Roger, earl of Clare, stores the castle of, 190.
— Maelgwn, son of Rhys, gets possession of the castle of, 254.
— Maelgwn, son of Rhys, completes the castle of, 258.
— burnt by him, 262.
Dinevwr, Rhys, son of Gruffudd, takes possession of the castle of, 198.
— Rhys and Maredudd, the sons of the lord Rhys, reduce the castle of, 240.
— the youngest sons of the lord Rhys take possession of the castle of, 252.
— won by Gruffudd, son of Rhys, from his brother Maelgwn, 260.
— young Rhys invests the castle of, 276.
— Rhys the Little, son of Rhys Mechyll, proceeds to, 342.
— young Rhys dies in the castle of, 358.
Dingeraint, Gilbert, son of Rickert, builds a castle at, 104.
Dinweleir (Dinweileir), Cadell, son of Gruffudd, reduces the castle of, 168.
— Maredudd and Rhys, the sons of Gruffudd, son of Rhys, repair the castle of, 180.
— earl Rheinallt, the earl of Bristol, the earl of Clare, two other earls, Cadwalader, son of Gruffudd, Howel and Cynan, encamp at the castle of, 194.

Diserth in Tegeingl, king Henry III. fortifies the castle of Carreg, near, 328.
Dolvorwyn, Llywelyn, son of Gruffudd, visits the castle of, 358.
— the earl of Lincoln and Roger Mortimer besiege the castle of, 364.
Dor, the bishop of Bangor received into the monastery of, 324.
Drought, excessive, 336.
Dubkynt, the battle of, 14.
Dublin, the people of, devastate Ireland and Mona, 20.
— devastated by the Scots, 32.
— Brian, king of all Ireland, and other kings, are stirred up against, 34.
— the Pagans of, capture Gruffudd, son of Llywelyn, 40.
— certain Germans make their escape from Owain, son of Gruffudd, to, 166.
— king Henry II. awaits the arrival of ships from, 202.
— Rickert, earl of Terstig, son of Gilbert Strongbow, gets possession of, 208.
Dunwallon, is slain by the men of Iago and Ieuav, sons of Idwal, 22.
Dunwallon, king of Strath Clyde, goes to Rome, 26.
Dwnchath, son of Brian, dies on his way to Rome, 44.
Dwrngarth, king of Cornwall, is drowned, 14.
Dyganwy, is burnt by lightning, 10.
— the castle of, destroyed by the Saxons, 10.
— the earl of Caerleon builds the castle of, 264.
— Llywelyn, son of Iorwerth, reduces the castle of, 278.
— king Henry III. comes to, 330, 344.
— the barons of England, siding with the Welsh against Edward I., purpose to destroy the castle of, 350.
Dyryslwyn, Maredudd, son of Rhys the Hoarse, dies in the castle at, 358.
Dyved, devastated by Godfrey, son of Harold, 28.

E E 2

Dyved—*cont.*
    devastated by Edwin, son of Einon, and Eclis the Great, 30.
    devastated by the Pagans, 32, 40.
    devastated, 36.
    devastated by Gruffudd, son of Llywelyn, 42.
    ravaged by the French, 46.
    seized by the French, 54.
    the castles of, demolished by the Britons, 56.
    left a desert, 56.
    the half of, given by king Henry I. to Iorwerth, son of Bleddyn, 70.
    taken by the king from Iorwerth, and given to a certain cavalier named Saer, 74.
    king Henry I. sends the Flemings to inhabit, 80.
    pillaged by the companions of Owain, son of Cadwgan, 102.
    left by Cedivor, son of Goronwy, full of Flemings, French, and Saxons, 128.
    Cadwalader, son of Rhys, killed in, 232.
    the Welsh get possession of, 282, 284.
    three cantrevs of, allotted to Maelgwn, son of Rhys, 288.
    Llywelyn, son of Iorwerth, leads his army against the Flemings of, 300.

Dyvi and Aeron, Rhys and Owain, the sons of Gruffudd, consent that king John should have the territory between, 270.

Dyvnwal, obtains the castle of Abergavenny through treachery from the men of king Henry II., 218.

Dyvnwal, son of Howel, dies, 22.

Dyvnwal, son of Tewdwr, dies, 6.

E.

Earthquake, a great, 2, 54, 256, 332, 362

Easter, the time of, as observed in the British church, altered by the command of Elbod, 6.

Eclipse, of the moon, 8, 12.
    of the sun, 8, 162, 232, 236.

Eclis the Great, a Saxon prince, devastates the kingdoms of Maredudd, son of Owain, 30.

Edbalt, king of the Saxons, dies, 6.

Edelfled, queen, dies, 20.

Edelred, son of Edgar, expelled from his kingdom by Swain, son of Harold, 34.

Edelstan, king of the Saxons, dies, 20.

Edeyrnion, Owain Gwynedd and Cadwalader, sons of Gruffudd, Rhys, son of Gruffudd, Owain Cyveiliog, Iorwerth the Red, the sons of Madog, son of Maredudd, and the two sons of Madog, son of Idnerth, move their armies to, 200.

Edgar, king of the Saxons, collects a large fleet at Caerleon upon Usk, 26.
    his death, 26.

Edmund, son of king Henry III., seized by the earls and barons of England, who were seeking the restoration of the good laws and customs of the land, 352.
    leads an army to Llanbadarn, and begins to build a castle at Aberystwyth, 368.
    bestows his cousin Eleanor in marriage on Llywelyn, son of Gruffudd, 370.

Edward, son of king Henry III., born, 326.
    the kingdom of England entrusted to his care, 338.
    left by his father in Gascony for the purpose of guarding it, 338.
    goes to survey his castle and lands in Gwynedd, 340.
    burns some of the towns in Gwynedd, 350.
    falls out with the earls and barons of England, 350.
    is seized by the earls and barons, 352.

Edward, son of king Henry III.—*cont.*
  collects a vast army of earls, barons, and knights against Simon Montford, 352.
  marches to London, and attacks it, 354.
  reigns after his father, 358.
  consecrated king of England, 360.
  appoints a council in London, in which new institutions are established, 362.
  summons Llywelyn, son of Gruffudd, to do homage to him, 362.
  bears the charge of Llywelyn's nuptial festivities, 362.
  appoints a council at Worcester, in which he designs an expedition against Wales, 364.
  is reconciled to Gruffudd and Cynan, sons of Maredudd, and Llywelyn, son of Owain, 366.
  retains Cynan, son of Maredudd, and Rhys Wyndod with him at court, 366.
  receives the homage of Rhys, son of Maredudd, Rhys Wyndod, Gruffudd and Cynan, sons of Maredudd, and Rhys, son of Maelgwn, 368.
  leads an army to the midland district, and fortifies a castle at Flint, 368.
  proceeds to Rhuddlan, and fortifies it, 368.
  sends a part of his army to Mona, 368.
  makes peace with Llywelyn, son of Gruffudd, and receives his homage, 368, 370.
  orders Owain the Red, Owain, son of Gruffudd, and Gruffudd, son of Gwenwynwyn, to be released from prison, 370.
  bestows his cousin Eleanor in marriage on Llywelyn, 370.
  orders a new coinage, 370.
Edward, son of Malcolm, killed by the French, 56.
Edward, son of Malcolm, dies, 80.

Edwin, son of Einon, devastates the kingdoms of Maredudd, son of Owain, 30.
Edwin, son of Howel, dies, 22.
Edwin, son of Maredudd, is killed by the sons of Cynan, 38.
Egg, an, in a time of dearth, sold for three halfpence, 268.
Eilad, arrives in Britain, 36.
Einon, son of Anarawd, makes an attack upon the castle of Humfrey, 192.
  is slain in his sleep by Walter, son of Llywarch, his own man, 198.
Einon, son of Cadwgan, holds a portion of his brother Owain's share of Powys, after the death of the said Owain, 138.
  makes an attack upon the castle of Uchtryd, 140.
  requested to come to the assistance of Howel, son of Ithel, against the sons of Owain, son of Edwin, 142.
  is made war upon by king Henry I., 146.
  his death, 150.
Einon, son of Caradog, is slain, 266.
Einon Clud, seized by his brother Cadwallon, son of Madog, 194.
  goes with Rhys, son of Gruffudd, to the court of king Henry II. at Gloucester, 224.
  is slain, 230.
Einon, son of Cynan, dies, 232.
Einon, son of Howel, devastates Gower, 24, 26.
  his territory devastated by the Saxons under the command of Alvryd, 28.
  is treacherously killed by the nobles of Gwent, 28.
Einon, son of Owain, kills Cadwgan, son of Gruffudd, 156.
Einon, of Porth, is killed by his brother, 236.
Einon, son of Rhys, of Gwerthrynion, goes to the court of king Henry II. at Gloucester, 226.
Einon the Saxon, made abbot of Strata Florida, 372.

Elbod, archbishop of Gwynedd, alters the time of Easter, 6.
his death, 8.
Eleanor, who had been betrothed to Llywelyn, son of Gruffudd, sails for Gwynedd, 362.
is married to Llywelyn at Worcester, 370.
gives birth to a daughter, who was named Gwenllian, 364.
dies in childbirth, and is buried at Llanvaes in Mona, 364.
Elen, wife of Howel the Good, dies, 20.
Elfryt, king of the Saxons, dies and is buried at Damnan, 4.
Elise, son of Madog, endeavours to bring about a peace with Gwenwynwyn, 258.
Elisse, son of Cyngen, acts treacherously towards his brother Griffri, 10.
Elstan, king of the Saxons, dies, 18.
Elvael, subjected a second time by the French, 166.
the cantrev of, left by Giles de Bruse, for Walter, son of Gruffudd, who had subdued it, 282.
king Henry III. builds Pain's castle in, 318.
the men of, plundered by William, son of Gwrwared, 338.
Emlyn, Llywelyn, son of Iorwerth, fights against the castle of, 286.
the cantrev of, allotted to Maelgwn, son of Rhys, 288.
Emma, dame, sister of the king of England, is married to David, son of Owain, 224.
Empress, the, daughter of Henry I., arrives in England for the purpose of subduing the kingdom for Henry, her son, 152.
Emri, son of Simon Montford, sails with Eleanor his sister, for Gwynedd, 362.
is seized and imprisoned by the gate keepers of Haverford, 362.
is released from the king's prison, and takes a journey to Rome, 364.
England, devastated by the Normans, 16.

England—*cont.*
Cnute, son of Swain, takes possession of the kingdom of, 34.
William the Bastard gets possession of the kingdom of, 44.
the south of, brought under the sway of Stephen of Blois, 156.
prince Henry, grandson of Henry I., succeeds to the throne of, 182.
Christianity interdicted in the whole kingdom of, 262.
king John makes the kingdom of, tributary to the pope, 278.
English, the, attack the Welsh, and put them to flight, 252.
Maelgwn, son of Rhys, sells Aberteivi, the key of all Wales, for a trifling value, to the, 254.
of the North, quarrel with king John, 280.
a naval fight between them and the French, 298.
upwards of twelve hundred killed by the Welsh in one day, 350.
take possession of the territory of Rhys, son of Maelgwn, son of the lord Rhys, 368.
Entris, devastates Menevia, 34.
Ernulf, a disturbance between him and king Henry I., 66.
tries to make peace with the Gwyddelians, 68.
demands the daughter of Murtart, king of Ireland, in marriage, 68.
goes with his men to receive his wife, 72.
delivers up his castle to the king, and quits the kingdom, 72.
puts to flight the knights sent by king Henry I. to subdue Normandy, 78.
Eryri, the mountains of, ravaged by the Saxons, 10.
Owain, son of Cadwgan, retires to the mountains of, 114.
Llywelyn, son of Iorwerth, removes his property to the mountain of, 266.
king John proceeds towards the mountain of, 268.

Esham (or Evesham), the battle of, 352.
Euelvre, granted by king Henry II. to Rhys, son of Gruffudd, 212.
Euerys, bishop of Menevia, dies, 20.
Evilfre, death of, 40.
Extreme unction, 156, 160, 168, 206.

F.

F, a Sunday letter, 332.
Failure of provision, in Ireland, 16.
    in the camp of Henry II. on the Berwyn mountains, 200.
    compels Gruffudd, son of Llywelyn, to return home after he had gone to meet William Marshall near Caermarthen, 312.
Famine, 32.
    in the territory of Maredudd, son of Owain, 32.
    in Ireland, 316.
Farthings, to be made round, by order of Edward I., 370.
Fasting and prayer, the mole-like vermin in Ireland driven away by means of, 18.
    the Britons, when threatened by William Rufus, turn to God in, 60.
Fat, Anselm the, bishop of Menevia, dies, 332.
    Hugh the, commands French troops against Gwynedd, 60.
    Hugh the, dies, 66.
Ferers, earl, 314.
Ferna, Diermid, king of Leinster, buried in the city of, 208.
Fernvail, son of Idwal, dies, 6.
Feryll the bard, 244.
Festival, a grand, given by the lord Rhys at the castle of Aberteivi, 228.
Fiddler, a son to Cibon the, obtains the victory in instrumental song at the said festival, 228.
Finant, the battle of, 12.
Fine weather, extraordinary, 288.
Fineable, Iorwerth, son of Bleddyn, adjudged to be, 76.
Fish, abundance of, at Aberystwyth, 262.

Fitz Walter, Robert, taken in battle, 296.
Flanders, a nation from, sent to inhabit Dyved by king Henry I., 80.
    king Henry II. collects a vast army of the choice warriors of, 200.
    the earl of, delivered by the king of England to the king of France as a pledge in respect of Thomas, archbishop of Canterbury, 208.
    the earl of, assists young Henry, son of Henry II., to harrass his father's territory, 222.
    the earl of, accompanies king John on his voyage to Poictou, 278.
    a terrible war breaks out between it and Poictou, 278.
    Otho, emperor of Rome, driven to flight from, 280.
    the earl of, captured at Vernon, 280.
Fleet, a, fails coming from Ireland to South Wales, 42.
    from Ireland, endangers South Wales, 42.
Flemings, William Brabant, an old man of the, killed by some companions of Owain, son of Cadwgan, 102.
    attacked by Gruffudd, son of Rhys, 122.
    dwelling in Dyved, 121.
    dwelling in Blaen Porth Hodnant, 128.
    pursue Owain, son of Cadwgan, and kill him, 138.
    oppose Owain and Cadwalader, sons of Gruffudd, and their confederates, in Ceredigion, 158.
    take to flight, according to their usual custom, 160.
    attack the castle of Caermarthen, 168.
    spoiled and slaughtered, 198.
    attack the castle of Cilgerran, 202.
    attack Howel and Maelgwn, the sons of Rhys, killing some of their men and putting others to flight, 238.
    opposed by Llywelyn, son of Iorwerth, 300.
    send messengers to Llywelyn, son of Iorwerth, to sue for peace, 300.
    Llywelyn concludes a truce with them, 306.

Flesh, horse, considered a dainty by the army of king John, when short of provisions at Dyganwy, 266.
Flint, king Edward I. fortifies a castle at, 368.
Flood, a, in the Nile, which prevents the Christians from going to Babylon, 308.
a destructive, 336.
Foolish young men from all parts of the country join Gruffudd, son of Rhys, 124, 126.
Foulke, builds a castle for king John at Aberystwyth, 270.
seneschal of Cardiff, is ordered by the king to compel Rhys the Hoarse to deliver up the castle of Llanymddyvri and the district to the sons of Gruffudd, son of Rhys, or to retire into exile, 274.
joins young Rhys, 274.
Foulke Bruse, a flank movement made from the army commanded by, 296.
France, Pepin the Elder, king of, dies, 4.
a war between the king of, and Henry I., king of England, 142.
peace concluded between them, 144.
Louis, king of, goes to the holy war, 172.
a contention between the king of, and Henry II., on account of the murder of Thomas, archbishop of Canterbury, 208.
the king of, sends messengers to Henry II., 216.
king Henry II. proceeds to, 218.
Philip, king of, goes to the holy war, 234.
war between Phillip, king of, and king John, 278.
the former obtains the victory, 280.
a truce concluded between the two kings, 280.
Louis, son of Phillip, sends for assistance from, 298.
peace concluded between Henry III. and Louis, son of the king of, 302.
Louis sails for, 302.
Louis, king of, dies, 314.

France—*cont.*
Henry III. sails for, 316, 328.
the king of, proceeds to Jerusalem, 334.
Henry III. sails for, to confer with the king, 346.
Simon Montford sails for, to seek aid from his relations and friends, 354.
Louis, king of, and his son, die, 358.
Frederick, the emperor, seizes cardinal Otto, and several other ecclesiastics, 328.
French, the, kill Maredudd, son of Owain, 46.
ravage Ceredigion and Dyved, 46.
kill Rhys, son of Tewdwr, 56.
take possession of Dyved, 56.
kill Malcolm, son of Dwnchath, king of the Scots, and Edward, his son, 54, 56.
go against Dyved, and are slain by the Britons at Celli Carnant, 58.
lead their forces against Gwynedd for the third time, 60.
enter the isle of Mona, 60.
attacked by Magnus, king of Germany, on the coast of Mona, 62.
reduce the country, 62.
are opposed a second time by the Gwyneddians, under the command of Owain, son of Edwin, 62.
flock to Henry, brother of William Rufus, and in conjunction with the Saxons appoint him king in England, 64.
many of them killed by Howel, son of Goronwy, 76.
treacherously kill Howel, son of Goronwy, 76.
a discord between them and Madog, son of Rhirid, 94.
Owain, son of Cadwgan, and Madog, son of Rhirid, commit many crimes in the country of the, 96.
an army of, under Gilbert, a prince of Cornwall, sent against the Welsh, 114.
the manner of, to deceive people, 120.
attacked by Gruffudd, son of Rhys, 122.

INDEX. 441

French, the—*cont.*
summon to them Owain, son of Caradog, Maredudd, son of Rhydderch, and his sons Maredudd and Owain, and test their fidelity to king Henry I., 124.
left in Dyved by Cedivor, son of Goronwy, 128.
the manner of, to do every thing by stratagem, 132.
attack a portion of the army that followed Gruffudd, son of Rhys, his uncle Rhydderch, son of Tewdwr, and his sons, Maredudd and Owain, 134.
from Caerleon assist the sons of Owain, son of Edwin, against Howel, son of Ithel, 142.
undeservedly accuse Gruffudd, son of Rhys, who is consequently driven from the land given to him by the king, 152.
from Aber Nedd to Aber Dyvi, oppose Owain and Cadwalader, sons of Gruffudd, 158.
attack the castle of Caermarthen, 168.
a battle between them and the men of Mona, who are victorious, 188.
a large number of the, join Rheinallt against Rhys, son of Gruffudd, 192.
Einon Clud delivered to the, 194.
garrison in Ceredigion expelled by the Welsh, 198.
from Pembroke attack the castle of Cilgerran, 202.
an army of, under Owain Cyveiliog, attack the castle of Caereinion, 204.
get possession of Caerleon, and drive away from there Iorwerth and Howel his son, 224.
seize Gwladus, the wife of Seisyll, and kill his son Cadwalader, 226.
an army of, collected by Maelgwn, son of Rhys, which is defeated by Rhys and Owain, sons of Gruffudd, 264.
an army of, collected by young Rhys, with which he gains the castle of Llanymddyvri, 276.

French, the—*cont.*
get possession of the city of Lincoln, 294.
are put to flight, 296.
a naval fight between them and the English near the efflux of the Thames, in which the English are victorious, 298.
Fruit, great scarcity of, 336.
Furneuale, Gerald de, killed in battle, 298.

G.

Gamage, Pain, taken and imprisoned by David, son of Gruffudd, 372.
Garthgrugyn, the castle of, fortified by Maelgwn the Little, 328.
Garthmaelog, the battle of, 4.
Gascony, furnishes choice warriors for the army of Henry II., 200.
Henry III. returns from, leaving his son Edward to guard it, 338.
Gelart, seneschal of Gloucester, fortifies the castle of Buellt, 366.
Gelli, taken by Giles de Bruse, 282.
king John proceeds to, 292.
burnt by Llywelyn, son of Iorwerth, 318.
Gemaron, the castle of, repaired by Hugh, son of Raulf, 166.
Genau y Glyn, the men of, retire to Gwynedd with Rhys, son of Maelgwn, 368.
Gerald de Furneuale, killed in battle, 298.
Gerald, the steward of Pembroke, ravages the boundaries of Menevia, 58, 60.
sent to Ireland to demand the daughter of king Murtart in marriage for Ernulf, 68.
the custody of the castle of Pembroke granted to him, 76.
founds the castle of Little Cenarch, 82.
his castle burnt, and his wife carried away by Owain, son of Cadwgan, 84.
incites an army of Flemings to pursue after Owain, 138.

Gerald, the steward of Pembroke—*cont.*
　his sons fight against Owain and Cadwalader, the sons of Gruffudd, 158.
　they command a large army of French and Flemings in their attack upon the castle of Caermarthen, 168.
Gerard, bishop of Hereford, succeeds to the archiepiscopal see of York, 66.
Germans, the, blind Cadwalader, son of Gruffudd, 164.
Germany, Cnute, son of Swain, takes possession of, 34.
　Eilav flees into, 38.
　Magnus, king of, comes as far as Mona, with the view of gaining the country, 62, 72.
　he makes depredations on the shores of Britain, 74.
　Henry I. marries the daughter of a prince of, 146.
　the emperor of, takes the cross, and proceeds to Jerusalem, 172.
　the king of, and his two sons, support king Henry III. and his son Edward on the plains of Lewes, 350.
Gewissi, death of Alvryd, king of the, 18.
Gilbert, earl of Clare, is killed in battle, 296.
Gilbert, a prince of Cornwall, commands an army against the Welsh, 114.
Gilbert, son of Gilbert, subdues Dyved, and erects the castle of Caermarthen and the castle of Mabudrut, 166.
　his death, 176.
Gilbert, abbot of Gloucester, consecrated bishop of Hereford, 176,
Gibert, earl of Pembroke, obtains through treachery the castle of Morgan, son of Howel, in Mechain, 324.
　restores it, for fear of Llywelyn, son of Iorwerth, 324.
Gilbert, son of Rickert, his character, 104.
　Henry I. gives him the land of Cadwgan, son of Bleddyn, 104.
　takes possession of the said land, 104.
　builds a castle near the efflux of the river Ystwyth, and another near Aberteivi, 104.

Gilbert, son of Rickert—*cont.*
　accuses Owain, son of Cadwgan, before the king, 112.
　his death, 142.
Giles de Bruse, sends his brother Robert to Brecheiniog, 282.
　goes there himself, and obtains possession of Aberhodni, Maes Hyveidd, Gelli, Blaenllyvni, and the castle of Buellt, without any opposition, 282.
　makes peace with the king, 284.
　his death, 286.
Glamorgan, devastated by Maredudd, son of Owain, 30.
Glasygrug, the followers of Gruffudd, son of Rhys, encamp at, 130.
Glen of Teyrnon, a religious society established in the, 230.
Gloucester, Gwalter, the high constable of, protects the people who fled before Ithel and Madog, sons of Rhirid, and Llywarch, son of Trahaiarn, 88.
　Rhys, son of Gruffudd, and other chieftains, go to the court of king Henry II. at, 224.
　Gelart, seneschal of, fortifies the castle of Buellt, 266.
　Giles, bishop of Hereford, dies at, 286.
　David, son of Llywelyn, goes to, to do homage to Henry III., 328.
Glumaen, son of Abloec, killed, 30.
Glywysig, ravaged by Cadweithen, 14.
Godfrey, son of Harold, devastates Mona, and by great craft subjugates the whole island, 24.
　devastates Lleyn and Mona, 26.
　devastates Dyved and Menevia, 28.
　at the head of the black host devastates Mona, 28.
Godrich, king of Man, his sons aid Rhodri, son of Owain, in the subjugation of the isle of Mona, 238.
Gorchwyl, death of bishop, 18.
Goronwy, son of Cadwgan, engaged in the battle of Camddwr, 48.
　his death, 66.
Goronwy, son of Ednyved, death of, 356.
　his character, 356.

INDEX. 443

Goronwy and (father of, according to *C. D.*) Howel, receive a grant of the Vale of Tywi, Cydweli, and Gower from king Henry I., 74.
Goronwy, son of Owain, accused by the son of Hugh, earl of Caerleon, 112.
    is requested by Owain, son of Cadwgan, to combine with Gruffudd, son of Cynan, against their enemies, 114.
    killed by his nephew Cadwallon, son of Gruffudd, 152.
Goronwy, son of Rhys, taken through treachery, and dies in prison, 74.
Gorwennydd, devastated by Owain, 22.
Gower, devastated by Einon, son of Owain, 24.
    devastated by Edwin, son of Einon and Eclis the Great, 30.
    devastated by the French, 56.
    granted by king Henry I. to Iorwerth, son of Bleddyn, 70.
    is taken from Iorwerth, and given to Howel and (son of, *C.D.*) Goronwy, 74.
    a castle in, burnt by Gruffudd, son of Rhys, 126.
    devastated by Maredudd and Rhys, the sons of Gruffudd, 180.
    all its castles reduced by young Rhys, 284.
    Llywelyn, son of Iorwerth, leads an army to, 300.
    all its castles destroyed by Rhys the Hoarse, 302.
Greece, pilgrims from Wales drowned on the sea of, 166.
Gregory IX., pope, releases the bishop of Bangor from his diocese, 324.
    sends a legate to England, 326.
    the emperor Frederick makes war against, 328.
Gregory X., pope, holds a general council in Lyons, 360.
Griffri, son of Cyngen, slain through the treachery of his brother Elisse, 10.
Griffri, son of Gwyn, death of, 182.
Griffri, son of Trahaiarn, killed, 80.

Grove of Celynog (Cyveiliog, *C.*) the Great, the, devastated by Howel, son of Ieuav, and the Saxons, 26.
Gruffudd, son of Cadwgan, attacks the castle of Uchtryd, son of Edwin, 140.
    his death, 236.
Gruffudd, son of Cynan, fights against the men of Iago and of Mona, 48.
    retreats to Ireland, for fear of the treachery of his own men, 60.
    returns from Ireland, 62.
    obtains Mona, 62.
    accused by the son of Hugh, earl of Caerleon, 112.
    enters into a mutual agreement with Goronwy, son of Owain, that no one should make reconciliation with their enemies without the other, 114.
    is desired by Alexander, son of Malcolm, and the earl of Caerleon, to make peace with king Henry I., 114.
    sends messengers to the king, to seek peace from him, 116.
    is sent for by the king, and desired to bring to him Gruffudd, son of Rhys, alive or dead, 120.
    sends men to force Gruffudd, son of Rhys, out of the church of Aberdaron, whither he had fled for sanctuary, but is prevented by the bishops, 122.
    requested by the men of Powys to join them against the king, 146.
    sends his sons Cadwalader and Owain with a large army into Meirionydd, 150.
    his death, 160.
    his power and greatness, 160.
Gruffudd, son of Cynan, son of Owain, dies at Aberconway, 254.
    his renown, 254.
Gruffudd, son of Cynan, captured in battle, 266.
Gruffudd, son of Gwenwynwyn, refuses to unite with David, son of Llywelyn, 330.

Gruffudd, son of Gwenwynwyn—*cont.*
    the whole of his territory, except the castle of Trallwng, and part of the Vale of Severn, with a little of Caereinion, subdued by Llywelyn, son of Gruffudd, and his confederates, 342.
    is driven from his territory into banishment, 344.
    destroys the castle of Gwyddgrug, 350.
    acts treacherously towards the messengers of Llywelyn, 360.
    all his territory subdued by Llywelyn, 360.
    seeks to reconquer his territory by the help of the earl of Lincoln and Roger Mortimer, 364.
    released from the prison of Llywelyn, by the command of the king, 370.
Gruffudd, son of Idnerth, cuts off the French at Aber Llech, 58.
Gruffudd, son of Ivor, son of Meurug, goes to the court of king Henry II., at Gloucester, 226.
Gruffudd, son of Ivor, is slain, 270.
    his character, 270.
Gruffudd, son of Llywelyn, son of Iorwerth, a dispute between him and his father, 306.
    having disposed his army in battle array, awaits the coming of his father, 306.
    is exhorted to deliver himself and his property up to the will of his father, 308.
    deprived by his father of the cantrev of Meirionydd, and comot of Ardudwy, 308.
    sent by his father with a large army to oppose William Marshall, 312.
    fights against William Marshall near Caermarthen, 312.
    lack of provision compels him to return home, 312.
    is sent by his father to intercept William Marshall at Carnwyllon, 314.
    is liberated, having been six years in prison, 322.

Gruffudd, son of Llywelyn—*cont.*
    deprived of Arwystli, Ceri, Cyveiliog, Mawddwy, Mochnant, and Caereinion by his brother David, 326.
    attempts to escape from the king's prison in London, 330.
    falls and breaks his neck, 330.
    his body removed from London to Aberconway, and buried there, 334.
Gruffudd, son of Llywelyn, son of Seisyll, governs after Iago, king of Gwynedd, 38.
    overcomes the Saxons and other nations in many battles, 38, 40.
    his victory at Rhyd y Groes, 40.
    depopulates Llanbadarn, 40.
    obtains the government of South Wales, and dispossesses Howel, son of Edwin, of his territory, 40.
    overcomes Howel, and captures his wife in the battle of Pen Cadeir, 40.
    is himself captured by the Pagans of Dublin, 40.
    again opposes and defeats Howel, son of Edwin, 40.
    Gruffudd and Rhys, sons of Rhydderch, act treacherously towards him, 42.
    revenges himself upon the men of the Vale of Tywi, 42.
    kills Gruffudd, son of Rhydderch, 42.
    defeats the Saxons under Reinolf at Hereford, 42.
    destroys their fortress and burns the town, 42.
    allies himself with Magnus, king of Germany, and ravages the dominions of the Saxons, 44.
    slain through the treachery of his own men, 44.
    his character for bravery, 44.
Gruffudd, son of Madog, son of Gruffudd Maelor, slain by his brother Maredudd, 326.
Gruffudd, son of Madog, declines joining David, son of Llywelyn, 330.
    is reconciled to Llywelyn, son of Gruffudd, 344.
    his death and burial, 356.

Gruffudd Maelor, king of Powys, dies and is buried, 236.
his character, 236.
Gruffudd, son of Maredudd, son of Bleddyn, attacks the castle of Uchtryd, 140.
obtains Cyveiliog, with Mawddwy and half of Penllyn, 140.
kills his cousin Ithel, son of Rhirid, 152.
his death, 154.
Gruffudd, son of Maredudd, son of the lord Rhys, archdeacon of Ceredigion, dies, 330.
Gruffudd, son of Maredudd, son of Owain, restores the middle comot to his brother Cynan, 358.
is reconciled to king Edward I., 366.
takes the town and castle of Aberystwyth, 372.
Gruffudd, son of Owain, slain by the men of Ceredigion, 20.
Gruffudd, son of Rhiwallon, slain by Rhys, son of Tewdwr, 50.
Gruffudd, son of Rhydderch, acts treacherously towards Gruffudd, son of Llywelyn, 42.
is slain by him, 42.
Gruffudd, son of Rhys, son of Gruffudd, succeeds his father in the government of his dominions, 248.
is seized by his brother Maelgwn, and sent to the prison of Gwenwynwyn, who sends him to an English prison, 250.
liberated by the English, 252.
gets possession of his share of his territory, except the castles of Aberteivi and Ystrad Meurug, 254.
possesses himself through treachery of the castle of Cilgerran, 254.
his death and burial, 256.
his sons win Llanymddyvri and Dinevwr from their uncle Maelgwn, 260.
they receive a portion of Ceredigion above Aeron from their uncle Llywelyn, son of Iorwerth, 262.

Gruffudd, son of Rhys, son of Tewdwr, arrives in Dyved from Ireland, 118.
is accused to king Henry I., 118.
goes to Gruffudd, son of Cynan, with the view of saving his life, 118.
flees for sanctuary to the church of Aberdaron, 122.
makes an attack upon a castle near Arberth, and burns it, 122.
burns the outwork of the castle of Llanymddyvri, 122.
sends his companions to attack a castle near Aberteivy, who having burnt the outworks and killed a few men, are compelled to retreat, 122.
is joined by young men from all parts of the country, 124.
commits great depredations on every side, 124.
attacks the castle of Caermarthen, and burns the outer ward, 126.
burns a castle in Gower, 126.
attacks Blaen Porth Hodnant, but without much success, 128.
prepares to attack the castle of Aberystwyth, but is defeated by the French, 132, 134.
Owain, son of Cadwgan, pursues after him, 136.
kills Gruffudd, son of Trahaiarn, 150.
having been unjustly accused by the French, is expelled from the land which the king had given him, 152.
assists Owain and Cadwalader, the sons of Gruffudd, in their expedition, 158.
his death, 160.
his character, 160.
Gruffudd, son of Seisyll, slain, 226.
Gruffudd, abbot of Strata Florida, settles with king Henry III. in respect of a debt which the monastery owed, 334.
Gruffudd, son of Trahaiarn, killed by Gruffudd, son of Rhys, 150.
Gruffudd, abbot of Ystrad Marchell, death of, 244.
Gwrgeneu, the abbot, death of, 206.

Gwrgeneu, son of Seisyll, treacherously killed by the sons of Rhys the Saxon, 50.

Gwalchmai, Maelgwn, son of Rhys, compared to, 236.

Gwalter, high constable of Gloucester, affords his protection to the country people, when Ithel and Madog, sons of Rhirid, Llywarch, son of Trahaiarn, and Uchtryd, son of Edwin, were hunting after Owain and Cadwgan his father, 88.

Gwarthav, the cantrev of, alloted to Maelgwn, son of Rhys, 288.

Gweithen, the battle of, 14, 16.

Gwenllian, daughter of Llywelyn, birth of, 364.
taken prisoner to England, 364.
made a nun against her own will, 364.

Gwenllian, daughter of young Maelgwn, death and burial of, 338.

Gwenllian, daughter of Rhys, son of Gruffudd, death of, 236.
her character, 236.

Gwenllwg, devastated by the Normans, 16.
the Britons of, resist the domination of the French, 58.
Iorwerth, son of Owain, of, attacks Caerleon, 222.

Gwennottyll, the battle of, 48.

Gwent, devastated by the Normans, 16.
the Britons of, resist the domination of the French, 58.
many of the chieftains of, are slain, 226.
a great slaughter of the good people of, 226.

Gwent Iscoed, attacked by Howel, son of Iorwerth, 222.

Gwenwynwyn, son of Owain Cyveiliog, kills Owain, son of Madog, 232.
his castle in Trallwng Llywelyn attacked by Henry, archbishop of Canterbury and justice of all England, 242.
regains the castle, 244.

Gwenwynwyn, son of Owain Cyveiliog—*cont.*
his family accompany Maelgwn, son of Rhys, to Aberystwyth, and subjugate the town and castle, 250.
sends Gruffudd, son of Rhys, to an English prison, 250.
meditates the restoration of their ancient rights to the Welsh, 252.
certain hostages released from the prison of, 254.
is opposed by Llywelyn, son of Iorwerth, 258.
Elise, son of Madog, endeavours to bring about a peace with him, 258.
terms of peace concluded between him and Llywelyn, 258.
wins (loses, *E.*) the castle of Llanymddyvri and the castle of Llangadog, 258, 260.
seized by king John at Shrewsbury, 262.
repossesses himself of his dominion by the assistance of king John, 264.
is summoned by the king to aid him against Llywelyn, son of Iorwerth, 266.
joins Llywelyn against the English, 270.
absolved by pope Innocent from his oath of fidelity to the king of England, 272.
accompanies Llywelyn on his expedition, 288.
makes peace with the king, 290.

Gwerthrynion, the Welsh fight against the castle of, 256.
wrested from Roger Mortimer by Llywelyn, son of Gruffudd, 342.

Gweun y Nygyl, battle of, 48.

Gwgawn, son of Gwriad, is slain, 22.

Gwgawn, son of Meurug, is drowned, 14.

Gwgawn, son of Meurug, forms a plot against Howel, son of Goronwy, 76.
takes him, 78.

Gwiu, the black Normans come to, 16.

Gwion, bishop of Bangor, dies, 236.
  his character, 236.
Gwladus the Dark, daughter of Llywelyn, son of Iorwerth, and wife of Sir Randulph Mortimer, dies, 336.
Gwladus, daughter of Gruffudd, son of Llywelyn, and wife of the lord (young, *B.C.*) Rhys, dies, 348.
Gwladus, daughter of Rhiwallon, 82.
Gwladus, wife of Seisyll, is captured by the French, 226.
Gwlvac, deprived of his eyesight, 32.
Gwrgant, son of Cadwgan, 138.
Gwrgant, son of Rhys, a poet, slain by the men of Ivor, son of Meurug, 188.
Gwriad, killed by the Saxons, 16.
Gwriad, deprived of his eyesight, 32.
Gwrmid, devastates Lleyn, 26.
Gwyddelians, Rhys, son of Tewdwr, collects a fleet of the, 52.
  gives to them a large sum of money, 52.
  Ernulf seeks assistance from them, 68.
  their savage manners compel Madog, son of Rhirid, to quit Ireland, 104.
  being disappointed of their hire, they make many captures, 164.
Gwyddgrug, the castle of, destroyed by the men of Owain, son of Gruffudd, 172.
  the castle of, destroyed by Gruffudd, son of Gwenwynwyn, 350.
Gwyn, the sons of, killed, 24.
Gwynedd, the black Normans come to, 16.
  subdued by Maredudd, son of Owain, 28.
  the sons of Meurug make an inroad into, 30.
  Cynan, son of Howel, reigns in, 32.
  Iago, son of Idwal, succeeds to the government of, 38.
  held by Bleddyn, son of Cynvyn, 46.
  the Britons demolish the castles of the French in, 56.

Gwynedd—*cont.*
  the French lead their armies into, 56, 60.
  king Henry I. collects an army against, 112.
  falls into the possession of David, son of Owain, 224.
  his brother Rhodri expels David out of, 224.
  the men of, obtain the victory in vocal song at the festival in the castle of Aberteivi, 228.
  a religious society from Strata Florida removes to Rhedynog Velen in, 232.
  king John builds many castles in, 268.
  these are destroyed by Llywelyn, son of Iorwerth, except Dyganwy and Rhuddlan, 270.
  all the wise men of, summoned to Aberdovey about the partition of land, 288.
  Llywelyn, son of Maelgwn, dies on his estate in, 318.
  king Henry III. takes hostages from David, son of Llywelyn, on account of, 328.
  Maelgwn the Little flees into, 331.
  Edward, son of king Henry III., takes a survey of his castles and lands in, 340.
  Llywelyn, son of Gruffudd, returns from South Wales to, 346, 348.
  traversed by Edward, who burns some of the towns, 350.
  Emri, son of Simon Montford, and Eleanor his sister, sail for, 362.
  Llywelyn, brother of Rhys Wyndod, and Howel and (son of, *C.D.*) Rhys the Hoarse, quit their territories and retire into, 366.
  Rhys, son of Maelgwn, retires into, 368.
Gwyneddians, bravery of the, 36.
  pursue Rein the Scot, 36.
  their kingdom ruled over by Trahaiarn, son of Caradog, 48.
  kill Cynvrig, son of Rhiwallon, 48.
  rise against the French, 62.

Gwynion, Rhys, son of Gruffudd, dismantles and burns the castle of the the son of, 198.
the comot of the son of (Mabwynion) allotted to Maelgwn, son of Rhys, 288, 290.
Gwynionydd, the comot of, allotted to Maelgwn, son of Rhys, 288, 290.
Gwys, Cadell, son of Gruffudd, and his brothers, with William, son of Gerald, and his brothers, raise an army against the castle of, 172.
the castle of, obtained through treachery by Howel the Saxon, 238.
the castle of, destroyed, and the town burnt, by Llywelyn, son of Iorwerth, 306.
Gwytherin, the battle of, 16.

H.

Hainault, the earl of, joins king John on his expedition to Poictou, 278.
Otho, emperor of Rome, driven from, 280.
Harold, king of Denmark, meditates the subjection of the Saxons, 44.
Harold, son of earl Godwin, puts him to death, 44.
deprived of his kingdom and life by William the Bastard, 44.
Haverford, invested by Llywelyn, son of Iorwerth, 300.
burnt by him, 306.
the gate keepers of, seize and imprison Emri, son of Simon Montford, and his sister Eleanor, 362.
Hayarndrud, a monk of Bardsey, death of, 34.
Hayarddur, son of Mervyn, drowned, 22.
Hector, the lord Rhys compared to, 246.
Heilin, the battle of, 4.
Heinuth, son of Bledri, death of, 16.
Helygi, 360.
Hennyrth, son of Clydog, death of, 20.
Henry, son of Arthen, an eminent teacher, dies, 198.

Henry Beaumont, his castle near Abertawy attacked by the men of Gruffudd, son of Rhys, 122.
Henry, duke of Burgundy, delivered as a pledge by Henry II. to the king of France in respect of the archbishop of Canterbury, 208.
Henry, son of Cadwgan, receives a hundred marks from king Henry I., 96.
Henry I., king of England, succeeds to the throne, 64.
marries Mahalt, daughter of Malcolm, king of Prydyn or Scotland, 64.
raises Gerard, bishop of Hereford, to the archbishopric of York, 66.
reinstates Anselm in the see of Canterbury, 66.
dissension between him and Robert, earl of Shrewsbury, and his brother Ernulf, 66.
assembles an army and invests the castle of Arundel, 68.
takes the castle of Bliv, 68.
proceeds to the castle of Brygge, 68.
invites the Welsh princes to his assistance against the earls, 70.
makes grants of territory to Iorwerth, son of Bleddyn, 70.
permits earl Robert to quit the kingdom, 72.
breaks his engagement with Iorwerth, and takes from him Dyved, which he gives to the cavalier Saer, and the Vale of Tywi, Cydweli, and Gower, which he gives to Howel and (son of, C.D.) Goronwy, 74.
expels the cavalier Saer from Pembroke, and grants the custody of the castle to Gerald the steward, 76.
sends knights to subdue Normandy, 78.
himself sails over, 80.
captures earl Robert and his cousin William, 80.
reduces the whole of Normandy, 80.
sends a certain nation from Flanders to occupy Dyved, 80.
receives Cadwgan, son of Bleddyn, and suffers him to dwell in a hamlet

Henry I.—*cont.*
    which he had obtained with his wife, 92.
    restores Ceredigion to Cadwgan, upon the payment of a hundred pounds, 92.
    offers on certain conditions to liberate Iorwerth, son of Bleddyn, from prison, 96.
    gives the land of Cadwgan, son of Bleddyn, to Gilbert, son of Rickert, 104.
    retains Cadwgan at his court, and allows him twenty-four pence towards his expenditure, 104.
    gives Powys to Cadwgan, and is reconciled to Owain his son, 108.
    grants to Maredudd, son of Bleddyn, the custody of the land of his brother Iorwerth, until Owain should return to the country, 110.
    gives the land to Owain on receiving pledges and the promise of much money, 110.
    seizes and imprisons earl Robert, 110.
    leads an army against Gwynedd and Powys, 112.
    sends out three different armies, commanded respectively by himself, Alexander, son of Malcolm, and the son of Hugh, earl of Caerleon, 114.
    arrives with his retinue at Mur Castell, 114.
    sends messengers to Owain, requiring him to make peace, 114.
    goes to Normandy, 118.
    returns from Normandy, 118.
    summons Gruffudd, son of Cynan, to him, and induces him with many promises to endeavour to secure Gruffudd, son of Rhys, 120.
    his great power and success, 128.
    sends for Owain, son of Cadwgan, and persuades him to expel Gruffudd, son of Rhys, 134.
    remains in Normandy, because of the war between him and the king of France, 142.

Henry I.—*cont.*
    having made peace with the king of France, he sets sail for England, 144.
    encounters a dreadful storm at sea, in which his children and retinue are shipwrecked and drowned, 146.
    marries the daughter of a prince of Germany, 146.
    raises an immense army against the men of Powys, 146.
    is struck by an arrow, 148.
    is alarmed, and proposes to enter into terms of peace with Maredudd, son of Bleddyn, and the sons of Cadwgan, 148, 150.
    returns from Normandy, having made peace with his enemies, 152.
    his death in Normandy, 156.

Henry II., king of England, obtains the throne, 182.
    leads an immense army to the plains of Caerleon, or Chester, against Gwynedd, 184.
    proceeds through the wood of Cennadlog to meet Owain, prince of Gwynedd, 186.
    a battle fought between him and the sons of Owain, 186.
    marches to Rhuddlan, 186.
    many of his warriors land in Mona, and pillage several of the churches, 188.
    makes peace with Owain, 188.
    is opposed by Rhys, son of Gruffudd, alone, 188.
    summons Rhys to him, and receives him into peace, 190.
    deceives Rhys as to his promises, 190.
    disregards Rhys's complaints, 190.
    proceeds to South Wales against Rhys, 192.
    returns to England, 192.
    proceeds beyond sea, 192.
    moves an army against South Wales, 198.
    having received hostages from Rhys, he returns to England, 198.
    leads his army back into Wales, 200.

Henry II.—cont.
  encamps for three days at Rhuddlan, 200.
  returns to England, and collects a vast army of the choice warriors of England, Normandy, Flanders, Anjou, Gascony, and Scotland, against the Welsh, 200.
  proceeds to Oswestry, 200.
  moves his army to the woods of the Vale of Ceiriog, 200.
  encamps on the Berwyn mountains, 200.
  overtaken by a dreadful storm, 200, 202.
  moves to the open plains of England, 202.
  orders the hostages that had been previously delivered up to him to be blinded, 202.
  moves his army to Caerleon or Chester, and encamps there for several days, 202.
  returns to England, 202.
  instigates the murder of Thomas, archbishop of Canterbury, 208.
  contention between him and the king of France on that account, 208.
  denies that it was by his counsel the murder was perpetrated, and refuses to go to Rome, 210.
  is alarmed on account of the apostolical excommunication, and returns to England, 210.
  summons to him all the princes of England and Wales under the pretext of subduing Ireland, 210.
  receives the lord Rhys into his friendship, 210.
  proceeds to South Wales, 210.
  captures Iorwerth, son of Owain, upon the river Usk, 210.
  proceeds with a large army into Pembroke, 212.
  gives Ceredigion, the Vale of Tywi, Ystlwyv, and Euelvre to the lord Rhys, 212.
  goes on a pilgrimage to Menevia, 212.

Henry II.—cont.
  makes there an offering of two choral caps for the singers, and a handful of silver, 214.
  dines with David, the bishop, 214.
  receives some horses from Rhys, 214.
  releases Howel, son of Rhys, who had been with him as hostage, 214.
  sets sail for Ireland, 216.
  remains there during the winter, 216.
  returns from Ireland, 216.
  arrives at Pembroke, where he remains during Easter, 216.
  has an interview with Rhys, 218.
  returns to England, 218.
  sends for Iorwerth, son of Owain, to come and speak to him about peace, 218.
  promises a certain sum of money to his son Henry for his private expenses, 220.
  appoints men to watch his son, 220.
  receives Howel, son of Rhys, honourably, whom his father had sent with the view of serving the king, 222.
  goes to the holy war, 234.
  his death, 234.
Henry, son of Henry II., slain in a battle with the men of Mona, 188.
Henry, son of Henry II., desires a loan from his father, to meet his personal expenses, 220.
  is reconciled to his father, 224.
  his death, 232.
Henry III., king of England, succeeds to the throne, 292.
  is consecrated king by the bishop of Bath, 294.
  his knights hold a council at Oxford to treat of peace with Louis, son of the king of France, and the men of the North, 294.
  having come to no agreement, his men attack his allies, 294.
  they prevail against the French and the North men at Lincoln, 296.
  is reconciled with Rheinallt de Bruse, 298.

INDEX. 451

Henry III—*cont.*
peace declared between him and Louis of France, 302.
the terms of the peace, 302.
leads a powerful army against Llywelyn, son of Iorwerth, and his confederates, 316,
encamps at Ceri, 316.
fights against the Welsh, 316.
returns to England, having received the homage of some of the princes, and concluded terms of peace with Llywelyn, 316.
sails for France with the view of asserting his right as to Normandy, Anjou, and Poictou, 316.
returns to England, 318.
builds Pain's Castle in Elvael, 318.
a dispute between him and Rickert Marshall, earl of Pembroke, 320.
marries the daughter of the earl of Provence, 324.
a son is born to him, who is named Edward, 326.
receives the homage of David, son of Llywelyn, at Gloucester, 328.
assembles an army with a view of subduing the princes of Wales, 328.
fortifies the castle of Carreg, near Diserth, 328.
takes hostages from David, son of Llywelyn, on account of Gwynedd, 328.
cites him to London, 328.
sails for Poictou, with the view of obtaining from the king of France his right as to his lands, 328.
tarries with his queen at Bourdeaux, 328.
returns from Bourdeaux, 330.
assembles the power of England and Ireland for the purpose of conquering Wales, 330.
comes to Dyganwy, and fortifies the castle, 330.
returns to England, having lost a vast portion of his army, 330.

Henry III—*cont.*
sends Nicholas de Myles, Maredudd, son of Rhys the Hoarse, and Maredudd, son of Owain, to dispossess Maelgwn the Little, 332.
settles with Gruffudd, abbot of Strata Florida, in respect of a debt which the monastery owed, 334.
permits the abbot of Strata Florida and the abbot of Aberconway to remove the body of Gruffudd, son of Llywelyn, from London to the latter place, 334.
sails for Bourdeaux, having commended the kingdom to the care of Edward his son, Rickert earl of Cornwall, his brother, and the queen, 338.
returns from Gascony, having left Edward there to guard it, 338.
brings a large army to Dyganwy, 344.
returns to England, 344.
sails for France to confer with the king, 346.
a disturbance between him and his son Edward on the one side and the earls and barons on the other, 350.
arrives on the plains of Lewes with the view of seizing the earls and barons, 350.
he himself and his two sons are seized by them, 352.
is set at liberty, 352.
collects a large army from England for the purpose of attacking the castle of Celli Wrda, occupied by Simon Montford, 354.
marches to London against Llywelyn, son of Gruffudd, who had taken possession of the city, 354.
peace confirmed between him and Llywelyn, 354.
the terms and conditions of peace, 356.
his death, 358.
Henry Pictot, lord of Ewias, 314.
Henry, emperor of Rome, character and death of, 78.
Hercules, Rhys, son of Gruffudd, compared to, 246.

F F 2

452 INDEX.

Hereford, the battle of, 6.
  Gruffudd, son of Llywelyn, marshals his troops at, 42.
  Gerard, bishop of, succeeds to the see of York, 66.
  Milo, earl of, slain, 164.
  Gilbert, abbot of Gloucester, consecrated bishop of, 176.
  Roger, earl of, dies, 184.
  the seneschal of, commanded by king John to compel Rhys the Hoarse to deliver up the castle of Llanymddyvri and the district to the sons of Gruffudd, son of Rhys, or to quit the country, 274.
  king John comes to, 292.
  Giles, bishop of, makes peace with king John, 284.
  the earl of, slain in battle, 296.
  the earl of, gets possession of Brecheiniog, 364.
Herwald, bishop of Llandaf, death of, 80.
Heurun, bishop of Menevia, death of, 40.
Hiraethwy, the battle of, 38.
Hirbarth, Constantine, son of Iago, killed in the battle of, 28.
Hirmawr, killed by the Pagans, 22.
Hirvryn, the comot of, allotted to Maelgwn, son of Rhys, 288.
Hoedlyw, son of Cadwgan, the son of Elstan, 140.
Holywell, the earl of Caerleon builds the castle of, 264.
Honorius III., succeeds as pope, 292.
Horses, Rhys, son of Gruffudd, stipulates to give three hundred, to king Henry II., 210.
  he sends him eighty-six, of which the king selects thirty-six, 212, 214.
Hospital, master of the, leads an army of Christians to Damietta, 304.
Hot summer, 4, 22.
Howel, defeats his brother Cynan in battle, 10.
  subdues the isle of Mona, expelling his brother Cynan therefrom, 10.
  driven from Mona, (Man, D.), 10.
  driven to Man, 10.
  dies at Rome, 16.

Howel, slain by Caradog, son of Gruffudd, 50.
Howel, son of Cadwalader, hanged in England, 272.
Howel, son of Edwin, holds the government of South Wales, 38.
  dispossessed of his territory by Gruffudd, son of Llywelyn, 40.
  conquered by Gruffudd in the battle of Pen Cadeir, 40.
  his wife captured, 40.
  vanquishes the Pagans who were ravaging Dyved, 40.
  meditates the devastation of South Wales, 40.
  is slain, 40.
Howel, son of Edwin (Owain, C. D. E.), king of Glamorgan, death of, 40.
Howel the Good, goes to Rome, 20.
  death of, 22.
Howel, son of Goronwy, fights against the castle of Pembroke, 58.
  (C.D.) receives the Vale of Tywi, Cydweli, and Gower from king Henry I., 74.
  driven from his dominions, 76.
  commits depredations and kills many of the French, 76.
  is killed through treachery by the French, 76.
  manner of his death, 78.
Howel, son of Gruffudd, expels his uncle, Maredudd, son of Cynan, from Meirionydd, 256.
  summoned by Llywelyn, son of Iorwerth, to join him against the English, 266.
  takes a part in Llywelyn's expedition, 286.
  his death and burial, 294.
  his character, 294.
Howel, son of Idnerth, urges Gruffudd, son of Rhys, to undertake an expedition against Ceredigion, 126, 128.
Howel, son of Ieuav, devastates the grove of Celynog (Cyveiliog, C.) the Great, 26.

Howel, son of Ieuav—*cont.*
  conquers the territory of Iago, son of Idwal, 26.
  kills Constantine, son of Iago, in the battle of Hirbarth, 26.
  devastates Cyveiliog the Great, 26.
  kills many of Alvryd's men, 28.
  killed by the Saxons, 28.

Howel, son of Ieuav, or Ieuan, son of Owain, gets possession of the castle of Tavalwern in Cyveiliog, through treachery, 196.
  commands the men of Arwystli in pursuit of Owain Gwynedd, 196.
  his death and burial, 232.
  his (son's, *C.D.E.*) death, 250.

Howel, son of Iorwerth, destroys the town of Caerleon, and devastates the country, 212.
  destroys the territory of king Henry II. as far as Hereford and Gloucester, 218.
  attacks Gwent Iscoed, subdues the whole country, except the castle, and takes hostages of the chief men of the country, 222.
  seizes Owen Pencarwn, his uncle, blinds and castrates him, 224.
  is driven out of Caerleon by the French, 224.

Howel, son of Ithel, goes to Ireland, 62.
  a dissension between him and the sons of Owain, son of Edwin, 142.
  death of, 144.

Howel, bishop of Llanelwy, death and burial of, 332.

Howel, son of Madog, slain, 162.

Howel, king of Man, death of, 10.

Howel, son of Maredudd, governs in South Wales, 38.

Howel, son of Maredudd, son of Bleddyn, killed by some one unknown, 162.

Howel, son of Maredudd of Brecheiniog, joins the expedition of Owain and Cadwalader, the sons of Gruffudd, 158.

Howel, son of Maredudd of Glamorgan, a fugitive among the mountains, 332.

Howel, son of Maredudd, son of Rhydderch, slain by the machination of Rhys, son of Howel, 162.

Howel, son of Meurug, constable of Roger Mortimer's new castle in Maelienydd, slain, with his wife, sons, and daughters, 348.

Howel, son of Owain, seizes Cadwalader, son of Gruffudd's, share of Ceredigion, and burns his castle at Aberystwyth, 164.
  ravages Aberteivi, 166.
  takes the castle of Caermarthen, 168.
  is invited to aid Cadell, Maredudd, and Rhys, sons of Gruffudd, and William, son of Gerald, and his brothers, in their attack upon the castle of Gwys, 172.
  invited under the promise of a reward to fight for the king, (*D.*), 172.
  defends the castle, (*D.*), 172.
  is successful in his attack upon the castle, 174.
  a dissension between him and his uncle Cadwalader, 174.
  calls out the men of Meirionydd, 174.
  attacks the castle of Cadwalader in Cynvael, and takes it, 174.
  captures his cousin Cadvan, son of Cadwalader, and seizes his land and castle, 178.
  the whole of Ceredigion, except one castle, taken from him (given to him, *D.*) by Cadell, Maredudd, and Rhys, the sons of Gruffudd, 178.
  obtains by force the castle of Llanrhystud, and burns it, killing the garrison, 178.
  repairs the castle of the son of Humfrey in the Vale of Calettwr, 180.
  encamps at the castle of Dinweleir, 194.
  ordered by king Henry II. to be blinded, 202.
  killed by his brother David, 206.

Howel, son of Rhys, goes with his brother Gruffudd to Gruffudd, son of Cynan, for protection from Henry II., 120.
his former imprisonment and subsequent escape, 120.
Howel, son of Rhys the Hoarse, quits his territory, and proceeds to Gwynedd to Llywelyn, son of Gruffudd, 366.
Howel the Saxon, son of Rhys, released by king Henry II., having been previously retained by him as hostage, 214.
sent by his father to serve the king beyond sea, 222.
is honourably received by the king, 222.
obtains the castle of Gwys through treachery, 238.
captures Philip, son of Gwys, the keeper of the castle, with his wife and two sons, 238.
permits his family and the family of Maelgwn, his brother, to demolish the castle of Llanuhadein, 238.
releases his father from prison, 240.
stabbed at Cemaes by the men of Maelgwn, his brother, 260.
his death and burial, 260.
Hubert, archbishop of Canterbury, dies, 260.
his dignity, 260.
Hugh, his injuries to the Britons, 70.
Hugh, the castle of, taken by young Rhys, 284.
Hugh, earl of Caerleon, the son of, accuses Gruffudd, son of Cynan, and Goronwy, son of Owain, 112.
purposes to exterminate all the Britons, 112.
commands an army under king Henry I., 114.
Hugh the Fat, leads a troop of French against Gwynedd, 60.
is wounded in the face by Magnus, king of Germany, 62.
his death, 66.
Hugh de Lacy, king John takes their land and castles from the sons of, 262, 264.

Hugh de Mortimer, seizes Rhys, son of Howel, and puts him in prison, 166.
Hugh, son of Raulf, repairs the castle of Gemaron, and conquers Maelienydd, 166.
Hugh de Say, marshals his cavalry against the Welsh, 242.
Humfrey, the castle of, burnt by the sons of Gruffudd, son of Cynan, 162.
the castle of the son of, repaired by Howel, son of Owain, 180.
the castle of, stored by Roger, earl of Clare, 190.
the castle of, attacked by Einon, son of Anarawd, 192.

I.

Iago, Gruffudd, son of Cynan, fights against the men of, 48.
Iago, son of Idwal, ravages Dyved, 22.
deprives his brother Ieuav of his eyes, 24.
expelled from his territory, 26.
is captured and his territory conquered, 26.
Iago, son of Idwal, holds the government of Gwynedd, 38.
is slain, 38.
Idwal, the sons of, fight against the sons of Owain, son of Howel, in the battle of Carno, 22.
his sons fight against the sons of Howel, in the battle of Conwy, 22.
they devastate Ceredigion, 22.
they reign at the time when the great snow happened, 24.
their kingdoms ravaged by the Saxons 24.
Idwal, is slain, 26.
Idwal, son of Meurug, is slain, 32.
Idwal, son of Rhodri, killed by the Saxons 20.
Idwal, son of Rhodri, killed, 24.
Idwallon, death of, 12.
Idwallon, son of Einon, death of, 26.

Ieuan, earl of Caerleon, death of, 326.
Ieuan, son of Dyvnwal, imprisoned in the castle of Abergavenny, 218.
Ieuan, high priest of Llanbadarn, dies, 160.
Ieuan, son of Owain, expels Maredudd, son of Llywarch, from his country, 154.
  slain by the sons of Llywarch, son of Owain, his cousin, 154, 156.
Ieuan, son of Seisyll, obtains the castle of Abergavenny, through treachery, from the men of king Henry II., 218.
Ieuav, son of Idwal, ravages Dyved, 22.
  blinded by his brother Iago, 24.
  imprisoned and hanged, 24.
Igmond, comes to the isle of Mona, and fights the battle of Rhos Meilon, 18.
Innocent III., pope, absolves Llywelyn, son of Iorwerth, Gwenwynwyn, and Maelgwn, son of Rhys, from their oath of fidelity to the king of England, 272.
  releases the interdict of the kingdom, 280.
  his death, 292.
Innocent, pope, intercedes for the liberation of Eleanor, 362.
Insects, a destructive swarm of, 220.
Ionathal, prince of Abergeleu, dies, 12.
Ionaval, son of Meurug, killed by Cadwallon, son of Ieuav, 28.
Iorwerth, son of Bleddyn, invited by Robert, earl of Shrewsbury, and Ernulf, his brother, to aid them against Henry I., 68.
  invited by the promise of a larger reward to join the king, 70.
  receives from the king a grant of Powys, Ceredigion, and the half of Dyved, 70.
  despoils the territory of earl Robert, 70.
  makes peace with his brothers, and shares the dominion between them, 72.
  confines his brother Maredudd in the king's prison, 74.

Iorwerth, son of Bleddyn—*cont.*
  gives his brother Cadwgan the territory of Ceredigion, and a part of Powys, 74.
  is disappointed by the king, who departs from his engagement with him, 74.
  cited to Shrewsbury, fined, and cast into prison, 76.
  his character, 76.
  stipulates with the king for his release, 96.
  his message to Owain and Madog, 96, 98.
  takes measures to pursue them, 98.
  repairs to the court of the king, 102.
  is plotted against by Madog, with the assistance of Llywarch's accomplices, and killed, 106, 108.
Iorwerth, son of Llywarch, killed by Llywelyn, son of Owain, in Powys, 154.
Iorwerth, bishop of Menevia, proposes terms of peace to Llywelyn, son of Iorwerth, 300.
  buries the body of Maredudd, son of Rhys, 316.
Iorwerth, son of Nudd, killed in battle, 144.
Iorwerth, son of Owain, killed, 156.
Iorwerth, son of Owain, governs the land of Caerleon, 188.
  taken by king Henry II. on the river Usk, 210.
  destroys the town of Caerleon, and devastates the country, 210, 212.
  sent for by the king to confer with him on the subject of peace, 218.
  destroys the territory of the king as far as Hereford and Gloucester, 218.
  attacks Caerleon, 222.
  attacks Gwent Iscoed, 222.
  subdues the whole country, 222.
  driven by the French from Caerleon, 224.
  recovers Caerleon, 226.
Iorwerth the Red, son of Maredudd, burns the castle of Yale, 188.
  leads an army against Henry II., 200.
  driven from his people and his territory in Mochnant, 204.

Iorwerth, abbot of Tal y Llychen, made bishop of Menevia, 284.
Ireland, a mortality in, 2.
rains blood in, 4.
arrival of the Pagans in, 8.
failure of provisions in, 16.
devastated by the people of Dublin, 20.
a fleet fails coming from, to South Wales, 42.
a fleet from, endangers South Wales, 42.
Rhys, son of Twdwr, retreats into, 52.
Cadwgan, son of Bleddyn, and Gruffudd, son of Cynan, retreat into, 60.
Howel, son of Ithel, goes to, 62.
Cadwalader, son of Gruffudd, collects a fleet from, and lands at Abermenai, 164.
Rickert, earl of Terstig, sails for, 208.
king Henry II. goes to, 216.
returns from, 216.
king John goes to, 262.
William Marshall, earl of Pembroke, sails for, 310.
Irish, a slaughter of the, at Aber Tywi, 40.
Iscoed, Gruffudd, son of Rhys, proceeds to, 128.
Isles, the Pagans of the, demolish Menevia, 54.
Ithel, son of Gruffudd, killed in the battle of Mechain, 46.
Ithel, king of Gwent, slain by the men of Brecheiniog, 12.
Ithel, son of Rhirid, incited by Rickert, bishop of London, to seize Owain, son of Cadwgan, 86.
seizes the portion of Powys belonging to Cadwgan and his son Owain, 92.
demanded by king Henry I. as hostage in respect of the release of Iorwerth, son of Bleddyn, 96.
liberated from the king's prison, 150.
slain by his cousin Gruffudd, son of Maredudd, 152.
Ithel, abbot of Ystrad Marchell, death of, 232.

Ivor, son of Alan, king of Armorica, reigns as chief or prince in Britain, 2.
his death, 2.
Ivor, son of Idnerth, cuts off the French at Aber Llech, 58.
Ivor, son of Meurug, the men of, treacherously kill Morgan, son of Owain Gwynedd, 188.
Ivor, of Porth Talarthi, dies, 32.
Iweryd, mother of Owain and Uchtryd, the sons of Edwin, king of Tegeingl, 140.

J.

Jeffrey, bishop of Llandaf, death of, 184.
Jeffrey, bishop of Menevia, death of, 118.
Jeffrey, bishop of Menevia, death of, 280.
Jerusalem, Robert, brother of Henry I., returns victoriously from, 64.
Morgan, son of Cadwgan, dies on his return from, 154.
pilgrims to, are drowned, 166.
Louis, king of France, proceeds to, 172.
subdued by the Saracens and the Jews, 234.
Baldwin, archbishop of Canterbury, goes to, 236.
an earthquake at, 256.
several crusaders go to, 304.
Jerusalem, king of, leads the Christians to Damietta, 304.
Jerusalem, patriarch of, comes to England to request aid from king Henry II. against the Jews and Saracens, 232.
leads the Christians to Damietta, 304.
Jews and Saracens, threaten the destruction of Jerusalem, 232.
take possession of the Cross, and subdue Jerusalem, 234.
Joan, dame, daughter of king John, and wife of Llywelyn, son of Iorwerth, dies at Aber, 324.
is buried in a new cemetery on the side of the strand, 324.

INDEX. 457

John, fortifies the castles of Menevia and Buellt, 330.
John, cardinal, arrives in England, and holds a council, 260.
John, king of England, succeeds to the throne, 254.
    banishes William Bruse, his son William, and their wives and grandsons, to Ireland, 262.
    seizes Gwenwynwyn at Shrewsbury, 262.
    goes with an immense army to Ireland, 262.
    dispossesses the sons of Hugh de Lacy of their land and castles, 262, 264.
    having received homage of all in Ireland, and captured the wife of William Bruse, and young William, and his wife, son, and daughter, he returns to England, 264.
    makes preparations for the subjugation of Gwynedd, 266.
    comes to Dyganwy, 266.
    having suffered great privations and losses, he returns to England, 268.
    is deprived of the Midland district by Llywelyn, son of Iorwerth, Gwenwynwyn, and Maelgwn, son of Rhys, 272.
    commands the seneschal of Hereford, and Foulke, the seneschal of Cardiff, to compel Rhys the Hoarse to deliver up the castle of Llanymddyvri and the district to the sons of Gruffudd, son of Rhys, or to quit the country, 274.
    does penance for the wrongs which he had committed against the church, 276.
    recalls the archbishop of Canterbury and the other bishops and scholars from exile, 278.
    makes his kingdom a tributary of the Roman see, 278.
    sails for Poictou with a large army, 278.
    makes a truce of seven years with the king of France, 280.

John, king of England—*cont.*
    returns to England, 280.
    pays many of their losses to the clergy, 280.
    a disturbance between him and his barons, 280.
    the Welsh rise against him, 282.
    loses London into the hands of the men of the North, 282.
    makes peace with Gwenwynwyn, 290.
    secures the rivers and harbours against the approach of Louis, the son of the French king, 292.
    flees towards Winchester and the Vale of the Severn, 292.
    burns the town of Winchester lest it should fall into the hands of Louis, and fortifies the castle, 292.
    proceeds to Hereford, 292.
    requires the Welsh princes to enter into terms of peace with him, 292.
    proceeds to Gelli and Maes Hyveidd, burns the towns, and demolishes the castles, 292.
    ravages and destroys Oswestry, 292.
    dies at Newark, 292.
    his body conveyed to Worcester, where it is buried, near the grave of St. Dunstan, 292.
Joseph, bishop of Llandaf, death of, 40.
Joseph, bishop of Menevia, death of, 44.

K.

Kent, Worgan consecrated in, by archbishop Ancellin, 80.

L.

Lacy, Hugh de, his sons dispossessed of their land and castles by king John, 262.
Lateran church, a general council held at, 286.

Leinster, the men of, oppose Brian, king of all Ireland, and his allies, 34.
Diermid, king of, dies, 208.
Lewes, the king of England and the king of Germany meet on the plains of, 350.
Lincoln, the North men and the French under Louis, take possession of the city of, 294.
it is retaken by the English under William Marshall, earl of Pembroke, and others, 296.
Lincoln, the bishop of, dies, 324.
Lincoln, the earl of, with Roger Mortimer, leads an army to Castle Baldwin, 364.
they besiege the castle of Dolvorwyn, and gain it, 364, 366.
Little Cenarch (Cengarth, *D.*), founded by Gerald, the steward of Pembroke, 82.
Llanarthneu, capture of Rhys the Hoarse at, 316.
Llanbadarn, devastated by the Pagans, 30.
depopulated by Gruffudd, son of Llywelyn, son of Seisyll, 40.
Ieuan, the high priest of, dies, 160.
Mahalt de Bruse dies at, 266.
Maredudd, son of Owain, dies at, 252.
Llanbadarn the Great, the church of, burnt, 344.
Llandaf, Joseph, bishop of, dies at Rome, 40.
Herwald, bishop of, dies, 80.
Uchtryd, bishop of, dies, 176.
Jeffrey, bishop of, dies, 184.
Llandeilo, burnt by Rhys the Hoarse, 276.
Llandeilo the Great, Rhys the Hoarse dies at, 320.
Llandinam, Owain Gwynedd moves an army as far as, 196.
Llandydoch, devastated by the Pagans, 30.
a battle near, between Rhys, son of Tewdwr, and Gruffudd, son of Maredudd, 54.

Llanddewi Brevi, the sanctuary of Dewi at, defiled and laid waste, 90.
Llanegwad, the castle of, subdued by young Rhys, 258.
Llanegwestl, the monastery of, founded by Madog, son of Gruffudd Maelor, 256.
Gruffudd, son of Madog, buried at, 356.
Llanelwy, Adam, bishop of, dies, 230.
Abraham, bishop of, dies, 320.
Howel, bishop of, dies, 332.
Llanerch Aeron, death of Maelgwn, son of Rhys, at, 318.
Llangadog, the castle of, won by (from, *E.*) Maelgwn, son of Rhys, and Gwenwynwyn, son of Owain Cyveiliog, 258.
taken possession of by Rhys the Little, 262.
burnt by Rhys and Owain, sons of Gruffudd, 262.
Llangarvan, devastated by the Pagans, 30.
Llan Geneu, the castle of, reduced and taken, 344.
Llangiwg, Llywelyn, son of Iorwerth, encamps at, 300.
Llangors, Trahaiarn the Little seized on his passage through, 250.
Llangwm, battle near, between the sons of Meurug and Maredudd, 32.
Llanilltud, devastated by the Pagans, 30.
Llanrhystud, a castle at, constructed by Cadwalader, son of Gruffudd, 176.
the castle conquered by the sons of Gruffudd, son of Rhys, 178.
Llanrwst, the action of Conwy at, between the sons of Idwal and the sons of Howel, 22.
Llanstephan, the castle of, burnt by the sons of Gruffudd, son of Cynan, 162.
conquered by the sons of Gruffudd, son of Rhys, 168.
taken possession of by Rhys, son of Gruffudd, 234.
demolished by Llywelyn, son of Iorwerth, 286.

Llanstephan—*cont.*
   destroyed by Llywelyn, son of Gruffudd, and his associates, 344.
Llanuhadein, the castle of, taken by Rhys, son of Gruffudd, 236.
   demolished by permission of Howel the Saxon, son of Rhys, son of Gruffudd, 238.
Llanvaes, the battle of, in Mona, 10.
   the monastery of, built by Llywelyn, son of Iorwerth, in honour of his wife Joan, 326.
Llanvihangel Gelynrod, death of Gwenllian, daughter of young Maelgwn, at, 338.
Llanweithenog, devastated by Godfrey, son of Harold, 28.
Llanwenog, the battle of, 28.
Llanymddyvri, the castle of, attacked by Gruffudd, son of Rhys, 122.
   subdued by Rhys, son of Gruffudd, 190.
   taken possession of by Gruffudd, son of Rhys, 256.
   obtained by the family of young Rhys, son of Gruffudd, 258.
   obtained through devices, by Gwenwynwyn and Maelgwn, son of Rhys, 258.
   won from Maelgwn, son of Rhys, 258, 260.
   taken possession of by Rhys the Hoarse, 264.
   strengthened by Rhys the Hoarse, 276.
   yielded to young Rhys, 276.
   allotted to Maelgwn, son of Rhys, 288.
   Maredudd, son of Gruffudd, dies in, 358.
Llawdden, nephew of Gurgeneu the abbot, slain by Cynan and Owain Gwynedd, 206.
Lleyn, devastated by the sons of Abloec, 24.
   devastated by Gwrmid, 26.
   devastated by Constantine, son of Iago, and Godfrey, son of Harold, 26.

Lleyn—*cont.*
   Cadwalader and Owain, sons of Gruffudd, remove all their property from Meirionydd into, 150.
   subdued by Llywelyn, son of Iorwerth, 256.
   the cantrev of, conceded to Owain the Red, 370.
Llwyn Pina, Owain, prince of Gwynedd, encamps in front of, 186.
Llych Crei, the battle of, 52.
Llychwr, the castle of, reduced by young Rhys, 284.
Llywarch, son of Hennyth, dies, 18.
Llywarch, son of Owain, deprived of his eyes, 28.
Llywarch, son of Owain, son of Edwin, a dissension between him with his brothers, and Howel, son of Ithel, 142.
   slaughtered in battle with Howel and his allies, 144.
Llywarch, son of Trahaiarn, his aid promised to Ithel and Madog, sons of Rhirid, against Owain, son of Cadwgan, by Rickert, bishop of London, 86.
   plots with Madog, son of Rhirid, against Iorwerth, son of Bleddyn, 106.
   his land invaded by the family of Maredudd, son of Bleddyn, 110.
   joined by king Henry I., with Owain, son of Cadwgan, in an expedition against Gruffudd, son of Rhys, 134.
   his territory ravaged by Maredudd, son of Bleddyn, and others, 152.
Llywelyn, son of Cadwallon, unjustly seized and blinded by his brothers, 232, 234.
Llywelyn, son of Cadwgan, takes part in a battle at Camddwr, 48.
   and in the battle of Gwennottyll, 48.
   killed by the men of Brecheiniog, 62.
Llywelyn, son of Cedivor, defeated and slain by Rhys, son of Tewdwr, 54.

Llywelyn, son of Gruffudd, awaits the hostile arrival of his brothers, 340.
captures and imprisons Owain the Red, 340.
takes possession of the territory of Owain and David, 340.
listens to the complaints of the Welsh nobles, 340.
in company with Maredudd, son of Rhys the Hoarse, invades the Midland country, 340.
takes Meirionydd to himself, 342.
gives the part of Ceredigion, which belonged to Edward, with Buellt, to Maredudd, son of Owain, 342.
restores his territory to Maredudd, son of Rhys the Hoarse, 342.
wrests Gwerthrynion from Roger Mortimer, 342.
in company with Maredudd, son of Rhys the Hoarse, and Maredudd, son of Owain, invades the territory of Gruffudd, son of Gwenwynwyn, 342.
destroys the castle of Bydydon, 342.
destroys the castle of Aber Torran, Llanstephan, Arberth, and Maenclochog, 344.
subdues Cemaes, 344.
is reconciled to Gruffudd, son of Madog, 344.
enters Buellt, 346.
takes it, with the exception of the castle, from Roger Mortimer, 346.
returns to Gwynedd, 346.
his men gain the castle of Buellt by a night onset, and destroy it, 346.
receives Owain, son of Maredudd of Elvael, into peace, 346.
comes with a large army to Maelienydd, 348.
receives the homage of the men of Maelienydd, 348.
permits Roger Mortime to return back, 348.
goes to Brecheiniog, 348.
returns to Gwynedd, 348.

Llywelyn, son of Gruffudd—*cont.*
becomes prince of all Wales, 352.
confederates with earl Clare, 354.
peace formed between him and king Henry III., 354.
terms of the compact, 356.
visits the castle of Dolvorwyn, 358.
upbraids Gruffudd, son of Gwenwynwyn, with his deceit and disloyalty, 360.
takes from him Arwystli and thirteen townships of Cyveiliog, and carries his eldest son Owain with him to Gwynedd, 360.
sends messengers to Gruffudd, son of Gwenwynwyn, who orders them to be imprisoned, 360.
fights against the castle of Trallwng, and subdues all the territory of Gruffudd, 360.
summoned by the king to do homage to him, 362.
refuses to go to the king, 362.
returns to Wales, 362.
espouses Eleanor, daughter of Simon Montford, 362.
sends messengers in vain to the court of the king about forming peace, 364.
comes to the king at Rhuddlan, and makes his peace with him, 370.
is invited to London, 370.
does homage to the king, 370.
having remained a fortnight in London, returns home, 370.
marries Eleanor in the great church at Worcester, 370.
returns with his wife to Wales, 370.
Llywelyn, son of Iorwerth, combines with Rhodri, son of Owain, and the sons of Cynan, against David, son of Owain Gwynedd, 240.
captured by Gwenwynwyn, 250.
subdues the cantrev of Lleyn, 256.
raises an army from Powys, against Gwenwynwyn, 258.
peace concluded between him and Gwenwynwyn, 258.

INDEX.   461

Llywelyn, son of Iorwerth—*cont.*
  returns happily after conquering the castle of Bala, 258.
  David, son of Owain, banished out of Wales by him, 258.
  takes possession of Gwenwynwyn's territory, castles, and courts, 262.
  repairs Aberystwyth, and takes to himself the cantrev of Penwedig, 262.
  gives the rest of Ceredigion above Aeron to the sons of Gruffudd, son of Rhys, 262.
  the castle of Dyganwy demolished by him, 264.
  ravages the territory of the earl of Caerleon, 264.
  makes cruel attacks upon the English, 266.
  king John is enraged against him, 266.
  disposes his army and property for the campaign with John, 266.
  sends his wife to make peace with the king, 268.
  confederates with the Welsh princes against the king, 270.
  is absolved by pope Innocent from the oath of fidelity to the king, 272.
  reduces the castles of Dyganwy and Rhuddlan, 278.
  invests Shrewsbury, and receives possession of the town and castle, 282.
  is joined by Maelgwn, and Owain, son of Gruffudd, in Gwynedd, 284.
  his daughter married to Rheinallt de Bruse, 286.
  collects a vast army to Caermarthen, 286.
  razes its castle to the ground, 286.
  demolishes the castles of Llanstephan, and Talacharn and St. Clare, 286.
  fights against the castle of Emlyn in Ceredigion, 286.
  receives the homage of the men of Cemaes, 286.
  the castle of Trevdraeth is delivered to him, 286.

Llywelyn, son of Iorwerth—*cont.*
  and the castles of Aberystwyth and Cilgerran, 286.
  returns victorious, with the confederate princes, 286.
  witnesses a partition of land between Maelgwn, son of Rhys, and Rhys the Hoarse and others, 288.
  strives to recal Gwenwynwyn to his allegiance to him, 290.
  enters Powys, and makes war on Gwenwynwyn, 290.
  becomes angry with Rheinallt de Bruse, 298.
  invades Brecheiniog, and attacks Aberhodni, 298.
  makes peace with the men of Aberhodni, and takes five hostages from them, 300.
  conducts his army to Gower, over the Black Mountain, 300.
  encamps at Llangiwg, 300.
  gives the castle of Senghenydd to Rheinallt de Bruse, who had surrendered to him, 300.
  leads his army towards Dyved, against the Flemings, 300.
  met at Cevn Cynwarchan, by messengers from the Flemings, 300.
  invests Haverford, 300.
  receives terms of peace from Iorwerth, bishop of Menevia, 300.
  Caermarthen and Aberteivi put under his custody, 302.
  advises young Rhys, and all the princes, to do homage to the king, 304.
  his daughter Margaret married to John de Bruse, 304.
  summons the princes of Wales, 306.
  collects a vast army against the Flemings of Rhos and Pembroke, 306.
  attacks the castle of Arberth, 306.
  obtains it by force, 306.
  destroys the castle of Gwys, and burns the town, 306.
  comes to Haverford, and burns the town, 306.

462 INDEX.

Llywelyn, son of Iorwerth—*cont.*
goes round Rhos and Deugleddyv, 306.
makes a truce with the Flemings, 306.
returns home joyful and happy, 306.
a dispute engendered between him and his son Gruffudd, 306.
collects an army against Gruffudd, 306.
threatens to take revenge upon him and his men, 306.
is exhorted to receive his son in peace, 308.
is reconciled to him, 308.
takes from him the cantrev of Meirionydd and comot of Ardudwy, 308.
begins to build a castle therein, 308.
goes to Aberystwyth, 308.
obtains possession of the castle and the territory attached to it, 308.
is, with the earls and barons of the marches, summoned by the king to Shrewsbury, 308.
is reconciled to young Rhys, 308.
relinquishes Aberteivi in his favour, 308.
gives a part of young Rhys's territory to Maelgwn, son of Rhys, 310.
sends Gruffudd, his son, with a large army to oppose William Marshall, earl of Pembroke, 312.
proceeds to Mabudrud, 314.
prepares to oppose the king, 316.
attacks his enemies, 316.
receives the castle of Buellt and a large sum of money for the liberation of young William Bruse, 316.
peace formed between him and the king, 316.
hangs William Bruse, 318.
burns the town and castle of Baldwin, Maes Hyveidd, Gelli, and Aberhodni, 318.
reduces Caerleon to ashes, 318.
casts the castles of Nedd and Cydweli to the ground, 318.
proceeds to Brecheiniog, 320.

Llywelyn, son of Iorwerth—*cont.*
destroys all the castles and towns, 320.
fights against the castle of Aberhodni for a month, 320.
burns the town of Colunwy, 320.
subjugates the Vale of Teveidiog, 320.
burns Trallwng and Oswestry, and razes the Red Castle to the ground, 320.
builds a monastery at Llanvaes, in honour of his wife, 326.
divests Maredudd, son of Madog, of his territory, 326.
dies, and is buried at Aberconway, 326.
his good works, 326.
Llywelyn, son of Madog, kills Stephen, son of Baldwin, 180.
is killed, 194.
Llywelyn, son of Maelgwn, dies, 318.
is buried at Aberconway, 318.
Llywelyn, son of Maredudd, a confederate prince with Llywelyn, son of Iorwerth, in his expedition to South Wales, 288.
Llywelyn, son of Owain, blinded by his uncle, Maredudd, son of Bleddyn, 154, *bis.*
kills Iorwerth, son of Llywarch, 154.
kills Maredudd, son of Llywarch, 154.
his death, 202.
his character, 202.
Llywelyn, son of Owain, reconciled to the king, 366.
placed by Pain as a youth in ward, 366, 368.
Llywelyn, son of young Rhys, and Howel, son of Rhys the Hoarse, go to Gwynedd, 366.
Llywelyn, son of Seisyll, kills Aeddan, son of Blegywryd, and his four sons, 34.
makes war against Rein the Scot, 36.
signally defeats him at Aber Gwyli, 36.
extent of his dominion, and prosperity of his reign, 36.

INDEX. 463

London, taken possession of by Henry I. on the death of William Rufus, 64.
  a council held in, for the purpose of confirming the laws of the churches 228.
  taken by the North men from king John, 282.
  the bishop of, dies, 324.
  David, son of Llywelyn, cited to, by king Henry III., 328.
  earl Clare marches with a vast army to, 354.
  takes it through the treachery of the burgesses, 354.
  is attacked by king Henry III., 354.
  king Henry III. interred in the new monastery in, 358.
  king Edward I. appoints a council in, 362.
Lough Garmon, the castle at, gained by Robert, son of Stephen, and Diermid, son of Murchath, 206.
Louis, king of France, joins a crusade to Jerusalem, 172.
  messengers from, come to king Henry II., 216.
Louis, son of Phillip, king of France, is sent by his father to Poictou, to meet king John, 278.
  comes to England with a great multitude, 290.
  receives homage from the earls and barons, at London, 292.
  takes the castle of Winchester, 292.
  a treaty of peace and compact with him discussed in a council at Oxford, 294.
  sails for France, 294.
  returns to England with a small retinue, 294.
  desists from attacking the castle of Canterbury, 298.
  comes to London, and sends to France for help, 298.
  pacification declared between him and Henry, king of England, 302.
  its terms, 302.
  sails for France, 302.

Louis (supra), king of France, and his three brothers, proceed with an immense army towards Jerusalem, 334.
  proceeds to the city of Damietta, 334.
  that city is given up to him, 334.
  taken by the Saracens, 334.
  compelled to restore Damietta to them, 334.
  regains it, 336.
  returns from his pilgrimage, 338
Lucius, succeeds Alexander in the papacy, 230.
  his death, 232.
Ludlow, Llywelyn, son of Iorwerth, and William Marshall, appear before the council of the king and archbishop at, 314.
Lwmbert, assumes the bishopric of Menevia, 14.
  his death, 20.

M.

Mabudrud, Llywelyn, son of Iorwerth, proceeds with his army to, 314.
Mabwynion, (son of Gwynion), the castle of, dismantled and burnt by Rhys, son of Gruffudd, 198.
  the comot of, alloted to Maelgwn, son of Rhys, 290.
Macmael Minbo, slain in a sudden onset, 46.
  his fame and power, 46.
Mactus the monk, death of, 40.
Madog, son of Bleddyn, assists his brothers in expelling Rhys, son of Tewdwr, from his territory and kingdom, 52.
  slain, with his brothers, in the battle of Llych Crei, 52.
Madog, son of Cadwgan, holds a share of Powys after his brother Owen's death, 138.
  invited by Howel, son of Ithel, to assist him against the sons of Owain, son of Edwin, 142.

Madog, son of Cadwgan—*cont.*
    aids in the defeat of the latter, 144.
    is opposed by king Henry I., 146.
Madog, son of Gruffudd Maelor, founds the monastery of Llanegwestl in Yale, 254, 256.
    summoned by king John to Caerleon, to join his army against Llywelyn, son of Iorwerth, 266.
    confederates with Llywelyn against the king, 270.
    his death and burial, 324.
    his character, 324.
Madog, son of Idnerth, joins the expedition of Owain and Cadwalader, sons of Gruffudd, 158.
    his death, 162.
    his two sons join Owain Gwynedd against Henry II., 200.
Madog, son of Llywarch, killed by his cousin Meurug, son of Rhirid, 156.
Madog, son of Maelgwn, hanged in England, 272.
Madog, son of Maredudd, builds the castle of Oswestry, and gives Cyveiliog to his nephews, Owain and Meurug, the sons of Gruffudd, 176.
    prepares to rise against Owain Gwynedd, 178.
    constructs a castle at Caereinion in the vicinity of Cymmer, 184.
    encamps between the army of king Henry II. and the army of Owain Gwynedd, 186.
    his death, 194.
    his character, 194.
    his sons assist Owain Gwynedd against Henry II., 200.
Madog, son of Rhirid, requested by Rickert, bishop of London, to secure Owain, son of Cadwgan, or to expel him and his father out of the country, 86.
    encamps at Rhyd Cornnec, 88.
    seizes the portion of Powys which belonged to Cadwgan and Owain, 92.

Madog, son of Rhirid—*cont.*
    a discord between him and the French, 94.
    seeks and obtains the friendship of Owain, son of Cadwgan, 94.
    with Owain, commit many crimes, 96.
    remonstrated with by Iorwerth, son of Bleddyn, 98.
    set upon by the men of Meirionydd, 100.
    goes into Powys, 100.
    goes to Ireland with Owain, 104.
    returns from Ireland, not being able to endure the savage manners of the Gwyddelians, 104.
    proceeds to Powys, but is not received kindly by his uncle Iorwerth, 106.
    forms a plot against his uncle, and makes a night attack upon him, 106.
    plots against Cadwgan, son of Bleddyn, and slays him, 108.
    taken prisoner by the family of Maredudd, son of Bleddyn, 110.
    blinded by Owain, son of Cadwgan, 112.
Madog, son of Rhys, escapes from his father's prison, 236.
    blinded by Anarawd, his brother, 238.
Mael Mordav, heads the men of Leinster against Brian, king of Ireland, 34.
Maelgwn, son of Cadwalader, death of, 250.
Maelgwn, son of Cadwallon, the sons of, take part in the expedition of Llywelyn, son of Iorwerth, to South Wales, 288.
Maelgwn the Little, son of Maelgwn, fights against Caermarthen, 322.
    completes the castle of Trev Ilan, 322.
    fortifies the castle of Garthgrugyn, 328.
    compelled to flee into Gwynedd, 332.
    retires into the mountains and wilds, 332.
Maelgwn, son of Maelgwn, son of Rhys, burns Aberteivi, and slays the burgesses, 318.
    breaks down the bridge, 318.

Maelgwn, son of Maelgwn, son of Rhys—*cont.*
    comes to Owain, son of Gruffudd, and the men of Llywelyn, 318.
    accompanied by them, breaks the castle with engines, 318.
    dies, and is buried at Strata Florida, 344.

Maelgwn, son of Owain, banished into Ireland by his brother David, 222.
    taken and imprisoned by the same, 224.

Maelgwn, son of Rhys, ravages and burns Tenby, 234.
    his character, 234.
    seized by his father, and imprisoned, 236.
    escapes from prison, 236.
    his family gain the castle of Ystrad Meurug, 238.
    and demolish the castle of Llanuhadein, 238.
    are attacked and put to flight by the Flemings, 238.
    gives the castle of Ystrad Meurug to his brothers, 238.
    assists his brothers in imprisoning his father, 240.
    deceived by his brother Howel, who releases his father, 240.
    his castle of Nyver demolished by the sons of Cadwallon, 240.
    subjugates, with the family of Gwenwynwyn, the town and castle of Aberystwyth, 248, 250.
    imprisons his brother Gruffudd, 250.
    takes Aberteivi and the castle of Ystrad Meurug, after his brother Gruffudd had gone into an English prison, 252.
    swears to deliver Aberteivi castle to Gruffudd, 254.
    disregards his oath, 254.
    gets possession of the castle of Dincirth, 254.
    sells Aberteivi for a trifling value to the English, 254.

Maelgwn, son of Rhys—*cont.*
    wins (loses, *E.*) the castle of Llanymddyvri and the castle of Llangadog, 258, 260.
    completes the castle of Dineirth, 258.
    his men treacherously stab his brother Howel, 260.
    loses Llanymddyvri and Dinevwr, the keys of all his dominions, 260.
    instigates an Irishman to kill Cedivor, son of Griffri, 260.
    constructs the castle of Abereinion, 262.
    razes the castle of Ystrad Meurug to the ground, and burns Dineirth and Aberystwyth, for fear of Llywelyn, son of Iorwerth, 262.
    makes peace with king John, 264.
    encamps at Cilcenin with a vast army of French and Welsh, 264.
    his army attacked and put to flight by Rhys and Owain, the sons of Gruffudd, 264.
    disgracefully flies on foot, 266.
    joins the army of the king, 266.
    is sent against the sons of Rhys, son of Gruffudd, 268.
    repairs to Penwedig, 268.
    repents of his terms with the king, and demolishes the new castle at Aberystwyth, 270.
    his territory ravaged by Rhys and Owain, 270.
    is absolved by pope Innocent of his oath of fidelity to the king of England, 272.
    becomes reconciled with his nephew, young Rhys, and proceeds with him to Dyved, 282.
    proceeds to Gwynedd, to Llywelyn, son of Iorwerth, 284.
    joins the expedition of Llywelyn to South Wales, 288.
    a partition of land between him and his brother Rhys the Hoarse and Rhys and Owain, sons of Gruffudd, at Aberdovey, 288.
    his allotments enumerated, 288.

Maelgwn, son of Rhys—*cont.*
   obtains from Llywelyn, son of Iorwerth, a part of the territory of Rhys, son of Gruffudd, deceased, 310.
   dies at Llanerch Aeron, and is buried at Strata Florida, 318.

Maelienydd, the men of, kill some persons who were fleeing to Arwystli, 88.
   conquered the second time by Hugh, son of Raulf, 166.
   Roger Mortimer leads an army to, 240.
   the castle of, fortified by Roger Mortimer, 330.
   the men of, pay homage to Llywelyn, son of Gruffudd, 348.

Maelog the Crooked, slain in the battle of Dineirth, 18.

Maelsalacheu, death of, (A.D. 860), 12.

Maenclochog, burnt by the Welsh, 284.
   burnt by Llywelyn, son of Gruffudd, and his companions, 344.

Maes Hyveidd, devastated by Maredudd, (A.D. 990), 30.
   burnt by the lord Rhys, 242.
   obtained possession of by Giles de Bruse, 282.
   king John proceeds to, burns the town, and demolishes the castle, 292.
   burnt by Llywelyn, son of Iorwerth, 318.
   the castle of, repaired by Rickert, earl of Pembroke, 320.

Maesydog, the battle of, between the Britons and Picts, 6.

Magnus, son of Harold, king of Germany, comes to England, and ravages the dominions of the Saxons, 44.
   comes as far as Mona, with the view of possessing himself of the countries of the Britons, 62.
   attacks the French, and then leaves the borders of the country, 62.
   comes a second time to Mona, and cuts down much timber, 72.
   returns to the isle of Man, and builds there three castles, which he fills with his own men, 72.

Magnus, son of Harold—*cont.*
   sends to Ireland to demand the daughter of Murchath for his son, 72.
   commits depredations on the coasts of Britain, 74.
   fights against the Britons, and is killed in battle, 74.

Mahalt de Bruse, mother of the sons of Gruffudd, dies at Llanbadarn the Great, 266.

Mahalt, daughter of Malcolm, king of Prydyn, married to Henry I., 64.

Maig, son of Ieuav, killed, 28.

Malcolm, son of Dwnchath, king of the Picts and Albanians, or Scots, killed by the French, 54, 56.

Mallaen, the comot of, allotted to Maelgwn, son of Rhys, 288.

Man, isle of, an earthquake in, 2.
   Howel driven from (to, *E.*) Man, 10.
   Howel, king of, dies, 10.
   devastated by Swain, son of Harold, 32.
   Gruffudd, son of Cynan, fights against the men of, 48.
   Magnus, king of Germany, builds castles in, 72.
   his son set up as king in, 72.

March, a great snow in the month of, 24.

Maredudd, son of Bleddyn, invited to the assistance of Robert, earl of Shrewsbury, and his brother, against king Henry I., 68.
   confined by his brother Iorwerth in the king's prison, 74.
   escapes from prison, and returns to his country, 80.
   requests the king to give him the land of his brother Iorwerth, 110.
   sends his family on an expedition to the land of Llywarch, son of Trahaiarn, 110.
   delivers Madog, son of Rhirid, into the hands of Owain, son of Cadwgan, 112.
   seeks the friendship of the king, 114.
   counsels Owain to repair to the king, 116.

Maredudd, son of Bleddyn—*cont.*
   is requested by Howel, son of Ithel to come to his assistance, 142.
   after a battle with the sons of Owain, son of Edwin, returns home, 144.
   opposed by king Henry I., 146.
   sends archers to intercept the king, 148.
   is reconciled to the king, 150.
   expels his nephew Maredudd, son of Cadwgan, 150.
   ravages the territory of Llywarch, son of Trahaiarn, 152.
   mutilates his nephew Llywelyn, son of Owain, 154.
   his death, 156.
   his character, 156.

Maredudd, son of Cadwgan, expelled by his uncle Maredudd, son of Bleddyn, 150.
   killed by his brother Morgan, 152.

Maredudd, son of Caradog, dies, 270.

Maredudd, son of Cynan, taken and imprisoned, 252.
   expelled by Llywelyn, son of Iorwerth, 256.
   expelled from Meirionydd, by his nephew Howel, son of Gruffudd, 256.

Maredudd, king of Dyved, dies, 8.

Maredudd, son of Edwin, holds the government of the South, 38.
   is killed by the sons of Cynan, 38.

Maredudd, son of Gruffudd, killed in the battle of Mechain, 46.

Maredudd, son of Gruffudd, custodian of the castle of Caermarthen, repels the French and Flemings who had come to attack the castle, 168.
   his courage, 170.
   raises an army against the castle of Gwys, 172.
   subdues Ceredigion as far as Aeron, 178.
   takes the whole of Ceredigion from (grants it to, *D.*) Howel, son of Owain, 178.
   repairs the castle of Ystrad Meurug, 180.
   fights against the castle of Aberllychwr and burns it, 180.

Maredudd, son of Gruffudd—*cont.*
   repairs the castle of Dinweileir, 180.
   leads his forces to Penwedig, fights against the castle of Howel, and demolishes it, 180.
   attacks the castle of Aberavan, burns it, and kills the garrison, 182.
   his death, 182.
   his compassion, power, and justice, 182, 184.

Maredudd, son of Gruffudd, lord of Hirvryn, dies, and is buried at Strata Florida, 356, 358.

Maredudd, son of Howel, with others, burns the castle of Rickert de la Mere, the castle of Dinerth, and the castle of Caerwedros, 158.
   joins the second expedition of Owain and Cadwalader, 158.
   slain by the sons of Bleddyn, son of Cynvyn, 162.

(Son of, *E.*), Maredudd, son of, (and, *D.*), Howel, Caer Offa falls before, 196.

Maredudd, son of Llywarch, expelled from his country by Ieuan, son of Owain, 154.
   killed by him, (by Llywelyn, son of Owain, *C.*), 154.
   his cruelty, 154.

Maredudd, son of Llywelyn of Meirionydd, dies, 338.

Maredudd, son of Madog, killed by Hugh de Mortimer, 168.

Maredudd, son of Madog, son of Gruffudd Maelor, kills his brother Gruffudd, 326.
   divested of his territory by Llywelyn, son of Iorwerth, 326.

Maredudd, son of Owain, kills Cadwallon, son of Ieuav, 28.
   pays to the black Pagans a tribute of a penny for each person, 30.
   devastates Maes Hyveidd, 30.
   his kingdoms devastated by Edwin, son of Einon, and Eclis the Great, 30.
   hires the Pagans, and devastates Glamorgan, 30.

Maredudd, son of Owain—*cont.*
  his son dies, 30.
  a great famine in his territory, 32.
  his death and renown, 32.
Maredudd, son of Owain, governs South Wales, 46.
  killed by Caradog, son of Gruffudd, 46.
Maredudd, son of Owain, receives from Llywelyn, son of Gruffudd, the part of Ceredigion which belonged to Edward, son of Henry III., 342.
  subdues the greater part of the territory of Gruffudd, son of Gwenwynwyn, 342.
  invades Rhos, 344.
  goes to Emlyn to speak with Maredudd, son of Rhys, and Patrick de Sayes, 346.
  dies at Llanbadarn the Great, and is buried at Strata Florida, 352, 354.
  his dignity, 352.
Maredudd Redhead, kills his cousin Meurug, son of Adam, in his sleep, 206.
Maredudd, son of Rhydderch, kindly receives certain fugitives in the Vale of Tywi, 88.
  assists the garrison of Llanymddyvri castle against Gruffudd, son of Rhys, 122.
  summoned by the French, and his fidelity to king Henry I. tested, 124.
  makes an indiscreet sally, 130.
Maredudd, son of Rhys, ordered by king Henry II. to be deprived of his sight, 202.
  subjugates through treachery the castle of Dinevwr and the castle of Cantrev Bychan, 240.
  seized and imprisoned by his father at Ystrad Meurug, 240.
  dies, and is buried at Whitland, 326.
Maredudd, son of Rhys, slain at Carnwyllon, 256.
  his character, 256.
Maredudd, son of the lord Rhys, archdeacon of Ceredigion, dies at Pont Stephan, 316.
  buried at Menevia, 316.

Maredudd, son of Rhys the Hoarse, invades the midland country, 340.
  receives his territory from Llywelyn, son of Gruffudd, 342.
  subdues most of the territory of Gruffudd, son of Gwenwynwyn, 342.
  reconciled to his nephew, Rhys Mechyll the Little, 344.
  attacks Trevdraeth, and demolishes the castle, 344.
  invades Rhos, 344.
  takes and reduces the castle of Llan Geneu, 344.
  disregards his oath, 344, 346.
  seizes the men who had gone to speak with him at Emlyn, 346.
  dies in the castle at Dyryslwyn, and is buried at Whitland, 358.
Maredudd, son of Robert, of Cydewain, joins the army of Llywelyn, son of Iorwerth, 266, 270, 288.
  dies, after taking the religious habit, at Strata Florida, 330.
Margaret, daughter of Llywelyn, son of Iorwerth, married to Rhys the Hoarse, 304.
Margaret, daughter of Maelgwn, and wife of Owain, son of Robert, dies, 340.
Margaret, wife of Malcolm, prays that she may not survive her husband and son, 56.
  her death, 56.
Mark, son of Harold, devastates and subjugates Mona, 24.
Marshall, earl, goes to Jerusalem as a crusader, 304.
Marshall, Rickert, earl of Pembroke, repairs the castle of Maes Hyveidd, 320.
  a dispute between him and king Henry III., 320.
  enters into treaty with Llywelyn, son of Iorwerth, and joins his army, 320.
  is stabbed in Ireland, 322.
Marshall, Walter, sent by the English to fortify Aberteivi, 328.

INDEX.   469

Marshall, William, fights against Cilgerran, and subdues it, 260.
   invited to assist the garrison of Lincoln, 294.
   fights against Caerleon, and takes it, 302.
   sails to Ireland, 310.
   returns with a vast fleet, 312.
   the castle of Aberteivi delivered up to him, 312.
   also the castle of Caermarthen, 312.
   fights against Gruffudd, son of Llywelyn, 312.
   repairs the castle of Caermarthen, and begins to build the castle of Cilgerran, 312.
   appears at Ludlow before the council of the king and archbishop, 314.
   slain at Carnwyllon, 314.
   his heirs obtain their patrimony in peace, 330.
Mathraval, in Powys, subdued by Llywelyn, son of Iorwerth, and his confederates, 270.
Mawddwy, falls to the share of Gruffudd, son of Maredudd, 140.
   taken by David, son of Llywelyn, from his brother Gruffudd, 326.
Mechain, the battle of, 46.
Meilir, son of Rhiwallon, slain by Rhys, son of Tewdwr, 50.
Meilyr, son of Owain, killed by his nephew Cadwallon, son of Gruffudd, 152.
Meirchion, son of Rhys, kills his cousin Rhydderch, son of Caradog, 48.
Meirionydd, subjugated by Maredudd, son of Owain, 28.
   the men of, oppose Owain and Madog, 100.
   falls to the share of the sons of Cadwgan, son of Bleddyn, 140.
   Einon, son of Cadwgan, holds a part of, 150.
   the men of, called out by Howel and Cynan, sons of Owain, 174.
   a dispute about the cantrev of, between Llywelyn, son of Iorwerth, and his son Gruffudd, 306.

Meirionydd—*cont.*
   taken by Llywelyn from Gruffudd, 308.
Meivod, the church of St. Mary at, consecrated, 184.
   Madog, son of Maredudd, buried at, 194.
   Gruffudd Maelor buried at, 236.
Menegyd, in Mona, the battle of, 14.
Menevia, burnt, 10.
   destroyed, 18.
   devastated by Godfrey, son of Harold, 28.
   devastated by the Pagans, 30, 46, 50.
   devastated by Edwin, son of Einon, and Eclis the Great, 30.
   depopulated by the Pagans, 32.
   devastated by the Saxons, 34.
   demolished, 36.
   William the Bastard goes on a pilgrimage to, 50.
   its boundaries ravaged by Gerald the steward, 58, 60.
   its ancient rights asserted by bishop Bernard, 176.
   king Henry II. goes on a pilgrimage to, 212.
   makes an offering there, 214.
   Maredudd, son of Rhys, buried in, 316.
   Rhys the Hoarse buried in, 322.
   the castle of, fortified by John, 330.
   N.B. The bishops of Menevia are referred to under their proper names.
Mercia, the Gwyneddians pursue Rein the Scot, and destroy the country as far as, 36.
Mere, Rickert de la, the castle of, burnt by Owain and Cadwalader, sons of Gruffudd, and others, 158.
Mervyn the Freckled, death of, 12.
   his son killed by the Pagans, 18.
Meurug, killed by the Saxons, 12.
Meurug, the sons of, make an inroad into Gwynedd, 30.
   a battle between the sons of, and Maredudd, near Llangwm; the former victorious, 32.

Meurug, son of Adam, of Buellt, killed in his sleep by his cousin Maredudd Redhead, 206.
Meurug, son of Arthvael, killed, 34.
Meurug, bishop of Bangor, dies, 196.
Meurug Barach, hanged in England, 272.
Meurug, son of Cadell, kills his brother Clydog, 20.
Meurug, son of Cadvan, death of, 24.
Meurug, abbot of Cwm Hir, dies, 232.
Meurug, son of Gruffudd, receives Cyveiliog from his uncle Madog, son of Maredudd, 176.
— escapes from prison, 184.
Meurug, son of Howel, captured by the Pagans, 38.
Meurug, son of Idwal, falls sick, 26.
Meurug, son of Madog (Meurug Tybodiad), killed through the treachery of his own men, 168.
Meurug, bishop of Menevia (A.D. 840), 12.
Meurug, son of Rhirid, kills his cousin Madog, son of Llywarch, 156.
— is mutilated, 156.
Meurug, son of Rhys, born of the latter's own niece, the daughter of his brother Maredudd, 220.
Meurug, son of Trahaiarn, killed, 80.
Mevenydd, the comot of, subjugated by Pain, son of Patrick, 366.
— conquered by Gruffudd, son of Maredudd, 372.
Midland District, king Edward I. leads his army to the, 368.
Milk and butter turned to blood, 4.
Milo, earl of Hereford, killed by an arrow while hunting, 164.
Mochnant, divided between Owain Cyveiliog and Owain the Little, 204.
— taken by Llywelyn, son of Iorwerth, from his brother Gruffudd, 326.
Mona, the isle of, subdued by Howel, 10.
— Cynan, his brother, expelled by him from, 10.
— Howel driven from, 10.
— the battle of Llanvaes in, 10.

Mona—*cont.*
— ravaged by the black Pagans, 12.
— the battle of Menegyd in, 14.
— the battle on Sunday in, 14.
— devastated by the people of Dublin, 20.
— subjugated by Godfrey, son of Harold, 24.
— devastated by him, 26, 28.
— subjugated by Maredudd, son of Owain, 28.
— devastated by the Pagans on Ascension Thursday, 32.
— Gruffudd, son of Cynan, fights against the men of, 48.
— the French encamp against, 60.
— Magnus, king of Germany, comes in ships as far as, 62.
— obtained by Gruffudd, son of Cynan, 62.
— Magnus comes a second time to, 72.
— Cadwallon expelled from, by his brother Owain, 180.
— some of king Henry II.'s men land in, and pillage several of the churches, 186, 188.
— a battle between them and the men of, 188.
— subdued by David, son of Owain Gwynedd, 222.
— David is expelled out of, by his brother Rhodri, 224.
— subjugated by Rhodri, 238.
— king Edward I. sends a great part of his army into, which burns much of the country and takes away muc of the corn, 368.
Montford, Simon, and his son, fall in the battle of Evesham, 352.
— his two sons escape from the king's prison, 354.
Moon, turns of a bloody colour, 4.
— turns black on Christmas day, 8.
Mor, son of Gwyn, dies, 32.
Morcheis, bishop of Bangor, dies, 20.
Moretania, William of, opposes king Henry I., 78.
Morgan, death of, 26.

Morgan, son of Cadwgan, opposed by king Henry I., 146.
kills Maredudd, his brother, 152.
dies at Cyprus, 154.
Morgan, son of Caradog, goes to the king's court at Gloucester, 226.
Morgan, son of Howel, the castle of, obtained by Gilbert, earl of Pembroke, 324.
declines to join David, son of Llywelyn, 330.
Morgan, son of Maredudd, slain, 230.
Morgan, son of Owain, kills Rickert, son of Gilbert, 156.
is killed through treachery by the men of Ivor, son of Meurng, 188.
Morgan, son of Rhys, dies after taking the religious habit at Strata Florida, 336.
Morgan, son of Seisyll, aids in destroying the town of Caerleon, and devastating the country, 212.
Morganwg, devastated by the Normans, 16.
Morgeneu, bishop, killed by the Pagans, 32.
Morgeneu, bishop of Menevia, dies, 38.
Mortality, in all Britain, 2, 176.
in Ireland, 2.
among the cattle in Britain, 10, 30.
among the men through famine, 30.
among the army of king Henry II. in Ireland, 216.
in Britain and the borders of France, 244.
in Damietta, 304.
Mortimer, Sir Hugh de, seizes Rhys, son of Howel, and confines him in prison, 166.
kills Maredudd, son of Madog, 168.
Mortimer, Ralph, death of, 332.
Mortimer, Sir Randulph, Gwladus the Dark, wife of, dies, 336.
Mortimer, Roger, comes into Maelienydd, expels the sons of Cadwallon, and builds the castle of Camaron, 240.
marshals his army against the Welsh, 242.
fortifies the castle of Maelienydd, 330.

Mortimer, Roger—*cont.*
loses Gwerthrynion, 342.
Llywelyn, son of Gruffudd, takes from him the whole of Buellt, except the castle, 346.
comes to the support of his castle in Maelienydd, 348.
is permitted by Llywelyn to return back, 348.
leads an army against Castle Baldwin, 364.
Morvran, abbot of Whitland, refuses to do homage to Howel and Cynan, 174.
Mur Castell, king Henry I. comes to, 114.
Murchath, the daughter of, demanded by Magnus, king of Germany, for his son, 72.
kindly receives Owain, son of Cadwgan, 22.
Murcherdach, the supreme king of Ireland, dies, 144.
his prosperity and success, 144.
Muregan, king of Leinster, dies of a fatal disorder, 18.
Murtart, his daughter, demanded in marriage by Ernulf, 68.
sends his daughter with armed assistance to Ernulf, 68.
Mwrchath, son of Brian, stirred up against Dublin, 34.
Myddvai, the manor of, allotted to Maelgwn, son of Rhys, 288.
Myles, Nicholas de, sent by king Henry III. to dispossess Maelgwn the Little, 332.
Myles, Roger, left by Edmund and Pain as constable at Aberystwyth, and to protect the country, 368.
Myrddin, his prophecies, 2, 370.

N.

Nanheudwy, Cadwgan, son of Gruffudd, killed at, 156.
Nannau of Meirionydd, the situation of Cymmer, 252.

Nant yr Ariant, the castle of, allotted to young Rhys and his brother Owain, the sons of Gruffudd, 290.

Nant Nyver, death of Cynan of, 14.

Nedd, the castle of, demolished by Llywelyn, son of Iorwerth, 318.

Nest, and her two sons and daughter, taken away from her husband Gerald by Owain, son of Cadwgan, 84.

her children restored to their father, 86.

Nestor, Rhys, son of Gruffudd, compared to, 246.

New Castle upon Usk, Henry II. invites Iorwerth, son of Owain, to an interview with him at, 218.

Newark, king John dies at, 292.

Nichol, son of bishop Gwrgant, succeeds to the see of Llandaf, 176.

Nicholas de Myles, sent by king Henry III. to dispossess Maelgwn the Little, 322.

Night, becomes as light as day, 4.

Nile, overflow of the, 308.

Normandy, king William Rufus goes to, 56.

earl Robert goes to, 72.

king Henry I. sends knights to subdue, 78.

himself sails over and reduces the country, 80.

Henry I. dies in, 156.

king Henry II. collects an army of the choice warriors of, against Wales, 200.

his right to, asserted by king Henry III., 316.

Normans, the, devastate England, Brecheiniog, Morganwg, Gwent, Buellt, and Gwenllwg, 16.

defeated by Owain and Cadwalader, 160.

join the army of Rheinallt against the lord Rhys, 192.

Normans, the black, come a second time to Castle Baldwin, 16.

North, a disturbance between king John and the English of the, 280.

they take from him the city of London, 282.

North—*cont.*

the men of the, and the French, get possession of the city of Lincoln, 294.

are defeated and put to flight, 296.

Nyver, the castle of, taken by the lord Rhys, 236.

it is demolished by the sons of Cadwallon, 240.

O.

Octobonus, the pope's legate, confirms peace between king Henry III. and Llywelyn, son of Gruffudd, 354.

Offa, king, destroys the South Wales men, 6.

the South Wales men devastate the island as far as, 6.

spoils the Britons in summer time, 8.

his territory devastated by the Welsh, 8.

causes the Dyke bearing his name to be made, 8.

his death, 8.

Osbric, king of the Saxons, dies, 4.

Osney, Adam, bishop of Llanelwy, buried in the monastery of, 230.

Oswestry, the castle of, built by Madog, son of Maredudd, 176.

king Henry II. arrives at, 200.

destroyed by king John, 292.

Other, comes to Britain, 18.

Otho, emperor of Rome, wages war upon Philip, king of France, 278.

is put to flight, 280.

Otter, commands an Irish fleet, 164.

Otto, the cardinal, seized by the emperor Frederick, 328.

Owain of Brithdir, dies, 250.

Owain, son of Cadwgan, kills (killed by Cadwgan, *C.D.*), 80.

Owain, son of Cadwgan, invited by his father to a Christmas feast, 82.

visits Nest, wife of Gerald the steward, 82.

carries her and her two sons and daughter away, 84.

INDEX. 473

Owain, son of Cadwgan—*cont.*
  restores the children, 86.
  is pursued by Ithel and Madog, sons of Rhirid, 88.
  flees to a ship at Aberdovey, 88.
  goes to Ireland, 92.
  his portion of Powys seized by Madog and Ithel, 92.
  returns from Ireland, 94.
  enters into terms of friendship with Madog, 94.
  commits many crimes in the country of the French, and in England, 96.
  is pursued by Iorwerth, son of Bleddyn, 98.
  encounters the men of Meirionydd, and ravages their country, 100.
  proceeds to Ceredigion, 102.
  goes again to Ireland, 104.
  is reconciled to king Henry I., and recalled, 108.
  receives the land of his uncle Iorwerth, on certain conditions, 110.
  deprives Madog, son of Rhirid, of his sight, 112.
  is accused to the king, 112.
  removes to the mountains of Eryri, 114.
  requested by the king to make peace with him, but he declines, 114, 116.
  he ultimately makes peace with him, 116.
  accompanies the king to Normandy, 118.
  is desired by the king to pursue Gruffudd, son of Rhys, 134.
  is pursued by the Flemings, and slain, 138.
Owain, son of Caradog, summoned by the French, 124.
  his fidelity to king Henry I. put to the test, 124.
  slain in an attack made upon the castle of Caermarthen by Gruffudd, son of Rhys, 126.
Owain, son of Cynan, combines with Llywelyn, son of Iorwerth, against David, son of Owain, 240.

Owain Cyveiliog, advances against king Henry II., 200.
  obtains Mochnant above the Cataract, 204.
  is opposed and put to flight by Owain and Cadwalader, the son of Gruffudd, and others, 204.
  comes with an army of the French against the castle of Caercinion, 204.
  is opposed by Rhys, son of Gruffudd, and compelled to submit, 210.
  dies at Ystrad Marchell, the monastery which he himself had founded, 250.
Owain, son of Dyvnwal, slain, 30.
Owain, son of Dyvnwal, slain, 34.
Owain, son of Edwin, commands the Gwyneddian army against the French, 62.
  dies after a long illness, 76.
Owain, son of Gruffudd, dies, 44.
Owain, son of Gruffudd, dies, 66.
Owain, son of Gruffudd, son of Cynan, sent by his father with a large army to Meirionydd, and removes the men and their property into Lleyn, 150.
  undertakes an expedition into Ceredigion, 156, 158.
  his eulogy, 158.
  burns the castles of Walter de Bec, Aberystwyth, Rickert de la Mere, Dinerth, and Caerwedros, 158.
  goes a second time to Ceredigion, 158.
  fights with the Flemings and Normans, and conquers them, 160.
  returns with much spoil, 160.
  is opposed by his brother Cadwalader with an Irish fleet, 164.
  they are reconciled, 164.
  attacks the Germans and put them to flight, 164, 166.
  his grief for the loss of his son Rhun, 170.
  is consoled upon the fall of the castle of Gwyddgrug or Mold, 172.
  builds a castle in Yale, 176.

Owain, son of Gruffudd, son of Cynan—*cont.*
   expels his brother Cadwalader from Mona, 180.
   unites with his brother and Rhys, son of Gruffudd, son of Rhys, against Owain Cyveiliog, and puts him to flight, 204.
   besieges the castle of Rhuddlan, and demolishes it, together with the castle of Prestatyn, 204, 206.

Owain, son of Gruffudd, son of Gwenwynwyn, taken by Llywelyn, son of Gruffudd, with him to Gwynedd, 360.
   (*A*) released from the prison of Llywelyn by command of the king, 37.

Owain, son of Gruffudd, son of Madog, wins Caer Offa, 196.

Owain, son of Gruffudd Maelor, dies, 250.

Owain, son of Gruffudd, son of Maredudd, receives Cyveiliog from his uncle Madog, son of Maredudd, 176.

Owain, son of Gruffudd, son of Rhys, attacks and burns the castle of Llangadog, 262.
   attacks and defeats the army of Maelgwn, son of Rhys, 264.
   declines making peace with king John, 268.
   consents to do so on certain conditions, 270.
   repairs to the court of the king, and is received by him as a friend, 270.
   ravages the territory of Maelgwn, son of Rhys, 270.
   marshals his forces against Rhys the Hoarse, 274.
   proceeds to Gwynedd, to Llywelyn, son of Iorwerth, 284.
   joins the expedition of Llywelyn, 288.
   a partition of land between him and others at Aberdovey, 288.
   the castles of Aberteivi and Nant yr Ariant, with three cantrevs of Ceredigion, allotted to him and his brother Rhys, 290.

Owain, son of Gruffudd, son of Rhys—*cont.*
   rises against his uncle and wrests from him the whole of Buellt, except the castles, 298.
   obtains part of his deceased brother's territory, 310.
   fights against the castle of Aberteivi, 320.
   proceeds against Aber Mynyw and burns it, slaying the garrison, 320.
   fights for three months against Caermarthen, 322.
   dies at Strata Florida, 322.
   his good qualities, 322.

Owain Gwynedd, imprisons his son Cynan, 178.
   is opposed by Madog, son of Maredudd, king of Powys, 178.
   mutilates his nephew Cunedda, 180.
   his nephew Rhys, son of Gruffudd, prepares to fight against him, 184.
   encamps at Basingwerk, with the view of fighting with king Henry II., 184.
   retreats to Cil Owain, 186.
   makes peace with the king, 188.
   delivers Einon Clud to the French, 194.
   his grief at the loss of the castle of Tavalwern, which fell into the hands of Howel, son of Ieuav, 196.
   his joy at his victory over Howel, son of Ieuan, 196.
   repairs the castle, 196.
   ravages Tegeingl, and removes the people to the Vale of Clwyd, 198.
   encamps at Corwen against the king, 200.
   destroys Basingwerk, 204.
   proceeds against the castles of Rhuddlan and Prestatyn, which he burns, 204, 206.
   his death, 206.
   his character, 206.

Owain, son of Howel, a battle between his sons and the sons of Idwal at Carno, 22.
   devastates Gorwennydd, 22.
   his death, 30.

Owain, son of Iorwerth, destroys the town of Caerleon, and ravages the country, 212.
    killed by a man attached to the earl of Bristol, 218.
Owain the Little, son of Madog, drives Iorwerth the Red from his territory in Mochnant, 204.
    obtains Mochnant below the Cataract, 204.
    receives Caereinion from Owain and Cadwalader, the sons of Gruffudd, 204.
    slain at Careghova, 232.
    his character, 232.
Owain, son of Maredudd, dies, 10.
Owain, son of Maredudd, lord of Cydewain, dies, 348.
Owain, son of Maredudd, of Elvael, makes peace with the lord Llywelyn, 346.
Owain, son of Maredudd, son of Owain, restores the middle comot to his brother Cynan, 358.
    dies and is buried at Strata Florida, 362.
Owain, son of Maredudd, son of Robert of Cydewain, dies, 324.
Owain Pencarwn, seized by Howel, son of Iorwerth, 224.
Owain, king of the Picts, dies, 6.
Owain the Red, son of Gruffudd, son of Llywelyn, reigns after David, son of Llywelyn, 332.
    divides the dominion with his brother Llywelyn, 332
    a dissension between him and his brother Llywelyn, 338.
    seized and imprisoned, and his territory taken by Llywelyn, 340.
    released from prison by command of king Edward I., 370.
Owain, son of Rhydderch, makes an indiscreet sally, 130.
Owain (son of Gruffudd, *D. E.*), son of Rhys, dies at Strata Florida, 236.
Owain, son of Robert, obtains Cydewain, 335.

Oxford, Adam, bishop of Llanelwy, dies at, 230.
    a council held at, in which it was treated of peace between the knights of king Henry III. and Louis, son of the French king, and the men of the North, 294.

P.

Pagans, their first arrival in Ireland, 8.
    strangle Cyngen, 12.
    the black, ravage Mona, 12.
    demolish Caer Alclut, 14.
    kill the son of Mervyn, 18.
    kill Hirmawr and Anarawd, the sons of Gwriad, 22.
    devastate Towyn, 22.
    devastate Llanbadarn, Menevia, Llanilltud, Llangarvan, and Llandydoch, 30.
    hired by Maredudd to join him in devastating Glamorgan, 30.
    devastate the isle of Mona, 92.
    depopulate Menevia, and kill bishop Morgeneu, 32.
    devastate Dyved, 32.
    capture Meurug, son of Howel, 38.
    vanquished by Howel, son of Edwin, while they were devastating Dyved, 40.
    of Dublin, capture Gruffudd, son of Llywelyn, 40.
    devastate Menevia and Bangor, 46, 50.
    of the Isles, demolish Menevia, 54.
Pain, son of Patrick de Says, leads an army to Caermarthen and Ceredigion, 364.
    is reconciled to Rhys, son of Maredudd, and Rhys Wyndod, 366.
    subjugates to king Edward I. the comots of Anhunog, Mevenydd, and the middle comot in Upper Aeron, 366.
    places Llywelyn, son of Owain, as a youth in guardianship, 366.
    goes to England, 368.

Pain's Castle, attacked and compelled to surrender by Rhys, son of Gruffudd, 242.
fought against for nearly three weeks by Gwenwynwyn, 252.
left by Giles de Bruse for Walter, son of Gruffudd, who had subdued it, 282.
built by king Henry III., 318.
Paris, Rhys, son of Gruffudd, compared to, 246.
Patrick de Sayes, the seneschal of king Henry III. at Caermarthen, breaks the truce, and seizes the men who had gone to speak with him, 346.
is slain, 346.
Pembroke, Uchtryd, son of Edwin, and others, fight against the castle of, 58.
the builder of the castle of, 66.
seized upon by Ernulf, 68.
built a second time by Gerald the steward, 82.
king Henry II. proceeds to, 212.
Penardd, falls to the share of Cynan, son of Maredudd, 360.
Pencader (Pen Cadeir), the battle of, 40.
king Henry II. arrives at, 198.
Pencelli (Pen Gelli), Robert de Bruse takes possession of the castle of, 282.
Owain, son of Gruffudd, and others, reduce the castle of, 320.
Pencoed, the fight of, 4.
Penharddlech, the castle of, reduced by David, son of Gruffudd, 372.
Penllwynog, allotted to Maelgwn, son of Rhys, 288.
Penllyn, half of it allotted to Gruffudd, son of Maredudd, and the other half to the sons of Cadwgan, son of Bleddyn, 140.
Penmon, devastated by Mark, son of Harold, 24.
Pennaeth Bachwy, Alexander, son of Malcolm, and the son of Hugh, earl of Caerleon, arrive at, 114.

Penwedig, Maredudd and Rhys, sons of Gruffudd, lead their forces to, 180.
the cantrev of, taken by Llywelyn, son of Iorwerth, for himself, 262.
the seneschal of Cardiff, and Rhys and Maelgwn, sons of the lord Rhys, move their armies to, 268.
the cantrev of, conquered by Rhys, son of Maelgwn, 372.
Pepin, the elder, king of France, dies, 4.
Percy, earl, killed in the battle of Lincoln, 296.
Peter, abbot, death of, 232.
Philip, king of France, takes the cross, 234, 236.
Otho, emperor of Rome, makes war upon, 278.
sends his son Louis to Poictou, with an army to meet the king of England, 278.
forms a truce for seven years with king John, 280.
Philip, son of Gwys, keeper of the castle of Gwys, with his wife and two sons, captured by Howel the Saxon, 238.
Philip the Red, the thirteenth abbot of Strata Florida, dies, 372.
Pictot, Henry, lord of Ewias, 314.
Pilgrimage, William the Bastard goes to Menevia on a, 50.
king Henry II. goes to Menevia on a, 212.
Louis, king of France, returns from his, 338.
Pilgrims from Wales, drowned on the sea of Greece in going with the cross to Jerusalem, 166.
Plague, a great, in the month of March, 24.
Poer, Randulph de, killed by the youths of Winchester, 230.
Poictou, king John sails for, 278.
king Henry II. sails for France to assert his right to, 316.
king Henry III. sails for, to obtain from the king of France his right as to the lands which he had taken from him, 328.

INDEX. 477

Port Lachi, taken in the first attack by Rickert, earl of Terstig, 208.
Powys, the kingdom of, taken by the Saxons into their possession, 10.
  held by Bleddyn, son of Cynvyn, 46.
  a portion of, taken by Cadwgan, son of Bleddyn, 62.
  given by king Henry I. to Iorwerth, son of Bleddyn, during the king's life, 70.
  a part of it given by Iorwerth to his brother Cadwgan, 74.
  given by the king, on the death of Iorwerth, to Cadwgan, son of Bleddyn, 108.
  king Henry I. raises an immense army against the men of, 146.
  he levies ten thousand head of cattle as a tribute upon, 150.
  Llywelyn, son of Iorwerth, raises an army against Gwenwynwyn from, 258.
Prestatyn, the castle of, burnt by Owain and Cadwalader, and the lord Rhys, 206.
Prodigies, raining blood, 4.
  milk and butter turned to blood, 4.
  the moon turns of a bloody colour, 4.
  the night becomes as light as day, 4.
  the moon turns black on Christmas day, 8.
  vermin of a mole-like form, fall from heaven, 16, 18.
  a wonderful star, of immense light, emitting a beam behind as thick as a column, 78.
Proverbs, British, 36, 136.
Prydyn (or North Britain), men from, in the army of Henry II., 200.
  the grand festival at Aberteivi proclaimed a year beforehand throughout Wales, England, Ireland, and, 228.
  the king of, dies, 336.
  his only son succeeds to the dominion of, 336.
Pwll Dyvach, the battle of, 40.
Pwll Gwdyg, the battle of, 48.

Pyrs, succeeds David in the see of Menevia, 228.
  his death, 254.

R.

Racline, destroyed, 8.
Rain of blood in Britain and Ireland, 4.
Ralph Mortimer, death of, 332.
Randulf, earl of Caerleon, prepares to rise against Owain Gwynedd, 178.
  his death, 182.
Randulf (or Randulph) de Poer, killed by the youths of Winchester, 230.
Razon the steward, his castle in Ystrad Peithyll burnt, 130.
  solicits aid from the garrison of Ystrad Meurug, to enable him to defend the castle of Aberystwyth, against Gruffudd, son of Rhys, 130.
Red Castle, razed to the ground by Llywelyn, son of Iorwerth, 320.
Rein, king of Dyved, dies, 8.
Rein the Scot, pretends to be the son of king Maredudd, and causes himself to be named king, 36.
  is received by the men of the South as their lord, 36.
  Llywelyn, son of Seisyll, makes war upon him, 36.
  defeated by the Gwyneddians at Aber Gwyli, 36.
Reinolf, commands a Saxon army against Gruffudd, son of Llywelyn, 42.
  is defeated, 42.
Remission, a general, to the churches of England and Wales, 280, 302.
Rhaiadr Gwy, a castle erected at, by the lord Rhys, 230.
  a second time, 240.
  demolished by the sons of Cadwallon, 240.
Rhedynog Velen, the convent of Strata Florida removed to, 232.
Rheims, Rickert, abbot of Clerynaut, killed in a monastery near, 226.

Rheinallt, son of king Henry II., encamps at Dinweleir against the lord Rhys, 192.

Rheinallt de Bruse. *See* Bruse, Rheinallt de.

Rheinallt de Cressy, killed in the battle of Lincoln, 298.

Rhirid, imprisoned in the castle of Abergavenny, 218.

Rhirid, son of Bleddyn, with his brothers, Madog and Cadwgan, expel Rhys, son of Tewdwr, from his kingdom, 52.

killed in the battle of Llych Crei, 52.

Rhirid, son of Iestin, slain, 252.

Rhirid, son of Iorwerth, king Henry I. demands hostages from, in respect of the liberation of his father Iorwerth, 96.

Rhirid, son of Owain, a dissension between him and Howel, son of Ithel, 142.

slain by his nephew Cadwallon, son of Gruffudd, 152.

Rhiwallon, son of Cynvyn, slain in the battle of Mechain, 46.

Rhodri (the Great), killed by the Saxons, 16.

avenged in the battle of Conwy, 16.

Rhodri, son of Howel, dies, 22.

Rhodri, son of Howel, slain, 252.

Rhodri, son of Idwal, slain, 24.

Rhodri Molwynog, succeeds to the British throne after Ivor, son of Alan, 2.

the battle of Heilin with, 4.

his death, 6.

Rhodri, son of Owain, taken and confined in fetters by his brother David, for seeking to obtain from him a share of his father's patrimony, 224.

escapes from prison, and expels David out of Mona and Gwynedd, 224.

subjugates the isle of Mona, 238.

is expelled by the sons of Cynan, son of Owain Gwynedd, 238.

(son of Cynan, *D.*) joins Llywelyn, son of Iorwerth, and others, against David, son of Owain Gwynedd, 240.

Rhos, the cantrev of, seized by the Flemings, 80.

the proprietary inhabitants of, expelled by them, 82.

invaded by Llywelyn, son of Iorwerth, 306.

Rhoshir, a church in, pillaged by king Henry II.'s men, 188.

Rhos Meilon in Mona, the battle of, 18.

Rhuddlan, a battle at, 8.

king Henry II. proceeds to, 186.

he purposes to erect a castle there, and encamps there three nights, 200.

Owain and Cadwalader, princes of Gwynedd, and the lord Rhys, prince of South Wales, proceed against the castle of, which they demolish, 204, 206.

the castle of, reduced by Llywelyn, son of Iorwerth, 278.

king Edward proceeds to, and fortifies, 368.

Llywelyn, son of Gruffudd, makes peace with the king at, 368.

Rhun, son of Owain, dies, 170.

his character and appearance, 170.

Rhuvoniog, the kingdom of, taken by the Saxons, 10.

Rhyd Cornnec, Madog and Ithel, sons of Rhirid, encamp at, 88.

Rhyd y Gors, the founder of the castle of, 58.

the castle of, stored by Rickert, son of Baldwin, 76.

under the conservancy and in the custody of Howel, son of Goronwy, 76.

Rhyd y Groes, a battle at, fought by Llywelyn, son of Seisyll, 38.

Rhydderch, bishop, death of, 24.

Rhydderch, son of Caradog, rules over South Wales, 48.

joins in the battle of Camddwr, 48.

killed by his cousin Meirchion, 48.

Rhydderch, son of Hennyth, beheaded in Arwystli, 18.

INDEX. 479

Rhydderch, son of Iestin, assumes the government of South Wales, 38.
killed by the Scots, 38.
his sons take part in the battle of Hiraethwy, 38.

Rhydderch, son of Tewdwr, his fidelity to king Henry I. put to the test, 124.
makes an indiscreet sally, 130.

Rhydderch, abbot of the White House, dies, 232.

Rhys, doctor, of Caer Rhiw, (Richard de Caerin, C.), consecrated by the pope bishop of Menevia, 342.

Rhys, son of Gruffudd, (called frequently in the Chronicle the lord Rhys), fights against the castle of Lianstephan, and conquers it, 168.
raises an army against the castle of Gwys, 172.
subdues Ceredigion as far as Aeron, 178.
takes the whole of Ceredigion, except the castle of Pengwern, from Howel, son of Owain, 178.
conquers the castle of Llanrhystud, 178.
repairs the castle of Ystrad Meurug, 180.
enters Gower, burns the castle of Aberllychwr, and devastates the country, 180.
repairs the castle of Dinweileir, 180.
invades Penwedig, and demolishes the castle of Howel, 180.
his sons attack the castle of Tenby, and deliver it to the keeping of William, son of Gerald, 182.
lays waste the castle of Ystrad Cyngen, 182.
attacks and burns the castle of Aberavan, 182.
ravages Cyveiliog, 182.
holds, in trust with Maredudd, the possessions of his brother Cadell, 182.
leads an army to Aberdovey with the intention of fighting against Owain Gwynedd, 184.

Rhys, son of Gruffudd—cont.
makes a castle there, 184.
prepares alone to wage war with king Henry II., 188.
confederates all South Wales and his friends as far as the woods of the Vale of Tywi, 188.
repairs to the king's court, and unwillingly makes peace with him, 190.
Walter Clifford carries a booty out of his territory, 190.
he is refused satisfaction by the king, 190.
subdues the castle of Llanymddyvri, 190.
makes an attack upon certain castles in Ceredigion, and burns them, 192.
frequently opposes the king, 192.
subdues and burns the castles which the French had built across Dyved, 192.
fights against Caermarthen, 192.
is opposed by Rheinallt, son of king Henry, 192.
assembles his men on the mountain of Cevn Rhestr, 192.
concludes a truce with his enemies, 194.
delivers hostages to the king, 198.
takes possession of Cantrev Mawr and the castle of Dinevwr, 198.
enters the territory of Roger, earl of Clare, 198.
dismantles and burns the castle of Aber Rheidiol and the castle of Mabwynion, and reconquers the whole of Ceredigion, 198.
spoils the Flemings, 198.
joins the allied princes against the king at Oswestry, 200.
encamps at Corwen, 200.
attacks the walls of Aberteivi and its castle, 202.
seizes the castle of Cilgerran, and imprisons Robert, son of Stephen, 202.

480 INDEX.

Rhys, son of Gruffudd—*cont.*
    vanquishes Owain Cyveiliog, 204.
    recovers Tavalwern, 204.
    besieges the castle of Rhuddlan, 204.
    burns it, and the castle of Prestatyn, 206.
    assembles an army against Owain Cyveiliog, 210.
    compels him to submit and to deliver hostages, 210.
    enters into friendship with the king, 210.
    the king gives him Ceredigion, the Vale of Tywi, Ystlwyv, and Euelvre, 212.
    builds the castle of Aberteivi with stone and mortar, 212.
    gives to the king several horses, 212, 214.
    obtains favour with the king, 214.
    has an interview with him at Talacharn, 218.
    appointed justice over the whole of South Wales, 218.
    sends his son Howel to the king beyond sea, to abide at his court and to serve him, 222.
    goes to the court of the king at Gloucester, 226.
    takes with him all the princes of South Wales who had been in opposition to the king, 226.
    holds a grand festival in the castle of Aberteivi, 228.
    erects the castle of Rhaiadr Gwy, 230.
    made war against by the sons of Cynan, son of Owain Gwynedd, 230.
    takes possession of the castles of St. Clare and Aber Corran and Llanstephan, 234.
    seizes and imprisons his son Maelgwn, 236.
    builds the castle of Cydweli, 236.
    builds the castle of Rhaiadr Gwy the second time, 240.
    seized by his sons and imprisoned, 240.
    released by his son, Howel the Saxon, 240.

Rhys, son of Gruffudd—*cont.*
    collects an army and attacks Caermarthen, which he burns to the ground, except the castle, 240.
    marches against the castle of Colwyn, subdues, and burns it, 242.
    moves his army to Maes Hyveidd, and burns it, 242.
    gains a signal victory over Roger Mortimer and Hugh de Say, 242.
    attacks Pain's castle in Elvael, and compels it to surrender, 242.
    relinquishes it by an agreement with William Bruse, 242.
    his death, 244.
    his character, 244, 246.
    Latin verses composed upon his death, 246.
    Latin verses on his tomb, 248.
    his youngest sons take possession of the castle of Dinevwr, 252.

Rhys (young), son of Gruffudd, son of Rhys, subdues the castle of Llanegwad, 258.
    attacks the castle of Llangadog, and burns it, 262.
    attacks the army of Maelgwn victoriously, 264.
    refuses to make peace with the king, 268.
    the consequences thereof, 268.
    makes peace, and gives up to the king the territory between the Dyvi and Aeron, 270.
    repairs to the court of king John, who receives him as a friend, 270.
    ravages Lower Aeron, the territory of Maelgwn, son of Rhys, 270.
    petitions the king for a share of his father's inheritance, 274.
    fails to obtain satisfaction from Rhys the Hoarse, in compliance with the king's command, 274.
    collects a vast army out of Brecheiniog against Rhys the Hoarse, 274.
    encamps at Trallwng Elgan, 274.
    obtains a victory over him, 274.

INDEX.

Rhys (young), son of Gruffudd, son of Rhys—*cont.*
    proceeds to attack the castle of Dinevwr, invests, and wins it, except one tower, 276.
    moves his army to Llanymddyvri, and obtains the castle, 276.
    is reconciled to his uncle Maelgwn, 282.
    collects an immense army, obtains possession of Cydweli and Carnwyllon, and burns the castle, 284.
    reduces the castle of Llychwr, 284.
    also the castle of Hugh, 284.
    proceeds to the castle of Ystum Llwynarth in Senghenydd, which he obtains, 284.
    having reduced all the castles of Gower, he returns home, 284.
    joins the expedition of Llywelyn, son of Iorwerth, 288.
    a partition of land between him and others at Aberdovey, 288.
    his allotment, 290.
    rises with his brother Owain against their uncle, and wrests from him the whole of Buellt, except the castle, 298.
    arbitrates between Llywelyn, son of Iorwerth, and the men of Aberhodni, 300.
    leads a body of men through the river Cleddyv, with the view of attacking the town of Haverford, 300.
    goes to the court of the king to render him homage, 304.
    falls out with Llywelyn, son of Iorwerth, 308.
    separates from him, and joins William Marshall, earl of Pembroke, 308.
    repairs to the court of the king, and complains of the insult offered to him by Llywelyn, 308.
    is reconciled to Llywelyn, son of Iorwerth, 308.
    dies, and is buried in Strata Florida, 310.
    his character, 310.

Rhys the Hoarse, takes possession of the castle of Llangadog, 262.
    obtains possession of the castle of Llanymddyvri, 264.
    summoned by king John to join his army against Gwynedd, 266.
    commanded by the king to go against the sons of Rhys, son of Gruffudd, son of Rhys, to compel them to surrender, or to retire out of the kingdom, 268.
    repents of his terms with the king, and demolishes the new castle at Aberystwyth, 270.
    refuses to obey the king's commands, 274.
    fights with Rhys and Owain, sons of Gruffudd, and Foulke, the seneschal of Cardiff, and is defeated, 274.
    strengthens the castle of Dinevwr with men and arms, 276.
    burns Llandeilo, 276.
    strengthens the castle of Llanymddyvri and retires to his brother Maelgwn, 276.
    is seized at Caermarthen, and put into the king's prison, 278.
    liberated upon giving hostages, 284.
    is one of the princes who took a part in Llywelyn's expedition, 288.
    a partition of land between him and others at Aberdovey, 288.
    his allotment, 290.
    entrusted by Llywelyn, son of Iorwerth, with the custody of the castle of Senghenydd, 300.
    destroys the castle of Senghenydd, and all the castles of Gower, 302.
    expels the English out of that country, and replaces them with Welshmen, 302.
    marries the daughter of the earl of Clare, 304.
    warns Gruffudd, son of Llywelyn, against the treachery of the burgesses of Cydweli, 312.
    sent by Llywelyn to Carnwyllon to intercept William Marshall, 314.

Rhys the Hoarse—*cont.*
    captured at Llanarthneu by his son Rhys the Little, 316.
    is liberated for the castle of Llanymddyvri, 316.
    dies at Llandeilo the Great, 322.
    buried in Menevia, 322.

Rhys, son of Howel, co-operates with Owain and Cadwalader, sons of Gruffudd, in burning the several castles of Rickert de la Mere, Dinerth, and Caerwedros, 158.
    slays Howel, son of Maredudd, son of Rhydderch, 162.
    seized and imprisoned by Sir Hugh de Mortimer, 166.

Rhys the Little, son of Rhys Mechyll, recovers the castle of Carreg Cennen, 334.
    aided by the barons and knights of England, goes to Caermarthen, 342.
    enters the castle of Dinevwr, and is seized by the garrison, 342.
    goes to Emlyn to speak with Maredudd, son of Rhys the Hoarse, and Patrick de Sayes, 346.
    dies in the castle of Dinevwr, 358.
    is buried at Tal y Llycheu, 358.

Rhys, son of Maelgwn, hanged at Shrewsbury by Robert Vepont, 272.

Rhys, son of Maelgwn, dies, and is buried at Strata Florida, 338.

Rhys, son of Maelgwn, makes his submission to king Edward I. by the hand of Roger Mortimer, 366.
    in company with four others, pays homage to the king at Worcester, 368.
    retires to Gwynedd, to Llywelyn, for fear of being taken by the English at Llanbadarn, 368.
    his territory taken possession of by the English, 368.
    takes possession of the town and castle of Aberystwyth, 372.
    conquers the cantrev of Penwedig, 372.

Rhys, son of Maredudd, exchanges comots with his brother Cynan, and obtains Penardd for himself, 360.
    reconciled to Pain, son of Patrick, 366.
    goes to the court of king Edward to offer his homage and oath of allegiance, 366.

Rhys Mechyll the Little, reconciled to his uncle Maredudd, son of Rhys, 344.
    attacks Trevdraeth, and demolishes the castle, 344.
    invades Rhos, 344.
    marches to Glamorgan, and reduces the castle of Llan Geneu, 344.

Rhys, son of Owain, kills Bleddyn, son of Cynvyn, 46.
    holds the government of South Wales, 48.
    is engaged in the battle of Camddwr, 48.
    also in the battle of Gwennottyll, 48.
    becomes a fugitive, 50.
    slain by Caradog, son of Gruffudd, 50.

Rhys, son of Rhydderch, acts treacherously towards Gruffudd, son of Llywelyn, 42.

Rhys, son of Rhys, advises his father to imprison his brother Maelgwn, 236.
    subjects the castles of Dinevwr and Cantrev Bychan, 240.
    imprisoned with Maredudd, by his father, at Ystrad Meurug, 240.
    joins the expedition against Rhys and Owain, sons of Gruffudd, 268.

Rhys the Saxon, treacherously kills Gurgenen, son of Seisyll, 50.

Rhys, son of Tewdwr, slays Caradog, Gruffudd, and Meilir, the sons of Rhiwallon, in the battle on Carn mountain, 50.
    expelled from his territory and kingdom by the sons of Bleddyn, son of Cynvyn, 52.
    is victorious at the battle of Llych Crei, 52.
    pays a vast sum of money to the Scottish and Irish mariners who had come to his assistance, 52.
    killed by the French of Brecheiniog, 54.

INDEX. 483

Rhys Wyndod, reconciled to Pain, son of Patrick, 366.
 goes to offer his homage to king Edward I., 366.
 retained by the king, 366.
 returns from the court of the king, 368.
Rhystud, the castle of, stored by Roger, earl of Clare, 190.
Richard I., crowned king of England, 234.
 seized and put in prison by a certain earl as he was returning from Jerusalem, 236.
 an extensive tax levied for his ransom, 236.
 wounded and killed, 254.
Rickert, son of Baldwin, stores the castle of Rhyd y Gors, 76.
Rickert, of Caer Rhiw, bishop of Menevia, dies, 370.
Rickert, archbishop of Canterbury, dies, 232.
Rickert, earl of Clare, dies, 348.
Rickert, abbot of Clerynaut, killed in a monastery near Rheims, 226.
Rickert, earl of Cornwall, entrusted with the care of the kingdom by king Henry III., 338.
Rickert, bishop of London, steward of the king at Shrewsbury, seeks to revenge an insult done to Gerald the steward, 86.
 counsels Ithel and Madog, sons of Rhirid, to seize or expel Owain, son of Cadwgan, 86.
 Cadwgan seeks to make peace with the king through, 92.
 desires Madog to seize the men who had committed wrongs against the king, 94.
 is requested by Madog to give him certain lands, 108.
Rickert Marshall. See Marshall, Rickert.
Rickert de la Mere, the castle of, burnt by Owain and Cadwalader, the sons of Gruffudd, and others, 158.
Rickert, earl of Pembroke, repairs the castle of Maes Hyveidd, 320.
 stabbed in battle, and dies, 322.

Rickert, son of Ponson, Gruffudd, son of Rhys, burns the outwork of the castle of, 122.
Rickert, earl of Terstig, son of Gilbert Strongbow, sails for Ireland, 208.
 attends king Henry II. at Menevia, 214.
Rites of the Church administered to the dying, 156, 160, 166, 194, 206, 266, 310.
Robert, bishop of Bangor, seized in his church, 268.
 ransomed for two hundred hawks, 268.
Robert, earl of Bethlehem, encounters the knights sent by Henry I. to subdue Normandy, 78.
 seized by the king, and imprisoned, 110.
 his son makes war against the king, 110.
Robert the Crookhanded, Bledri, son of Cedivor, appointed to keep the castle of, 126.
Robert Fitz Walter, taken in the battle of Lincoln, 296.
Robert, son of king Henry I., dies, 174.
Robert, brother of king Henry III., killed, 334.
Robert, bishop of Hereford, dies, 176.
 his character, 176.
Robert, son of Llywarch, dies, 208.
Robert, son of Martin, opposes Owain and Cadwalader, sons of Gruffudd, and their auxiliaries, 158.
Robert de Rupel, killed in the battle of Lincoln, 296.
Robert, earl of Shrewsbury, dissension between him and king Henry I., 66.
 seizes upon the castles of Arundel, Bliv, Brygge, and Shrewsbury, 68.
 his territory spoiled, 70.
 obtains permission from the king to quit the kingdom, 72.
 opposes the knights sent by the king to subdue Normandy, 78.
Robert, son of Stephen, taken and imprisoned by the lord Rhys, 202.
 released from prison, 206.
 taken to Ireland by Diermid, son of Murchath, 206.

H H 2

Robert Vepont, hangs Rhys, son of Maelgwn, at Shrewsbury, 272.

Robert, son of William the Bastard, his kingdom in Normandy defended by William Rufus during his absence in Jerusalem, 56.

returns victorious from Jerusalem, 66.

Roch, Hugh de, killed in the battle of Lincoln, 296.

Roger, earl of Clare, his hostile expedition to Ceredigion, 190.

his territory invaded by Rhys, son of Gruffudd, 198.

Roger Clifford, lord of the castle of Penharddlech, taken and imprisoned by David, son of Gruffudd, 372.

Roger, earl of Hereford, dies, 184.

Roger, son of Hugh the Fat, succeeds his father as earl of Caerleon, 66.

Roger Mortimer. *See* Mortimer, Roger.

Roger Mortimer, succeeds his father, 332.

Roger Myles, left by Edmund and Pain as constable of Aberystwyth, and to protect the country, 368.

Rome, Cadwalader the Blessed, dies at, 2.

Cyngen, king of Powys, dies at, 12.

Howel dies at, 16.

Dunwallon, king of Strath Clyde, goes to, 26.

Joseph, bishop of Llandaf, dies at, 40.

Dwnchath, son of Brian, dies on his way to, 44.

Henry, emperor of, dies, 78.

Henry II. ordered to appear at, to make satisfaction for the death of the archbishop of Canterbury 208.

a cardinal from, attends a council in London for confirming the laws of the churches, 228.

a general council held at the Lateran church in, 286.

a cardinal from, aids in the translation of the remains of Thomas the Martyr, 304.

a cardinal from, sent to England as the pope's legate, 326.

Thomas, bishop of Menevia, returns from the court of, 338.

Emri takes a journey to the court of, 364.

Rufus, William, succeeds to the throne of England, 52.

goes to Normandy to defend the kingdom of his brother Robert, during his absence in Jerusalem, 56.

raises an army against the Britons, 58.

is unsuccessful, 58.

leads a large army a second time against the Britons, but is unsuccessful, 60.

is killed, 60.

his body ordered to be conveyed to Winchester for burial, 64.

Rymney, Maredudd, son of Owain, killed on the banks of the river, 46.

Rythmarch the Wise, son of bishop Sulien, dies, 62.

his character, 62.

S.

Saer, receives Dyved from king Henry I., 74.

expelled by the king from Pembroke, 76.

Saracens, the, threaten the destruction of Jerusalem, 232.

and the Jews subdue Jerusalem, 234.

a battle in Spain between the Christians and, 272.

Damietta restored to, 310.

convey the Christians to Acre, 310.

take king Louis, 334.

for his liberation he is constrained to restore Damietta to, 334.

a great number of, killed by Louis, 336.

Sarur (Sayrebus, *C.*), the earl of, invites Otho, emperor of Rome, his nephew, to his assistance, 278.

captured at Vernon, 280.

Satubin, bishop of Menevia, dies, 12.

Saxons, the, gain the crown of Britain, 2.

a battle at Hereford between the Britons and, 6.

kill Caradog, king of Gwynedd, 8.

ravage the mountains of Eryri, and take the kingdom of Rhuvoniog, 10.

Saxons, the—*cont.*
   destroy the castle of Dyganwy, 10.
   take the kingdom of Powys, 10.
   kill Meurug, 12.
   kill Rhodri and his brother Gwriad, 16.
   devastate Strath Clyde, 20.
   kill Cadwgan, son of Owain, 22.
   ravage the kingdoms of the sons of Idwal, 24.
   devastate the Grove of Celynog (Cyveiliog, *C.*) the Great, 26.
   devastate Brecheiniog, and all the territory of Einon, son of Owain, 28.
   kill Howel, son of Ieuav, through treachery, 28.
   kill Caradog, son of Rhydderch, 38.
   pursued and destroyed by Gruffudd, son of Llywelyn, 38.
   vanquished in a battle with Gruffudd, son of Llywelyn, at Hereford, 42.
   their dominions ravaged by Magnus, son of Harold, king of Germany, 44.
   appoint Henry I. king in England, 64.
   inhabit Dyved, 128.
   ravaged and killed by the men of Gruffudd, son of Rhys, 128.
   N.B. The kings of the Saxons are referred to under their proper names.
Scandinavia, Magnus, king of Germany, makes depredations on the shores of, 74.
Scots, the, devastate Dublin, 32.
   kill Rhydderch, son of Iestyn, 38.
   auxiliaries to Trahaiarn, son of Caradog, 50.
   receive a large sum of money from Rhys, son of Tewdwr, for assistance rendered to him, 52.
Seisyll, son of Dyvnwal, seized treacherously by king Henry II.'s men, and imprisoned in the castle of Abergavenny, 218.
   goes to the court of the king at Gloucester, 226.

Seisyll, son of Dyvnwal—*cont.*
   slain through the treachery of the lord of Brecheiniog, in the castle of Abergavenny, 226.
Senghenydd, the castle of, destroyed in the expedition of Llywelyn, son of Iorwerth, 288.
   the castle of, given to Rheinallt de Bruse by Llywelyn, 300.
   it is destroyed by Rhys the Hoarse, 302.
Shrewsbury, the castle of, seized by Robert, earl of Shrewsbury, 68.
   Iorwerth, son of Bleddyn, cited to, 74.
   king John seizes Gwenwynwyn at, 262.
   Rhys, son of Maelgwn, hanged at, 272.
   invested by Llywelyn, son of Iorwerth, 282.
   king Henry III. summons Llywelyn and the earls and barons of the marches to, 308.
Simon, archdeacon of Cyveiliog, dies, 180.
   his character, 180.
Sitruc, son of Abloec, king of Dublin, a battle between him and Brian, king of all Ireland, 34.
Snow, a great, in the month of March, 24.
   on the calends of January, which remained until the feast of St. Patrick, 42.
Solomon, a maxim of, 126.
South Wales, the men of, destroyed by king Offa, 6.
   the devastation of, contemplated by Howel, son of Edwin, 40.
   laid waste, 42.
   endangered by a fleet from Ireland, 42.
   held by Maredudd, son of Owain, son of Edwin, 46.
   confederates with Rhys, son of Gruffudd, 188, 200.
   king Henry II. leads an army into, 192, 198.

South Wales—*cont.*
  the same king proceeds again to, 210.
  the lord Rhys appointed justice of all, 218.
  Christianity rendered free to the men of, 302.
  subjected to king Edward I., 366.
St. Clare, the castle of, taken by the lord Rhys, 234.
  the castle of, demolished by Llywelyn, son of Iorwerth, 286.
St. David (St. Dewi), the shrine of, stolen out of the church, and completely despoiled, 52, 54.
  certain wicked men carry away booty from the precincts of, 90, 92.
  king Henry II. makes an offering at Menevia for the singers in serving God and, 214.
St. Dunstan, king John buried at Worcester, near the grave of, 292.
St. Mary's church at Meivod, consecrated, 184.
St. Mary's church in Mona, pillaged by the men of king Henry II., 188.
St. Michael, the church of, consecrated, 4.
St. Padarn, booty carried out of the precincts of, 92.
  indecencies committed in the church of, 130.
  Sulien, an adopted son of the church of, 166.
St. Paul, king John gives his kingdom to, 278.
St. Peter, likewise to, 278.
  the church of, in Mona, pillaged by the men of king Henry II., 188.
Star, a, of wonderful appearance, 78.
Stephen, son of Baldwin, killed by Llywelyn, son of Madog, 180.
Stephen, king, of Blois, takes the crown of England by force, 156.
  his death, 182.
Stephen, archbishop of Canterbury, raises the body of Thomas the Martyr, 304.

Stephen, the constable, opposes Owain and Cadwalader, 158.
Storm, a violent and destructive, 220.
Strange, John, the younger, bailiff of Castle Baldwin, makes a night attack upon Ceri and Cydewain, 348, 350.
  pursued by the Welsh, 350.
  burns the barn of Aber Miwl, 350.
Strata Florida, the monastery of, established, 202.
  monks of, removed to Rhedynog Velen in Gwynedd, 232.
  the abbot of, permitted by king Henry III. to have the body of Gruffudd, son of Llywelyn, 334.
  he and the abbot of Aberconway remove it to Aberconway, 334.
  the great bell of, bought, 340.
  the same consecrated by the bishop of Bangor, 340.
  the bishop of Menevia sings mass in, 372.
  deaths and burials in, 226, 232, 236, 256, 260, 266, 310, 314, 318, 322, 330, 336, 338, 344, 354, 356, 358, 362, 372.
Strath Clyde, devastated by the Saxons, 20.
Subin, the wisest of the Scots, dies, 16.
Sulien, bishop of Menevia, assumes the bishopric, 46.
  resigns it, 50.
  takes it a second time, 50.
  resigns it again, 52.
  his death, 54.
  his character, 54.
Sulien, son of Rythmarch, dies, 166.
  his character, 166.
Sunday, the battle on, in Mona, 14.
Swain, son of Harold, devastates the isle of Man, 32.
  expels Edelred, son of Edgar, from his kingdom, and reigns in his stead, 34.
  his death, 34.

T.

Tal y Llycheu, Iorwerth, abbot of, made bishop of Menevia, 284.
   young Rhys, son of Rhys Mechyll, buried at, 358.
Talacharn, interview between king Henry II. and Rhys, son of Gruffudd, at, 218.
   the castle of, demolished by Llywelyn, son of Iorwerth, and his confederates, 286, 288.
Talargan, king of the Picts, killed by the Britons in the battle of Maesydog, 6.
Tavalwern, the castle of, obtained through treachery by Howel, son of Ieuav, 196.
   won by Owain and Cadwalader, the sons of Gruffudd, and their confederates, 204.
Tegeingl, ravaged by David, son of Owain Gwynedd, 198.
   Owain and Cadwalader, sons of Gruffudd, and the lord Rhys, move their armies against the castle of Rhuddlan in, 204.
   king Henry III. fortifies the castle of Carreg in, 328.
Temple, the master of, leads an army of Christians to Damietta, 304.
Tenby, the men of, hurt Cadell, son of Gruffudd, 180.
   the castle of, attacked and taken by the sons of Rhys, 182.
   ravaged and burnt by Maelgwn, son of Rhys, 234.
Terdeilach, king of Conach, dies, 184.
Terdelach, king of the Scots or Gwyddelians, dies, 52.
Tewdwr, son of Beli, dies, 6.
Tewdwr, son of Einon, slain in a battle near Llangwm, 32.
Teyrnon, a religious society established in the Glen of, 230.

Theobald, son of Theobald, duke of Burgundy, delivered as hostage by Henry II., to the king of France, in respect of the archbishop of Canterbury, 208.
Theobald, earl of Burgundy, aids prince Henry in harassing the territory of his father the king, 222.
Thomas, archbishop of Canterbury, murdered, 208.
   his character, 208.
   translation of his remains, 304.
Thomas, bishop of Menevia, returns from the court of Rome, 338.
Thomas, archbishop of York, dies, 66.
Thunderstorms, violent, 10, 220.
Tours, Henry, son of king Henry II., borrows money from the burgesses of, 220.
Towyn, devastated by the Pagans, 24.
Trahaiarn, son of Caradog, rules over Gwynedd, 48.
   a battle between him and Gruffudd, at Bron yr Erw, 48.
   wins the battle of Pwll Gwdyg, 48.
   slain in the battle on Carn Mountain, 50.
Trahaiarn, son of Ithel, invites Gruffudd, son of Rhys, to undertake an expedition into Ceredigion, 128.
Trahaiarn the Little, of Brecheiniog, seized and fettered, 250.
   his character, 250.
Trallwng Elgan, young Rhys encamps at, 274.
Trallwng Llywelyn, Cadwgan, son of Bleddyn, arrives in, 108.
   the castle of Gwenwynwyn in, attacked by Henry, archbishop of Canterbury, and others, 242.
   burnt by Llywelyn, son of Iorwerth, 320.
   Llywelyn, son of Gruffudd, sends messengers to Gruffudd, son of Gwenwynwyn, to the castle of, 360.
   the castle destroyed by Llywelyn, 360.

Trevdraeth, the castle of, destroyed by Llywelyn, son of Iorwerth, and his confederates, 286, 288.
— attacked, and the castle demolished by Llywelyn, son of Gruffudd, Maredudd, son of Rhys, and Rhys Mechyll the Little, 344.
Tribute of ten thousand head of cattle, levied upon Powys, by king Henry I., 150.
Tryffin, son of Rein, death of, 10.
Turkyll, the son of, commands a fleet from Ireland, come to the assistance of Cadwalader, son of Gruffudd, 164.
Two thousand men blinded, 28.
Tyrell, Walter, unwittingly kills William Rufus in hunting, 64.
Tywi, William Marshall marches against Gruffudd, son of Llywelyn, through the, 312.
— a bridge made over it by Maelgwn the Little, Rhys the Hoarse, and others, who were fighting against Caermarthen, 322.
Tywi, Vale of. *See* Vale.

U.

Ubis, devastates Menevia, 34.
Uchtryd, son of Edwin, fights against the castle of Pembroke, and ravages the whole country, 58.
— invites the country people to come to him for protection, when Ithel and Madog, the sons of Rhirid, and Llywarch, son of Trahaiarn, were endeavouring to secure Owain and Cadwgan, 88.
— his address to Madog and his brother, 88.
— they accuse him of flattery and cunning, 90.
— his sons invite the men of Meirionydd to assist them in expelling Owain and Madog out of their land, 100.

Uchtryd, son of Edwin—*cont.*
— the castle of, attacked by Einon, son of Cadwgan, and Gruffudd, son of Maredudd, 140.
— fights against Howel and Maredudd, and the sons of Cadwgan, 142.
— the building of the castle of the son of, 166.
Uchtryd, bishop of Llandaf, dies, 176.
— his character, 176.
Uereu, bishop, death of, 20.
Ulysses, Rhys, son of Gruffudd, compared to, 246.
Urbanus III., succeeds to the see of Rome, 232.
Usk, Iorwerth, son of Owain, taken by king Henry II. on the river, 210.
Ussa, son of Llawr, dies, 20.

V.

Vale of Ceiriog, king Henry II. moves his army into the, 200.
Vale of Clwyd, David, son of Owain Gwynedd, removes the people of Tegeingl, with their cattle, into the, 198.
— Peter, abbot, dies in the, 232.
Vale of Severn, king John retreats towards the, 292.
Vale of Teveidiog, subjugated by Llywelyn, son of Iorwerth, 320.
Vale of Tywi, devastated by Anarawd, 16.
— treachery of the men of, 42.
— devastated by Gruffudd, son of Llywelyn, 42.
— the chieftains and noblemen of, conspire to the death of Bleddyn, son of Cynvyn, 46.
— devastated by the French, 56.
— granted to the son of Baldwin, 70.
— granted to Howel and (son of, *C. D.*) Goronwy, 74.
— Owain, son of Cadwgan, and Llywarch, son of Trahaiarn, lead their forces to it, against Gruffudd, son of Rhys, 134.

INDEX. 489

Vale of Tywi—*cont.*
  Rhys, son of Gruffudd, confederates with the South Walians as far as the woods of the, 188.
  granted by king Henry II. to the lord Rhys, 212.
  parts of, allotted to Maelgwn, son of Rhys, 288.
Vepont, Robert, hangs Rhys, son of Maelgwn, at Shrewsbury, 272.
Vermin of a mole-like form, devour the food in Ireland, 16, 18.
Vernon, the earls of Flanders, Boleyn, and Sayrebus, captured at, 283.
Verses, Latin, on the death of Rhys, son of Gruffudd, 246.
  on his tomb, 248.
Vesey, Simon de, slain in battle, 296.
Ville, Bryan de, goes on a crusade to Jerusalem, 304.
Vortigern of Repulsive Lips, Myrddin's prophecy to, 2.

W.

Wales, pilgrims from, drowned on the sea of Greece, 166.
  Aberteivi considered as the key of, 254.
  the expulsion of David, son of Owain, out of, 258.
  king John goes into, 268.
  the nobles of, swear fidelity to Llywelyn, son of Gruffudd, 344.
  king Henry III. allows Llywelyn to receive the homage of the barons of, 356.
  and that they should henceforth be called princes of, 356.
  king Edward I. designs three armies against, 364.
Wallis, Thomas, bishop of Menevia, death of, 340.
Walter de Bec, the castle of, burnt by Owain and Cadwalader, sons of Gruffudd, 158.

Walter, son of Gruffudd, retains Pain's castle, the castle of Colwyn, and the cantrev of Elvael, 282.
Walter, son of Llywarch, kills Einon, son of Anarawd, in his sleep, 198.
Walter, son of Rhirid, kills Cadwgan, son of Maredudd, 198.
Weather, extraordinarily fine, throughout the winter and spring, until Ascension Thursday, when it became very tempestuous, 220.
  unusually fine, 288.
Welsh, the, devastate the territory of Offa, 8.
  soldiers in the army of Rheinallt, son of king Henry, 192.
  all the, combine to expel the French garrisons, 198.
  a few chosen, oppose king Henry II. in the Vale of Ceiriog, 200.
  distrustful of the French, 226.
  they raze the castle of Llanubadein to the ground, 238.
  the restoration of their ancient rights contemplated by Gwenwynwyn, 252.
  they fight against the castle of Gwerthrynion, and burn it to the ground, 256.
  they rise against king John, 282.
  obtain possession of nearly all Dyved, 282, 284.
  men placed by Rhys the Hoarse, to dwell in Gower, 302.
  pursue the English, and slay upward of twelve hundred, 350.
  are slain near Colunwy by John Strange, 350.
Welsh princes, make peace with king Henry II., 188.
  make peace with king John, 268.
  collect a vast army to Caermarthen, 286.
  return to their countries happy and victorious, 286.
  invited to be present at a partition of land between Maelgwn, son of Rhys, and Rhys the Hoarse, his brother, and Rhys and Owain, sons of Gruffudd, 288.

Welsh princes—*cont.*
  most of them invited by Llywelyn, son of Iorwerth, to make war upon Gwenwynwyn, 290.
  summoned by king John, to enter into compact with him, 292.
White Castle, taken possession of by Robert de Bruse, 282.
White House, the lord Rhys arrives at the, 212.
  death of Cynan, abbot of the, 226.
  death of Rhydderch, abbot of the, 232.
  burial of Cadwalader, son of Rhys, at the, 232.
  a religious society from, removes to Ireland, 314.
Whitland (White House), Maredudd the Blind, buried at, 326.
Whitland in Ireland, a religious society from the White House settles at, 314.
Wiciew, Einon Clud escapes from, 194.
Wilfre, takes the bishopric resigned the third time by Sulien, 52.
William, son of Aed, commands an army of French and Flemings against the castle of Caermarthen, 168.
William, son of Baldwin, dies, 58.
William the Bastard, kills Harold and obtains the kingdom of England, 44, 46.
  goes on a pilgrimage to Menevia, 50.
  his death, 52.
  his fame, power, and riches, 52.
William Brabant, a Fleming, killed, 102.
William, son of Gerald, raises an army against the castle of Gwys, 172.
  the castle of Tenby delivered into his custody, 182.
William, son of Gwrwared, seneschal to king Henry III. over the land of young Maelgwn, spoils the men of Elvael, 338.
William of London (de Londres), leaves his castle and property through fear of Gruffudd, son of Rhys, 126.

William of Moretania (Brittany, *C.*), opposes and defeats the knights sent by Henry I. to subdue Normandy, 78, 80.
  seized and imprisoned by the king, 80.
William, son of Orc, opposes Owain and Cadwalader, sons of Gruffudd, and their confederates, 158.
William Rufus. *See* Rufus.
William, son of William Bruse, banished into Ireland, by king John, 262.
  his wife, son, and daughter captured by the king, 264.
  put to death with his mother in the castle of Windsor, 264.
Winchester, the body of William Rufus ordered to be conveyed to, 64.
  Henry, brother of William Rufus, secures the royal riches at, 64.
  the youths of, kill Randulf de Poer, and many knights with him, 230.
  the town of, burnt, and the castle fortified by king John, 292.
  the castle attacked, and taken by Louis, son of the king of France, 292.
  retaken by the men of the king, 294.
  the bishop of, dies, 326.
  the marriage of Llywelyn and Eleanor solemnized at, 362.
Windsor, the wife and son of William Bruse put to death in the castle of, 264.
Worcester, king John buried at, 292.
  the bishop of, dies (A.D. 1236), 324.
  a council appointed at, in which king Edward I. designs three armies against Wales, 364.
  king Edward I., and Edmund his brother, bestow their cousin Eleanor on Llywelyn, at the door of the great church in, 370.
Worgan, succeeds Herwald as bishop of Llandaf, 80.

Y.

Yale, a castle in, built by Owain, son of Gruffudd, 176.
the castle burnt by Iorwerth the Red, 188.
the monastery of Llanegwestl in, founded by Madog, son of Gruffudd Maelor, 256.
York, a dispute between the archbishop of, and the archbishop of Canterbury, 228.
Yspwys, a battle between the French and Cadwgan, son of Bleddyn, in the wood of, 56.
Ystas the historian, 244.
Ystiwyv, granted by king Henry II. to Rhys, son of Gruffudd, 212.
Ystrad Antarron, Gruffudd son of Rhys, and his uncle Rhydderch, arrive in disorder at, 132.
Ystrad Cyngen, the castle of, devastated by Rhys, son of Gruffudd, 182.
Ystrad Marchell, Ithel, abbot of, dies, 232.
Gruffudd, abbot of, dies, 244.
Owain Cyveiliog dies at, 250.
Ystrad Meurug, Razon, the castellaine of Aberystwyth castle, requests assistance from the garrison of, 130.
the castle of, burnt by the sons of Gruffudd, son of Cynan, 162.
the castle of, repaired by Cadell, Maredudd, and Rhys, sons of Gruffudd, 180.
Roger, earl of Clare, stores the castle of, 190.
the castle of, taken by the family of Maelgwn, son of Rhys, 238.
given by Maelgwn to his brothers, 238.
Rhys and Maredudd seized by their father, the lord Rhys, at, 240.
the castle of, taken by Maelgwn, son of Rhys, 252.
he razes it to the ground, 262.
Ystrad Peithyll, the castle of Razon, situated at, 130.
Ystum Llwynarth, young Rhys marches towards the castle of, 284.
Ystwyth, a castle built by Gilbert, son of Rickert, near the efflux of the river, 104.
the castle of Aberystwyth, situated on a hill shelving down to the river, 132.

LONDON:
Printed by GEORGE E. EYRE and WILLIAM SPOTTISWOODE,
Printers to the Queen's most Excellent Majesty.
For Her Majesty's Stationery Office.

LIST OF WORKS

PUBLISHED

By the late Record and State Paper Commissioners, or under the Direction of the Right Hon. the Master of the Rolls, which may be had of Messrs. Longman and Co.

PUBLIC RECORDS AND STATE PAPERS.

ROTULORUM ORIGINALIUM IN CURIA SCACCARII ABBREVIATIO. Henry III.—Edward III. *Edited by* HENRY PLAYFORD, Esq. 2 vols. folio (1805—1810). *Price,* boards, 12s. 6d. each, or 25s.

CALENDARIUM INQUISITIONUM POST MORTEM SIVE ESCAETARUM. Henry III.—Richard III. *Edited by* JOHN CALEY AND J. BAYLEY, Esqrs. 4 vols. folio (1806—1808 ; 1821—1828), boards: vols. 2 and 3, separately, *price,* boards, each 21s.; vol. 4, boards, 24s.

NONARUM INQUISITIONES IN CURIA SCACCARII, temp. Edward III. *Edited by* GEORGE VANDERZEE, Esq. 1 vol. folio (1807), boards. *Price,* 18s.

LIBRORUM MANUSCRIPTORUM BIBLIOTHECÆ HARLEIANÆ CATALOGUS. Vol. 4. *Edited by* The Rev. T. H. HORNE, (1812) folio, boards. *Price* 18s.

ABBREVIATIO PLACITORUM, Richard I.—Edward II. *Edited by* The Right Hon. GEORGE ROSE, AND W. ILLINGWORTH, Esq. 1 vol. folio (1811), boards. *Price* 18s.

LIBRI CENSUALIS vocati DOMESDAY-BOOK, INDICES. *Edited by* Sir HENRY ELLIS. Small folio (1816), boards (Domesday-Book, vol. 3). *Price* 21s.

LIBRI CENSUALIS vocati DOMESDAY, ADDITAMENTA EX CODIC. ANTIQUISS. *Edited by* Sir HENRY ELLIS. Small folio (1816), boards (Domesday-Book, vol. 4). *Price* 21s.

[C. P.]

STATUTES OF THE REALM, in very large folio. Vols. 4 to 11, including 2 vols. of Indices (1810—1828). *Edited by* Sir T. E. TOMLINS, JOHN RAITHBY, JOHN CALEY, and WM. ELLIOTT, Esqrs. *Price* 31s. 6d. each.

⁎⁎* The Alphabetical and Chronological Indices may be had separately, *price* 30s. each.

VALOR ECCLESIASTICUS, temp. Henry VIII., Auctoritate Regia institutus. *Edited by* JOHN CALEY, Esq., and the Rev. JOSEPH HUNTER. Vols. 4 to 6, folio (1810, &c.), boards. *Price* 25s. each.

⁎⁎* The Introduction is also published in 8vo. cloth. *Price* 2s. 6d.

ROTULI SCOTIÆ IN TURRI LONDINENSI ET IN DOMO CAPITULARI WESTMONASTERIENSI ASSERVATI. 19 Edward I.—Henry VIII. *Edited by* DAVID MACPHERSON, JOHN CALEY, AND W. ILLINGWORTH, Esqrs., and the Rev. T. H. HORNE. 2 vols. folio (1814—1819), boards. *Price* 42s.

"FŒDERA, CONVENTIONES, LITTERÆ," &c.; or, Rymer's Fœdera, A.D. 1066—1391. New Edition, Vol. 2, Part 2, and Vol. 3, Parts 1 and 2, folio (1821—1830). *Edited by* JOHN CALEY and FRED. HOLBROOKE, Esqrs. *Price* 21s. each Part.

DUCATUS LANCASTRIÆ CALENDARIUM INQUISITIONUM POST MORTEM, &c. Part 3, Ducatus Lancastriæ. Calendar to the Pleadings, &c. Henry VII.—Ph. and M.; and Calendar to Pleadings, 1—13 Elizabeth. Part 4, Calendar to Pleadings to end of Elizabeth. *Edited by* R. J. HARPER, JOHN CALEY, and WM. MINCHIN, Esqrs. Part 3 (or Vol. 2) (1827—1834), *price* 31s. 6d.; and Part 4 (or Vol. 3), boards, folio, *price* 21s.

CALENDARS OF THE PROCEEDINGS IN CHANCERY IN THE REIGN OF QUEEN ELIZABETH, to which are prefixed examples of earlier proceedings in that Court from Richard II. to Elizabeth, from the originals in the Tower. *Edited by* JOHN BAYLEY, Esq. Vols. 2 and 3 (1830—1832), boards, each, folio, *price* 21s.

PARLIAMENTARY WRITS AND WRITS OF MILITARY SUMMONS, together with the Records and Muniments relating to the Suit and Service due and performed to the King's High Court of Parliament and the Councils of the Realm. Edward I., II. *Edited by* Sir FRANCIS PALGRAVE. (1830—1834). Vol. 2, Division 1, Edward II., 21s.; Vol. 2, Division 2, 21s.; Vol. 2, Division 3, folio, boards, *price* 42s.

ROTULI LITTERARUM CLAUSARUM IN TURRI LONDINENSI ASSERVATI. 2 vols. folio (1833—1844). The first volume commences A.D. 1204 to 1224. The second volume 1224—1227. *Edited by* THOMAS DUFFUS HARDY, Esq. Together, *price* 81s. cloth; or the volumes may be had separately. Vol. 1, *price* 63s. cloth; Vol. 2, cloth, *price* 18s.

THE GREAT ROLLS OF THE PIPE FOR THE SECOND, THIRD, AND FOURTH YEARS OF THE REIGN OF KING HENRY THE SECOND, 1155—1158. *Edited by* the Rev. JOSEPH HUNTER. 1 vol. royal 8vo. (1844), cloth. *Price* 4s. 6d.

THE GREAT ROLL OF THE PIPE FOR THE FIRST YEAR OF THE REIGN OF KING RICHARD THE FIRST, 1189—1190. *Edited by* the Rev. JOSEPH HUNTER. 1 vol. royal 8vo. (1844), cloth. *Price* 6s.

PROCEEDINGS AND ORDINANCES OF THE PRIVY COUNCIL OF ENGLAND, commencing 10 Richard II.—33 Henry VIII. *Edited by* Sir N. HARRIS NICOLAS. 7 vols. royal 8vo. (1834—1837), cloth 98s.; or any of the volumes may be had separately, cloth. *Price* 14s. each.

ROTULI LITTERARUM PATENTIUM IN TURRI LONDINENSI ASSERVATI, A.D. 1201 to 1216. *Edited by* THOMAS DUFFUS HARDY, Esq. 1 vol. folio (1835), cloth. *Price* 31s. 6d.

*** The Introduction is also published in 8vo., cloth. *Price* 9s.

ROTULI CURIÆ REGIS. Rolls and Records of the Court held before the King's Justiciars or Justices. 6 Richard I.—1 John. *Edited by* Sir FRANCIS PALGRAVE. 2 vols. royal 8vo. (1835), cloth. *Price* 28s.

ROTULI NORMANNIÆ IN TURRI LONDINENSI ASSERVATI, A.D. 1200—1205. Also from 1417 to 1418. *Edited by* THOMAS DUFFUS HARDY, Esq. 1 vol. royal 8vo. (1835), cloth. *Price* 12s. 6d.

ROTULI DE OBLATIS ET FINIBUS IN TURRI LONDINENSI ASSERVATI, tempore Regis Johannis. *Edited by* THOMAS DUFFUS HARDY, Esq. 1 vol. royal 8vo. (1835), cloth. *Price* 18s.

EXCERPTA E ROTULIS FINIUM IN TURRI LONDINENSI ASSERVATIS. Henry III., 1216—1272. *Edited by* CHARLES ROBERTS, Esq. 2 vols. royal 8vo. (1835, 1836), cloth, *price* 32s.; or the volumes may be had separately, Vol. 1, *price* 14s.; Vol. 2, cloth, *price* 18s.

FINES SIVE PEDES FINIUM SIVE FINALES CONCORDIÆ IN CURIA DOMINI REGIS. 7 Richard I.—16 John (1195—1214). *Edited by* the Rev. JOSEPH HUNTER. In Counties. 2 vols. royal 8vo. (1835—1844), together, cloth, *price* 11s.; or the volumes may be had separately, Vol. 1, *price* 8s. 6d.; Vol. 2, cloth, *price* 2s. 6d.

ANCIENT KALENDARS AND INVENTORIES (THE) OF THE TREASURY OF HIS MAJESTY'S EXCHEQUER; together with Documents illustrating the History of that Repository. *Edited by* Sir FRANCIS PALGRAVE. 3 vols. royal 8vo. (1836), cloth. *Price* 42s.

DOCUMENTS AND RECORDS illustrating the History of Scotland, and the Transactions between the Crowns of Scotland and England; preserved in the Treasury of Her Majesty's Exchequer. *Edited by* Sir FRANCIS PALGRAVE. 1 vol. royal 8vo. (1837), cloth. *Price* 18s.

ROTULI CHARTARUM IN TURRI LONDINENSI ASSERVATI, A.D. 1199—1216. *Edited by* THOMAS DUFFUS HARDY, Esq. 1 vol. folio (1837), cloth. *Price* 30s.

REGISTRUM vulgariter nuncupatum "The Record of Caernarvon," e codice MS. Harleiano, 696, descriptum. *Edited by* Sir HENRY ELLIS. 1 vol. folio (1838), cloth. *Price* 31s. 6d.

ANCIENT LAWS AND INSTITUTES OF ENGLAND; comprising Laws enacted under the Anglo-Saxon Kings, from Æthelbirht to Cnut, with an English Translation of the Saxon; the Laws called Edward the Confessor's; the Laws of William the Conqueror, and those ascribed to Henry the First; also, Monumenta Ecclesiastica Anglicana, from the 7th to the 10th century; and the Ancient Latin Version of the Anglo-Saxon Laws; with a compendious Glossary, &c. *Edited by* BENJAMIN THORPE, Esq. 1 vol. folio (1840), cloth. *Price* 40s.

——— 2 vols. royal 8vo. cloth. *Price* 30s.

ANCIENT LAWS AND INSTITUTES OF WALES; comprising Laws supposed to be enacted by Howel the Good; modified by subsequent Regulations under the Native Princes, prior to the Conquest by Edward the First; and anomalous Laws, consisting principally of Institutions which, by the Statute of Ruddlan, were admitted to continue in force. With an English Translation of the Welsh Text. To which are added a few Latin Transcripts, containing Digests of the Welsh Laws, principally of the Dimetian Code. With Indices and Glossary. *Edited by* ANEURIN OWEN, Esq. 1 vol. folio (1841), cloth. *Price* 44s.

——— 2 vols. royal 8vo. cloth. *Price* 36s.

ROTULI DE LIBERATE AC DE MISIS ET PRÆSTITIS, Regnante Johanne. *Edited by* THOMAS DUFFUS HARDY, Esq. 1 vol. royal 8vo. (1844), cloth. *Price* 6s.

DOCUMENTS ILLUSTRATIVE OF ENGLISH HISTORY in the 13th and 14th centuries, selected from the Records in the Exchequer. *Edited by* HENRY COLE, Esq. 1 vol. fcp. folio (1844), cloth. *Price* 45s. 6d.

MODUS TENENDI PARLIAMENTUM. An Ancient Treatise on the Mode of holding the Parliament in England. *Edited by* THOMAS DUFFUS HARDY, Esq. 1 vol. 8vo. (1846), cloth. *Price* 2s. 6d.

REPORTS OF THE PROCEEDINGS OF THE RECORD COMMISSIONERS, 1800 to 1819, 2 vols., folio, boards. *Price* 5l. 5s. From 1819 to 1831 their proceedings have not been printed. A third volume of Reports of their Proceedings, 1831 to 1837, folio, boards, 8s. 3 vols. together, boards. *Price* 5l. 13s.

THE ACTS OF THE PARLIAMENTS OF SCOTLAND. 11 vols. folio (1814–1844). Vol. I. *Edited by* THOMAS THOMSON and COSMO INNES, Esqrs. *Price* 42s.

⁎ Also, Vols. 4, 7, 8, 9, 10, 11, 10s. 6d. each Vol.

THE ACTS OF THE LORDS OF COUNCIL IN CIVIL CAUSES. A.D. 1478—1495. *Edited by* THOMAS THOMSON, Esq. Folio (1839). *Price* 10s. 6d.

THE ACTS OF THE LORDS AUDITORS OF CAUSES AND COMPLAINTS. A.D. 1466—1494. *Edited by* THOMAS THOMSON, Esq. Folio (1839). *Price* 10s. 6d.

REGISTRUM MAGNI SIGILLI REGUM SCOTORUM in Archivis Publicis asservatum. A.D. 1306—1424. *Edited by* THOMAS THOMSON, Esq. Folio (1814). *Price* 15s.

ISSUE ROLL OF THOMAS DE BRANTINGHAM, Bishop of Exeter, Lord High Treasurer of England, containing Payments out of His Majesty's Revenue, 44 Edward III., 1370. *Edited by* FREDERICK DEVON, Esq. 1 vol. 4to. (1835), cloth. *Price* 35s.

—— Royal 8vo. cloth. *Price* 25s.

ISSUES OF THE EXCHEQUER, containing similar matter to the above, temp. Jac. I., extracted from the Pell Records. *Edited by* FREDERICK DEVON, Esq. 1 vol. 4to. (1836), cloth. *Price* 30s.

—— Royal 8vo. cloth. *Price* 21s.

ISSUES OF THE EXCHEQUER, containing like matter to the above, extracted from the Pell Records; Henry III. to Henry VI. inclusive. *Edited by* FREDERICK DEVON, Esq. 1 vol. 4to. (1837), cloth. *Price* 40s.

—— Royal 8vo. cloth. *Price* 30s.

LIBER MUNERUM PUBLICORUM HIBERNIÆ, ab an. 1152 usque ad 1827; or, The Establishments of Ireland from the 19th of King Stephen to the 7th of George IV., during a period of 675 years; being the Report of Rowley Lascelles, of the Middle Temple, Barrister-at-Law. Extracted from the Records and other authorities, by Special Command, pursuant to an Address, an. 1810, of the Commons of the United Kingdom. With Introductory Observations by F. S. THOMAS, Esq. (1852.) 2 vols. folio. *Price* 42s.

NOTES OF MATERIALS FOR THE HISTORY OF PUBLIC DEPARTMENTS. By F. S. THOMAS, Esq. Demy folio (1846). *Price* 10s.

HANDBOOK TO THE PUBLIC RECORDS. By F. S. THOMAS, Esq. Royal 8vo. (1853.) *Price* 12s.

STATE PAPERS DURING THE REIGN OF HENRY THE EIGHTH. 11 vols. 4to. (1830—1852) completing the work in its present form, with Indices of Persons and Places to the whole. *Price* 5*l.* 15*s.* 6*d.*

Vol. I. contains Domestic Correspondence.
Vols. II. & III.—Correspondence relating to Ireland.
Vols. IV. & V.—Correspondence relating to Scotland.
Vols. VI. to XI.—Correspondence between England and Foreign Courts.

** Any Volume may be purchased separately, *price* 10*s.* 6*d.*

MÔNUMENTA HISTORICA BRITANNICA, or, Materials for the History of Britain from the earliest period. Vol. 1, extending to the Norman Conquest. Prepared, and illustrated with Notes, by the late HENRY PETRIE, Esq., F.S.A., Keeper of the Records in the Tower of London, assisted by the Rev. JOHN SHARPE, Rector of Castle Eaton, Wilts. Finally completed for publication, and with an Introduction, by THOMAS DUFFUS HARDY, Esq., Assistant Keeper of Records. (Printed by command of Her Majesty.) Folio (1848). *Price* 42*s.*

HISTORICAL NOTES RELATIVE TO THE HISTORY OF ENGLAND; embracing the Period from the Accession of King Henry VIII. to the Death of Queen Anne inclusive (1509 to 1714). Designed as a Book of instant Reference for the purpose of ascertaining the Dates of Events mentioned in History and in Manuscripts. The Name of every Person and Event mentioned in History within the above period is placed in Alphabetical and Chronological Order, and the Authority from whence taken is given in each case, whether from Printed History or from Manuscripts. By F. S. THOMAS, Esq., Secretary of the Public Record Office. 3 vols. 8vo. (1856.) *Price* 40*s.*

CALENDARS OF STATE PAPERS.

[IMPERIAL 8vo.   *Price* 15*s.* each Volume.]

CALENDAR OF STATE PAPERS, DOMESTIC SERIES, OF THE REIGNS OF EDWARD VI., MARY, ELIZABETH, 1547—1580, preserved in the State Paper Department of Her Majesty's Public Record Office. *Edited by* ROBERT LEMON, Esq., F.S.A. 1856.

CALENDAR OF STATE PAPERS, DOMESTIC SERIES, OF THE REIGN OF JAMES I., preserved in the State Paper Department of Her Majesty's Public Record Office. *Edited by* MARY ANNE EVERETT GREEN. 1857—1859.
- Vol. I.—1603—1610.
- Vol. II.—1611—1618.
- Vol. III.—1619—1623.
- Vol. IV.—1623—1625, with Addenda.

CALENDAR OF STATE PAPERS, DOMESTIC SERIES, OF THE REIGN OF CHARLES I., preserved in the State Paper Department of Her Majesty's Public Record Office. *Edited by* JOHN BRUCE, Esq., V.P.S.A. 1858.
- Vol. I.—1625-1626.
- Vol. II.—1627-1628.

CALENDAR OF THE STATE PAPERS relating to SCOTLAND, preserved in the State Paper Department of Her Majesty's Public Record Office. *Edited by* MARKHAM JOHN THORPE, Esq., of St. Edmund Hall, Oxford. 1858.
- Vol. I., the Scottish Series, of the Reigns of Henry VIII., Edward VI., Mary, Elizabeth, 1509—1589.
- Vol. II., the Scottish Series, of the Reign of Queen Elizabeth, 1589—1603; an Appendix to the Scottish Series, 1543—1592; and the State Papers relating to Mary Queen of Scots during her Detention in England, 1568—1587.

In the Press.

CALENDAR OF THE STATE PAPERS RELATING TO IRELAND, preserved in the State Paper Department of Her Majesty's Public Record Office. *Edited by* H. C. HAMILTON, Esq.

CALENDAR OF STATE PAPERS, DOMESTIC SERIES, OF THE REIGN OF CHARLES I., preserved in the State Paper Department of Her Majesty's Public Record Office. *Edited by* JOHN BRUCE, Esq., V.P.S.A.
    Vol. III.

In Progress.

CALENDAR OF THE STATE PAPERS, DOMESTIC SERIES, OF THE REIGN OF CHARLES II., preserved in the State Paper Department of Her Majesty's Public Record Office. *Edited by* MARY ANNE EVERETT GREEN.

THE CHRONICLES AND MEMORIALS OF GREAT BRITAIN AND IRELAND DURING THE MIDDLE AGES.

[ROYAL 8vo. *Price 8s. 6d.* each Volume.]

1. THE CHRONICLE OF ENGLAND, by JOHN CAPGRAVE. *Edited by* the Rev. F. C. HINGESTON, M.A., of Exeter College, Oxford.
2. CHRONICON MONASTERII DE ABINGDON. Vols. I. and II. *Edited by* the Rev. J. STEVENSON, M.A., of University College, Durham, and Vicar of Leighton Buzzard.
3. LIVES OF EDWARD THE CONFESSOR. I.—La Estoire de Seint Aedward le Rei. II.—Vita Beati Edvardi Regis et Confessoris. III.—Vita Æduuardi Regis qui apud Westmonasterium requiescit. *Edited by* H. R. LUARD, M.A., Fellow and Assistant Tutor of Trinity College, Cambridge.
4. MONUMENTA FRANCISCANA; scilicet, I.—Thomas de Eccleston de Adventu Fratrum Minorum in Angliam. II.—Adæ de Marisco Epistolæ. III.—Registrum Fratrum Minorum Londoniæ. *Edited by* the Rev. J. S. BREWER, M.A., Professor of English Literature, King's College, London, and Reader at the Rolls.
5. FASCICULI ZIZANIORUM MAGISTRI JOHANNIS WYCLIF CUM TRITICO. Ascribed to THOMAS NETTER, of WALDEN, Provincial of the Carmelite Order in England, and Confessor to King Henry the Fifth. *Edited by* the Rev. W. W. SHIRLEY, M.A., Tutor and late Fellow of Wadham College, Oxford.
6. THE BUIK OF THE CRONICLIS OF SCOTLAND; or, A Metrical Version of the History of Hector Boece; by WILLIAM STEWART. Vols. I., II., and III. *Edited by* W. B. TURNBULL, Esq., of Lincoln's Inn, Barrister-at-Law.
7. JOHANNIS CAPGRAVE LIBER DE ILLUSTRIBUS HENRICIS. *Edited by* the Rev. F. C. HINGESTON, M.A., of Exeter College, Oxford.
8. HISTORIA MONASTERII S. AUGUSTINI CANTUARIENSIS, by THOMAS OF ELMHAM, formerly Monk and Treasurer of that Foundation. *Edited by* C. HARDWICK, M.A., Fellow of St. Catharine's Hall, and Christian Advocate in the University of Cambridge.
9. EULOGIUM (HISTORIARUM SIVE TEMPORIS), Chronicon ab Orbe condito usque ad Annum Domini 1366; a Monacho quodam Malmesbiriensi exaratum. Vol. I. *Edited by* F. S. HAYDON, Esq., B.A.

10. MEMORIALS OF KING HENRY THE SEVENTH: Bernardi Andreæ Tholosatis de Vita Regis Henrici Septimi Historia; necnon alia quædam ad eundem Regem spectantia. *Edited by* J. GAIRDNER, Esq.

11. MEMORIALS OF HENRY THE FIFTH. I.—Vita Henrici Quinti, Roberto Redmanno auctore. II.—Versus Rhythmici in laudem Regis Henrici Quinti. III.—Elmhami Liber Metricus de Henrico V. *Edited by* C. A. COLE, Esq.

12. MUNIMENTA GILDHALLÆ LONDONIENSIS; Liber Albus, Liber Custumarum, et Liber Horn, in archivis Gildhallæ asservati. Vol. I., Liber Albus. *Edited by* H. T. RILEY, Esq., M.A., Barrister-at-Law.

13. CHRONICA JOHANNIS DE OXENEDES. *Edited by* Sir H. ELLIS, K.H.

14. A COLLECTION OF POLITICAL POEMS FROM THE ACCESSION OF EDWARD III. TO THE REIGN OF HENRY VIII. Vol. I. *Edited by* T. WRIGHT, Esq., M.A.

15. The "OPUS TERTIUM" and "OPUS MINUS" of ROGER BACON. *Edited by* the Rev. J. S. BREWER, M.A., Professor of English Literature, King's College, London, and Reader at the Rolls.

16. BARTHOLOMÆI DE COTTON, MONACHI NORWICENSIS, HISTORIA ANGLICANA (A.D. 449—1298). *Edited by* H. R. LUARD, M.A., Fellow and Assistant Tutor of Trinity College, Cambridge.

17. The BRUT Y TYWYSOGION, or, The Chronicle of the Princes of Wales; and the ANNALES CAMBRIÆ. *Edited by* the Rev. J. WILLIAMS AB ITHEL.

In the Press.

THE REPRESSER OF OVER MUCH BLAMING OF THE CLERGY. By REGINALD PECOCK, sometime Bishop of Chichester. *Edited by* C. BABINGTON, B.D., Fellow of St. John's College, Cambridge.

RICARDI DE CIRENCESTRIA SPECULUM HISTORIALE DE GESTIS REGUM ANGLIÆ. (A.D. 447—1066.) *Edited by* J. E. B. MAYOR, M.A., Fellow and Assistant Tutor of St. John's College, Cambridge.

THE ANGLO-SAXON CHRONICLE. *Edited by* B. THORPE, Esq.

LE LIVERE DE REIS DE BRITTANIE. *Edited by* J. GLOVER, M.A., Chaplain of Trinity College, Cambridge.

RECUEIL DES CRONIQUES ET ANCHIENNES ISTORIES DE LA GRANT BRETAIGNE A PRESENT NOMME ENGLETERRE, par JEHAN DE WAURIN. *Edited by* W. HARDY, Esq.

THE WARS OF THE DANES IN IRELAND : written in the Irish language. *Edited by* the Rev. Dr. TODD, Librarian of the University of Dublin.

MUNIMENTA GILDHALLÆ LONDONIENSIS ; Liber Albus, Liber Custumarum, et Liber Horn, in archivis Gildhallæ asservati. Vol. II., Liber Custumarum. *Edited by* H. T. RILEY, Esq., M.A., Barrister-at-Law.

A COLLECTION OF ROYAL AND HISTORICAL LETTERS DURING THE REIGNS OF HENRY IV., HENRY V., AND HENRY VI. *Edited by* the Rev. F. C. HINGESTON, M.A., of Exeter College, Oxford.

EULOGIUM (HISTORIARUM SIVE TEMPORIS), Chronicon ab Orbe condito usque ad Annum Domini 1366 ; a Monacho quodam Malmesbiriensi exaratum. Vol. II. *Edited by* F. S. HAYDON, Esq., B.A.

A COLLECTION OF POLITICAL POEMS FROM THE ACCESSION OF EDWARD III. TO THE REIGN OF HENRY VIII. Vol. II. *Edited by* T. WRIGHT, Esq., M.A.

ORIGINAL LETTERS AND PAPERS ILLUSTRATIVE OF THE HISTORY OF ENGLAND DURING THE FIFTEENTH CENTURY. *Edited by* the Rev. J. STEVENSON, M.A., of University College, Durham, and Vicar of Leighton Buzzard.

A COLLECTION OF SAGAS AND OTHER HISTORICAL DOCUMENTS relating to the Settlements and Descents of the Northmen on the British Isles. *Edited by* GEORGE W. DASENT, Esq., D.C.L. Oxon.

DESCRIPTIVE CATALOGUE OF MANUSCRIPTS RELATING TO THE EARLY HISTORY OF GREAT BRITAIN. *Edited by* T. DUFFUS HARDY, Esq.

In Progress.

HISTORIA MINOR MATTHÆI PARIS. *Edited by* Sir F MADDEN, K.H., Chief of the MS. Department of the British Museum.

POLYCHRONICON RANULPHI HIGDENI, with Trevisa's Translation.

January 1860.

Made in the USA
Monee, IL
16 September 2023

42840216R00326